General Liability Insurance Coverage

General Liability Insurance Coverage

Key Issues in Every State

Fifth Edition

Volume I

Randy Maniloff
Jeffrey Stempel
Margo Meta

ISBN: XXXXXXXXXX
ISBN 13: XXXXXXXXXXXXX

Note to Readers
This publication is designed to provide accurate and authoritative information in regard to the subject matter covered. It is based upon sources believed to be accurate and reliable and is intended to be current as of the time it was written. It is sold with the understanding that the publisher and authors are not engaged in rendering legal, accounting, or other professional services. If legal advice or other expert assistance is required, the services of a competent professional person should be sought. Also, to confirm that the information has not been affected or changed by later developments, traditional legal research techniques should be used, including checking primary sources where appropriate.

Dedication

To Lisa and Ella— whom I love without terms, conditions, limitations, or exclusions

– R.J.M.

To Ann, Ryan, Shanen, and Reed— The Ultimate Coverage Team

– J.W.S.

To Jonel – my greatest source of inspiration

– M.E.M.

About the Authors

Randy J. Maniloff is an attorney at White and Williams, LLP in Philadelphia. He concentrates his practice in the representation of insurers in coverage disputes over primary and excess obligations under a host of policies, including commercial general liability and various professional liability policies. Mr. Maniloff is an adjunct professor, teaching insurance law, at Temple University Beasley School of Law. Mr. Maniloff publishes *Coverage Opinions* [CoverageOpinions.info], an electronic newsletter that addresses recent insurance coverage developments, looks at the lighter side of the law and features interviews with the nation's most unique, accomplished and celebrated lawyers. For the past twenty years, Mr. Maniloff has published a year-end article that addresses the ten most significant insurance coverage decisions of that year. Mr. Maniloff has published dozens of articles addressing a variety of insurance coverage subjects, is a frequent lecturer at industry seminars and has been quoted on insurance coverage topics by such media as *The Wall Street Journal, The New York Times, USA Today, Dow Jones Newswires and Associated Press*. He has also published numerous editorials in *The Wall Street Journal* addressing various legal issues. Mr. Maniloff received his B.S., with distinction, in 1988 from Pennsylvania State University and his J.D. in 1991 from Temple University School of Law in Philadelphia.

 Jeffrey W. Stempel, the Doris S. & Theodore B. Lee Professor of Law, teaches legal ethics, civil procedure, insurance, and contracts at the William S. Boyd School of Law, University of Nevada Las Vegas. He is the author or co-author of many law journal articles and six previous books, including *Fundamentals of Litigation Practice* (2014), *Fundamentals of Pretrial Litigation* (11th ed. 2020), *Principles of Insurance Law* (5th ed. 2020), *Stempel and Knutsen on Insurance Coverage* (4th ed. 2016), and *Foundations of the Law* (1994). A member of the bar in both Minnesota and Nevada, he served on the State Bar of Nevada Committee on Ethics and Professional Responsibility and the Bar's Ethics 2000 Committee. Prior to joining the UNLV law faculty in 1999, he taught at Florida State University College of Law and Brooklyn Law School and has been a practicing attorney and judicial clerk. He is a graduate of the University of Minnesota and the Yale Law School.

Margo E. Meta is an attorney at White and Williams, LLP. She focuses her practice on advising major property and casualty insurance companies on complex insurance coverage issues under general and professional liability, homeowner's liability, commercial property and excess policies. Ms. Meta has handled a wide variety of coverage and litigation matters, including construction defect (with related risk transfer issues), premises and product liability, business interruption, educator's legal liability, sexual misconduct, rescission and bad faith. Prior to joining White and Williams, Ms. Meta served as Associate General Counsel for Universal Property and Casualty Insurance Company. Ms. Meta received her B.A., with the highest distinction, from the University of Pittsburgh and her J.D. from Rutgers Law School.

Acknowledgments

Just as it perhaps "takes a village" to raise a child, a book-length project inevitably is based on the work of many persons in addition to the named authors. Support from White and Williams, LLP and the William S. Boyd School of Law at the University of Nevada Las Vegas was essential. In addition, our spouses and children displayed more than their usual extraordinary patience and tolerance regarding our fascination with insurance coverage matters.

We have both benefited enormously from the lawyers, legal scholars, insurance claims professionals, and clients with whom we have worked over the years. Their insights and opportunities to engage in real-world insurance disputes have been in many ways the backbone of our understanding of the often complex (and usually state-variant) issues of insurance coverage law. Although this group is by definition too numerous for giving adequate recognition to all of its members, certain persons stand out for their support and the degree to which their scholarship and practice has enriched our understanding of insurance coverage and other areas of law.

Randy thanks his parents, whose love, unwavering support, and reminder to never forget the lesson of Coca-Cola have brought him to this point; his wife, Lisa, and daughter, Ella, for their love, unwavering support and sacrifice; his many colleagues at White and Williams who helped shoulder his burden during this project; Dana Genovese, his fantastic secretary; Shane Morris, Drexel University Law School, Class of 2021, who served as a research assistant on this 5th edition; Brenda and Howard Axel, for being such supportive and understanding in-laws; Gale White, for her tremendous support for this project; Celestine Montague for her friendship and sharing the JG moment; Lauren McHale for her friendship and humor; Erin Hadley for her infinite wisdom; Cara Vecchione, Ocean City, N.J. pizza soulmate; Spencer D. Schwartz, for a lifetime of friendship; Peggy Killeen for her confidence placed in him; Randy Spencer, the funniest stand-up comic he knows, for his levity during the rough spots; Margo Meta for her tremendous work on this edition and, of course, Jeff Stempel, for the privilege of working with one of the true deans of the coverage bar. Lastly, Randy is tremendously grateful to the readers of *Coverage Opinions* for their loyalty to the newsletter and this book.

In addition to his family, Jeff thanks David McClure, Jeanne Price, and the entire crew of the Weiner-Rogers Law Library as well as Deans John White, Nancy Rapaport, and Dan Hamilton and the Boyd School of Law administration and students as well as Ken Abraham, Aviva Abramovsky, Josh Aiklen, Mike Aylward, Amy Bach, Vanita Banks, Gene Backus, Tom Baker, Owen Barcala, Bill Barker, Jim Barker, Roger Baron, John Benedict, Denise Bradshaw, Natalie Baughman, Hazel Beh, Larry Berman, Michelle Boardman, John Buchanan, Pat Byrne, Patrick Carty, Mike Cashman, Drew Cass, Elizabeth Coleman, Dennis Connolly, Pete Christenson, Curtis Coulter, Bob Cusamano, Mark Derewetsky, Cary Donham, Rob Dotson, Kevin Dreher, Robert Eglet, Cory Eschweiler, Susan Field, Jim Fischer, Kelsey Fischer, Laura Foggan, Gary Fye, Shannon Gallo, David Gardner, Scott Godes, David Goodwin, Teri Greenman, Ken Grunfeld, Steve Guy, Rick Hagstrom, Yong Han, Laird Hart, Marjorie Hauf, Gary Haugen, Paul Hejmanowski, Roger Henderson, Helmut Heiss, David Herr, Dallas Horton, Michel Horton, Bob Hughes, Rachel Hutchinson, David Hyman, Mark Jackson, Bob Jerry, Cindy Jordano, George Kappus, Ken Katel, Anne Kelley, Dennis Kennedy, John Kennedy, Erik Knutsen, Jennifer Kokes, Christian Lang, Tim Law, Gene Leverty, Pat Leverty, Barry Levin, Jenapher Lin, Kyle Logue, Phil Lorenzo, Allen Kaercher, George Kappus, E.J. Kotalik, Annette Mann, Ryan Manning, Mike Marick, Rob Martin, Leo Martinez, Lorelie Masters, Bill Maupin, Charlie McCrea, Dan McFadden, Jeff Mikoni, Graham Mills, Mike Mills, Tony Mirenda, Jay Mootz, David Mulliken, Jim Murphy, Melanie Grande Murrieta, Brad Myers, Farhan Naqvi, Tom Newman, Barry Ostrager, Alan Packer, Mark Packman, Johnny Parker, Steve Parsons, Noel Paul, Steve Pearson, Marty Pentz, Alicia Portillo, Paul Powell, Dennis Prince, Mike Prough, Mark Plumer, Mike Raibman, Jerry Randolph, Jeff Raskin, Jim Reece, Joe Regalia, Doug Richmond, Brad Richardson, John Rivkin, Mark Rubeinstein, Adam Scales, Dan Schwarz, Peter Seligman, Matt Sharp, John Shugrue, Charles Silver, Hank Sorrett, Christian Smith, Wendy Smith, Rick Stempel, Larry Stewart, Alex SugzdaRick Swedloff, Peter Swisher, Kent Syverud, Danielle Tarmu, Bob Thavis, Jeff Thomas, Todd Touton, David Torrey, Carolyn Upton, Bob Vannah, Tamara Vannah, Manfred Wandt, Peter Wedge, Kristina Weller, Jeff Whittington,

Jim Whitmire, Sabrina Wibicki, Kathleen Wilde, Herb Wilkins, Bob Works, Kendelee Works, Ryan Works, Cara Xidis – and in particular – no surprise – Randy Maniloff. From the annual "Top Ten" cases to a seemingly endless supply of Coverage Opinions and the more than occasional op-ed piece, Randy is a true public intellectual of insurance and an important resource for anyone toiling in this field.

Margo thanks her parents and brother for their unwavering and never ending support; her husband, Jonel, for his encouragement and uplifting attitude; Gale White, who helped her find her path and who has generously shared her wisdom and experience; Anthony Miscioscia, who is always excited to discuss a unique coverage issue and whose support and encouragement are unparalleled; her colleagues at White and Williams who provide new challenges every day and who encourage her to step outside her comfort zone; Professor Jay Feinman, of Rutgers Law School, who taught her that (despite prevailing beliefs) insurance can be fun and interesting; Jeff Bartolino, who influenced her to pursue the career she loves and who is always ready for a good grammar joke; Michelle Federer, Adam Smith, Jen Morales, Angela Highland, Kizzy Ferrer and Kelly Phelan who are examples of true friendship; and most especially Randy Maniloff, a true mentor who is always willing to share his vast knowledge and without whom none of this would be possible.

Randy Maniloff
Jeff Stempel
Margo Meta

July 2021

Preface

Those involved with insurance claims, such as risk managers, brokers, insurance company claims professionals, and coverage counsel all respond to a new claim scenario with the same three words: Is it covered? [That may also be the last time that they agree on anything.] General liability insurance claims are complex, and the answer to that three-word question can be vexing.

On one hand, insurance is a business built on standardization. The vast majority of insurance policies are standardized documents, particularly for property/casualty risks, where the leading forms—including the commercial general liability (CGL) policy—are authored by the Insurance Services Office (ISO). But despite the relative uniformity of policies, states can differ widely in their interpretation and application of insurance policies. Whether a claim is covered under a CGL policy can depend a great deal on whether the case arises on one side of the mountain or river or another.

But despite this uncertainty, general liability claims, even the most challenging, usually involve one or more schools of thought that govern their resolution. The task for courts is often to identify and examine these various schools and decide in which one they want to enroll. This process, while convenient, leads to fractures among states over how to handle the most important coverage issues. This can be so even in the case of claims that involve virtually identical policy language and facts. In this book, we identify the various schools of thought that govern the most important coverage issues, and provide the type of state-specific knowledge that is essential to enable counsel, claims professionals, and all those involved in a claim to more efficiently and accurately assess a coverage controversy.

In some instances, this book will provide the answer with as much certainty as possible—such as a situation where the instant claim involves facts and policy language that are not materially different from those that have been addressed by the relevant state supreme court. In other instances, the answer will be less clear—such as situations where the law is unsettled or the instant claim involves facts or policy language that can be distinguished from otherwise settled law. But even where the book cannot provide certainty to the "is it covered" question, it will provide guidance on the issues that must be resolved to get to that answer. This may also enable the stakeholders in the claim to handicap their chances of prevailing.

With these two volumes, the reader is armed with the tools to address the key coverage issues of the day for each state. Although the book is aimed at attorneys and insurance professionals with some degree of experience, it is accessible to entry-level readers as well. Chapter 1 provides an overview of the CGL policy and the general ground rules of insurance law and policy construction. In addition, each chapter contains an overview of the nature, background, development, and competing schools of thought concerning the issue addressed in that chapter's fifty-state survey of the law. Most important, however, readers will get a comprehensive state-by-state summary of relevant law on the coverage issue, including the latest cases and developments.

This book has its roots in our own frustrations when addressing areas of insurance law. Although there are several good treatises on insurance law, many of which include listings of many cases, none had the sort of thorough, nuanced, and specific state-by-state focus of the critical issues that can best aid the insurance professional and claims attorney in knowing and understanding the law applicable to a particular dispute. We hope to bridge that gap—not to mention in a convenient fashion.

The viewpoints expressed are not necessarily those of White and Williams, LLP, the University of Nevada Las Vegas, or any of its clients or constituents. Indeed, because of the collaborative nature of this book, the views expressed herein may not be held by both authors. The same holds true for the employers or home institutions of any additional contributors. Notwithstanding this disclaimer, we have endeavored to "play it straight" throughout this book and to keep our own preferences out of our reporting of the state of the law of key coverage issues. State-by-state case law is reported impartially, without any intent to slant descriptions in favor of policyholders, insurers, brokers, or others with a stake in coverage disputes.

The fifth edition of this book was updated generally from mid-2020 to mid-2021. The coverage landscape is constantly changing. And rapidly so. New decisions arrive constantly – even after chapters were completed. Therefore, by its very nature, a book of this sort can never be completely current. Care should be taken to ensure that the law is current at the time that it is being examined.

We hope you will find the book a useful, perhaps even essential, addition to the coverage toolbox. But never lose sight that this is a reference book (a hopefully dog-eared one) and not a substitute for a subscription to Lexis or the advice of experienced counsel. We welcome questions or comments.

Randy J. Maniloff
White and Williams, LLP
Philadelphia, PA
215-864-6311
maniloffr@whiteandwilliams.com

Jeffrey W. Stempel
Doris S. & Theodore B. Lee Professor of Law
William S. Boyd School of Law–UNLV
Las Vegas, NV
702-895-2361
jeff.stempel@unlv.edu

Margo Meta
White and Williams, LLP
Philadelphia, PA
215-864-6219
metam@whiteandwilliams.com

July 2021

Table of Contents (Volume I)

Table of Contents (Volume II)

CHAPTER

1

Commercial General Liability Insurance–An Overview

The Structure and Development of General Liability Coverage

Liability coverage provides the policyholder and others insured under the policy with protection, including a defense, against lawsuits and liability that may result in judgments or settlements. The most common type of liability insurance is "general" liability insurance that provides protection for bodily injury or property damage claims that arise from the alleged negligence of the policyholder.

The commercial general liability (CGL) policy is the dominant general liability policy in the United States. In addition to providing coverage for "bodily injury" and "property damage" claims generally sounding in negligence, the standard CGL form also provides coverage for "personal injury" claims such as defamation or invasion of privacy and "advertising injury" claims such as when the policyholder's advertising infringes another's copyright.

The extent of coverage, of course, is defined by the insuring agreement as tailored by various exclusions contained in the CGL form. But the question oftentimes does not end there. In addressing insurance construction and coverage, it is important to note that state law can differ dramatically on how the policy language is interpreted. It is not unusual for virtually identical facts and policy language to result in a finding of no coverage whatsoever in one state and full coverage in another. Consequently, choice-of-law methodology in a given state can have an enormous impact on the ultimate resolution of a coverage dispute, as demonstrated in this book.

This book focuses on state-by-state treatment of important CGL coverage issues. By "coverage," we mean the question whether the insurance policy is obligated to provide protection under the facts and circumstances of the claim. While the specifics of more specialized types of liability insurance—such as Directors and Officers, Errors and Omissions, and Professional Liability—are outside the scope of this book, some of the CGL issues addressed in this volume are relevant to these other forms of liability insurance.

The language of the CGL policy and case law have long dominated the determination of liability coverage. In May 2018, the American Law Institute ("ALI") finalized a Restatement of the Law of Liability Insurance. This eight-year project provides a rule book, of sorts, addressing many important issues concerning liability insurance, including several that are subjects in this book. *See* Chapter 21 for a discussion of the relatively new ALI Restatement. The eyes of the coverage community have been focused on the Restatement, waiting to see how is may affect judicial decisions concerning the availability of liability insurance. As discussed in Chapter 21, courts are starting, albeit slowly, to answer the question.

For the most part, liability insurance provides protection against these claims without regard to the fault or blameworthiness of the policyholder so long as the policyholder did not intend to harm the claimant or the policyholder's conduct does not trigger a specific fault-based exclusion such as one forbidding coverage if the injury is the result of criminal acts by the policyholder.

Liability insurance is a relatively recent development, one most scholars define as beginning with general accident and specific risk liability policies sold to manufacturers and merchants in the late nineteenth century. Liability coverage expanded significantly with automobile liability policies in the late nineteenth and early twentieth centuries. These policies were arranged to provide coverage for damages against the policyholder resulting from an "accident." Liability insurance expanded to other areas gradually but took root as a form of commercial insurance protection in the 1920s and 1930s. The liability policies of that era continued to define coverage in terms of claims arising out of an "accident."

Early liability policies also tended to be policies designed to provide coverage against liability for a particular premises or operations hazards of the policyholder. Employers Liability Insurance was created to cover claims for work-related injuries and today continues but in modified form as an adjunct to workers compensation policies. Public Liability Insurance came into use and covered claims made against policyholders by injured customers or passersby, the type of classic "slip-and-fall" claims that are staples of the first-year torts class. Public Liability Insurance was reasonably broad in scope but not as comprehensive as the modern CGL policy. There was also Owners, Landlords, and Tenants liability insurance, Manufacturers' Public Liability Insurance, Contractor's Public Liability Insurance, as well as more narrow insurance products such as Elevator Liability Insurance and Product Liability Insurance. Separate liability insurance for contractors and builders also developed and was commonly called Owners' Protective Liability Insurance or Contractors'

Protective Liability Insurance. *See generally* ELMER W. SAWYER, COMPREHENSIVE LIABILITY INSURANCE (1943).

Prior to the advent of the CGL policy, various specific types of liability insurance were each sold and purchased as separate insurance policies. This presented difficulties for both insurers and policyholders. Insurers disliked the increased potential for adverse selection by policyholders, who might purchase only a coverage more likely to be needed while refusing to buy other coverages, thereby depriving insurers of potential premium dollars. It also raised pricing problems and issues of fairness in that some customers subsidized the coverages of others. It was also thought that presenting this much choice to some policyholders would encourage unduly risky behavior as policyholders gambled on the types of coverages they would need. Rating the multiple coverages was also difficult because of the narrow focus of risk assumed and the smaller pools of premiums for collection and investment.[1] In response to the problems of splintered policies and coverages, the liability insurance industry developed the CGL policy.

In the late 1930s and early 1940s, insurers began offering a "comprehensive" commercial liability policy that also included a "duty to defend" claims irrespective of whether the claims were meritorious. This provided the policyholder not only indemnity protection for adverse judgments or settlements but also with legal representation to defend the claim. *See* Chapter 5 for a discussion of the Duty to Defend.

The standard form CGL policy provides that the insurer controls the litigation and resolution of the claim and will supply counsel. That the insurer selects counsel has led to numerous disputes between insurers and policyholders that are unsatisfied with the insurer's choice. In addition, the relationship between attorney, policyholder, and insurer can lead to significant legal ethics issues for counsel— for which a complex body of law has developed. States vary in their responses to these situations. These issues are addressed in Chapter 6. For further information in these areas, *see* ALLAN WINDT, INSURANCE CLAIMS AND DISPUTES § 4.19 (5th ed. 2007); JEFFREY W. STEMPEL, STEMPEL ON INSURANCE CONTRACTS § 10.07[B] (3d ed. 2006 & Supp. 2009); RONALD E. MALLEN & JEFFREY M. SMITH, LEGAL MALPRACTICE §§ 30:3–5 (4th ed. 1996).

The initials CGL initially stood for "comprehensive" general liability policy. Insurers subsequently renamed the CGL a "commercial" general liability policy to avoid the implication that the CGL covered "everything" (or more than the insurer intended). The CGL policy was still written on an accident basis until 1966,

---

1 *See* ELMER W. SAWYER, COMPREHENSIVE LIABILITY INSURANCE (1943).

when the "occurrence" language was introduced (although "occurrence" coverage for "bodily injury" was the subject of an advisory endorsement in the late 1950s). During the 1980s, CGL coverage, particularly for product liability, was increasingly written on a claims-made basis,[2] but the occurrence-basis form remains most popular. The first standardized CGL form, crafted by the National Bureau of Casualty and Surety Underwriters and the Mutual Casualty Insurance Rating Bureau, was issued in 1941.[3] A revised standard form CGL issued in 1943 became widely used. The CGL policy was again revised in 1947 and significantly revised in 1955, 1966, 1973, and 1986.[4] Still further versions of the CGL policy followed, this time more frequently and with less significant changes. The two rating bureaus that crafted the CGL policy eventually merged into the Insurance Services Office (ISO), an organization that continues today and is responsible for the more recent revisions to the CGL policy.

The original CGL policy provided coverage where injury giving rise to a liability claim was "caused by accident." The term "accident" was not defined in the original CGL policy, the 1943 CGL form, the 1947 form, or the 1955 form. Courts were divided significantly on the question whether an injury-producing event must be discrete and isolated in order to constitute an "accident." The majority of courts concluded that an "accident" need not be confined in time and space and could be an injury-producing event taking place over a longer time span.

Many insurers were opposed to this judicial trend, arguing that an "accident" needed to be an event confined in time and space.[5] During the 1955 to 1966 period, these insurers either came to change their views or to accept the judicial interpretation of the "accident" trigger of coverage as inevitable. In addition, some individual insurers were offering "occurrence" basis coverage that was an attractive competing product because it clearly provided coverage for liability that resulted from ongoing conditions. In response, as part of the insurance industry's 1966 revision to the stan-

---

2 *See* Donald S. Malecki & Arthur L. Flitner, Commercial General Liability (8th ed. 2005) (describing revisions of CGL during past thirty years and current structure and content of CGL).

3 *See* Sawyer, *supra* note 1.

4 *See* Eugene R. Anderson, Jordan S. Stanzler, & Lorelie S. Masters, Insurance Coverage Litigation § 1.02 (2d ed. 2000) (also noting less significant revisions in 1988, 1990, and 1993).

5 *See, e.g.,* John J. Tarpey, *The New Comprehensive Policy: Some of the Changes,* 33 Ins. Couns. J. 223 (1966) ("The principal reason given for revision of the policies was adverse court decisions.").

dard CGL policy, the term "occurrence" was substituted for the term "accident," with an "occurrence" being defined as "an accident, including injurious exposure to conditions, which results, during the policy period, in bodily injury or property damage neither expected nor intended from the standpoint of the insured."

The fundamental requirement of the CGL policy, that bodily injury and property damage must occur during the policy period (although such requirement is no longer located in the definition of "occurrence"), has led to an enormous amount of coverage litigation. This seemingly simple question can sometimes be far from it, as evidenced by the fact that this issue is the subject of not just one, but two, chapters in this book. *See* Chapters 16 and 17.

Under the terms of an occurrence basis CGL policy, the insurer ordinarily establishes a limit of its liability, generally known as a "per occurrence" limit, which is usually set forth on the declarations page of the CGL policy and constitutes the maximum amount that the CGL insurer will pay for any one occurrence. Today, most occurrence basis CGL policies also provide an "aggregate limit" that sets forth the maximum amount of the CGL insurer's liability irrespective of the number of occurrences. However, aggregate limits for general liability claims did not become part of the standard ISO form until 1986. For products hazard coverage, however, insurers had employed aggregate limits well prior to the 1980s, largely because of the greater risk of cascading liability that was effectively beyond the control of the policyholder or insurer once products were in the field or structures were in use by third parties. That the limit of the CGL policy's liability is provided on a "per occurrence" basis had led to much litigation over the "number of occurrences" at issue in a claim. In many cases, more "occurrences" means more limits of liability available. *See* Chapter 9.

The Organization of the CGL Form

The CGL policy, like most insurance policies, has a relatively targeted objective for insuring risks. It is designed to protect commercial entities from litigation and liability arising out of their business operations. The CGL policy is not designed to guarantee the quality of the policyholder's work or the successful completion of its business activities. *See* Chapter 12 for a discussion of the dispute between insurers and policyholders over coverage for faulty workmanship.

Because even broad coverages are at some point limited in scope, an effective risk management plan for businesses (and for individuals) usually includes a package of coverages that match up and may even overlap. Effective risk-management leaves no "gaps" in the coverage of purchased policies unless the policyholder consciously intends to self-insure or "go bare" as to the risk that falls in the gap. A general liability policy will accordingly seek to cover only general liability. More specific liabilities that may be seen by the underwriters as presenting different sorts of risks are often excluded from the CGL but usually can be insured through the purchase of another type of policy.

The boundary disputes between the CGL policy and other forms of insurance coverage can become vexing where the loss is of a type that either does not clearly fall on one side of the line or where the policyholder can make a nonfrivolous argument that it reasonably expected coverage or that the loss at issue is properly characterized as a claim stemming from general operations. Commentators may refer to some of these cases as involving "tough" exclusions or policy language. Both policyholder and insurer may have good arguments for or against coverage.

Organizationally, the CGL policy has a declarations page giving the basic information summary of the policy, usually including the policyholder(s) and insurer names (and entities comprising any syndicates on the risk), the limits of insurance, the coverage period, and the premiums charged. The declarations page may also list the various forms that make up the policy, although it has become popular to relegate the list of forms to its own page—evidence, no doubt, that insurance policies are growing in size. Indeed, the 1955 version of the standard CGL form was five pages and the most current one is more than three times this length.

Until the late 1960s, CGL policies were written with an annual policy period and hence obvious annualized limits on the policy. Aggregate limits and multiyear policy periods began to arrive in the late 1960s and 1970s and were common by the 1980s. In coverage actions involving older policies (e.g., asbestos or environmental liability actions), there can arise a question whether the limits of a multiyear policy are annualized or apply only once for the entire multiyear period (usually three years). There is mixed case law on the issue, with some cases taking the view that a multiyear declarations page has a "plain meaning" that makes the limit a collective three-year limit rather than three one-year limits. Regarding the CGL language, one commentator has concluded: "[w]here a contract is issued for a period of three years, the limits of the insurer's liability apply separately to each *consecutive* annual period thereof."[6]

---

6 C. A. KULP & JOHN W. HALL, CASUALTY INSURANCE 143 (4th ed. 1968).

Section I of the CGL policy outlines its "coverages": Coverage A for "bodily injury and property damage liability"; Coverage B for "personal and advertising injury liability"; and Coverage C for "medical payments" available in connection with bodily injury claims. Each of the three coverages has its own "insuring agreement" setting forth the nature of the coverage and the insurer's obligation as well as a list of exclusions that apply to that particular coverage.

By length and verbiage alone, bodily injury and property damage is clearly the focus of the CGL.

Section II of the CGL defines who is an "insured," and Section III sets forth the "limits of insurance," making reference to the declarations page for the precise dollar amounts of the policy in question. An important, but to some extent implicit, concept in liability insurance is that the CGL policy ordinarily covers actions by third parties seeking monetary relief but does not provide coverage for purely injunctive claims against the policyholder.

Section IV establishes a number of CGL conditions that the policyholder must satisfy to successfully invoke coverage (e.g., notice and cooperation) as well as "other insurance" ground rules for coordination of coverage. Failure to give prompt notice of a claim is a commonly litigated issue in insurance disputes as is allocation of responsibility among insurers (and insurers and policyholders). *See* Chapters 3 and 18 respectively.

Finally, in Section V, one finds the definitions of the policy. These provisions are often more than cosmetic. For example, Section V of the CGL form defines such important terms as "personal and advertising injury," "bodily injury," "property damage," and "occurrence." Although any phrase in a policy can become important in particular litigation, coverage litigation often focuses on the meaning of a definition or exclusion in dispute.

As noted above, much coverage litigation involves claims for occurrences of bodily injury. The CGL defines bodily injury as "bodily injury [to be sure, insurance policies have their share of redundancies], sickness, or disease sustained by a person, including death resulting from any of these at any time," while an occurrence "means an accident, including continuous and repeated exposure to substantially the same general harmful conditions." However, "accident" is not defined. CGL Coverage Part A brings the two terms together by stating that the coverage applies only if the bodily injury or property damage "is caused by an 'occurrence' that takes place in the coverage territory" and if the bodily injury or property damage "occurs during the policy period."

The Coverage A exclusion list includes many of the classic sticking points of insurance coverage litigation: the expected or intended exclusion; contractual liabilities; alcohol-induced injury; pollution; vehicular injuries (auto insurers are supposed to cover this); war; the "owned property" exclusion; and exclusions for the insured's own work and product. These exclusions may prompt the policyholder to characterize a claim as sounding in something other than bodily injury. The Coverage B exclusions are fewer in number and tend to focus on intentional conduct, breach of contract, and date of conduct. But, of course, one reason the exclusion list can be so short is because Coverage B itself is not nearly so expansive as Coverage A.

Construction and Interpretation of Insurance Policies: Rules of Policy Construction Generally

Because insurance policies are contracts, the general rules of contract formation and construction apply to the CGL form. Relatively little insurance litigation concerns issues of contract formation. In almost all coverage disputes, there is no question that a policy was issued (the exception being life or health insurance conditional receipt cases or property insurance binder cases in which a claim is made for a loss that took place during the underwriting process, and the insurer contests whether there is coverage during this period under the terms of the conditional receipt). There is also a significant amount of insurance litigation concerning possible rescission of an issued policy on grounds of fraud or misrepresentation. For the most part, however, cases involve whether an admittedly operative policy provides coverage for a particular third party's claim against the policyholder or other person or entity that qualifies as an "insured" under the policy.

In construing insurance policies, courts strive to give effect to the intent of the parties. Normally, the text of the agreement provides the best indication of that intent. Consequently, clear policy text will usually be enforced unless the term is unconscionable or violates a statute, regulation, or public policy as announced by courts or legislatures. To be unconscionable, an insurance policy provision must be unreasonably favorable to one side or the agreement obtained through misconduct. Many courts require a showing of both this latter "procedural" unconscionability as well as "substantive" unconscionability in that the provision is too one-sided. Disputes also arise over clear policy text when insureds argue that the policy is "illusory" because it excludes coverage for a significant portion of the insured's operations. Insureds arguing that a policy is illusory often face a demanding standard as courts often reject the argument when the policy provides some coverage in some fashion—even if not what the insured in essence needed from the policy.

Because insurance is so heavily regulated, a policy term approved by or permitted by regulators is unlikely to be deemed substantively unconscionable. Policyholders have had more success contending that insurance policy provisions violate public policy. For example, auto insurance provisions limiting coverage may be held to unduly undermine state requirements that all drivers have adequate liability insurance because of the strong state policy in demanding at least minimal financial responsibility by drivers. Public policy arguments are less successful in CGL litigation because the policies are not usually required by law and are by definition purchased by often sophisticated businesses rather than less sophisticated consumers. However, the insurability of punitive damages under the CGL policy often gives rise to public policy arguments. *See* Chapter 19.

Even when text is reasonably clear, a court may examine other evidence of party intent or the purpose of the insurance policy in order to inform its construction of disputed words in the policy. For the most part, however, courts consider intent or purpose seriously only when the words are unclear. If a policy term is ambiguous, then the general rule of *contra proferentem* ("against the drafter") is that the language will be construed against the party that authored the problematic language and in favor of the nondrafter.

As Maniloff likes to say in jest, all policyholders seem to "speak Latin" in coverage cases as they are often quick to invoke the principle of *contra proferentem*, arguing that contested language is sufficiently ambiguous such that it should be construed to favor them rather than the insurer, who is almost always the author of the policy, particularly in the case of CGL policies. Although all courts follow the *contra proferentem* principle, various jurisdictions and individual judges vary in their eagerness to invoke the maxim. A few courts will immediately rule against the insurer if ambiguity is shown. A few are highly resistant to conceding any textual ambiguity and will conduct extensive linguistic analysis seeking to find the true meaning of text that initially may seem unclear.

Most courts take a middle approach. If policy text is not clearly and easily read to resolve a dispute, the court then examines extrinsic evidence of party intent and policy purpose, perhaps looking at underwriting documents, promotional material, correspondence, e-mails, drafting history, claims history, or other material in an attempt to resolve textual ambiguity. Only if these other indicia of meaning fail does the court usually use the ambiguity principle or *contra proferentem* as a tiebreaker to decide the case. In a small number of cases, such as when a policyholder or its broker authors or insists upon certain language in the policy, the ambiguity principle may actually favor the insurer.

For more extensive discussion of contract doctrine and insurance policy construction, *see generally* Joseph M. Perillo, Calamari and Perillo on Contracts (6th ed. 2009); Barry R. Ostrager & Thomas R. Newman, Handbook on Insurance Coverage Disputes (14th ed. 2008); Jeffrey W. Stempel, Stempel on Insurance Contracts (3d ed. 2006 & Supp. 2010); Emeric Fischer, Peter Nash Swisher, & Jeffrey W. Stempel, Principles of Insurance Law Ch. 2 (3d ed. 2004 and Supp. 2006); E. Allan Farnsworth, Contracts (4th ed. 2004); Eugene Anderson, Jordan Stanzler, & Lorelie S. Masters, Insurance Coverage Litigation (2d ed. 2004); Peter Kalis, Thomas M. Reiter, & James R. Segerdahl, Policyholder's Guide to Insurance Coverage § 10.04 (1997 & Supp. 2004).

Occurrence Policies as Contrasted with Claims-Made Policies

An occurrence basis policy operates differently from a claims-made policy. Under the occurrence basis CGL, an action seeking damages against the policyholder for bodily injury or property damage is covered if it results from an occurrence and causes such injury or damage during the policy period. The triggering point is the time of the alleged injury or damage. If the claimant is successful in demonstrating the time of loss alleged, the CGL insurer on the risk at that time must provide coverage for the damages obtained (absent the applicability of an exclusion or the exhaustion of policy limits). Once a CGL policy is "triggered," the insurer remains on the risk even if the injury continues into a subsequent policy period. The key point is the time of the precipitating injury. The occurrence (e.g., negligence, defective manufacture) need not take place at the same time as the injury. For example, negligent manufacture may cause harm that does not take place for years. But when it does, the occurrence CGL policy on the risk *at that time* is triggered. Consequently, occurrence CGL policies are sometimes described as providing almost unlimited "prospective" coverage. As noted, this "timing" issue can be more complex than it seems. *See* Chapters 16 and 17.

By contrast, a claims-made CGL is not triggered until there is a claim made and reported to the insurer during the policy period—even if the claim is based on long-ago events. In theory, this could make the claims-made CGL provide almost unlimited retroactive coverage. Insurers avoid such unlimited retroactive coverage by including a "retroactive date," which provides that the insurance will not cover claims caused in whole or in part by occurrences taking place prior to the retroactive date.

Another significant difference between occurrence and claims-made policies is their treatment of late notice. While prejudice is almost always required for an insurer to disclaim coverage for late notice under an occurrence policy, the opposite is usually true in the case of claims-made policies.

Coverage for Claims of "Bodily Injury"

Because of the frequency of litigation over Coverage A (bodily injury and property damage), the contours of bodily injury and property damage coverage are also comparatively well established. For example, a shorthand aphorism describing CGL coverage is that bodily injury coverage is construed to extend to tort claims against the policyholder but not to breach of contract liability. However, this aphorism can be misleading. For example, the CGL policy provides coverage for liability assumed under certain types of contracts.

There is also some division over the question whether bodily injury coverage includes damages for emotional distress. Most courts read the term "bodily injury" to require at least some detectible physical injury in order to trigger coverage,[7] although the term has been described as ambiguous.[8] Many courts have found that pure emotional injury qualifies as bodily injury when there is physical manifestation of the emotional injury, such as chest pains. A perhaps obvious point that can occasionally be forgotten is that "bodily injury" must involve a human body. The extent to which emotional injury may qualify as bodily injury is the subject of Chapter 11.

---

7 *See, e.g., Jacobsen v. Farmers Mut. Ins. Co.*, 87 P.3d 995, 999 (Mont. 2004) ("We … conclude that the term "bodily injury" as defined in [the instant policy], is limited to physical injury to a person caused by an accident and does not include emotional and psychological injuries stemming therefrom"); *SL Indus., Inc. v. American Motorists Ins. Co.*, 128 N.J. 188, 205, 607 A.2d 1266, 1275 (1992); *National Cas. Co. v. Great Southwest Fire Ins. Co.*, 833 P.2d 741, 746 (Colo. 1992). *See generally* OSTRAGER & NEWMAN § 7.03[a].
8 *See, e.g., Lavanant v. General Accident Ins. Co. of Am.*, 79 N.Y.2d 623, 630, 584 N.Y.S.2d 744, 747, 595 N.E.2d 819, 822 (1992).

Coverage for "Property Damage"

Similarly, the meaning of "property damage" under Coverage A of the basic CGL policy is also viewed as relatively well settled. For example, numerous cases hold that the property damage alleged must affect tangible property. Economic losses such as those connected with investments or anticipated profits do not count.[9] However, where economic loss occurs as a fairly traceable consequence of tangible physical injury, property damage coverage is likely to be available.

Exclusions from Bodily Injury and Property Damage Coverage

Although the scope of the insuring agreement of the CGL is quite broad, the typical CGL form contains a list of exclusions significantly restricting coverage for "bodily injury" and "property damage" claims. Among the standard exclusions are:

- Expected or Intended injury or damage
- Liability assumed in a contract or agreement (but with significant exceptions)
- Liquor Liability
- Workers Compensation claims
- Employer's Liability
- Pollution (*see* Chapters 14 and 15)
- Aircraft, Automobile, or Watercraft claims
- Claims arising from the transportation of mobile equipment
- Claims arising out of war, including civil war, insurrection, rebellion, or revolution
- Claims for damage to the policyholder's own property
- Claims for damage to the policyholder's own product

---

9 *See, e.g., Kazi v. State Farm Fire & Cas. Co.*, 24 Cal. 4th 871, 103 Cal. Rptr. 2d 1, 15 P.3d 223 (2001) (impairment of easement is not claim alleging physical injury to tangible property); *Miller v. Triad Adoption & Counseling Servs., Inc.*, 65 P.3d 1099 (N.M. App. 2003) (financial injury not property damage); *Whitman Corp. v. Commercial Union Ins. Co.*, 782 N.E.2d 297 (Ill. App. 2002) (economic injury from breach of asset purchase agreement not property damage); *Scottsdale Ins. Co. v. International Protective Agency, Inc.*, 19 P.3d 1058 (Wash. App. 2001) (where restaurant sued security agency over negligent admission of a minor, which led to loss of liquor license, restaurant had not stated a claim for property damage against policyholder security agency).

- Claims for damage to the policyholder's own work (heavily litigated in construction defect cases, with an exception "if the damaged work or the work out of which the damage arises was performed on your [the insured's] behalf by a subcontractor")
- Damage to "Impaired Property" or property that was not physically injured
- Product recall
- Personal and Advertising Injury (which is covered, subject to its own set of exclusions, in Part B of the policy, as discussed below)
- Loss of electronic data; and
- Telephone Consumer Protection Act ("junk fax") claims or other statutes that prohibit or limit the distribution of material

The Parameters of Personal Injury and Advertising Injury Coverage

The bulk of modern liability insurance coverage litigation has centered on the "bodily injury" and "property damage" coverage of the standard commercial general liability policy, when it occurred, what constitutes an "occurrence" under that coverage, and whether certain key exclusions in Part A of the CGL form are applicable. Increasingly, policyholders have focused on the other facets of the CGL, particularly the advertising injury and personal injury coverages. For the most part, this has been an effort to find coverage for claims that, at first blush, had traditionally been viewed as excluded bodily injury claims or uninsured events. The policyholder effort to expand the scope of the CGL, through a common law of claims characterized as personal injury or advertising injury matters, has enjoyed some success.

The standard CGL defines "personal and advertising injury" as injury that arises out of one or more of the following offenses:

(a) False arrest, detention, or imprisonment;
(b) Malicious prosecution;
(c) The wrongful eviction from, wrongful entry into, or invasion of the right of private occupancy of a room, dwelling, or premises that a person occupies, committed by or on behalf of the owner, landlord, or lessor;
(d) Oral or written publication, in any manner, of material that slanders or libels a person or organization or disparages a person's or organization's goods, products, or services;

(e) Oral or written publication, in any manner, of material that violates a person's right of privacy;

(f) The use of another's advertising idea in your "advertisement"; or

(g) Infringing upon another's copyright, trade dress, or slogan in your "advertisement."

Unlike the CGL itself and the "bodily injury" and "property damage" provisions of Coverage A, which is broadly drafted, personal and advertising injury coverage is written more narrowly, with focus on specified risks. However, where a loss arises out of one of the claimed enumerated offenses, emotional injury is usually covered.[10]

The personal injury provisions of Part B of the CGL contain exclusions for:

- Knowing violation of rights of another;
- Material published with knowledge of falsity;
- Material first published prior to the policy period;
- Criminal acts;
- Contractual liability;
- Breach of contract;
- Failure of goods to measure up to promised quality;
- Wrong description of prices;
- Infringement of copyright, patent, trademark, or trade secret;
- Insureds in media and internet type businesses;
- Electronic chatrooms or bulletin boards;
- Unauthorized use of another's name or product;
- Pollution (added to the policy form as a reaction to judicial decisions that found pollution liability claims to fall under the "trespass" or "wrongful entry" portion of personal injury coverage), including a specific exclusion for pollution-related expenses such as government-mandated cleanup;
- War; and
- Telephone Consumer Protection Act ("junk fax") claims or other statutes that prohibit or limit the distribution of material.

---

10 *See, e.g., Artcraft of N.H., Inc. v. Lumberman's Mut. Cas. Co.*, 126 N.H. 844, 497 A.2d 1195, 1196 (1985).

In general, courts have taken a relatively strict view of personal and advertising injury coverage, reading the enumerated items strictly and construing other actions according to their similarity or "fit" with the covered torts. This approach of confined construction of the coverage has been tested by policyholder efforts to obtain coverage for sexual harassment claims,[11] discrimination claims,[12] breach of contract claims,[13] and pollution-related claims[14] and has raised whether the "wrongful entry" provisions apply to claims that a policyholder is unfairly usurping another's property rights.

Courts generally have required that there be some selling or promotion or marketing of a product to third parties in order to fall within the coverage for advertising injury. Courts divide as to whether there must be "mass media" type of advertising or whether any sales promotion is sufficient to fall within coverage in view of the insurance industry's failure to use a more explicit and narrow definition of advertising in the CGL.[15] The current CGL definition of an "advertisement" is surprisingly

---

11 *See* OSTRAGER & NEWMAN, § 7.04[A] (12th ed. 2004).

12 *See, e.g.*, *Groshong v. Mutual of Enumclaw Ins. Co.*, 329 Or. 303, 985 P.2d 1284 (1999) (prospective tenant's claim of discrimination by policyholder landlord in failing to rent unit does not fall within CGL personal injury coverage for "wrongful eviction" or "invasion of the right of private occupancy" because claimant never had acquired possession and thus could not be evicted nor have right of occupancy invaded). *Accord Westfield Ins. Group v. J.P.'s Wharf, Ltd.*, 859 A.2d 74 (Del. 2004); *Rockgate Mgmt Co. v. CGU Ins., Inc.*, 88 P.3d 798 (Kan. Ct. App. 2004).

13 *See, e.g.*, *Holly Mountain Resources, Ltd. v. Westport Ins. Corp.*, 104 P.3d 725 (Wash. Ct. App. 2005) (claims of timber trespass and breach of contract not covered under property damage Part A of CGL form, which had specific timber trespass exclusion; policyholder apparently did not argue for personal injury or advertising injury coverage); *City of Arvada v. CIRSA*, 988 P.2d 184 (Colo. App. 1999), *aff'd*, 19 P.3d 10 (Colo. 2001) (tenant's suit for breach of contract, interference with prospective contractual relations, and misappropriation of business opportunity does not come within personal injury coverage as "infringement of property" (the contract); third-party claim sounds in breach of contract rather than interference with possessory right and is therefore outside scope of CGL). *See also Robinson Helicopter Co., Inc. v. Dana Corp.*, 34 Cal. 4th 979, 102 P.3d 268 (Cal. 2004) (economic loss doctrine does not bar tort of misrepresentation in connection with sale of product and performance of contract; cases like this may lead to subsequent coverage litigation).

14 *See, e.g.*, *Connecticut Specialty Ins. Co. v. Loop Paper Recycling, Inc.*, 824 N.E.2d 1125 (Ill. Ct. App. 2005) (absolute pollution exclusion bars personal injury coverage). *But see Brucia v. Hartford Accident & Indem.*, 307 F.Supp. 2d 1079 (N.D. Calif. 2003) (successful use of personal injury section of CGL to obtain coverage in pollution case). State divergence in application of both the absolute pollution exclusion and its predecessor qualified pollution exclusion is discussed later in this book.

15 *See Hameid v. National Fire Ins. of Hartford*, 31 Cal. 4th 16, 71 P.3d 761 (2003) (advertising

not all that helpful in resolving the dispute. It provides that an advertisement is "a notice that is broadcast or published to the general public or specific market segments" about the policyholder's business "for the purpose of attracting customers or supporters." The definition expressly includes electronic postings and certain portions of websites. This language can be read as including business marketing such as kiosk postings, distribution of handbills, or similar "narrowcasting" sorts of advertising/marketing/solicitation, but insurers generally contend that these sorts of marketing efforts are not "advertisements."

To be covered, the claims made against the policyholder must arise from advertising activity.[16] A highly attenuated connection to advertising is not sufficient to create coverage.[17] If courts were to view any advertisement connected to a tort claim as triggering coverage, the same logic would make product liability claims covered under the advertising injury provisions of the policy (Coverage B), rather than the bodily injury policy provisions (Coverage A), any time the offending product was advertised. Although efforts to shoehorn intellectual property claims into advertising injury are not as stretched (the advertising has a greater relation to public perceptions of product identity than it bears to the product's physical danger to users), the link is uncomfortably close for many courts.

A battle has emerged over the availability of personal and advertising injury coverage for data breaches -- such as when personally identifiable information is made public on account of a web site, computer system or retailer's point of purchase credit card terminals being hacked. Such hacking claims follow an overall rise in privacy litigation on account of advances in technology.

Policyholders generally argue that CGL coverage is owed, for losses resulting from the failure to maintain the security of personal information, because it satisfies

---

connotes widespread activity directed to public at large); *Monumental Life Ins. Co. v. United States Fid. & Guar. Co.*, 94 Md. App. 505, 617 A.2d 1163, *cert. denied*, 330 Md. 319, 624 A.2d 491 (1993) (advertising must be public to qualify as advertising within common sense of the word); *Smartfoods, Inc. v. Northbrook Prop. & Cas. Co.*, 35 Mass. App. Ct. 239, 618 N.E.2d 1365 (1993) (letter sent to third party may have discussed product attributes but was not advertising).

16 *See Sentry Ins. v. R. J. Weber Co.*, 2 F.3d 554 (5th Cir. 1993) (applying Texas law); *Bank of the West v. Superior Ct.*, 2 Cal. 4th 1254, 1276–1277, 10 Cal. Rptr. 2d 538, 552-553, 833 P.2d 545, 559–560 (1992).

17 *See The Frog, Switch & Mfg. Co., Inc. v. Travelers Ins. Co.*, 193 F.3d 742, 744 (3d Cir. 1999) (applying Pennsylvania law) ("This case involves allegations that the insured stole various ideas and then advertised the results of that theft; the question is whether the advertising converts the theft into 'advertising injury.' We conclude that it does not.").

the definition of "personal and advertising injury" for "[o]ral or written publication, in any manner, of material that violates a person's right of privacy." Insurers generally reject this argument and have been marketing separate, stand-alone policies, specifically designed to cover data breaches and other "cyber" risks. The CGL coverage debate may be short-lived, or at least not go on forever, as insurers have been incorporating data breach exclusions into CGL policies. Insurers contend that the adoption of such exclusions is not an admission that data breaches are otherwise covered under CGL policies, but, rather, it is a clarification that data breaches are not so covered. On-going coverage disputes for data breaches under the CGL, and, eventually, under separate data breach policies, can be expected. In addition, litigation has emerged under Crime policies, addressing whether they afford coverage for e-mail "spoofing" claims, such as when an insured is duped into wiring money to someone posing as a person known to the insured.

Choice of Law for Coverage Disputes

Steven M. Klepper[1]

Any attempt to use this book's various fifty-state surveys begs a threshold question: *Which* state's law do I use? Since claims and lawsuits do not always arise in the same state in which the insurance policy was issued, the answer is not always obvious.

For several reasons, few insurance coverage professionals likely place choice of law on their list of favorite issues. Thanks to its complexity, choice of law can be time-consuming (or tedious) to analyze. Even worse, it is not unusual that, even after this time-consuming or tedious analysis is complete, policyholders and insurers still cannot say for certain which state's law applies. And then throw in that some courts may consider applying different state's laws to different issues in the same case or treat choice of law differently between bad faith and interpretation of a policy provision. Some coverage issues combine generally undisputed facts with well-defined legal tests to lead to reasonable predictability of the outcome. Choice of law is not one of these.

With that said, there are thankfully two main situations where the reader can skip this chapter. First, if the policy declarations show an address for the named insured and the broker in one state, the person seeking coverage is the named insured (or some other entity in that same state), and the claim arose and the underlying lawsuit are pending in that same state, then that state's law should control absent some unusual circumstance. Even in this situation, creative advocacy can lead to anomalous results, such as *TPLC v. United Nat. Ins. Co.*, 796 F. Supp. 1382 (D. Colo. 1992), *aff'd*, 44 F.3d 1484 (10th Cir. 1995), in which the policyholder convinced the court to apply the law of Pennsylvania, where the *insurer* was domiciled,

---

1 Mr. Klepper is a principal at Kramon & Graham, P.A., focusing his practice on appellate advocacy and insurance coverage. He authored this chapter, as it appeared in the first three editions of this book. Authors Maniloff and Stempel revised and updated the chapter for the fourth and this fifth edition.

instead of the law of Colorado, where the policyholder was domiciled, to the question whether the insurer needed to demonstrate prejudice to disclaim coverage on the basis of late notice.

Second, if the substantive law is the same in all jurisdictions whose law could possibly apply, there is no need to undertake a choice-of-law analysis. "When certain contacts involving a contract are located in two or more states with identical local law rules on the issue in question, the case will be treated for choice-of-law purposes as if these contacts were grouped in a single state." Restatement (Second) of Conflict of Laws § 186 (1971), cmt. c. *See, e.g., Glidden Co. v. Lumbermens Mut. Cas. Co.*, 861 N.E.2d 109, 115 (Ohio 2006); *Talen v. Employers Mut. Cas. Co.*, 703 N.W.2d 395, 408–09 (Iowa 2005). Although courts sometimes use the term "false conflict" to describe a situation in which two jurisdictions' laws are identical, the term "no conflict" more accurately applies. *Hammersmith v. TIG Ins. Co.*, 480 F.3d 220, 229–30 (3d Cir. 2007). The term "false conflict" connotes that, upon application of a Second Restatement–type analysis, a court has determined that "only one jurisdiction's governmental interests would be impaired by the application of the other jurisdiction's laws." *Id.* at 229 (quoting *Lacey v. Cessna Aircraft Co.*, 932 F.2d 170, 187 (3d Cir. 1991)). If more than one jurisdiction has an interest in applying its own law, a "true conflict" exists, requiring a court to weigh those competing interests. *Id.* at 230.

To decide if a choice-of-law analysis is necessary, the parties must consider all jurisdictions where a coverage action could be brought and then analyze how each of those states would resolve choice of law—with a state court applying its own choice-of-law rule and a federal court applying the choice-of-law rule of the state in which it sits. *Klaxon Co. v. Stentor Elec. Mfg. Co.*, 313 U.S. 487, 496 (1941). Restatement (First) of Conflict of Laws § 332 (1934); Restatement (Second) of Conflict of Laws § 6 (1971).

The party invoking another state's law bears the burden of establishing a material difference from forum law; otherwise, the court will apply forum law. *See, e.g., Excess Underwriters at Lloyd's v. Frank's Casing Crew & Rental Tools, Inc.*, 246 S.W.3d 42, 53 (Tex. 2008); *Pekin Ins. Co. v. XData Solutions, Inc.*, No. 1-10-2769, 2011 Ill. App. LEXIS 1056 (Ill. App. Ct. Sept. 30, 2011) (federal decisions predicting Indiana law insufficient to establish actual conflict between Illinois and Indiana law). In a case involving coverage under multiple policies, a separate choice-of-law analysis is necessary as to each policy. *In re Liquidation of Midland Ins. Co.*, 947 N.E.2d 1174, 1180–82 (N.Y. 2011).

In theory, two provisions of the U.S. Constitution—the "full faith and credit" clause of Article IV and the "due process" clause of the Fourteenth Amendment—limit a state's ability to apply its own law to an insurance contract. But the U.S. Supreme Court has adopted a standard so permissive that, in practice, choice of law rarely raises constitutional concerns. "[F]or a State's substantive law to be selected in a constitutionally permissible manner, that State must have a significant contact or significant aggregation of contacts, creating state interests, such that choice of its law is neither arbitrary nor fundamentally unfair." *Allstate Ins. Co. v. Hague*, 449 U.S. 302, 312–13 (1981).

Until the 1970s, virtually all courts resolved choice-of-law disputes by applying the common law doctrine of *lex loci contractus*, which is Latin for "the law of the place of the contract." Under this doctrine, "a contract is governed by the law of the jurisdiction within which the contract is made." *Lifestar Response of Ala., Inc. v. Admiral Ins. Co.*, 17 So. 3d 200, 213 (Ala. 2009). While many states dismiss *lex loci contractus* as an outdated nineteenth-century doctrine, a substantial number of states, all of which have running water, continue to apply the rule. See the state summaries for Alabama, Arkansas, Florida, Georgia, Kansas, Maryland, New Mexico, North Carolina, Oklahoma, South Carolina, Tennessee, and Virginia. The Supreme Court of Florida conceded that *lex loci contractus* is inflexible but defended that inflexibility as "necessary to ensure stability in contract arrangements." *State Farm Mut. Auto. Ins. Co. v. Roach*, 945 So. 2d 1160, 1164 (Fla. 2006). Under *lex loci contractus*, the law of the state where the insurer delivered the policy to the named insured ordinarily will control. *Admiral Ins. Co. v. G4S Youth Servs.*, 634 F. Supp. 2d 605, 611–12 (E.D. Va. 2009).

The vast majority of jurisdictions have abandoned *lex loci contractus* in favor of the flexible "most significant relationship" analysis set forth in the American Law Institute's Restatement (Second) of Conflict of Laws, usually called the "Second Restatement" for short. The overarching framework of that analysis appears at Section 6, which provides that, absent a controlling statutory directive regarding choice of law, courts look to:

(a) the needs of the interstate and international systems, (b) the relevant policies of the forum, (c) the relevant policies of other interested states and the relative interests of those states in the determination of the particular issue, (d) the protection of justified expectations, (e) the basic policies underlying the particular field of law, (f) certainty, predictability and uniformity of result, and (g) ease in the determination and application of the law to be applied.

Restatement (Second) of Conflict of Laws § 6. As a matter of practical application to insurance contracts, however, the "underlying principles or guideposts" of Section 6 are of "secondary importance" to the more specific provisions of Sections 188 and 193. *Zurich Am. Ins. Co. v. Goodwin*, 920 So. 2d 427, 433–34 (Miss. 2006).

Section 193 enunciates the cardinal rule for insurance contracts:

> The validity of a contract of fire, surety or casualty insurance and the rights created thereby are determined by the local law of the state which the parties understood was to be the principal location of the insured risk during the term of the policy, unless with respect to the particular issue, some other state has a more significant relationship … to the transaction and the parties, in which event the local law of the other state will be applied.

Restatement (Second) of Conflict of Laws § 193.

Second Restatement jurisdictions frequently disagree whether a liability policy, applying to injury occurring anywhere in the United States, has a "principal location of the insured risk," and, if so, where that risk is located. Some courts, usually in the context of coverage for environmental contamination, find that each state where a claim arises is the principal location of the insured risk. *Reichhold Chems., Inc. v. Hartford Acc. & Indem. Co.*, 703 A.2d 1132, 1138 (Conn. 1997). Decisions involving environmental contamination may have rested on considerations that do not apply in other contexts. *Fantis Foods, Inc. v. N. River Ins. Co.*, 753 A.2d 176, 178 (N.J. Super. Ct. App. Div. 2000). Other courts have reasoned that the policyholder's principal place of business, as the place where the policyholder faces the ultimate economic risk, doubles as the principal location of the insured risk. *Babcock & Wilcox Co. v. Arkwright-Boston Mfg. Mut. Ins. Co.*, 867 F. Supp. 573, 580 (N.D. Ohio 1992).

More frequently, courts hold that there is no principal location of the insured risk under a policy covering the insured's liability in any state where a claim may arise. *Compagnie des Bauxites de Guinee v. Argonaut-Midwest Ins. Co.*, 880 F.2d 685, 690 (3d Cir. 1989). Indeed, a comment to Section 193 provides that "the location of the risk has less significance … where the policy covers a group of risks that are scattered throughout two or more states," and that a court should instead look to the considerations that govern choice of law for contracts generally. Restatement (Second) of Conflict of Laws § 193 cmt. b.

Section 188 sets forth these general considerations, which govern in the absence of a principal location of the insured risk, or which in some cases may even outweigh the principal location of the insured risk. These considerations include: "(a) the place of contracting, (b) the place of negotiation of the contract, (c) the place of performance, (d) the location of the subject matter of the contract, and (e) the domicil, residence, nationality, place of incorporation and place of business of the parties." Restatement (Second) of Conflict of Laws § 188. Because these factors focus on the relationship of the parties to the contract at the time of contracting, they will in most cases point to the state where the policyholder maintained its principal place of business during the policy period. *See, e.g., St. Paul Fire & Marine Ins. Co. v. Bldg. Constr. Enters., Inc.,* 526 F.3d 1166, 1168–69 (8th Cir. 2008); *Certain Underwriters at Lloyd's v. Foster Wheeler Corp.,* 822 N.Y.S.2d 30, 35 (Sup. Ct. App. Div. 2006); *Liggett Group, Inc. v. Affiliated FM Ins. Co.,* 788 A.2d 134, 138 (Del. Super. Ct. 2001).

Whatever approach a court takes to choice of law, a court's analysis frequently leads back to the application of its own law. But, as the Supreme Court of North Dakota observed, applying forum law to protect "North Dakota residents whenever North Dakota has any contacts with a controversy … is the kind of 'chauvinistic parochialism' sought to be avoided by modern choice-of-law analysis." *Plante v. Columbia Paints,* 494 N.W.2d 140, 142 (N.D. 1992) (quoting Robert A. Leflar, *The Nature of Conflicts Law,* 81 COLUM. L. REV. 1080 (1981)).

Sometimes, albeit rarely, a liability policy will contain a clause specifying which state's law governs the interpretation of the policy. The Second Restatement, however, is much less friendly toward choice-of-law clauses than one might anticipate: "Effect will frequently not be given to a choice-of-law provision in a contract of fire, surety, or casualty insurance which designates a state whose local law gives the insured less protection than he would receive under the otherwise applicable law." Restatement (Second) of Conflicts of Law § 193 cmt. e. *See, e.g., Industrial Indem. Ins. Co. v. United States,* 757 F.2d 982 (9th Cir. 1985) (declining to apply Illinois choice-of-law clause to policy having no relationship to Illinois).

It is important to review a state's statutes, not just its case law, to determine applicable law. In California, for instance, a statute has long provided that a "contract is to be interpreted according to the law and usage of the place where it is to be performed; or, if it does not indicate a place of performance, according to the law and usage of the place where it is made." CAL. CIV. CODE § 1646. But only recently did California decisions addressing choice-of-law for liability policies begin to cite that statute or to recognize its effect on the analysis. *Compare Frontier Oil Corp. v. RLI Ins. Co.*, 63 Cal. Rptr. 3d 816, 836–37 (Ct. App. 2007), *and Costco Wholesale Corp. v. Liberty Mut. Ins. Co.*, 472 F. Supp. 2d 1183, 1197–98 (S.D. Cal. 2007), *with Downey Venture v. LMI Ins. Co.*, 78 Cal. Rptr. 2d 142, 164 (Ct. App. 1998). Montana and Oklahoma courts have treated identical statutes as a mere factor in a "most significant relationship" analysis, even though the Second Restatement expressly provides that the multifactor analysis applies only in the absence of a statutory directive on choice of law. Restatement (Second) of Conflicts of Law § 6. *See Bohannan v. Allstate Ins. Co.*, 820 P.2d 787, 797 (Okla. 1991) (applying 15 OKLA. STAT. ANN. § 162); *Tucker v. Farmers Ins. Exchange*, 215 P.3d 1, 7–8 (Mont. 2009) (citing cases addressing MONT. CODE ANN. § 28-3-102).

In any choice-of-law regime—statutory, *lex loci contractus*, or Second Restatement—different considerations may apply in disputes that turn on details of the performance of the insurer's contractual obligations, as opposed to whether an obligation exists in the first instance. Distinguishing Mississippi decisions looking to the law of the policyholder's headquarters to interpret the insurance contract, the Fifth Circuit held that Mississippi law governed whether an insurer faced a conflict of interest in controlling the defense of a Louisiana policyholder in a Mississippi tort action: "Mississippi's interest here involves the power of its courts to enforce its conflict of interest rules in litigation in order to protect parties and the judicial process." *Hartford Underwriters Ins. Co. v. Foundation Health Servs, Inc.*, 524 F.3d 588, 599 (5th Cir. 2008). Applying Kansas *lex loci contractus* decisions, the Tenth Circuit held that the law of Missouri, where a lawsuit was pending, governed details of the insurer's defense of its policyholder, but that the law of the policyholder's home state of Kansas governed whether an obligation arose to settle that lawsuit within policy limits. *Moses v. Halstead*, 581 F.3d 1248, 1252–54 (10th Cir. 2009).

The lesson is that whenever a policyholder headquartered in one state is sued or has a claim arise in a different state, there frequently will be room for argument as to which state's law applies to the interpretation of the insurance policy. If the two states have reached differing interpretations of the policy language at the center of the dispute, and if the two states have differing approaches to choice of law, the resulting uncertainty may force the insurer or the policyholder to file suit to determine the controlling law. *See generally* Steven M. Klepper, *Choice of Law for CGL Insurance Policies: Toward a Uniform Rule*, 45 TORT TRIAL & INS. PRAC. L.J. 31 (2009). In the event of coverage litigation, a party advocating the application of another state's law should raise that issue in a timely manner, at the risk of waiving such contention. *See, e.g., Wood v. Mid-Valley Inc.*, 942 F.2d 425, 426 (7th Cir. 1991).

50-State Survey: Choice of Law for Coverage Disputes

Alabama: An Alabama statute provides: "All contracts of insurance, the application for which is taken within this state, shall be deemed to have been made within this state and subject to the laws thereof." Code of Ala. § 27-14-22. "Alabama law follows the traditional conflict-of-law principles of *lex loci contractus*," under which "a contract is governed by the law of the jurisdiction within which the contract is made." *Lifestar Response of Ala., Inc. v. Admiral Ins. Co.*, 17 So. 3d 200, 213 (Ala. 2009). Thus, where the policyholder was a citizen of Georgia at the time of the issuance of the policy, Georgia law controlled even though the policyholder had moved to Alabama by the time of the accident. *Am. Interstate Ins. Co. v. Holliday*, 376 So. 2d 701, 702 (Ala. 1979). Where the parties stipulated that a CGL policy was executed in South Carolina, South Carolina law governed whether the insurer's issuance of a reservation of rights letter gave rise to an enhanced duty of good faith. *Twin City Fire Ins. Co. v. Colonial Life & Acc. Ins. Co.*, 839 So. 2d 614, 616–17 (Ala. 2002). However, the law of the state where the contract was formed does not govern if it is contrary to the forum state's fundamental public policy. *Stovall v. Universal Constr. Co.*, 893 So. 2d 1090, 1102 (Ala. 2004). *See also Gabriel v. Chartis Specialty Ins. Co.*, 2016 U.S. Dist. LEXIS 46137, at *5 (S.D. Ala. Apr. 6, 2015) ("A court follows the law of the state where the contract was formed unless that state's law is contrary to the forum state's fundamental public policy."); *Protective Life Ins. Co. v. Apex Parks Grp., LLC*, No. 1180508, 2020 Ala. LEXIS 129 (Ala. Sept. 18, 2020) ("The contract at issue -- the policy -- is governed by California law because the policy was issued and was delivered to Apex in California.") (citing *Lifestar*); *Rockhill Ins. Co. v. Southeastern Cheese Corp.*, No. 18-268, 2020 U.S. Dist. LEXIS 60995 (S.D. Ala. Apr. 7, 2020) ("[T]he parties' contractual choice of law in the Policy is not overridden by the choice of law provision in Section 27-14-22 unless the provision would violate Alabama public policy. Thus, Missouri law applies because the Policy's choice of law provision does not violate Alabama public policy.").

Alaska: The Supreme Court of Alaska applies the contractual choice-of-law provisions of Section 188 of the Second Restatement. *Long v. Holland America Line Westours, Inc.*, 26 P.3d 430, 432–33 (Alaska 2001). An Alaska District Court, noting that Alaska employs a Second Restatement analysis, applied Alaska law to an E&O policy issued to an Alaska-based real estate broker. *CNA Ins. Co. v. Lightle*, 364 F. Supp. 2d 1068, 1072 (D. Alaska 2005) ("Although it is not known where the parties entered or negotiated the policy, Alaska is where the policy is to be performed, where its subject matter is located, and where Realty Executives is incorporated. Those contacts with Alaska require that the court interpret the policy under Alaska law."). In *Johnson v. RLI Ins. Co.*, No. 14-00095, 2016 U.S. Dist. LEXIS 24253, at *9-11 (D. Alaska Feb. 29, 2016), the federal district court applied a Second Restatement analysis, noted that "the law of a different forum may apply to different issues in a case," and concluded that Arizona law governed the interpretation of the policy and North Dakota law governed "all issues of performance, including the bad faith and punitive damages claims." *Id.* at *11. *See also Allstate Ins. Co. v. Progressive Direct Ins. Co.*, No. 18-00173, 2019 U.S. Dist. LEXIS 163481 (D. Alaska July 2, 2019) ("Pursuant to Alaska substantive law, Alaska courts apply the law specified in choice-of-law provisions except when '(1) Alaska's law would apply under Restatement § 188 in the absence of an effective choice of law; (2) Alaska has a materially greater interest in the issue; and (3) the application of [another state's] law would offend a fundamental policy of Alaska.' [*Long v. Holland Am. Line Westours, Inc.*] The parties do not argue and the Court does not find that these conditions are satisfied in this instance. Accordingly, the Court will apply Washington law when interpreting the Progressive policy."

Arizona: Arizona courts apply an analysis under the Second Restatement. *Beckler v. State Farm Mut. Auto. Ins. Co.*, 987 P.2d 768, 771 (Ariz. Ct. App. 1999) (applying § 193 and § 6) ("Considering the weight given to the principal location of the risk, we find it appropriate to apply Arizona law. We do not find that Nebraska's concerns and interests are sufficient to invoke the § 193 exception cited by the dissent."). *See also Jahnke v. Fed. Ins. Co.*, No. 06-0795, 2008 Ariz. App. LEXIS 221, at *14-15 (Ariz. Ct. App. Apr. 15, 2008) (applying § 188) ("As we have previously acknowledged, Arizona has a strong interest in providing recovery for injured residents. Yet, the state of Pennsylvania has a more significant relationship to the parties for purposes of the coverage determination in this case. Federal and the Sternsons entered the Policy, which contains terms specific to Pennsylvania, in Pennsylvania, and application of Pennsylvania law would protect their justified expectations. Moreover, there are no relevant Arizona public policies that would require us to reject Pennsylvania law and Pennsylvania has an interest in having insurance contracts entered in its state interpreted in accordance with its law. Further, applying Pennsylvania law is reasonable, results in uniformity and it may be applied with the same ease as Arizona law."); *P.F. Chang's China Bistro, Inc. v. Fed. Ins. Co.*, No. 15-01322, 2016 U.S. Dist. LEXIS 70749, at *8 (D. Ariz. Mar. 31, 2016) ("Arizona adheres to Restatement (Second) of Conflict of Laws § 193 (1971), which states that insurance contracts are generally governed by the local law of the state which the parties understood was to be the principal location of the insured risk during the term of the policy. *Beckler v. State Farm Mut. Auto. Ins. Co.*, 195 Ariz. 282, 286, 987 P.2d 768, 772 (App. 1999). Since the principal location of the insured was in Arizona and the insurance agreement was entered into in Arizona, Arizona law governs the enforcement of the Policy."); *Bell v. Great Am. Ins. Co.*, No. 1 CA-CV 07-0445, 2008 Ariz. App. Unpub. LEXIS 346 (Ariz. Ct. App. July 31, 2008) (applying Arizona law in action addressing coverage under Texas policy for Arizona additional insured who built homes only in Arizona); *Smith v. Hughes Aircraft Co. Corp.*, 783 F. Supp. 1222, 1228 (D. Ariz. 1991) (applying law of California as policyholder's headquarters and as the location of the greatest part of the risk), *rev'd in part on other grounds*, 22 F.3d 1432, 1436 (9th Cir. 1993) (declining to reach choice-of-law question); *White v. Evanston Ins. Co.*, 15-00980, 2017 U.S. Dist. LEXIS 67431, *15-16 (D. Ariz. May 1, 2017) ("[N]either party to the contract is domiciled in California, but the parties to the contract agreed that the Policy would cover the California Event. Moreover, the accident occurred in California, and to the extent Defendant may have a duty to defend, that duty would arise in in California. Therefore, even though Defendant is an Illinois domiciliary, and the Policy was entered into in West Virginia, no state other than California has a more significant relationship to the transaction or the parties.") (reaching the conclusion that California law applied under both § 188 and § 193); *Empire Fire & Marine Ins. Co. v. Patton*, No. 17-02159, 2018 U.S. Dist. LEXIS 199540 (D. Ariz. Nov. 26, 2018) ("On balance, the factors of § 188 weigh in favor of the application of California law. And while Mandalia points out that Arizona has a special interest in litigation where a victim was injured in Arizona, the Court has already acknowledged that the car accident is not the transaction at issue between these two parties. Arizona has little interest in a contractual dispute where the contract was executed in California and neither party to the contract is an Arizona resident."); *Labertew v. Chartis Prop. Cas. Co.*, 363 F. Supp. 3d 1031 (D. Ariz. 2019) (undertaking a detailed Restatement analysis to determine the location of the insured risk and the state with the most significant relationship to the contract and the parties).

Arkansas: Arkansas courts apply a "most significant relationship" test under Section 188 of the Second Restatement. *Scottsdale Ins. Co. v. Morrowland Valley Co., LLC*, 411 S.W.3d 184, 189-90 (Ark. 2012). Applying that test, the Supreme Court of Arkansas held that Arkansas law controlled coverage under a CGL policy issued to an Arkansas-headquartered policyholder with respect to farms located in Tennessee and Arkansas, notwithstanding that the underlying claim arose on a Tennessee farm. *Id. See also Simmons Foods, Inc. v. Indus. Risk Insurers*, No. 13-5204, 2014 U.S. Dist. LEXIS 192574, at *5 (W.D. Ark. June 6, 2014) ("With regard to contract cases in general, the Arkansas Supreme Court has considered the 'significant relationship test' in determining choice of law questions. The factors to consider are: '(1) the place of contracting; (2) the place of negotiation of the contract; (3) the place of performance; (4) the location of the subject matter of the contract; and (5) the domicile, residence, nationality, place of incorporation, and place of business of the parties.' [citing *Morrowland*] In this case, the policy was negotiated and issued to Plaintiff in Arkansas. Plaintiff is an Arkansas corporation. The policy insured multiple locations, including many within Arkansas. While the particular loss in question occurred in Oklahoma, the remaining choice of law factors weigh heavily in favor of applying Arkansas law.") (*affirmed in part and reversed in part on other grounds*, 863 F.3d 792 (8th Cir. 2017)); *Boyd v. Cog Marketers*, No. 19-00323, 2020 U.S. Dist. LEXIS 250615 (E.D. Ark. Dec. 16, 2020) (contractual dispute, but not coverage) (examining five factors set out in *Morrowland* and concluding that, while several states were implicated in the dispute, Michigan law would govern as it is where the defendant was headquartered, and, thus, "emerges as the consistent center of gravity for the events surrounding each claim in this case").

California: A California choice-of-law statute provides that a "contract is to be interpreted according to the law and usage of the place where it is to be performed; or, if it does not indicate a place of performance, according to the law and usage of the place where it is made." Cal. Civ. Code § 1646. Apparently overlooking this statute, a number of decisions from the 1990s applied a Second Restatement § 193 analysis, holding that a "liability insurance policy issued on a nationwide basis may be construed in accordance with the law of the jurisdiction in which a particular claim arises. ... Thus, the same policy language may receive different construction and application in different jurisdictions." *Downey Venture v. LMI Ins. Co.*, 78 Cal. Rptr. 2d 142, 164 (Ct. App. 1998). *See Stonewall Surplus Lines Ins. Co. v. Johnson Controls, Inc.*, 17 Cal. Rptr. 2d 713, 719–21 (Ct. App. 1993) (applying law of California, where car battery was manufactured and injured California resident, not law of insured manufacturer's home state of Wisconsin). More recent decisions, however, have held that the California choice-of-law statute controls in contract actions. In *Frontier Oil Corp. v. RLI Ins. Co.*, 153 Cal. App. 4th 1436 (2007), the court examined § 1646 is detail and explained that "[a] contract 'indicate[s] a place of performance' within the meaning of section 1646 if the contract expressly specifies a place of performance <u>or</u> if the intended place of performance can be gleaned from the nature of the contract and its surrounding circumstances." *Id.* at 1443. An intermediate appellate decision held that, with respect to endorsements to a Texas-made CGL policy specifically covering certain California locations, the policy contemplated California law as the place of performance of the insurer's defense obligation, and that California law controlled over Texas law in determining whether an underlying California pollution lawsuit triggered a defense obligation. *Id.* at 836–37. *See also Am. Motorists Ins. Co. v. Thomson Inc.*, No. B226068, 2011 Cal. App. Unpub. LEXIS 6537 (Cal. Ct. App. Aug. 29, 2011) (unpublished) ("place of performance" under § 1646 was state where each of policyholder's film processing sites was located, and California law therefore controlled coverage for contaminated site in California). But a California federal decision, finding that a CGL policy covering multistate risks failed to specify a place of performance, held that Connecticut law controlled coverage for bodily injury sustained in Pennsylvania, where the insurer delivered the policy to the insured's Connecticut-based parent corporation in Connecticut. *Costco Wholesale Corp. v. Liberty Mut. Ins. Co.*, 472 F. Supp. 2d 1183, 1197–98 (S.D. Cal. 2007). *See also Global Décor, Inc. v. Cincinnati Insurance Company*, No. 11-2602, 2011 U.S. Dist. LEXIS 64529, at *10-11 (C.D. Calif. June 16, 2011) ("Here, despite its broad coverage territory the Policy includes Illinois endorsements, entitled 'Illinois Changes — Known Injury or Damage,' that modify both the commercial general liability and the umbrella coverage. As in *Frontier*, these endorsements 'clearly demonstrate that the parties intended the policy to provide coverage for' Plaintiffs operations in Illinois."); *Ameron International Corp. v. American Home Assurance Co.*, No. 11-1601, 2011 U.S. Dist. LEXIS 61486, at *12 (C.D. Calif. June 6, 2011) (holding that California law applied to a liability policy issued in California and a construction defect action pending in Hawaii) ("Unlike the policy at issue in *Frontier Oil*, the policies in this case do not expressly provide coverage for a fixed location in Hawaii or any other state. Instead, the policies provide coverage for all property damage caused by an occurrence taking place anywhere in the United States and elsewhere. Nor do any endorsements to the policies indicate that the parties contemplated that Hawaii would be the place of performance for the policies. In fact, the only state-specific endorsements to the policies relate to California"); *Shanze Enters. v. Am. Cas. Co. of Reading, PA*, No. 14-02623, 2015 U.S. Dist. LEXIS 27877, at *11-12 (E.D. Cal. Mar. 5, 2015) ("This court agrees that the California Supreme Court would apply Civil Code § 1646, rather than the general governmental interests test, in the circumstances of this case. The statute's more specific provisions and status as legislative enactment support its applicability in cases of contract interpretation. And by requiring the court to determine whether a contract 'indicate[s] a place of performance,' Cal. Civ. Code § 1646, the statute bolsters 'the fundamental goal of contract interpretation' under California law: 'to give effect to the mutual intent of the parties as it existed at the time of contracting.'") ("[A]pplying the California choice-of-law rule to the contract at issue in this case, it points to Texas law, regardless of whether the parties' agreement contemplates performance in a specific location. First, assuming the agreement applies all over the world, as Shanze suggests, then it would functionally apply in no specific location or jurisdiction, and section 1646 would require application of the law 'of the place where it [was] made." Cal. Civ. Code § 1646. The parties negotiated and executed their agreement in Texas, thus Texas law applies."); *One Call Med., Inc. v. Nat'l Fire & Marine Ins. Co.*, 401 F. Supp. 3d 994 (E.D. Cal. 2019) (noting that California uses two choice-of-law tests -- § 1646 and common-law "governmental interest test"); *Scottsdale Ins. Co. v. Dickstein Shapiro LLP*, No. 18-02893, 2019 U.S. Dist. LEXIS 133045 (C.D. Cal. Aug. 1, 2019) ("courts have suggested that § 1646 is limited to matters of contract interpretation" and the "governmental interest" test "is to be used for choice-of-law issues other than contract interpretation") (applying in detail the "governmental interest" test).

Colorado: The Supreme Court of Colorado has adopted the Second Restatement in selecting the law governing contracts. *Wood Bros. Homes, Inc. v. Walker Adjustment Bur.*, 601 P.2d 1369, 1372–73 (Colo. 1979) (looking to § 188 and to subsequent sections that "apply to specific types of contracts"); *Ackerman v. Foster*, 974 P.2d 1, 3 (Colo. Ct. App. 1998) (applying § 193 to automobile insurance contract, finding that California law applied, even though purported omnibus insured moved to Colorado). The Colorado Court of Appeals, citing *Wood Brothers* for the proposition that it adopted the most significant relationship approach for contract actions, held that, under a homeowner's policy issued to Colorado policyholders with respect to a Colorado home, Colorado law controlled the application of the policy's liability coverage to a Florida lawsuit alleging that the policyholders' son, while a student in Florida, violated Florida privacy laws. *Fire Ins. Exchange v. Bentley*, 953 P.2d 1297, 1300 (Colo. Ct. App. 1998) ("all significant contacts are in Colorado"). In a rare decision to find that the law of the insurer's home state controlled an insurance coverage dispute, the Tenth Circuit held that Pennsylvania law controlled the question of whether a Pennsylvania insurer asserting a late-notice defense needed to show prejudice to disclaim coverage for a Missouri lawsuit alleging that a Colorado-based policyholder defectively manufactured a pacemaker. *Telectronics, Inc. v. United Nat. Ins. Co.*, 796 F. Supp. 1382, 1389–90 (D. Colo. 1992), *aff'd sub nom.*, *TPLC, Inc. v. United Nat. Ins. Co.*, 44 F.3d 1484, 1490–91 (10th Cir. 1995). *See also Berry & Murphy, P.C. v. Carolina Cas. Ins. Co.*, 586 F.3d 803 (10th Cir. 2009) (finding that Colorado law applied to construction of legal malpractice policy because the "contract was apparently negotiated and entered into in Colorado and the insured's place of business is in Colorado"); *Dish Network Corp. v. Arch Specialty Ins. Co.*, 734 F. Supp. 2d 1173, 1177–78 (D. Colo. 2010) (Colorado law controlled coverage for California litigation under CGL policy issued to corporation headquartered in Colorado); *Nicholls v. Zurich Am. Ins. Group*, 244 F. Supp. 2d 1144, 1152 (D. Colo. 2003) (Colorado law controlled construction of directors' and officers' liability policy issued with respect to Colorado-based corporation, even though the policy was issued by California-based producer to California-based broker); *Kipling v. State Farm Mut.*, 774 F.3d 1306, 1310-12 (10th Cir. 2014) (noting that Colorado applies a Second Restatement analysis to contract actions and a bad faith claim against an insurer sounds in tort); *Okland Constr. Co. v. Phoenix Ins. Co.*, No. 11-02652, 2014 U.S. Dist. LEXIS 28803, at *14-15 (D. Colo. Mar. 6, 2014) ("Utah's more remote connections to the circumstances of this case further lead me to conclude that Colorado has a greater interest in its outcome than Utah. Colorado's interest this case is further demonstrated by the fact that Colorado has enacted extensive laws, including C.R.S. §§ 10-3-1115 & 1116, to regulate insurance practices within its borders. Since Travelers and Everest are licensed to transact business in Colorado and in fact specifically insured risks located in Colorado, it was certainly foreseeable that they would be subject to Colorado law."); *Bowers v. Buckeye State Mut. Ins. Co.*, No. 18-00496, 2019 U.S. Dist. LEXIS 4040 (D. Colo. Jan. 9, 2019) (undertaking detailed analysis of Restatement provisions) ("[A]lthough Colorado and Kansas both have strong interests in having their law applied, Kansas' interest is stronger. Application of Kansas law best protects the expectations of the parties to the underlying insurance contract. Kansas was the state in which the contract was executed. The subject matter of the contract was understood by the parties to be principally located in Kansas, Defendant relied on that information when it entered into the contract, and the named insured was a Kansas resident.") (also noting that where "a forum's conflict of laws rules refer to the law of another jurisdiction, courts will not apply the foreign law if it is contrary to the strong public policy of the forum"); *Pharmacists Mut. Ins. Co. v. NAMIC Ins. Co.*, No. 18-0791, 2020 U.S. Dist. LEXIS 203853 (D. Colo. Oct. 31, 2020) ("[T]he re-insurance relationship between Pharma and NAMIC, like the insurance relationship between ITT and the employee, existed from a contract that was formed and intended to be performed outside of Colorado. And as in *ITT* [*Specialty Risk Servs. v. Avis Rent a Car Sys.*, 985 P.2d 43 (Colo. Ct. App. 1998)] other states, like Iowa and Indiana, have a greater interest in ensuring that policies of re-insurance between their own residents are properly executed than does Colorado, whose interest in the Pharma-NAMIC policy is minimal.").

Connecticut: Applying a Second Restatement analysis to CGL policies, the Supreme Court of Connecticut has adopted a presumption in favor of the application of the law of the state where "the bulk of the contracting transactions took place," unless, under the factors enumerated in Sections 6 and 188 of the Second Restatement, another state has a more significant interest in the controversy. *Interface Flooring Sys., Inc. v. Aetna Cas. & Sur. Co.*, 804 A.2d 201, 206 (Conn. 2002). Thus, the law of Georgia, as the place where the policyholder maintained its headquarters and several manufacturing facilities during the policy period, controlled coverage for pre-tender defense costs under a CGL policy. *Id.* at 205–08. In a dispute regarding uninsured motorist coverage, the Supreme Court of Connecticut recently reaffirmed the applicability of the Second Restatement test and undertook a detailed analysis of the interplay between §§ 193, 188 and 6. *Gen. Acc. Ins. Co. v. Mortara*, 101 A.3d 942 (Conn. 2014) (applying law of state where vehicle was principally garaged). *See also Liberty Mut. Ins. Co. v. Harco Nat'l Ins. Co.*, 990 F. Supp. 2d 194, 200 (D. Conn. 2013) (applying law of New York, the location of policyholder's headquarters, rather than law of Connecticut, the situs of underlying wrongful death). The Supreme Court of Connecticut found this presumption to be overcome in the context of coverage for environmental contamination, finding that the location of the polluted waste site is presumed to control. *Reichhold Chems., Inc. v. Hartford Acc. & Indem. Co.*, 703 A.2d 1132, 1138 (Conn. 1997) (applying law of Washington as place of contaminated site rather than law of New York as policyholder's headquarters). Like most states, Connecticut does not consider the insurer's domicile to be a significant contact. *Interface*, 804 A.2d at 207. A Connecticut trial court decision held that New York law governed an insurer's duty to defend a New York policyholder in an antitrust action, and that Connecticut law governed the duty to defend its Connecticut subsidiary; because neither party challenged the point on appeal, the Connecticut Supreme Court affirmed that holding. *QSP, Inc. v. Aetna Cas. & Sur. Co.*, 773 A.2d 906, 912 n. 8 (Conn. 2001). A Connecticut federal court held that the fact that a policy covered a number of risks nationwide was not a bar to the application of Massachusetts law for immovable risks in Massachusetts. *Dominion Energy, Inc. v. Zurich Am. Ins. Co.*, No. 13-156, 2015 U.S. Dist. LEXIS 25795 (D. Conn. Mar. 3, 2015). "*Reichhold* holds, in square opposition to Zurich's suggestion, that a policy's coverage of immovable risks in more than one state does not affect the application of section 193's special presumption with respect to lawsuits arising out of any given risk: if the law to be applied with respect to each is different in different cases, so be it." *Id.* at *13-14. *See also First State Ins. Co. v. Am. Home Assur. Co.*, 463 F. Supp. 3d 298 (D. Conn. 2020) ("With respect to liability insurance contracts, the starting point is § 193 of the Restatement (Second), which creates a rebuttable presumption in favor of the state where the insured risk is located. In order to overcome the presumption, another state's interest must outweigh those of the state where the insured risk is located and must be sufficiently compelling to trump the § 193 presumption.") (quoting *Reichhold*).

Delaware: In *In re Viking Pump, Inc.*, 148 A.3d 633, 651 (Del. 2016), the Supreme Court of Delaware, without analysis, held that it agreed with the choice of law conclusion reached by the Chancery Court in *Viking Pump, Inc. v. Century Indem. Co.*, 2 A.3d 76 (Del. Ch. Ct. 2009), which used a Second Restatement analysis and stated: "In cases like these, where a company obtains insurance for risks and operations in a variety of jurisdictions, Delaware courts have placed great weight on where an insured has its headquarters as the 'situs which link[s] all the parties together.' This judgment is reinforced by the intuition that an insured's headquarters staff is typically heavily involved in the contracting, negotiation, and performance of an insurance contract. In this case, Houdaille's headquarters takes on even more importance because its operations were widely spread throughout the United States. At its peak, Houdaille had several facilities in different states and therefore Houdaille's headquarters appears to be the only common link between the operations that Liberty Mutual and the Excess Insurers were insuring." *Id.* at 87-88.

In *Liggett Group, Inc. v. Affiliated FM Ins. Co.*, 788 A.2d 134, 137–44 (Del. Super. Ct. 2001), the Superior Court of Delaware, addressing coverage for over 1,000 tobacco health-related lawsuits, under in excess of 100 liability insurance policies issued over a 28-year span, applied a Second Restatement analysis to hold that the law of North Carolina controlled. The policyholder maintained its principal place of business in North Carolina for most of the relevant period, and the manufacturing operations and marketing functions giving rise to the alleged liability were centered in North Carolina for the entire period. The fact that many of the policies were negotiated through New York brokers was a relatively insignificant contact that did not require the application of New York law. *See also Annestella v. GEICO Gen. Ins. Co.*, No. K13C-11-027, 2015 Del. Super. LEXIS 346, at *6-7 (Del. Super. Ct. June 15, 2015) ("Delaware follows the Restatement (Second) Conflict of Laws's 'most significant relationship' test when resolving choice of law issues. Choice of law issues involving insurance coverage are resolved by analyzing the relevant contacts set forth in sections 188 (dealing with general contractual issues) and 193 (dealing specifically with fire, surety, and casualty insurance contracts) of the Restatement. These contacts must also be evaluated in light of the principles set forth in section 6 of the Restatement.").

The Supreme Court of Delaware recently addressed choice of law, in the insurance context, in *Certain Underwriters at Lloyds v. Chemtura Corp.*, 160 A.3d 457 (Del. 2017) and *Travelers Indem. Co. v. CNH Indus. Am.*, No. 420 2017, 2018 Del. LEXIS 334 (Del. July 16, 2018). In both instances the court undertook detailed analyses under the Restatement. The *Chemtura* Court held: "[T]his Court adopts the approach used by the Superior Court and the Court of Chancery on many occasions when confronted by similar problems. Because Uniroyal and its successors obtained an overall set of insurance coverage addressing risks across all of its operations, and because New York was the principal place of business for Uniroyal at the beginning of the coverage and there were a number of contacts with New York over time after the beginning of the coverage, this Court determines that the most significant relationship among the parties for this insurance program and its contracts is New York, and so New York law should be applied to resolve this contract dispute. This is based, in part, on the sensible understanding that a company's headquarters staff is usually heavily involved in managing insurance programs that cover the entire company." *Id.* at 470. The *CNH Indus.* Court examined *Chemtura* and held: "[A]pplying the law where each Tenneco subsidiary was located could allow 'the meaning of the contract[s] to vary arbitrarily.' Applying the law of Texas, which has the most significant relationship to the parties and the dispute, maintains 'certainty, predictability and uniformity' in interpreting the insurance contracts and provides 'ease in the determination and application of the law.'" *Id.* at *13. "The presumption in § 193, which states that '[t]he validity of a contract of . . . insurance and the rights created thereby are determined by the local law of the state which the parties understood was to be the principal location of the insured risk during the term of the policy'. . . . does not apply to policies [that] provide broad-based coverage across many jurisdictions for a company's enterprise-wide risks." *Id.* at *8. "[W]hen addressing a comprehensive insurance program, § 193's presumption is, at best, directionally helpful but arguably not conclusive. Rather, § 188's factors are the most appropriate way to determine the appropriate law." *Id.* at *9.

District of Columbia: The Court of Appeals of the District of Columbia, applying a "governmental interest" test under the Second Restatement, held that Colorado law controlled coverage for a series of lawsuits alleging that a brewery marketed alcohol to minors. The policyholder was based in Colorado, and the policy contained Colorado amendatory endorsements. The District's only connection to the dispute was that one of the four underlying lawsuits was filed in its courts. *Adolph Coors Co. v. Truck Ins. Exchange*, 960 A.2d 617, 620–21 (D.C. Cir. 2008). The court described the "governmental interest" test as follows: "Where a contract is silent on the matter, we conduct a 'governmental interest' analysis to determine which jurisdiction's law controls the interpretation and enforcement of the contract. This analysis requires us to consider several factors, including: (1) the place of contracting; (2) the place of negotiation of the contract; (3) the place of performance; (4) the location of the subject matter of the contract; (5) the residence and place of business of the parties; and (6) the principal location of the insured risk." *Id.* at 620. *See also Chicago Ins. Co. v. Paulson & Nace, PLLC*, 37 F. Supp. 3d 281 (D.D.C. 2014) (applying law of D.C., where insured law firm was headquartered, to decide coverage under legal malpractice policy for claim in Virginia) (*affirmed* 783 F.3d 897 (D.C. Cir. 2015)); *Potomac Elec. Power Co. v. Cal. Union Ins. Co.*, 777 F. Supp. 968, 973 (D.D.C. 1991) (applying law of the District, as the place of the policyholder's headquarters, rather than law of Maryland, the site of the underlying environmental contamination); *Cincinnati Ins. Co. v. All Plumbing, Inc. Serv., Parts Installation*, 983 F. Supp. 2d 162, 166 (D.D.C. 2013) ("Where no true conflict exists" between the law of two interested jurisdictions, "a court applies the law of the District of Columbia by default."); *Feld v. Fireman's Fund Ins. Co.*, 206 F. Supp. 3d 378 (D.D.C. 2016) ("D.C. employs the 'governmental interest' test to determine which state's law to apply.

The test involves a two-step inquiry: identify the governmental policy underlying the applicable law and then determine which state's policy would be most advanced by having its_law applied to the facts of the case. For insurance contracts, there is a presumption that the governing law is the 'local law of the state which the parties understood was to be the principal location of the insured risk during the term of the policy, unless with respect to the particular issue, some other state has a more significant relationship.' Restatement (Second) of Conflict of Laws § 193 (1971). D.C. courts look at six factors to determine whether another state has 'a more significant relationship': (1) the place of contracting; (2) the place of negotiation of the contract; (3) the place of performance; (4) the location of the subject matter of the contract; (5) the residence and place of business of the parties; and (6) the principal location of the insured risk.") (citations omitted); *Am. Nat'l Ins. Co. v. JPMorgan Chase & Co.*, 164 F. Supp. 3d 104, 108 (D.D.C. 2016) (characterizing's D.C.'s choice of law test as a blend between a "governmental interests analysis" and a "most significant relationship" test); *21st Century N. Am. Ins. Co. v. Nationwide Gen. Ins. Co.*, No. 14-00557, 2015 U.S. Dist. LEXIS 46390 (D.D.C. Apr. 9, 2015) (examining the factors set out in *Adolph Coors* to determine which state had a more substantial interest); *Rockhill Ins. Co. v. Hoffman-Madison Waterfront, LLC*, 417 F. Supp. 3d 50 (D.D.C. 2019) ("Both parties presume that District of Columbia of law applies. That presumption is correct for two reasons. District of Columbia law is appropriate in this case because the place of performance and the insured risk is in the District of Columbia.") (citing *Adolph Coors*).

Florida: The Supreme Court of Florida has "long adhered to the rule of lex loci contractus," which "provides that the law of the jurisdiction where the contract was executed governs the rights and liabilities of the parties in determining an issue of insurance coverage." *State Farm Mut. Auto. Ins. Co. v. Roach*, 945 So. 2d 1160, 1164 (Fla. 2006) (automobile coverage). The place of execution is usually where the policy was delivered to the policyholder. *Mid-Continent Cas. Co. v. Basdeo*, 742 F. Supp. 2d 1293, 1322 (S.D. Fla. 2010). Florida courts have carved out a narrow exception to the *lex loci* rule, for the purpose of necessary protection of a Florida citizen, or to enforce some paramount rule of public policy. "This has become known as the public policy exception. It requires *both* a Florida citizen in need of protection *and* a paramount Florida public policy." *Roach* at 1165 (emphasis in original); *see also USF&G v. Liberty Surplus Insurance Company*, No. 6:06-cv-1180-Orl-31UAM, 2007 U.S. Dist. LEXIS 77004 (M.D. Fla. Oct. 15, 2007) ("Although *Roach* was an automobile insurance case, the court did not in any way suggest that its pronouncements were limited to such policies."). The Eleventh Circuit predicted that Florida courts would, with respect to a multiple-risk policy providing liability and other coverage for nightclubs located in multiple states, apply a Second Restatement analysis under which coverage would depend on the law in which each club was located. *Shapiro v. Associated Int'l Ins. Co.*, 899 F.2d 1116, 1119–20 (11th Cir. 1990). No Florida state court has adopted *Shapiro*, and one Florida District Court decision held that *Shapiro* was restricted to the multirisk policy at issue. *CNL Hotels & Resorts, Inc. v. Houston Cas. Co.*, 505 F. Supp. 2d 1317, 1320–21 (M.D. Fla. 2007) (applying *lex loci contractus* to directors and officers liability policy). *See Embroidme.com, Inc. v. Travelers Prop. Cas. Co. of Am.*, 992 F. Supp. 2d 1259, 1263 (S.D. Fla. 2014) (Florida law applied where CGL policy declarations listed policyholder's Florida address, notwithstanding that one of six scheduled locations was in Massachusetts) (*affirmed with no choice of law discussion*, 845 F.3d 1099 (11th Cir. 2017)). In 2008, the Eleventh Circuit certified to the Supreme Court of Florida the question whether *lex loci contractus* applied to a construction defect coverage dispute regarding a commercial general liability policy issued in Massachusetts to a contractor headquartered there, *see U.S. Fid. & Guar. Co. v. Liberty Surplus Ins. Corp.*, 550 F.3d 1031, 1034–35 (11th Cir. 2008), but the parties settled before resolution of that question. *See Wausau Underwriters Ins. Co. v. Danfoss, LLC*, No. 14-14420, 2015 U.S. Dist. LEXIS 144828, at *21 (S.D. Fla. Oct. 26, 2015) ("Subsequent to *Shapiro*, in *Roach*, the Florida Supreme Court strongly endorsed the *lex loci contractus* doctrine without expressly limiting its holding to automobile insurance contracts, emphasizing: 'We have never retreated from our adherence to this rule in determining which state's law applies in interpreting contracts.' (citing *Roach*) Accordingly, this Court concludes that the Florida Supreme Court would apply the doctrine of *lex loci contractus* in determining what law governs the instant controversy."); *Sun Capital Partners, Inc. v. Twin City Fire Ins. Co.*, No. 12-81397, 2015 U.S. Dist. LEXIS 102445, at *14-20 (S.D. Fla. Aug. 5, 2015) (addressing in detail what is the "last act" under Florida's *lex loci contractus* doctrine); *Remedios v. Nat'l Fire & Marine Ins. Co.*, No. 19-21559, 2019 U.S. Dist. LEXIS 148498 (S.D. Fla. Aug. 29, 2019) (declining to apply the "public policy exception" to *lex loci contractus* – which applies Florida law, despite place of execution -- as there was no "paramount rule of public policy" at issue); *Prime Time Sports Grill, Inc. v. DTW 1991 Underwriting Ltd.*, No. 20-771, 2020 U.S. Dist. LEXIS 237338 (M.D. Fla. Dec. 17, 2020) ("When the contract deals with an insurance policy, the locus contractus is generally the state where the insured executed the insurance application."); *Riverside Apts. of Cocoa, LLC v. Landmark Am. Ins. Co.*, No. 18-1639, 2020 U.S. Dist. LEXIS

247984 (M.D. Fla. Dec. 4, 2020) (based on *lex loci contractus*, applying Georgia law, where the binder was issued) ("The Court seriously doubts that the legislature's regulation of surplus lines insurers implies a desire for Florida's general contract law to govern all disputes arising from surplus lines policies. Moreover, an implication to that effect will not suffice. If the legislature intended to abandon *lex loci contractus* in cases involving surplus lines insurance contracts, it needed to indicate such change clearly.").

Georgia: Georgia courts adhere to the common law rule of *lex loci contractus*, under which the law of the place of the delivery of the insurance contract controls. *General Tel. Co. of Southeast v. Trimm*, 311 S.E.2d 460 (Ga. 1984) (discussing history of *lex loci contractus* dating back to 1847). *See also O'Neal v. State Farm Mut. Auto. Ins. Co.*, 533 S.E.2d 781, 782 (Ga. Ct. App. 2000); *OneBeacon Am. Ins. Co. v. Catholic Diocese of Savannah*, 477 F. App'x 665, 669 (11th Cir. 2012); *Lima Delta Co. v. Global Aerospace, Inc.*, 752 S.E.2d 135 (Ga. Ct. App. 2013) (for purposes of *lex loci contractus*, the place in which the policy is delivered may be a place other than the insured's address on the policy) (policy delivered by insurer to Atlanta office of independent broker resulted in application of Georgia law); *Travelers Prop. Cas. Co. of Am. v. Cont'l Cas. Co.*, 226 F. Supp. 3d 1359 (N.D. Ga. 2017) ("Georgia follows the traditional choice of law rule of *lex loci contractus*, under which the validity, form, and effect of insurance contracts are governed by the law of the place where the contract was made. Insurance contracts are considered 'made' at the place where the contract was delivered to the insured. It is not disputed that both the Travelers Policies and Continental Policies were delivered to CKS at its offices in Atlanta, Georgia. Accordingly, the insurance coverage issues are controlled by Georgia law.") (citations omitted); *Owners Ins. Co. v. Brown*, No. 19-219, 2020 U.S. Dist. LEXIS 77369 (S.D. Ga. May 1, 2020) ("As is relevant here, Georgia law considers an insurance contract to be made where it is delivered. Here, both insurance policies contain cover letters addressed to Defendants at their Georgia addresses, and there is no indication that Defendants received the policies at any other location. Thus, Georgia law applies to Defendants' anticipatory breach of contract claim."). In *Mt. Hawley Ins. Co. v. East Perimeter Pointe Apts., LP*, No. 19-13824, 2021 U.S. App. LEXIS 15932 (11th Cir. May 27, 2021), the court, citing *Trimm*, noted that *lex loci contractus* has been Georgia's choice of law rule, governing contracts, since 1847. However, in interpreting *lex loci contractus*, the court concluded that "the Georgia Supreme Court has made it clear that *lex loci contractus* only permits Georgia courts to consider a foreign state's law when it involves its statutes or judicial decisions on those statutes. *Coon v. Med. Ctr., Inc.*, 300 Ga. 722, 797 S.E.2d 828, 833-34 (Ga. 2017). Where a foreign state has adopted the English common law and there is no statute from that state to govern a contractual dispute, the outcome of the dispute can then only be determined by that state's common law. And when a foreign state's common law is in play, Georgia courts and federal courts in Georgia will apply the common law as expounded by the courts of Georgia, not the common law of that foreign state." *Id.* at *12. Applying this rule, the court concluded that Georgia law controlled in late notice-prejudice dispute regardless of which state the policies had been delivered in (the Court did not rule on this issue), as the notice-prejudice rule was a product of common law.

Hawaii: "Hawaii's choice-of-law approach creates a presumption that Hawaii law applies unless another state's law would best serve the interests of the states and persons involved." *Mikelson v. United Services Auto. Ass'n*, 111 P.3d 601, 607 (Haw. 2005) ("This court has moved away from the traditional and rigid conflict-of-laws rules in favor of the modern trend towards a more flexible approach looking to the state with the most significant relationship to the parties and subject matter. This flexible approach places primary emphasis . . . on deciding which state would have the strongest interest in seeing its laws applied to the particular case. Hence, this court has said that the interests of the states and applicable public policy reasons should determine whether Hawai'i law or another state's law should apply. The pre-ferred analysis, [then] in our opinion, would be an assessment of the interests and policy factors involved with a purpose of arriving at a desirable result in each situation."). The Supreme Court of Hawaii, relying on that approach, rather than on the Second Restatement, held that Hawaii had the strongest interest in coverage for environmental contamination in Hawaii, notwithstanding that California was the place of contracting and the principal place of business of the insurer and the policy-holder. *Del Monte Fresh Produce (Haw.), Inc. v. Fireman's Fund Ins. Co.*, 183 P.3d 734, 740–41 & n.12 (Haw. 2007). *See Ingalls v. Gov't Employees Ins. Co.*, 903 F. Supp. 2d 1049, 1056 (D. Haw. 2012) (noting state's rejection of strict Second Restatement analysis); *Allied World Surplus Lines Ins. Co. v. Haw. Med. Serv. Ass'n*, No. 17-00156, 2017 U.S. Dist. LEXIS 160496 (D. Haw. Sept. 27, 2017) ("Review of the Policies demonstrates that Hawaii is the state with the most significant interest in having its laws applied. Defendant HMSA is a company organized and existing under the laws of the State of Hawaii with its principal place of business in Hawaii."); *Hanover Ins. Co. v. Anova Food, LLC*, 173 F. Supp. 3d 1008 (D. Hawaii 2016) (detailed analysis of numerous choice of law factors) ("There are no facts alleged that demonstrate that the patent infringement and false advertising claims alleged in the Underlying Lawsuit were exclusive to Hawaii. The alleged injury did not occur only within the State of Hawaii. Nothing in the contents of the policies suggests that Hawaii is the state with the most significant relationship to the insurance contracts at issue. There are no references to Hawaii law or provisions directed specifically to locations in Hawaii."); *Dengler v. Horace Mann Ins. Co.*, No. 17-68, 2018 U.S. Dist. LEXIS 234111 (D. Haw. Feb. 22, 2018) ("This Court concludes that Idaho has the strongest interest in seeing its law applied in the instant case because: the Denglers obtained the Policies in Idaho; and Plaintiff and B.P.D. reside in Idaho. Although the accident in question occurred in Hawai'i, B.P.D. was merely a transient visitor to Hawai'i at the time of the accident."); *Puna Geothermal Venture v. Allianz Global Risks US Ins. Co.*, No. 19-00451, 2019 U.S. Dist. LEXIS 211661 (D. Haw. Dec. 5, 2019) (addressing the scope of a choice of law provision in a policy).

Idaho: Idaho applies the "most significant relationship" test of the Second Restatement. *Ryals v. State Farm Mut. Auto. Ins. Co.*, 1 P.3d 803, 805–06 (Idaho 2000) (Idaho law controlled coverage for New York accident, under policy issued in Idaho, with respect to vehicle principally garaged in Idaho). The Idaho District Court held that, where the named insured under a CGL policy was headquartered in Idaho, the insured risk was work performed at job sites in Idaho, the named insured acquired the policy in Idaho through an Idaho insurance producer, the policy was issued in Idaho, one of the additional insured endorsements was for an Idaho development company, the policy reflected an Idaho address, and the accident occurred in Idaho, Idaho law controlled, even though the putative "additional insured" was based in Idaho and the underlying plaintiff was a Washington resident. *Nautilus Ins. Co. v. Pro-Set Erectors, Inc.*, 928 F. Supp. 2d 1208, 1218 (D. Idaho 2013). *See also Harmon v. State Farm Mut. Auto. Ins. Co.*, 394 P.3d 796 (Idaho 2017) (upholding a choice of law provision in a policy).

Illinois: In determining the law governing an insurance policy, the Supreme Court of Illinois looks to "the location of the subject matter, the place of delivery of the contract, the domicile of the insured or of the insurer, the place of the last act to give rise to a valid contract, the place of performance, or other place bearing a rational relationship to the general contract." *Lapham-Hickey Steel Corp. v. Protection Mut. Ins. Co.*, 655 N.E.2d 842, 845 (Ill. 1995). Thus, in a dispute under a liability component of an all-risk policy, insuring property in six different states, the law of Illinois, as the policyholder's home state, controlled whether an insurer was obligated to defend a claim for pollution at a Minnesota site. *Id.* Illinois intermediate appellate decisions generally have applied the law of the policyholder's home state in determining the law governing CGL policies. *Water Applications & Sys. Corp. v. Bituminous Cas. Corp.*, 986 N.E.2d 124, 136 (Ill. App. Ct. 2013); *Liberty Mut. Fire Ins. Co. v. Woodfield Mall, L.L.C.*, 941 N.E.2d 209, 216 (Ill. App. Ct. 2010) (declining to follow pre *Lapham-Hickey* appellate decisions that gave "undue weight to the location of the insured risk in Illinois" and applying law of the policyholder's home state to a "commercial general liability policy insuring all the locations of a major, nationwide retail chain"); *Maremont Corp. v. Cheshire*, 681 N.E.2d 548, 551 (Ill. App. Ct. 1997) ("Other than being the location of the polluted site, South Carolina had nothing to do with the negotiating, purchasing, delivering or performing of the insurance policies."). Where there is no conflict between the law of Illinois and of another state, an Illinois court applies forum law. *Landmark Am. Ins. Co. v. NIP Grp., Inc.*, 962 N.E.2d 562, 570 (Ill. App. Ct. 2011). To establish a true conflict with Illinois law and another state's law, it is insufficient for a party to cite federal district court decisions predicting the other state's law. *Bridgeview Health Care Ctr., Ltd. v. State Farm Fire & Cas. Co.*, 10 N.E.3d 902, 906 (Ill. 2014). In *Cincinnati Ins. Co. v. Northridge Builders, Inc.*, No. 12-9102, 2015 U.S. Dist. LEXIS 132165 (N.D. Ill. Sept. 30, 2015), an Illinois federal court addressed coverage under a CGL policy, for a contractor with a principal place of business in Illinois, for construction defects to a home it built in Indiana. In determining that Illinois law applied, the court stated: "Parallels between this case and *Lapham-Hickey* should be obvious: Northridge is an Illinois corporation with most of its business in Illinois, the Policies were delivered in Illinois and the Policies covered sites in three states. Precisely the same concerns that animated *Lapham-Hickey* point strongly (and indeed conclusively) in favor of a finding that Illinois law applies." *Id.* at *10. Further, the court explained that "only one consideration listed in *Lapham-Hickey* weighs in favor of the application of Indiana law to the Policies -- that the site of the insured loss is in Indiana -- and furthermore because *Lapham-Hickey* (and *Liberty Mut.* as well) [*Liberty Mut. Fire Ins. Co. v. Woodfield Mall, L.L.C.*, 941 N.E.2d 209 (Ill. Ct. App. 2010)] deemphasized the importance of that very consideration under facts closely analogous to those presented here, the law of Illinois unquestionably governs the interpretation of the Policies." *Id.* at *11. *See also Cincinnati Ins. Co. v. Chapman*, 55 N.E.3d 74, 83 (Ill. Ct. App. 2016) ("The record shows that at the time the policy was renewed in 2006, Phoenix was an Indiana corporation with a single office in Mt. Vernon, Indiana, while Cincinnati is an Ohio corporation with its principle place of business in Cincinnati, Ohio. The record does not indicate whether Phoenix was licensed to conduct business in Illinois. The only connection to Illinois is that the alleged fax from the underlying lawsuit was sent to an Illinois resident. Moreover, the place bearing a rational relationship to the insurance contract is Indiana. Accordingly, Indiana law must govern the insurance agreement between Cincinnati and Phoenix.") (citing *Lapham-Hickey*); *Bull v. Ill. Union Ins. Co.*, No. 16-11446, 2017 U.S. Dist. LEXIS 119479 (N.D. Ill. July 31, 2017) ("Per Illinois's choice-of-law rules, New York law controls because the policy was delivered in New York to U.S. Coachways, a New York corporation which operated its business in New York."). However, in *Frankenmuth Mut. Ins. Co. v. Hockey Cup, LLC*, No. 18-8142, 2019 U.S. Dist. LEXIS 160278 (N.D. Ill. Sept. 20, 2019), the court cited, among other authorities, the test from *Lapham-Hickey* and concluded that New York law governed, despite the policy being issued in Illinois: "Where the insured company conducts business nationwide...the location of the insured risk is the place where the insured's liability actually arises. . . . In this case, as in *Moonlight Design* [*Western Am. Ins. Co. v. Moonlight Design, Inc.*, 95 F. Supp. 2d 838 (N.D. Ill. 2000)], A&R and Dewey's liability arose in New York. While is true that the insureds are domiciled in Illinois and that the insurance contract was delivered in this state, the NHL Suit was filed in New York by entities headquartered in that state; it asserts claims under federal and New York state law; and it challenges defendants' use of the NHL's intellectual property in marketing and sales conducted in New York and elsewhere. . . . In view of the 'special emphasis' Illinois law gives to the location of the risk, *Society of Mount Carmel*, 643 N.E. at 1287, I conclude that New York law governs the interpretation of the policy at issue." *Hockey Cup* at *3-4.

Indiana: The Supreme Court of Indiana, applying Section 193 of the Second Restatement, has held that an "insurance policy is governed by the law of the principal location of the insured risk during the term of the policy." *Dunn v. Meridian Mut. Ins. Co.*, 836 N.E.2d 249, 251 (Ind. 2005). The Supreme Court of Indiana brought some long-needed clarity to how that principle applies to a CGL policy covering risks in multiple states, resolving a conflict between intermediate appellate decisions. Indiana courts apply a uniform-contract-approach, under which the law of a single state governs all issues in a coverage case. *Nat'l Union Fire Ins. Co. of Pittsburgh, Pa. v. Standard Fusee Corp.*, 940 N.E.2d 810, 815 (Ind. 2010). The controlling law is that of the principal location of the insured risk or, if there is no principal location, the law of the state with the most intimate contacts with the insurance contract. *Id.* at 815–16. "The general development of Indiana's choice-of-law rules leads us to conclude that the uniform-contract-interpretation approach is more consistent with our jurisprudence, as it applies a single state's law to the entire contract. In the 65 years since *W.H. Barber Co.* [*v. Hughes*, 63 N.E.2d 417 (Ind. 1945)], we have followed a choice-of-law rule in contracts cases that contemplates contacts in multiple states but applies only the law of the state with the most intimate contacts. . . . We see no reason why pollution sites in multiple states should be treated any differently than other contacts." *Id.* at 815. *Standard Fusee*, following a Second Restatement § 188 analysis, held that, where a CGL policy covered one polluted site in Maryland and one in Indiana, and where the insured's corporate headquarters had always been in Maryland, Maryland was the principal location of the insured risk. *Id.* at 816. The *Standard Fusee* decision left open the possibility that in certain cases, where the number of insured sites was greater in one state than in any other, the principal location of the insured risk could differ from the state of the policyholder's headquarters. *Id.* (citing *Am. Employers Ins. Co. v. Coachmen Indus., Inc.*, 838 N.E.2d 1172, 1181 (Ind. Ct. App. 2005)). In *Northern Assur. Co. of Am. v. Thomson Inc.*, 996 N.E.2d 785, 797 (Ind. Ct. App. 2013), the Indiana Court of Appeals, following a Second Restatement analysis under *Standard Fusee*, held that California law applied to determining coverage where two of the three pollution sites at issue were located in California, the cleanup was directed by the California EPA, all of the policies were issued at a California address and the broker involved in procuring the policies was in California). ("The only connection with Indiana that these policies have is that Thomson, a corporation with long-established ties to Indiana, acquired Technicolor's assets in 2000, decades after the policies were issued and years after most of the alleged pollution would have occurred."). *See also Landis + GYR Inc. v. Zurich American Ins. Co.*, No. 16-82, 2019 U.S. Dist. LEXIS 6964 (N.D. Ind. Jan. 15, 2019) (undertaking a lengthy and detailed Restatement analysis and applying New York law to some policies and Connecticut law to others) ("Landis has provided some evidence to show that the bulk of Landis's operations occurred in Indiana. However, Landis was headquartered in New York and Connecticut and the vast majority of evidence indicates that the place of contracting and negotiation occurred in New York."); *Cincinnati Ins. Co. v. Sohacki*, No. 20A-MI-1823, 2021 Ind. App. Unpub. LEXIS 343 (Ind. Ct. App. April 27, 2021) ("The insured company, Joint Venture, is an Illinois limited-liability company with its principal place of business in Illinois. The Policy was issued in Illinois and contains references to Illinois law, and the Nelsons reside in Illinois. Because the insured risks—here Joint Venture and the Nelsons—reside in Illinois, we conclude the principal location of the insured risk is Illinois.") ("The main contact with Indiana here was the location of the accident. But given the case's strong ties to Illinois, the location of the accident is not dispositive.").

Iowa: The Supreme Court of Iowa applies Sections 188 and 193 of the Second Restatement to questions of coverage under insurance contracts. *Gabe's Constr. Co., Inc. v. United Capitol Ins. Co.*, 539 N.W.2d 144, 146–47 (Iowa 1995). *Gabe's* rejected the contention that Minnesota law governed an Iowa general contractor's claim for coverage as an additional insured under a Minnesota subcontractor's CGL policy with respect to bodily injury sustained at an Iowa construction site. Because the "general liability coverage applied separately to each insured," and because the general contractor sought coverage under an endorsement issued solely with respect to the Iowa job site, the principal location of the insured risk was Iowa. *Id.* Distinguishing *Gabe's* as construing an endorsement "specifically limited to coverage of one project in one state," a federal court applied Iowa law to a commercial property policy covering an Iowa company's properties in multiple states, even though the dispute involved a property in Florida. *Weitz Co., LLC v. Lexington Ins. Co.*, 982 F. Supp. 2d 975, 990 (S.D. Iowa 2013). If a party does not sufficiently plead and prove that another state's law controls, an Iowa court will apply Iowa law. *Talen v. Employers Mut. Cas. Co.*, 703 N.W.2d 395, 408–09 (Iowa 2005). In *Travelers Prop. Cas. Co. of Am. v. Flexsteel Indus.*, 847 N.W.2d 237, 2014 Iowa App. LEXIS 277 (Iowa Ct. App. 2014) the Court of Appeal of Iowa undertook a detailed choice of law analysis, under § 193, for purposes of interpreting a pollution exclusion (and did so as well as under § 188 and arrived at the same result). Weighing these competing arguments, the court held that Indiana law applied: "All agree that that the key determination under this provision is the 'principal location of the risk.' Flexsteel argues the principal location is Indiana. It notes that '[t]he only sites for which [it] seeks coverage are located in Indiana; the only lawsuits for which [it] seeks a defense were filed in Indiana; and the only allegations against Flexsteel relate to its alleged conduct in Indiana.' Travelers counters that '[w]here as here, the liability policies are multiple-risk policies covering a national, publicly traded company conducting business in virtually all fifty states, there is no principal location of the risk, and Section 193 carries little or no weight in the analysis.'" *Id.* at *11-12. *See also Weitz Co., LLC v. Lexington Ins. Co.*, 982 F. Supp. 2d 975, 991-92 (S.D. Iowa 2013) ('This Court is unconvinced that the location of the underlying project, and the claimed damage in Florida outweigh the contacts with Illinois. The location of where a risk subsequently manifests into a claim has little to do with the risk's principal location at the time the contract is entered into. . . . Here, Lexington/Allied were insuring against the risk of injury to Hyatt's real and personal property throughout the United States and Territories. The principal location of the risk at the time of contracting was not Florida. In fact, Weitz concedes the fact that 'Lexington/Allied provided property insurance to Hyatt for numerous properties nationwide — covering hundreds of millions, if not billions, of dollars of construction and physical assets — on an annual basis.' Furthermore, Iowa courts place less weight on the location of an accident or claimed damage, and instead, rely on the place of contracting and the negotiation of the contract to determine choice-of-law questions.") (*affirmed with no choice of law discussion*, 786 F.3d 641 (8th Cir. 2015)).

Kansas: The Kansas Supreme Court has held, in cases not involving CGL policies, that "Kansas follows the general rule that the law of the state where the insurance contract is made controls." *Safeco Ins. Co. of Am. v. Allen*, 941 P.2d 1365, 1372 (Kan. 1997). Applying that principle to a CGL policy, the Kansas Court of Appeals held that the place of the delivery to the policyholder was the state where the contract was made. *Cent. Power Sys. & Servs., Inc. v. Universal Underwriters Ins. Co.*, 319 P.3d 562, 566 (Kan. Ct. App. 2014). Surveying Kansas *lex loci contractus* decisions, the Tenth Circuit recognized that the First Restatement sometimes looks to the law of the place of performance, but "only when the question goes to the manner and method of performance." *Moses v. Halstead*, 581 F.3d 1248, 1252 (10th Cir. 2009). Construing that exception narrowly, the Tenth Circuit held that the law of Missouri, where a lawsuit was pending, governed details of the insurer's defense of its policyholder, but that the law of the policyholder's home state of Kansas governed whether an obligation arose to settle that lawsuit within policy limits. *Id.* at 1252–54. *See also Greene v. CSAA Fire & Cas. Ins. Co.*, No. 16-4144, 2017 U.S. Dist. LEXIS 149668, at *5 (D. Kan. Sept. 15, 2017) ("Under Kansas law, insurance contracts are governed by the law of the state where the contract was made.") (citing *Allen*); *Sexton v. Am. Nat'l Prop. & Cas. Co.*, No. 14-2384, 2015 U.S. Dist. LEXIS 97365, at *10 (D. Kan. July 27, 2015) ("Kansas courts apply the Restatement (First) of Conflict of Laws when determining choice of law issues. If a contract dispute goes to the substance of the obligation, the Court should apply *lex loci contractus*, or the law of the state where the contract was made. Generally, a cause of action for bad faith conduct against an insurer relating to the duty to defend or settle goes to the substance of the obligation. Although it appears that the parties agree that their dispute goes to the substance of the contract and that the law of the state where the contract was made should therefore control this action, the parties disagree on where the contract was made."); *Bedivere Ins. Co. v. Blue Cross & Blue Shield of Kan., Inc.*, No. 18-2371, 2019 U.S. Dist. LEXIS 171308 (D. Kan. Sept. 30, 2019) ("The insured is a Kansas entity, with a Kansas address on the policy, and the insurance policies at times reference Kansas law within them. The court thus applies Kansas law."); *Wood v. Safeco Ins. Co. of Am.*, No. 20-2222, 2021 U.S. Dist. LEXIS 49642 (D. Kan. Mar. 17, 2021) ("[T]he Tenth Circuit [*Moses v. Halstead*, 581 F.3d 1248 (10th Cir. 2009)] has predicted that the Kansas Supreme Court would follow the law of the place of contracting on a claim alleging an insurer's bad faith refusal to settle.").

Kentucky: The Supreme Court of Kentucky applies Sections 188 and 193 of the Second Restatement to questions of coverage under insurance contracts. *Lewis v. Am. Family Ins. Group*, 555 S.W.2d 579, 581–82 (Ky. 1977); *State Farm Mut. Auto. Ins. Co. v. Hodgkiss-Warrick*, 413 S.W.3d 875, 879 (Ky. 2013). Applying Kentucky choice-of-law principles to coverage under a construction manager's professional liability policy for defective work on a Kentucky golf course, the Sixth Circuit held that Tennessee law applied because the policy "was issued to Tennessee citizens, was negotiated by a Tennessee citizen with an insurance agent located in Tennessee, and was issued by an insurer authorized to do business in Tennessee." *Security Ins. Co. v. Kevin Tucker & Assocs., Inc.*, 64 F.3d 1001, 1006 (6th Cir. 1995). *See also Cincinnati Ins. Co. v. Crossmann Communities P'ship*, No. 05-470-KSF, 2008 U.S. Dist. LEXIS 25188 (E.D. Ky. Mar. 28, 2008) (applying same analysis to CGL policy issued to Indiana-based general contractor); *Lacrosse v. Owners Ins. Co.*, No. 2015-000418, 2016 Ky. App. LEXIS 204, at *7 (Ky. Ct. App. Dec. 22, 2016) (Kentucky's general choice-of-law rule [noting that it is the Second Restatement's "most significant relationship" test] is only disregarded when Kentucky's public policy clearly overwhelmingly disfavors application of the foreign state's law."); *Grange Prop. & Cas. Co. v. Tenn. Farmers Mut. Ins. Co.*, 445 S.W.3d 51, 56 (Ky. Ct. App. 2014) ("Since the issue here is the construction and application of the Tennessee insurance contract, the above-enumerated factors far outweigh Grange's arguments that Kentucky law should apply since the accident occurred in Kentucky while Pruitt was driving a vehicle, insured by Grange, as an employee of a Kentucky company. In our estimation, the significant transaction is not the accident but the interpretation of the UM coverage provided by Tennessee Farmers' insurance contract. Thus, we conclude that Tennessee law, rather than Kentucky law, governs the insurance contract dispute.") (noting no distinction in the rule because the dispute was between two insurance companies); *Woods v. Std. Fire Ins. Co.*, 411 F. Supp. 3d 397 (E.D. Ky. 2019) ("Notwithstanding the outcome of the most significant relationship test,

Woods contends that Kentucky law should apply as a matter of public policy. It is true that Kentucky courts may refuse to apply the law of another jurisdiction when application of said law will result in enforcement of contractual provisions that contravene Kentucky's public policy."). *But see Asher v. Unarco Material Handling, Inc.*, 737 F. Supp. 2d 662, 667–74 (E.D. Ky. 2010) (Kentucky law governed Kentucky subcontractor's claim for coverage as additional insured under CGL policy issued to Illinois general contractor); *South Fifth Towers, LLC v. Aspen Ins. UK, Ltd.*, 763 Fed. Appx. 401 (6th Cir. 2019) ("Admittedly, the insurance policy was issued in New York, South Fifth obtained it through a New York broker, and South Fifth is a New York citizen. However, the building's location and Kentucky's strong choice-of-law bias outweigh these New York connections. Thus, we will use Kentucky law to interpret the policy.").

Louisiana: Under the Louisiana Civil Code, "an issue of conventional obligations is governed by the law of the state whose policies would be most seriously impaired if its law were not applied to that issue." LA. CIV. CODE ANN. art. 3537. The Court of Appeals of Louisiana held that the law of Belgium, not Louisiana, governed coverage for an asbestosis injury claim involving asbestos products delivered across the United States and Canada. Louisiana was merely "one location among many that could be considered the object of the contract. … A contrary conclusion could subject this policy to 50 different interpretations based on the state in which a plaintiff files suit, thereby destroying any predictability or uniformity of application." *Murden v. ACandS, Inc.*, 921 So. 2d 165, 172 (La. Ct. App. 2005). *See also Norfolk S. Corp. v. Cal. Union Ins. Co.*, 859 So. 2d 167, 181 (La. Ct. App. 2003) (CGL policies "intended to provide indemnity to [policyholder] for liability arising out of the conduct of its business, regardless of the location of the risk"); *In re FEMA Trailer Formaldehyde Prods. Liab. Litig.*, 780 F. Supp. 2d 514, 520–23 (E.D. La. 2011) (law of policyholder's home state of Florida, not law of Louisiana, governed coverage for Louisiana claims against procurer of modular housing units for victims of Hurricane Katrina); *Kirschenbaum v. Spraggins*, 752 F. Supp. 2d 728, 740–41 (E.D. La. 2010) (finding, even though parties assumed Louisiana law controlled coverage for Louisiana injury, that governing law was that of policyholder's Pennsylvania headquarters); *Contreras v. Vesper*, 214 So. 3d 898, 902 (La. Ct. App. 2016) ("Since the insurance policy at issue was issued in Mississippi and the accident occurred in Louisiana, Plaintiffs contend we must first determine whether Mississippi or Louisiana law governs. Under La. C.C. art. 3537, 'an issue of conventional obligations is governed by the law of the state whose policies would be most seriously impaired if its laws were not applied to that issue.'"); *Endurance Am. Specialty Ins. Co. v. Dual Trucking & Transp., LLC*, No. 17-1293, 2018 U.S. Dist. LEXIS 180359 (E.D. La. Oct. 22, 2018) ("Louisiana has a substantial interest in the uniform application of its laws governing insurance contracts issued in this state. Montana has an interest in providing a remedy for torts that occur in Montana, but the particular dispute in this case involves the interpretation and enforcement of the policy issued in Louisiana. The Court finds Louisiana law applies."); *Q Clothier New Orleans LLC v. Twin City Fire Ins. Co.*, No. 20-1470, 2021 U.S. Dist. LEXIS 78244 (E.D. La. April 23, 2021) ("defendant does not indicate how Texas's policies would be impaired if this Court were not to apply Texas); LA. CIV. CODE ANN. art. 3537 was effective on Jan. 1, 1992. Thus, caution should be used if examining earlier cases.

Maine: The Maine Supreme Judicial Court, applying a Second Restatement analysis, held that Maine law governed CGL coverage for a New Hampshire–based contractor doing business in Maine, New Hampshire, and Vermont, with respect to the construction of a school located in Maine. *Baybutt Constr. Corp. v. Commercial Union Ins. Co.*, 455 A.2d 914 (Me. 1983), *rev'd on other grounds*, *Peerless Ins. Co. v. Brennon*, 564 A.2d 383 (Me. 1989). "In a multiple risk policy which, as in the instant case, was clearly intended to afford comprehensive liability in the three states of Maine, New Hampshire and Vermont, the authorities have treated such policies in respect to the location of a particular risk in one of the states covered by the contract as if a separate policy had been issued to cover only the risks in that state. The rationale for such a holding is based on the fact that the location of the insurance risk in a particular state pinpoints the jurisdiction that has the greatest interests in the contract and any issues arising therefrom. Thus, the rights of the insured and the responsibility of the insurer under their insurance contract in this case must be determined under Maine law." *Id.* at 919. "In no way in the instant case can the mere fact … that the construction company was a New Hampshire corporation and that the insurance contract was issued in New Hampshire be considered of greater significance, whether by reason of state contact or governmental interest, than the location, here in Maine, of the insured risk." *Id.*at 918. *See also Ted Berry Co. v. Excelsior Ins. Co.*, 997 F. Supp. 2d 66, 67 (D. Me. 2014) ("The insurance policy was issued in Maine through a Maine agent. The damage for which the insured seeks coverage occurred to a municipality in New Hampshire. If I were to ignore that earlier agreement [reached by the parties that Maine law applies] and apply Maine choice-of-law principles, I would probably find that New Hampshire law applies to this dispute." (citing *Baybutt*). *But see Am. Employers' Ins. Co. v. DeLorme Pub. Co., Inc.*, 39 F. Supp. 2d 64, 72 (D. Me. 1999) ("Maine law is applicable because the insured's risk—the business of [the insured]—is located in Maine.").

Maryland: Although Maryland follows the *lex loci contractus* rule, the Court of Appeals of Maryland, the state's highest court, has recognized the "limited *renvoi*" exception, under which Maryland will apply its own law to an insurance contract made in another state if and only if that other state's choice-of-law rules favor the application of Maryland law. *Am. Motorists Ins. Co. v. ARTRA Group, Inc.*, 659 A.2d 1295, 1304 (Md. 1995). Thus, Maryland law governed CGL coverage for pollution in Maryland where, although the insurance contract was formed in Illinois, the Maryland Court of Appeals determined that an Illinois court would apply the law of Maryland. *Id.* at 1302–03. For purposes of the *lex loci contractus* rule, the fact that a policyholder is headquartered in a particular state, or that a contract was countersigned in a particular state, is not dispositive in determining the "last act necessary" to give the policy binding effect. *See TIG Ins. Co. v. Monongahela Power Co.*, 209 Md. App. 146, 166 (2012), *aff'd*, 86 A.3d 1245 (Md. 2014). The rule of *ARTRA Group* was reiterated in *Perini/Tompkins Joint Venture v. Ace Am. Ins. Co.*, 738 F.3d 95 (4th Cir. 2013): "Under certain circumstances, however, Maryland choice of law rules follow the renvoi doctrine, an exception to the *lex loci contractus* rule. Under this exception, a Maryland court may disregard the rule of *lex loci contractus* and apply Maryland law, if 1) Maryland has the most significant relationship, or, at least, a substantial relationship with respect to the contract issue presented; and 2) The state where the contract was entered into would not apply its own substantive law, but instead would apply Maryland substantive law to the issue before the court." *Id.* at 100-101. In *Brownlee v. Liberty Mut. Fire Ins. Co.*, 175 A.3d 697 (Md. 2017), Maryland's highest court observed that, as an exception to *lex loci contractus*, Maryland law still governs when the law of the otherwise applicable state is contrary to a strong Maryland public policy. *Id.* at 701. "Nevertheless, for Maryland public policy to override the *lex loci contractus* rule, the public policy must be very strong and not merely a situation in which Maryland law is different from the law of another jurisdiction." *Id.* The court held that "[a]bsent a legislative affirmation that pollution exclusion clauses are against public policy, we decline to declare that Georgia's law violates Maryland's public policy. Therefore, Georgia's interpretation of the pollution exclusion clause governs here." *Id.* at 712. *See also Balt. Scrap Corp. v. RLI Ins. Co.*, 493 F. Supp. 3d 433 (D. Md. 2020) (using *lex loci contractuts* and applying Maryland law, where the policy was apparently entered into).

Massachusetts: Applying the Second Restatement, the Supreme Judicial Court of Massachusetts held that New York law governed coverage for asbestos claims against a New York manufacturer because whether "there is a duty to defend or to indemnify under a nationwide comprehensive general liability policy as to such a claim should not depend on the law of the jurisdiction governing that particular claim but rather should be determined by the law governing the interpretation of the insurance policy and its issuance." *W.R. Grace & Co. v. Hartford Acc. & Indem. Co.*, 555 N.E.2d 214, 221–22 (Mass. 1990). *See also W.R. Grace & Co. v. Md. Cas. Co.*, 600 N.E.2d 176, 179 (Mass. App. Ct. 1992) (applying law of New York, rather than law of Massachusetts, where environmental contamination occurred), *rev. denied*, 604 N.E.2d 35 (Mass. 1992). More recently, a Massachusetts appeals court, following a lengthy choice of law analysis under Second Restatement § 188 and § 193, held: "[D]espite the fact that the underlying claims involved in this case arose in Rhode Island in connection with a Rhode Island operating company, we believe the insurance contracts as a whole, and the circumstances connected to their issuance, point toward the application of Massachusetts law. . . . Where relevant contacts and considerations are balanced, or nearly so, we are inclined to resolve the choice by choosing that law which would carry out and validate the transaction in accordance with intention, in preference to a law that would tend to defeat it. We conclude that the intention of the parties to the OneBeacon insurance contracts was uniformity of coverage, so that the operations of multiple companies were insured as a single risk under a single policy, at a reduced cost. We think application of Massachusetts law provides the uniformity that was sought by EUA and its operating companies when they contracted together for comprehensive insurance coverage." *OneBeacon America Insurance Company v. Narragansett Electric Company*, 57 N.E.3d 18, 23-24 (Mass. App. Ct. 2016). *See also NES Equip. Servs. Corp. v. Acadia Ins. Co.*, No. 14-1064, 2016 Mass. Super. LEXIS 367 (Mass. Super. Ct. Sept. 30, 2016) (citing *W.R. Grace* (1990) and *Narragansett Electric* and concluding that Maryland law applied as negotiation and procurement of liability policy took place there) ("Such a result produces coherent interstate insurance coverage; appears to conform to justified expectations; offers the prospect of certainty, predictability, and uniformity of result; provides relative ease in the determination and application of the governing law; and looks to the law of the [s]tate which, as to the legal issues involved, has the most significant relationship with the transaction and the parties."); *Phoenix Ins. Co. v. Ragnar Benson Constr. LLC.*, 404 F. Supp. 3d 427 (D. Mass. 2019) ("[W]hile an underlying tort claim might properly be resolved under the laws of the State where the injury occurred, the obligation of an insurer to defend and indemnify against that claim is more appropriately determined by reference to the insurance contract itself and the circumstances of its issuance.") (quoting *Narragansett Electric*). *But see Stonewall Ins. Co. v. Travelers Cas. & Sur. Co.*, 677 F. Supp. 2d 420, 422 (D. Mass. 2010) (without citing *W.R. Grace* decisions, holding that Texas law governed an insurer's claim for contribution under a policy issued to a Florida-based parent corporation because the subsidiary at issue was based in Texas, the majority of defense costs were incurred in Texas, and a Texas law firm generated over 70 percent of the defense costs).

Michigan: The Supreme Court of Michigan applied a Second Restatement analysis to determine the law governing a contract. *Chrysler Corp. v. Skyline Indus. Servs., Inc.*, 528 N.W.2d 698, 703 (Mich. 1995). Intermediate state appellate decisions have applied Section 193 to insurance policies. *Farm Bur. Ins. Co. v. Abalos*, 742 N.W.2d 624, 626–27 (Mich. Ct. App. 2007) (law of Michigan, where vehicle was principally garaged, controlled coverage under automobile policy with respect to accident in Ohio). A Michigan District Court, engaging in an extensive choice-of-law analysis, held that the law of a single state governs the construction of an insurance contract under the Second Restatement and, therefore, Michigan law controlled coverage under a Michigan-based corporation's CGL policy for environmental contamination occurring in California. *Aetna Cas. & Sur. Co. v. Dow Chem. Co.*, 883 F. Supp. 1101, 1104–10 (E.D. Mich. 1995). *See also Mill's Pride, Inc. v. Continental Ins. Co.*, 300 F.3d 701, 708–09 (6th Cir. 2002) (law of Ohio, as policyholder's headquarters and place of negotiation of policy, controlled coverage under CGL policy for Michigan trademark action, where settlement with underlying Michigan plaintiff ended any Michigan interest in contract dispute); *Wausau Underwriters Ins. Co. v. Reliable Transp. Specialists, Inc.*, No. 15-12954, 2016 U.S. Dist. LEXIS 103103, at *8 (E.D. Mich. Aug. 5, 2015) (discussing *Chrysler Corp.* and undertaking a Second Restatement analysis) ("Although the insured risk was one of many within a multiple risk policy, it is considered insured by a single policy for the purposes of the choice-of-law analysis. Because the insured risk was garaged and contemplated to be insured in Michigan, any contract disputes arising out of the Wausau Policy will be governed by Michigan law."); *Whitehouse Condo. Group, LLC v. Cincinnati Ins. Co.*, 569 Fed. Appx. 413, 415 (6th Cir. 2014) ("The insurance policy here has no choice-of-law provision, so we must consider the following five factors, as instructed by the Michigan Supreme Court: place of contracting, place of negotiation, place of performance, location of the subject-matter of the contract, and place of incorporation of the parties.") (citing case law that cites Second Restatement § 188); *Nat'l Cont'l*

Ins. Co. v. Aiazbekov, 818 Fed. Appx. 468 (6th Cir. 2020) ("As in *Abalos*, the relevant Restatement factors favor the state of contracting, not the state where the accident occurred. And as in *Mill's Pride*, uniformity concerns favor that state too.").

Minnesota: Minnesota applies the "significant contacts test" for choice-of-law analyses, "which consists of the following choice-influencing factors: (1) Predictability of results; (2) Maintenance of interstate and international order; (3) Simplification of the judicial task; (4) Advancement of the forum's governmental interest; and (5) Application of the better rule of law." *Nodak Mut. Ins. Co. v. American Family Mut. Ins. Co.*, 604 N.W.2d 91, 94 (Minn. 2000). The Court of Appeals of Minnesota found that it "strains credulity to believe that either party to this contract of insurance could have intended" that "the law of each state where [the policyholder's] properties are located could potentially control," held that the law of either the policyholder's home state of Minnesota or of the insurer's home state of Illinois, not the law of Georgia, as the site of environmental contamination, controlled the interpretation of an "owned property" exclusion in an environmental impairment liability policy. *Cargill, Inc. v. Evanston Ins. Co.*, 642 N.W.2d 80, 89–90 (Minn. Ct. App. 2002) (proceeding to find no conflict between Minnesota and Illinois law). *See also Hawkins, Inc. v. Am. Int'l Specialty Lines Ins. Co.*, No. A07-1529, 2008 Minn. App. Unpub. LEXIS 1218, at *12-13 (Minn. Ct. App. Oct. 14, 2008) ("[A]s we held in *Cargill*, a case that involved a dispute over whether the costs of cleaning a polluted site owned by an insured were covered under an environmental impairment liability policy, the only applicable laws through which a court may interpret the terms of an insurance policy when the policy contains no choice-of-law provision are the laws of the parties' home states."); *St. Paul Mercury Ins. Co. v. N. States Power Co.*, No. A07-1775, 2009 Minn. App. Unpub. LEXIS 977, at *18 (Minn. Ct. App. Aug. 25, 2009) ("While Wisconsin undoubtedly has a strong interest in cleaning up the NSP-WI sites, it has comparatively minimal interest in determining who should pay for the cleanup of that contamination. As in *Cargill*, the insurance contracts involve insurers and insureds in multiple states, and it would similarly 'strain[ ] credulity' to conclude that the law of each state where insured properties are located would necessarily control insurance coverage.") (undertaking an analysis of the five choice of law factors); *Nat'l Union Fire Ins. Co. v. Donaldson Co.*, 272 F. Supp. 3d 1099 (D. Minn. 2017) ("[T]he Minnesota Court of Appeals has held that when an insurance contract covering national risks does not contain a choice-of-law provision, if any states are to be involved in a choice-of-law analysis, it should be . . . the home states of the parties to the litigation. This rule ensures predictability of results; otherwise, an insurer's duties to the insured would vary based solely on the forum in which a plaintiff sues the insured. It strains credulity to believe that either party to [a] contract of insurance could have intended such a result." (citations and internal quotes omitted).

Mississippi: Although a statute provides that "[a]ll contracts of insurance on property, lives, or interests in this state shall be deemed to be made therein," MISS. CODE ANN. § 83-5-7, modern Mississippi choice-of-law decisions do not cite this statute. The Supreme Court of Mississippi has held that Sections 188 and 193 of the Second Restatement determine the law governing the construction of an insurance contract, with Section 188 assuming greater importance outside the context of coverage for "immovables and chattel whose location [is] geographically localized." *Zurich Am. Ins. Co. v. Goodwin*, 920 So. 2d 427, 434 (Miss. 2006). Thus, Iowa law governed coverage for an accident in Mississippi under a commercial automobile policy issued to an Iowa-based policyholder with respect to a fleet of trucks mostly garaged in Iowa. *Id.* at 436–37 ("The public policy, of adequate compensation to injured [Mississippi] motorists is not strong enough to override the contracting parties' expectations of which state's substantive law will apply."). A Mississippi District Court held that the law of Texas, as the location of the policyholder's headquarters and thirteen of its plants, or the law of Iowa, as the state of contracting and the location of four covered plants, controlled CGL coverage for environmental contamination at the single covered plant in Mississippi, even though Mississippi was also the policyholder's state of incorporation. *Employers Mut. Cas. Co. v. Lennox Int'l, Inc.*, 375 F. Supp. 2d 500, 508–09 (S.D. Miss. 2005). *Cf. Hartford Underwriters Ins. Co. v. Foundation Health Servs, Inc.*, 524 F.3d 588, 599 (5th Cir. 2008) (distinguishing decisions involving interpretation of insurance contracts, finding that Mississippi had primary interest in whether insurer faced a conflict of interest in controlling the defense of a Louisiana policyholder in Mississippi tort action); *See also Progressive Gulf Ins. Co. v. Farve*, No. 13-287, 2014 U.S. Dist. LEXIS 11545, at *12-13 (S.D. Miss. Jan. 30, 2014) ("The Mississippi Supreme Court has adopted section 193. But it has also explained that the location of the risk is irrelevant for consideration of the question of coverage when dealing with movable property like commercial tractors. As explained by the Fifth Circuit, '§ 193 is pertinent only if there is, in fact, a single state which can be identified as the principal location of the risks insured by a policy.' *Hartford Underwriters Ins. Co.*, 524 F.3d at 594. [*Hartford Underwriters Ins. Co. v. Found. Health Servs.*, 524 F.3d 588 (5th Cir. 2008)] Because section 193 does not apply, the Court looks to section 188, which provides that the law that has the most significant relationship to the transaction and the parties should be applied."); *Progressive Gulf Ins. Co. v. Farve*, No. 13-287, 2014 U.S. Dist. LEXIS 11545 (S.D. Miss. Jan. 30, 2014) ("[T]he statute [§ 83-5-7] does not displace Mississippi's center-of-gravity test."); *Nat'l Union Fire Ins. Co. v. Petco Petroleum Corp.*, No. 12-00165, 2013 U.S. Dist. LEXIS 157612, at *29-30 (S.D. Miss. Nov. 4, 2013) ("Although Mississippi has an interest in Richardson's underlying tort claims, Illinois has the greatest interest in the interpretation of Petco's insurance policies given Petco's strong presence in Illinois. The 'certainty' factor also weighs in favor of applying Illinois law. If the law of the state where a claim happens to arise applies to the notice issue, the effect of the timing of a notice of claim would potentially vary from claim to claim. It is unlikely that Petco and the Insurance Companies intended such a result. Because none of the § 6 factors rebut the presumption that Illinois law applies to the notice issue, Illinois law shall govern the issue."); *Smith v. Church Mut. Ins. Co.*, 254 So. 3d 57 (Miss. 2018) ("Courts of this state will not give effect to the substantive law of another state if to do so would be 'offensive to the deeply ingrained or strongly felt public policy of the state.'") (quoting *Boardman v. United Servs. Auto. Assoc.*, 470 So. 2d 1024 (Miss. 1985)). While it involves an auto policy, *Boardman* is a go-to decision for Mississippi courts addressing choice of law.

Missouri: The Supreme Court of Missouri held that Pennsylvania was the principal location of the insured risk under Section 193 of the Second Restatement, and that Pennsylvania law therefore governed coverage for asbestos claims, where Pennsylvania was the place of the policyholder's incorporation, of its insurance department, of its brokers, and of the delivery of the policies. *Viacom, Inc. v. Transit Cas. Co.*, 138 S.W.3d 723, 725 (Mo. 2004) (en banc). The Eighth Circuit held that, in a lawsuit against a Missouri contractor for defective work in Kansas, Missouri law controlled. It rejected the contention that an endorsement creating separate limits of liability for each project was the equivalent of creating a separate Kansas-specific policy controlled by Kansas law. *St. Paul Fire & Marine Ins. Co. v. Bldg. Constr. Enters., Inc.*, 526 F.3d 1166, 1168–69 (8th Cir. 2008). *See Doe Run Res. Corp. v. Certain Underwriters at Lloyd's London*, 400 S.W.3d 463, 473 (Mo. Ct. App. 2013) (Missouri was principal location of insured risk under policy issued to Missouri-headquartered company, covering sites predominantly in Missouri); *Kerns v. Alliance Indem. Co.*, 515 S.W.3d 254, 266 (Mo. Ct. App. 2017) (applying a Second Restatement analysis) ("Here, all parties to the accident were Kansas residents, the accident occurred in Kansas, and the policy at issue covers vehicles garaged only in Kansas. It appears that the sole connection to Missouri involved is that the rental vehicle Cherity Kerns was driving was registered in Missouri. Thus, it is clear that under a conflict-of-laws analysis, Kansas law governs this dispute."); *Am. Railcar Indus. v. Hartford Ins. Co.*, No. 13-778, 2014 U.S. Dist. LEXIS 11388, at *8-10 (E.D. Mo. Jan. 30, 2014) (applying a Second Restatement analysis and holding that "[b]ecause Mr. Tedder brought a workers' compensation claim and tort action against plaintiff in Arkansas arising out of his injury at plaintiff's Arkansas facility, the Court will determine the rights and obligations of the parties under the Policy in accordance with Arkansas law") ("[T]he parties entered into a workers' compensation and employers' liability policy that contemplated liability at ARI's workplaces in a fixed set of enumerated states. This is not a case in which the policy was designed to cover commercial operations wherever they happened to occur, including projects that had not begun when the policy was delivered. ARI's covered workplaces were located in several states, but these workplaces were fixed. The policy expressly identified these several states as the location of the insured risk by specifically listing the states of these workplaces.") (*aff'd* 847 F.3d 970 (8th Cir. 2017) but with no discussion of choice of law). *But see Thunder Basin Coal Co. v. Zurich Am. Ins. Co.*, 943 F. Supp. 2d 1010, 1013 (E.D. Mo. 2013) (holding, without citing foregoing authorities, that Wyoming law governed policy covering facilities in multiple states because "the risk at issue in this case involves a single facility located in Wyoming"). At issue in *Butterball, LLC v. Great Am. E&S Ins. Co.*, No. 18-5074, 2019 U.S. Dist. LEXIS 175423 (W.D. Mo. July 9, 2019) was an environmental liability policy covering 175 specified properties in 9 different states. The court held that Missouri law governed because the insured risk involved real property located in Missouri. "The Policy insures multiple real properties, located in multiple states. Comment f of § 193 addresses this precise scenario. Under Comment f, the court treats the Policy as if it involved multiple policies, each insuring an individual risk." *Id.* at *8. "[I]f the policy covers general liability spread across multiple states -- from which the parties could not reasonably be expected to anticipate which states' law would govern their dispute -- Comment b indicates that the factors in § 188 apply." *Id.* at *9. Tort choice-of-law principles generally govern claims of bad faith. *W. Am. Ins. Co. v. RLI Ins. Co.*, 698 F.3d 1069, 1073 (8th Cir. 2012); *Am. Guar. & Liab. Ins. Co. v. U.S. Fid. & Guar. Co.*, 668 F.3d 991, 996 (8th Cir. 2012).

Montana: A Montana statute provides that a "contract is to be interpreted according to the law and usage of the place where it is to be performed or, if it does not indicate a place of performance, according to the law and usage of the place where it is made." MONT. CODE ANN. § 28-3-102. The Supreme Court of

Montana overruled decisions suggesting that a Second Restatement analysis could supplant that statute. *Tidyman's Mgmt. Servs. Inc. v. Davis*, 330 P.3d 1139 (Mont. 2014) (Montana law governed directors and officers liability policy, issued to Washington corporation with its principal place of business in Montana). If the law of two different jurisdictions produces the same result, there is a "false conflict," and the court need not engage in a choice-of-law analysis. *Newman v. United Fire & Cas. Co.*, 995 F. Supp. 2d 1125, 1130 (D. Mont. 2014), *aff'd on other grounds* 668 Fed. Appx. 816 (9th Cir. 2016)). *See also Nat'l Sur. Corp. v. Mack*, No. 15-35, 2015 U.S. Dist. LEXIS 167634, at *11-12 (D. Mont. Dec. 15, 2015) ("[T]he Underlying Proceeding was filed in Montana. The wrongful conduct alleged against Mack in the Underlying Proceeding occurred partially in Montana. The debtors that Mack allegedly helped defraud are Montana residents, and Mack allegedly knew harm would be suffered in Montana. Like in *Mitchell* [*v. State Farm Ins. Co.*, 68 P.3d 703 (Mont. 2003)] Mack will receive the benefit of his insurance policy in Montana. Mack is receiving a defense in the Underlying Proceeding before the United States Bankruptcy Court for the District of Montana. If Mack prevails in the instant case, National Surety will indemnify Mack against the possible judgment rendered by the Bankruptcy Court. Because of the statutory directive found at Mont. Code Ann. § 28-3-102, the Court should not analyze the factors found at Restatement § 188(2). The insurance contract is being performed in Montana; therefore, Montana law will govern its interpretation in relation to the Underlying Proceeding."); *Homesite Ins. Co. v. Frost*, No. 20-00024, 2020 U.S. Dist. LEXIS 163535 (D. Mont. Sept. 8, 2020) (addressing Mont. Code Ann. § 28-3-102 and concluding that Montana law governed) ("[T]he Policy insures real property located within Montana and provides Mr. Frost with property damage and personal liability coverage for claims arising anywhere in the world, including Montana. As such, this Court concludes that Montana is an anticipated place of performance under the Policy.").

Nebraska: The Supreme Court of Nebraska applies Sections 188 and 193 of the Second Restatement to questions of coverage under insurance contracts. *Johnson v. U.S. Fid. & Guar. Co.*, 696 N.W.2d 431, 441–42 (Neb. 2005). A Nebraska District Court held that, under a policy issued to an Illinois parent corporation, Nebraska law controlled coverage for a Nebraska-based subsidiary (also a named insured) held liable for a polluted site in Nebraska: "Nebraska has the most significant interest in determining who will pay for the cleanup of a contaminated site within the state's borders." *Lindsay Mfg. Co. v. Hartford Acc. & Indem. Co.*, 911 F. Supp. 1249, 1254 (D. Neb. 1995), *rev'd on other grounds*, 118 F.3d 1263, 1265 (8th Cir. 1997) (agreeing that Nebraska law controlled). *See also First Neb. Trust Co. v. Greb (Estate of Greb)*, 848 N.W.2d 611, 622 (Neb. 2014) ("For the resolution of conflict of laws involving contracts, this court has adopted the Restatement (Second) of Conflict of Laws § 188. Under the Restatement, in the absence of an effective choice of law by the parties, a court is to consider several contacts in determining the law applicable to an issue. These contacts include (1) the place of contracting; (2) the place of negotiation of the contract; (3) the place of performance; (4) the location of the subject matter of the contract; and (5) the domicile, residence, nationality, place of incorporation, and place of business of the parties."); *Ameritas Life Ins. Corp. v. Fed. Ins. Co.*, No. 16-3006, 2017 U.S. Dist. LEXIS 216440 (D. Neb. Oct. 25, 2017) ("Under Nebraska's conflict-of-law rules, courts look to principles of contract formation, not—as Ameritas suggests here—the location of the alleged loss."); *Fed. Ins. Co. v. COR Clearing, LLC*, 328 F. Supp. 3d 956 (D. Neb. 2018) (applying law of the state of the insurer's location) ("[T]he last act necessary to make the contract binding was Federal's acceptance of the application for the bond. Although a close question, after analyzing the issue under § 188 the Court concludes New Jersey has a more significant relationship to the transaction and the parties than Nebraska.").

Nevada: The Supreme Court of Nevada applied Sections 188 and 193 of the Second Restatement to questions of coverage under insurance contracts. *Progressive Gulf Ins. Co. v. Faehnrich*, 327 P.3d 1061, 1063 (Nev. 2014). A Nevada District Court decision held that, notwithstanding a provision that the policies conformed to Illinois law, Nevada law governed the construction of healthcare liability policies issued to a Nevada rest home through a Nevada broker and covering risks located only in Nevada. *Prime Ins. Syndicate, Inc. v. Damaso*, 471 F. Supp. 2d 1087, 1094–95 (D. Nev. 2007). Two other Nevada District Court decisions have held that, in the context of environmental contamination within the state, Nevada had the most significant interest in the availability of insurance for remedial measures. *Mont. Refining Co. v. Nat. Union Fire Ins. Co.*, 918 F. Supp. 1395, 1397 (D. Nev. 1996); *Pioneer Chlor Alkali Co., Inc. v. Nat. Union Fire Ins. Co.*, 863 F. Supp. 1237, 1241 (D. Nev. 1994) (applying Texas choice-of-law rules after transfer from Southern District of Texas). A Nevada District Court decision held that tort choice-of-law principles governed a claim for bad faith. *Vignola v. Gilman*, 854 F. Supp. 2d 883, 888 (D. Nev. 2012). *See also Starr Indem. & Liab. Co. v. Young*, No. 14-00239, 2016 U.S. Dist. LEXIS 109886, at *9-11 (D. Nev. Aug. 17, 2016) (undertaking a Second Restatement analysis, for purposes of a general liability policy, but also noting that "applying another state's law must not violate a strong public policy of Nevada) (applying Nevada law) (as part of Second Restatement analysis: "The insurance policy specifically lists Young as a participating member in the insurance policy, and Young's address is in North Las Vegas, Nevada. Further, Young was employed as a massage therapist by Massage Envy in Nevada. The Court therefore finds that the place of performance of the contract was Nevada."); *Humes v. Acuity*, No. 17-01778, 2020 U.S. Dist. LEXIS 116116 (D. Nev. July 1, 2020) (undertaking Restatement analysis and concluding that South Dakota law applied) ("[T]he fact that the injury, treatment, and claim investigation occurred in Nevada is not dispositive: if the location of an accident were enough to apply a state's law, then laws would be applied according to the fortuity of where the accident occurred rather than by the provisions of the insured's policy. As Acuity puts it, this case involves the breach of the contract drafted in and entered into within the State of South Dakota, not the motor vehicle accident itself.").

New Hampshire: The Supreme Court of New Hampshire applied Sections 188 and 193 of the Second Restatement to questions of coverage under insurance contracts. *Cecere v. Aetna Ins. Co.*, 766 A.2d 696, 698–700 (N.H. 2001) ("Particularly in the context of insurance contracts, we have found that the State which is the principal location of the insured risk bears the most significant relationship to the contract, in the absence of an express choice of law by the parties. This rule articulates the fundamental contract policy of giving effect to the intention of the parties and their reasonably justified expectations, and promotes predictability of results, which is of foremost concern in contracts cases.") (citations and internal quotes omitted). Applying these principles to a CGL policy issued to a Massachusetts-based company that sold and maintained forklifts, the court held that Massachusetts law governed coverage for a forklift accident occurring in New Hampshire. Massachusetts was the principal location of the insured risk because the CGL policy "was intended to insure [the policyholder], rather than its customers, from liability." *Marston v. U.S. Fid. & Guar. Co.*, 609 A.2d 745, 748 (N.H. 1992). A New Hampshire District Court applied the same analysis to CGL coverage for contamination from a manufacturing facility in New Hampshire, finding that the law of the policyholder's home state of Massachusetts controlled. *See also K.J. Quinn & Co., Inc. v. Continental Cas.*, 806 F. Supp. 1037, 1041 (D.N.H. 1992) ("The fact that one of [the policyholder's] facilities was located in New Hampshire does not dictate the application of New Hampshire law to this policy any more than would be the case with the law of Missouri or the several provinces of Canada where other [of its] facilities are located."). *But see Cadell v. XL Specialty Ins. Co.*, No. 11-394, 2012 U.S. Dist. LEXIS 85239, at

*7-8 (D.N.H. June 20, 2012) ("In holding [in *Cecere*] that Massachusetts law applied, however, the court noted that the dealership conducted operations only in Massachusetts and that 'its insurance policy is designed to insure bodily injury or property damage resulting from activities located primarily upon the garage site.' The court further noted that its 'conclusion in this case rests substantially, if not entirely, on the unique nature of garage insurance policies.' Here, in contrast to *Cecere*, UOR had various locations, including one in New Hampshire. The Policy was an automotive insurance policy, not a garage policy, and it covered vehicles registered and garaged in other states. Therefore, unlike in *Cecere*, the principal location of the insured risk was in multiple states, including at least Connecticut and New Hampshire. . . . Accordingly, because the Policy was an automotive insurance policy covering vehicles located in different states, and because the truck involved in the accident was registered and garaged in New Hampshire, the primary location of the insured risk in this case was New Hampshire. Therefore, the court will interpret the Policy under New Hampshire law.").

New Jersey: The Supreme Court of New Jersey applies Sections 188 and 193 of the Second Restatement to determine the law governing a CGL policy. A trio of 1998 decisions from New Jersey's top court, expressing a preference for applying the law most favorable to coverage for environmental contamination, rejected the notion that the law of a single state controls the construction of a CGL policy. *Pfizer, Inc. v. Employers Ins. of Wausau*, 712 A.2d 634, 642–43 (N.J. 1998) (law of policyholder's home state of New York controlled, except that, in event of demonstrated conflict with law of any of nineteen states where contamination occurred, law of site controlled coverage for that site); *HM Holdings, Inc. v. Aetna Cas. & Sur. Co.*, 712 A.2d 645, 649 (N.J. 1998) (where, although policies had no connection to New Jersey at time of contracting, policyholder subsequently moved from New York to New Jersey, "New Jersey law or the law of the waste sites should govern the late-notice issues," but if "the law of the waste sites is similar to New York's, it should yield to New Jersey's unless the insurance companies are domestic companies of the waste sites"); *Unisys Corp. v. Ins. Co. of N. Am.*, 712 A.2d 649, 652–53 (N.J. 1998) (construing CGL policies issued to New York policyholder, holding that "in the case of New Jersey sites, New Jersey law should govern; in the case of the other sites, the law of the waste sites should govern if it differs from New Jersey's"). Subsequent intermediate appellate authority indicates that the Second Restatement analysis applies differently outside the context of coverage for environmental contamination, but that analysis remains malleable and unpredictable. *DeMarco v.*

Stoddard, 84 A.3d 965, 978 (N.J. Super Ct. App. Div. 2014) (policy issued to cover medical practice in New Jersey and Rhode Island governed by New Jersey law in action by New Jersey patients, notwithstanding that Rhode Island was the state of contracting) (*reversed on other grounds*, 125 A.3d 367 (N.J. 2015)) and noting that a conflict of laws did not arise because there was not a substantive difference between the potentially applicable laws); *Fantis Foods, Inc. v. N. River Ins. Co.*, 753 A.2d 176, 178 (N.J. Super. Ct. App. Div. 2000) (under New Jersey policyholder's general liability policy issued with respect to buildings located in several states, law of New York controlled coverage for imminent collapse of particular building in New York). *See Lonza, Inc. v. Everest Reinsurance Co.*, No. A-0170-03T1, 2006 N.J. Super. Unpub. LEXIS 1001 (N.J. Super. Ct. App. Div. May 16, 2006) ("when the 'subject matter of the insurance is an operation or activity' and when 'that operation or activity is predictably multistate, the significance of the principal location of the insured risk [under § 193] diminishes. …' In such situations, the governing law is that of the state with the dominant significant relationship according to the principles set forth in Restatement section 6") (applying § 193 to environmental contamination). In *Mega Constr. Corp. v. XL Am. Group*, 684 Fed. Appx. 196 (3rd Cir. 2017), the Third Circuit applied Pennsylvania law to a coverage dispute involving construction defects, despite the policy being issued to the insured contractor in New Jersey: "The insured risk in this case — Mega's construction work — took place in Pennsylvania during much of the relevant coverage period, May 2009 to May 2011. During that time Mega worked alongside other contractors to construct the 300+-unit apartment complex in Pennsylvania. 'Accidents' with potential to cause 'property damage' at this project were going to occur at the construction site in Pennsylvania, not in New Jersey. Thus the parties reasonably understood Pennsylvania to be the insured risk's principal location. Pennsylvania law governs unless New Jersey has a more significant relationship under *Restatement* § 6." *Id.* at 199. *See also First Mercury Ins. Co. v. Markowitz*, No. 12-06527, 2014 U.S. Dist. LEXIS 62961, at *19-22 (D.N.J. May 7, 2014) ("In this case, the factors of section 188 of the Restatement point decisively to a finding that New York law applies to the contract and issue before the Court. First, the policy was issued to Markowitz at a New York address to cover a New York law practice of an attorney who is licensed to practice only in New York. The policy was also issued under the New York Surplus Lines Law. Resp. The Court finds that the place of contracting, factor (a), was New York state, meaning that its laws are presumptively applicable.") ("As for the section 6 factors, the Court agrees with First Mercury: 'New Jersey has absolutely no interest in this coverage dispute which involves a Policy issued to a New York insured, at a New York address, to cover New York operations.' And though the underlying transaction involved New Jersey properties, the reasonable expectations of the parties also point to New York: 'First Mercury could have in no way anticipated that an attorney who was solely admitted in New York would have represented a client who was purchasing New Jersey properties,' and 'Markowitz, an attorney only admitted in New York and no other jurisdiction' could not 'have any reasonable expectation that New Jersey law apply to the Policy.'").

In *Continental Ins. Co. v. Honeywell International, Inc.*, 188 A.3d 297 (N.J. 2018), the New Jersey Supreme Court addressed choice of law concerning coverage for thousands of asbestos bodily injury claims pending nationwide. The court, following a review of the state's choice of law history and a detailed Restatement analysis, concluded that the law of Michigan – the location of the original insured to whom the policies were issued – did not apply. Instead, following a complex analysis, the court concluded that New Jersey law applied. The court rejected the insurers' argument that the analysis begins with "Restatement § 193 and its presumption that the law of the place of contracting applies." *Id.* at 317. Instead, "[t]he conflicts analysis here should center on Restatement §§ 188 and 6." *Id.* at 318. "Having already abandoned the place of contracting (here Michigan) as the presumptive starting point, we adhere to the observation in Restatement § 188 cmt. e. on subsection (2), that '[s]tanding alone, the place of contracting is a relatively insignificant contact.' That is particularly true where, as here, the insured risk is not site-specific. The place of negotiation (again Michigan) can be of importance, as recognized in the Restatement's comment to § 188. However, two stronger considerations under § 188, applied to this matter, combine to point toward New Jersey. Here, the place of performance, § 188(c), and the domicile, residence, and places of incorporation and of business of the parties, § 188(e), all point to New Jersey. The latter takes into account enduring characteristics and deserves to be a starting point in the analysis. Further, heavy weight must be given to the nature of the insured risk and its site, or to an otherwise performance-related location consideration. New Jersey is the longstanding domicile of the insured in this litigation (since 1983). Honeywell is the successor to the rights of Bendix under the insurance contract. As such, Honeywell's place of domicile and business (New Jersey) is easily determined at the time coverage is invoked due to litigation, triggering the terms of the insurance contract for these products liability claims. Relatedly, New Jersey is also the place of performance for the contractual defense and indemnification of Honeywell in this litigation involving long-tail claims on an occurrence policy for a predecessor's products cast into the national marketplace. Even before the New Jersey-based Honeywell became the successor to Bendix, New Jersey was integrally involved in Bendix's business operations. It is no stranger to the dispute." *Id.* at 318.

New Mexico: The Supreme Court of New Mexico has generally adhered to the *lex loci contractus* rule, applying the law of the state of contracting in insurance disputes, but it has applied a Second Restatement "most significant relationship" test in certain cases that require a flexible approach. *Ferrell v. Allstate Ins. Co.*, 188 P.3d 1156, 1173 & n.3 (N.M. 2008) ("We conclude that the Restatement (Second) is a more appropriate approach for multi-state contract class actions."). New Mexico courts further deviate from *lex loci contractus* where the law of the state of contracting contravenes New Mexico public policy. *State Farm Mut. Auto. Ins. Co. v. Ballard*, 54 P.3d 537, 542 (N.M. 2002) ("step down" provision of automobile policy void as against New Mexico public policy). *See also Valencia v. Colo. Cas. Ins. Co.*, 560 F. Supp. 2d 1080, 1085–86 (D.N.M. 2007) (applying Colorado law to Colorado policy because insured had not "advanced a public policy ground sufficient to overcome the general rule" of *lex loci contractus*). *See also Anczarski v. Travelers Indem. Co.*, No. 16-0856, 2017 U.S. Dist. LEXIS 110166, at *69-70 (D.N.M. July 17, 2017) ("The Supreme Court of New Mexico has recognized one exception to the *lex loci contractus* rule. *See State Farm Mut. Auto. Ins. Co. v. Ballard*, 2002-NMSC-030, 132 N.M. 696, 54 P.3d 537, 539. To overcome the rule favoring the place where a contract is executed, there must be a countervailing interest that is fundamental and separate from general policies of contract interpretation. Application of the rule must result in a violation of fundamental principles of justice before applying New Mexico law rather than the law of the jurisdiction where the contract was signed. *See Reagan v. McGee Drilling Corp.*, 1997-NMCA-014, ¶ 9, 23 N.M. 68, 933 P.2d 867, 869 ('The threshold . . . is whether giving effect to another state's policies would 'violate some fundamental principle of justice, some prevalent conception of good morals, some deep-rooted tradition of the common weal' of the forum state.'). This exception applies only in extremely limited circumstances.") (citations omitted); *Delgado v. Liberty Mut. Fire Ins. Co.*, No. 15-196, 2017 U.S. Dist. LEXIS 204700 (D.N.M. Dec. 13, 2017) ("The Court will apply the *lex loci contractus* rule because it is workable in this case and because, as one court in this District has noted, for almost 30 years 'case law in the Tenth Circuit and New Mexico have [sic] held that New Mexico applies *lex loci contractus*.'"); *Miller v. Cincinnati Ins. Co.*, 323 F. Supp. 3d 1253 (D.N.M. 2018) (addressing whether a time-to-sue provision in a policy "would so offend New Mexico public policy that its application would violate fundamental principles of justice and require overriding the presumption that" the law where the policy was issued applied).

New York: The Court of Appeals of New York, the state's highest court, applies Sections 188 and 193 of the Second Restatement to CGL policies. *Zurich Ins. Co. v. Shearson Lehman Hutton, Inc.*, 642 N.E.2d 1065, 1068–69 (N.Y. 1994). The law of the policyholder's domicile normally controls the choice-of-law analysis for a CGL policy "'where it is necessary to determine the law governing a liability insurance policy covering risks in multiple states, the state of the insured's domicile should be regarded as a proxy for the principal location of the insured risk.'" *In re Liquidation of Midland Ins. Co.*, 947 N.E.2d 1174 (N.Y. 2011) (quoting *Certain Underwriters at Lloyd's v. Foster Wheeler Corp.*, 822 N.Y.S.2d 30, 35 (Sup. Ct. App. Div. 2006), *aff'd*, 6 N.E.2d 500 (N.Y. 2007)) (in dispute regarding coverage for asbestos liabilities in multiple states, New Jersey law governed New Jersey–based policyholder's CGL policies, which were negotiated in New York). *See also Liberty Surplus Ins. Corp. v. Nat. Union Fire Ins. Co.*, 888 N.Y.S.2d 35, 36 (Sup. Ct. App. Div. 2009) (law of Connecticut governed as state of policyholder's principal place of business); *Avrio Group Surveillance Solutions, Inc. v. Essex Ins. Co.*, 790 F. Supp. 2d 89, 96–97 (W.D.N.Y. 2011) ("because [the policyholder] is domiciled in Maryland, and no other state has significant relationship to the insurance contract or its parties, New York law requires the court construe the CGL Policy according to Maryland law"); *Fed. Ins. Co. v. Am. Home Assur. Co.*, 664 F. Supp. 2d 397, 404–05 (S.D.N.Y. 2009) (Florida law governed CGL policies where Florida-based parent was named insured); *Md. Cas. Co. v. Continental Cas. Co.*, 332 F.3d 145, 153–55 (2d Cir. 2003) (law of policyholder's home state of New York controlled CGL coverage for environmental contamination in multiple states); *Utica Mut. Ins. Co. v. Munich Reinsurance Am., Inc.*, 976 F. Supp. 2d 254, 262 (N.D.N.Y. 2013) (applying same analysis to reinsurance contract). *Cf. Homestead Vill. Assoc., L.P. v. Diamond State Ins. Co.*, 818 F. Supp. 2d 642, 647 (E.D.N.Y. 2011) (applying law of New York to policy negotiated and delivered in New Jersey because all insured premises were in New York, and because policy contained endorsements specific to New York). State appellate courts have reached differing decisions whether, in a dispute if a person qualifies as an "additional insured," the controlling law should be that of the named insured's headquarters. *Compare QBE Ins. Corp. v. Adjo Contracting Corp.*, 976 N.Y.S.2d 534, 548 (Sup. Ct. App. Div. 2013) (applying law of named insured's Pennsylvania headquarters), *with Ill. Nat'l Ins. Co. v. Zurich Am. Ins. Co.*, 969 N.Y.S.2d 11, 12 (Sup. Ct.

App. Div. 2013) (applying New York law because parties, in adding person as "additional insured" for particular site, "understood … that the 'principal location of the insured risk' was in New York, where the work took place," rather than in Maryland, where named insured was headquartered); *see also Narragansett Elec. Co. v. Am. Home Assur. Co.*, 921 F. Supp. 2d 166, 177 (S.D.N.Y. 2013) (looking to first named insured's headquarters, rather than to headquarters of subsidiary named insureds who happened to be sued); *FC Bruckner Assocs., L.P. v. Fireman's Fund Ins. Co.*, 944 N.Y.S.2d 84, 85 (Sup. Ct. App. Div. 2012) (same); *Fireman's Fund Ins. Co. v. Great Am. Ins. Co.*, 822 F.3d 620, 642-45 (2d Cir. 2016) ("Critical to a sound analysis, however, is selecting the contacts that obtain significance in the particular contract dispute. The New York Appellate Divisions have repeatedly recognized that where the insured risk is scattered throughout multiple states, [New York] courts … deem the risk to be located principally in one state, namely, in the state of the *insured's domicile* at the time the policy was issued, and thus have held that the state of the insured's domicile should be regarded as a proxy for the principal location of the insured risk. These courts have noted that [t]he state of the insured's domicile is a fact known to the parties at the time of contracting, and … application of the law of that state is most likely to conform to their expectations.") (citations and internal quotes omitted; emphasis in original) (coverage under EPL policy for Mississippi insured) ("Because the parties' understanding and the insured's domicile favor application of Mississippi law, while the other choice of law factors do not favor the law of any one particular state, Mississippi has the 'most significant relationship to the transaction and the parties,' such that Mississippi law governs the EPI Policy."); *QBE Ins. Corp. v Adjo Contr. Corp.*, No. 2011-04611, 2014 N.Y. App. Div. LEXIS 7270, at *33-34 (N.Y. App. Div. Oct. 29, 2014) ("Because the subject policy covered risks in multiple states, and because Erie's and Penn National's named insured was domiciled in Pennsylvania, it is appropriate to apply that state's law."); *Ben Weitsman & Son of Scranton, LLC v. Hartford Fire Ins. Co.*, No. 16-0780, 2018 U.S. Dist. LEXIS 22970 (N.D.N.Y. Feb. 13, 2018) ("[I]n a proper case, a foreign State's sufficiently compelling public policy could preclude an application of New York law otherwise indicated by the grouping of contacts analysis, particularly where New York's policy is weak or uncertain."); *Cartagena v. Homeland Ins. Co.*, No. 19-628, 2019 U.S. Dist. LEXIS 219044 (S.D.N.Y. Dec. 16, 2019) ("Where the insured risk is scattered throughout multiple states, New York courts deem the risk to be located principally in the state of the insured's domicile at the time the policy was issued."); *Arch Specialty Ins. Co. v. Ellas Heating & Cooling Inc.*, No. 19-3314, 2020 U.S. Dist. LEXIS

124535 (E.D.N.Y. July 13, 2020) ("Under New York's choice of law rules, the focus in a contract dispute is on the contract's 'center of gravity,' which, in an insurance contract dispute, is 'generally the state where the insured risk is located.'").

North Carolina: North Carolina courts adhere to the common law doctrine of *lex loci contractus*, which "mandates that the substantive law of the state where the last act to make a binding contract occurred, usually delivery of the policy, controls the interpretation of the contract." *Huber Engineered Woods, LLC v. Canal Ins. Co.*, 690 S.E.2d 739, 743 (N.C. Ct. App. 2010) (quoting *Fortune Ins. Co. v. Owens*, 526 S.E.2d 463, 465–66 (N.C. 2000)); *Fed. Ins. Co. v. S. Lithoplate, Inc.*, 7 F. Supp. 3d 579 (E.D.N.C. 2014). Nevertheless, pursuant to N.C. Gen. Stat. § 58-3-1, which provides that "[a]ll contracts of insurance on property, lives, or interests in this State shall be deemed to be made therein … and are subject to the laws thereof," North Carolina law may control "where a close connection exists between [North Carolina] and the interests insured by an insurance policy." *Fortune*, 526 S.E.2d at 466 (Florida law controlled automobile policy issued to cover vehicle principally garaged in Florida at time of contracting, even though policyholder had temporary address in North Carolina at the time of North Carolina accident, because mere presence in state insufficient to trigger statute) (citing *Collins & Aikman Corp. v. Hartford Acc. & Indem. Co.*, 436 S.E.2d 243 (N.C. 1993) (applying North Carolina law to policy made in California because vast majority of insured fleet of trucks were principally garaged in North Carolina)). *See also NAS Sur. Group v. Precision Wood Prods., Inc.*, 271 F. Supp. 2d 776, 780 (M.D.N.C. 2003) ("The North Carolina courts have explicitly held that where the fortuity of an accident within the state is the only connection to the state, that is not sufficient to make North Carolina's law applicable."); *Naylor Concrete Constr. Co. v. Mid-Continent Cas. Co.*, 754 S.E.2d 259 (N.C. Ct. App. 2014) ("Although the provisions of N.C. Gen. Stat. § 58-3-1 apply in the event that 'a close connection exists between this State and the interests insured by an insurance policy,' 'the mere presence of the insured interests in this State at the time of an accident does not constitute a sufficient connection to warrant application of North Carolina law.' (quoting *Fortune*). The undisputed information contained in the present record establishes that Defendant is an Oklahoma corporation which is not registered to do business in North Carolina and that the policy in question in this proceeding was both issued and delivered in Oklahoma. For that reason, the only connection between the policy at issue and this State is the fact that the Dillard's store at which Ms. Marshall was injured is located in North Carolina. According to *Fortune*, such a connection does not suffice to establish that North Carolina law should be applied for the purpose of resolving the dispute between the parties. As a result, given that the traditional '*lex loci*' rule remains applicable in this jurisdiction and that the policy in question in this case was 'made' in Oklahoma, we agree with the parties that we are required to apply Oklahoma law in determining whether the trial court erred by granting summary judgment in favor of Defendant."); *Certain Interested Underwriters v. Am. Realty Advisors*, No. 16-940, 2017 U.S. Dist. LEXIS 185842 (E.D.N.C. Nov. 9, 2017) ("[A]ny consequences for localization under section 58-3-1 is immaterial where localization is no part of the analysis in a contract containing an enforceable choice of law clause."); *Am. Realty Advisors v. Lexington Ins. Co.*, No. 18CVS5171, 2019 NCBC LEXIS 59 (N.C. Super. Ct. Sept. 10, 2019) (addressing in detail the inter-relationship between *lex loci contractus* and § 58-3-1 and "due process constrains applying Section 58-3-1 unless North Carolina has a 'close connection' to the insured loss). The law of the state of the injury controls choice-of-law for a tort claim of bad faith. *Martinez v. Nat'l Union Fire Ins. Co.*, 911 F. Supp. 2d 331, 336 (E.D.N.C. 2012).

North Dakota: North Dakota applies the "significant contacts approach ... in cases with 'multi-state factual contacts.'" *Schleuter v. N. Plains Ins. Co.*, 772 N.W.2d 879, 885 (N.D. 2009) (quoting *Plante v. Columbia Paints*, 494 N.W.2d 140, 142 (N.D. 1992)). In an action addressing coverage for an explosion in North Dakota allegedly caused by defective paint, Washington law controlled the construction of a CGL policy issued to the Washington-based policyholder to cover its retail and manufacturing functions in five states. The parties were "more likely to have thought that the coverage provided would be determined in accordance with the law of Washington, where the contract was negotiated, the policy was delivered, and the premiums were paid, than in accordance with the law of any other state." *Plante*, 494 N.W.2d at 143. "The most compelling North Dakota contact here is that the injured parties are North Dakota residents. Protecting North Dakota residents whenever North Dakota has any contacts with a controversy, however, is the kind of 'chauvinistic parochialism' ... sought to be avoided by modern choice-of-law analysis." *Id.* (quoting Robert A. Leflar, *The Nature of Conflicts Law*, 81 Colum. L. Rev. 1080 (1981)). *See also Am. Fire & Cas. Co. v. Hegel*, 847 F.3d 956, 961 (8th Cir. 2017) (undertaking a detailed Second Restatement analysis) ("[T]he primary thrust of *Plante* is that when insurance coverage is at issue, the location of the accident has 'less significance' when the policy covers risks that are scattered throughout two or more states."); *Great West Cas. Co. v. XTO Energy, Inc.*, No. 16-387, 2019 U.S. Dist. LEXIS 797 (D.N.D. Jan. 3, 2019) ("First, the court identifies the relevant contacts which might logically influence the decision of which law to apply. Second, the court applies the five choice-influencing 'Leflar factors' to determine which state has the more significant interest in the outcome of the litigation. The five Leflar factors are: (1) predictability of results; (2) maintenance of interstate and international order; (3) simplification of the judicial task; (4) advancement of the forum's governmental interests; and (5) application of the better rule of law.") ("Predictability of result favors application of the law of the state where the policy was negotiated and issued. Maintenance of interstate order is not an issue and the Court will have no difficulty applying the law of either state. Montana has a greater interest in regulating the relationship between a Nebraska insurance company and a Montana insured than does North Dakota. Courts rarely give consideration to which state has 'the better rule of law' as sometimes different laws are just different. The Court concludes based on the facts of this case, that Montana has more significant contacts and interests in the insurance contract at issue than North Dakota. Thus, the Court will apply Montana law.").

Ohio: The Supreme Court of Ohio applies Sections 188 and 193 of the Second Restatement to determine the law governing an insurance contract. *Ohayon v. Safeco Ins. Co.*, 747 N.E.2d 206, 211 (Ohio 2001) (automobile policy). Ohio intermediate appellate decisions have reached divergent results in applying the Second Restatement analysis to CGL policies. *Compare Gen. Acc. Ins. Co. v. Ins. Co. of N. Am.*, 590 N.E.2d 33, 36–37 (Ohio Ct. App. 1990) (law of Ohio, as headquarters of policyholder and additional insureds, governed coverage for defective coke battery installed at plant in Maryland), *and Nationwide Ins. Co. v. Phelps*, 2003-Ohio-497, 2003 Ohio App. LEXIS 497 (Ohio Ct. App. Jan. 31, 2003) (law of West Virginia, where insured homebuilder was located and performed most work, governed coverage for claim arising out of a house built in Ohio), *with Morton Int'l, Inc. v. Aetna Cas. & Sur. Co.*, 666 N.E.2d 1163, 1167–68 (Ohio Ct. App. 1995) (applying law of Washington, as location of polluted site, rather than law of Pennsylvania, as state of contracting and policyholder's headquarters). Ohio federal decisions have reached similarly divergent results. *Compare Babcock & Wilcox Co. v. Arkwright-Boston Mfg. Mut. Ins. Co.*, 867 F. Supp. 573, 580 (N.D. Ohio 1992) ("the principal location of the insured risk … is the principal location of that insured's assets"), *with Int'l Ins. Co. v. Stonewall Ins. Co.*, 863 F. Supp. 599 (S.D. Ohio 1994) (insured risk "was the possibility of adverse tort judgments against [the policyholder], a risk that necessarily depends upon the law of the state that governs the tort claim"), *aff'd*, 86 F.3d 601, 606 (6th Cir. 1996). *See also Irondale Indus. Contractors, Inc. v. Va. Sur. Co., Inc.*, 754 F.

Supp. 2d 927, 931 (N.D. Ohio 2010) ("Although [policyholder] is headquartered in Alabama—which weighs in favor of applying Alabama law—all other factors weigh in favor of applying Ohio law: the policy endorsement at issue here is specific to Ohio, relates only to work occurring in Ohio, covers [policyholder's] Ohio employees and, importantly, the injury forming the basis of this action occurred in Ohio."); *McCarty v. Nat'l Union Fire Ins. Co.*, No. 15-247, 2016 U.S. Dist. LEXIS 39526, at *8-9 (S.D. Ohio Mar. 25, 2016) (undertaking a Second Restatement analysis) ("The location of the subject matter of the insurance policy is Ohio because Pedraza was licensed to practice law in Ohio and his practice was based in Springfield, Ohio. The location of Pedraza and his law practice carries significant weight because, given the nature of the policy, it is where the parties should have reasonably expected to have been drawn into court to resolve any claims against the policy."); *Maxum Indem. Co. v. Drive West Ins. Servs.*, 630 Fed. Appx. 599, 604-05 (6th Cir. 2015) (undertaking a Second Restatement analysis) ("The insurance contract at issue in this case was between Mulberry, a California corporation, and Maxum, a Delaware corporation with its principal place of business in Georgia. Mulberry negotiated the contract and entered into it from California. Maxum would have tendered any payment under the contract to Mulberry in California, but the lawsuits it chose not to defend were filed in state and federal courts located in Ohio. The fraudulent quotes and binders at issue in those suits were apparently issued to owners of properties in a variety of jurisdictions. Weighing the Restatement factors, we deem California to have had the most significant relationship to the Maxum Policy, the parties to it, and performance under its terms."); *Hartford Accident & Indem. Co. v. FFP Holdings LLC*, 490 F. Supp. 3d 1226 (N.D. Ohio Sept. 28, 2020) (undertaking detailed and fact-intensive Restatement analysis in the context of coverage for environmental property damage with several policies and various states at issue).

Oklahoma: An Oklahoma statute adopts the *lex loci contractus* rule, providing that "[a] contract is to be interpreted according to the law and usage of the place where it is to be performed, or, if it does not indicate a place of performance, according to the law and usage of the place where it is made." 15 OKLA. STAT. § 162. The Supreme Court of Oklahoma has "carved an exception to application of the *lex loci contractus* rule for choice-of-law questions in motor vehicle insurance cases that deal with conflicting state laws." *Bernal v. Charter County Mut. Ins. Co.*, 209 P.3d 309, 315 & n.25 (Okla. 2009) (citing *Bohannan v. Allstate Ins. Co.*, 820 P.2d 787, 795–97 (Okla. 1991)). "In those instances, the traditional *lex loci contractus* rule governs the validity, interpretation, application and effect of the motor vehicle insurance contracts *except* where (1) the provisions would violate Oklahoma public policy or (2) the facts demonstrate another jurisdiction has the most significant relationship to the subject matter and the parties." *Id.* at 315–16 (emphasis in original). This hybrid First Restatement/Second Restatement approach appears to be limited by its terms to automobile insurance. The *lex loci contractus* rule appears to continue to apply to CGL policies. *Bituminous Cas. Corp. v. St. Clair Lime Co.*, 69 F.3d 547 (Table) (10th Cir. Oct. 27, 1995). *See also Cudd Pressure Control, Inc. v. N.H. Ins. Co.*, 645 Fed. Appx. 733, 740-41 (10th Cir. 2016) ("In the context of applying Oklahoma's choice-of-law rules, we have previously explained that the language of Okla. Stat. tit. 15, § 162 'compels a reading which restricts application of the law of the place of performance of a contract to cases in which the *place of performance is indicated in the contract.*' However, we have also noted under Oklahoma law that courts may discern 'the implied intent of contracting parties that the law of a certain jurisdiction control their contractual obligations from their conduct or from certain language in the contract.' In addition, we have recognized that the specification of a place for payment of premiums and benefits under an insurance policy evinces a designation of a location as the place of performance. Nevertheless, when the language of the contract does not directly *or* implicitly indicate a place of performance, we will resort to applying the law of the state of contracting.") (quoting *Rhody v. State Farm Mut. Ins. Co.*, 771 F.2d 1416 (10th Cir. 1985)) (emphasis in original); *Harlow v. Golden Rule Ins. Co.*, No. 15-1313, 2018 U.S. Dist. LEXIS 39972 (W.D. Okla. Mar. 12, 2018) ("The contract here does not indicate a place of performance. Therefore, the Court must look to the law of the place where the contract was made. When there is no indication in the contracts text where performance is to occur, the *lex loci contractus rule* - the law of the place where the contract is made - will govern.") (addressing 15 Okla. Stat. § 162); *Starr Surplus Lines Ins. Co. v. Cushing Hosp., LLC*, No. 20-0651, 2021 U.S. Dist. LEXIS 53350 (W.D. Okla. Mar. 22, 2021) ("When an insurance contract does not indicate the place of performance, the law of the state in which the insurance contract is delivered is deemed to be the place where the contract is made and, therefore, the law of that state governs interpretation of the contract. Delivery of the instrument is its completion; thus, where an instrument is signed in one state and delivered in another, the law of the latter governs since the contract is made in the latter state.") (addressing 15 Okla. Stat. § 162 and factors that evidence place of delivery).

Oregon: An Oregon statute governs choice of law in contracts cases: "To the extent that an effective choice of law has not been made by the parties pursuant to

ORS 15.350 or 15.355, or is not prescribeed by ORS 15.320, 15.325, 15.330, 15.335 or 15.380, the rights and duties of the parties with regard to an issue in a contract are governed by the law, in light of the multistate elements of the contract, that is the most appropriate for a resolution of that issue. The most appropriate law is determined by: (1) Identifying the states that have a relevant connection with the transaction or the parties, such as the place of negotiation, making, performance or subject matter of the contract, or the domicile, habitual residence or pertinent place of business of a party; (2) Identifying the policies underlying any apparently conflicting laws of these states that are relevant to the issue; and (3) Evaluating the relative strength and pertinence of these policies in: (a) Meeting the needs and giving effect to the policies of the interstate and international systems; and (b) Facilitating the planning of transactions, protecting a party from undue imposition by another party, giving effect to justified expectations of the parties concerning which state's law applies to the issue and minimizing adverse effects on strong legal policies of other states." ORS § 15.360. *See IBC Mfg. Co. v. Berkshire Hathaway Specialty Ins. Co.*, No. 16-00908, 2016 U.S. Dist. LEXIS 115240 (D. Ore. Aug. 29, 2016) ("Oregon's applicable choice of law statute sets forth a multi-factor test for determining the 'most appropriate law' to be applied when the contracting parties have not selected their choice of law."); *Tech. Sec. Integration, Inc. v. Philadelphia Indem. Ins. Co.*, No. 14-01895, 2015 U.S. Dist. LEXIS 100317 (D. Or. May 27, 2015) ("Given the absence of a choice-of-law clause in the CGL Policy, the Court must turn to ORS § 15.360 in order to determine the appropriate state law to apply.") ("The ORS § 15.360 factors weigh in favor of applying Washington state law here. On the one hand, Oregon has relevant connections with the parties to this case. This coverage dispute stems from counterclaims against Plaintiff filed by an Oregon resident in Oregon federal court. In addition, Plaintiff elected to file this breach of contract action against Defendant, a Pennsylvania corporation, in Oregon federal court. On the other hand, however, none of the parties that participated in the underlying transaction (i.e., entering into the insurance contract) are residents of Oregon."), *affd* 710 Fed. Appx. 753 (9th Cir. 2018) (addressing the factors in § 15.360) ("TSI, a Washington corporation, negotiated the contract using a Washington broker. Philadelphia sent policy declarations to TSI's Washington address. While the contract lacks a forum selection clause, it provides that arbitration will take place in Washington, and that the proceedings are governed by the local rules and procedures of Snohomish County, Washington. The Oregon rules also require courts to 'identify[ ] the policies underlying any apparently conflicting laws' of the proposed forums, and to consider 'the relative strength and pertinence of those policies.' A Washington statute prohibits mandatory arbitration agreements in insurance contracts, while Oregon lacks any analogous provision."); *Scheel v. GuideOne Mut. Ins. Co.*, No. 15-01112, 2016 U.S. Dist. LEXIS 39947 (D. Ore. Mar. 24, 2016) (citing § 15.360 and also addressing Restatement § 188 in determining which state has the "most significant relationship" in deciding choice of law) ("Here, nearly all of the factors weigh in favor of applying the law of Canada. The PAU [Power of Attorney and Authorization] was executed and negotiated between Canada and GuideOne. Further, the PAU's subject matter pertains exclusively to the minimum liability limits to which GuideOne will be held while its policyholders operate automobiles in Canadian territory. The place of performance is also Canada, as the heightened minimum liability limits apply only while GuideOne's policyholders operate insured vehicles on Canadian highways. Although the Policy at issue in this case was issued in Oregon, Oregon has little to no connection to the PAU or its purpose. Thus, the law of British Columbia should apply to determine the effect of the PAU.") (*aff'd* 741 Fed. Appx. 523 (9th Cir. 2018)).

Pennsylvania: For purposes of choice of law, governing casualty insurance contracts, Pennsylvania looks to the *Second Restatement of Conflicts of Laws* § 193 as the starting point. It provides that the law of the state that the parties understood was to be the principal location of the insured risk governs, unless some other state has a more significant relationship under the principles stated in § 6. Comment b to *Restatement* § 193 explains that the location of the insured risk under the contract should generally be given greater weight than any other single contact. However, the importance of the principal location of the insured risk diminishes if the policy covers a group of risks that are scattered throughout two or more states. In that situation, the location of the risk has less significance, and the location of the insured and the place where the policy was negotiated, become the most significant contacts. *Hammersmith v. TIG Ins. Co.*, 480 F.3d 220, 232-33 (3d Cir. 2007). There is, however, a paucity of state-court authority. *See Specialty Surfaces Int'l, Inc. v. Cont'l Cas. Co.*, 609 F.3d 223, 232–37 (3d Cir. 2010) ("Where, as here, the sole interest of both jurisdictions is in enforcing the intent of the parties, we believe Pennsylvania's choice of law rules would favor giving primary weight to the jurisdiction providing the context in which the decision making parties negotiated their agreement. Accordingly, in this case, we believe that the place of contracting, the place of negotiation, and the parties' principal places of business are the most important contacts when determining which state's law should be applied. In short, Pennsylvania law was the context in which the parties negotiated and expressed the agreement they had reached."); *Travelers Prop. Cas. Co. of Am. v. Chubb Custom Ins. Co.*, 864 F. Supp. 2d 301, 312 (E.D. Pa. 2012) (undertaking detailed Second Restatement analysis) ("Although Indiana has an interest in ensuring its residents enjoy adequate defense and compensation in tort actions, Pennsylvania's interest in regulating insurance contracts made in Pennsylvania, and issued to Pennsylvania corporations that transact all of their business from their Pennsylvania headquarters is paramount. Therefore, because Pennsylvania has the most significant relationship with the insurance contracts at issue, and the greatest government interest in seeing its laws enforced, this Court will apply Pennsylvania law."); *Cincinnati Ins. Co. v. Jerry Ellis Constr.*, No. 14-155, 2016 U.S. Dist. LEXIS 75405, at *14 (W.D. Pa. June 9, 2016) (undertaking a detailed Second Restatement analysis) ("Weighing the above factors on a 'qualitative scale,' it is clear that Indiana has a more significant relationship to the insurance contract than Pennsylvania. (citing *Hammersmith*). Indeed, the only connection Pennsylvania has to this dispute is that [Gadley] resides, and [the claim] occurred, in Pennsylvania. Similarly, Plaintiff has alleged that the insurance policy at issue is governed by and is to be interpreted under Indiana law. Thus, because we are [primarily] concerned with [the] contract of insurance, and, as to the insurance policy, [Indiana] has the most significant contacts."); *Castlepoint Nat'l Ins. Co. v. Ins. Co. of the Pa.*, No. 14-0792, 2015 U.S. Dist. LEXIS 62525, at *8-9 (M.D. Pa. May 13, 2015) ("Pennsylvania applies a flexible, interest/contacts methodology under the *Restatement (Second) Conflict of Laws*, to contract choice of law questions, bearing in mind that we are concerned with the contract of insurance and not the underlying tort. (citing *Hammersmith*). Pennsylvania applies Section 193 of the *Restatement (Second) of Conflict of Laws* when the insured has a principal place of insured risk, stating the rights created thereby are determined by the local law of the state which the parties understood was to be the principal location of the insured risk during the term of the policy."); *H.J. Heinz Co. v. Starr Surplus Lines Ins. Co.*, 675 Fed. Appx. 122 (3d Cir. 2017) (policy's service-of-suit endorsement does not supersede its choice-of-law provision); *State Auto Prop. & Cas. Ins. Co. v. Moser*, No. 589 MDA 2017, 2018 Pa. Super. Unpub. LEXIS 1471 (Pa. Super. Ct. May 7, 2019) (addressing choice of law for insurability of punitive damages) ("Because Maryland is the state of issuance for the applicable insurance policies, we hold that Maryland law applies for purposes of ascertaining the rights of the parties."); *Am. Guar. & Liab. Ins. Co. v. Law Offices of Richard C. Weisberg*, No. 19-05055, 2021 U.S. Dist. LEXIS 44329 (E.D. Pa. Mar. 9, 2021) (undertaking a very lengthy choice of law analysis, for a legal malpractice policy, applying the Restatement and *Hammersmith*) ("[W]e similarly find it significant that Weisberg, a resident of Pennsylvania at the time the contract was formed, was required to provide notice under a Pennsylvania policy that was issued and delivered in Pennsylvania. Weighing these contacts on a qualitative scale, we find that Pennsylvania has a more significant relationship to the insurance policy and this action than Texas or Arizona.").

Rhode Island: Rhode Island law, concerning choice of law, in insurance coverage disputes, is sparse. The Rhode Island Supreme Court, in *Baker v. Hanover Ins. Co.*, 568 A.2d 1023 (R.I. 1990), citing its cases from 1927 and 1938, stated: "In the case at bar we are dealing with a policy of insurance [automobile] executed and delivered in the Commonwealth of Massachusetts to a Massachusetts corporation whose principal place of business is located in South Attleboro, Massachusetts. Consequently the construction of this policy must be determined in accordance with Massachusetts law." *Id.* at 1025. *See Michaud v. Merrimack Mut. Fire Ins. Co.*, No. 94-0175B, 1994 U.S. Dist. LEXIS 19930 (D.R.I. Nov. 16, 1994) ("Rhode Island law applies. The Rhode Island rule is that the law of the place of contracting governs all questions of contract interpretation. Here the Policy was issued by a Rhode Island agency to a Rhode Island insured.") (citing, among others, *Baker*); *Insurance Co. of North America v. Kayser-Roth Corp.*, No. PC 92-5248, 1999 R.I. Super. LEXIS 66 (R.I. Super. Ct. July 29, 1999) (addressing liability policies and claims for environmental property damage) ("It is undisputed that New York is where the policies were brokered and accepted. While the location of the insured premises and the events leading to trigger of coverage took place in Rhode Island, it seems clear that New York law ought to be applied to the parties' contractual relations.") (citing *Baker*); *Hartford Cas. Ins. Co. v. A&M Assocs.*, 200 F. Supp. 2d 84 (D.R.I. 2002) (applying an "interest weighing" approach and holding that Massachusetts law governed a CGL policy, issued in Massachusetts to a Massachusetts-based contractor, in a dispute regarding coverage for allegedly defective construction work in Rhode Island); *Charette v. Commerce Ins. Co.*, No. 10-249, 2013 U.S. Dist. LEXIS 15923 (D.R.I. Feb. 6, 2013) ("Rhode Island follows an interest-weighing approach to determine the law that applies in a given situation. In applying the interest-weighing approach, the Court reviews a series of factors to determine the law of the state that bears the most significant relationship to the event and the parties. Defendant does not write insurance policies for Rhode Island residents. In the instant case, the insurance policy was issued in Massachusetts to a Massachusetts resident by a Massachusetts corporation. In the case of insurance contracts, the Rhode Island Supreme Court has held that when the insured is a Massachusetts corporation doing business in Massachusetts, and the contract is executed and delivered in Massachusetts, Massachusetts law governs the interpretation of the contract.").

South Carolina: Section 38-61-10 of the South Carolina Code provides that "[a]ll contracts of insurance on property, lives, or interests in this State are considered to be made in the State and all contracts of insurance the applications for which are taken within the State are considered to have been made within this State and are subject to the laws of this State." In *Sangamo Weston, Inc. v. National Sur. Corp.*, 414 S.E.2d 127, 130 (S.C. 1992), the Supreme Court of South Carolina held that, under this statute, South Carolina law controlled CGL coverage for contamination at a site in South Carolina, even though the policy was made outside the state and covered the policyholder's risk of liability at locations through the country. *Id.* In cases not controlled by the statute, South Carolina courts look to the law of the state where the policy was delivered to the policyholder. *Companion Prop. & Cas. Ins. Co. v. Airborne Exp., Inc.*, 631 S.E.2d 915, 916 (S.C. Ct. App. 2006) (Georgia law controlled CGL policy delivered to Georgia corporation in Georgia). *See also Evanston Ins. Co. v. AJ's Elec. Testing & Serv.*, LLC, No. 15-01843, 2016 U.S. Dist. LEXIS 8144, at *10-11 (D.S.C. Jan. 26, 2015) (holding that South Carolina's modification of its traditional choice of law rules via § 38-61-10 "does not necessarily govern choice of law determinations in cases like this concerning the scope of coverage under insurance policies") ("Southern Substation is a Florida company with its principal place of business in Florida; it appears to have neither any employees nor any property in South Carolina. Moreover, even though the plaintiffs in the underlying action are South Carolina residents, the insurance policies at issue were formed in Florida. Therefore, this court concludes that under South Carolina's traditional choice of law determinations [insurance policy governed by the law of the state in which the policy was issued], Florida law applies in this action."); *Russell v. McGrath*, 135 F. Supp. 3d 427, 431-32 (D.S.C. 2015) (discussing choice of law in detail) ("However, § 38-61-10 does not automatically supplant the traditional doctrine of *lex loci contractus* in every case. . . . Indeed, courts have often held that § 38-61-10 is inapplicable, noting a lack of connection, interest or nexus to South Carolina, such that it could not be said that the 'property, lives, or interests' insured were located in South Carolina.") (contrasting *Sangamo*, where the property insured - a manufacturing facility - was permanently located in South Carolina and holding that insured's connection to South Carolina - part-time resident and paid income taxes there, but a permanent resident of, licensed by and registered in the state of Georgia -- was not significant enough to trigger application of § 38-61-10); *E. Bridge Lofts Prop. Owners Ass'n v. Crum & Forster Specialty Ins. Co.*, No. 14-2567, 2015 U.S. Dist. LEXIS 156947, at *12-13 (D.S.C. Nov. 2, 2015) ("Creekstone SC is a South Carolina entity that performed two construction projects in South Carolina. After these projects were completed, Creekstone SC did not consider doing any other projects. Creekstone SC is licensed only in South Carolina as a general contractor and this license expired in 2008. Thus, it appears that Creekstone SC was created for the sole purpose to perform two discrete construction projects in South Carolina. . . . To find S.C. Code Ann. § 38-61-10 inapplicable here would run counter to the intent of the South Carolina legislature. Accordingly, the Court finds that in light of Section § 38-61-10 and *Sangamo*, the CGL policies at issue fall under the scope of the South Carolina statute."); *Integon Nat'l Ins. Co. v. Gomez*, No. 19-02958, 2020 U.S. Dist. LEXIS 219237 (D.S.C. April 21, 2020) ("[T]he Policy was formed in Alabama. Section 38-61-10 does not apply because the Policy covers property, i.e., cars, that were garaged and primarily located in Alabama.").

South Dakota: A statute provides that a "contract is to be interpreted according to the law and usage of the place where it is to be performed or, if it does not indicate a place of performance, according to the law and usage of the place where it is made." S.D.C.L. § 53-1-4. The Supreme Court of South Dakota has held that, in an action to determine coverage under an insurance policy that does not specify a place of performance, the controlling law is that of the state of delivery of the policy, which is the last act necessary to complete the contract. *Great W. Cas. Co. v. Hovaldt*, 603 N.W.2d 198, 201 (S.D. 1999) (automobile policy). *See also St. Paul Reinsurance Co., Ltd. v. Baldwin*, 503 F. Supp. 2d 1255, 1261 (D.S.D. 2007) (applying § 53-1-4 and holding that South Dakota law controlled CGL policy delivered to South Dakota broker for South Dakota policyholder); *Larson v. Auto Owners Ins. Co.*, No. 12-4020, 2012 U.S. Dist. LEXIS 129846, at *7 (D.S.D. Dec. 12, 2012) (applying § 53-1-4 to an auto policy) ("Larson purchased the insurance policy from an agent located in Minnesota. At the time he purchased the policy, Larson was working and living in Minnesota, albeit only temporarily. Because the insurance contract was 'made' in Minnesota, Minnesota law applies to Larson's breach of contract claim.") (undertaking different choice of law analysis for purposes of bad faith claim); *Bell v. Young*, No. 16-04046, 2020 U.S. Dist. LEXIS 228636 (D.S.D. Dec. 4, 2020) ("[I]nterpretation of the settlement agreement is governed by South Dakota state law because the agreement was negotiated exclusively in South Dakota by residents of this state.") (non-insurance) (citing § 53-1-4 and *Hovaldt*).

Tennessee: "In Tennessee, absent a valid choice of law provision, the rights and obligations under an insurance policy are governed by the law of the state where the insurance policy was 'made and delivered.'" *Charles Hampton's A-1 Signs, Inc. v. Am. States Ins. Co.*, 225 S.W.3d 482, 485 n.1 (Tenn. Ct. App. 2006) (quoting *Ohio Cas. Ins. Co. v. Travelers Indem. Co.*, 493 S.W.2d 465, 467 (Tenn. 1973)). Thus, Missouri law controlled coverage under a Missouri subcontractor's CGL policy for defective welding on sign poles at restaurants located in multiple states. *Id. See also Hartford Cas. Ins. Co. v. Ewan*, 890 F. Supp. 2d 886, 892 (W.D. Tenn. 2012) (applying Mississippi law to CGL policies issued and delivered to policyholder in Mississippi); *Founders Ins. Co. v. Bentley Entm't, LLC*, 2013 U.S. Dist. LEXIS 100778, at *30 (M.D. Tenn. July 17, 2013) ("The insurance policy here [liquor liability] was delivered in Tennessee to insure a Tennessee business. Absent a showing of an explicit choice-of-law provision in the policy, the Court concludes that Tennessee law applies here where the insurance policy was issued and delivered in Tennessee."). A Tennessee statute modifies this *lex loci contractus* rule, providing that "[e]very policy of insurance, issued to or for the benefit of any citizen or resident of this state … shall be held as made in this state and construed solely according to the laws of this state." TENN. CODE § 56-7-102. However, in *NGK Metals Corp. v. Nat'l Union Fire Ins. Co.*, No. 04-56, 2005 U.S. Dist. LEXIS 40603 (E.D. Tenn. Apr. 29, 2005), the court noted that "[s]ince this statute was enacted in 1907, no court addressing the choice-of-law issue in an insurance contract dispute has applied § 56-7-102 instead of the traditional *lex loci* rule." *Id.* at *16. The court undertook an analysis of the impact of § 56-7-102 on its choice of law decision. Note that, in 2018, 2019 and 2021, the statute was updated to add provisions concerning policy interpretation, duty to defend, declaratory judgment actions and assignment. *See Progressive Specialty Ins. Co. v. Kim*, No. M2019-01998-COA-R3-CV, 2021 Tenn. App. LEXIS 108 (Tenn. Ct. App. Mar. 22, 2021) ("Under Tennessee law, an insurance policy which was not issued nor delivered in Tennessee is not a Tennessee contract, and thus is not controlled by Tennessee law. Here, Sanchez is a sole proprietorship operated in Birmingham, Alabama. Progressive issued and delivered the liability insurance coverage policy to Sanchez in Alabama. Thus, the insurance policy is an Alabama contract, and the substantive law of Alabama controls the determination of whether the insurance policy provides coverage for Sanchez in the underlying tort action.").

Texas: Although a Texas statute provides that "[a]ny contract of insurance payable to any citizen or inhabitant of this State by any insurance company or corporation doing business within this State shall be held to be a contract made and entered into under and by virtue of the laws of this State relating to insurance, and governed thereby," Tex. Ins. Code Art. 21.42, Texas courts apply that statute only to insurance policies delivered in Texas to Texas citizens in the course of insurers' Texas business. *Austin Bldg. Co. v. Nat. Union Fire Ins. Co.*, 432 S.W.2d 697, 701 (Tex. 1968) (applying Kansas law to policy negotiated in Kansas to cover Kansas property, even though insured was a Texas resident); *Scottsdale Ins. Co. v. National Emergency Servs., Inc.*, 175 S.W.3d 284, 292–93 (Tex. Ct. App. 2004) (statute inapplicable to medical liability policy where named insured not a Texas resident, even though Texas subsidiaries and physicians were insureds); *Reddy Ice Corp. v. Travelers Lloyds Ins. Co.*, 145 S.W.3d 337, 341 (Tex. Ct. App. 2004) (statute applied to CGL policy only if policyholder incorporated in Texas, even if principal place of business in Texas). *But see Am. Home Assur. Co. v. Safway Steel Prods. Co., Inc.*, 743 S.W.2d 693, 697 (Tex. Ct. App. 1987) (umbrella liability policy became payable to Texas citizens under Art. 21.42 upon entry of judgment against out-of-state policyholders). In cases where no statute controls, the Supreme Court of Texas employs a Second Restatement analysis to determine the law governing a contract. *Sonat Exploration Co. v. Cudd Pressure Control, Inc.*, 271 S.W.3d 228, 231 (Tex. 2008). Texas courts applying the Second Restatement to CGL policies generally have found that the governing law is that of the state where the policyholder maintained its principal place of business during the policy period, even if the injury occurred in a different state. *Reddy Ice*, 145 S.W.3d at 345–46 (under §§ 188 and 193, Texas law controlled CGL policy issued to policyholder headquartered in Texas and doing business mostly in Texas, even though dispute involved coverage for pollution at Louisiana site); *Pennzoil-Quaker State Co. v. Am. Int'l Specialty Lines Ins. Co.*, 653 F. Supp. 2d 690, 702–03 (S.D. Tex. 2009) (applying Texas law to pollution legal liability policy covering Texas policyholder as to sites in sixteen states, even though coverage dispute involved only Louisiana sites).

In *Markel Am. Ins. Co. v. Verbeek*, No. 14-00143, 2015 U.S. Dist. LEXIS 124134 (W.D. Tex. Sept. 17, 2015), the court addressed choice of law for purposes of a coverage dispute involving a D&O policy. The insurer argued that the "most significant relationship" test, outlined in Section 188 of the Restatement, should govern choice of law. However, the court stated that "these factors come into play only if no statutory mandate directs the application of Texas law." The court held: "Markel is an admitted lines insurer in Texas, and three of the four insureds under the D&O policy at issue are Texas residents. Of the Defendants participating in bringing the pending Motion for Partial Summary Judgment and Motions to Strike, at least one is a Texas resident. Therefore, Texas Insurance Code, Article 21.42 applies to direct the choice of Texas; substantive law in this case." *Id.* at *19-20. *See also ADI Worldlink, LLC v. RSUI Indem. Co.*, 2017 U.S. Dist. LEXIS 151106, at *18 (E.D. Tex. Aug. 16, 2017) (addressing the citizen or inhabitant requirement of § 21.42 in detail) ("In the instant case, Plaintiff argues Texas Insurance Code § 21.42 applies and mandates the Court's application of Texas law to the questions presented in this case. The Court disagrees. Initially, and as the authorities cited *supra* illustrate, a foreign corporation does not become a Texas 'citizen or inhabitant' within the meaning of § 21.42 by virtue of establishing its principal place of business in Texas."); *Aggreko v. Chartis Specialty Ins. Co.*, No. 16-297, 2018 U.S. Dist. LEXIS 239237 (E.D. Tex. Mar. 7, 2018) (undertaking detailed analysis under both § 21.42 and Restatement most significant relationship test; Texas law applied under both) ("Considering the factors as a whole and the respective strength of the contacts, the court concludes that Texas has the most significant relationship with the dispute and the case at bar. Given that the insured risk was located in Texas, the accident occurred in Texas, and the injured parties reside there, and the Covenant Not to Execute specifies the application of Texas law, Texas has the greatest interest in the matters at issue in this case. Further, the parties were aware of the location of the subject matter upon contracting for the insurance, as evidenced by the Rental Agreement for the Aggreko generator. The court has weighed these factors according to their relative importance, and, thus, Texas law will provide the applicable rules of decision for the matters under consideration in the instant motions."); *Frosch Holdco, Inc. v. Travelers Indem. Co.*, No. 20-1478, 2021 U.S. Dist. LEXIS 65994 (S.D. Tex. Feb. 11, 2021) (noting that, in the context of § 21.42, a corporation is an inhabitant only of the state where it is incorporated).

Utah: The Supreme Court of Utah applies Sections 188 and 193 of the Second Restatement to questions of coverage under insurance contracts. *Am. Nat. Fire Ins. Co. v. Farmers Ins. Exchange*, 927 P.2d 186, 188–92 (Utah 1996). *American National*, which involved an automobile policy, provides a strong indication that the law of a single state would control such a case: "To protect justified expectation and predictability of result as intended by Restatement of Conflict section 6, we must hold that the parties to an automobile insurance contract cannot change their bargain or have the bargain changed for them every time they drive across a state line." *Id.* at 192. The Court of Appeals of Utah applied Texas law where the insured's headquarters and the plant where asbestos inhalation allegedly occurred were located in Texas at the time of contracting. *One Beacon Am. Ins. Co. v. Huntsman Polymers Corp.*, 276 P.3d 1156, 1171-72 (Utah Ct. App. 2012). "Having considered the pertinent contacts under section 188, we conclude that Texas is the state with the most significant relationship to this contractual dispute. Because this case involves a multiple risk policy, the location of the insured risk is not wholly determinative here. Nonetheless, the location of the insured risk has considerable weight in the choice of law analysis because the insured risk 'can be located, at least principally, in a single state,' *see* Restatement (Second) of Conflict of Laws § 193 cmt. b (1971). That weight is enhanced because this is not a case where 'some other state has a more significant relationship ... to the [contract] and the parties' than Texas, *see id.* § 193. In particular, One Beacon has not persuaded us that Utah has a more significant relationship to this contractual dispute than Texas. Indeed, any relationship Utah has to this dispute as Huntsman's principal place of business and the actual place of performance is, in the end, fortuitous because those contacts only arise from the purchase of El Paso Products by Huntsman decades after the CGL insurance policy was issued and after the active relationship between the contracting parties had dissipated. Those contacts to Utah therefore carry much less weight in the overall most significant relationship analysis." *Id.* Some pre–*American National* decisions from Utah federal courts applied the law of Utah to CGL coverage for injury occurring in Utah. *See Anaconda Minerals Co. v. Stoller Chem. Co., Inc.*, 773 F. Supp. 1498, 1504 n.8 (D. Utah 1991) (finding that Second Restatement factors favored application of law of Utah, as location of polluted site, in CGL coverage dispute where parties did not brief choice of law); *Mountain Fuel Supply v. Reliance Ins. Co.*, 933 F.2d 882, 888 (10th Cir. 1991) (choosing between state of injury and state of negotiation of policies, as neither party looked to state of policyholder's headquarters). *See also Rupp v. Transcontinental Ins. Co.*, 627 F. Supp. 2d 1304, 1314–16 (D. Utah 2008) (applying tort choice-of-law principles of Second Restatement § 145 to find that Utah law governed claim for bad-faith failure to settle Utah lawsuit); *Mitchell v. Wells Fargo Bank*, 280 F. Supp. 3d 1261 (D. Utah 2017) ("Where two or more states have an interest in a dispute, Utah courts have applied the test in Section 188 of the Restatement (Second) of Conflict of Laws to analyze which state holds 'the most significant relationship' to the contractual dispute.") (non-insurance, but citing *American National*).

Vermont: The Supreme Court of Vermont applies the contractual choice-of-law provisions of Second Restatement § 188. *Pioneer Credit Corp. v. Carden*, 245 A.2d 891, 894 (Vt. 1968). Vermont federal decisions have applied conflicting Second Restatement analyses to CGL policies. One decision held that the law of Vermont—as the policyholder's headquarters, the place where the policies where negotiated and delivered, and the place where the policyholder did most of its business—governed coverage under CGL policies for pollution in Missouri. *Village of Morrisville Water & Light Dept. v. U.S. Fid. & Guar. Co.*, 775 F. Supp. 718, 723 (D. Vt. 1991). But a second decision expressly declined to follow *Village of Morrisville*, which it interpreted as applying a *lex loci contractus* approach: "While the traditional rule of 'lex loci contractus' may better apply to cases involving multiple sites, judicial economy and predictability dictate that in single site cases courts apply the law of the state where the site is located." *E.B. & A.C. Whiting Co. v. Hartford Fire Ins. Co.*, 838 F. Supp. 863, 865–66 (D. Vt. 1993), *disapproved on other grounds*, *Maska U.S., Inc. v. Kansa Gen. Ins. Co.*, 198 F.3d 74 (2d Cir. 1999). Although "the insurance policies were all negotiated, executed and paid for in states other than Vermont," Vermont, "as the state in which the toxic waste site is located … has the strongest interest in how the policies are interpreted because resolution of insurance issues impacts directly on Vermont environmental policies." *Id.* at 866. *Cf. City of Burlington v. Hartford Steam Boiler Inspection & Ins. Co.*, 190 F. Supp. 2d 663, 678 (D. Vt. 2002) (applying *E.B. & A.C. Whiting* site-specific approach to property policy). A Vermont federal court applied the *Morrisville* decision to a personal umbrella policy issued to a Vermont policyholder involved in a Massachusetts accident: "[I]f the issue is coverage, Vermont has the most significant relationship, because among other things, the Policy was obtained in Vermont through a Vermont insurance broker, the Policy was intended to comply with Vermont law, and the insureds reside in Vermont." *RLI Ins. Co. v. Klonsky*, 771 F. Supp. 2d 314, 329 (D. Vt. 2011). But the same decision, applying tort choice-of-law principles held that Massachusetts law applied to the injured party's bad faith claim because "[i]f the issue is claims handling, Massachusetts has the most significant relationship, because the accident occurred in Massachusetts, the injured party resides in Massachusetts, and much of the investigation and claims handling occurred in Massachusetts." *Id. See also Acadia Ins. Co. v. Welog, Inc.*, No. 15-102, 2017 U.S. Dist. LEXIS 108770, at *17-18 (D. Vt. July 11, 2017) (analyzing Restatement Second §§ 6, 188 and 193, distinguishing *E.B. & A.C. Whiting* and applying New Hampshire law) ("There is no suggestion in *E.B. & A.C. Whiting* that the plaintiff, a manufacturer of nylon bristle, conducted business in states other than Vermont or that the insurance policies in question insured risks at sites outside Vermont. The *only* location of insured risk identified in the case is the toxic site in Vermont. It is therefore unsurprising that the court, applying section 193, concluded that Vermont law applied to the interpretation of the insurance policies. In comparison, in this case, it is undisputed that the significant majority of WeLog's operations in general, and its logging business in particular, occurred not in Vermont but in New Hampshire.") (emphasis in original).

Virginia: Virginia adheres to the common law rule of *lex loci contractus*, under which an insurance policy is "governed by the law of the place where made." *Lexie v. State Farm Mut. Auto. Ins. Co.*, 469 S.E.2d 61, 63 (Va. 1996). *See CACI Int'l, Inc. v. St. Paul Fire & Marine Ins. Co.*, 566 F.3d 150 (4th Cir. 2009) (applying Virginia law to CGL policies delivered in Virginia to government contractor accused of torture and abuse at prison in Iraq). "Under Virginia law, a contract is made when the last act to complete it is performed, and in the context of an insurance policy, the last act is the delivery of the policy to the insured." *Resource Bankshares Corp. v. St. Paul Mercury Ins. Co.*, 407 F.3d 631, 635–36 (4th Cir. 2005). *See also Marks v. Scottsdale Ins. Co.*, 791 F.3d 448, 451 (4th Cir. 2015) ("In insurance cases, Virginia law looks to the law of the state where the insurance contract is written and delivered."); *Atl. Cas. Ins. Co. v. Connection Auto Sales, Inc.*, No. 20-275, 2020 U.S. Dist. LEXIS 241168 (E.D. Va. Dec. 22, 2020) (same); *Hopeman Bros., Inc. v. Cont'l Cas. Co.*, 307 F. Supp. 3d 433 (E.D. Va. 2018) ("At the time the policies were issued, Hopeman's headquarters was located in New York. Hopeman's New York business address is listed on the policies, and it paid insurance premiums from that state. Further, Hopeman used brokers located in New York to procure the policies, and it corresponded with these brokers from New York. Under Virginia's choice of law rules, these facts establish that the policies were written and delivered in New York, and therefore New York law governs their interpretation.").

Washington: "Since 1967, Washington courts have adhered to and applied the most significant relationship test to contract choice of law issues." *Mulcahy v. Farmers Ins. Co.*, 95 P.3d 313, 317 (Wash. 2004) (applying Second Restatement § 188). The Supreme Court of Washington has held that, for a CGL policy covering potential risk in multiple states, with the location of the risk therefore unidentifiable at the time of contracting, the "principal location of the insured risk" principle of Section 193 of the Second Restatement is inapplicable. *Fluke Corp. v. Hartford Acc. & Indem. Co.*, 34 P.3d 809, 815–16 (Wash. 2001). Thus, Washington law controlled coverage under a Washington-based policyholder's CGL policy with respect to a malicious prosecution action filed in California. *Id. See also N. Ins. Co. v. Allied Mut. Ins. Co.*, 955 F.2d 1353 (9th Cir. 1992) (applying same analysis to conclude that California law controlled question of whether insurer needed to pay for independent *Cumis* counsel for California-based policyholder in lawsuit in Washington); *Tilden-Coil Constructors, Inc. v. Landmark Am. Ins. Co.*, 721 F. Supp. 2d 1007, 1015 (W.D. Wash.

2010) (Washington law controlled insurer's obligation to pay settlement entered into by Washington policyholder in California litigation); *Milgard Mfg. v. Ill. Union Ins. Co.*, No. C10-5943, 2011 U.S. Dist. LEXIS 84023, at *16 (W.D. Wash. Aug. 1, 2011) (applying Washington law to a claim for coverage involving defective windows, manufactured by an insured in Washington, and installed in Oregon) ("The insurance policy in the present case is a multiple-risk policy with multiple coverage areas and without a choice-of-law provision. With multiple-risk insurance policies, there often will be no principal location for the insured risk. In such circumstances, the general, multi-factored test of Section 188, rather than the site-specific test of Section 193, typically controls. Milgard conducts business in several states and nothing in the policy indicates that the parties anticipated Oregon would be the primary location of the insured risks."). *But see Teck Metals, Ltd. v. Certain Underwriters at Lloyd's, London*, 735 F. Supp. 2d 1231, 1239–45 (E.D. Wash. 2010) (finding that Washington's interest in remediation of contamination outweighed interests of British Columbia, as place of contracting and location of most of insured sites and where insured had its operations) ("As legitimate an expectation by the insured, and the insurers for that matter, is that Washington law might apply to policies insuring risk worldwide where the alleged wrongful action and the alleged damage occurred in Washington, only a few miles from the Trail smelting operation. Furthermore, Washington's interest in remedying that damage is just as compelling as B.C.'s interest in protecting what it perceives to be the legitimate expectations of insurers who do business in that province. The most significant relationship test does not involve simply counting contacts. The relative policies and interests of the states in the subject matter of the contract must also be considered."); *Ingenco Holdings, LLC v. ACE Am. Ins. Co.*, 921 F.3d 803 (9th Cir. 2019) (undertaking lengthy Restatement analysis, examining numerous choice of law factors); *Safeco Ins. Co. v. McPartland*, No. C20-1049, 2021 U.S. Dist. LEXIS 82521 (W.D. Wash. Apr. 29, 2021) (undertaking Restatement analysis to determine which state's law governed duty to defend standard) (concluding that Oregon law applied as "most significant that the policy is an 'Oregon Renter's Policy' purchased to insure a residence in Oregon") (reaching conclusion, despite insured residing in Washington and purchasing policy from an agent in Washington, listing insured's address in Washington).

West Virginia: The Supreme Court of Appeals of West Virginia has adopted a hybrid of *lex loci contractus* and the Second Restatement—the law of the state of the formation of the insurance contract governs, unless another state has a more significant relationship to the transaction and the parties, or the law of the other state is contrary to West Virginia public policy. *Liberty Mut. Ins. Co. v. Triangle Indus., Inc.*, 390 S.E.2d 562, 566–67 (W. Va. 1990). Thus, New Jersey law governed coverage for a New Jersey corporation, which owned plants in multiple states, for a suit alleging that waste transported from its West Virginia plant contaminated a landfill in Ohio. The court reasoned that "it is infinitely more practicable to permit one policy to cover the numerous contracts rather than to require both [the policyholder] and the insurance companies to negotiate individual policies based upon each state where an insured risk is located." *Id. See also Joy Technologies v. Liberty Mut. Ins. Co.*, 421 S.E.2d 493, 496-97 (W. Va. 1992) ("The action in the present case arises out of the expenditures of monies for remediating damage caused by pollution to property in West Virginia, and it is rather clear that the pollution arose from operations which were conducted in West Virginia and involved a facility located in West Virginia. Thus, the injury occurred in West Virginia, the instrumentality of injury was located in West Virginia, and the forum selected to try the issues was West Virginia. These factors suggest that West Virginia has had a very significant relationship to the transaction and the parties. In fact, the relationship would appear to be more substantial than that of Pennsylvania, where the contract was formed."); *Mulvey Constr., Inc. v. Bituminous Cas. Corp.*, 571 F. App'x 150, 157 (4th Cir. 2014) (Virginia law governed CGL policy formed in Virginia, in dispute regarding coverage for accident in West Virginia); *APAC-Atl., Inc. v. Protection Servs., Inc.*, 397 F. Supp. 2d 792, 796–97 (N.D. W. Va. 2005) (in CGL coverage action arising out of motorist's death at highway construction site in West Virginia, law of Pennsylvania, as state where policy was issued to subcontractor, controlled whether general contractor was entitled to defense as additional insured); *Ohio Sec. Ins. Co. v. K R Enters.*, No. 15-16264, 2017 U.S. Dist. LEXIS 42011, at *8-9 (S.D. W. Va. Mar. 23, 2017) ("This general rule [*lex loci contractus* for choice of law for contracts] is subject to an exception. [I]n a case involving the interpretation of an insurance policy, made in one state to be performed in another, the law of the state of formation of the contract shall govern, unless another state has a more significant relationship to the transaction and parties, or the law of the other state is contrary to the public policy of this state.") ("Because the policy was issued in Virginia, the court begins with the presumption that Virginia law applies. No other state has a more significant relationship to the transaction and the parties than Virginia. The Ohio Security Policy identifies thirty-two K R Enterprise locations, six of which are located in West Virginia and twenty-six of which are located in Virginia. Furthermore, the court does not find (nor do defendants argue) that the law of Virginia is contrary to the public policy of West Virginia. Therefore, under the rule of *Triangle*, Virginia law should govern interpretation of the Ohio Security policy and there are good reasons for doing so."); *St. Paul Mercury Ins. Co. v. Nat'l Sur. Corp.*, No. 14-45, 2015 U.S. Dist. LEXIS 4363, at *13-14 (N.D. W.Va. Jan. 4, 2015) (addressing CGL policy) ("The injuries at issue in *Joy* are very different than the damages in the present case. In *Joy*, a manufacturing plant, located in West Virginia, emitted toxic pollution that caused both property damage to adjoining landowners and personal injuries to employees of the plant. Unlike *Joy*, the damages here are economic in nature, and no unforeseeable third parties suffered harm. . . . Moreover, the *Joy* Court held that West Virginia's public policy regarding the insurance policy exclusion at issue in the case was best served by applying West Virginia law. Here, the parties do not assert that West Virginia's public policy would be contravened by applying Missouri law."); *Ohio Sec. Ins. Co. v. K R Enters.*, No. 15-16264, 2017 U.S. Dist. LEXIS 42011 (S.D. W. Va. Mar. 23, 2017) ("Because the policy was issued in Virginia, the court begins with the presumption that Virginia law applies. No other state has a more significant relationship to the transaction and the parties than Virginia. The Ohio Security Policy identifies thirty-two K R Enterprise locations, six of which are located in West Virginia and twenty-six of which are located in Virginia. Furthermore, the court does not find (nor do defendants argue) that the law of Virginia is contrary to the public policy of West Virginia. Therefore, under the rule of *Triangle*, Virginia law should govern interpretation of the Ohio Security policy and there are good reasons for doing so."); *J.A. St. & Assocs., Inc. v. Bitco Gen. Ins. Corp.*, No. 17-0079, 2019 W. Va. LEXIS 205 (W. Va. May 1, 2019) (restating *Triangle Indus.*); *Main St. Am. Assur. Co. v. Posada*, No. 19-3, 2019 U.S. Dist. LEXIS 226656 (N.D. W. Va. Sept. 9, 2019) ("It is not disputed that the subject insurance policy was delivered to the insured, Posada, in Manassas, Virginia. The Policy also has several Virginia specific endorsements. The delivery and terms of the Policy indicate that the parties intended the insurance contract to be governed by Virginia law.").

Wisconsin: Wisconsin courts apply a "grouping-of-contacts" analysis that follows Sections 188 and 193 of the Second Restatement. *Utica Mut. Ins. Co. v. Klein & Son, Inc.*, 460 N.W.2d 763, 767 (Wis. Ct. App. 1990). Thus, Wisconsin law controlled coverage under a Wisconsin insurance broker's errors and omissions policy with respect to a lawsuit filed in Minnesota because the insured risk had its principal location at the insured's offices. *Id.* "The place of the accident is irrelevant in deciding which law governs a contract, including an insurance agreement." *Lampe v. Genuine Parts Co.*, 463 F. Supp. 2d 928, 935 (E.D. Wis. 2006). Nevertheless, a state appellate decision, applying Wisconsin law to a dispute regarding CGL coverage for a polluted site in Wisconsin, found that the policyholder's headquarters in Ohio weighed only "negligibly in favor of Ohio." *NCR Corp. v. Transp. Ins. Co.*, 823 N.W.2d 532, 538 (Wis. Ct. App. 2012). *See also Kender v. Auto-Owners Ins. Co.*, 793 N.W.2d 88, 94-95 (Wis. Ct. App. 2010) (auto policy) ("After considering the relevant contacts under the grouping of contacts rule [(a) the place of contracting, (b) the place of negotiation of the contract, (c) the place of performance, (d) the location of the subject matter of the contract, and (e) the domicile, residence, nationality, place of incorporation and place of business of the parties], we conclude that Minnesota has the more significant relationship with the Auto-Owners policy. The contract was executed and negotiated in Minnesota given that both Strom and its insurance agent are located there. The contract was performed in Minnesota (along with other states). In addition, the place most relevant to the subject matter of the contract is Minnesota as Strom was located there, and, most telling for our purposes, is the fact that the policy incorporated Minnesota-specific endorsements. The parties to the policy were Strom, a Minnesota corporation, and Auto-Owners, a Michigan insurance company. We agree with Enterprise that 'it is clear from the parties' inclusion of endorsements specifically adding Minnesota provisions to the insurance contract, that the parties to this contract expected Minnesota law to apply to its interpretation.'"); *Chesapeake Life Ins. Co. v. Parker*, No. 18-C-643, 2018 U.S. Dist. LEXIS 96699 (E.D. Wis. June 8, 2018) (life insurance) (Wisconsin courts apply the 'grouping-of-contacts' approach, which provides that insurance coverage is determined by the law of the jurisdiction with which the contract has its most significant relationship."); *West Bend Mut. Ins. Co. v. Travelers Prop. Cas. Co. of Am.*, No. 20-1600, 2021 U.S. Dist. LEXIS 68097 (E.D. Wis. Apr. 8, 2021) ("For contractual disputes, Wisconsin courts apply the 'grouping of contacts' rule, which requires considering several factors.") (citing *J3 Eng'g Grp., LLC v. Mack Indus. of Kalamazoo, LLC*, 390 F. Supp. 3d 946 (E.D. Wis. 2019) (non-insurance) which addresses choice of law in detail).

Wyoming: Wyoming has little authority on choice-of-law for insurance policies. Wyoming apparently applies a Second Restatement analysis. *Resource Tech. Corp. v. Fisher Scientific Co.*, 924 P.2d 972, 975 (Wyo. 1996). *See also Cal. Cas. & Fire Ins. Co. v. Brinkman*, 50 F. Supp. 2d 1157, 1166 (D. Wyo. 1999) (applying Wyoming law to automobile liability policy issued with respect to a vehicle principally garaged in Wyoming and involved in an accident in Colorado); *Act I, LLC v. Davis*, 60 P.3d 145, 149 (Wyo. 2002) (statute of frauds) ("The Second Restatement method is constructed around the principle that the state with the most significant contacts to an issue provides the law governing that issue. A court therefore conducts a separate choice-of-law analysis for each issue in a case, attempting to determine which state has the most significant contacts with that issue."); *Elworthy v. First Tenn. Bank*, 391 P.3d 1113 (Wyo. 2017) (contract, but not insurance policy) ("In analyzing choice of law questions, this Court uses the approach defined by the *Restatement (Second) of Conflict of Laws*."). Even where two jurisdictions apply different rules, there is no material conflict, as would require a choice-of-law analysis, unless the application of those differing rules is outcome-determinative. *Employers Mut. Cas. Co. v. Bartile Roofs, Inc.*, 618 F.3d 1153, 1170–71 (10th Cir. 2010). In *Carolina Cas. Ins. Co. v. Burlington Ins. Co.*, 951 F.3d 1199 (10th Cir. 2020), the Tenth Circuit, citing *Elworthy*, stated that Wyoming analyzes choice-of-law questions under the Second Restatement. However, finding no conflict, the court applied the forum state's law—Wyoming. *See Carolina Cas. Ins. Co. v. Burlington Ins. Co.*, No. 17-20, 2018 U.S. Dist. LEXIS 241859 (D. Wyo. May 11, 2018) for the court's application of the Second Restatement factors to conclude that Wyoming law applied.

CHAPTER
3

Late Notice Defense Under "Occurrence" Policies: Is Prejudice to the Insurer Required?

The typical first-party property policy requires that the policyholder give the insurer timely notice of a loss while the typical third-party liability policy similarly requires timely notice of a claim or suit against the policyholder. Although some policies state that notice should be given "immediately," "as soon as possible," or within a fixed time limit, the average policy speaks of prompt notice or notice "as soon as practicable."

The notice requirement is usually contained in the "Conditions" section of a policy and is sometimes described in technical legal terms as a "condition precedent" to coverage, i.e., an event that must take place before the other party to the contract (the insurer) has any obligations under the contract (the policy).

Historically, condition precedent requirements in contracts were fairly strictly enforced, and this was certainly the case with insurance policies until approximately the middle of the twentieth century. Under the traditional approach, if a policyholder's notice of a loss or claim was late, the policyholder had failed to satisfy the condition precedent of prompt notice, and the insurer was not obligated to defend or pay under the policy. This appears to have been the majority rule in the United States as late as 1960.

During the past sixty years, however, the legal landscape has completely shifted, with most states now holding that late notice defeats coverage *only if* the insurer has been materially prejudiced by the untimely notice—although there remain states strictly applying the traditional rule (as Arkansas did in 2010) as well as states with older traditional rule precedent that may or may not be followed in future cases. States differ on whether late notice creates a rebuttable presumption of prejudice or whether it is the insurer's burden to demonstrate prejudice. The bulk of states appear to place this burden on the insurer while others assume prejudice but permit policyholders to regain coverage if they can demonstrate lack of prejudice from late notice.

The burden of proof on the issue is usually the familiar "preponderance of the evidence" standard, which asks whether it is "more likely than not" that the insurer was prejudiced in its ability to investigate, evaluate, defend, settle, or pay a claim due to the late notice.

It should be stressed that in so-called "notice-prejudice rule" states, the prejudice to the insurer must be something more than mere inconvenience or additional effort. Rather, material prejudice is required, which is generally defined as an impact that strips the insurer of important substantive rights it would have had if the notice had been timely. If key evidence has been altered or destroyed and there is no reasonable alternative source of information (such as incident reports, documents, video footage, or adequate witness testimony), the insurer will generally be considered to have been materially prejudiced in its ability to adjust or defend a claim.

If, for example, a policyholder repairs a damaged roof and then notifies the insurer, the insurer may be considered to have been prejudiced because the damaged property is no longer in its original condition and the insurer cannot evaluate whether the repairs were reasonable in scope and cost. More dramatically, a liability insurer will generally be considered to have been materially prejudiced if a policyholder/defendant settles a claim or trial in the matter has concluded prior to the insurer's notification (although a few cases find even this to be insufficiently prejudicial). Similarly, a policyholder's agreement to arbitration of a claim that could have been litigated (or vice versa) may be considered sufficiently prejudicial to an insurer.

The primary rationale for the move from the "no prejudice rule" to the "notice-prejudice rule" is a desire to avoid unreasonable forfeiture of insurance policy benefits. If the insurer is not prejudiced, it is viewed as unfair to deprive the policyholder of the insurance coverage it had purchased—perhaps having paid premiums for decades—simply because of the "technicality" of late notice (and lateness is only a technicality absent prejudice). In addition, under general principles of contract law, failure to give prompt notice can be viewed as only an "immaterial" breach unless there is prejudice. Generally, an immaterial breach does not allow the other party to walk away from the contract but restricts it to seeking compensation for the consequences of breach. Absent significant prejudice to the insurer, there appear to be no such consequences for the breach of late notice.

Further, the fiduciary-like relation of insurer and policyholder prompts many courts to find it inappropriate for an insurer to deny coverage on late notice grounds unless there has been some sufficiently concrete harm to the insurer. A legal maxim of long standing is that "law abhors a forfeiture." Policyholder counsel have during the past few decades largely been successful in arguing that to deny coverage due to late notice in the absence of prejudice to the insurer is to work a forfeiture against the policyholder.

Another factor in the move to the notice-prejudice rule, at least for liability insurance, is the public policy of adequately compensating victims. If the policyholder/tortfeasor is stripped of otherwise applicable insurance for failing to give prompt notice, the injured victim suffers as much or more than the policyholder, perhaps leading to increased victim claims for public health or welfare benefits.

Against these arguments, insurer counsel defending the traditional rule point out that the insurance policy is often characterized as a unilateral or reverse-unilateral contract in which the policyholder performs first by paying the premium but the insurer is only required to perform if established conditions precedent take place. The typical insurance policy lists prompt notice as a condition that must occur before the promise is activated. Therefore, according to the traditional argument, late notice fails to satisfy an essential condition precedent to coverage and excuses the insurer from the contract regardless of prejudice and regardless of working a forfeiture upon the policyholder.

Regardless of the rule used in a given jurisdiction, there will always be the question whether notice is in fact "late." Even notice coming long after an accident may be considered timely if the policyholder had no reason to expect a claim. For example, a policyholder's houseguest may slip in the bathroom but seem fine. Months later, the guest may develop back pains or headaches and attribute them to the fall, bringing a claim. In this sort of case, the clock usually begins ticking (for late notice purposes) upon the policyholder's receipt of the claim rather than from the time of the guest's fall. However, specific insurance policy deadlines based on any incident may change this approach if the court does not view the notice requirements as confusing or unfair to the policyholder. In addition, the insurer may require notice of any event that *may* lead to a claim, strengthening the notice obligations contained in the policy.

As one might expect, common sense is usually the courts' guide in these areas. However, even notice years after an incident may not be "late" depending on the circumstances. Because law "abhors a forfeiture" of contract benefits, the traditional rule/"no prejudice required" jurisdictions often exhibit reluctance to label notice as "late," perhaps because to do so conclusively strips the policyholder of coverage.

Alternatively, even concededly late notice may also be considered excused under apt circumstances. For example, wind may blow off a roof of a home or burst plumbing may flood a neighbor's condominium on a lower floor. If the policyholder was not present at the time, most courts will suspend the running of the clock for late notice purposes, at least for some reasonable time and perhaps even until the policyholder becomes consciously aware of the problem. Conversely, insurers will argue, with mixed success, that the policyholder must take at least some steps to be reasonably informed about the condition of its property or the consequences of its business operations or property upon others.

The trend toward a prejudice requirement in occurrence-based insurance policies is in more than a little tension with the use of claims-made policy forms for many types of liability insurance. The claims-made form is particularly popular for Professional Liability (e.g., legal and medical malpractice), Errors and Omissions coverage generally, Directors and Officers liability insurance, and has seen intermittent use for General Liability insurance. Under the law of most states involving typical claims-made forms, there must be quite strict compliance with the deadlines set forth in the policy, which usually require that the policyholder give notice to the insurer of claims made against it during the policy period prior to the expiration of that same policy period or any extended reporting period provided in the policy. It is generally not necessary for the insurer to prove that it has been prejudiced by the policyholder's failure to comply with a claims-made policy's notice requirements. Indeed, it is not at all unusual for a state to place a demanding prejudice requirement on insurers seeking to disclaim coverage for late notice under occurrence basis policies but then do a complete about-face and allow the insurer to disclaim coverage for late notice under claims-made basis policies based on the slimmest of violations by the policyholder and without any showing of prejudice by the insurer. At the margin, however, notice regarding claims-made policies can become less cut-and-dried. This chapter deals only with notice regarding occurrence policies.

50-State Survey: Late Notice Defense Under "Occurrence" Policies: Is Prejudice to the Insurer Required?

Alabama: No prejudice required for primary insurers to successfully invoke the late notice defense, but excess insurers must show prejudice from late notice to defeat coverage. *See Midwest Emp'rs Cas. Co. v. E. Ala. Health Care*, 695 So. 2d 1169, 1173 (Ala. 1997) (workers' compensation claim involving an employee whose initial diagnosis after suffering an injury on the job was a sprained ankle, but later required back surgery due to a herniated disc; claim exceeded the primary insurance policy limits, and the excess insurer complained of late notice when it did not receive notice until two years after the initial injury; burden to prove prejudice in excess cases is on the insurer) (prejudice also may be a factor in determining whether notice is deemed to be late). "Alabama law is clear that notice provisions must be adhered to by the insured, and that compliance with them is a condition precedent to coverage. Prejudice to the insurer by late notice is presumed. … When determining whether an insured has satisfied the reasonable notice requirement, the Alabama Supreme Court has directed Alabama courts to consider only (1) the length of the delay; and (2) the existence or non-existence of an objectively reasonable excuse for the delay. Absence of actual prejudice to the insurer, even if true, is not a factor to be considered." *Sharp Realty & Mgmt., LLC v. Capitol Specialty Ins. Corp.*, No. CV-10-AR-3180-S, 2012 U.S. Dist. LEXIS 75353 (N.D. Ala. May 31, 2012) (citations omitted) (concluding insured's eight-month delay with no excuse unreasonable as a matter of law), *aff'd*, No. 12-13344, 2013 U.S. App. LEXIS 243 (11th Cir. Jan. 4, 2013); *see also Travelers Indem. Co. of Conn. v. Miller*, 86 So. 3d 338, 342 (Ala. 2011) (absent a reasonable excuse, notice after default judgment bars recovery). As with a primary insurer, "the length of the delay and the reasons for the delay also must be considered in the context of excess insurer's assertion of late notice. Alabama [courts] … impose an additional requirement upon an excess insurer; an excess insurer also must demonstrate that it was prejudiced by the late notice." *Lemuel v. Admiral Ins. Co.*, 414 F. Supp. 2d 1037, 1056 (M.D. Ala. 2006), *aff'd*, No. 2:03cv1101-D, 2007 U.S. App. LEXIS 380 (11th Cir. Jan. 9, 2007); *see also Overstreet v. Safeway Ins. Co. of Ala.*, 740 So. 2d 1053, 1059 (Ala. 1999) ("If the [excess] insurer fails to present evidence as to prejudice, then the insured's failure to give notice will not be a bar to his recovery" but finding prejudice and breach due to policyholder settlement of claim without insurer consent); *Arrowood Indem. Co. v. Macon Cnty. Greyhound Park, Inc.*, 757 F. Supp. 2d 1219, 1226 (M.D. Ala. 2010) (concluding that excess liability insurer had no duty to indemnify where insurer was not notified of underlying occurrence until two weeks after a jury entered a verdict against the insured) (granting summary judgment for insurer because insured did not have reasonable excuse for its failure to provide notice to insurer), *aff'd*, No. 3:08-cv-812-MEF, 2011 U.S. App. LEXIS 23892 (11th Cir. Nov. 29, 2011); *Auto-Owners Ins. Co. v. Small*, 2017 U.S. Dist. LEXIS 35119, No. 16-01042 (N.D. Ala. Mar. 13, 2017) ("To support its contention, Auto-Owners cites *Pharr v. Continental Casualty Co.*, 429 So. 2d 1018, 1019-20 (Ala. 1983) (eight-month delay unreasonable as a matter of law), and *Southern Guaranty Insurance Co. v. Thomas*, 334 So. 2d 879, 883 (Ala. 1976) (six-month delay unreasonable as a matter of law). These authorities are distinguishable, however, because, in *Pharr*, the insured provided no 'excuse for the delay,' and, in *Thomas*, the insured claimed that he thought the policy did not provide coverage and/or that he was not liable for the underlying accident. Accepting the non-movant's factual allegations as true, as this court must do, Small delayed providing notice to Auto-Owners because of his wife's stroke and his resulting responsibility to provide constant care for her until her death. Therefore, because the reasonableness of a delay is often a factual issue."); *Pa. Nat'l Mut. Cas. Ins. Co. v. J.F. Morgan Gen. Contrs., Inc.*, 79 F. Supp. 3d 1245 (N.D. Ala. 2015) (setting forth a discussion of numerous cases addressing late notice under Alabama law and holding that thirteen month delay in forwarding suit papers to insurer was unreasonable as a matter of law because no legitimate excuse for the delay was offered). The nature of Alabama's late notice test – presumably, the objectively reasonable excuse for the delay factor -- seems to lead to numerous decisions addressing the issue. They are fact driven and resort to the cases is recommended. *See State Farm Fire & Cas. Co. v. GHW, III*, 56 F. Supp. 3d 1210 (N.D. Ala. 2015); *Auto Owners Ins. Co. v. Guardian Builders, Inc.*, No. 11-04096, 2014 U.S. Dist. LEXIS 40203 (N.D. Ala. Mar. 24, 2015); *Evanston Ins. Co. v. The Break I Inc.*, No. 18-01197, 2019 U.S. Dist. LEXIS 113109 (N.D. Ala. July 9, 2019); *Evanston Ins. Co. v. Yeager Painting, LLC*, No. 16-02061, 2018 U.S. Dist. LEXIS 130316 (N.D. Ala. Aug. 3, 2018); *Communs. Unlimited Contr. Servs. v. Liberty Mut. Ins. Co.*, No. 18-00613, 2020 U.S. Dist. LEXIS 154048 (N.D. Ala. Aug. 25, 2020); ("[E]ven if CUI possessed a good-faith belief that a Comcast systems error was to blame for the missing equipment, CUI had 'reasonable grounds' to believe that Melcher could have been to blame instead. At that moment (2015), the timely-notice provision required CUI to inform Liberty Mutual about Comcast's chargeback and Comcast's suspicion that CUI employees were involved so that Liberty Mutual could begin its own investigation and potentially limit or disprove its liability. CUI's decision to wait more than two years to inform Liberty Mutual of the chargeback stripped Liberty Mutual of the chance to investigate the loss while the evidence was fresh.").

Alaska: Prejudice required. *See Weaver Bros., Inc. v. Chappel*, 684 P.2d 123, 125 (Alaska 1984) (finding that the insurer was not notified of the accident implicating the policy until six years after it occurred; because notice provision intended to protect the insurer from prejudice, prejudice must be demonstrated to deny coverage because of untimely notice) ("In the absence of prejudice, regardless of the reasons for the delayed notice, there is no justification for excusing the insurer from its obligations under the policy."). Burden to prove prejudice on insurer. *Id.*

at 126; *see also Estes v. Alaska Ins. Guar. Ass'n*, 774 P.2d 1315 (Alaska 1989) (finding a policy provision requiring action within one year of loss unenforceable absent prejudice to insurer from delay in a case where the policyholder reported fire loss one year and seven days after fire); *Tush v. Pharr*, 68 P.3d 1239, 1250 (Alaska 2003) (citing *Weaver* for the proposition that "absent prejudice, regardless of the reasons for the delayed notice, there is no justification for excusing the insurer from its obligations under the policy") (quotation omitted); *Allstate Ins. Co. v. Herron*, 634 F.3d 1101, 1112 (9th Cir. 2011) (applying Alaska law) (extending notice-prejudice to cooperation clauses); *Dietz-Clark v. HDR, Inc.*, No. 15-00035, 2015 U.S. Dist. LEXIS 141381 (D. Alaska Oct. 15, 2015), *aff'd*, 2017 U.S. App. LEXIS 16550 (9th Cir. Aug. 29, 2017) ("Alaska has a notice-prejudice rule that has developed through case law. Alaska's notice-prejudice rule, like California's rule, has been applied to extend contractual notice of claim deadlines absent a showing of prejudice by an insurer.") (citing *Weaver*); *Lynch & Kennedy Dry Goods, Inc. v. Am. Fire & Cas. Co.*, No. 17-00006, 2018 U.S. Dist. LEXIS 1739 (D. Alaska Jan. 2, 2018) (court "inclined to agree" with insurer that it is prejudiced, as a matter of law, when it receives notice of an action after its resolution, but deciding issue on different grounds: "There is nothing ambiguous about the [voluntary payments] provision. Consent is required before an insured can incur any costs or make any payments. Unlike the late notice defense, there is nothing to suggest prejudice must be shown before an insurer can rely on this provision.").

Arizona: Prejudice required. *See Lindus v. N. Ins. Co. of N.Y.*, 438 P.2d 311, 315 (Ariz. 1968) (involving a policyholder that waited two years to notify insurer of car accident but no prejudice resulted; insurer could not deny coverage) ("[A]n insurance company is not relieved of its contractual liability because of the insured's failure to give notice unless it can show that it has been prejudiced thereby."). Burden to prove prejudice on insurer. *Id.*; *see also Salerno v. Atl. Mut. Ins. Co.*, 6 P.3d 758 (Ariz. Ct. App. 2000) (policyholder failed to give notice of injury because she did not become aware coverage existed for her medical bills until after the time limit expired but insurer could not prove prejudice); *U.S. Fid. & Guar. Co. v. Powercraft Homes*, 685 P.2d 136 (Ariz. Ct. App. 1984) (finding that a delay in answer alone is insufficient prejudice); *Clark Equip. Co. v. Ariz. Prop. & Cas. Ins. Guar. Fund*, 943 P.2d 793 (Ariz. Ct. App. 1997) (applying notice-prejudice to cooperation provisions); *Penn-Am. Ins. Co. v. Sanchez*, 202 P.3d 472, 480 (Ariz. Ct. App. 2008) (citing *Lindus* for the rule that, in the absence of actual prejudice to the insurer, late notice will not bar the insured's claim); *City of Glendale v. Nat'l Union Fire Ins. Co.*, No. CV-12-380-PHX-BSB, 2013

U.S. Dist. LEXIS 45468 (D. Ariz. Mar. 28, 2013) (finding that a delay in providing notice alone is not sufficient to establish prejudice) ("Under Arizona law, an insurer is relieved of its coverage obligations if it has been substantially prejudiced by the insurer's breach of insurance policy conditions relating to timely notice."); *11333 Inc. v. Certain Underwriters at Lloyd's, London*, No. 14-02001, 2015 U.S. Dist. LEXIS 46498 (D. Ariz. April 9, 2015) (addressing the notice-prejudice rule in the context of a policy that the court concluded was neither occurrence nor claims made); *Racquet Club at Scottsdale Ranch Condo. Ass'n v. Phila. Indem. Ins. Co.*, No. 17-1215, 2019 U.S. Dist. LEXIS 10004 (D. Ariz. Jan. 22, 2019) (property case, but citing *Lindus* for this proposition: "Arizona case law does not support a rule that the timeliness of a notice depends solely on the date of loss, rather than the date when the insured actually or constructively knew of the loss.").

Arkansas: No prejudice required—if notice provision in policy sufficiently demarcated as a "condition precedent." *See Fireman's Fund Ins. Co. v. Care Mgmt., Inc.*, 361 S.W.3d 800 (Ark. 2010) (finding no coverage for medical malpractice claim where policyholder notified insurer more than two years after complaint served on policyholder). "In sum, it is well-settled law in Arkansas that an insured must strictly comply with an insurance policy provision requiring timely notice where that provision is a condition precedent to recovery. Failure to do so constitutes a forfeiture of the right to recover from the insurance company, regardless of whether the insurance company was prejudiced by the failure. On the other hand, if notice is not a condition precedent, the insurance company must show it was prejudiced by any delay in notice in order to be relieved of liability." *Id.* at 805 (overruling *Members Mut. Ins. Co. v. Benefield*, 499 S.W.2d 608 (Ark. 1973)); *see also D & D Parks Constr., Inc. v. Century Sur. Co*, No. 3:12-CV-03167, 2013 U.S. Dist. LEXIS 81141 (W.D. Ark. June 10, 2013) (granting summary judgment in favor of insurer because insured's failure to satisfy condition precedent of notice precluded insurer from an opportunity to investigate and defend the lawsuit before the entry of judgment); *Vaughn v. Shelter Mut. Ins. Co.*, 382 S.W.3d 736 (Ark. Ct. App. 2011) (granting summary judgment in favor of insurer because insured did not provide insurer with notice of settlement until twenty-eight days before it became effective and insured's policy required thirty days notice); *accord Am. Gen. Life Ins. Co. v. First Am. Nat'l Bank*, 716 S.W.2d 205 (Ark. Ct. App. 1986) (en banc) (reasoning that, because notice of disability within one year was a condition precedent to coverage, it was unreasonable for policyholder to give notice more than a year after accident and insurer could deny coverage); *Campbell & Co. v. Utica Mut. Ins. Co.*, 820 S.W.2d

284 (Ark. Ct. App. 1991) (en banc) (finding that an insurer must show prejudice in occurrence policy unless prompt notice is identified as a condition precedent to coverage). Burden to show prejudice on insurer if prejudice is required. *Id.* at 288. *But see Kimbrell v. Standard Ins.*, 207 F.3d 535 (8th Cir. 2000) (applying Arkansas law) (finding insurer estopped from using notice defense where its conduct induced policyholder's delay in providing notice); *Auto-Owners Ins. Co. v. Hambuchen Constr., Inc.*, No. 16-00005, 2016 U.S. Dist. LEXIS 160364 (E.D. Ark. Nov. 18, 2016) ("The Policy provides that if a claim or suit is brought against the insured, the insured must send Auto-Owners 'written notice of the claim or 'suit' as soon as practicable.' The Policy further provides that no person or organization has a right to coverage unless 'all of [the policy] terms have been fully complied with.' It is undisputed that the Lessmanns filed suit against Hambuchen on May 7, 2009 and that Auto-Owners learned about the lawsuit on August 11, 2015, when it received a letter from Hambuchen's attorney, advising that the Lessmanns had filed an amended complaint in state court. In light of the undisputed facts, the Court finds that Hambuchen failed to satisfy the notice provision of the Policy, as to the Lessmann lawsuit, which is a condition precedent to coverage."); *Columbia Ins. Group, Inc. v. Park Plus Mgmt. Co.*, No. 14-1025, 2015 U.S. Dist. LEXIS 63287 (W.D. Ark. May 14, 2015) ("No reasonable jury could find that notifying Columbia three years after the lawsuit was filed was 'as soon as practicable' when there were no extenuating circumstances in this case that would justify a three-year delay. Lett-Montgomery and Williamson simply believed that the CGL Policy had expired when it had not. Their own error and lack of diligence caused the three-year delay, and under these circumstances, that delay was not justified. Therefore, Lett-Montgomery and Williamson failed to satisfy the timely notice provision of the CGL policy, which is a condition precedent to coverage."); *Dowden v. Cornerstone Nat'l Ins. Co.*, No. 18-6123, 2020 U.S. Dist. LEXIS 92869 (W.D. Ark. May 28, 2020) (reviewing the facts at issue and rejecting insured's argument that insurer should not be able to disclaim coverage, based on late notice, on the basis that he was an "unsophisticated party").

California: Prejudice required. *See Clemmer v. Hartford Ins. Co.*, 587 P.2d 1098 (Cal. 1978) (finding that because insurer of murderer could show no prejudice in late notice from widow and son of a murder victim, insurer's defense of late notice failed) ("[P]rejudice must be shown with respect to breach of notice clause."); *see also Campbell v. Allstate Ins. Co.*, 384 P.2d 155, 156 (Cal. 1963) (holding there was insufficient evidence to show prejudice from late notice and insurer had to pay default judgment to persons injured by policyholder). Burden to prove prejudice on insurer. *Id.* at 157; *Rosen v. State Farm Gen. Ins. Co.*, 70 P.3d 351, 368–69 (Cal. 2003) (noting California's longstanding notice-prejudice rule); *Safeco Ins. Co. of Am. v. Parks*, 88 Cal. Rptr. 3d 730, 740 (Cal. Ct. App. 2009) (rejecting late notice defense in personal injury case where insurer failed to show actual prejudice) ("The insurer must show actual prejudice, not the mere possibility of prejudice."). For excess insurance, the judicial inquiry tends to focus on whether the policyholder acted reasonably in giving notice in view of the practicality that an excess insurance policy is generally implicated only by claims with a potential for sizeable recovery. *Providence Wash. Ins. Co. v. Container Freight, Inc.*, 68 Cal. Rptr. 2d 776 (Cal. Ct. App. 1997). "Lack of timely notice is a defense to coverage only if the insurer can prove substantial prejudice from the delay." *Doe v. Life Ins. Co. of N. Am.*, 737 F. Supp. 2d 1033, 1035 (N.D. Cal. 2010); *see also BEI Sensors & Sys. Co. v. Great Am. Ins. Co.*, No. C 09-5819 SBA, 2011 U.S. Dist. LEXIS 27996 (N.D. Cal. Mar. 4, 2011) (determining that insurer failed to meet its burden of proving that late notice resulted in prejudice) (noting that, although policyholder did not notify insurer of losses at the earliest possible time, the delay in notification did not reduce insurer's likelihood of garnering a better result); *Henderson v. Farmers Grp., Inc.*, 148 Cal. Rptr. 3d 385 (Cal. Ct. App. 2012) (holding insurer could not rely on defense resulting from failure to submit proof of loss defense without showing substantial prejudice, but finding insurer's failure to object to untimely notice of loss forfeited that defense); *Ins. Co. of Pa. v. Argonaut Ins. Co.*, No. 12 Civ. 6494 (DLC), 2013 U.S. Dist. LEXIS 110597 (S.D.N.Y. Aug. 6, 2013) (addressing California law) ("Under California law, an insurer may assert defenses based upon breach by the insured of a condition of the policy—such as a notice clause—but the breach cannot be a valid defense unless the insurer was substantially prejudiced thereby."); *Hoffman v. Am. Soc'y for Technion-Israel Inst. of Tech., Inc.*, No. 09-CV-2482, 2013 U.S. Dist. LEXIS 24149 (S.D. Cal. Feb. 21, 2013) ("California's 'notice-prejudice' rule provides that '[a] defense based on an insured's failure to give timely notice [of a claim] requires the insurer to prove that it suffered substantial prejudice.'"); *Graciano v. Mercury General Corp.*, 231 Cal. App. 4th 414 (2014) ("Where, as here, the insurer denies coverage, it may establish substantial prejudice only by demonstrating that, in the event that a timely tender of the defense [in the underlying action] had been made, it would have undertaken the defense. If the insurer asserts that the underlying claim is not a covered occurrence or is excluded from basic coverage, then earlier notice would only result in earlier denial of coverage. To establish actual prejudice, the insurer must show a substantial likelihood that, with timely notice, and notwithstanding a denial of coverage or reservation of rights, it would have settled the claim."); *Pitzer College v. Indian Harbor Ins. Co.*, 447 P.3d 669 (Cal. 2019) (concluding, in the context of a choice of law analysis, that California's notice-prejudice rule is a fundamental public policy of the state) ("Prejudice is a question of fact on which the insurer has the burden of proof. The insured's delay does not itself satisfy the burden of proof. The insurer establishes actual and substantial prejudice by proving more than delayed or late notice. It must show a substantial likelihood that, with timely notice, and notwithstanding a denial of coverage or reservation of rights, it would have settled the claim for less or taken steps that would have reduced or eliminated the insured's liability. In the context of third party coverage, for example, the insurer must show that timely notice would have enabled it to achieve a better result in the underlying third party action."); *Am. Bankers Ins. Co. v. Nat'l Fire Ins. Co.*, 488 F. Supp. 3d 892 (N.D. Cal. 2020) ("Although Travelers does not detail the specifics regarding lower defense rates or substantive arguments it could have brought on behalf of the City, the prejudice is plain where Travelers could not contribute at all to the settlement discussions."); *Travelers Prop. Cas. Co. of Am. v. 127 Bayo Vista Condo. Ass'n-Oakland*, No. 19-04697, 2021 U.S. Dist. LEXIS 101776 (N.D. Calif. May 28, 2021) ("The Court concludes that Travelers has not demonstrated that it is entitled to summary judgment on its late notice defense. Although Travelers contends that BVCA waived its right to challenge the defective service by filing the motion to set aside the default pursuant to California Code of Civil Procedure § 473 and not § 418.10, here Travelers assumed the defense before the briefing on the motion to set aside the default judgment was completed and prior to the hearing. Travelers could have moved to set aside the default and default judgment based on jurisdictional grounds. On the facts presented here, the Court cannot conclude that such a motion would have been futile.").

Colorado: Prejudice required. *See Clementi v. Nationwide Mut. Fire Ins. Co.*, 16 P.3d 223, 230 (Colo. 2001) (en banc) (holding that uninsured motorist carrier did not show prejudice when state trooper failed to give timely notice of injury so insurer could not deny coverage). "[I]nsurer prejudice should now be considered when determining whether noncompliance with a UIM policy's notice requirements vitiates coverage." *Id.* Burden to prove prejudice is usually on the insurer, but not always. *Id.; see also Friedland v. Travelers Indem. Co.*, 105 P.3d 639, 641 (Colo. 2005) (en banc) (extending notice-prejudice rule in *Clementi* to liability policies) (overruling *Marez v. Dairyland Ins. Co.*, 638 P.2d 286 (Colo. 1981)); *Lauric v. USAA Cas. Ins. Co.*, 209 P.3d 190, 193 (Colo. Ct. App. 2009) (remanding to reassess an uninsured motorist vehicle claim with a presumption of prejudice where the insured failed to notify the insurer until after settlement). "When an insured settles in breach of notice and consent-to-settle clauses, we conclude that there must be a presumption of prejudice." *Id.*; *Stresscon Corp. v. Travelers Prop. Cas. Co. of Am.*, 370 P.3d 140 (Colo. 2016) (declining to extend the notice-prejudice rule in *Friedland* to the insured's voluntary payment made in the face of a no-voluntary-payments clause) ("Much like the notice of claim provision in *Craft* [claims made policy], the contract clause at issue in this case, far from amounting to a mere technicality imposed upon an insured in an adhesion contract, was a fundamental term defining the limits or extent of coverage. This so-called 'no voluntary payments' clause clearly excluded from coverage any payments voluntarily made or obligations voluntarily assumed by the insured without consent, for anything other than first aid. The insurance policy emphatically stated that any such obligations or payments would be made or assumed at the insured's own cost rather than by the insurer."); *MarkWest Energy Partners, L.P. v. Zurich Am. Ins. Co.*, No. 15CA0770, 2016 Colo. App. LEXIS 956 (Colo. Ct. App. July 14, 2016) (discussing Colorado's late notice law in some detail and holding that its notice-prejudice rule applies even if the notice requirement is a condition precedent to coverage under an occurrence liability policy); *Children's Hosp. Colo. v. Lexington Ins. Co.*, No. 15-01904, 2017 U.S. Dist. LEXIS 56892 (D. Colo. April 13, 2017) (applying *Friedland* and concluding the insurer bears the burden of proving both unreasonably late notice and prejudice) ("AIG and Lexington failed to make any inquiry about the case, exhibit any desire to learn about, comment on, or participate in preparation and trial, or otherwise exercise any claimed right under the Policy to monitor or work with CHC's attorney in settlement negotiations, investigation, or trial. This failure completely undermines Lexington's speculative and unsupported position that it was prejudiced because with earlier notice it would have been able to avoid or mitigate the liability it now faces by resolving the Pressey lawsuit for less than the ultimate judgment entered against CHC."); *Holyoke Mut. Ins. Co. v. Cincinnati Indem. Co.*, No. 18-01853, 2019 U.S. Dist. LEXIS 88898 (D. Colo. May 28, 2019) ("Nor does CIC's prior actual knowledge of the claims against Cheesman preclude application of the no-voluntary payments clause where, as here, the insured undertook the obligations prior to obtaining a coverage decision from the insurer and without the insurer's knowledge or consent.") (discussing *Stresscon*); *First Mercury Ins. Co. v. Wonderland Homes*, No. 19-00915, 2020 U.S. Dist. LEXIS 200276 (D. Colo. Aug. 20, 2020) ("Since neither the facts nor legal issues here align with those in *Stresscon*, I find the Colorado Supreme Court's decision does not have the determinative effect for this case that First Mercury claims.").

Connecticut: Prejudice required. *See Arrowood Indem. Co. v. King*, 39 A.3d 712 (Conn. 2012) ("[T]he insurer bears the burden of proving, by a preponderance of evidence, that it has been prejudiced by the insured's failure to comply with a notice provision."), *answer to certified question conformed to* 699 F.3d 735, 739 n.3 (2d Cir. 2012) ("Not only did the Court settle Connecticut law that friendly social interactions do not excuse an insured's late notice of claim but it also took its response to our certified questions as an opportunity to overturn its earlier case law by placing the burden of proving prejudice, resulting from a delayed notice of an accident, on the insurer and relieving the insured of the obligation to prove an absence of prejudice."); *see also Palkimas v. State Farm Fire & Cas. Co.*, No. CV095022078S, 2013 Conn. Super. LEXIS 155 (Conn. Super. Ct. Jan. 17, 2013) (denying insured's summary judgment motion based on genuine dispute as to whether insured satisfied notice provision), *aff'd*, 91 A.3d 532 (Conn. App. Ct. 2014); *Prizio v. Lincoln Nat'l Life Ins. Co.*, No. 11-736, 2014 U.S. Dist. LEXIS 43886 (D. Conn. Mar. 31, 2014) (finding prejudice resulted where late-notice precluded insurer from investigating damages for three years); *State Farm Fire & Cas. Co. v. Yoel*, No. 03:13CV101, 2014 U.S. Dist. LEXIS 116743 (D. Conn. August 21, 2014) (addressing whether insurer was prejudiced by late notice with respect to locating witnesses); *Ellis v. Cty. Agency, Inc.*, No. 146017155S, 2017 Conn. Super. LEXIS 3466 (Conn. Super. Ct. May 25, 2017) ("Entry of a default judgment against an insured is evidence of prejudice as well as the lack of opportunity for the insurer to investigate a claim and to pursue a compromise or settlement."); *Zahoruiko v. Fed. Ins. Co.*, No. 15-474, 2017 U.S. Dist. LEXIS 28204 (D. Conn. Feb. 28, 2017) ("Connecticut requires two conditions to be satisfied before an insurer's duties can be discharged pursuant to the 'notice' provision of a policy: (1) an unexcused, unreasonable delay in notification by the insured; and (2) resulting material prejudice to the insurer. Thus, a policyholder who fails to give timely notice of an insurable loss does not forfeit his coverage if . . . his delay did not prejudice his insurer. [T]he insurer bears the burden of proving . . . that it has been prejudiced by the insured's failure to comply with a notice provision."); *Veilleux v. Progressive Northwestern Ins. Co.*, No. 16-2116, 2018 U.S. Dist. LEXIS 155861 (D. Conn. Sept. 13, 2018) (following lengthy discussion of notice facts at issue, concluding that there was a genuine issue of material fact whether insurer was materially prejudiced by the timing of the notice it received of the accident); *Zahoruiko v. Fed. Ins. Co.*, 717 Fed. Appx. 50 (2nd Cir. 2018) ("Zahoruiko's arguments that the district court improperly assumed prejudice and that Federal failed to carry its preponderance burden are equally meritless. Federal provided a declaration from a senior claim officer stating that Zahoruiko's failure to give notice until after default was entered denied it the opportunity to interview witnesses or participate in the defense or any proposed settlement of the claim."); *Allstate Ins. Co. v. Tenn*, No. 19-432, 2021 U.S. Dist. LEXIS 50687 (D. Conn. Mar. 18, 2021) (finding no prejudice) ("The altercation occurred on October 10, 2016, and Allstate was made aware of the potential for litigation on June 19, 2018. The state complaint was filed on October 8, 2018, three-and-a-half months after Allstate received notice of the incident. The three-month period after Plaintiff became aware of the potential for litigation and before the complaint was filed provided sufficient opportunity for it to investigate the claim and engage in settlement discussions with Defendants.").

Delaware: Prejudice required. *See Nationwide Mut. Ins. Co. v. Starr*, 575 A.2d 1083, 1088 (Del. 1990) (insurer must provide coverage in uninsured motorist claim even though claimant failed to promptly notify insurer of judgment against insured because insurer could not prove prejudice). "To prevail on its claim, [the insurer] must show both that the policy was breached and that it was prejudiced by the violation of the policy." *Id.* Burden to prove prejudice on insurer. *Id.*; *State Farm Mut. Auto. Ins. Co. v. Johnson*, 320 A.2d 345 (Del. 1974) (finding that where policyholder failed to show compliance with notice provision, insurer had burden of showing prejudice before coverage could be denied); *Falcon Steel Co., Inc. v. Md. Cas. Co.*, 366 A.2d 512 (Del. Super. Ct. 1976) (finding a nine-month delay unreasonable, but that the insurer must still provide coverage because insurer could not show prejudice because of delay); *Wilhelm v. Nationwide Gen. Ins. Co.*, No. 09C-07-155, 2011 Del. Super. LEXIS 407 (Del. Super. Ct. May 11, 2011) (concluding that eleven-year delay in notice violates "as soon as practicable" requirement in both the insurance policy and Delaware Code), *aff'd*, 29 A.3d 246 (Del. 2011). *See also In re IdleAire Techs. Corp.*, No. 08–10960 (KG), 2010 Bankr. LEXIS 436 (Bankr. D. Del. Feb. 17, 2010) (six-month delay in notifying insurer of product liability claim does not void coverage in absence of insurer showing of prejudice; notice-prejudice rule firmly established in Delaware); *Arrowood Indem. Co. v. Hartford Fire Ins. Co.*, 774 F. Supp. 2d 636, 654 (D. Del. 2011) (concluding that Delaware law does not require insurers to demonstrate prejudice before disclaiming coverage under a suit limitation provision) (finding insured misapprehended difference between suit limitation provision and notice of loss provision); *Northrop Grumman Innovation Sys. v. Zurich Am. Ins. Co.*, No. N18C-09-210, 2021 Del. Super. LEXIS 92 (Del. Super. Ct. Feb. 2, 2021) ("[A] sufficiently unreasonable or totally unjustified delay might, a fortiori, establish prejudice. As a result, though Delaware courts almost without fail articulate 'prejudice' as a required element, they nevertheless have on occasion treated prejudice as commensurate with delay where notice was required as soon as practicable but the insured's tardiness was unexcused as a matter of law. That's not too far from skipping a prejudice analysis altogether.").

District of Columbia: Prejudice not required. *Greenway v. Selected Risks Ins. Co.*, 307 A.2d 753, 756 (D.C. Cir. 1973) ("[I]t [is] abundantly clear that actual prejudice to the carrier is not a necessary element in the defense") (citation omitted); *see also AMTRAK v. Lexington Ins. Co.*, 445 F. Supp. 2d 37, 44 (D.D.C. 2006) ("The District's 'no prejudice' rule, for one, has not had time to atrophy, having been restated by the Court of Appeals as recently as 2001.") (holding that an excess insurer did not have to pay policyholder because "[n]otice provisions in insurance contracts are of the essence of the contract") (citing *Travelers Indem. Co. v. United Food & Commercial Workers Int'l Union*, 770 A.2d 978, 991 (D.C. Cir. 2001)), *aff'd*, No. 06-7158, 2007 U.S. App. LEXIS 24974 (D.C. Cir. 2007); *Capitol Specialty Ins. Corp. v. Sanford Wittels & Heisler, LLP*, 793 F. Supp. 2d 399, 408 (D.D.C. 2011) (applying District of Columbia law) ("Where the policy expressly makes compliance with its terms a condition precedent to liability on the part of the insurer, failure to comply with the notice provision will release the insurer of liability on the policy."); *Feld v. Fireman's Fund Ins. Co.*, 206 F. Supp. 3d 378 (D.D.C. 2016) ("In the District of Columbia . . . 'an insurer is not required to demonstrate actual prejudice before denying coverage on the basis of an insured's failure to comply with a contractual notice provision.'") (quoting *AMTRAK*), *vacated on other grounds*, 909 F.3d 1186 (D.C. Cir. 2018); *Zurich Am. Ins. Co. v. UIP Cos. LLC*, No. 19-1818, 2021 U.S. Dist. LEXIS 28115 (D.D.C. Feb. 16, 2021) ("[W]hether notice was given within a reasonable time depends on (1) what the insured could reasonably have believed was its obligation under the insurance policy, (2) what the insured could reasonably have believed about the seriousness of the injury and its liability for it, and (3) what the insured could reasonably have believed about the likelihood of a claim being made against it.") (citing *Starks v. North East Ins. Co.*, 408 A.2d 980 (D.C. Cir. 1979)) (undertaking detailed factual analysis to conclude that the insured "failed to show that any of the *Starks* factors justify its delay of seven to nine months in providing notice" of suit to the insurer; insurer not required to prove that it was prejudiced by untimely notice).

Florida: Prejudice required. *See Bankers Ins. Co. v. Macias*, 475 So. 2d 1216, 1218 (Fla. 1985) (finding that substantial prejudice was required in case involving a policy the insured tried to activate two years after a car accident). "If the insured breaches the notice provision, prejudice to the insurer will be presumed." *Id.*; *Tiedtke v. Fid. &*

Cas. Co. of N.Y., 222 So. 2d 206, 209 (Fla. 1969). Burden to prove absence of prejudice on policyholder. *Bankers Ins. Co.*, 475 So. 2d at 1218 (finding that presumption of prejudice against the insurer arises because of late notice; policyholder has burden of disproving); *Robinson v. Auto-Owners Ins. Co.*, 718 So. 2d 1283 (Fla. Dist. Ct. App. 1998) (same). "[P]rejudice to the insurer results if the untimely notice substantially disadvantages the insurer's ability to (1) investigate a claim, (2) defend a claim, (3) or to mitigate damages through settlement or early repairs." *Kendall Lakes Towers Condo. Ass'n, Inc. v. Pacific Ins. Co., Ltd.*, No. 10-24310, 2012 U.S. Dist. LEXIS 10749 (S.D. Fla. Jan 30, 2012) (finding an insured's subjective beliefs regarding damages and coverage insufficient to justify non-compliance with notice provision); *see also Liberty Mut. Ins. Grp. v. Cifuentes*, 760 So. 2d 230 (Fla. Dist. Ct. App. 2000) (finding that the insurer should be relieved of liability if insurer is prejudiced by the policyholder's failure to comply with the timely notice requirement); *Martinez-Claib v. Bus. Men's Assurance Co. of Am.*, No. 2:06-cv-479-FtM-34SPC, 2008 U.S. Dist. LEXIS 92016 (M.D. Fla. Sept. 9, 2008) (holding that the policyholder's disability insurance claim was barred where she waited two years to notify insurer of her disability), *aff'd*, No. 08-16681, 2009 U.S. App. LEXIS 23074 (11th Cir. Oct. 21, 2009). "Florida law provides that prejudice to the insurer is presumed 'when a policy makes a compliance with a written notice provision a condition precedent to the insurer's liability.'" *Id.*; *Kroener v. Fla. Ins. Guar. Ass'n*, 63 So. 3d 914, 916 (Fla. Dist. Ct. App. 2011) ("[W]e agree with the trial court's ruling that, as a matter of law, notice to the insurer of a claim of loss more than two years and two months after the loss occurred was not prompt notice; the untimely reporting of the loss violated the insurance policy and was sufficient to bar the claim."); *Hamid Mohebbi Pharm.D v. Founders Ins. Co.*, 41 F. Supp. 3d 1412 (S.D. Fla. 2014) ("The facts here are that Defendant could not protect its interests in the state court proceeding before or after entry of the default judgment because the insured failed to comply with the policy's notice requirement. As a matter of law, the insured's breach of the policy's notice requirement denied Defendant the opportunity to protect its interests in what resulted in an over half-a-million dollar judgment and prejudiced Defendant."); *1500 Coral Towers Condo. Ass'n v. Citizens Prop. Ins. Corp.*, 112 So. 3d 541 (Fla. Ct. App. 2013) ("Although the issue of whether an insured has overcome the presumption of prejudice caused by late notice is generally reserved for the trier of fact, it is appropriately raised on summary judgment where, as in this case, the insured fails to present evidence sufficient to rebut the presumption."); *Laquer v. Citizens Prop. Ins. Corp.*, 167 So. 3d 470 (Fla. Ct. App. 2015) ("A two-step analysis determines whether an insured's untimely reporting of loss results in the denial of coverage. The first step focuses on whether the insured provided timely notice. If the insured provided timely notice, of course, coverage cannot be denied. But even if the insured's notice was untimely, the insured has the ability to prove that the insurer was not prejudiced by the untimely notice. During this step, prejudice to the insurer is presumed and the insured bears the burden of proving otherwise."); *Rodriguez v. Liberty Mut. Fire Ins. Co.*, No. 16-21926, 2017 U.S. Dist. LEXIS 29519 (S.D. Fla. Mar. 2, 2017) ("Having found the notice late as a matter of law, there is a presumption that Liberty Mutual was prejudiced as a result of the delay. Plaintiffs have not tried to overcome the presumption or put forth evidence that Liberty Mutual was not prejudiced."); *Walton v. St. Paul Fire & Marine Ins. Co.*, No. 17-61391, 2018 U.S. Dist. LEXIS 136434 (S.D. Fla. Aug. 10, 2018) (setting forth lengthy case law discussion of Florida late notice) ("St. Paul indisputably had notice of the claim prior to entry of final judgment and had access to the record of defense provided to IAG by its counsel Ms. Cartwright and her law firm, as is evident from the evidence offered in this proceeding. There is no suggestion of anything 'materially different' that would have been disclosed to St. Paul if it were involved in the investigation earlier. Where an insurer has an opportunity to investigate a claim and deny it on other grounds than late notice, that effectively rebuts any presumption of prejudice arising from the late notice."); *Scott, Blane, & Darren Recovery, LLC v. Auto-Owners Ins. Co.*, 727 Fed. Appx. 625 (11th Cir. 2018) ("Here, Auto-Owners suffered substantial prejudice because Anova denied Auto-Owners the ability to attempt to negotiate a settlement of the California Suit and denied Auto-Owners the ability to examine the new state law claim advanced in the California Suit.").

Georgia: Prejudice may or may not be required. *Richmond v. Georgia Farm Bureau Mut. Ins. Co.*, 231 S.E.2d 245 (Ga. Ct. App. 1976) ("In many cases, as in this one, the notice condition is expressly made a condition precedent to the insurer's coverage or liability. These conditions are valid and must be complied with, absent a showing of justification. Where an insured has not demonstrated justification for failure to give notice according to the terms of the policy, and where the insurer has not waived compliance with the terms or any objections to the insured's failure, then the insurer is not obligated to provide either a defense or coverage. This is not a case of forfeiture. Moreover, there is no need for an insurer to prove it was prejudiced by an insured's failure to give notice. The valid condition precedent of notice 'as soon as practicable' is to be treated in this regard the same way as the condition precedent of forwarding to an insurer copies of the suit and summons."). Despite Georgia's reputation as a "no prejudice" state, the Court of Appeals applied a more nuanced approach in *Plantation Pipe Line Co. v. Stonewall Insurance Co.*, 780 S.E.2d 501 (Ga. Ct. App. 2015*), review denied* 2016 Ga. LEXIS 339 (Ga. 2016): "In keeping with the desire of the law to avoid forfeitures of coverage, the general rule is that a notice provision in an insurance policy is only considered a condition precedent to coverage if it expressly states that a failure to provide such notice will result in a forfeiture of the insured's rights or uses language which otherwise clearly expresses the intention that the notice provision be treated as a condition precedent. Where policy language does nothing more than require the insured to give notice of a particular event, [it] is insufficient to create a condition precedent." *Id.* at 511. Turning to the policy at hand, the court held that the notice provision did not expressly stipulate that compliance was a condition precedent to coverage. Thus, the court held that "the trial court erred in concluding that the Stonewall policy expressly made compliance with the notice provision a condition precedent to coverage and in ruling on that basis that Stonewall was not required to show prejudice." *Id. See also Progressive Mt. Ins. Co. v. Bishop*, 790 S.E.2d 91 (Ga. Ct. App. 2016) ("Bishop's policy contained a general provision requiring his full compliance with the policy's terms: 'We may not be sued unless there is full compliance with all the terms of this policy.' Progressive argues that the notice provision in Bishop's policy creates a condition precedent to coverage, particularly in the light of that general requirement that the insured must comply fully with the policy's terms before the insurer may be sued. We agree, as the policy predicated coverage on compliance with all the terms of the policy, which of course includes the notice provision. . . . In order to obtain coverage under his policy, therefore, Bishop must show that he complied with the notice provision or demonstrate justification for failing to do so."); *Cincinnati Ins. Co. v. Stone*, No. 19-02153, 2020 U.S. Dist. LEXIS 165378 (N.D. Ga. Sept. 10, 2020) (concluding that notice provision was a condition precedent and, even if prejudice were required, insurer may have suffered it: "By the time Plaintiff heard about the accident, the underlying lawsuit was eighteen months old and Defendant Gerow had already been deposed. This could reasonably be viewed as prejudicial because it deprived Plaintiff of the right to provide and to control the defense of the case during a substantial and critical portion of the litigation, including investigation of the claim, selection of counsel, theories of defense, conduct of discovery, and [preliminary] trial strategy."); *Auto Owners Ins. Co. v. Sapp*, No. 15-90, 2017 U.S. Dist. LEXIS 34201 (M.D. Ga. March 10, 2017) (concluding that notice provision was a condition precedent and "belief that the insured will not be held liable for the underlying incident is not sufficient to justify delay notice to the insurer"); *Johnson & Bryan, Inc. v. Utica Mut. Ins. Co.*, 741 Fed. Appx. 722 (11th Cir. 2018) ("Georgia courts . . . have determined that when a delay in notice is due to the insured's own negligence, the delay is unreasonable as a matter of law.") (citing *Plantation*).

Earlier cases cited in *Insurance Key Issues* should be considered with *Plantation Pipe Line Co.* and *Bishop* in mind. *Caldwell v. State Farm Fire & Cas. Ins. Co*, 385 S.E.2d 97, 99 (Ga. Ct. App. 1989) (holding that the notice requirement allows the insurer to prepare its defense while the facts are fresh and the witnesses are available); *Canadyne-Ga. Corp. v. Cont'l Ins. Co.*, 999 F.2d 1547, 1557 (11th Cir. 1993) (holding that Georgia law does not require an insurer to demonstrate prejudice to avail itself of a notice requirement). *See also Royer v. Murphy*, 625 S.E.2d 544, 545 (Ga. Ct. App. 2006) (holding that the insured's two-year delay in reporting an automobile accident was unreasonable and discharged the insurer's obligation). "[F]ailure to meet this condition precedent [providing notice] is fatal to [the] action." *Id.*; *Eells v. State Farm Mut. Auto. Ins. Co.*, 752 S.E.2d 70, 72 (Ga. Ct. App. 2013) (holding that oral or other notice inconsistent with a policy's notice requirement is insufficient) (notice of claim two years after car accident unjustified) ("It is well established that a notice provision expressly made a condition precedent to coverage is valid and must be complied with, absent a showing of justification."); *Travelers Indem. Co. v. Douglasville Dev.*, LLC, No. 1:07-CV-0410-JOF, 2008 U.S. Dist. LEXIS 71956 (N.D. Ga. Sept. 19, 2008) (involving a property damage dispute, the court found untimely notice; doubt as to coverage is not an excuse for not giving notice). "The Georgia courts have repeatedly held that where no valid excuse exists, failure to give written notice for periods in the range of four to eight months is unreasonable as a matter of law." *Id.*; *Ill. Union Ins. Co. v. Sierra Contr. Corp.*, 744 F. Supp. 2d 1349, 1351 (N.D. Ga. 2010) (determining that nine-month delay did not constitute notice "as soon as possible" and therefore insurer was not obligated to provide coverage or defense); *accord Cureton v. State Farm & Cas. Co.*, No. 4:12-CV-329 (CDL), 2014 U.S. Dist. LEXIS 4497 (M.D. Ga. Jan. 14, 2014) (finding insured's failure to disclose any reasonable excuse as to its six-month delay in providing notice of alleged theft unreasonable as a matter of law); *see also Am. Ins. Co. v. Evercare Co.*, 699 F. Supp. 2d 1361, 1366 (N.D. Ga. 2010) (objective standard applies in evaluating reasonableness of insured's excuse) (finding policyholder's explanation for nine-month late notice of competitor's Lanham Act claim unreasonable as a matter of law), *aff'd*, No. 10-12728, 2011 U.S. App. LEXIS 12188 (11th Cir. 2011). "Under Georgia law, 'timely notice to the insurer of a claim or occurrence is a condition precedent to the insurer's duty to defend or pay.'" *Id.* "The duty to provide notice is triggered when [the policyholder] knew or *should have known* that it might be liable for an occurrence that fell within [the policyholder's] coverage periods." *Id.* at 1367 (emphasis in original) (quoting *S.C. Ins. Co. v. Coody*, 957 F. Supp. 234, 237 (M.D. Ga. 1997)); *see also Forshee v. Emp'rs Mut. Cas. Co.*, 711 S.E.2d 28 (Ga. Ct. App. 2011) (addressing in detail that an insured is not required to foresee every possible claim, no matter how remote, that might arise from an event and give notice to the insurer; insured only required to act reasonably under the circumstances) ("The reasonableness of the failure of the Forshees to give notice sooner to Employers Mutual must be assessed from the perspective of a reasonable person in the circumstances in which the Forshees found themselves, not that of an omniscient being having the benefit of full and accurate information that emerged only later and the benefit of hindsight."); *Ill. Union Ins. Co. v. NRI Const. Inc.*, 846 F. Supp. 2d 1366, 1371 (N.D. Ga. 2012) (noting investigatory purpose of prompt notice provision) (rejecting insured's excuse and finding its two-year delay in notice regarding slip and fall unreasonable as a matter of law) ("[Insured] . . . cannot rely on the representations of its own insurance agent to excuse its failure to comply with the notice provision."); *Brit UW Ltd. v. Hallister Prop. Dev., LLC*, No. 1:11-CV-4396-JEC, 2014 U.S. Dist. LEXIS 32332 (N.D. Ga. Mar. 13, 2014) (finding insured's excuse as to its subjective beliefs legally insufficient and concluding two-year delay in providing notice unreasonable as a matter of law so as to bar coverage).

Hawaii: Prejudice required. *See Standard Oil Co. of Cal. v. Hawaiian Ins. & Guar. Co.*, 654 P.2d 1345, 1348 n.4 (Haw. 1982) (involving an insurer that failed to defend when heirs of plane crash victims sued policyholder; holding that for late notice to bar coverage, insurer must be prejudiced). "The function of the notice requirement … is simply to prevent the insurer from being prejudiced, not to provide a technical escape-hatch. …" *Id.* (suggesting insurer has the burden of proving prejudice); *see also Haw. Mmgt. Alliance Ass'n v. Ins. Comm'r*, 100 P.3d 952, 960 (Haw. 2004) (involving a dispute over attorney's fees after a cancer patient's successful claim for coverage; comparing independent review standards with late notice rules). "[A]n insurer will not be relieved of liability based on an insured's untimely notice of a claim unless the insurer demonstrates that it has been prejudiced as a result of the late notice." *Id.*; *Great Am. Ins. Co. v. Aetna Cas. & Sur. Co.*, 876 P.2d 1314, 1319 (Haw. 1994) (interpreting prejudice rule in *Standard Oil*) ("[T]his court appeared to suggest that even where the insurer can show untimely notice on the part of its insured, the insurer will additionally be required to show that it was prejudiced by the late notice in order to deny coverage under the policy."). *See also Ass'n of Apartment Owners of Imperial Plaza v. Fireman's Fund Ins. Co.*, 939 F. Supp. 2d 1059, 1064-65 (D. Haw. 2013) (addressing notice-prejudice rule in context of cooperation clause) ("Generally, an insurer seeking to avoid coverage because of an insured's breach of cooperation clause must prove (1) the existence of substantial prejudice and (2) the exercise of reasonable diligence to secure the insured's cooperation before it can deny coverage because of breach of a cooperation clause.").

Idaho: Prejudice may or may not be required. *See Viani v. Aetna Ins. Co.*, 501 P.2d 706, 713–14 (Idaho 1972) (holding that where policyholder failed to give notice of suit until after an adverse judgment was entered, no showing of prejudice was required; insurer prejudiced because it had no chance to defend the claims), *overruled in part on other grounds by Sloviaczek v. Estate of Puckett*, 565 P.2d 564 (Idaho 1977). *See also Sparks v. Transamerica Ins. Co.*, No. 96-36110, 1998 U.S. App. LEXIS 6848 (9th Cir. April 6, 1998) (no prejudice required; insured failed to demonstrate that the Idaho Supreme Court has abandoned its holding in *Viani*) ("Sparks' failure to provide any notice of the EPA's September 1989 letter to Transamerica for almost two years constitutes a material breach of the insurance contract and excuses Transamerica from providing a defense and indemnity."); *Blue Cross of Idaho Health Serv., Inc. v. Atl. Mut. Ins. Co.*, No. 1:09-CV-246-CWD, 2011 U.S. Dist. LEXIS 4892 (D. Idaho Jan. 19, 2011) ("Failure to comply with the notice of suit provisions, whether a complete failure until after judgment, or late notice … provides grounds upon which an insurer can refuse to honor its duty to defend, and consequently, its duty to indemnify.") (determining that four-month delay in notification of suit qualified as "late notice," but declaring that insurer's "words and conduct constitute[d] both waiver and estoppel of its right to assert late notice as a defense" because insurer's coverage letter in response to notice was ambiguous about interposition of defense, insurer delayed clarifying coverage position, and insurer did conduct some investigation and pay a portion of defense costs); *Hoffman v. Or. Mut. Ins. Co.*, No. CIV. 1:11-120 WBS, 2012 U.S. Dist. LEXIS 76090 (D. Idaho May 29, 2012) (applying *Axis Surplus Ins. Co. v. Lake CDA Dev. LLC*, No. CV-07-505-E-BLW, 2008 U.S. Dist. LEXIS 69020 (D. Idaho Sept. 10, 2008) in concluding that, under Idaho law, "[p]rejudice to the insurer is not material" in the determination of whether insured's late notice excused insurer's performance under policy) (noting that Idaho has not enacted any statutes or regulations that would require a showing of prejudice); *N. Pac. Ins. v. Gardner*, No. 11-00147, 2012 U.S. Dist. LEXIS 111783 (D. Idaho Aug. 6, 2012) (rejecting insured's argument that no prejudice resulted from late notice) (construing *Hoffman* to mean that Idaho law does not require a showing of prejudice where an insured fails to give notice of a suit or accident within reasonable time); *Evanston Ins. Co. v. Bosski, Inc.*, No. 14-00227, 2017 U.S. Dist. LEXIS 48177 (D. Idaho Mar. 28, 2017) ("Idaho courts make a distinction between substantial compliance and a complete failure to comply with a notice of suit condition. If the insured can demonstrate substantial compliance with the notice provision and a valid excuse for failing to meet a strict compliance standard, then the burden shifts to the insurer who must demonstrate both that the notice provision is a condition precedent to coverage and that it suffered prejudice in order to be relieved of liability. . . . In contrast, in situations in which there is a total failure to comply with a notice of suit provision, prejudice is essentially assumed. A complete breach of a notice of suit provision, such that an insurer is never made aware of the suit until after a judgment has been entered against the insured, is generally a total defense to liability."). *But see Union Warehouse & Supply Co. v. Ill. R.B. Jones, Inc.*, 917 P.2d 1300, 1306 (Idaho 1996) (regarding lack of cooperation defense, insurer must establish prejudice).

Illinois: Hybrid rule. Insurer need only show that notice was late to defeat coverage but whether the insurer was prejudiced is a factor in determining whether notice was sufficiently late to be fatal to coverage. *See Country Mut. Ins. Co. v. Livorsi Marine, Inc.*, 856 N.E.2d 338, 346 (Ill. 2006) (recognizing Illinois's notice/prejudice rule and holding that, even if there was no prejudice to the insurer, the policyholder must still give reasonable notice in accordance with the terms of the policy) (involving a trademark dispute and a finding that the insurer had no duty to defend or indemnify pursuant to a commercial general liability policy where the policyholder waited over twenty-one months to give notice). "[L]ack of prejudice may be a factor in determining ... whether a reasonable notice was given in a particular case yet it is not a condition which will dispense with the requirement." *Id.* at 343; *accord Simmon v. Iowa Mut. Cas. Co.*, 121 N.E.2d 509, 512 (Ill. 1954) (same). *See also Berglind v. Paintball Bus. Ass'n*, 921 N.E.2d 432, 441 (Ill. App. Ct. 2009) (finding that fact issues precluded summary judgment for insurer despite policyholder's eleven-month delay in giving notice when paintball facility sued by injured patron) ("[A] lengthy passage of time in notification is not an absolute bar to a claim of defense or indemnity under an insurance policy, even under the 'as soon as practicable' provision.") (finding that the factors relevant to determining whether notice was unreasonably late included "(1) the specific language of the policy's notice provision; (2) the degree of the insured's sophistication in the world of commerce and insurance; (3) the insured's awareness that an occurrence as defined under the terms of the policy has taken place; (4) the insured's diligence and reasonable care in ascertaining whether policy coverage is available once the awareness has occurred; and (5) any prejudice to the insurance company") (citing *Livorsi Marine*), *modified*, 930 N.E.2d 1036 (Ill. App. Ct. 2010); *Am. Standard Ins. Co. v. Slifer*, 919 N.E.2d 372, 374, 377 (Ill. App. Ct. 2009) (concluding that late notice strips an insured of coverage for failure to report 2002 hit-and-run fatality while driving insured vehicle where policyholder/perpetrator not apprehended and sued until 2007 and that the policy at issue required "prompt" notice of "an auto accident or loss" regardless of severity or existence of claim). *See, e.g., W. Am. Ins. Co. v. Yorkville Nat'l Bank*, 939 N.E.2d 288, 295 (Ill. 2010) (In 6-1 decision, supreme court reversed appellate court finding of notice twenty-seven months after defamation lawsuit against bank late as a matter of law and upheld fact-based trial court determination of sufficiently timely notice as "not against the manifest weight of the evidence."). Applying the *Livorsi Marine* factors, the *Yorkville Bank* Court found (1) the policy language inconclusive; (2) the Bank was a sophisticated policyholder, which weighed in favor of a late notice finding; (3) the Bank was aware of an occurrence, which weighed in favor of a late notice finding; (4) the Bank had been sufficiently diligent and had been misinformed by a broker and the insurer regarding coverage, a key factor weighing against a finding of late notice; and (5) that there was no showing of prejudice by the insurer, a factor militating against a finding of late notice. *Id.* at 293–96. Although notice was given shortly before scheduled trial, the insurer hurt its chances of prevailing on a late notice defense by failing to investigate and failing to seek a continuance. *Id.* at 295. "After considering all relevant factors, we find that, under the circumstances in the present case, Yorkville's written notice of the lawsuit to West American was given within a reasonable time and did not violate the notice provision in the Policy." *Id.* at 296. *See also Acuity v. Osler Indus., Inc.*, No. 1-11-0326, 2011 Ill. App. Unpub. LEXIS 1321 (Ill. App. Ct. May 9, 2011) (using the *Livorsi Marine* factors, the court reasoned that a nine-month delay in notice was unreasonable and insurer was entitled to refuse coverage); *accord Auto-Owners Ins. Co. v. Xtreme Auto Sales, Inc.*, No. 08 C 6608, 2011 U.S. Dist. LEXIS 11553 (N.D. Ill. Feb. 7, 2011) (finding that "insurer['s] notice of the accident approximately 47 months after the accident" constituted late notice); *First Chi. Ins. Co. v. Molda*, 948 N.E.2d 206, 213 (Ill. Ct. App. 2011) (discussing late notice and whether insurer was prejudiced by delay in notification); *Phila. Indem. Ins. Co. v. 1801 W. Irving Park, LLC*, No. 11 C 1710, 2012 U.S. Dist. LEXIS 115256 (N.D. Ill. Aug. 13, 2012) (finding absence of prejudice alone insufficient to render insured's ten month delay reasonable);

AIU Ins. Co. v. TIG Ins. Co., 934 F. Supp. 2d 594 (S.D.N.Y. 2013) (applying Illinois law) (holding reinsurer not required to prove prejudice in addition to late notice to refuse coverage) (finding notice of claim three years later unreasonable); *Nat'l Union Fire Ins. Co. of Pittsburgh, Pa. v. Petco Petroleum Corp.*, No. 412-00165, 2013 U.S. Dist. LEXIS 157612 (S.D. Miss. Nov. 4, 2013) (applying Illinois law) (noting that under Illinois law an insurer is not required to show prejudice to rely on a late notice defense and may prevail if other factors make notice late); *State Auto Prop. & Cas. Ins. Co. v. Brumit Servs.*, No. 17-1700, 2017 U.S. App. LEXIS 24920 (7th Cir. Dec. 11, 2017) (explaining why each of the five late notice factors weighed in favor of the insured's 21 month delay, in notifying its insurer, being unreasonable); *First Chi. Ins. Co. v. Molda*, 36 N.E.3d 400 (Ill. Ct. App. 2015) (discussing Illinois late notice law in general and concluding that insured's 31 month delay, in notifying its insurer, was not unreasonable); *Great Am. E&S Ins. Co. v. Power Cell LLC*, 356 F. Supp. 3d 730 (N.D. Ill. 2018) (addressing the five *Livorsi Marine* factors and concluding that insurer could not rely on late notice as a defense) (*e.g.*, "Zeus, a battery distributor, has never filed a lawsuit against any other company. It therefore bears little resemblance to the defendant in Yorkville, which was 'presumed to be sophisticated in the areas of commerce and insurance' because it is a bank."); *Towne Place Condo. Ass'n v. Phila. Indem. Ins. Co.*, No. 17-1561, 2019 U.S. Dist. LEXIS 121393 (N.D. Ill. July 22, 2019) ("Illinois courts will consider whether the insurer was prejudiced but will not permit a lack of prejudice to compensate for inexcusable delay.") ("insurer can prevail on a late notice defense without showing prejudice if the delay is extreme") (setting out several case examples).

Indiana: Prejudice required, but prejudice presumed if notice is late. *See Ind. Ins. Co. v. Williams*, 463 N.E.2d 257, 260–61 (Ind. 1984) (involving a policyholder that did not give notice of car accident until six months after it occurred; court held prejudice can be presumed from unreasonable delay in giving notice) ("The requirement of prompt notice gives the insurer an opportunity to make a timely and adequate investigation of all the circumstances surrounding the accident or loss. This adequate investigation is often frustrated by a delayed notice. Prejudice to the insurance company's ability to prepare an adequate defense can therefore be presumed by an unreasonable delay in notifying the company about the accident or about the filing of the lawsuit. This is not in conflict with the public policy theory that the court should seek to protect the innocent third parties from attempts by insurance companies to deny liability for some insignificant failure to notify."). The burden to prove a prima facie case of no prejudice is placed on the policyholder or third-party claimant, with the ultimate question of prejudice thereafter a question of fact. *Williams*, 463 N.E.2d at 260–61; *Wolf Lake Terminals, Inc. v. Mut. Marine Ins. Co.*, 433 F. Supp. 2d 933, 952 (N.D. Ind. 2005) (stating that the presumption of prejudice "is rebutted by evidence that the insureds' 'adequately safeguarded' the [insurers'] interests by assuming the defense of the contamination claims" made against policyholder). *See also P.R. Mallory & Co. v. Am. Cas. Co of Reading, Pa.*, 920 N.E.2d 736, 748–55 (Ind. Ct. App. 2010) (concluding that policyholder's delay of approximately twenty years in providing notice to insurers despite being aware of environmental contamination was unreasonably late and created presumption of prejudice that policyholder must factually rebut to obtain coverage; instant policyholder failed to shoulder burden, supporting summary judgment for insurer); *Askren Hub States Pest Control Servs., Inc. v. Zurich Ins. Co.*, 721 N.E.2d 270, 278–79 (Ind. Ct. App. 1999) (finding a delay of six months unreasonable); *Ind. Farmers Mut. Ins. Co. v. N. Vernon Drop Forge, Inc.*, 917 N.E.2d 1258 (Ind. Ct. App. 2009) (concluding that policyholder's delay of eighteen months in giving notice of contamination claims was unreasonably late but that it did not prejudice insurer when fact of contamination and identity of responsible party not in dispute; extent of injury unclear but can be determined at trial, with amount of insurer responsibility, if any, assessed accordingly); *Sheehan Constr. Co. v. Cont'l Cas. Co.*, 938 N.E.2d 685, 689 (Ind. 2010) (citing to *Williams* with favor and holding that insurer had no duty to indemnify where policyholder failed to give notice of underlying lawsuit for nearly two years); *Nat'l Union Fire Ins. Co of Pittsburgh, Pa. v. Mead Johnson & Co., LLC*, 735 F.3d 539, 544 (7th Cir. 2013) (applying Indiana law) (finding insured inexcusably failed to comply with notice provisions in CGL policy and excess policy, but holding factual issues existed as to whether insurer was prejudiced by late notice) ("Late notice does create a presumption of [prejudice], thereby shifting to the insured the burden of producing 'some evidence,' but probably does not shift the burden of persuasion."); *Didion v. Auto-Owners Ins. Co.*, 999 N.E.2d 108 (Ind. Ct. App. 2013) ("Indiana courts have been consistent in holding that there is no 'discovery rule' in the insurance context. In *Brunner v. Economy Preferred Insurance Co.*, 597 N.E.2d 1317 (Ind. Ct. App. 1992), we adopted the rule that, for purposes of notice provisions in insurance contracts, the insured's failure to discover the loss until some time after it occurred was immaterial."); *Landis+Gyr Inc. v. Zurich Am. Ins. Co.*, No. 16-82, 2018 U.S. Dist. LEXIS 173197 (N.D. Ind. Oct. 5, 2018) (concluding that insured did not rebut the presumption that insurer was prejudiced by notice given approximately 30 years after environmental remediation and negotiation with the state authorities occurred) ("Zurich contends that if it had received notice earlier it could have evaluated the claim and taken steps to mitigate the length and cost of the closure of the Sagamore site."); *Greene v. Westfield Ins. Co.*, 963 F.3d 619 (7th Cir. 2020) (citing *Tri-Etch, Inc. v. Cincinnati Ins. Co.*, 909 N.E.2d 997 (Ind. 2009)) for the proposition that "an insurance company can disclaim coverage only if it was prejudiced by lack of notice" and "late notice creates a rebuttable presumption of prejudice in favor of the insurer").

Iowa: Prejudice required. *See Grinnell Mut. Reinsurance Co. v. Jungling*, 654 N.W.2d 530, 542 (Iowa 2002) (holding that if policyholder cannot show substantial compliance with the notice requirement, prejudice is presumed) ("Unless the insured shows such substantial compliance [with a notice requirement], excuse, waiver, or lack of prejudice to the insurer, prejudice must be presumed."). Burden to prove lack of prejudice is on policyholder. *Grinnell*, 654 N.W. at 542; *see also Simpson v. U.S. Fid. & Guar. Co.*, 562 N.W.2d 627, 631–32 (Iowa 1997) (finding that, where policyholder can demonstrate excuse for late notice, burden to prove prejudice placed upon insurer); *Met-Coil Sys. Corp. v. Columbia Cas. Co.*, 524 N.W.2d 650, 654 (Iowa 1994) (same); *Fireman's Fund Ins. Co. v. ACC Chem. Co.*, 538 N.W.2d 259, 264 (Iowa 1995) (same); *Dico, Inc. v. Emp'rs Ins. of Wausau*, 581 N.W.2d 607, 614 (Iowa 1998) ("[A]n insured's lack of compliance with notice requirements can be determined as a matter of law when the delay is measured in terms of months and years."); *B & F Jacobson Lumber & Hardware, L.L.P. v. Acuity*, No. 13-0952, 2014 Iowa App. LEXIS 500 (Iowa Ct. App. Apr. 30, 2014) (concluding a factual question existed as to whether insurer was prejudiced by the ten-month delay in receiving notice of "additional" damage); *Mich. Millers Mut. Ins. Co. v. Asoyia, Inc.*, No. 11-00006, 2014 U.S. Dist. LEXIS 187329 (S.D. Iowa Apr. 24, 2014) ("Based on the testimony of those at the fire scene and those who contemporaneously investigated the fire, all of the physical evidence preserved from the Sunnyside fire, and witnesses statements and photographs from the fire scene, the jury had a reasonable basis for finding that Michigan Millers was not prejudiced by Asoyia's two-year delay in notifying it of the fire. None of the authorities offered by Michigan Millers are sufficiently analogous to require a holding that United Fire, as a matter of law, did not rebut the presumption of prejudice."), *aff'd* 793 F.3d 872 (8th Cir. 2015) ("To further rebut the presumption, United Fire presented testimony allowing a reasonable jury to conclude that—despite some potential obstacles—the carefully preserved evidentiary record, including photographs, witness statements, and stored physical evidence, would enable Michigan Millers to conduct a thorough and meaningful investigation of the fire, even two years after receiving notice.").

Kansas: Prejudice required. *See Atchison, Topeka & Santa Fe Ry. Co. v. Stonewall Ins. Co.,* 71 P.3d 1097, 1139 (Kan. 2003) (holding there is better reasoning in support of requiring prejudice than not requiring it and finding late notice defense unsuccessful in case involving request for indemnification for a large quantity of work-related injuries). "[U]ntimely notice … is not alone sufficient to excuse performance of the insurer or relieve the insurer of its obligation to provide coverage when coverage otherwise should be afforded. Kansas also requires a showing of actual prejudice as a result of the untimely notice." *Id.* at 1137; *Nat'l Union Fire Ins. Co. v. FDIC,* 957 P.2d 357, 368 (Kan. 1998) (applying the notice-prejudice rule to proof-of-loss requirements in a fidelity bond). "Given that insurance contracts are not negotiated agreements, no compelling reason appears for allowing the insurer to avoid performing a duty purchased by the insured's premium unless the insured's delay caused loss to the insurer." *Id.* at 368. Burden to prove prejudice on insurer. *Id. See also Sheldon v. Kan. Pub. Emps. Ret. Sys.,* 189 P.3d 554, 564–66 (Kan. Ct. App. 2008) (discussing varying approaches and rationales behind the late-notice defense in the context of a disability income dispute). "Policy provisions respecting notice of claim or occurrence should be liberally construed in favor of the insured." *Id.* at 564, *appeal after remand,* 277 P.3d 448 (Kan. Ct. App. 2012); *B.S.C. Holding, Inc. v. Lexington Ins. Co.,* No. 13-3142, 2014 U.S. App. LEXIS 4492 (10th Cir. Mar. 11, 2014) (applying Kansas law) (reversing district court's grant of summary judgment in favor of insurer) ("Even if the [insureds] had taken too long, the delay would only relieve [the insurer] of coverage if it showed substantial prejudice.") ("Under Kansas law, an insurer can show prejudice by presenting evidence that (1) its ability to investigate the claim has been lost; or (2) opportunities to negotiate settlement have been lost; or (3) opportunities to defend have been lost. But the insurer's generalizations about lost opportunities do not constitute a showing of actual prejudice because [a] rule that would recognize prejudice whenever the insurer's routine procedures were disrupted is one that improperly *presumes* prejudice simply from the insurer's lost opportunity to join and control the underlying defense. Rather, to demonstrate prejudice, the insurer must show that it would have handled some aspect of the investigation, discovery or defense differently and that with this change, [the insurer] likely could have either defeated the underlying claims or settled the underlying claims for a lower sum than what the insureds settled.") (emphasis in original). *See also Kannaday v. Ball,* No. 12-2742-RDR, 2014 U.S. Dist. LEXIS 3414 (D. Kan. Jan. 9, 2014) (applying notice-prejudice rule in context of cooperation provision); *Geer v. Eby,* 432 P.3d 1001 (Kan. 2019) ("When our focus is placed, as it must be in this case, squarely on the purpose behind notice-of-suit provisions—to enable the insurer to locate and defend the suit—prejudice to Key as a matter of law is evident. (citing *Atchison*). Eby did not notify Key of the litigation. Eby's failure to respond to the lawsuit resulted in default judgment. Had Key known of the lawsuit, it would have been under a duty to defend Eby in the litigation, which would have resulted in either a factual finding on liability or a settlement. As a direct result of Eby's breach of his notice-of-suit duty, Geer's allegation that Eby's negligence caused the accident was never tested or compromised."); *Auto-Owners Mut. Ins. Co. v. Bricks & Stones, LLC.*, No. 20-2365, 2021 U.S. Dist. LEXIS 107784 (D. Kan. June 9, 2021) ("DD&B has cited evidence from which a jury could infer that [Insurer] could have acted sooner and thereby avoided default judgment and defended the claim on the merits. With respect to the merits of the claims in the underlying suit, the court notes [Insurer] has not specified or explained what defenses [Insurer] was unable to assert as a result of the delay in notice.").

Kentucky: Prejudice required. *See Jones v. Bituminous Cas. Corp.*, 821 S.W.2d 798, 803 (Ky. 1991) (holding insurer could not deny coverage because of six-month delay before notification of explosion implicating policy because insurer could not prove prejudice). "We view the question of prejudice in terms of whether it is reasonably probable that the insurance carrier suffered substantial prejudice from the delay in notice." *Id. See also Best v. W. Am. Ins. Co.*, 270 S.W.3d 398, 405 (Ky. Ct. App. 2008) (finding that the insurer was still obligated to pay on an anti-theft automobile policy where the insured waited two months before providing notice). "[A]n insurer may not deny coverage because the insured failed to provide prompt notice of loss unless the insurer can prove that it is reasonably probable that it suffered substantial prejudice from the delay in notice." *Id.* (also suggesting that insurer presented no evidence of prejudice to the court). Burden to prove prejudice on insurer. *Jones*, 821 S.W.2d at 803. *See also Old Republic Ins. Co. v. Underwriters Safety & Claims, Inc.*, No. 3:05-CV-343-S, 2010 U.S. Dist. LEXIS 77812 (W.D. Ky. Aug. 2, 2010) (explaining, on remand from the Sixth Circuit, the Court of Appeals's holding that prejudice resulting from late notice cannot be proven by the insurer merely disclosing that it was not able to partake in any of the judicial proceedings, as the insurer must demonstrate that there was "some reasonable possibility that the outcome would have been different had it received notice"); *Murphy v. Fair*, No. 2012-CA-001117-MR, 2013 Ky. App. Unpub. LEXIS 602 (Ky. Ct. App. July 19, 2013) (affirming summary judgment for insurer based on insured's failure to assist instead of notice provision) ("While timely notice of the loss would ordinarily have

enabled [insurer] to take whatever steps it deemed necessary to protect its potential rights, [insurer] was entitled—under express terms of this policy—to rely upon
[insured] for assistance in preserving its ability to assert its rights."); *Metro. Direct
Prop. & Cas. Ins. Co. v. Farmer*, No. 17-40, 2019 U.S. Dist. LEXIS 125486 (E.D.
Ky. July 29, 2019) ("Based on the foregoing review of *Jones* and its progeny, the
Court finds that proof of substantial prejudice is 'conclusive,' and thus appropriate
for summary judgment, when an insurer shows either (1) that the outcome would
have been more favorable if it had received timely notice of the claim; or (2) that
the insurer was actually and substantially harmed by the delay in notice. However,
in this Court's opinion, it makes more sense to presume prejudice where there is
an unreasonable delay in notifying the insurer of a covered loss. Then, the insured
could rebut that presumption by producing evidence supporting that the insurer
was not prejudiced, and the issue would become one for the trier of fact. And a
minority of other jurisdictions agree that presuming prejudice is a better approach
when the insured does not reasonably provide timely notice.").

Louisiana: Prejudice may or may not be required. *See Miller v. Marcantel*, 221
So. 2d 557, 559 (La. Ct. App. 1969) (insurer suffered no prejudice when employee
failed to inform employer of accident implicating policy until five months later;
insurer could not deny coverage). "[U]nless the insurer is actually prejudiced by the
insured's failure to give notice immediately, the insurer cannot defeat its liability."
Id. Burden to prove prejudice on insurer. *Gully & Assocs. v. Wausau Ins. Cos.*, 536 So.
2d 816 (La. Ct. App. 1988); *Moskau v. Ins. Co. of N. Am.*, 366 So. 2d 1004, 1006-07
(La. Ct. App. 1978) ("Though notice of an accident comes a substantial amount of
time after it occurred, as long as the rights of the insurer are not prejudiced by the
delay, coverage still exists.") (citing *Jackson v. State Farm Mut. Auto. Ins. Co.*, 29 So.
2d 177 (La. 1946)). *See also State ex rel. Div. of Admin., Office of Risk Mgmt. v. Nat'l
Union Fire Ins. Co. of La.*, 984 So. 2d 91, 97 (La. Ct. App. 2008) (finding summary
judgment inappropriate where material questions of prejudice to the insurer were
not addressed) ("[A]n insurer cannot escape liability unless it suffers prejudice either
in fact or as a matter of law from the late notice."), *appeal after remand*, 56 So. 3d
1236, 1247 (La. Ct. App. 2011) (denying insurer's motion for summary judgment
because a five-year delay in notice was not enough for insurer to show prejudice);
In re Matter of Complaint of Settoon Towing, L.L.C., 720 F.3d 268, 277 (5th Cir. 2013)
(applying Louisiana law) ("[W]here notice is *not* a condition precedent to coverage,
an 'insurer cannot deny coverage merely because its insured failed to give notice of
loss as soon as practicable' without a showing of prejudice.") (quoting *Peavey Co. v.*

M/V ANPA, 971 F.2d 1168, 1172 (5th Cir. 1992)); *XL Specialty Ins. Co. v. Bollinger Shipyards, Inc.*, 57 F. Supp. 3d 728 (E.D. La. 2014), *aff'd on other grounds* 800 F.3d 178 (5th Cir. 2015) ("Since notice is not a condition precedent to recovery, XL can avoid liability on notice grounds only if it can show that it was prejudiced by Bollinger's failure to give timely notice. Under Louisiana law, it is extraordinarily difficult for an insurer to show actual prejudice from breach of a notice condition at the summary judgment stage. Insurers are not entitled to summary judgment based upon only the naked delay in notifying the insurer of the suits brought against the insured . . . absent unusual or aggravated circumstances, such as failure to provide notice until after trial on the merits."); *Anco Insulations, Inc. v. Nat'l Union Fire Ins. Co.*, 787 F.3d 276 (5th Cir. 2015) ("The general rule in Louisiana is that when the requirement of timely notice is not an express condition precedent [to insurance coverage], the insurer must demonstrate that it was sufficiently prejudiced by the insured's late notice in order to deny coverage. This general rule, however, is subject to an exception: When timely notice is an express condition precedent to coverage, Louisiana law enforces provisions of insurance contracts which require notice as a condition precedent *without* also requiring the insurer to make a particular showing of prejudice."). However, it seems less clear whether Louisiana state courts apply a rule that an insurer need not prove prejudice when timely notice is a condition precedent. *See Norfolk Southern Corp. v. Cal. Union Ins. Co.*, 859 So. 2d 167 (La. Ct. App. 2003) ("A review of the relevant law of Virginia and Louisiana indicates that there is a genuine conflict between the laws of the two states concerning the issue of the effect of late notice to the insurance company. Under Virginia law, the require-ment of timely notice of an accident or occurrence is a condition precedent to an insurance company's liability coverage and requires substantial compliance by the insured. When the failure to provide such notice is 'substantial and material,' the insurance company is not required to demonstrate that it was prejudiced by the lack of timely notice. (citations omitted) By contrast, under Louisiana law, a failure to provide timely notice does not act as a bar to coverage absent a showing of prejudice to the insurer. *See Kinchen v. Dixie Auto Insurance Company*, 343 So. 2d 263, 265 (La. App. 1st Cir.), denied 344 So. 2d 1057 (La. 1977).").

Maine: Prejudice required. *See Me. Mut. Fire Ins. Co. v. Watson*, 532 A.2d 686 (Me. 1987); *Lanzo v. State Farm Mut. Auto. Ins.*, 524 A.2d 47, 50 (Me. 1987) (con-cluding that notice a year and a half after an accident was adequate where insurer failed to show prejudice). "[T]o avoid liability as a result of a failure of notice, a lia-bility insurer must show that the notice provision was breached *and* that the insurer was prejudiced by the insured's delay." *Id.*; *accord Ouellette v. Me. Bonding & Cas. Co.*, 495 A.2d 1232, 1235 (Me. 1985); *Acadia Ins. Co. v. Keiser Indus., Inc.*, 793 A.2d 495 (Me. 2002). Burden to prove prejudice on insurer. *Marquis v. Farm Family Mut. Ins. Co.*, 628 A.2d 644, 649 (Me. 1993). *See also Jackson v. N. E. Ins. Co.*, No. 07–178, 2009 Me. Super. LEXIS 165 (Me. Super. Ct. Nov. 10, 2009) (insurer had duty to defend despite late notice of a vehicular accident claim because it was not prejudiced as it became aware of accident and had ability to investigate within two months of event even though default judgment entered against insured) (personal injury action arising under a commercial garage policy) ("The purpose of a notice provision … is to allow the insurer an opportunity to investigate the circumstances surrounding an accident giving rise to a claim reasonably soon after the accident has occurred."), *aff'd*, No. Cum-11-344, 2012 Me. Unpub. LEXIS 118 (Me. Oct. 4, 2012); *accord Michoud v. Mut. Fire, Marine & Inland Ins. Co.*, 505 A.2d 786, 787 (Me. 1986) (insurer failed to demonstrate prejudice despite learning of claim eight months after entry of default but before hearing on damages; insurer failed to participate in damages hearing despite knowledge of the claim); *Allen v. Nautilus Ins. Co.*, No. 12-0163, 2013 Me. Super. LEXIS 178 (Me. Super. Ct. Aug. 2, 2013) ("Nautilus has not demonstrated any prejudice by the insured's failure to give notice or by the delay in its receipt of notice of the lawsuit after the litigation had commenced. Notice to Nautilus occurred on or about April or May of 2008, nearly 10 months before the Judgment was entered on March 17, 2009. There was ample time for Nautilus to step in and defend its interests. Allen in his telephone call to Nautilus supplied sufficient information to enable Nautilus to locate and defend the suit against Lessard.").

Maryland: Prejudice required. *See Prince George's Cnty. v. Local Gov't Ins. Trust*, 879 A.2d 81, 93–95 (Md. 2005) (finding that a trust participating in an excess insurance pool is not required to indemnify the state in a police brutality suit because it successfully met its burden of proving prejudice) (finding prejudice as a matter of law where excess carrier did not receive notice until ten days after a large jury verdict). "[Insurer must] establish by a preponderance of the evidence that it suffered 'actual prejudice' from the lack of notice before [it] may deny coverage." *Id.* at 92; *accord Commercial Union Ins. Co. v. Porter Hayden Co.*, 698 A.2d 1167 (Md. 1997); *Sherwood Brands, Inc. v. Hartford Accident & Indem. Co.*, 698 A.2d 1078, 1084 (Md. 1997); *Allstate Ins. Co. v. State Farm Mut. Auto. Ins. Co.*, 767 A.2d 831, 840 (Md. 2001); *Prince George's Cnty. v. Local Gov't Ins. Trust*, 879 A.2d 81, 92–93 (Md. 2005); *St. Paul Fire & Marine Ins. Co. v. House*, 554 A.2d 404 (Md. 1989); *see also McNeill v.*

Md. Auto. Ins. Fund, 927 A.2d 418 (Md. Ct. Spec. App. 2007) (finding the insurer responsible for coverage in a tort action because the injured plaintiff did not have enough information to feasibly meet notice requirement); *Morse v. Erie Ins. Exch.*, 90 A.3d 512, 519 (Md. Ct. Spec. App. 2014) (noting that Maryland has followed a "prejudice rule" since 1964, by statute, and since 2005, as a matter of common law, and discussing both at length). "By its terms, § 19-110 requires an insurer to show actual prejudice only where the insurer disclaims liability coverage as a consequence of its insured's failure to cooperate with the insurer or failure to give the insurer required notice." *Id.* (internal quotations omitted), *aff'd Woznicki v. GEICO Gen. Ins. Co.*, 115 A.3d 152 (Md. 2015) ("Had the Legislature intended for § 19-110 to apply to an insured's noncompliance with a consent to settle clause, a notice of claim clause, a no-action clause, or any number of clauses commonly found in insurance policies, it certainly could have said so."); *see also Sherwood Brands, Inc. v. Great Am. Ins. Co.*, 13 A.3d 1268, 1288–89 (Md. 2011) (explaining Md. Code Ann., Ins. § 19-110); *Perini/Tompkins Joint Venture v. Ace Am. Ins. Co.*, 738 F.3d 95, 101 (4th Cir. 2013) (applying Maryland law) (concluding § 19-110 did not apply to insured's failure to obtain insurer's consent to settle in violation of no-action clause); *see also Minn. Lawyers Mut. Ins. Co. v. Baylor & Jackson, PLLC*, No. 12-1581, 2013 U.S. App. LEXIS 13235 (4th Cir. June 27, 2013) (applying Maryland law) (finding that the insurer proved actual prejudice). For a recent and comprehensive discussion of Maryland law concerning late notice, from its highest court, *see Nat'l Union Fire Ins. Co. v. Fund for Animals*, 153 A.3d 123 (Md. 2017): "The actual prejudice element requires that the harm be more than possible, theoretical, hypothetical, speculative, or conjectural. This Court has found actual prejudice in instances where the insured's breach has: precluded the insurer from establishing a legitimate jury issue or presenting potentially outcome-determinative evidence, hampered the insurer from presenting a credible defense, or impeded an insurer's right to involvement or participation in the litigation." *Id.* at 136. *See also Mora v. Lancet Indem. Risk Retention Grp., Inc.*, 773 Fed. Appx. 113 (4th Cir. 2019) ("[A]lthough the insurer does not have to overcome the almost insurmountable burden of proving that the verdict was the direct result of a lack of cooperation, it must show that the insured's failure to cooperate has, in a significant way, precluded or hampered it from presenting a credible defense to the claim. Under this standard, possible, theoretical, conjectural, or hypothetical prejudice does not suffice.").

Massachusetts: Prejudice required. *See Johnson Controls, Inc. v. Bowes*, 409 N.E.2d 185, 187 (Mass. 1980) (court departed from previous common law requiring that the insured follow strict compliance with contract provisions regarding notice, reasoning that an insurance contract is not a negotiated contract because the insurer dictates most terms aside from the monetary amount of coverage) (late notice defense unsuccessful where attorney provided untimely notice of professional negligence claim to legal malpractice insurer). "[W]here an insurance company attempts to be relieved of its obligations … on the ground of untimely notice, [it] will be required to prove both that the notice provision was in fact breached and that the breach resulted in prejudice to its position." *Id. See also Darcy v. Hartford Ins. Co.*, 554 N.E.2d 28 (Mass. 1990) (declining to apply a rebuttable presumption of prejudice where the delay in notice is "extreme") ("The proposed rule would tend to shift unfairly the burden of showing prejudice from the party in the best position, and with the most resources, to ascertain the existence of prejudice to the party who is least capable of investigating the likelihood that a claim, despite a delay in notice, can be adequately defended. In the process, the protections for which insurance was obtained and paid for, could be denied."); *Bellanti v. Boston Pub. Health Comm'n*, 874 N.E.2d 439, 447 (Mass. App. Ct. 2007) (noting that, while Massachusetts law is usually forgiving of late notice, prejudice is not required where written presentment to an executive officer required) ("In the context of presentment, however, it has been held that [i]t is irrelevant that the defendant may not have suffered any prejudice by reason of the lack of actual notice."). The insurer has the burden to prove prejudice and is also required to prove that the notice provision was in fact breached. *Id. See also Pilgrim Ins. Co. v. Molard*, 897 N.E.2d 1231, 1240 (Mass. App. Ct. 2008) (finding that an insurer must prove delayed notice, which materially prejudiced the company and that generalities and even extreme time delays are generally not sufficient to prove prejudice, the court found that further proceedings were required to decide if delayed notice was prejudicial where an injured taxicab passenger spent approximately eight months locating the negligent driver that caused her injuries); *Amica Mut. Ins. Co. v. Kahn*, No. 13-11416, 2014 U.S. Dist. LEXIS 111132 (D. Mass. Aug. 12, 2014) ("As a result of the late notice, plaintiff could not depose or examine under oath Solomont who experienced the bodily injuries subject to coverage. It also could not conduct a medical examination of her by a physician of its choosing to determine the scope and depth of her bodily injuries. Through no fault of its own, plaintiff therefore experienced a 'loss of critical evidence' (an IME) and testimony from a 'material witness' (Solomont) as a result of defendants' failure to notify plaintiff in a timely manner."); *Boyle v. Zurich Am. Ins. Co.*, 36 N.E.3d 1229 (Mass. 2015) ("When Zurich learned of the Boyles' lawsuit, the hearing to assess the Boyles' damages had not yet taken place. At that juncture, Zurich could have contacted C&N and arranged to enter an appearance on its behalf. Zurich could have requested a postponement of the damages hearing. It could have moved to have C&N's default set aside, pursuant to Mass. R. Civ. P. 55 (c). Even after a judgment had entered, Zurich could have moved to set the judgment aside, pursuant to rule 55 (c) and Mass. R. Civ. P. 60 (b). Most importantly, Zurich still could have resolved the Boyles' claim by offering to pay the policy limit of $50,000, an offer that, the judge found, the Boyles would have accepted. On these facts, the judge's conclusion that Zurich failed to present 'proof of actual prejudice,' was well founded."); *Nat'l Union Fire Ins. Co. v. Town of Norwood*, No. 16-11978, 2017 U.S. Dist. LEXIS 17812 (D. Mass. Feb. 8, 2017) (citing *Boyle* and concluding that insurer suffered no prejudice) ("No settlement was reached in the BEH action, and National Union does not allege that its ability to investigate the claims or present a defense in the BEH action has been compromised in any way. Nor does defendants' failed settlement effort preclude future efforts to settle the remaining claim with National Union's participation."); *Tiede v. Seneca Specialty Ins. Co.*, No. 17-10074, 2019 U.S. Dist. LEXIS 42185 (D. Mass. March 15, 2019) ("These breaches resulted in actual prejudice to Seneca. The investigation report prepared by Mark Adjustment in March 2011 suggests that Seneca had strong grounds on which it could have defended Tiede's lawsuit. Seneca was deprived of the opportunity to assert those arguments as it did not receive the information necessary to appear and defend until after the default had entered and the assessment of damages hearing had occurred.").

Michigan: There is authority placing Michigan in the majority group of states requiring prejudice to the insurer to make late notice an effective defense. *See Koski v. Allstate Ins. Co.*, 572 N.W.2d 636, 639 (Mich. 1998) (finding that the insurer was prejudiced, and thus relieved from obligation, where the policyholder did not provide notice until after entry of default judgment) (involving a personal injury allegedly covered by a homeowner's policy) ("[A]n insurer who seeks to cut off responsibility on the ground that its insured did not comply with a contract provision requiring notice immediately or within a reasonable time must establish actual prejudice to its position."). Burden to prove prejudice is on the insurer. *Id.* But subsequent case law appears to have placed Michigan in the smaller group of states that does not require prejudice in order for an insurer to avoid coverage due to late notice. *See DeFrain v. State Farm Mut. Auto. Ins. Co.*, 817 N.W.2d 504 (Mich. 2012). In *DeFrain*, the court, in a 4-3 decision, held that *Koski* had been limited by subsequent decisions, in effect restricting *Koski* to cases in which the notice provision was unclear. The notice provision in *DeFrain* clearly required notice of a hit-and-run accident to the police within 24 hours and to the insurer within 30 days and was enforced by the majority, which reasoned that "an unambiguous contractual provision providing for a shortened period of limitations is to be enforced as written unless the provision would violate law or public policy. A mere judicial assessment of 'reasonableness' is an invalid basis upon which to refuse to enforce contractual provisions. Only recognized traditional contract defenses may be used to avoid the enforcement of the contract provision." *DeFrain*, 817 N.W.2d at 512. "The critical distinction between this case and *Koski* lies in the language of the contractual provisions at issue. *Koski* involved a contractual provision that required the insured to 'immediately forward [to the insurer] any legal papers' relating to the accident, whereas the instant case involves a contractual provision requiring the insured to notify State Farm within 30 days of the accident. The holding in *Koski* imposed a prejudice requirement only on contractual provisions 'requiring notice immediately or within a reasonable time.' The Court did not purport to impose a prejudice requirement on contractual provisions requiring notice within a specified time such as 30 days. There is an obvious distinction between a contract provision requiring notice 'immediately' or 'within a reasonable time,' which are temporally imprecise terms, and one that requires notice 'within 30 days,' which could not be clearer. Thus, contrary to the suggestion in *Bradley* [*Bradley v. State Farm Mut. Auto. Ins. Co.*, 810 N.W.2d 386 (Mich. Ct. App. 2010)] and the rule preferred by the dissent, the prejudice requirement of *Koski* does not apply to *all* contracts. To the extent that *Bradley* improperly extended *Koski*, it is hereby overruled." *Id.* at 513-514 (emphasis in original). If the current division of the Justices should hold, Michigan has presumably become a state where failure to give notice voids coverage without inquiry regarding prejudice so long as the notice provision is sufficiently clear, with a specific number of days constituting an unambiguous provision. Under *DeFrain*, it remains possible that a very short notice provision (e.g., a week or less) might be deemed to violate public policy or be unconscionable. *But see Heath Williams & Opus Dev. v. Travelers Prop. & Cas. Co. of Am.*, No. 301454, 2012 Mich. App. LEXIS 1287 (Mich. Ct. App. June 28, 2012) (citing *Koski* for the proposition that "[t]he failure to comply with a notice requirement does not alleviate the insurer of its obligations under the insurance contract unless the insurer establishes that it was prejudiced by the insured's failure to provide timely notice" but not citing *Defrain* (decided one month earlier) anywhere in the decision.); *Stryker Corp. v. XL Ins. Co.*, 57 F. Supp. 3d 823 (W.D. Mich. 2014) ("*Koski's* prejudice requirement is limited to contractual provisions requiring notice immediately or within a reasonable time rather than a fixed time period. *DeFrain v. State Farm Mut. Auto. Ins. Co.*, 491 Mich. 359, 817 N.W.2d 504, 514 (Mich. 2012). The TIG Policy fits squarely within *Koski* because it requires the insured to provide 'prompt' notice and to 'immediately' send copies of documents.") (*reversed but not addressing notice*, 842 F.3d 422 (6th Cir. 2016)); *Tudor Ins. Co. v. PM Servs.*, No. 335841, 2018 Mich. App. LEXIS 3064 (Mich. Ct. App. Aug. 21, 2018) (stating that insurer must establish actual prejudice) (citing *Koski*).

Minnesota: Prejudice may or may not be required. *Reliance Ins. Co. v. St. Paul. Ins. Cos.*, 239 N.W.2d 922 (Minn. 1976) (involving an insured attorney who waited eighteen months before notifying insurer of claim, concluding that this did not render policies unenforceable absent showing of prejudice) (burden to prove prejudice on insurer). "One of the prime reasons for this type of liability insurance is to pay the damages caused by certain acts or omissions of the insured. Unfortunately, omissions are frequent, including omissions to immediately notify the insurer. The very nature of these peculiarities insured against indicates that this type of insurance is not only a contract between the insurer and the insured but also a contract for the benefit of the public. Therefore, we hold that despite delay in notification the insurers are required to afford coverage under their contracts in the absence of actual prejudice, should liability be otherwise shown according to the terms of the policies. We are not holding that in some cases such an extraordinary length of time between an event and notification would not be prejudicial in itself, but this factual setting is not one of those cases." *Id*. at 925. *See also Owatonna Clinic-Mayo Health Sys. v. Med. Protective Co. of Fort Wayne, Ind.*, 639 F.3d 806, 813 (8th. Cir. May 11, 2011) (applying Minnesota law) ("[G]eneral Minnesota jurisprudence … rejects technical and narrow objections to the existence of coverage, especially when it comes to matters of notice.") (holding that insurer received "appropriate notice" even though notice did not "include any names and addresses or detailed particulars of the injuries" as required in the policy because notification of "the time, place, and circumstances" involving the occurrence of injuries in question was sufficient); *Lexington Ins. Co. v. United Health Grp.*, No. 09-10504, 2011 U.S. Dist. LEXIS 14929 (D. Mass. April 18, 2011) (applying Minnesota law) (declaring that loss run reports were an insufficient form of notice and insurer was badly prejudiced from insufficient notice because policyholder settled claims without insurer's input); *O'Brien & Wolf, L.L.P. v. Liberty Ins. Underwriters, Inc.*, No. 11-3748, 2012 U.S. Dist. LEXIS 109089 (D. Minn. Aug. 3, 2012) (applying prejudice rule in context of cooperation clause) ("Prejudice can occur when the insurer loses its opportunity to protect its interests through investigation or control of the litigation."). However, in *Food Mkt. Merch., Inc. v. Scottsdale Indem. Co.*, 857 F.3d 783 (8th Cir. 2017), the court relied on *Sterling State Bank v. Virginia Sur. Co.*, 173 N.W.2d 342 (Minn. 1969) and held that, when notice is a condition precedent to coverage – and a requirement of notice "as soon as practicable" is not -- an insurer need not prove prejudice to disclaim coverage based on the insured's failure to comply with a notice requirement. Of note, the court described the notice provision as follows: "Here, the 'policy did not require notice to be given during the policy period, but instead only required that notice be given as soon as practicable,' but 'in no event later than sixty (60) days after the end of the Policy Period.' As such, it does not precisely fit the definition of a claims-made policy in Minnesota. Ultimately, classification of the policy is irrelevant to an analysis of the issue needing decision: did [Food Market] give notice as soon as practicable?" *Id.* at 786. *See also Bach v. Liberty Mut. Fire Ins. Co.*, No. A17-1814, 2018 Minn. App. Unpub. LEXIS 488 (Minn. Ct. App. June 11, 2018) (automobile no-fault claim) (insurer could not establish prejudice as there were no witnesses that it could not now interview) (distinguishing *Noon Realty, Inc. v. Aetna Insurance Co.*, 387 N.W.2d 465 (Minn. Ct. App. 1986), which involved an insurer's inability to interview witnesses following a seven year delay in notice).

Mississippi: Prejudice may or may not be required. *Bolivar Cnty. Bd. of Supervisors v. Forum Ins. Co.*, 779 F.2d 1081 (5th Cir. 1986) (applying Mississippi law) ("The Mississippi Supreme Court has, on a number of occasions, considered insurance policies requiring notice of claims 'as soon as practicable.' When an insurance policy requires as a condition precedent that notice be given to the insurer 'as soon as practicable,' such notice must be given within the time agreed upon unless the insured offers a reasonable excuse.") ("The policy here clearly and expressly provided that the giving of notice 'as soon as practicable' was a condition precedent to recovery. In view of the controlling Mississippi precedent, which this Court is bound to follow ... Forum was not required to prove that it suffered actual prejudice from Bolivar County's unreasonably delayed notice."); *Lawler v. Gov't Emps. Ins. Co.*, 569 So. 2d 1151 (Miss. 1990) ("County Line contends that Reliance cannot avoid its policy obligations, since in its view the company was not prejudiced by the delay. However, under the clear terms of the policy, prompt notice was made a condition precedent to Reliance's liability and under Mississippi law, the company is relieved of any policy obligations (at least as to the chancery lawsuit) regardless of the presence or absence of demonstrable prejudice."); *Farmers Ins. Exch. v. Sheffield*, No. 16-134, 2017 U.S. Dist. LEXIS 143038 (N.D. Miss. Sept. 5, 2017) ("Though an insured generally breaches its notice obligation by failing to provide notice until the eve of trial, the Mississippi Supreme Court has held that such breach may not provide grounds for the insurer to avoid liability unless that breach results in prejudice to the insurer. On the other hand, Courts have found that an insurer is not required to prove prejudice where the notice clause is considered a 'condition precedent' to coverage.") ("Insurers who wish to make notice a condition precedent must do so clearly. Because Plaintiff has not established that the notice was a condition precedent ["as soon as practicable"] it must show that it was actually prejudiced.") ("[T]hough Plaintiff has asserted its fears regarding witness's recollection of relevant facts and the presence of evidence, it has not cited to specific examples tending to show how it would be actually prejudiced in this matter."). *But see Travelers Indem. Co. v. Forrest Cnty.*, No. 14-22, 2016 U.S. Dist. LEXIS 89513 (S.D. Miss. July 11, 2016) ("Under Mississippi law, delay in giving notice is excusable under certain circumstances, but such delay must have occurred without fault or negligence on the part of the insured. (citing *Bolivar County Bd. of Supervisors*) [W]here an insurance policy requires notice as a condition precedent to coverage, coverage may still be allowed unless the insurer suffered prejudice due to delay; that prejudice is a question of fact.") (but relying on *Jackson v. State Farm Mut. Auto. Ins. Co.*, 880 So. 2d 336 (Miss. 2004), a notice case involving uninsured motorist coverage).

Missouri: Prejudice required. *See Tresner v. State Farm Ins. Co.*, 913 S.W.2d 7 (Mo. 1995) ("Missouri courts have consistently placed the burden on insurers to demonstrate that they are prejudiced by receiving late notice of a claim before allowing the companies to avoid coverage under a policy because of the late notice. (citations omitted). Prejudice to the insurer will not be presumed from the mere fact of an insured's delay in giving notice and the presence or absence of prejudice in this context is an issue of fact to be determined on the particular facts of each case."). *See also Weaver v. State Farm Mut. Auto. Ins. Co.*, 936 S.W.2d 818, 820–21 (Mo. 1997) (finding that delay alone was insufficient to prove prejudice in a case involving a policyholder that waited a year before requesting benefits from an uninsured motorist policy) ("[T]he insurer must establish prejudice to forfeit the coverage to which the insured would otherwise be entitled."); *Billings Mut. Ins. Co. v. Cameron Mut. Ins. Co.*, 229 S.W.3d 138, 148 (Mo. Ct. App. 2007) (engaging in a detailed explanation of late notice policy and holding that the insurer suffered prejudice where insured failed to provide notice of a house fire until after jury verdict.) ("A showing of untimely notice is not enough; the insurer must also prove that it was prejudiced by that late notice."). Burden to prove prejudice on insurer. *Weaver*, 936

S.W.2d at 821; *Bolin v. Progressive Nw. Ins. Co.*, No. 2:07CV0049 AGF, 2009 U.S. Dist. LEXIS 30234 (E.D. Mo. Apr. 9, 2009) (concluding that a fifteen-month delay in reporting motorcycle accident insufficient to show prejudice) ("[S]howing of untimely notice [by an insured] is not enough; the insurer must also prove that it was prejudiced by that late notice."); *Clarinet, LLC v. Essex Ins. Co.*, No. 4:10 CV 1686, 2012 U.S. Dist. LEXIS 7300 (E.D. Mo. Jan. 23, 2012) ("Clarinet's failure to notify or at least attempt to obtain consent from Essex prejudiced Essex in that Essex was foreclosed from investigating the extent of damage to the Switzer Building, the need for stabilization and/or demolition prior to demolition, or seeking more favorable demolition or stabilization contract terms."), *aff'd* 712 F.3d 1246 (8th Cir. 2013); *Green Tree Servicing, LLC v. Chi. Title Ins. Co.*, 499 S.W.3d 771 (Mo. Ct. App. 2016) ("The determination of whether an insured provided prompt notice to its insurer is normally an issue of fact, but it may become a question of law where all reasonable persons would conclude that notice or proof was not given or made within [a reasonable time]. Next, we must determine whether, as a matter of law, Respondent was prejudiced by Appellant's failure to comply. The burden of proof regarding compliance with the Policy's notice requirement is on the Appellant insured, and the burden of proof regarding prejudice is on the Respondent insurer.") (quoting *Tresner*); *Lurie v. Commonwealth Land Title Co., LLC*, 558 S.W.3d 583 (Mo. Ct. App. 2018) ("[Insurer] has demonstrated actual prejudice by Appellant's failure to tender prompt notice of his litigation. The specific provisions of the Policy regarding [Insurer's] control of litigation and counsel and Appellant's unexcused failure to give notice within a reasonable time as a matter of law terminates [Insurer's] liability on the Policy for Appellant's attorney's fees accrued from his lawsuits against Polinsky."); *Northrop Grumman Guidance & Elecs. Co. v. Emplrs. Ins. Co. of Wausau*, 612 S.W.3d 1 (Mo. Ct. App. 2020) (setting forth numerous reasons why insurers suffered substantial prejudice from insured's late notice of claim).

Montana: Prejudice required. *See Steadele v. Colony Ins. Co.*, 260 P.3d 145, 151 (Mont. 2011) ("[B]ecause Colony did not receive notice of the claim, Colony was prejudiced in that it was deprived of the ability to investigate, to locate witnesses, to appoint counsel, to engage in discovery, to negotiate a settlement, and to develop a trial strategy. Finally, we observe that this is not a case where the insured failed to notify its carrier by a few days or where the failure to notify was *de minimis*. Rather, here, MCHC failed to notify Colony for months after having been served with the Steadeles' summons and complaint."). While the Supreme Court of Montana stated in its decision that Colony had been prejudiced, the court did not address whether prejudice is a requirement, in general, for an insurer to disclaim coverage based on late notice. As the facts here made for a relatively easy finding of prejudice–Colony was not notified of the claim until two months after a default judgment had been entered against its insured–the court's statement about prejudice could have been a reference to simply the matter at hand. Further, Colony itself argued that it had been prejudiced. *Id.* at 148. In addition, the *Steadele* Court described the policy's notice provision as being in plain English and simple, clear and easy to understand. *Id.* at 150. The court also cited *LaBonte v. Mut. Fire & Lightning Ins. Co.*, 241 P. 631, 635 (Mont. 1925) for the proposition that notice requirements are a condition precedent and failure to comply will bar recovery under the policy, unless the condition is waived by the insurer. *Steadele*, 260 P.3d at 150. In *Atlantic Casualty Ins. Co. v. Greytak*, 350 P.3d 63 (Mont. 2015), the Supreme Court of Montana clarified any confusion that may have existed over the meaning of *Steadele*. "An insured's technical or illusory failure to comply with obligations of a policy will not automatically terminate coverage, and an insurer who does not receive timely notice required by the terms of an insurance policy must demonstrate prejudice from that lack of notice in order to avoid the obligation to provide defense and indemnification of the insured. This rule applies whether the claim arises from the insured . . . or from a third party claiming damages as in the present case. The purpose of the notice-prejudice rule is to protect the insured or those claiming through the insured from a loss of insurance coverage over a technical violation of the policy when that violation is of no prejudicial consequence to the insurer. Nothing in *Steadele* should be construed to provide for any contrary rule. At the same time, a policy may include notice requirements, and an insured who fails to provide required notice to the insurer does so at his or her peril. If the insurer is able to show prejudice arising from the lack of notice, the insured may not be covered by the policy, as in *Steadele*." *Id.* at 67. *See also Contractors Bonding & Ins. Co. v. Sandrock*, 321 F. Supp. 3d 1205 (D. Mont. 2018) ("Notwithstanding that Sandrock argues that '[t]he case was far from over' when Sandrock's broker first provided notice in October 2016, the court in The Casino Case at that point had already entered judgment on liability against Sandrock, and the validity of the judgment had been affirmed on appeal. Sandrock's failure to notify the Plaintiff went far beyond a mere technical violation of the policies. The notice, provided only after judgment was entered, prevented any opportunity to investigate the facts, find witnesses, hire counsel, undertake discovery, negotiate a settlement, or devise a strategy for trial."); *Baadsgaard v. Safeco Ins. Co.*, No. 19-75, 2020 U.S. Dist. LEXIS 201225 (D. Mont. Sept. 21, 2020) (citing

Greytak for the proposition that Montana applies the notice-prejudice rule) ("Here, Safeco did not receive notice of Plaintiffs' state court lawsuit until after a settlement had been reached and a consent judgment had been entered in favor of the Plaintiffs. Safeco suffered prejudice. Safeco was deprived of the ability to appoint counsel, to engage in discovery, to negotiate a settlement, and to develop a trial strategy. Safeco was also deprived of the opportunity to defend Gamas under a reservation of rights and file a declaratory judgment action to discern whether coverage existed under the auto policy it had issued to Gamas, based on the allegations in Plaintiffs' state court complaint.") (For court's additional discussion of prejudice suffered by Safeco, *see* 2020 U.S. Dist. LEXIS 235643 (D. Mont. Dec. 15, 2020)).

Nebraska: Prejudice required. *See Herman Bros., Inc. v. Great W. Cas. Co.*, 582 N.W.2d 328, 334–35 (Neb. 1998) ("Courts in a substantial number of jurisdictions, Nebraska included, have taken the position that in order to escape liability or the duty to defend on account of an insured's unreasonable and unexcused delay in giving notice of a claim, a liability insurer is required to show that it was prejudiced. Therefore, we adhere to the proposition that where there is no evidence of collusion and it is not shown that the insurer has been prejudiced in its handling of the claim, the failure to give timely notice is not a defense to the claim.") (concluding that the insurer was prejudiced when insured waited twenty months before giving notice under a contract term that required notice "as soon as practicable" and that insurer did not have adequate notice to be able to "meaningfully protect its interests"). *See also Steffensmeier v. Le Mars Mut. Ins. Co.*, 752 N.W.2d 155, 161 (Neb. 2008) (concluding that the insurer was prejudiced where it did not receive notice of a pending lawsuit in time to intervene) ("[P]rejudice from an unreasonable and unexcused delay in giving notice of a claim 'is established by examining whether the insurer received notice in time to meaningfully protect its interests.'"). Burden to prove prejudice on insurer. *Herman Bros. Inc.*, 582 N.W.2d at 334–35; *MFA Mut. Ins. Co. v. Sailors*, 141 N.W.2d 846 (Neb. 1966) ("The purpose of the cooperation clause is to prevent collusion between the injured and the insured and to facilitate the handling of claims by the insurer. Where there is no evidence of collusion between the injured and the insured and it is not shown that the insurer has been prejudiced in its handling of the claim, we think the better rule is that the breach of the policy is not a defense."). *Accord Dutton-Lainson Co. v. Cont'l Ins. Co.*, 716 N.W.2d 87, 102 (Neb. 2006) ("In order to escape liability or the duty to defend on account of an insured's unreasonable and unexcused delay in giving notice of claim, a liability insurer is required to show that it was prejudiced. Prejudice is established by examining whether the insurer received notice in time to meaningfully protect its interests.") (involving an insurer's contesting indemnification of environmental cleanup costs; court concluded summary judgment was inappropriate where insurer failed to prove prejudice caused by lack of notice), *appeal after remand* 778 N.W.2d 433 (Neb. 2010); *Mefferd v. Sieler & Co.*, 676 N.W.2d 22, 28 (Neb. 2004) (notice after default judgment results in prejudice as a matter of law); *Rent-A-Roofer, Inc. v. Farm Bureau Prop. & Cas. Ins. Co.*, 869 N.W.2d 99 (Neb. 2015) ("Given the similarity in purpose between notice provisions and voluntary payments provisions, we find that it is proper to maintain the prejudice requirement when an insurer seeks to avoid the policy for breach of a voluntary payments provision.") ("[P]rejudice may be shown as a matter of law where the insured's settlement deprived the insurer of the opportunity to protect its interests in litigation or participate in the litigation and settlement discussions.").

Nevada: Prejudice required. The Supreme Court of Nevada held that an insurer must show prejudice before it may properly deny coverage to an insured based on late notice of a claim. *Las Vegas Metro. Police Dep't v. Coregis Ins. Co.*, 256 P.3d 958, 965 (Nev. 2011). In reaching its decision, the court acknowledged its prior ruling in *State Farm Mutual Auto. Ins. Co. v. Cassinelli*, 216 P.2d 606 (Nev. 1950), which rejected a notice-prejudice rule. However, as the *Coregis* Court noted, "*Cassinelli* has since been abrogated by NAC [§] 686A.660(4) and abrogated *sub silentio* by *Las Vegas Star Taxi, Inc. v. St. Paul [Fire & Marine] Ins. [Co.]*, 714 P.2d 562 (1986)." *Coregis Ins. Co.*, 256 P.3d at 964. Indeed, NAC § 686A.660(4), which was adopted in 1980 by the Nevada Department of Commerce, Division of Insurance, states in part that "[n]o insurer may ... require a claimant to give written notice of loss or proof of loss within a specified time or seek to relieve the insurer of the obligations if the requirement is not complied with, *unless the failure to comply prejudices the insurer's rights.*" *Coregis Ins. Co.*, 256 P.3d at 964 (emphasis added by court). In further support of its now official notice-prejudice rule, the *Coregis* Court reasoned that "[t]he majority of jurisdictions since 1950 have adopted a notice-prejudice rule," and "equitable[] principles support placing the burden to prove prejudice on the insurer because it is trying to deny its obligations under a contract of adhesion." *Id.* Moreover, this notice-prejudice rule, as the court asserted, "recognize[s] the difficulty the insured party would face in trying to prove that the insurer was not prejudiced and recognize[s] that the insurer is in the better position to prove that it was prejudiced by late notice." *Id.* "In accordance with the majority of jurisdictions and with the express language of NAC 686A.660(4), we adopt a notice-prejudice rule: in order for an insurer to deny coverage of a claim based on the insured party's late notice of that claim, the insurer must show (1) that the notice was late and (2) that it has been prejudiced by the late notice. Prejudice exists where the delay materially impairs an insurer's ability to contest its liability to an insured or the liability of the insured to a third party." *Coregis Ins. Co.*, 256 P.3d at 964 (citation and internal quotations omitted). *See also Big-D Constr. Corp. v. Take It For Granite Too*, 917 F. Supp. 2d 1096, 1114-15 (D. Nev. 2013) (citing *Coregis* and denying insurer's summary judgment motion because it did not show that earlier notice would have affected its determination as to coverage); *Pennymac Holdings, LLC v. Fid. Nat'l Ins. Co.*, 423 P.3d 608 (Nev. 2018) ("[E]ven assuming PennyMac failed to give Fidelity National timely notice of an adverse claim, Fidelity National cannot establish prejudice on a motion to dismiss. Prejudice arises where the delay materially impairs an insurer's ability to contest its liability to an insured or the liability of the insured to a third party. The issue of prejudice is an issue of fact, and as a general rule, questions of prejudice are best left to the trier of fact.").

New Hampshire: Prejudice required. *See Dover Mills P'ship v. Commercial Union Ins. Cos.*, 740 A.2d 1064, 1067 (N.H. 1999) (holding that the three factors considered in determining if delay bars a claim are (1) length of delay, (2) reasons for the delay, and (3) prejudice to the insured). Burden to prove prejudice is on the insurer. *See id.* at 1066–67; *see also Wilson v. Progressive N. Ins. Co.*, 868 A.2d 268, 271 (N.H. 2005) (finding that a seven month delay in reporting a hit-and-run accident in itself insufficient to show prejudice); *Lumbermens Mut. Cas. Co. v. Oliver*, 335 A.2d 666, 668 (N.H. 1975) (finding that policyholder had burden to prove that notice was given as soon as reasonably possible). *See also Sleeper Vill., LLC v. NGM Ins. Co.*, No. 09-44-PB, 2010 U.S. Dist. LEXIS 105053 (D.N.H. Oct. 1, 2010) (citing *Dover* for proposition that "New Hampshire insurance law … provides that a claim for coverage under an occurrence-based liability insurance policy will not be defeated by late notice of a claim unless the insured [*sic*] can establish that it was prejudiced by the late notice"); *Ohio Mut. Ins. Group v. Wilbur*, No. 2015-0538, 2016 N.H. LEXIS 98 (N.H. Apr. 25, 2016) ("[E]ven assuming the delay was substantial, and that Wilbur's purported reason did not excuse the delay, we disagree with the trial court that Ohio Mutual was prejudiced by the delay.") (discussing and comparing *Dover*) (providing various reasons why the insurer was not prejudiced by a seven month delay in an insured's provision of notice); *Nautilus Ins. Co. v. Gwinn Design & Build*, No. 18-633, 2018 U.S. Dist. LEXIS 208437 (D.N.H. Dec. 11, 2018) ("Nautilus contends that it was prejudiced by Gwinn's failure to provide notice because the delay prevented it from responding to Stanton's claims. Specifically, due to the delay, Nautilus lost the opportunity to resolve the matter with Stanton before suit was brought and then lost the opportunity to present a defense in the suit. Gwinn defaulted, which resulted in an uncontested judgment.") (concluding that insurer established prejudice and rejecting argument that insurer cannot claim prejudice because it did not file a motion to reconsider a default judgment until five months after it knew of the suit and the judgment).

New Jersey: Prejudice required, but recognized as "appreciable prejudice." *See Cooper v. Gov't Emps. Ins. Co.*, 237 A.2d 870, 874 (N.J. 1968) (finding late notice defense unavailing because policyholders acted in good faith as they reasonably believed a claim would not arise, and no prejudice resulted from delay) (holding that the burden to prove prejudice is on insurer) ("[A]lthough the policy may speak of the notice provision in terms of 'condition precedent,' ... nonetheless what is involved is a forfeiture, for the carrier seeks, on account of a breach of that provision, to deny the insured the very thing paid for. This is not to belittle the need for notice of an accident, but rather to put the subject in perspective. Thus viewed, it becomes unreasonable to read the provision unrealistically or to find that the carrier may forfeit the coverage, even though there is no likelihood that it was prejudiced by the breach. To do so would be unfair to insureds. It would also disserve the public interest, for insurance is an instrument of a social policy that the victims of negligence be compensated. To that end companies are franchised to sell coverage. We should therefore be mindful also of the victims of accidental events in deciding whether a forfeiture should be upheld."). *See also Jackson v. N.J. Idem. Ins. Co.*, No. A-5296-09T3, 2011 N.J. Super. Unpub. LEXIS 1951 (N.J. Super. App. Div. July 20, 2011) ("New Jersey has long required a showing of prejudice before a contract of insurance may be avoided."); *British Ins. Co. of Cayman v. Safety Nat'l Cas.*, 335 F.3d 205, 207 (3d Cir. 2003) (applying New Jersey law) (predicting that New Jersey law will require a reinsurer to show prejudice to prevail on a late notice defense); *Hager v. Gonsalves*, 942 A.2d 160, 163 (N.J. Super. Ct. App. Div. 2008) (concluding that the prejudice standard used for notice also applies to the duty of cooperation in a case where insured and person injured in an automobile accident failed to cooperate with insurer efforts to gather information) ("[T]he carrier may not forfeit the bargained-for protection unless there are both a breach of the notice provision and a likelihood of appreciable prejudice."); *Martin v. Fireman's Fund Ins. Co.*, No. A-4206-09T1, 2011 N.J. Super. Unpub. LEXIS 1041 (N.J. Super. Ct. App. Div. Apr. 28, 2011) (holding that insurer was appreciably prejudiced after insured waited four years to notify insurer of injuries he sustained in an accident, resulting in insurer's inability to intervene in insured's lawsuit against the tortfeasor); *State Nat'l Ins. Co. v. Camden*, No. 08-5128, 2014 U.S. Dist. LEXIS 43229 (D.N.J. Mar. 31, 2014) (discussing late notice in detail and extending the "appreciable prejudice" rule to insured's breach of an "adequate defense and investigation" condition); *Travelers Cas. & Sur. Co. v. Becton Dickinson & Co.*, No. 14-4410, 2016 U.S. Dist. LEXIS 90550 (D.N.J. July 12, 2016) ("The Court has found no New Jersey case, nor have Plaintiffs cited to any, in which a New Jersey court has ruled that the appreciable prejudice standard would not be applied in a case brought pursuant to an 'occurrence-based' policy.") (no exception to the appreciable prejudice standard for a sophisticated insured or policy that is not one of adhesion); *Nat'l Union Fire Ins. Co. of Pittsburgh, P.A. v. Becton, Dickinson & Co.*, No. 14-4318, 2018 U.S. Dist. LEXIS 14558 (D.N.J. Jan. 30, 2018) ("Courts consider two main factors in determining whether an insurer incurred appreciable prejudice. The first is whether substantial rights have been irretrievably lost by virtue of the failure of the insured to notify the carrier in a timely fashion. This factor requires the insurer to establish more than the mere fact that it cannot employ its normal procedures in investigating and evaluating the claim. Rather, the insurer must show that substantial rights have been irretrievably lost. The second factor considers the likelihood that the insurer would have been successful in defending against the injured party's claim if it had received timely notice.") (citations omitted); *Harleysville Preferred Ins. Co. v. E. Coast Painting & Maint., LLC*, No. 16-860, 2019 U.S. Dist. LEXIS 135295 (D.N.J. Aug. 12, 2019) ("[T]he loss of evidence alone does not constitute prejudice where other evidence exists with which an insurer can defend a claim."); *D'Andrea Constr. Co. v. Old Republic Gen. Ins. Corp.*, No. A-5126-18T2, 2020 N.J. Super. Unpub. LEXIS 2088 (N.J. Super. Ct. App. Div. Nov. 4, 2020) ("Everest was not named as a defendant potentially liable for the defense and indemnity of Crumley's claim until more than seven years after the accident, almost four years after settlement, and three years after plaintiffs filed this declaratory judgment action. We agree Everest was prejudiced by the delay in notification. The trial court found ACE, Lloyd's and Aspen had no motive to develop proofs that would defeat a loading and unloading claim, and that although Everest was able to depose Monitzer in 2016, he acknowledged that his memory of the event was not as clear as it had been in 2010.").

New Mexico: Prejudice required. *See Found. Reserve Ins. Co. v. Esquibel*, 607 P.2d 1150, 1152 (N.M. 1980) (insured breached an auto policy's notice, cooperation and concealment of fraud provisions) ("The risk-spreading theory of liability should operate to afford to affected members of the public -- frequently innocent third persons -- the maximum protection possible consonant with fairness to the insurer. If we were to hold otherwise, a windfall for the insurer at the expense of the public would result. We hold that the insurer must demonstrate substantial prejudice as a result of a material breach of the insurance policy by the insured before it will be relieved of its obligations under a policy.") (burden to prove prejudice on insurer); *Roberts Oil Co. v. Transamerica Ins. Co.*, 833 P.2d 222 (N.M. 1992) (applying *Esquibel* in the context of an insured's breach of a voluntary payments clause) ("[E]ven when there has been a substantial and material breach of the insured's obligation and a resulting failure of a condition precedent to the insurer's liability, that breach and nonoccurrence of condition does not discharge the insurer absent a showing that the insurer has been substantially prejudiced."); *Whelan v. State Farm Mut. Auto. Ins. Co.*, 329 P.3d 646 (N.M. 2014) (addressing "time-to-sue provisions") ("Because avoiding prejudice is the purpose of notice provisions, under our law the enforceability of a contract provision limiting when a claim for benefits under the contract can be brought by an insured depends on whether the insurer has been prejudiced by the insured's failure to comply with such a provision."); *Raja v. Ohio Sec. Ins. Co.*, 305 F. Supp. 3d 1206 (D.N.M. 2018) (addressing *Esquibel* and *Roberts* in the context of an insured's obligation to comply with policy conditions).

New York: New York traditionally followed the rule that no prejudice was required for late notice to defeat coverage. New York law is replete with case law making this point. In January 2009, New York enacted § 3420(a) of the New York Insurance Law to require that liability insurance policies covering bodily injury or destruction of property, issued or delivered in New York, contain a provision that provides, "that failure to give any notice… within the time prescribed therein shall not invalidate any claim made by the insured, injured person, or any other claimant, unless the failure to provide timely notice has prejudiced the insurer… ." *See* NY CLS Ins § 3420(a)(5). "[T]he burden of proof shall be on: (i) the insurer that it has been prejudiced, if the notice was provided within two years of the time required under the policy; or (ii) the insured, injured person or other claimant to prove that the insurer has not been prejudiced, if the notice was provided more than two years after the time required under the policy." NY CLS Ins § 3420(c)(2)(A). However, "an irrebuttable presumption of prejudice shall apply if, prior to notice, the insured's liability has been determined by a court of competent jurisdiction or by binding arbitration; or if the insured has resolved the claim or suit by settlement or other compromise." NY CLS Ins § 3420(c)(2)(B). Resort to the complete text of the statute is advised. *See also Hernandez Castillo v. Prince Plaza, LLC,* 981 N.Y.S.2d 906 (N.Y. Sup. Ct. 2014) (interpreting and discussing § 3420 in detail). Notably, in *Indian Harbor Ins. Co. v. City of San Diego,* 586 Fed. Appx. 726 (2d Cir. 2014), the Second Circuit clarified that § 3420(a)(5) has not changed the common law of New York, stating: "[W]e reject the City's argument that the amendment to § 3420 created a new public policy, and thus changed the common-law no-prejudice rule. If the New York legislature had intended to change the common law for all policies, it could have done so. … Moreover, numerous cases have continued to apply the common-law no-prejudice rule after § 3420(a)(5) came into effect on January 17, 2009, where the criteria under the statute had not been met." *See also Freeway Co., LLC v. Technology Ins. Co., Inc.,* 31 N.Y.S.3d 467 (N.Y. App. Div. 2016) ("Technology was not required to show that it was prejudiced as a result of plaintiff's late notice, because the subject policy was issued before Insurance Law § 3420 was amended to provide that an insurer could disclaim coverage based on untimely notice only if it was prejudiced by the untimely notice. The amendment expressly applies to policies issued on or after its effective date, January 17, 2009."); *Aspen Ins. UK Ltd. v Nieto.,* 27 N.Y.S.3d 52 (N.Y. App. Div. 2016) ("[W]hether there existed a good faith belief that the injured party would not seek to hold the insured liable [to justify untimely notice] and whether that belief was reasonable, are questions of fact for the factfinder."); *Kleinberg v Nevele Hotel, LLC,* 8 N.Y.S. 3d 484 (N.Y. App. Div. 2015) ("Because an injured party is allowed by law to provide notice to an insurance company, he or she is also generally held to any prompt notice condition precedent of a policy. However, such an injured party can overcome an insurance company's failure to receive timely notice—which would otherwise vitiate coverage—by a demonstration that he or she did not know the insurer's identity despite his or her reasonably diligent efforts to obtain such information."); *Strauss Painting, Inc. v Mt. Hawley Ins. Co.,* 26 N.E.3d 218 (N.Y. 2014) ("We have long held that a policyholder's timely notice to a broker does not constitute the notice contemplated by the insurance policy since a broker is normally the agent of the insured and notice to the ordinary insurance broker is not notice to the liability carrier.") (nothing in the "record supported the proposition that the insurer and broker had a relationship sufficiently close to suggest that service to the broker was effectively service to the insurer"); *Harleysville Worcester Ins. Co. v. Wesco Ins. Co.,* 752 Fed. Appx. 90 (2d Cir. 2019) ("[A] generalized assertion of prejudice is insufficient to establish Wesco was 'materially impair[ed]' in its ability to defend M&T. While Wesco need not show that there would have been a different outcome, it must identify something it could have done differently in discovery, at summary judgment, or at mediation; or identify different defenses or strategies it could have pursued."); *United States Underwriters Ins. Co. v. ITG Dev. Group, LLC*, 294 F. Supp. 3d 18 (E.D.N.Y. 2018) (notice more than two years late and insured could not establish that insurer had not been prejudiced) (citing Magistrate's recommendation: "ITG 'no longer had [any] records [of the incident] and could not provide [Plaintiff] with any type of lease agreement, occurrence report, contact or any other pertinent information regarding the loss occurrence of October 7, 2010.'").

North Carolina: Prejudice required. *See Great Am. Ins. Co. v. C.G. Tate Constr. Co.*, 279 S.E.2d 769 (N.C. 1981) (*Great American I*) ("The effect of this decision is to create a three-step test for determining whether the insurer is obliged to defend. When faced with a claim that notice was not timely given, the trier of fact must first decide whether the notice was given as soon as practicable. If not, the trier of fact must decide whether the insured has shown that he acted in good faith, *e.g.*, that he had no actual knowledge that a claim might be filed against him. If the good faith test is met the burden then shifts to the insurer to show that its ability to investigate and defend was materially prejudiced by the delay."). Then, in *Great American II* (*Great Am. Ins. Co. v. C.G. Tate Constr. Co.*, 340 S.E.2d 743 (N.C. 1986)), the North Carolina high court further expended on the three-step test: "[T]he first step in the *Great American* test simply requires the trial court to determine whether there has been any delay in notifying the insurer. In most instances, unless the insurer's allegations that notice was not timely are patently groundless, this first part of the test is met by the fact that the insurer has introduced the issue to the court." *Id.* at 747. *Great American II* went on to discuss the good faith test: "Certainly, if the insured knows that he is liable or even that he will possibly be held liable, or that others claim that he is at fault, an untimely delay in notification of the insured is a delay without good faith. The good faith test is phrased in the conjunctive: both knowledge *and* the deliberate decision not to notify must be met for lack of good faith to be shown. If the insured can show that either does not apply, then the trial court must find that the insured acted in good faith." *Id. Kubit v. MAG Mut. Ins. Co.*, 708 S.E.2d 138 (N.C. Ct. App. 2011) ("When faced with a claim that notice was not timely given, the trier of fact must first decide whether the notice was given as soon as practicable. If not, the trier of fact must decide whether the insured has shown that he acted in good faith, *e.g.*, that he had no actual knowledge that a claim might be filed against him. If the good faith test is met the burden then shifts to the insurer to show that its ability to investigate and defend was materially prejudiced by the delay.") ("Since plaintiffs have apparently never made any argument that they did not knowingly and purposefully fail to notify Travelers from July 2006 through March 2007, the good faith test is not met. Thus, the burden does not shift to Travelers to show that its ability to investigate and defend was materially prejudiced by the delay."); *Foremost Ins. Co. v. Raines*, 784 S.E.2d 236 (N.C. Ct. App. 2016) (discussing *Great American I* and *Great American II* and concluding that insurer met its burden to prove that it was materially prejudiced by insured's delay in notice when there was a default judgment obtained against the insured which could not be set aside); *Nationwide Mut. Ins. Co. v. Wahome*, No. 15-601, 2019 U.S. Dist. LEXIS 156668 (E.D.N.C. Sept. 13, 2019) (discussing *Great American I* and *Great American II*) ("Plaintiffs ability to defend in the underlying lawsuit was prejudiced by the admissions and this prejudice was material in that virtually all liability was conceded. Collins, the attorney retained to represent plaintiff in the underlying litigation, testified that the failure to be able to deny the request for admissions, in effect, destroyed the potential liability defense and the underlying lawsuit for purposes of J. Wahome became a damages-only case."); *Pa. Nat'l Mut. Cas. Ins. Co. v. JJA Constr., Inc.*, No. 18-00266, 2019 U.S. Dist. LEXIS 86637 (W.D.N.C. May 23, 2019) ("[I]f the insured establishes that it acted in good faith, then the burden shifts to the insurer to show that it was prejudiced by the delay. Some relevant factors in determining whether the insurer has been prejudiced by the delay are: (1) the availability of witnesses; (2) the ability to discover other information regarding the incident; (3) the existence of official reports concerning the occurrence; (4) the preparation and preservation of demonstrative and illustrative evidence; and (5) the ability of experts to reconstruct the scene and the occurrence."); *Penn Nat'l Mut. Cas. Ins. Co. v. Viking Pizza*, No. 17-1155, 2020 U.S. Dist. LEXIS 131981 (M.D.N.C. July 27, 2020) (undertaking an extensive analysis of the tests in *Great American I* and *Great American II*) ("Penn National may have suffered some prejudice as a result of the delay, but it still had time and resources to defend 'the claim in question.' The burden is on the insurer to prove they suffered a 'material prejudice' as a result of delayed notification. Penn National has not provided evidence that meets that burden as a matter of law.").

North Dakota: Prejudice required. *See Finstad v. Steiger Tractor, Inc.*, 301 N.W.2d 392, 398 (N.D. 1981) ("Although the group insurance policy in the instant case provides that written notice of claim must be given to Stuyvesant, the policy does not expressly provide for a forfeiture or any other consequence upon failure to give such notice within the time period specified in the policy. In accord with the rationale expressed by the New Jersey Supreme Court in *Cooper* and in accord with the foregoing principles of interpretation, we conclude that failure to provide a timely notice of claim to Stuyvesant as required by the insurance policy will result in a forfeiture of benefits to Finstad only if Stuyvesant can demonstrate that such failure resulted in a likelihood of appreciable prejudice to Stuyvesant so as to constitute a material breach of contract justifying a discharge of Stuyvesant's liability."). *See also Hasper v. Ctr. Mut. Ins. Co.*, 723 N.W.2d 409, 416 (N.D. 2006) ("A UIM insurer that "seeks to deny coverage based upon the insured's failure to notify the insurer of a proposed settlement with the tortfeasor must demonstrate that it suffered actual prejudice resulting from the lack of notice.") ("The insurer must demonstrate an actual, rather than theoretical, impairment of [its] ability to recover through subrogation, and UIM coverage should not be denied on the basis of a merely technical breach that has no effect on the insurer's ability to recover through subrogation. Because the purpose of consent-to-settle clauses is almost exclusively to protect the insurer's subrogation rights against the party released, such clauses should not be enforced to deny the UIM claim [w]hen the insurers subrogation rights are unaffected by the settlement."). Burden to prove prejudice on insurer. *Finstad*, 301 N.W.2d at 398; *Blackburn, Nickels & Smith, Inc. v. Nat'l Farmers Union Prop. & Cas. Co.*, 482 N.W.2d 600 (N.D. 1992) ("Aetna also asserts that Smith should not be able to recover, because he did not provide timely notification to Aetna of the accident and did not comply with other 'conditions precedent to coverage' as required by the policy. The disposition of this issue is controlled by our decision in *Kippen v. Farm Bureau Mutual Insurance Company*, 421 N.W.2d 483 (N.D. 1988), where we held that the insureds were not precluded from recovering benefits by their failure to notify the insurance company of a settlement agreement, because the insurance company had not provided them with a copy of the policy or other documentation.").

Ohio: Prejudice required but prejudice presumed from late notice. *See Ferrando v. Auto-Owners Mut. Ins. Co.*, 781 N.E.2d 927, 944–45 (Ohio 2002) (reviewing case law in Ohio and other jurisdictions and noting "modern trend" in favor of notice-prejudice rule, with most jurisdictions requiring insurer to show prejudice; also applying similar analysis to consent to settle provisions and preservation of insurer's subrogation rights) ("[W]e hold that when an insurer's denial of UIM coverage is premised on the insured's breach of a prompt notice provision in a policy of insurance, the insurer is relieved of the obligation to provide coverage if it is prejudiced by the insured's unreasonable delay in giving notice. An insured's unreasonable delay in giving notice is presumed prejudicial to the insurer absent evidence to the contrary.")

(burden to prove absence of prejudice on policyholder); *See also Champion Spark Plug Co. v. Fid. & Cas. Co. of N.Y.*, 687 N.E.2d 785, 791 (Ohio Ct. App. 1996) (concluding that a delay of one year before notifying insurer of possible liability for pollution cleanup failed to meet policy requirements of notification "as soon as possible" where policyholder gave no reasonable explanation for an unreasonable delay; prejudice was presumed with potential for rebuttal by the policyholder); *Thomas v. Nationwide Mut. Ins. Co.*, 895 N.E.2d 217, 230 (Ohio Ct. App. 2008) (concluding that lower court erred in giving a directed verdict where reasonable minds could differ as to insurer prejudice where policyholder called her insurer after an accident but did not submit written notice as required by her policy). In *Pennsylvania General Insurance Co. v. Park-Ohio Industries*, 930 N.E.2d 800 (Ohio 2010), the Ohio Supreme Court applied the state's law of notice in an allocation matter. Pursuant to *Goodyear Tire & Rubber Co. v. Aetna Casualty & Surety Co.*, 769 N.E.2d 835 (Ohio 2002), Ohio is an "all sums" state (see Chapter 18 regarding state-by-state difference regarding allocation of insurer responsibility in cases of consecutively triggered policies) that allows a policyholder facing claims implicating several policy periods of multiple triggered policies to approach particular insurers for coverage, with the targeted insurer then permitted to seek pro rata contribution from other triggered insurers. In the 2010 *Park-Ohio* opinion, the court addressed the issue of whether insurers facing an indemnity request could assert a late notice defense and concluded that they could—but that such defenses would not be successful unless the insurer was prejudiced by the delay. In what may be a departure from the general law of late notice, the *Park-Ohio* opinion can be read as suggesting that in multiyear contribution cases of this sort, the insurer bears the burden to show prejudice from any delay in seeking contribution. On the merits, the *Park-Ohio* Court found that the delay in notifying the insurers was not unreasonable and was "as soon as practicable" under the circumstances of the long-tail asbestos liability at issue in the underlying case. 930 N.E.2d at 808. "If the failure to notify non-targeted insurers pursuant to the relevant insurance policies results in prejudice to the nontargeted insurers, then the nontargeted insurers will not be required to contribute to the targeted insurer. In cases in which the nontargeted insurers have not been prejudiced by a failure to notify, the equitable nature of the all sums approach requires that those nontargeted insurers will still be liable in a contribution action brought by the targeted insurer." *Id.* at 807. [*But see Canton Drop Forge*, discussed below.] *See also Kelley v. State Farm Mut. Auto. Ins. Co.*, No. 98749, 2013 Ohio App. LEXIS 514 (Ohio Ct. App. Feb. 21, 2013) (two-and-one-half year delay in asserting a claim prejudiced insurer); *Burlington Ins.*

Co. v. PMI Am., Inc., 862 F. Supp. 2d 719, 737-38 (S.D. Ohio 2012) ("An insured's failure to give its insurer notice in a timely fashion bars coverage because notice provisions in insurance contracts are conditions precedent to coverage.") (citing *Goodyear Tire & Rubber Co.*) ("[A]n unexcused significant delay may be unreasonable as a matter of law.") (citing *Ormet Primary Aluminum Corp. v. Emp'rs Ins. of Wausau*, 725 N.E.2d 646 (Ohio 2000)); *W. Res. Mut. Cas. Co. v. OK Café & Catering, Inc.*, No. 9-12-45, 2013 Ohio App. LEXIS 3489 (Ohio Ct. App. Aug. 5, 2013) ("As a result of OK Café's failure to forward copies of the complaint and summons to Western Reserve as required by the CGL Policy, Western Reserve did not receive notice of Cooperider's lawsuit until it was too late. Had Western Reserve received copies of the complaint and summons as the CGL Policy had designed, it could have further investigated Cooperider's claim, determined the relative fault of the parties involved, and, most importantly, hired counsel for OK Café who would have assisted OK Café in responding to the complaint and avoiding default judgment."); *Burlington Ins. Co. v. Eden Cryogenics LLC*, 126 F. Supp. 3d 947 (S.D. Ohio 2015) ("The Court finds that a period of four months and a few days does not constitute an unreasonable delay and, in any case, Burlington was not prejudiced by the delay. Defendants not only notified Burlington while the litigation was still pending, the notice was received in the incipient stages of the litigation. Burlington was, therefore, provided with a meaningful opportunity to investigate the claims, to determine whether the underlying claims implicated the .... [insurance] agreement and to otherwise protect its interest."); *McCruter v. Travelers Home & Marine Ins. Co.*, No. 2019-L-167, 2021 Ohio App. LEXIS 483 (Ohio Ct. App. Feb. 22, 2021) ("The Supreme Court of Ohio has created a two-step analysis to be applied in determining whether coverage may be avoided based upon late notice. First, the court must determine whether the insured's notice was timely. This determination is based on asking whether the insurer received notice within a reasonable time in light of all the surrounding facts and circumstances. If the insurer did not receive reasonable notice, the next step is to inquire whether the insurer was prejudiced. Unreasonable notice creates a presumption of prejudice to the insurer, which the insured bears the burden of evidence to rebut.") (citing *Ferrando*); *Canton Drop Forge, Inc. v. Travelers Cas. & Sur. Co.*, No. 18-01253, 2021 U.S. Dist. LEXIS 45535 (N.D. Ohio Mar. 11, 2021) (rejecting insured's attempt to use *Park-Ohio* to defeat a late notice defense and limiting *Park-Ohio* to its unique facts).

Oklahoma: Prejudice required. *See Fox v. Nat'l Sav. Ins. Co.*, 424 P.2d 19, 25 (Okla. 1967) (policyholder waited six months to notify insurer of car accident implicating policy; court remanded case because lower court did not assess whether the insurer satisfied its burden of proving prejudice). "We think it is in accord with the public policy of this State, and the majority of better reasoned authorities on insurance policies like the one involved here, to place the burden upon the insurer to show prejudice from non-compliance with the policy's provisions concerning written notice, where the evidence shows that the insurer has received actual notice, or knowledge, of an accident or a potential claim arising out of it, and covered by the policy[.]" *Id.; Indep. Sch. Dist. No. 1 of Tulsa Cnty. v. Jackson*, 608 P.2d 1153, 1155 (Okla. 1980) ("In this case, Mid-Continent received no notice of the pending lawsuit, nor did it receive notice that default judgment would be taken. The insurance policy specifically stated that notice must be provided. Mid-Continent was prejudiced because it did not have the opportunity to present its defense."); *Melton Truck Lines, Inc. v. Indem. Ins. Co. of N. Am.*, No. 04-263, 2006 U.S. Dist. LEXIS 43179 (N.D. Okla. June 26, 2006) ("The provision of notice to an insurer under an insurance contract is a condition precedent to coverage. It is clear from the record before the court that a question of fact remains as to the timeliness of the notice provided to IINA. Further, pursuant to Oklahoma law, an insurer must also demonstrate prejudice from lack of notice. The issue of prejudice is also a matter which must be determined by the trier of fact.") (citing *Fox*); *Safeco Ins. Co. v. Estate of Speck*, No. 20-238, 2020 U.S. Dist. LEXIS 147462 (N.D. Okla. Aug. 17, 2020) (citing *Indep. Sch. Dist. No. 1*) ("Safeco does not allege prejudice due to the alleged late notice. The record reflects a motion for default judgment is pending in the state civil action and an answer has been filed on behalf of Taylor. In his response to the motion for default, Taylor explained that the answer was not filed late due to the extensions mandated by the Oklahoma Supreme Court and the Court of Criminal Appeals due to the Covid pandemic. It is premature to request this Court to make a finding of prejudice resulting from the lack of or late notice of the incident, claim and judicial proceedings when prejudice cannot be determined due to the current status of the state proceedings."); *Hiland Partners Holdings, LLC v. Nat'l Union Fire Ins. Co.*, 475 P.3d 869 (Okla. Ct. App. 2020) (concluding that an insurer is required to show prejudice when it asserts an insured has breached the voluntary payments clause; "Immaterial or mere technical failures to comply with the clause are insufficient to waive or relieve an insurer of liability.").

Oregon: Prejudice required. *See Lusch v. Aetna Cas. & Sur. Co.*, 538 P.2d 902, 904 (Or. 1975) (en banc) ("[W]e conclude that the first inquiry should be whether the notice of accident was received in time for the insurer to make a reasonable investigation and adequately protect its interest and that of the insured. Stated conversely, the first inquiry should be whether the insurer was prejudiced by the insured's failure to give earlier notice of the accident. If notice from any source was sufficiently timely so that the insurer could adequately investigate and protect itself, thereby suffering no prejudice, the insurer is bound to fulfill its policy obligations. Whether the insured acted reasonably is immaterial. However, if the insurer could not adequately investigate or otherwise protect itself, thereby suffering prejudice, then the relevant inquiry is whether the insured acted reasonably in failing to give notice at an earlier time. If the insured did act reasonably, the insurer is obligated to perform."). *See also Emp'rs Ins. of Wausau v. Tektronix, Inc.*, 156 P.3d 105, 112 (Or. Ct. App. 2007) (concluding that late notice cases require two inquiries: (1) was the insurer prejudiced by the late notice and (2) was the insured's delay in reporting reasonable). "If the insured does not give notice immediately after the accident or if notice is given by a third party, the initial question should be whether the notice is given in time for the insurer to adequately investigate the potential claim and thus protect itself and the insured." Id. Burden to prove prejudice on insurer. *Halsey v. Fireman's Fund Ins. Co.*, 681 P.2d 168 (Or. Ct. App. 1984); *Lusch*, 538 P.2d at 904; *see also Smagala v. Sequoia Ins. Co.*, 969 F. Supp. 2d 1271, 1282 (D. Or. 2013) ("On this record the Court concludes Sequoia has established it was prejudiced by Plaintiffs' failure to notify it of the alleged collapses until November 15, 2012. The Court also concludes Plaintiffs have not established their failure to notify Sequoia of the collapses until November 15, 2012, was reasonable."); *Artisan & Truckers Cas. Co. v. John Zaccar Cranley Nw. Pilot Car Serv.*, No. 13-00389, 2014 U.S. Dist. LEXIS 330 (D. Or. Jan. 3, 2014) ("When an insured fails to give immediate notice to its insurer of a possible claim, the viability of the insurer's policy obligation turns on a two-part inquiry: (1) whether the insurer was prejudiced by the delayed notice; and (2) if the insurer was prejudiced, whether the insured acted reasonably in failing to give notice at an earlier time. The insurer has the burden of demonstrating prejudice.") ("Because Plaintiffs do not show any prejudice caused by Sue Cranley's delayed notice as required under Oregon law, this Court need not determine whether the delay was reasonable. Thus, the Court concludes Plaintiffs cannot avoid the duty to defend or to indemnify Sue Cranley on the ground that she provided untimely notice of the accident."); *Gerke v. Travelers Cas. Ins. Co. of Am.*, 815 F. Supp. 2d 1190, 1201 (D. Or. 2011) ("In each of the above cases where Oregon courts have required the insurer to show prejudice, it has been when the insurer seeks to invoke the insured's non-cooperation as a defense to its denial of coverage, thereby barring the insured's recovery. None of these cases address whether the insurer must show prejudice when it seeks to preclude the insured from bringing suit until the insured has complied with all the policy conditions that allow the insurer to make a decision regarding coverage.") ("[T]he court concludes that the Travelers Policies' EUO provisions serve as a conditions precedent to Gerke's ability to bring suit."); *Great Am. All. Ins. Co. v. SIR Columbia Knoll Assocs. L.P.*, No. 18-00908, 2020 U.S. Dist. LEXIS 162401 (D. Or. Sept. 4, 2020) ("'Under Oregon law an insurer may deny coverage on the basis of an insured's failure to give timely notice of the claim if the insurer satisfies a two-part inquiry regarding prejudice and reasonableness. *Smagala v. Sequoia Ins. Co.*, 969 F. Supp. 2d 1271, 1282 (D. Or. 2013). The first question is whether the insurer was prejudiced by the insured's conduct. The second question is whether the insured acted reasonably. Prejudice may be shown if the insurer did not receive the notice with sufficient time 'to make a reasonable investigation and adequately protect its interest and that of the insured.' *Lusch v. Aetna Cas. & Surety Co.*, 272 Or. 593, 599, 538 P.2d 902 (1975).") (denying summary judgment in first-party property policy dispute) (insurer offered no argument as to how or why destructive testing or alleged repairs affected its ability to perform a reasonable investigation and insured may have provided notice, within a reasonable period of time, under the circumstances).

Pennsylvania: Prejudice required. *See Brakeman v. Potomac Ins. Co.*, 371 A.2d 193, 196 (Pa. 1977) (departing from prior decisions and holding that an insurer must prove breach of notice provision and prejudice as a result of that breach to avoid coverage obligation). "[T]he insurance company will be required to prove that the notice provision was in fact breached and that the breach resulted in prejudice to its position." *Id.* at 198. "[A] reasonable notice clause is designed to protect the insurance company from being placed in a substantially less favorable position than it would have been in had timely notice been provided, e. g., being forced to pay a claim against which it has not had an opportunity to defend effectively. In short, the function of a notice requirement is to protect the insurance company's interests from being prejudiced. Where the insurance company's interests have not been harmed by a late notice, even in the absence of extenuating circumstances to excuse the tardiness, the reason behind the notice condition in the policy is lacking, and it follows neither logic nor fairness to relieve the insurance company of its obligations under the policy in such a situation." *Id.* at 197. *See also Metal Bank of Am., Inc. v. Ins. Co. of N. Am.*, 520 A.2d 493 (Pa. Super. Ct. 1987) ("Even assuming that the appellant was not required to give notice of the events on which it based its claim until

1977, the appellees were nevertheless prejudiced by delay of five years in receiving notice. During these five years the insurers were precluded from the extensive investigations, negotiations and litigation which occurred, and the appellees were given no opportunity to control the situation or even participate."); *Vanderhoff v. Harleysville Ins. Co.*, 997 A.2d 328, 335 (Pa. 2010) ("[W]e conclude that before an insurer can deny uninsured motorist benefits resulting from an accident involving a phantom vehicle, the insurer must demonstrate prejudice due to the failure of an insured to notify the insurer"), *aff'd*, 78 A.3d 1060 (Pa. 2013) (showing of prejudice due to late notice of phantom vehicle did not require proof of what insurer would have found if notice was timely); *Pac. Emplrs. Ins. Co. v. Global Reinsurance Corp.*, No. 09–6055, 2011 U.S. Dist. LEXIS 54825 (E.D. Pa. May 23, 2011) (reviewing the history of notice-prejudice law in Pennsylvania and predicting that the Pennsylvania Supreme Court would require a showing of prejudice for reinsurance policies); *Nationwide Mut. Fire Ins. Co. v. Nova Real Estate LLC*, No. 09-0303, 2011 U.S. Dist. LEXIS 20601 (E.D. Pa. Mar. 1, 2011) ("Nationwide has demonstrated that the receiving of post-settlement notice put it at a significant disadvantage and placed it in a substantially less favorable position than it would have been in had timely notice been provided. This is precisely the type of harm reasonable notice clauses are designed to prevent. We are satisfied that Nationwide has suffered a loss of substantial defense opportunities and a likelihood of success if those opportunities had been available."); *Berko Inv., LLC v. State Nat. Ins. Co., Inc.*, No. 08-2609, 2010 U.S. Dist. LEXIS 73144 (E.D. Pa. July 21, 2010) (holding that insurer was prejudiced after insured replaced entire damaged roof before the insured notified the insurer of the damage, as such action effectively prevented the insurer "from inspecting the roof and determining the cause and origin of the damage, and what repairs were required"); *Brethren Mut. Ins. Co. v. Velez*, No. 06-1961, 2008 U.S. Dist. LEXIS 46675 (M.D. Pa. June 13, 2008) ("[The insurer's] litany of harm, although impressive, does not show that the probable outcome of this matter has been altered to its disadvantage by reason of untimely notice. There is no evidence that the matter could have been settled at an amount lower than could be negotiated now. There is no indication of the loss of evidence to the detriment of the defense. While Brethren Mutual undoubtedly would prefer to assume control over the defense as soon as possible, there is no concrete evidence that it has been harmed by the untimely notification from its insureds. As our Court of Appeals noted, the 'right to associate in the defense of a claim is too amorphous and cannot itself constitute prejudice, unless [the insurer] can demonstrate that earlier notice would probably have led to a more advantageous result."); *Burke-Dice v. Gov't Emples. Ins. Cos.*, No. 17-3198, 2017 U.S. Dist. LEXIS 129858 (E.D. Pa. Aug. 5, 2017) (discussing Pennsylvania's unsettled law on what constitutes prejudice in the UM context and concluding that "what might constitute prejudice, and the manner of proving one was prejudiced by an insured's untimely notice, vary significantly depending on the circumstances of the case"); *J.P. Jenks, Inc. v. Commerce & Indus. Insurance Co.*, No. 15-cv-00155, 2017 U.S. Dist. LEXIS 21663 (W.D. Pa. Feb. 16, 2017) ("Defendant cites cases where courts have found prejudice as a matter of law when notice was not provided until after a claim was fully litigated or settled. *See, e.g., Metal Bank of Am., Inc. v. Ins. Co. of N. Am.*, 360 Pa. Super. 350, 520 A.2d 493 (Pa. Super. Ct. 1987). Unlike these cases, however, Defendant had an opportunity to defend the identical claim when it was filed in Pennsylvania."); *NVR, Inc. v. Motorists Mut. Ins. Co.*, 371 F. Supp. 3d 233 (W.D. Pa. 2019) (undertaking extensive discussion in concluding that insurer was prejudiced by late notice) ("Even if NVR strategically withheld notice from MMIC, the law remains clear: the record must demonstrate that MMIC was actually prejudiced by NVR's late notice in order for it to avoid its obligations to defend and/or indemnify under the Policy.").

Rhode Island: Prejudice required. *Pickering v. American Employers Ins. Co.*, 282 A.2d 584 (R.I. 1971) ("We find the reasoning in *Cooper* [*see* New Jersey] to be most persuasive. We do not believe that a technical breach of the notice provisions in a policy should bar an insured from recovering the benefits for which he has paid. We include within the term 'notice' such items as the furnishing of a proof of claim and a copy of the summons and complaint. Since we have seen fit to overrule that part of *Sherwood Ice Co.*, [100 A. 572 (R.I. 1917)] which speaks about the lack of prejudice, we deem it proper to remand this case to the Superior Court where the insurer may, if it wishes, seek to show how and in what manner the four-month delay in the giving of notice and/or the lack of the proof of claim and the suit papers have worked to its prejudice."); *Pa. Gen. Ins. Co. v. Becton*, 475 A.2d 1032, 1035 (R.I. 1984) ("The medical records reveal that Becton was discharged by her physician on April 25, 1977, and that she only returned to him on April 10, 1979, for a routine checkup. The insurer therefore would have been required to investigate three-year-old injuries that had not been treated in over two years. While the mere passage of time is not sufficient to establish prejudice, the finding by the trial justice in this case that the insurer was prejudiced because of its inability adequately to investigate Becton's claim is supported by the facts."); *Avco Corp. v. Aetna Cas. & Sur. Co.*, 679 A.2d 323 (R.I. 1996) (finding that insurer's unrebutted claim of prejudice established sufficient prejudice); *IDC Prop., Inc. v. Chi. Title Ins. Co.*, 974 F. Supp. 2d 87 (D.R.I. 2013) ("While written notice was not prompt, undisputed evidence indicates that Chicago was aware of the litigation giving rise to IDC's claims before IDC provided formal written notice. However, the record before this Court does not indicate precisely when Chicago was aware. Nor does the record contain evidence regarding what Chicago did when it became aware that a claim might exist, i.e., whether Chicago undertook an investigation, considered participating in pre-litigation discussions, or evaluated intervening in the litigation. In addition, Chicago has not set forth undisputed facts regarding the harmfulness of the opportunities it asserts it lost due to the late written notice. Given the record at this time, a genuine issue of material fact exists regarding whether Chicago was prejudiced by IDC's failure to provide prompt written notice."); *Mathews v. Travelers of Mass.*, No. 2016-4145, 2019 R.I. Super. LEXIS 81 (R.I. Super. Ct. June 28, 2019) ("Travelers was prejudiced because without contact with DaSilva, there was only a limited amount its assigned counsel could do to protect DaSilva, and by extension, Travelers, from having default entered. This distinguishes this case from *Boyle* [*v. Zurich American Insurance Company*, 36 N.E.3d 1229 (Mass. 2015)], wherein the insurer had opportunities to prevent judgment from entering against its insured or to have the judgment set aside and chose not to do so.").

South Carolina: Prejudice required. *See Vt. Mut. Ins. Co. v. Singleton*, 446 S.E.2d 417 (S.C. 1994) ("Where the rights of innocent parties are jeopardized by a failure of the insured to comply with the notice requirements of an insurance policy, the insurer must show substantial prejudice to the insurer's rights.") ("The purpose of a notification requirement is to allow for investigation of the facts and to assist the insurer in preparing a defense.") (concluding that insurer failed to show substantial prejudice to defeat coverage when policyholder waited four months to report eye injury implicating homeowners policy); *Berenyi, Inc. v. Landmark Am. Ins. Co.*, No. 09-01556, 2010 U.S. Dist. LEXIS 3018 (D.S.C. Jan. 14, 2010) ("The court also finds that Landmark has failed to meet its burden of showing that it has been substantially prejudiced by any delay in Berenyi's notification of the Claim. As stated by Berenyi, Landmark has been provided sufficient time to investigate the facts and to prepare a defense; that no default judgment has been entered; and that until Landmark denied a defense to Berenyi, it had defended the action, controlled the litigation, and hired experts."); *Jessco, Inc. v. Builders Mut. Ins. Co.*, No. 10-1215, 2012 U.S. App. LEXIS 6502 (4th Cir. Mar. 29, 2012) (applying South Carolina law) (finding that prejudice to the insurer may not be presumed in rejecting insurer's unsupported allegations of prejudice arising from insured's delay in notice); *Wiedeman v. Canal Ins. Co.*, No. 15-4182, 2017 U.S. Dist. LEXIS 84673 (N.D. Ga. June 2, 2017) (applying S.C. law) ("Based on Auto-Owners' unambiguous litigation position, it is unlikely Auto-Owners would have investigated the Collision even if it had received prompt notice of it. Under these circumstances, the Court finds Auto-Owners failed to show 'substantial prejudice' to its rights resulting from any failure of prompt notice."); *Founders Ins. Co. v. Richard Ruth's Bar & Grill LLC*, 761 Fed. Appx. 178 (4th Cir. 2019) ("Founders did not receive notice of Kehagias' lawsuit until the Ruths were in default in the underlying action. Kehagias then refused to waive the default after Founders undertook its defense obligations under the Policies, and the state court denied the Ruths' motion to set aside the default. Because Founders was unable to obtain relief from default, Founders did not have the opportunity to properly investigate the case, to raise defenses to the lawsuit or to negotiate a settlement without the handicap of the default position. This, in turn, led to the entry of a five million dollar default judgment against the Ruths. The Ruths' attorney appealed, but the Ruths instructed their attorney to withdraw the appeal after they assigned Kehagias their rights against Founders. Based on these facts, we find there is no genuine issue of material fact as to whether Founders' rights were substantially prejudiced by the Ruths' failure to provide notice of the lawsuit and copies of the legal papers. Therefore, summary judgment is appropriate in favor of Founders."); *Neumayer v. Phila. Indem. Ins. Co.*, 831 S.E.2d 406 (S.C. 2019) (addressing history of state's late notice law) ("We hold the circuit court erred in ruling that section 38-77-142(C) invalidates the standard notice clause contained in this insurance policy. While *Shores* [*v. Weaver*, 433 S.E.2d 913 (S.C. Ct. App. 1993)] requires an insurer to provide the statutorily-mandated minimum coverage, an insurer may continue to invoke notice clauses to deny coverage above the statutory limits, providing the insurer can prove that it was substantially prejudiced by its insured's failure to comply with the provision.").

South Dakota: Prejudice required. *See Fort Pierre v. United Fire & Casualty Co.*, 463 N.W.2d 845 (S.D. 1990) ("An unexcused delay by the insured in giving notice to the insurer of [a loss] does not relieve the insurer of its obligation to defend and indemnify unless the delay operates materially to prejudice the insurer's ability to investigate and defend. (several citations omitted) The traditional position, that the failure to strictly comply with notice requirements releases an insurer from its obligation to defend and indemnify an insured, is based on the inaccurate and outdated view that insurance policies are private contracts in the traditional sense. As the Pennsylvania Supreme Court has explained [*see* Pennsylvania - *Brakeman*]: 'Such a position fails to recognize the true nature of the relationship between insurance companies and their insureds. An insurance contract is not a negotiated agreement; rather its conditions are by and large dictated by the insurance company to the insured.'"); *Auto-Owners Ins. Co. v. Hansen Housing, Inc.*, 604 N.W.2d 504, 513 (S.D. 2000) (finding insurer prejudiced given insured's failure to give prompt notice of proof of loss where insured waited two years to notify insurer of burglary). "Where the insurance company's interests have not been harmed by a late notice, even in the absence of extenuating circumstances to excuse the tardiness, the reason behind the notice condition in the policy is lacking." *Id.*; *Union Pac. R.R. v. Certain Underwriters at Lloyd's London*, 771 N.W.2d 611 (S.D. 2009) (concluding insurer was prejudiced and granting insurer summary judgment due to policyholder's late notice, which occurred after cleanup of site pursuant to EPA pressure and after seven-figure expenditures by policyholder) ("[Insurer] articulated specific facts and reasons for the claim of actual prejudice and demonstrated that its interests were actually harmed."); *McElgunn v. Cuna Mut. Ins. Soc.*, 700 F. Supp. 2d 1141, 1156 (D.S.D. 2010) (rejecting insurer's argument that "[u]nder South Dakota law, the notice requirements … should not be strictly enforced unless the delay in notification has prejudiced the insurer's ability to defend a claim" by citing to the recognition of the notice-prejudice rule in *Hansen Housing* and *Union Pac. R.R.*).

Tennessee: Prejudice required. *See Alcazar v. Hayes*, 982 S.W.2d 845, 856 (Tenn. 1998) (departing from previous precedent) ("[We believe that the rebut-table presumption rule is the soundest approach in the context of an uninsured/underinsured motorist policy as it provides the best balance between the competing interests. . . . Therefore, once it is determined that the insured has failed to provide timely notice in accordance with the insurance policy, it is presumed that the insurer has been prejudiced by the breach. The insured, however, may rebut this presumption by proffering competent evidence that the insurer was not prejudiced by the insured's delay."); *Am. Justice Ins. Reciprocal v. Hutchison*, 15 S.W.3d 811, 818 (Tenn. 2000) (extending the rebuttable presumption of prejudice in *Alcazar* to breach of notice provision in a general liability insurance policy); *Everest Nat'l Ins. Co. v. Rest. Mgmt. Grp.*, No. E2010-01753-COA-R3-CV, 2011 Tenn. App. LEXIS 199 (Tenn. Ct. App. Apr. 25, 2011) (holding that insurer was prejudiced and did not have a duty to defend or indemnify insured after insured waited five months to inform insurer of the occurrence even though it knew of the event and probable litigation, as an insured cannot wait "until it is convinced of the merits of a potential claim") ("One of the factors to be considered in determining prejudice is whether there have been 'physical changes in the location of the accident during the period of the delay.' In the present case, it is undisputed that RMG made repairs to the parking lot where Mr. Evans fell, even though it knew there were 'issues' about Mr. Evans' fall, before it ever gave Everest notice of the claim. We agree with the trial court that RMG's alteration of the site demonstrates prejudice to Everest."); *Lester v. Allstate Prop. & Cas. Ins. Co.*, No. 12-299, 2013 U.S. Dist. LEXIS 101380 (E.D. Tenn. July 18, 2013) (granting summary judgment for insurer based on insured's failure to rebut the presumption of prejudice by competent evidence) (insured failed to submit to an EUO), *aff'd*, 743 F.3d 469 (6th Cir. 2014); *Knight v. Provident Life & Accident Ins. Co.*, No. 12-01226, 2014 U.S. Dist. LEXIS 14149 (M.D. Tenn. Feb. 5, 2014) (citing *Alcazar* and *Hutchison* for the viewpoint that "the failure to comply with a notice provision does not result in a forfeiture of an insurance policy, if the insurer is not prejudiced by the delay"); *Christian v. Auto-Owners Ins. Co.*, No. 13-CV-339, 2016 U.S. Dist. LEXIS 53405 (E.D. Tenn. Apr. 21, 2016) ("In addition to showing a lack of cooperation, an insurer must also have been prejudiced in order to defeat liability under the policy. The burden to show prejudice does not fall on the insurer. Instead, the insured's failure to perform a duty under an insurance policy gives rise to a rebuttable presumption that the insurance company has been prejudiced. However, the insured can rebut the presumption of prejudice by presenting 'competent evidence.'"); *Scottsdale Ins. Co. v. Alarm Co., LLC*, No. 14-2636, 2016 U.S. Dist. LEXIS 41891 (W.D. Tenn. Mar. 30, 2016) ("In sum, though the language at issue here, 'as soon as practicable,' should be read to give insurance claimants 'more or less free play,' the court has little trouble concluding as a matter of law that it does not give Defendants the right to delay notice for years without explanation or justification. Further, it does not allow insured entities to hide, by omission, conduct that would lead an insurer to reassess its decision to assume an insured's risk."); *United States Specialty Ins. Co. v. N602DW, LLC*, No. 16-02092, 2017 U.S. Dist. LEXIS 166127 (M.D. Tenn. Oct. 5, 2017) ("[T]he Owner has not presented any 'competent evidence' to rebut the presumption that the Owner's three-year delay in making its claim prejudiced Specialty Insurance. Because the Owner delayed in discovering the missing engine bracket and avionics, Specialty Insurance cannot identify when the alleged-theft occurred, witnesses to the alleged-theft, or whether there was other evidence of the alleged-theft.").

   Texas: Prejudice required. *See PAJ, Inc. v. Hanover Ins. Co.*, 243 S.W.3d 630, 636–37 (Tex. 2008) (finding prejudice when insured jewelry manufacturer did not notify insurer of copyright infringement suit brought against it until six months after litigation commenced). "[A]n insured's failure to timely notify its insurer of a claim or suit does not defeat coverage if the insurer was not prejudiced by the delay." *Id.*; *Harwell v. State Farm Mut. Auto. Ins. Co.*, 896 S.W.2d 170, 174 (Tex. 1995) ("The insured's failure to notify the insurer of a suit against her does not relieve the insurer from liability for the underlying judgment unless the lack of notice prejudices the insurer."); *Hernandez v. Gulf Grp. Lloyds*, 875 S.W.2d 691, 694 (Tex. 1994) (concluding that breach of notice provision was an immaterial breach of insurance contract unless insurer was prejudiced). Burden of proving prejudice on insurer. *See PAJ*, 243 S.W.3d at 636–37; *see also E. Tex. Med. Ctr. Reg'l Healthcare Sys. v. Lexington Ins. Co.*, No. 6:04-CV-165, 2011 U.S. Dist. LEXIS 18918 (E.D. Tex. Feb. 25, 2011) (explaining the history of Texas notice-prejudice law and concluding that insurer was not prejudiced even though policyholder did not give notice until eight months after being named in a lawsuit); *Lennar Corp. v. Markel Am. Ins. Co.*, 413 S.W.3d 750 (Tex. 2013) (Boyd, J., concurring) (discussing, in detail, the five cases where the court has directly addressed the prejudice requirement over the past forty years: (1) *Members Mut. Ins. Co. v. Cutaia*, 476 S.W.2d 278 (Tex. 1972); (2) *Hernandez*; (3) *PAJ*; (4) *Prodigy Commc'n Corp. v. Agric. Excess & Surplus Ins. Co.*, 288 S.W.3d 374 (Tex. 2009); and (5) *Fin. Indus. Corp. v. XL Specialty Ins. Co.*, 285 S.W.3d 877 (Tex. 2009)). *See also Hamilton Prop. v. Am. Ins. Co.*, No. 3:12-CV-5046-B, 2014 U.S. Dist. LEXIS 91882 (N.D. Tex. July 7, 2014) (finding that insured waiting nineteen to twenty-seven months before notifying insurer compromised the reliability and availability of evidence necessary to investigate the claim so as to prejudice the insurer); *Berkley Reg'l Ins. Co. v. Phila. Indem. Ins. Co.*, 600 Fed. Appx. 230 (5th Cir. 2015) (agreeing with the court in *Berkley I* (690 F.3d 342 (5th Cir. 2012)) that insurer was prejudiced because it "lost the ability to do any investigation or conduct its own analysis of the case, as well as the ability to 'join in' Nautilus's evaluation of the case. The court also noted that Philadelphia lost a seat at the mediation table and found its rights were lost, leaving Philadelphia holding the bag for more than $700,000 in excess liability if Berkley prevails. Lastly, the *Berkley I* court disagreed with the notion that Philadelphia could have meaningfully participated on appeal as a means to show lack of prejudice."); *Gonzalez v. Phila. Indem. Ins. Co.*, 663 Fed. Appx. 302 (5th Cir. 2016) ("As we recognized in *Berkley I* and *Berkley II*, this post-settlement notice deprived Philadelphia of valuable, bargained-for rights, including the rights to investigate the facts and parties to the settlement, participate in the settlement negotiations, and pursue subrogation. It makes no difference that *Berkley* dealt with post-verdict notice; the insurer loses the same valuable rights when it receives post-settlement notice."); *Certain Underwriters at Lloyd's v. Lowen Valley View, LLC*, No. 16-0465, 2017 U.S. Dist. LEXIS 114468 (N.D. Tex. June 21, 2017) (setting forth detailed factual explanation to support conclusion that insurer was delayed by late notice of a claim for roof damage caused by hail) (*aff'd on other grounds* 892 F.3d 167 (5th Cir. 2018)); *NES Rentals v. Arch Specialty Ins. Co.*, No. 19-00015, 2020 U.S. Dist. LEXIS 166494 (N.D. Tex. Sept. 11, 2020) ("Notice, and a demand for defense and indemnity, was provided only after the claims had been settled, precluding Arch from participating in the defense in any way, including consulting and consenting with respect to the settlements. . . . [T]he Court finds Arch was prejudiced as a matter of law by NES's failure to comply with the policy provisions and is relieved of liability under the policy."); *Ryan Law Firm, LLP v. New York Marine & Gen. Ins. Co.*, No. 19-629, 2020 U.S. Dist. LEXIS 125904 (W.D. Tex. July 16, 2020) (addressing breach of a consent-to-settle provision with a lengthy discussion of Texas law on the issue) ("NYM's contention, like the insurer's argument in *Lennar*, essentially is that if NYM had been involved in the final settlement negotiations, it would have received a better result. As the *Lennar* court found, this is a question of fact, not of law. There is no evidence that Finish Line was willing to settle the case for a lower amount.") (*Magistrate's report and recommendation adopted at* 2020 U.S. Dist. LEXIS 205615 (W.D. Tex. Sept. 9, 2020)).

Utah: Prejudice required. *See* Utah Code Ann. § 31A-21-312 ("Every insurance policy shall provide that: (a) when notice of loss is required separately from proof of loss, notice given by or on behalf of the insured to any authorized agent of the insurer within this state, with particulars sufficient to identify the policy, is notice to the insurer; and (b) failure to give any notice or file any proof of loss required by the policy within the time specified in the policy does not invalidate a claim made by the insured, if the insured shows that it was not reasonably possible to give the notice or file the proof of loss within the prescribed time and that notice was given or proof of loss filed as soon as reasonably possible. (2) Failure to give notice or file proof of loss as required by Subsection (1)(b) does not bar recovery under the policy if the insurer fails to show it was prejudiced by the failure." …). *See also State Farm Mut. Auto. Ins. Co. v. Green*, 89 P.3d 97, 104 (Utah 2003) ("Generally, if an insured in Utah fails to provide notice or proof of loss to its insurer as required by the terms of an insurance policy, the insurer may not deny recovery to the insured unless the insurer was prejudiced by the failure. Utah Code Ann. § 31A-21-312(2) (2001). There is no reason why the rule should be harsher to the insured in the context of a settlement that could affect an insurer's subrogation rights. The actual prejudice rule strikes an appropriate balance between protecting an insurer's interests and avoiding forfeiture of coverage when an insurer has not been harmed."); *Busch Corp. v. State Farm Fire & Cas. Co.*, 743 P.2d 1217 (Utah 1987) (finding a five-year delay in providing notice prejudicial as a matter of law) (listing as reasons for insurer prejudice: no opportunity to investigate, examine the scene, take photographs, interview witnesses or take statements, or possibly settle the lawsuit and employ their own counsel); *8665 N. Cove, LLC v. Am. Family Mut. Ins. Co.*, No. 12-237, 2014 U.S. Dist. LEXIS 86579 (D. Utah June 19, 2014) (finding prejudice resulted based on notice over two and a half years late, which deprived insurer of the opportunity to investigate the damages properly or participate in repair decisions), *aff'd* 612 Fed. Appx. 492 (10th Cir. 2015) ("[W]e reject North Cove's contention that the district court ignored § 31A-21-312(2) in its analysis. Although the court did not specifically cite the statute, it repeatedly explained in its decision that American Family suffered prejudice from the untimely notice.").

Vermont: Prejudice required. *See Coop. Fire Ins. Ass'n of Vt. v. White Caps, Inc.*, 694 A.2d 34, 38 (Vt. 1997) ("We conclude, therefore, that the modern rule represents the better reasoned approach. The contract of insurance not being a truly consensual arrangement, and the penalty being a matter of forfeiture, we think it appropriate to abandon the strict contract analysis of *Houran* [*v. Preferred Accident Ins. Co.*, 195 A. 253 (Vt. 1937)]. We hold, instead, that an insurer may not forfeit its insured's protection unless it demonstrates that the notice provision was breached, and that it suffered substantial prejudice from the delay in notice. This is consistent not only with the modern trend among jurisdictions, but also with the current Vermont rule governing an insured's breach of the standard covenant of cooperation.") (finding that, because insurer failed to prove substantial prejudice from policyholder restaurant's eighteen-month delay in giving notice of slip-and-fall incident implicating policy, insurer could not deny coverage). "When faced with a claim for coverage, it is not sufficient for the carrier to merely sit back and engage in cursory investigation, seeking excuses for lack of information." *Id.* at 39; *see also Northshire Commc'n, Inc. v. AUI Ins. Co.*, 811 A.2d 216, 220 (Vt. 2002) (holding five-year notice delay substantially prejudiced insurer) ("Northshire's five-year delay in providing AIU with notice left AIU with no opportunity to investigate the claim; there had been little discovery on Rothschild's counterclaims and discovery had been emphatically closed by the court. AIU's attempts to learn the status of the litigation were met with misinformation and apparently deliberate obfuscation. Unlike the insurance provider in White Caps, AIU did not merely sit back and engage in cursory investigation. Therefore, finding that AIU's position relative to the underlying claim against Northshire was substantially prejudiced by Northshire's breach of the prompt-notice provision is consistent with our decision in *White Caps*."); *Smith v. Nationwide Mut. Ins. Co.*, 830 A.2d 108, 114 (Vt. 2003) (extending notice-prejudice rule in *White Caps* to cooperation/assistance clauses); *Hardwick Recycling & Salvage, Inc. v. Acadia Ins. Co.*, 869 A.2d 82 (Vt. 2004) (holding that insurer was required to provide defense in environmental cleanup case because insurer did not prove prejudice occurred where policyholder waited five years to make a claim) (prejudice is usually a question for the trier of fact and insurer entitled to additional discovery on the issue); *Creller v. MMG Ins. Co.*, No. 53-10-16, 2017 Vt. Super. LEXIS 135 (Vt. Super. Ct. Aug. 28, 2017) ("There is no reason to conclude, if confronted with a consent to settle clause in a UIM or UM policy that the Vermont Supreme Court would take a different approach [than *White Caps*]. In both situations the claimant is an insurer's customer who has paid a premium. Even with a reasonably founded contract notice/ consent provision, when there is breach that results in no harm to the insurer, the technical breach should not work a contract forfeiture.").

Virginia: No prejudice required. *See State Farm Fire & Cas. Co. v. Scott*, 372 S.E.2d 383, 385 (Va. 1988) ("When a violation of the notice requirement is substantial and material, the insurer is not required to show that it has been prejudiced by the violation. An absence of prejudice, however, is a circumstance to be considered on the question of the materiality of the information which it is claimed the insured failed to give.") (allowing the jury to consider prejudice when deciding whether a ten-week delay in reporting an uninsured motorist claim was a breach of the notice provision, but finding that the insurer does not have to show prejudice to deny coverage where late notice is established). *See also State Farm Fire & Cas. Co. v. Walton*, 423 S.E.2d 188 (Va. 1992) (holding that a prolonged delay in notification alone may breach an insurance policy even absent a showing of prejudice); *Atlas Ins. Co. v. Chapman*, 888 F. Supp. 742, 746 (E.D. Va. 1995) (four-month delay in notice without excuse constitutes substantial and material breach of notice provision); *Nationwide Mut. Fire Ins. Co. v. Overstreet*, 568 F. Supp. 2d 638, 645 (E.D. Va. 2008) ("[I]t is no defense to a claim that notice was untimely to say that the insured subjectively did not understand his policy might be implicated."); *Dabney v. Augusta Mut. Ins. Co.*, 710 S.E.2d 726 (Va. 2011) (concluding that, although it is well-settled in Virginia that notice is a condition precedent, notice as "soon as practical" is not a fixed standard, and where there are extenuating circumstances, lengthy delays may be excusable) (determining that insurer did not receive timely notice due to confusion caused by policyholder's death and estate administration, but holding that late notice was excused because of the extenuating circumstances); *State Farm Fire & Cas. Co. v. Wallace*, No. 13-00027, 2014 U.S. Dist. LEXIS 13056 (W.D. Va. Feb. 3, 2014) ("In determining the reasonableness of an insurer's notice, the Virginia Supreme Court follows an objective standard, requiring that an insurer be notified whenever it should reasonably appear to the insured that the policy may be implicated. Failure to give timely notice will not be excused when the insured *subjectively* concludes that coverage under the policy will not be implicated or is ignorant of the notice provisions.") (emphasis in original) (finding delay material and substantial so as to relieve insurer's obligation under the policy based on insured's duty to give notice arising over a year before notice was actually given); *Citizens Ins. Co of Am. v. Ung*, No. 13-1978, 2014 U.S. Dist. LEXIS 22885 (E.D. Pa. Feb. 24, 2014) (applying Virginia law) (citing *Dabney* for the proposition that a fixed number of days does not determine reasonableness) ("There are three factors that bear upon the materiality of a breach of the notice provision of an insurance policy ... : (1) reasonableness of the delayed notice; (2) the amount of prejudice suffered by the insurer as a result of the delay; and (3) the length of time that elapsed before notice was given.") (citations omitted); *E Dillon & Co. v. Travelers Cas. & Sur. Co. of Am.*, No. 14-00070, 2015 U.S. Dist. LEXIS 76295 (W.D. Va. June 12, 2015) (summarizing Va. late notice law) ("Even if there were no prejudice [court concluded that there was] however, the length of the delay alone is sufficient to conclude that E Dillon materially breached the Policy's condition of coverage. The two-year delay in this case far exceeds delays that have been found unreasonable as a matter of law in Virginia. Virginia courts have generally held that notice given beyond 75 days, without a reasonable excuse, is untimely, and a delay of 601 days is beyond the outer limits of reasonableness."); *Builders Mut. Ins. Co. v. Wedge Constr.*, 423 F. Supp. 3d 253 (E.D. Va. 2019) (addressing liability policy and concluding that fifteen month delay was "unreasonable, unjustified, and of a significant duration," and, thus, "both substantial and material and constituted a breach of the notice provisions of the insurance policy) ("Furthermore, in Virginia, notice provisions of this kind constitute a 'condition precedent to recovery.'").

Washington: Prejudice required. In *Or. Auto Ins. Co. v. Salzberg*, 535 P.2d 816, 819 (Wash. 1975) (en banc), the Supreme Court of Washington held that "sound public policy requires that an alleged breach of a cooperation clause may be considered substantial and material, and may effect a release of an insurer from its responsibilities *only* if the insurer was actually *prejudiced* by the insured's actions or conduct. The requirement of a showing of prejudice would pertain irrespective of whether the cooperation clause could be said to be a covenant or an express condition precedent and, in this regard, the burden of proof is upon the insurer." (emphasis in original). Subsequent cases in Washington have treated *Salzberg* as a late notice case as well. *See Olds-Olympic v. Commercial Union*, 918 P.2d 923 (Wash. 1996) ("In *Salzberg* we held a late notice will release an insurer from its responsibilities only if the insurer was actually prejudiced by the insured's actions or conduct."); *Mut. of Enumclaw Ins. Co. v. USF Ins. Co.*, 191 P.3d 866 (Wash. 2008) ("We hold that in order to show prejudice, the insurer must prove that an insured's breach of a notice provision had an identifiable and material detrimental effect on its ability to defend its interests. The rule will manifest itself differently depending on the kind of prejudice an insurer claims. If the insurer claims that its own counsel would have defended differently, it must show that its participation would have materially affected the outcome, either as to liability or the amount of damages. If the insurer claims that it was deprived of the ability to investigate, it must show that the kind of evidence that was lost would have been material to its defense. This rule effectuates the longstanding *Salzberg* rule that the insurer has the burden of proving actual and substantial prejudice."); *Staples v. Allstate Ins. Co.*, 295 P.3d 201 (Wash. 2013) ("Prejudice will be presumed only in 'extreme cases.'"); *Terhune Homes, Inc. v. Nationwide Mut. Ins. Co.*, No. C13-789, 2014 U.S. Dist. LEXIS 70361 (W.D. Wash. May 9, 2014) (rejecting the argument that prejudice should be presumed as a matter of law under the circumstances presented (notice five years after suit filed and two years after judgment entered) "because the Washington Supreme Court was presented with similar factual circumstances as to timing, and concluded that prejudice had not been demonstrated as a matter of law"); *Port of Longview v. Arrowood Indem. Co.*, No. 46654-6-11, 2016 Wash. App. LEXIS 3100 (Wash. Ct. App. Dec. 21, 2016) ("The Supreme Court in *Mutual of Enumclaw* noted that Washington courts have relied on many factors when evaluating prejudice from late notice, and provided a nonexhaustive list of these factors: [1] Were damages concrete or nebulous? [2] Was there a settlement or did a neutral decision maker calculate damages; what were the circumstances surrounding the settlement? [3] Did a reliable entity do a thorough investigation of the incident? [4] Could the insurer have eliminated liability if given timely notice? [5] Could the insurer have proceeded differently in the litigation?"); *Am. Alternative Ins. Corp. v. Goodwill of the Olympics & Rainier Region*, No. C17-5978, 2020 U.S. Dist. LEXIS 7258 (W.D. Wash. Jan. 15, 2020) ("American cites no facts establishing that it was precluded from investigating any relevant aspect of the underlying claim. Similarly, American cites no facts to establish that it was prejudiced by the trial court's imposition of liability as a sanction for Goodwill's failure to timely disclose evidence.").

West Virginia: Prejudice may or may not be required. *See Colonial Ins. Co. v. Barrett*, 542 S.E.2d 869, 875 (W. Va. 2000) ("In cases which involve liability claims against an insurer, several factors must be considered before the Court can determine if the delay in notifying the insurance company will bar the claim against the insurer. The length of the delay in notifying the insurer must be considered along with the reasonableness of the delay. If the delay appears reasonable in light of the insured's explanation, the burden shifts to the insurance company to show that the delay in notification prejudiced their investigation and defense of the claim. If the insurer can produce evidence of prejudice, then the insured will be held to the letter of the policy and the insured barred from making a claim against the insurance company. If, however, the insurer cannot point to any prejudice caused by the delay in notification, then the claim is not barred by the insured's failure to notify."). *See also Dairyland Ins. Co. v. Voshel*, 428 S.E.2d 542, 545 (W. Va. 1993) ("[R]egardless of the language used [in the policy] … the courts are generally in agreement that reasonable notice is sufficient.") ("In this case, no explanation was given which would make an almost two-year delay appear reasonable. Further, Dairyland presented evidence of prejudice caused by the delay."); *State Farm Mut. Auto. Ins. Co. v. Milam*, 438 F. Supp. 227, 232 (S.D. W. Va. 1977) ("The test to apply is whether the insurer would be in a better position … [if] it [had] been furnished notice within a reasonable time."); *Arch Specialty Ins. Co. v. Go-Mart, Inc.*, No. 2:08–0285, 2009 U.S. Dist. LEXIS 120490 (S.D. W. Va. Dec. 28, 2009) (insurer was unduly prejudiced as a matter of law where convenience store/policyholder waited thirty-two months to provide notice of a customer's injuries) ("When the delay is determined to be unreasonable, prejudice need not be determined" through fact adjudication and court may find prejudice to insurer as a matter of law); *FA Mgmt., Inc. v. Great Am. Ins. Co. of N.Y.*, No. 13-25, 2014 U.S. Dist. LEXIS 75912 (N.D. W. Va. June 4, 2014) ("[T]he West Virginia Supreme Court noted that [t]he particular language used in the automobile insurance policy as to the time in which notice must be given is not controlling; regardless of the language used, whether 'immediate,' 'prompt,' 'forthwith,' 'as soon as practicable' or words of similar import, the courts are generally in agreement that reasonable notice is sufficient. In this case, the insurance contract required the plaintiff to provide 'prompt notice' which falls within those 'words of similar import' as set forth above. As such, because the plaintiff has requested a jury trial, the reasonableness of the plaintiff's either nine or 12 month delay would be a question for the jury, as would the question of whether or not the defendant was prejudiced by such delay."); *Travelers Indem. Co. v. U.S. Silica Co.*, 788 S.E.2d 286 (W. Va. 2015) ("[W]e conclude that U.S. Silica has failed to demonstrate that its explanation for its significant delay in notifying Travelers of the silica claims was reasonable—both because the delay was substantial and because its proffered reason to excuse its delay, *i.e.*, that it was unaware of the subject policies, is not reasonable. Absent a demonstration of reasonableness, the burden does not shift to the insurer to prove that it was prejudiced by the delayed notice, and the inquiry necessarily ends with a finding that coverage is precluded by the insured's failure to comply with the policy's notice provision."); *Clarendon National Ins. Co. v. Marushia*, No. 16-0562, 2017 W. Va. LEXIS 469 (W. Va. June 9, 2017) ("Respondent Marushia's claims against the Commission arose in 2003 and were the subject of Respondent Marushia's underlying action filed against the Commission in 2005. However, petitioner did not receive notice of Respondent Marushia's claims until October of 2012, nine years following the accident. As satisfaction of the notice provision in an insurance policy is a condition precedent to coverage for the policyholder, and as no such notice was herein provided to petitioner, an award of summary judgment in favor of petitioner was proper.") (also noting that insured did not provide an explanation of the reason for failing to provide notice); *Rich v. First Mercury Ins. Co.*, 482 F. Supp. 3d 511 (S.D.W.Va. 2020) (setting forth detailed explanation why a three year delay was unreasonable; therefore, insurer not required to show that it was prejudiced as the result of the untimely notice).

Wisconsin: Prejudice required. WIS. STAT. § 631.81(1): "Provided notice or proof of loss is furnished as soon as reasonably possible and within one year after the time it was required by the policy, failure to furnish such notice or proof within the time required by the policy does not invalidate or reduce a claim unless the insurer is prejudiced thereby and it was reasonably possible to meet the time limit." In addition, Wis. Stat. § 632.26 provides: "Every liability insurance policy shall provide: (a) That notice given by or on behalf of the insured to any authorized agent of the insurer within this state, with particulars sufficient to identify the insured, is notice to the insurer. (b) That failure to give any notice required by the policy within the time specified does not invalidate a claim made by the insured if the insured shows that it was not reasonably possible to give the notice within the prescribed time and that notice was given as soon as reasonably possible. (2) Failure to give notice as required by the policy as modified by sub. (1) (b) does not bar liability under the policy if the insurer was not prejudiced by the failure, but the risk of nonpersuasion is upon the person claiming there was no prejudice." *See Gerrard Realty Corp. v. Am. States Ins. Co.*, 277 N.W.2d 863 (Wis. 1979) (applying Wis. Stat. § 631.81) ("We interpret sec. 631.81, Stats., as providing that an insured's notice is not deemed untimely and precluding recovery against the policy if the notice is furnished as soon as reasonably possible within one year of the time notice is required by the terms of the insurance policy, and the insurer is unable to prove prejudice or that it was possible to give notice within the time limit required in the policy. However, sec. 631.81 does not address situations, as in the instant case, where notice is given more than one year after the time in which notice is required by the policy provisions. Thus, we hold that where notice is given more than one year after the time required by the policy, there is a rebuttable presumption of prejudice and the burden of proof shifts to the claimant to prove that the insurer was not prejudiced by the untimely notice."); *Fireman's Fund Ins. Co. v. Bradley Corp.*, 660 N.W.2d 666 (Wis. 2003) ("The Insurance Company has consistently maintained no coverage existed. Even if the lack of timely notice placed the Insurance Company in a difficult litigation position, the clear and uncontroverted evidence in the record is that the timing of Bradley's notice would not have changed the Insurance Company's decision to deny its duty to defend. Thus we conclude as a matter of law that the Insurance Company suffered no prejudice. Bradley carried its burden to prove lack of prejudice."); *Int'l Flavors & Fragrances, Inc v. Valley Forge Ins. Co.*, 738 N.W.2d 159, 162 (Wis. Ct. App. 2007) (concluding, following detailed analysis, that insurer was not prejudiced where it received notice of a multiple personal injuries caused by exposure to "butter popcorn flavoring" before trial was imminent). "[F]ailure to provide timely notice as required by the policy does not defeat coverage unless the insurer is prejudiced thereby." *Id.* "Prejudice to the insurer is a serious impairment of the insurer's ability to investigate, evaluate, or settle a claim, determine coverage, or present an effective defense, resulting from the unexcused failure of the insured to provide timely notice. An insurer suffers prejudice when it has been denied the opportunity to have input into the manner in which the underlying claim is being defended. *Id.* at 163; *Lewis v. Wolter Bros. Builders, Inc.*, No. 2009AP2037-AC, 2010 Wisc. App. LEXIS 215 (Wis. Ct. App. Mar. 24, 2010) (concluding that insurer was prejudiced by late notice where it lost ability to participate in legal proceedings such as filing motions or obtaining discovery); *Ansul, Inc. v. Emp'rs Ins. Co. of Wausau*, 826 N.W.2d 110 (Wis. Ct. App. 2012) (finding prejudice as a matter of law resulted from insured's failure to notify because facts showed some potentially relevant evidence had been lost); *Old Republic Ins. Co. v. Liberty Mut. Fire Ins. Co.*, 138 F. Supp. 3d 1013 (E.D. Wis. 2015) (setting forth a detailed explanation of prejudice sustained by the insurer on account of insured's late notice); *Shugarts v. Mohr*, 909 N.W.2d 402 (Wis. 2018) ("[T]he operative event triggering the notice requirement in the Shugarts' UIM policy is the tender of the tortfeasor's underlying policy limit. We further conclude that Wis. Stat. § 631.81(1) does not apply to the UIM policy provision at issue. Consequently, we determine that the Shugarts provided Allstate with timely proof of their UIM claim as the policy language dictates."); *Grigg v. Aarrowcast, Inc.*, 909 N.W.2d 183 (Wis. Ct. App. 2018) ("[T]he record conclusively shows the lack of any prejudice stemming from the alleged nearly two-year delay in notice because Hudson does not argue it would have provided a defense of Grigg upon receiving earlier notice.").

Wyoming: Prejudice required. In *Century Sur. Co. v. Jim Hipner, LLC*, 377 P.3d 784 (Wyo. 2016) the Wyoming Supreme Court answered in the affirmative the following question certified to it by the Eight Circuit Court of Appeals: "W]hether, under Wyoming law, an insurer must be prejudiced before being entitled to deny coverage when the insured has failed to give notice 'as soon as practicable.' Many states have expressly adopted a notice-prejudice rule under which an insurer will only be able to disclaim coverage if it demonstrates it was actually prejudiced by late notice. *See* 46A C.J.S. Insurance § 1769. To date, Wyoming has not. *Id.* at 785. In adopting a prejudice requirement, the *Hipner* court undertook a thorough examination of late notice law nationally, including its history, and rested its decision on: the unequal bargaining power between insurer and insured, including that insurance policies are contracts of adhesion, the public interest in compensating accident victims, including innocent third parties and preventing insurers from reaping undeserved windfalls. After adopting the notice-prejudice rule, the court turned to the insurer's argument that its policy specifically excluded coverage unless the insured notified the insurer "as soon as practicable . . . whether [the insurer] [is] prejudiced or not." The *Hipner* Court held that an insurer cannot contract around the prejudice requirement and such policy language was void as against public policy. Thus, the court adopted a two-step approach to an insurer's claim of late notice. "This approach requires a preliminary determination that an insured's notice was untimely, in violation of the notice requirement contained in the insurance policy. The question of the timeliness of the insured's delay in providing notice will depend upon a number of factors, including, but not limited to, the language of the notice requirement in the policy, the timing of the notice, the insured's knowledge of the underlying facts and ability to provide notice, the sophistication of the parties, the type of insurance at issue, and the reasonableness of any delay. Once it is determined that notice was untimely, a court should then turn to the question of whether the insurer was prejudiced by that delay. If the insurer was prejudiced, then the insurer will be relieved of its obligation to provide coverage." *Id.* at 791. Following the Supreme Court's decision, the Eighth Circuit concluded that the insurer had not been prejudiced: "Century's argument fails because Century does not show how the four-month delay in receiving notice actually prevented it from taking any meaningful investigatory steps that it would have done had there been no delay. This is because Century chose not to investigate once it received the investigative materials from Great West. If Century believed that something was missing after receiving the investigative materials, it could have launched its own investigation or followed up with Great West's investigation, but it chose not to." *Century Sur. Co. v. Jim Hipner LLC*, 842 F.3d 606, 612 (8th Cir. 2016). *See also Artisan & Truckers Cas. Co. v. Neron Logistics LLC*, No. 18-2220, 2021 U.S. Dist. LEXIS 27171 (S.D. Ill. Feb. 12, 2021) (applying Wyoming law) ("Based on the record before the Court, it is difficult to see what actual prejudice ATCC has or will suffer as a consequence of the late notice. Even a 27-month delay in providing notice of lawsuit can be reasonable where the insurance company has sufficient information to locate and defend the suit. ATCC asserts that it was unable to investigate the occurrence. But it identifies no question of fact with respect to the occurrence or liability and does not suggest what additional investigation is necessary.").

CHAPTER

4

Coverage for Pre-Tender Defense Costs

As the previous chapter demonstrated, insurers have generally not fared well in their efforts to be relieved of policy obligations on the basis that their insured did not provide notice of a claim in a timely manner. First, as a starting point, even when claims are reported months after they should have been, that is oftentimes *not late enough* to serve as a breach of the policy's notice requirement. What's more, even when a claim *is* sufficiently tardy, to qualify as having formally breached the policy's notice requirement, the insurer must usually prove that it was prejudiced by the insured's delayed notification in order for such breach to serve as a basis to exclude coverage. And prejudice is frequently difficult for insurers to establish. For these reasons, insurers have had a difficult go at it when attempting to disclaim coverage for defense and indemnity on the basis that their insured did not provide notice of a claim in a timely manner.

But there is a close cousin (sibling, even) to late notice where insurers' fortunes have been significantly different. There are times when an insurer is not seeking to completely disclaim coverage for defense and indemnity on account of late notice. Rather, the insurer is only asserting that is has no obligation to reimburse its insured for defense costs incurred by the insured *prior to* the time that the insured placed the insurer on notice of the claim. These are referred to in coverage circles as "pre-tender defense costs." And unlike their unimpressive results in disclaiming all coverage for defense and indemnity on the basis of late notice, insurers have done remarkably well in avoiding any obligation to pay for pre-tender defense costs.

The difference between late notice and pre-tender defense costs, even within the same state, can be dramatic. For example, New Jersey sets a very high burden on insurers seeking to disclaim coverage for defense and indemnity on the basis of late notice—requiring a likelihood of appreciable prejudice. *See Cooper v. Gov't Employees Ins. Co.*, 237 A.2d 870 (N.J. 1968). But when the issue is pre-tender defense costs, New Jersey law takes a one-hundred-and-eighty-degree turn, holding that an insurer is only obligated to pay for that portion of the defense costs arising after it was informed of the facts triggering the duty to defend—and no showing of prejudice is required. *SL Indus., Inc. v. Am. Motorists Ins. Co.*, 607 A.2d 1266, 1272 (N.J. 1992). Several examples abound of states whose standards between late notice and pre-tender defense are diametric.

Late notice and pre-tender defense costs seem remarkably similar. So why have insurers been so much more successful when it comes to pre-tender defense costs? In general, some courts are unwilling to saddle an insurer with an obligation to pay for defense costs that it had no ability to control. Other courts conclude that the duty to defend does not arise until the insurer receives notice of the claim. *See Dreaded, Inc. v. St. Paul Guardian Ins. Co.*, 904 N.E.2d 1267, 1273 (Ind. 2009) ("The function of a notice requirement is to supply basic information to permit an insurer to defend a claim. The insurer's duty to defend simply does not arise until it receives the foundational information designated in the notice requirement. Until an insurer receives such enabling information, it cannot be held accountable for breaching this duty."); *Domtar, Inc. v. Niagara Fire Ins. Co.*, 563 N.W.2d 724, 739–40 (Minn. 1997) ("[A]n insured does not invoke its insurer's duty to defend until it properly tenders a defense request. Logically, then, an insurer cannot be held responsible for defense costs incurred prior to the tender of the defense request giving rise to the insurer's duty to defend, the diligence of the insured notwithstanding."); *SL Indus., supra* ("[I]f the insured does not properly forward the information to the insurance company, the insured cannot demand reimbursement from the insurer for defense costs the insurer had no opportunity to control."). Some courts rule in favor of insurers on the basis that an insured that incurs defense costs, prior to providing notice to the insurer, has breached the policy's "voluntary payments" provision. *E & L Chipping Co. v. The Hanover Ins. Co.*, 962 S.W.2d 272, 278 (Tex. Ct. App. 1998).

The critical factor to insurers' success, when it comes to pre-tender defense costs, is the rejection by courts of the requirement that the insurer prove that it was prejudiced by the insured incurring such costs. *See Am. Mut. Liability Ins. Co. v. Beatrice Co.*, 924 F. Supp. 861, 873–74 (N.D. Ill. 1996) (applying Massachusetts law) (concluding that the prejudice requirement that attached to the notice rule did not apply to pre-tender defense costs because "[t]he prejudice requirement was adopted to prevent complete forfeiture based upon technical failure of the insured to provide timely notice" whereas "enforcement of the rule that pre-tender defense cost are not recoverable does not result in complete forfeiture of an insured's right to recover fees").

Not all courts, however, have eliminated the prejudice requirement before an insurer can avoid an obligation for pre-tender defense costs. *See Griffin v. Allstate*

Ins. Co., 29 P.3d 777 (Wash. Ct. App. 2001). But even when prejudice is required, it may be found based on an insured's retention of counsel who charges higher rates or fails to pursue appropriate strategies. *Id.*

Pre-tender defense costs can be no small issue. While a claim that is reported late by three or four months may offer no basis to an insurer for a late notice disclaimer, a significant amount of defense costs may have been incurred during this pre-notice period—especially since litigation can be very active in the initial stages. Even a claim that is only a few weeks late in being reported could have rung up some meaningful defense costs during the pre-notice period. For this reason, the question whether coverage is available for pre-tender defense costs arises in numerous claim contexts—many more than whether late notice serves as a basis for disclaiming all coverage for defense and indemnity.

50-State Survey: Coverage for Pre-Tender Defense Costs

Alabama: No instructive authority.

Alaska: No instructive authority.

Arizona: The Ninth Circuit Court of Appeals, interpreting Arizona law, held that no coverage was owed to an insured for pre-tender defense costs. *Research Corp. v. Westport Ins. Corp.* 289 Fed. Appx. 989, 993–94 (9th Cir. 2008). "Here, Research was served with the Johnson complaint in September 2001, but did not tender the claim to Westport for six months. During that time, substantial fees were incurred. Under the express terms of the policy, Research failed to fulfill its duties precedent to coverage by failing to give immediate notice of the claim and by not obtaining prior written consent before incurring defense costs. Research argues that Westport did not suffer actual prejudice. However, Westport was prejudiced by this breach because it was deprived of its exclusive right to assign counsel, thus potentially avoiding what it now considers to be unreasonable attorneys fees." *Id.* at 994. *See also Landmark Am. Ins. Co. v. Shurwest LLC*, No. 19-04743, 2020 U.S. Dist. LEXIS 167774 (D. Ariz. July 23, 2020) (rejecting the insured's argument that it was entitled to reimbursement of defense costs prior to the date of formal tender because "an insured is only entitled to post-tender defense costs, irrespective of prejudice" to the insurer).

Arkansas: No instructive authority.

California: The Court of Appeal of California held that an insurer was not responsible for paying an insured's pre-tender expenses because the general liability policy's "no voluntary payments provision ... bar[red] reimbursement for pre-tender expenses based on the reasoning that until the defense is tendered to the insured, there is no duty to defend." *Tradewinds Escrow, Inc. v. Truck Ins. Exch.*, 118 Cal. Rptr. 2d 561, 565 (Cal. Ct. App. 2002). "[W]here the insured has failed to demand a defense and relinquish control over the case, it cannot expect the quid pro quo of pre-tender voluntary payments, expenses, or other obligations incurred by the insured pre-tender without the insurer's consent." *Id.* "[A] separate showing of prejudice is not part of the equation in evaluating denial of pre-tender costs." *Id.* at 566. "However, even if the policy contains a no voluntary payments provision, pre-tender expenses are not barred if they were incurred involuntarily. Generally, voluntariness is a question of fact." *Id.* at 565. The court suggested that examples of involuntariness may be when the insured is unaware of the identity of the insurer or when urgency of time pressures requires the insured to expend money pre-tender. *Id.* at 566; *see also Am. Nat. Red Cross v. St. Paul Travelers, Inc.*, 293 Fed. Appx. 512, 513 (9th Cir. 2008) (applying California law) ("An insurer generally has no duty to defend an insured until the insured tenders his defense. [citing *Tradewinds*] However, an exception exists where the insured was unaware of the existence or contents of the policy and was therefore unable to tender."); *Columbia Cas. Co. v. Gordon Trucking, Inc.*, 758 F. Supp. 2d 909, 918 (N.D. Cal. 2010) ("California's rule [enforcing the "No Voluntary Payment" clause] protects an insurer's right to control the defense because it encourages insureds to quickly tender defense to their insurer and discourages insureds from exercising any control of the defense after tender."); *Burgett, Inc. v. American Zurich Ins. Co.*, 875 F. Supp. 2d 1125 (E.D. Cal. 2012) (rejecting argument that insurer who declines to accept a defense after tender will subsequently be obligated to pay pre-tender expenses because insurer owed a duty to defend); *Diamond Blue Enterprises v. Cont'l Ins. Co.*, No. 254256, 2015 Cal. App. Unpub. LEXIS 2614 (Cal. Ct. App. Apr. 15, 2015) (reiterating *Tradewinds* and concluding that the insured did not timely investigate insurance and incur costs before he could identify the insurer); *County of Stanislaus v. Travelers Indem. Co.*, 142 F. Supp. 3d 1065 (E.D. Cal. 2015) (addressing pre-tender in the context of site investigation costs associated with an environmental property damage claim); *Celerity Educ. Grp. v. Scottsdale Ins. Co.*, No. 17-03239, 2019 U.S. Dist. LEXIS 17744 (C.D. Cal. Feb. 4, 2019) (insurer not obligated for pre-tender defense costs; addressing issue in the context of a director's and officer's policy and voluntary payments provision); *Wei v. Stewart Title Guar. Co.*. No. B278636, 2018 Cal. App. Unpub. LEXIS 2612 (Cal. Ct. App. Apr. 19, 2018) ("It is irrelevant when the fees were incurred. The policy requires that the fees be approved by Stewart Title, which they were not. Under the terms of the policy, Stewart Title was not obligated to pay any fees it did not approve in advance, whether they were incurred pre-tender or afterwards"); *Anheuser-Busch v. State Farm Mut. Auto Ins. Co.*, No. 19-6018, 2020 U.S. Dist. LEXIS 199291 (C.D. Cal. Sep. 11, 2020) (noting that, although the general rule provides that "[a]n insurer's duty to defend arises upon tender and they have no obligation to pay pre[-]tender fees and costs which they would not have been responsible for anyway," there is an exception where the duty to defend "arise[s] upon receipt of 'constructive notice' of the contractual duty to defend"); *Premier Constr. & Remode v. Mesa Underwriters Special Ins. Co.*, No. 18-2582, 2020 U.S. Dist. LEXIS 168120 (C.D. Cal. July 8, 2020) (stating that an "insurer's liability for pre-tender defense costs is a question of fact where an issue exists as to whether payments were 'voluntary' within the meaning of voluntary payments provision") (finding that insureds were not entitled to reimbursement for pre-tender defense costs because they could "point to no extraordinary circumstances causing the delay [in tendering the defense], nor [could] they argue they were unaware of the insurance or lacked documentation of the Policy"); *Zurich Am. Ins. Co. v. N.Y. Marine & Gen. Ins. Co.*, No. 09-288, 2021 Del. Super. LEXIS 144 (Del. Super. Ct. Feb. 8, 2021) (applying California law) (noting that a "no-voluntary-payments" provision bars reimbursement for pre-tender expenses, but that pre-tender expenses may be recoverable if incurred involuntarily) (examples of involuntarily incurred defense costs include situations in which "the insured is unaware of the identity of the insurer or the contents of the policy," "the insured must respond to the lawsuit to avoid default" or "the urgency of time pressures requires the insured to expend money pre-tender under duress").

Colorado: No instructive authority. *But see Holyoke Mut. Ins. Co. v. Cincinnati Indem. Co.*, No. 18-018523, 2019 U.S. Dist. LEXIS 88898 (D. Colo. May 28, 2019) (holding that a "no-voluntary payments clause" barred Holyoke's claim for contribution from Cincinnati - who provided limited additional insured coverage to Holyoke's insured - for defense costs because Holyoke's insured "incurred the defense and indemnification costs at issue without seeking approval from—or even affirmatively tendering a claim to" Cincinnati.).

Connecticut: No instructive authority. *But see Steadfast Ins. Co. v. Purdue Frederick Co.*, No. X08CV020191697, 2004 Conn. Super. LEXIS 2650 (Conn. Super. Ct. Sept. 14, 2004) (noting that the Connecticut Superior Court's decision in *Interface Flooring Systems v. Aetna Cas. & Sur. Co.*, which applied Georgia law, and held that no coverage was owed for pre-tender defense costs, and which was affirmed by the Connecticut Supreme Court, was "cogently reasoned") (*see* Georgia, *infra*); *MacDermid, Inc. v. Travelers Indem. Co.*, No. 12-6067744, 2017 Conn. Super. LEXIS 937 (Conn. Super. Ct. May 19, 2017) (discussing *Interface Flooring*) ("[W]hether or not prejudice may be presumed as a matter of law, this court concludes that under the particular facts in this case, Travelers has satisfied its burden of showing that there are no material facts in dispute as to its having been prejudiced.") ("If the 'no voluntary payments' provision is ignored, Travelers' expectations from the insurance contract are completely eradicated, while MacDermid receives the full benefit of its contractual expectations, and more. Travelers' *right* to manage and control the defense of the claim and thereby define the nature and scope of the indemnity is transformed into a nondiscretionary *obligation* to reimburse the insured.") (emphasis in original).

Delaware: The Superior Court of Delaware, while discussing whether an insurer had a duty to defend after an insured failed to "expressly request a defense before filing suit," noted "that there is generally no duty to pay pre-tender defense costs." *Liggett Group, Inc. v. Affiliated FM Ins. Co.*, No. Civ. A. 00C-01-207 (Del. Super. Ct. Sept. 21, 2001). *See also Abrams v. RSUI Indemnity Co.*, No. 16-4886, 2017 U.S. Dist. LEXIS 127227 (S.D.N.Y. Aug. 10, 2017) (applying Delaware law) ("The policy repeatedly makes clear that any costs incurred without the consent of the defendant are not covered under the policy. And the plaintiffs have failed to establish that Delaware, as a matter of law, would stray from the well-established principle that pre-notice defense expenses are generally not covered, irrespective of prejudice."); *Abrams v. RSUI Indemnity Co.*, 272 F. Supp. 3d 636 (S.D.N.Y. 2017) (lengthy discussion of Delaware law) ("Delaware law would enforce the plain terms of the D&O Policy, and the plaintiffs' argument that Delaware law would likely require the defendant to show prejudice before disclaiming pre-notice defense expenses is without merit."); *Solera Holdings, Inc. v. XL Specialty Ins. Co.*, 213 A.3d 1249 (Del. Super. Ct. 2019) (finding that the implied prejudice requirement that Delaware courts apply to consent-to-settle clauses applies) ("[C]onsent-to-settle and consent-to-defense provisions are meant to allow the insurer a meaningful opportunity to participate in litigation and to protect the insurer from prejudice, but a strict interpretation of either provision would lead to forfeiture of coverage. Implying the prejudice requirement in both circumstances protects an insured who has breached a consent provision from the harsh result of forfeiture, but only if the insured can prove by competent evidence a lack of prejudice to the insurer.").

District of Columbia: No instructive authority. *See* Maryland. "When District of Columbia law is silent, it has been the practice of the federal courts in this Circuit to turn to the law of Maryland for historical and geographical reasons." *Gray v. American Exp. Co.*, 743 F.2d 10, 17 (D.C. Cir. 1984).

Florida: A Florida District Court held that "under the plain language of the Policy ('No insured will, except at that insured's own cost, voluntarily make a payment, assume any obligation, or incur any expense, other than for first aid, without our consent.') there is no coverage for the defense costs incurred without Travelers' knowledge and not at Travelers' request." *Embroidme.com, Inc. v. Travelers Property Cas. Co. of America*, 992 F. Supp. 2d 1259 (S.D. Fla. 2014), *affirmed* 845 F.3d 1099 (11th Cir. 2017) ("*Beville* [*Nationwide Mut. Fire Ins. Co. v. Beville*, 825 So. 2d 999 (Fla. Ct. App. 2002)] addressed a coverage defense, which was the insurer's assertion of a general policy provision requiring an insured to provide prompt notice of a lawsuit to its insurer. An insured's non-compliance with that provision gives an insurer a defense to coverage that otherwise exists. *Beville* never held, nor could it, that an insured was entitled to coverage on matters that are expressly excluded by the policy. And as we have earlier explained, Travelers is not relying on a coverage defense; it is relying on an exclusion from coverage contained in the policy provision that expressly excludes reimbursement for expenses that an insured unilaterally incurs without the prior consent of the insurer. That provision states that 'no insured will, except at that insured's own cost, voluntarily make a payment, assume any obligation, or incur any expense, other than for first aid, without our consent.' This provision clearly excludes any voluntary payments made by an insured without the insurer's permission. It is an exclusion from coverage, and there is no dispute that EmbroidMe disregarded it.").

Georgia: The Eleventh Circuit Court of Appeals, applying Georgia law and relying on *O'Brien Family Trust v. Glen Falls Ins. Co.*, 461 S.E.2d 311 (Ga. Ct. App. 1995), held that an insured could not recover pre-tender defense costs where the policy was "silent on the issue of pre-tender expenses but included[] terms that require[d] the insured to provide notice of potential claims 'as soon as practicable' and to forward all papers connected with lawsuits 'immediately.'" *Elan Pharm. Research Corp. v. Employers Ins. of Wausau*, 144 F.3d 1372, 1381–82 (11th Cir. 1998); *see also Interface Flooring Sys., Inc. v. Aetna Cas. & Sur. Co.*, 804 A.2d 201, 208–11 (Conn. 2002) (applying Georgia law) ("The policies here require that the insured: (1) forward legal papers related to claims or lawsuits 'immediately' to the insurer; and (2) provide written notice of lawsuits or claims to the insurer 'as soon as reasonably possible' or 'as soon as practicable.' It is undisputed that, in the present case, the plaintiff did not comply with these conditions until some six months following the resolution of the Milliken action. Pursuant to the rule set forth in *O'Brien Family Trust* and applied in *Elan Pharmaceutical Research Corp.*, namely, that an insurer's duty to defend a lawsuit is not triggered until these conditions are complied with, and that an insured is precluded from recovering any expenses incurred in defending a lawsuit prior to such compliance, we conclude that the trial court properly determined that the defendant in the present case is not liable for costs the plaintiff incurred in defending the Milliken action."); *Allied Prop. & Cas. Ins. Co. v. Bed Bath & Beyond, Inc.*, No. 12-1265, 2014 U.S. Dist. LEXIS 156062 (N.D. Ga. Nov. 4, 2014) (addressing pre-tender defense costs in the context of an additional insured and holding that "[t]he insurers had actual notice of the underlying actions and had not demonstrated that they were prejudiced by any alleged lateness of additional insureds' election of coverage. In the present case, Allied was on notice of the claims for which [the additional] seeks coverage, and Allied has shown no prejudice arising from late notice of the election of coverage.").

Hawaii: The Supreme Court of Hawaii held that an insurer's "duty to defend [the insured did] not include the duty to contribute to defense costs incurred before [the insurer] had notice of the claim against [the insured]." *Great Am. Ins. Co. v. Aetna Cas. & Sur. Co.*, 876 P.2d 1314, 1315 (Haw. 1994). The court concluded that the insured "waived any claim against [the insurer] to contribute to defense costs incurred before [insurer] had notice of the claim." *Id.* at 1319; *see also Allstate Ins. Co. v. Gadiel*, No. 07-00565, 2008 U.S. Dist. LEXIS 90923 (D. Haw. Nov. 7, 2008) (denying insurer's motion for summary judgment that it was not obligated for pre-tender defense costs because the insurer failed to meet its burden of production as it "merely recited[] the 'voluntary payment provision' language, potentially but not necessarily relevant Hawaii law, and non-dispositive case law from other jurisdictions").

Idaho: A District Court of Idaho determined that, under the circumstances before it, a mere delay in notice did not preclude recovery of pre-tender defense costs, but that the insurer was nonetheless not obligated to reimburse its insured for pre-tender defense costs because such costs were incurred voluntarily, and the insured's policy contained a voluntary payment clause. *Blue Cross of Idaho Health Serv. v. Atlantic Mut. Ins. Co.*, No.1:09-CV-246 (D. Idaho Jan. 19, 2011). Based on Idaho's adherence to "equitable principles" and the California Court of Appeal's decision in *Tradewinds Escrow, Inc. v. Truck Ins. Exch.*, 188 Cal. Rptr. 2d 561 (Cal.

Ct. App. 2002), the court concluded that voluntary payment provisions prevent an insured from recovering pre-tender defense costs where the insured "simply took its time notifying the insurer" because "until the defense is tendered to the insurer, there is no duty to defend." *Id.* at 21. (internal quotation and citation omitted). Nevertheless, pre-tender expenses are not barred if they were incurred involuntarily, such as where the insured is unaware of the identity of the insurer or was compelled to incur pre-tender defense costs immediately to protect its legal interests. *Id.; see also Huntsman Advanced Materials, LLC v. OneBeacon Am. Ins. Co.*, No. 08–229, 2011 U.S. Dist. LEXIS 81672 (D. Idaho July 21, 2011) (determining that voluntary payment provisions "have been held to bar an insured from recovering defense costs incurred," but holding that "it is possible [that] some of the costs incurred by [the insured] were incurred out of necessity and before [the insurer] could have made a coverage determination" and "if this is the case, [the insured] would have a right to have those costs reimbursed") (reconsideration denied on pre-tender issue at No. 108-229, 2012 U.S. Dist. LEXIS 19053 (D. Idaho Feb. 13, 2012)).

Illinois: The Appellate Court of Illinois held that an insured was not entitled to pre-tender defense costs because the insurer was prejudiced as a result of the insured "defending … the … complaint for more than a year prior to the … policy becoming effective and … not giving[] notice of the suit to [the insurer] until almost 2 ½ years after it was filed." *Fire Ins. Co. v. G. Heileman Brewing Co.*, 747 N.E.2d 955, 968 (Ill. App. Ct. 2001). "A voluntary payment provision provides that an insurer will not be held liable for expenses voluntarily incurred by an insured before tendering defense of a suit to the insurer. … An insurer seeking to avoid responsibility because of a breach of this clause must show prejudice." *Id. See also Westfield Ins. Co. v. Indem. Ins. Co. of N. Am.*, No. 14-3040, 2020 U.S. Dist. LEXIS 6548 (C.D. Ill. Jan. 15, 2020) ("A tender of a defense within a reasonable time effectively requires an insurer to pay all the defense costs, even those incurred before the date of the tender of the defense.") (citing *West American Ins. Co. v. Yorkville Nat. Bank*, 939 N.E.2d 288 (Ill. 2010)).

Indiana: The Supreme Court of Indiana, differentiating the situation where insurers attempt to "completely disclaim … policy obligations" due to late notice, held that an insurer—regardless of whether prejudice existed—was not obligated to reimburse its insured for defense costs and expenses incurred before the insured notified the insurer of the suit because an insurer's duty to defend does not arise until notice of the claim has been received. *Dreaded, Inc. v. St. Paul Guardian Ins. Co.*, 904 N.E.2d 1267, 1273 (Ind. 2009). "The function of a notice requirement is to supply basic information to permit an insurer to defend a claim. The insurer's duty to defend simply does not arise until it receives the foundational information designated in the notice requirement. Until an insurer receives such enabling information, it cannot be held accountable for breaching this duty." *Id.*; *see also Great N. Ins. Co. v. Precision Plastics of Indiana, Inc.*, 910 N.E.2d 1288, at *7 (Table) (Ind. Ct. App. 2009) ("[T]he trial court's requirement of prejudice in its order, which was issued prior to the *Dreaded* opinion, is contrary to the subsequent holding in *Dreaded*. Notice of an occurrence or claim triggers the duty to defend on the part of the insured. Here, it is undisputed that the tender of notice did not occur until 1991 even though the discovery of the contamination occurred in 1989. Thus, the Insurance Company's duty to defend Precision did not begin until February 19, 1991."); *Travelers Ins. Companies v. Maplehurst Farms, Inc.*, 953 N.E.2d 1153 (Ind. Ct. App. 2011) (discussing *Dreaded* and holding that insurer was not obligated to pay pre-tender defense costs); *Meridian Mut. Ins. Co. v. Majestic Block & Supply Inc.*, 1 N.E.2d 173 (Ind. Ct. App. 2013) (applying *Dreaded* and stating that under the late notice doctrine, insurer was not liable for pre-tender defense costs); *Roman Catholic Archdiocese of Indiana v. Travelers Ins. Co.*, No. 12-1246, 2013 U.S. Dist. LEXIS 32702 (S.D. Ind. Mar. 7, 2013) (citing *Dreaded* and *Travelers* and holding that notice to insurer after case had been resolved precluded insurer's responsibility for prior defense fees and costs); *T.R. Bulger v. Indiana Ins. Co.*, No. 46D03-0709-388, 2014 Ind. Super. LEXIS 209 (Ind. Super. Ct. May 1, 2014) (reiterating *Maplehurst* [2011] and stating that "[t]he policies at issue also contain a voluntary payments clause, which provides that the insured will not incur any expense without prior approval except at his own cost. Indiana law provides that an insurer is not liable when an insured breaches a voluntary payment clause by not obtaining the insurer's consent prior to incurring the expense."); *Travelers Cas. & Sur. Co. of Am. v. Maplehurst Farms*, 18 N.E.3d 311 (Ind. Ct. App. 2014) (holding that "the trial court erred when it interpreted *Travelers Ins. Cos. v. Maplehurst Farms, Inc.*, 953 N.E.2d 1153 (Ind. Ct. App. 2011) to require Travelers to pay costs that were incurred as a result of [a] [s]ettlement. As a result, the trial court erred by granting summary judgment to Maplehurst."); *Arcelormittal Ind. Harbor LLC v. Amex Nooter, LLC*, No. 15-195, 2018 U.S. Dist. LEXIS 542 (N.D. Ind. Jan. 3, 2018) (stating rule from *Dreaded* and addressing the timing of various defense costs in determining any payment obligation).

   Iowa: No Instructive authority.

   Kansas: No instructive authority.

Kentucky: The Sixth Circuit Court of Appeals, applying Kentucky law, noted that "Kentucky's general pronouncement on late notice is very persuasive authority that Kentucky would continue to place the burden on the insurer to show prejudice due to late notice rather than assuming prejudice as many other jurisdictions have for pre-tender defense costs." *Travelers Prop. Cas. Co. v. Hillerich & Bradsby Co.*, 598 F.3d 257, 274 (6th Cir. 2010). This potential stance, as the Sixth Circuit acknowledged, would contradict most other jurisdictions that "do not allow recovery for pre-tender costs because those are deemed waived by the insured, especially when an insurance contract prohibits voluntary payments without the consent of the insurer, and so no showing of prejudice is required on the part of the insurer." *Id.* at 273. The court declined to resolve the issue before it, however, because the insured had tendered the claim to the insurer "before its duty to defend arose." *Id.*

Louisiana: The Court of Appeal of Louisiana held that an insured was not entitled to recover defense costs incurred "prior to the notification date" because an "insurer's duty to provide a defense does not arise until the insurer receives notice of the litigation." *Gully & Assoc., Inc. v. Wausau Ins. Co.*, 536 So. 2d 816, 817–18 (La. Ct. App. 1988). The court recognized that an insurer can only escape its duty to defend as a result of an insured's late notice if the insurer can show prejudice, but concluded that the prejudice requirement is not applicable to the issue of pre-tender defense costs because the insurer is not attempting to deny coverage completely. *Id.* at 818. Furthermore, in making its decision, the court emphasized that the insured's policy required it to "immediately forward to the company every demand, notice, summons or other process received by him or his representative." *Id.*; *see also Transcon. Pipe Line Corp v. Nat'l Union Fire Ins. Co.*, 378 F. Supp. 2d 729, 738–39 (M.D. La. 2005) (citing *Gully* for the proposition that "an insurer's duty to provide a defense does not arise until the insurer receives notice of the litigation, regardless of whether the insurance company is prejudiced by the late notice") (quotations omitted from original); *Anco Insulations, Inc. v. AIG Premier Ins. Co.*, No. 7-657, 2013 U.S. Dist. LEXIS 27550 (M.D. La. Feb. 28, 2013) (holding that insurer was not required to reimburse insured for legal fees and costs incurred before insured tendered suits to insurer) (*affirmed* 787 F.3d 276 (5th Cir. 2015)); *Liberty Mut. Ins. Co. v. Jotun Paints, Inc.*, No. 07-3114, 2009 U.S. Dist. LEXIS 2164 (E.D. La. Jan. 13, 2009) (indicating that prejudice is required for an insurer to disclaim coverage for pre-tender defense costs) ("Liberty does not direct the Court to any policy language or authority stating that the insurer is only obligated to pay those defense costs incurred *after* a duty to defend arises. Liberty's motion does not present the question of whether it owes defense costs from a particular date onward. When a duty to defend commences and what that duty entails are obviously distinct questions.") (emphasis in original); *Adventure Harbor Estates, LLC v. LeBlanc*, No. 12-1848, 2014 U.S. Dist. LEXIS 112889 (E.D. La. Aug. 13, 2014) ("In this case the LeBlancs waited nearly a year to notify Allstate of the suit that was filed against them individually. Thus, there is no argument to be made in this case that exigencies forced the LeBlancs to incur expenses to defend the suit before Allstate could step in to provide a defense. In the interim between being sued and finally notifying Allstate about the lawsuit, the LeBlancs retained the attorney of their choice, which was their prerogative to do, but under the clear terms of the policy they had to exercise that prerogative at their own cost. Allstate is entitled to judgment as a matter of law as to the pre-notice attorney's fees and expenses.") (suggesting that, based on *Peavey Co. v. M/V ANPA*, 971 F.2d 1168 (5th Cir. 1992), lack of coverage for pre-tender defense costs must be supported by policy language).

Maine: No instructive authority.

Maryland: The Court of Appeals of Maryland held that an insurer was obligated to reimburse the insured "for the pre-notice fees and expenses incurred by [the insured], which the jury found to be reasonable." *Sherwood Brands, Inc. v. Hartford Accident and Indem. Co.*, 698 A.2d 1078, 1087 (Md. 1997). However, the Maryland high court's decision addressed the issue under various scenarios. "If the insurer declines to defend solely because, in its view, the claim is not even potentially within the policy coverage and the court ultimately agrees with that view, there is no obligation to reimburse the insured for any litigation expenses, whether incurred before or after the notice was given. The timing of the notice has no bearing on the issue. If, on the other hand, as occurred here, the court concludes that the claim *was* potentially within the policy coverage and that, as a result, the insurer *did* breach its duty to defend, the insurer is liable for all damages incurred by the insured as a result of that breach." *Id.* at 1086 (emphasis in original). The court also concluded that an insurer that prospectively assumes a defense, but refuses to reimburse pre-notice defense costs, must prove that it was prejudiced in order to do so. *Id.* In so deciding, the court was persuaded that § 482 of the Maryland Code controlled. *Id.* Section 482 is now MD Code, Insurance § 19-110, which provides: "An insurer may disclaim coverage on a liability insurance policy on the ground that the insured or a person claiming the benefits of the policy through the insured has breached the policy by failing to cooperate with the insurer or by not giving the insurer required notice only if the insurer establishes by a preponderance of the evidence that the lack of cooperation or notice has resulted in actual prejudice to the insurer." *See also Baker's Express, LLC v. Arrowpoint Capital Corp.*, No. ELH-10-2508, 2012 U.S. Dist. LEXIS 135418 (D. Md. Sept. 20, 2012) (citing *Sherwood* and reaffirming evaluation of insured's ability to collect pre-tender defense costs based on whether insurer was prejudiced by late tender and if fees incurred were reasonable).

Massachusetts: A District Court of Massachusetts held that an insured was not entitled to recover pre-tender defense costs after the insured delayed notifying its insurer of ongoing litigation for almost one year. *Managed Health Care Sys., Inc. v. St. Paul Fire & Marine Ins. Co.*, No. Civ.A.98CV10831, 2001 U.S. Dist. LEXIS 18302 (D. Mass. Sept. 28, 2001). "MHCS's policy required it to give St. Paul notice of any claims against it, and when faced with a claim the policy instructed MHCS not to 'assume any financial obligation or pay out any money without [St. Paul's] consent.' The plaintiffs breached these terms by waiting almost a year before notifying St. Paul of Foster's suit and by deciding to pay their attorney in excess of $200,000 to defend against the suit without St. Paul's approval. By giving St. Paul no notice during the first year of the suit, the plaintiff left St. Paul with no power to affect the course and cost of the litigation during that time. Under *Augat [v. Liberty Mut. Ins. Co.*, 571 N.E.2d 357 (Mass. 1991)] St. Paul should not have to pay for the portion of the Foster suit it had no opportunity to influence." *See also Am. Mut. Liability Ins. Co. v. Beatrice Co.*, 924 F. Supp. 861, 873–74 (N.D. Ill. 1996) (applying Massachusetts law) (concluding that the prejudice requirement that attached to the notice rule did not apply to pre-tender defense costs because "[t]he prejudice requirement was adopted to prevent complete forfeiture based upon technical failure of the insured to provide timely notice" whereas "enforcement of the rule that pre-tender defense cost are not recoverable does not result in complete forfeiture of an insured's right to recover fees"); *Myers v. The Travelers Indem. Co.*, No. 11-40157, 2014 U.S. Dist. LEXIS 40944 (D. Mass. Mar. 27, 2014) (assuming that pre-tender costs are recoverable absent a showing of prejudice and holding that insurer was prejudiced by insured's late notice) ("Travelers was materially prejudiced by their inability to have any input as to managing the clean up and/or associated costs.") *But see Liberty Mut. Ins. Co. v. The Black & Decker Corp.*, 383 F. Supp. 2d 200, 207 (D. Mass. 2004) ("The widely-followed late notice doctrine under which post-notice costs are recoverable absent prejudice, but pre-notice costs are *per se* excluded, is in tension with the underpinnings of Massachusetts's analysis of the notice clause. … I predict that the Supreme Judicial Court, if confronted with these arguments, would find that pre-notice defense costs are recoverable absent prejudice."); *Pacific Ins. Co., Ltd. v.*

Eaton Vance Management, 260 F. Supp. 2d 334, 343–44 (D. Mass. 2003) (holding that prejudice required to disclaim coverage for pre-tender defense costs under policy in which insurer explicitly delegated the duty to defend to insured, asking only that it be given the opportunity to consent, with consent not to be unreasonably withheld) ("There is thus nothing unfair about requiring Pacific to pay for the Pre-Tender Costs where Pacific would have consented had it been asked."); *Dominion Energy, Inc. v. Zurich Am. Ins. Co.*, No. 13-00156, 2016 U.S. Dist. LEXIS 32980 (D. Conn. March 15, 2016) (applying Massachusetts law) (distinguishing other cases that precluded coverage for pre-tender defense costs on the basis that the insured had notice of the lawsuit shortly after it was filed).

Michigan: A District Court of Michigan held that an insurer was "only obligated to pay defense costs from the date the [insureds] requested a defense." *Century Indem. Co. v. Aero-Motive Co.*, 318 F. Supp. 2d 530, 544 (W.D. Mich. 2003). In reaching its conclusion, the court rejected the argument that "an insurer is liable for pre-tender defense costs … where the insured fails to allege that the insurer created a conflict of interest situation" because "[a] contrary result would essentially turn an insurer's defense obligation into a duty to reimburse, without affording the insurer the opportunity to control the defense and settlement of the underlying obligation." *Id.* See also *AMI Entertainment Network, Inc. v. Zurich American Ins. Co.*, 526 Fed. Appx. 635 (6th Cir. 2013) (citing *Aero-Motive* and concluding that insurer was not liable for insured's defense fees and costs incurred before insurer had notice of underlying case); *Flint Auto Auction, Inc. v. Univ. Underwriters Ins. Co.*, No. 12-14793, U.S. Dist. LEXIS 172555 (E.D. Mich. Dec. 9, 2013) (citing *AMI Entertainment* and holding that insurer did not have to reimburse insured for pre-tender defense costs because insureds did not notify insurer promptly or by required method of notification).

Minnesota: The Supreme Court of Minnesota held that an insured could not recover pre-tender defense costs after it delayed for seven months tendering the defense of an environmental cleanup claim to its insurer. *Domtar, Inc. v. Niagara Fire Ins. Co.*, 563 N.W.2d 724, 739–40 (Minn. 1997). The court reasoned that "an insured does not invoke its insurer's duty to defend until it properly tenders a defense request. Logically, then, an insurer cannot be held responsible for defense costs incurred prior to the tender of the defense request giving rise to the insurer's duty to defend, the diligence of the insured notwithstanding. While there may be, as we implied in *SCSC [v. Allied Mut. Ins. Co.*, 536 N.W.2d 305 (Minn. 1995)], circumstances justifying a departure from the general rule, we do not find such compelling circumstances present in this case." *Id.* at 739. The court was not pursued to rule differently on the basis that Domtar's delay was on account of spending several months searching its insurance records. *Id.* See *also Continental Ins. Co. v. Daikin Applied Ams. Inc.*, No. 17-552, 2019 U.S. Dist. LEXIS 143049 (D. Minn. Aug. 14, 2019) (following *Domtar* and rejecting the insured's argument that the pre-tender rule affects a forfeiture) ("At least one case has found that a bad faith denial of coverage could render an insurer liable for pre-tender costs. *See Gopher Oil Co. v. Am. Hardware Mutual Ins. Co.*, 588 N.W.2d 756, 771 (Minn. App. 1999). But Daikin Applied has not pointed to evidence that would suggest that Continental engaged in a bad faith denial of coverage.").

Mississippi: No instructive authority.

Missouri: The Missouri Court of Appeals held that an insurer need not prove that it was prejudiced to disclaim coverage for pre-tender defense costs. *Doe Run Resources Corp. v. American Guarantee & Liability Ins.*, No. ED103026, 2016 Mo. App. LEXIS 964 (Mo. Ct. App. Sept. 27, 2016), *rev'd on other grounds*, 531 S.W.3d 508 (Mo. 2017). The court distinguished a late notice defense for all coverage versus for defense costs: "Doe Run nevertheless argues, as the trial court asserted, that '[e]ven had Doe Run failed to comply with purported tender obligations prior to March 16, 2012. . . St. Paul can disallow defense costs only if it proves actual and substantial prejudice,' but we disagree because the cases cited by Doe Run and the trial court for this principle in fact do not stand for it, but instead stand for an entirely separate rule that in cases where an insurer disclaims *all* coverage because the insured has allegedly breached a 'late notice' or 'cooperation' clause, the insurer must establish prejudice to avoid coverage on those grounds. Here, St. Paul has disclaimed coverage of only a portion of Doe Run's defense costs, and denying Doe Run coverage of such costs in the absence of prejudice here would not amount to a 'forfeiture' of Doe Run's CGL policy coverage from St. Paul in any of the underlying lawsuits. Thus, St. Paul need not show prejudice." (emphasis in original). *See also Process Controls Int'l, Inc. v. Commercial Union Ins. Co.*, 16 S.W.3d 593, 593 (Mo. Ct. App. 2000) (affirming, without discussing, a trial court decision holding that an insurer did not need to show prejudice before a claim for pre-tender defense costs could be barred); *Post Holdings v. Liberty Mut. Fire Ins. Co.*, No. 18-1741, 2020 U.S. Dist. LEXIS 49594 (E.D. Mo. Mar. 23, 2020) (finding that insurer had no obligation to reimburse insured for any pre-tender defense costs) (unique facts and citing no law).

Montana: No instructive authority.

Nebraska: The Supreme Court of Nebraska, following a review of the issue nationally, stated that "[c]ourts around the country differ in their approach to voluntary payments provisions. Some states find that an insured's failure to comply with a voluntary payments provision means that the insurer is not liable to the insured under the policy, and do not require the insurer to be prejudiced as a result of the settlement. Other states still require the insurer to show prejudice resulting from the breach of the voluntary payments provision, but presume prejudice as a matter of law where the insurer did not have an opportunity to participate in the defense or the settlement process." *Rent-A-Roofer, Inc. v. Farm Bureau Prop. & Cas. Ins. Co.*, 869 N.W.2d 99 (Neb. 2015). The Supreme Court joined the camp that requires prejudice, noting that, "[g]iven the similarity in purpose between notice provisions and voluntary payments provisions, we find that it is proper to maintain the prejudice requirement when an insurer seeks to avoid the policy for breach of a voluntary payments provision." However, the court found that the insurer was in fact prejudiced: "An insurer cannot fail in defending a suit that it has no knowledge of. In this case, we conclude that this complete denial of Farm Bureau's opportunity to engage in the defense, take part in the settlement discussions, or consent to the settlement agreement was prejudicial as a matter of law to Farm Bureau and find that Farm Bureau is not liable for defense costs.").

Nevada: No instructive authority.

New Hampshire: No instructive authority.

New Jersey: The Supreme Court of New Jersey held that an insurer is only obligated to pay "for that portion of the defense costs arising after it was informed of the facts triggering the duty to defend." *SL Indus., Inc. v. Am. Motorists Ins. Co.*, 607 A.2d 1266, 1272 (N.J. 1992). In reaching its conclusion, the court reasoned "that the duty to defend is triggered by facts *known* to the insurer." *Id.* (emphasis in original). "[I]f the insured does not properly forward the information to the insurance company, the insured cannot demand reimbursement from the insurer for defense costs the insurer had no opportunity to control." *Id.* at 200; *see also Chem. Leaman Tank Lines, Inc. v. Aetna Cas. and Sur. Co.*, 817 F. Supp. 1136, 1158–61 (D.N.J 1993) (citing *Cooper v. Gov't Employees Ins. Co.*, 237 A.2d 870 (N.J. 1968) to demonstrate the difficult burden of proving late noticce generally because of the requirement to establish "that the insurer suffered a likelihood of appreciable prejudice" while, in contrast, discussing *SL Indus.* and holding that an insurer is not obligated to reimburse an insured for defense costs prior to the time that it received notice of the claim).

New Mexico: No instructive authority.

New York: A District Court of New York held that an insurer was not liable for defense costs incurred by its insured until it received notice of the claim. *Smart Style*

Ind. Inc. v. Pa. Gen. Ins. Co., 930 F. Supp. 159, 164 (S.D.N.Y. 1996). The court recognized that an insurer's "duty to defend is triggered by the filing of a complaint containing allegations that could possibly bring the action within the scope of coverage provided by the insurance company" and that, as a result, "the insurer will be liable for defense costs from the time that the duty was triggered." (internal citation and quotation omitted). *Id.* at 163. However, the insured's policy contained a "voluntary payments" clause that prohibited the insured from incurring any expense without the insurer's consent. *Id.* Accordingly, the court determined that the insurer had an obligation to pay the insured's defense costs only after it was notified of the underlying action. *Id.* at 164. Nonetheless, the court also acknowledged that a voluntary payments clause cannot prohibit an insured from incurring any expense without the insurer's explicit approval—providing, as an example, the insured's need to respond to a complaint on a timely basis. *Id.* at 163; see also *New York Marine and Gen. Ins. Co. v. Lafarge North America, Inc.*, 599 F.3d 102, 122 (2nd Cir. 2010) (applying New York law) (holding, in the context of an emergency situation, that it was reasonable for insured to act quickly to hire a law firm in order to minimize exposure to damages before receiving consent from or giving notice to insurer and insured was entitled to recover from insurer the legal fees it incurred); *Consol. Edison of N.Y. v. Lexington Ins. Co.*, No. 14-6547, 2015 U.S. Dist. LEXIS 121573 (S.D.N.Y. Sept. 9, 2015) (noting that "[r]ecently there has developed a narrow exception to this default rule [that the insurer is liable for defense costs from the time that the complaint is filed]: when an insurance policy contains a so-called 'voluntary payments' provision, which bars an insured from making a payment, assuming an obligation or incurring an expense in connection with the defense of a claim without the insurer's consent, the duty to defend may not be triggered by the filing of a complaint. Such clauses are enforceable, just like any other clauses in an insurance policy. However, they 'cannot literally be read as prohibiting an insured from incurring *any* expense without the explicit prior approval of the insurer. Rather, the clause must be construed according to the reasonable expectations of the insured.'") (quoting *Smart Style*); *Merendino v. Costco Wholesale Corp.*, No. 154010/12, 2016 N.Y. Misc. LEXIS 1835 (May 6, 2016) (no coverage owed for additional insured's pre-tender defense costs; additional insured required to tender to the insurer and tender to named insured is not sufficient); *Greater N.Y. Mut. Ins. Co. v. State Natl. Ins. Co., Inc.*, No. 155444/16, 2019 N.Y. Misc. LEXIS 6824 (N.Y. Sup. Ct. Dec. 6, 2019) ("[W]hen an insurer is in breach of its obligation to defend, the appropriate remedy is to reimburse the insured for any and all legal costs incurred in defending the underlying action. . . .

Reimbursement of defense costs is determined by the date the insurer received tender.") (citing *Bovis Lend Lease LMB v Royal Surplus Lines Ins. Co.*, 806 N.Y.S.2d 53 (1st Dept. 2005)).

North Carolina: A District Court of North Carolina held that an insurer was not liable for paying its insured's legal fees incurred prior to the insurer's date of notice. *WM. C. Vick Constr. Co. v. Pennsylvania Nat. Mut. Cas. Ins. Co.*, 52 F. Supp. 2d 569, 596 (E.D.N.C. 1999). "Although this court has found no North Carolina case on point, given the absence of contractual language requiring the insurer to pay for pre-notification legal expenses, and the fact that North Carolina's courts have long recognized the validity of notice provisions in insurance contracts … [the insurer] should not be held liable for any defense costs incurred by Plaintiff prior to being notified of the underlying arbitration claims against [the insured]." *Id.* The court was persuaded by decisions holding that a contrary result would require the insurer to pay defense costs that it had no opportunity to control. *Id.*; *see also Kubit v. MAG Mut. Ins. Co.*, No. COA09-1056, 2011 N.C. App. LEXIS 482 (N.C. Ct. App. Mar. 15, 2011) (adopting the "majority rule" by holding that "the duty to defend is triggered when the insurer receives notice of the underlying complaint"); *Westfield Ins. Co. v. Weaver Cooke Constr., LLC*, 383 F. Supp. 3d 566 (E.D. N.C. 2019) (acknowledging rule from *Vick Constr.* but concluding that insurer had an obligation for pre-tender defense because it breached the duty to defend).

North Dakota: No instructive authority.

Ohio: The Court of Appeals of Ohio held that an insurer was not obligated to pay the defense costs incurred by its insured prior to the insurer receiving notice of the claim because the insured breached its obligations under the policy by failing to timely notify the insurer of the claim. *Dover Lake Park, Inc. v. Scottsdale Ins. Co.*, No. 21324, 2003 Ohio App. LEXIS 2973 (Ohio Ct. App. June 25, 2003). The court distinguished the scenario involving pre-tender defense costs with other Ohio cases dealing with late notice in general, by concluding that "the prejudice inquiry … has no application to a determination of whether [the insured's] late notice relieved [the insurer] of its obligation under the policy to provide reimbursement for [the insured's] pre-tender fees and litigation expenses."

Oklahoma: No instructive authority.

Oregon: The Court of Appeals of Oregon held, in a situation that could be analogous to a claim for pre-tender defense costs, that an insurer had no duty to defend its insured because the suit's original complaint supported the insurer's position that it had no duty to defend, and the insured failed to provide the amended complaint to the insurer. *Oregon Ins. Guar. Assoc. v. Thompson*, 760 P.2d 890, 893 (Or. Ct. App. 1988). "Without having knowledge that the counterclaim had been amended in a manner that could affect its contractual duty, [the insurer] had no reason or basis on which to reconsider its initial decision not to defend." *Id.* Moreover, the court concluded that "when the duty to defend is at issue, the matter of prejudice from an insured's failure to give notice of the claim is irrelevant." *Id.* at 894. *See also Century Indem. Co. v. Marine Group, LLC*, No. 08-1375, 2015 U.S. Dist. LEXIS 22507 (D. Or. Feb. 25, 2015) ("In light of existing Oregon case law, as well as opinions by this district and the Ninth Circuit applying similar law, the court is convinced that, given the opportunity, Oregon courts would agree with the teachings of the treatises and prohibit the recovery [sic] defense costs incurred prior to formal tender of the underlying action to the insurer. Accordingly, the court finds Marine does not have a claim against any of the Insurers for defense costs incurred prior to tender of defense of the Remediation."); *Siltronic Corp. v. Employers Ins. Co.*, No. 11-1493, 2015 U.S. Dist. LEXIS 4287 (D. Or. Jan. 14, 2015) (quoting *Thompson*) ("When the duty to defend is at issue, the matter of prejudice from an insured's failure to give notice of the claims is irrelevant.").

Pennsylvania: A Pennsylvania District Court held that an insurer was not relieved of an obligation to pay for pre-tender defense costs unless it could prove that it suffered actual prejudice from the untimely notice. *Rite Aid Corp. v. Liberty Mut. Fire Ins. Co.*, No. 1:CV-03-1801, 2006 U.S. Dist. LEXIS 57094 (M.D. Pa. Aug. 14, 2006). In making its determination, the court concluded that the same principles underlining its stance on late notice in general should be applied to pre-tender defense costs, stating that "the function of a notice requirement is to protect the insurance company's interests from being prejudiced" and "[w]here the insurance company's interests have not been harmed by a late notice, even in the absence of extenuating circumstances to excuse the tardiness, the reason behind the notice condition in the policy is lacking, and it follows neither logic nor fairness to relieve the insurance company of its obligation under the policy in such a situation." The court found persuasive the Tenth Circuit's decision in *TPLC, Inc. v. United Nat. Ins. Co.*, 44 F.3d 1484 (10th Cir. 1995), which applied Pennsylvania law, and held that, in the absence of an insurer showing prejudice, the duty to defend includes the duty to reimburse reasonable pre-tender defense costs. *Id.*; *see also Dale Corp. v. Cumberland Mut. Fire Ins. Co.*, No. 09-1115, 2010 U.S. Dist. LEXIS 65052 (E.D. Pa. June 30, 2010) (following *Rite Aid Corp.* and holding that the insurer's duty to defend arose prior to insured's tender of notice because the insurer could not show any prejudice arising from the late notice); *Commerce & Indus. Ins. Co. v. Century Sur. Co.*, No. 19-3635, 2020 U.S. App. LEXIS 14082 (6th Cir. Apr. 30, 2020) (applying Pennsylvania law) (no obligation for defense costs incurred before a complaint was filed that triggered insurer's defense obligation); *Westminster Am. Ins. Co. v. Spruce 1530, LLC*, No. 19-539, 2020 U.S. Dist. LEXIS 106534 (E.D. Pa. Jun. 17, 2020) (citing *Rite Aid Corp.* and noting that "courts applying Pennsylvania law have not unanimously embraced the argument that an insurer's duty to defend 'only arises after notice'") (court unable to find "any case in which an insurer was required to reimburse pre-notice costs despite having no ongoing duty to defend"); *NVR, Inc. v. Motorists Mut. Ins. Co.*, 371 F. Supp. 3d 233 (W.D. Pa. 2019) (noting that NVR contravened the policy's no voluntary payment provision which unambiguously applied to "thousands of dollars of pre-tender expenses in the form of legal fees and other costs" in a matter which had been "litigated for over three years before NVR gave MMIC any indication that it desired or expected a defense").

Rhode Island: A District Court of Rhode Island held that an insurer was only liable for paying insured's defense costs that were incurred after it was notified of the underlying litigation. *Michaud v. Merrimack Mut. Fire Ins. Co.*, No. 94-0175B, 1994 U.S. Dist. LEXIS 19930 (D.R.I. Nov. 16, 1994). The court reasoned that, becausemaxu the insured "voluntarily incurred legal expenses for their defense in the … action without [the insurer's] consent in clear violation of unambiguous policy language[,]" … the insureds "are now hard pressed to justify reimbursement for *all* defense costs and expenses since the initiation of the … action." (emphasis in original).

South Carolina: A District Court of South Carolina addressed whether the insurer was obligated to provide coverage for pre-tender defense costs and concluded that "an insurer's duty to defend arises upon the filing of the underlying complaint, and late notice from the insured does not excuse the insurer from complying with its duty to defend except where the insurer can show prejudice." *Episcopal Church in So. Carolina v. Church Ins. Co. of Vt.*, 53 F. Supp. 3d 816 (D.S.C. 2014). The court reasoned that "under South Carolina law, the duty to notify is merely a covenant that, absent a showing of prejudice, does not excuse the insurer from complying with its duty to defend." On the specific issue at hand, the court predicted that "the South Carolina Supreme Court would join [other] … courts and hold that, absent a showing by the insurer of substantial prejudice caused by the insured's late notice, an insurer who breached its duty to defend will be liable for reasonable costs of defense incurred both before and after notice."

South Dakota: No instructive authority.

Tennessee: A District Court of Tennessee held that an insured was entitled to recover pre-tender fees and expenses because the insurer did not experience any prejudice as a result of the insured's late notice. *Smith & Nephew, Inc. v. Fed. Ins. Co.*, No. 02-2455, 2005 U.S. Dist. LEXIS 49058 (W.D. Tenn. Dec. 12, 2005). The court concluded that "a prejudice analysis should apply to both the existence of a duty to defend after late notice, as well as to whether that duty includes pre-notice costs," because a state like Tennessee concludes that "notice is not a condition precedent to coverage." "While it is logically consistent to find that a duty to defend does not arise until notice is provided in a state that holds notice to be a condition precedent to the duty to defend, the same is not true for a state, like Tennessee, which holds the duty exists independent of notice. In a state where the duty to notify is merely a covenant that, absent a showing of prejudice, does not excuse the insurer from complying with its duty to defend, the logic of such a holding becomes significantly attenuated, for it creates a time gap between the insurer's right to control the defense and its duty to provide one."

Texas: The Court of Appeals of Texas held, "based on the [voluntary payment] provision, that [the insureds] cannot recover the costs of defending the [underlying lawsuits], since they failed to notify the insurers of the suits pursuant to the policy provisions, and since they voluntarily undertook such costs and payments." *E & L Chipping Co. v. The Hanover Ins. Co.*, 962 S.W.2d 272, 278 (Tex. Ct. App. 1998). The court declined to accept the insureds' argument that the insurer was required to prove that it was prejudiced. *Id.*; *see also 15625 Ft. Bend Ltd. v. Sentry Select Ins. Co.*, No. H-12-0600, 2014 U.S. Dist. LEXIS 34673 (S.D. Tex. Mar. 13, 2014) (citing *E & L Chipping* and holding that insurer did not have to pay any defense costs or attorney's fees incurred by insured before insured provided notice of suit to insurer); *Coastal Ref. & Mktg. v. U.S. Fid. and Guar. Co.*, 218 S.W.3d 279, 294 (Tex. Ct. App. 2007) (citing *E & L Chipping* for the proposition that "[b]ecause an insurer's duty to defend is triggered by notice, the insurer has no duty to reimburse the insured for defense costs incurred before the insured gave the insurer notice of the lawsuit"); *Protectors Ins. & Fin. Servs., LLC v. Lexington Ins. Co.*, No. H-12-3469, 2013 U.S. Dist. LEXIS 130338 (S.D. Tex. Sep. 12, 2013) (citing *Coastal Ref. & Mktg.* and concluding that insurer did not have to reimburse insured for legal expenses incurred before date insurer received tender of suit); *Princeton Excess & Surplus Lines Ins. Co. v. Maxum Indem. Co.*, No. 18-2705, 2019 U.S. Dist. LEXIS 164272 (S.D. Tex. Aug. 5, 2019) (contribution claim between insurers) ("Princeton requests 100% of post-tender fees and costs. Princeton is only entitled to its defense costs from the time Maxum's duty to defend arose and a tender request had been made.").

Utah: A District Court of Utah held that, "as a matter of law, [insurers] are not liable for any litigation expenses incurred prior to tender of defense to them." *Crist v. Ins. Co. of N. Am.*, 529 F. Supp. 601, 603 (D.C. Utah 1982). In reaching its determination, the court reasoned that "[t]he insurer's duty to defend corresponds to the insured's duty to relinquish control of the defense, and one cannot arise without the other." *Id.* at 603. "Plaintiffs counter that because the defendants refused to defend, they cannot now be heard to complain that tender was untimely, and argue that the failure to award these expenses constitutes a windfall for the defendants. The responsibility of promptly notifying their respective insurers and tendering to them their defense of the action, however, rested with the insureds. Any windfall would on the contrary result from requiring the defendants to bear the burden of the defense prior to their knowledge of the action." *Id.* at 604.

Vermont: No instructive authority.

Virginia: A District Court of Virginia held that an insurer was not obligated to provide coverage for pre-tender defense costs, but with no discussion of the prejudice issue. *Lessard v. Cont'l Cas. Co.*, No. 14-63, 2014 U.S. Dist. LEXIS 115953 (E.D. Va. Aug. 19, 2014). The court held: "Plaintiff gave notice of the dispute underlying his insurance Claim to Defendant to his prior carrier, Travelers, on February 1, 2011, and Wells Fargo filed its lawsuit in August 2011. [Continental Casualty] received notice from the Plaintiff on January 24, 2012 - nearly a year from the date Plaintiff notified Travelers and nearly five months from the commencement of Wells Fargo's suit. Since it was unaware of the Claim, [Continental Casualty] had no say in how Plaintiff was handling the defense or the fees incurred from it, exceeding $475,000 in defense costs before [Continental Casualty] was notified. The undisputed length of time between Plaintiff being on notice of the Claim and Plaintiff notifying [Continental Casualty] contravenes the basis for the policy's 'as soon as practicable' provision. Moreover, Plaintiff's conclusory excuse for late notice - his belief that the Wells Fargo lawsuit lacked merit - does not evince a genuine dispute of material fact over whether notice was made as soon as practicable." *Id.* at *12-13.

Washington: The Supreme Court of Washington held that "the duty to defend arises not at the moment of tender, but upon the filing of a complaint alleging facts that could potentially require coverage. . . . Accordingly, an insured can recover pre-tender fees and costs except where a late tender prejudiced the insurer." *National Sur. Corp. v. Immunex Corp.*, 297 P.3d 688 (Wash. 2013) (concluding that, unless insurer could show prejudice, insured could recover pre-tender defense costs despite the fact that tender was delayed several years and insured was "on the eve of settling…a lawsuit" when it finally provided notice). A pre-*Immunex* decision addressed what may be prejudice. The Court of Appeals of Washington held that, "subject to policy based defenses, an insurer is liable for fees and costs incurred before the insured tenders defense of a covered claim." *Griffin v. Allstate Ins. Co.*, 29 P.3d 777, 779 (Wash. Ct. App. 2001). The court emphasized that, for late notice in general, "the duty to defend arises upon the filing of a covered complaint, and the duty is not excused by late notice unless the insurer is prejudiced." *Id.* at 781. Applying this proposition on late notice to pre-tender defense costs, the court concluded that the insurer "must also prove actual prejudice … even assuming [the insurer] could prove breach of the voluntary payment provision." *Id.* at 783. Accordingly, because the insurer had not demonstrated any type of prejudice, the insureds were entitled to pre-tender defense costs, despite the existence of a voluntary payment provision. *Id.* "This is not to say that insureds may freely conduct their own litigation and then seek reimbursement. Allstate's promise is to defend through counsel of its own choosing. Prejudice to the insurer may follow from an insured's retention of counsel who may charge higher rates or fail to pursue appropriate strategies. Prejudice may be more difficult to show where an insured is forced to incur expense before tender can be made, but the issue is still factual." *Id.* at 782.

West Virginia: No instructive authority. A District Court of West Virginia noted that "[t]he Supreme Court of Appeals of West Virginia has not addressed certain contested legal issues" such as "liability for pre-tender defense costs." *Cardinal Cas. Co. v. S.E.C.U.R.E.*, 842 F. Supp. 899, 902 (S.D.W.V. 1994). The court refrained from providing any guidance on the issue, however, as it felt "reluctant to address questions of first impression of state law, particularly when those answers could adversely affect the rights of numerous state litigants whose interests are not represented or protected here." *Id.*

Wisconsin: The Supreme Court of Wisconsin held that an insurer, even though it breached its duty to defend, was not liable for defense costs incurred by the insured until after the insured tendered the defense to the insurer. *Towne Realty, Inc. v. Zurich Ins. Co.*, 548 N.W.2d 64, 68 (Wis. 1996). In reaching its determination, the court concluded that an insurer "can only be liable for damages which 'naturally flow' from its breach of a contractual *duty*" and an insurer's duty to defend only arises when it is "put on notice that there was a claim against the insureds." *Id.* "Any expenses which the [i]nsureds incurred before [the notice to insurers], unless specifically allowed by the contract, cannot flow from [the insurer's] breach of this duty." *Id. See also Dhein v. Frankenmuth Mut. Ins. Co.*, 950 N.W.2d 861 (Wis. Ct. App. 2020) (citing *Towne Realty* for the proposition that an insured is not entitled to recover pre-tender defense costs).

Wyoming: No instructive authority.

CHAPTER

5

Duty to Defend Standard:
"Four Corners" or Extrinsic Evidence?

If coverage issues were stocks, the duty to defend would be Blue Chip. Just as investors purchase such stocks in hopes of steady and consistent returns, the rules concerning an insurer's duty to defend have long been unwavering.

This is why it comes as a surprise to no one when a court states that the duty to defend is broader than the duty to indemnify. After all, this has been the case for decades. *Goldberg v. Lumber Mut. Cas. Ins. Co. of N.Y.*, 77 N.E.2d 131, 133 (N.Y. 1948) ("The courts have frequently remarked that the duty to defend is broader than the duty to pay."). Likewise, it does not make news when a court declares that an insurer is obligated to defend even groundless, false, or fraudulent claims. This too has been the case for a very long time. *Patterson v. Standard Accident Ins. Co.*, 144 N.W. 491, 492 (Mich. 1913) (describing a provision in an automobile liability policy that obligated the insurer to defend any suits alleging injuries and demanding damages even if the allegations or demands were "wholly groundless, false or fraudulent"). Still another duty to defend truism is that "the appropriate starting point" for such a determination are the allegations contained in the complaint filed against the insured. *Essex Ins. Co. v. Fieldhouse, Inc.*, 506 N.W.2d 772, 775 (Iowa 1993). And, of course, no citation is needed for the test for determining an insurer's duty to defend: whether a claim in the complaint is potentially covered under the policy.

Given that these principles are so universally held, they are not candidates for a fifty-state survey. Any such survey would be the proverbial broken record. But there is a duty to defend issue about which courts do not agree. While all courts may begin their duty to defend determination by reviewing the complaint filed against the insured and comparing it to the policy, they often part ways on whether such examination also ends there. There is wide variation between courts over whether, and, if so, the extent to which, information contained outside the complaint— so-called "extrinsic evidence"—can be considered when deciding if an insurer's duty to defend has been triggered. Such wide disparity between the states concerning this issue, makes it an appropriate one for a fifty-state survey.

In some states, the answer is simple—No. Courts are not permitted to consider extrinsic evidence when evaluating whether an insurer is obligated to defend. This is sometimes referred to as the "complaint" rule, "comparison test," "four corners" rule, or "eight corners" rule. *Pompa v. Am. Family Mut. Ins. Co.*, 520 F.3d 1139, 1145 (10th Cir. 2008) (applying Colorado law). While the rule is, by definition, constraining, it is applied with adherence to certain principles that are designed to benefit policyholders. Where there is some doubt as to whether the complaint against the insured alleges a risk insured against, that doubt should be resolved in favor of the insured. *Pac. Ins. Co. v. Liberty Mut. Ins. Co.*, 956 A.2d 1246, 1255 (Del. 2008). Further, any ambiguity in the pleadings should be resolved against the insurer. *Id.*

Depending on the situation, a rule that limits a court's duty to defend determination to only a comparison between the complaint and the policy can favor policyholders or insurers. For example, the Supreme Court of Connecticut's application of the "four corners" rule favored a policyholder in *Hartford Casualty Insurance Co. v. Litchfield Mutual Fire Insurance Co.*, 876 A.2d 1139, 1144 (Conn. 2005). The court held that an insurer was obligated to defend an insured if the complaint alleged a covered claim, *even if* the insurer obtained information from the insured or anyone else that the claim was not in fact covered. On the other hand, the Supreme Court of Pennsylvania's adherence to the "four corners" rule in *Kvaerner Metals Div. of Kvaerner U.S., Inc. v. Commercial Union Ins. Co.*, 908 A.2d 888, 895 (Pa. 2006) resulted in the opposite outcome for the policyholder. Here the policyholder was denied a defense because the court would not consider extrinsic evidence that the lower court concluded triggered a defense obligation.

In *West Hills Dev. Co. v. Chartis Claims, Inc.*, 385 P.3d 1053 (Or. 2016), the Supreme Court of Oregon observed that "[o]n its face, the four-corners rule seems clear. Applying that rule to real world complaints, however, can create more of a challenge. In particular, a complaint may not definitively allege the facts that ultimately will determine whether a claim is covered by the policy." *Id.* at 1059.

While many states adhere to the "four corners" rule, about twice as many do not and have concluded that extrinsic evidence can be considered by a court in its duty to defend determination. *Miller v. Westport Ins. Corp.*, 200 P.3d 419, 424 (Kan. 2009) (quoting *Spivey v. Safeco Ins. Co.*, 865 P.2d 182, 188 (Kan. 1993)) ("If these known or reasonably discoverable extrinsic facts give rise to potential liability on the insured's part, the insured (sic) has a duty to defend … . This approach has become known as the 'extrinsic evidence' approach or rule. Under [this] approach, the insurer's duty to defend still hinges on the potential for coverage, but the universe of information from which that potential must be ascertained is much greater [than the universe used in an approach limited to the 'eight corners' of a pleading and the applicable insurance policy].") (alteration in original).

It is seems simple enough to determine the number of states that apply each approach. Then how to explain this: In *Water Well Solutions Serv. Group Inc. v. Consol. Ins. Co.*, 881 N.W.2d 285 (Wis. 2016), a dissenting Justice on the Supreme Court of Wisconsin noted that 31 states have exceptions to the four corners rule. Three weeks later a Tennessee federal court stated that "[i]t is accepted in the overwhelming majority of jurisdictions that the obligations of a liability insurance company to defend an action brought against the insured by a third party is to be determined solely by the allegations contained in the complaint in that action." *Medicus Ins. Co. v. ERx Grp., LLC*, No. 15-205, 2016 U.S. Dist. LEXIS 95809, at *9 (E.D. Tenn. July 22, 2016) (quoting *St. Paul Fire and Marine Ins. Co. v. Torpoco*, 879 S.W.2d 831, 835 (Tenn. 1994)).

Courts that have rejected the "four corners" rule have done so based on various rationales. New York's highest court was troubled by the "four corners" rule, reasoning that the denial of a defense, notwithstanding the existence of extrinsic evidence proving that a defense was owed, would eliminate the breadth of the duty to defend. *Fitzpatrick v. Am. Honda Motor Co.*, 575 N.E.2d 90, 92 (N.Y. 1991) ("[W]here the insurer is attempting to shield itself from the responsibility to defend despite its actual knowledge that the lawsuit involves a covered event, wooden application of the 'four corners of the complaint' rule would render the duty to defend narrower than the duty to indemnify—clearly an unacceptable result. For that reason, courts and commentators have indicated that the insurer must provide a defense if it has knowledge of facts which potentially bring the claim within the policy's indemnity coverage.").

Courts have also rejected the "four corners" rule on the basis that notice pleading often provides few facts upon which to assess an insurer's duty to defend. *Talen v. Employers Mut. Cas. Co.*, 703 N.W.2d 395, 406 (Iowa 2005); *but see Transcon. Ins. Co. v. Jim Black & Assocs., Inc.*, 888 So. 2d 671, 675 (Fla. Dist. Ct. App. 2004) ("Even under the more liberal federal pleading requirements, a third-party plaintiff's claims against an insured should be sufficiently described to allow a determination of whether a duty to defend arises under the allegations of the complaint.").

The permissibility of extrinsic evidence to establish an insurer's duty to defend has also been justified on the basis that liability insurance is in effect "litigation insurance" to protect the insured from the expense of defending suits brought against it. *Aetna Cas. & Sur. Co. v. Cochran*, 651 A.2d 859, 865 (Md. 1995). Therefore, "[a]llowing an insured the opportunity to establish a defense to tort allegations which may provide a potentiality of coverage under an insurance policy prior to the insured incurring expenses associated with maintaining a defense in that tort action is precisely what the insured bargained for under the insurance contract." *Id.* This rationale is tied to an insured's reasonable expectations that the insurer will defend it whenever there is a potential for coverage. *Id.*; *see also Ball v. Wilshire Ins. Co.*, 221 P.3d 717, 723 (Okla. 2009) ("The defense duty is measured by the nature and kinds of risks covered by the policy as well as by the reasonable expectations of the insured.").

Extrinsic evidence has also been permitted in a duty to defend determination "to avoid permitting the pleading strategies, whims, and vagaries of third party claimants to control the rights of parties to an insurance contract." *M. Mooney Corp. v. U.S. Fid. & Guar. Co.*, 618 A.2d 793, 797 (N.H. 1992).

Some states that have adopted an exception to the "four corners" rule sometimes refuse to apply such exception when extrinsic evidence is sought to be used by an insurer to deny a defense that is otherwise owed under the four corners of the complaint. *Woo v. Fireman's Fund Ins. Co.*, 164 P.3d 454, 459 (Wash. 2007) ("The insurer may not rely on facts extrinsic to the complaint to deny the duty to defend—it may do so only to trigger the duty."); *see also Dairy Road Partners v. Island Ins. Co., Ltd.*, 992 P.2d 93, 113 (Haw. 2000) (noting a split of authority nationally on the permissibility of an insurer's use of extrinsic evidence to disclaim a duty to defend and concluding that the majority forbid it).

But even when courts permit an insurer to use extrinsic evidence to disclaim a defense, they sometimes do so narrowly—allowing consideration of extrinsic evidence solely in specific situations. For example, the Supreme Court of Hawaii held that an insurer may only disclaim a duty to defend based on extrinsic facts by showing that none of such facts relied upon might be resolved differently in the underlying lawsuit. *Dairy Road Partners*, 992 P.2d at 117 n. 17 ("One example of an extrinsic fact upon which an insurer might rely pursuant to the new rule arises when an insurer argues that an occurrence was outside of the effective period of the policy. In such a case, the factual issue regarding the parameters of the effective period of the policy would not normally be subject to dispute in the underlying action."); *see also Pompa v. Am. Family Mut. Ins. Co.*, 520 F.3d 1139, 1147 (10th Cir. 2008) (applying Colorado law) (predicting that the Supreme Court of Colorado would adopt an exception to the complaint rule, explaining that "[w]hen the extrinsic facts relied on by the insurer are relevant to the issue of coverage, but do not affect the third party's right of recovery, courts occasionally have held that the insurer may refuse to defend third-party actions, even though the allegations in the complaint suggest that coverage exists") (quotation and internal citation omitted).

Another example of extrinsic evidence being permissible to disclaim a defense, but narrowly so, is where a complaint pleads "negligence," but, despite such label, the conduct at issue was unquestionably intentional. *Peerless Ins. Co. v. Viegas*, 667 A.2d 785, 788–89 (R.I. 1995) (holding that, notwithstanding that the duty to defend is determined by the "pleadings test," an insurer was not obligated to defend an insured that sexually abused a minor, even if the allegations in the complaint were described in terms of negligence).

Some courts may also permit the consideration of extrinsic evidence, as a basis to disclaim a defense obligation, when such evidence addresses a threshold issue concerning coverage under the policy. *Nateman v. Hartford Cas. Ins. Co.*, 544 So. 2d 1026, 1027 (Fla. App. Ct. 1989) ("While, as a general rule, the obligation to defend an insured against an action, whether groundless or not, must be measured and determined by the allegations of the petition rather than the outcome of the litigation, an obvious exception must be made in those instances where, notwithstanding allegations in the petition to the contrary, the insurer successfully urges the alleged insured is not in fact an insured under the policy.").

While the use of extrinsic evidence to disclaim a defense is oftentimes, at most, permitted solely in narrow circumstances, courts often speak in broad terms when addressing the allowance of extrinsic evidence to establish an insurer's defense obligation. However, such pronouncements are sometimes general and lacking in guidance. *Talen*, 703 N.W.2d at 406 (Iowa 2005) ("The scope of inquiry [for the duty to defend] … [includes] the pleadings of the injured party and any other admissible and relevant facts in the record.") (citations and internal quotation omitted); *Am. Bumper & Mfg. Co. v. Hartford Fire Ins. Co.*, 550 N.W.2d 475, 481 (Mich. 1996) ("The insurer has the duty to look behind the third party's allegations to analyze whether coverage is possible."); *Garvis v. Employers Mut. Cas. Co.*, 497 N.W.2d 254, 258 (Minn. 1993) (stating that the determination of the duty to defend includes consideration of facts of which the insurer is "aware"); *Farmland Mut. Ins. Co. v. Scruggs*, 886 So. 2d 714, 719 n.2 (Miss. 2004) (holding that, in determining whether an insurer has a duty to defend, an insurer may consider those "true facts [that] are inconsistent with the complaint," the insured brought to the insurer's attention);

Peterson v. Ohio Cas. Group, 724 N.W.2d 765, 773–74 (Neb. 2006) (finding that a duty to defend exists where the "actual facts" reveal such a duty exists); *Am. Gen. Fire & Cas. Co. v. Progressive Cas. Co.*, 799 P.2d 1113, 1116 (N.M. 1990) ("The duty of an insurer to defend arises from the allegations on the face of the complaint or from the known but unpleaded factual basis of the claim."); *State Farm Fire & Cas. Co. v. Harbert*, 741 N.W.2d 228, 234 (S.D. 2007) ("[T]he issue of whether an insurer has a duty to defend is determined by … 'other evidence of record.'").

Courts also vary in the nature of the insurer's effort that is required to obtain extrinsic evidence that could trigger a defense obligation. *Scottsdale Ins. Co. v. MV Transp.*, 115 P.3d 460, 466 (Cal. 2005) ("[T]hat the precise causes of action pled by the third party complaint may fall outside policy coverage does not excuse the duty to defend where, under the facts alleged, reasonably inferable, or otherwise known, the complaint could fairly be amended to state a covered liability."); *Colonial Oil Indus. v. Underwriters Subscribing to Policy Nos. TO31504670 & TO31504671*, 491 S.E.2d 337, 338–39 (Ga. 1997) ("The insurer is under no obligation to independently investigate the claims against its insured … A different rule, however, applies when the complaint on its face shows no coverage, but the insured notifies the insurer of factual contentions that would place the claim within the policy coverage."); *Garvis*, 497 N.W.2d at 258 ("[I]f the insurer is aware of facts indicating that there may be a claim, either from what is said directly or inferentially in the complaint, or if the insured tells the insurer of such facts, or if the insurer has some independent knowledge of such facts, then the insurer must either accept tender of the defense or further investigate the potential claim."); *Revelation Indus., Inc. v. St. Paul Fire & Marine Ins. Co.*, 206 P.3d 919, 926 (Mont. 2009) (holding that insurers are not required to "look at facts beyond the allegations in the complaint" and that those that do, "do so at their own risk as they will be required to defend and/or indemnify based on the information discovered"); *Waste Mgmt. of Carolinas, Inc. v. Peerless Ins. Co.*, 340 S.E.2d 374, 377–78 (N.C. 1986) (finding that an insurer's investigation includes investigation into any facts it "knows or could reasonably ascertain"); *First Bank of Turley v. Fid. & Deposit Ins. Co.*, 928 P.2d 298, 303 (Okla. 1996) ("The insurer's defense duty is determined on the basis of information gleaned from the petition (and other pleadings), from the insured and from other sources available to the insurer at the time the defense is demanded.").

As these decisions demonstrate, whether an insurer is in the "four corners" or "extrinsic evidence" camp is only the first duty to defend question—and the easiest one. Where the complexity arises is when it comes to extrinsic evidence states and determining the nature of such evidence to be considered by the insurer, as well as the manner in which such evidence is obtained by the insurer. These are oftentimes extremely fact-intensive determinations with case law providing guidance but not a definitive answer.

50-State Survey: Duty to Defend Standard: "Four Corners" or Extrinsic Evidence?

Alabama: The Supreme Court of Alabama held that the determination of the duty to defend is not limited to the allegations in the complaint. *Hartford Cas. Ins. Co. v. Merchs. & Farmers Bank*, 928 So. 2d 1006, 1009–10 (Ala. 2005) ("Whether an insurance company owes its insured a duty to provide a defense in proceedings instituted against the insured is determined primarily by the allegations contained in the complaint. If the allegations of the injured party's complaint show an accident or an occurrence within the coverage of the policy, then the insurer is obligated to defend, regardless of the ultimate liability of the insured. However, this Court has rejected the argument that the insurer's obligation to defend must be determined solely from the facts alleged in the complaint in the action against the insured.") (citations and internal quotation omitted). "[I]f there is any uncertainty as to whether the complaint alleges facts that would invoke the duty to defend, the insurer must investigate the facts surrounding the incident that gave rise to the complaint in order to determine whether it has a duty to defend the insured." *Blackburn v. Fid. & Deposit Co. of Md.*, 667 So. 2d 661, 668 (Ala. 1995). *See also Pharmacists Mut. Ins. Co. v. Godbee Med. Distribs., Inc.*, 733 F. Supp. 2d 1281, 1285 (M.D. Ala. 2010) ("[T]he Alabama Supreme Court has never held that, even though the allegations of the complaint *do* allege a covered accident or occurrence, the courts may consider evidence outside the allegations to disestablish the duty to defend.") (citation and internal quotation omitted) (emphasis in original); *Am. Safety Indem. Co. v. T.H. Taylor, Inc.*, No. 2:10cv48, 2011 U.S. Dist. LEXIS 33267 (M.D. Ala. Mar. 29, 2011) ("[I]t is the allegations in the complaint, not the legal phraseology, that determine whether an insurer has a duty to defend its insured in the action. Indeed, if the allegations are irreconcilable with a legal theory ... asserted in the complaint, the allegations, not the mere assertion of the legal theory, determine an insurer's duty to defend.") (citations and internal quotes omitted); *Cool Temp, Inc. v. Pa. Nat'l Mut. Cas. Ins. Co.*, 148 So. 3d 448 (Ala. Ct. Civ. App. 2013) ("Because Pilkerton's allegations against Cool Temp in his complaint in the underlying suit were not covered under the policy and because there is no evidentiary support for Pilkerton's initial contention that his injuries were not related to his employment with Cool Temp, PNMCIC had no duty to investigate further. We hold that the trial court properly concluded that PNMCIC had no obligation under the policy to provide Cool Temp with a defense to Pilkerton's tort and contract claims[.]"); *Mid-Continent Cas. Co. v. Advantage Med. Elecs, LLC*, 196 So. 3d 238 (Ala. 2015) (extensively quoting *Merchs. & Farmers Bank*); *Owners Ins. Co. v. GTR, Inc.*, 461 F. Supp. 3d 1190 (M.D. Ala. 2020) (addressing duty to defend by examining various sources of extrinsic evidence to determine if "bodily injury" or "property damage" took place during the policy period); *Elite Refreshment Servs. LLC v. Liberty Mut. Grp., Inc.*, No. 19-00425, 2020 U.S. Dist. LEXIS 14627 (N.D. Ala. 2020) ("The Court does not have to look beyond the allegations of the underlying complaint in this instance because in its complaint in this action, Elite Refreshment has not alleged facts that could be proved by admissible evidence to establish a post-January 31, 2017 employment practice that would trigger coverage.").

Alaska: The Supreme Court of Alaska held that the determination of the duty to defend is not limited to the allegations in the complaint. *Great Divide Ins. Co. v. Carpenter*, 79 P.3d 599, 616 (Alaska 2003) ("The allegations of the complaint provide the initial guide to whether an insurance company has a duty to defend. The duty to defend arises if the complaint on its face alleges facts which, standing alone, give rise to a possible finding of liability covered by the policy. If the complaint does not contain allegations indicating coverage, there is nonetheless a duty to defend if facts underlying the complaint are within, or potentially within, the policy coverage and are known or reasonably ascertainable by the insurer.") (citations and internal quotation omitted). Extrinsic evidence may not be resorted to by an insurer to disclaim a defense that is otherwise owed based on the complaint. *Afcan v. Mut. Fire, Marine & Inland Ins. Co.*, 595 P.2d 638, 645 (Alaska 1979) ("[E]ven though facts extrinsic to the pleadings may show that there will be no ultimate liability under the policy, if the complaint on its face alleges facts which, standing alone, give rise to a possible finding of liability covered by the policy, the insured has the contractual right to a proper defense at the expense of the insurer."). *See also Makarka ex rel. Makarka v. Great Am. Ins. Co.*, 14 P.3d 964, 970 (Alaska 2000) ("[W]here coverage turns solely on the interpretation of policy language that has never been reviewed by this court, that fact alone is not enough to create a possibility of coverage that required a defense. Given the level of scrutiny directed at an insurer's decision not to provide coverage, insurers who accurately interpret their policies and give their insureds timely notice of the reason why there is no coverage are not required to provide a defense merely because we have yet to interpret that particular policy language."); *Williams v. GEICO Cas. Co.*, 301 P.3d 1220 (Alaska 2013) ("Generally, an insurer's duty is determined by the policy, which is interpreted according to the parties' reasonable expectations in light of the language of the policy as a whole, as well as extrinsic evidence and applicable case law. An insurer's duty to defend exists where vagaries of law and fact are sufficient to create the potential that an insured will incur covered liability."); *State Farm Fire & Cas. Co. v. Millman*, 413 F. Supp. 3d 940 (D. Alaska 2109) (while courts can consider extrinsic evidence, it made no difference because the complaint allegations "mirror the undisputed" facts at issue).

Arizona: The Court of Appeals of Arizona held that the determination of the duty to defend is not limited to the allegations in the complaint. *U.S. Fid. & Guar. Corp. v. Advance Roofing & Supply Co., Inc.*, 788 P.2d 1227, 1231 (Ariz. Ct. App. 1989) (quoting *Kepner v. W. Fire Ins. Co.*, 509 P.2d 222, 224 (Ariz. 1973)) ("[T]he duty to defend should focus on the facts rather than solely upon the allegations of the complaint, and that there was no duty to defend where the alleged facts ostensibly bring the case within the policy coverage but other facts which are not reflected in the complaint plainly take the case outside the policy coverage.") (citation and internal quotation omitted); *see also Lennar Corp. v. Auto-Owners Ins. Co.*, 151 P.3d 538, 547 (Ariz. Ct. App. 2007) ("Even assuming the complaint did not otherwise identify any specific subcontractor as negligent sufficient to create in its insurer an obligation to defend Lennar as an additional insured, according to Arizona law, once an insured makes some factual showing that the suit is actually one for damages resulting from events that fall under policy terms, an insurer has a duty to investigate those facts and provide a defense when indicated."); *City of Glendale v. National Union Fire Ins. Co.*, No. 12–380, 2013 U.S. Dist. LEXIS 45468 (D. Ariz. Mar. 29, 2013) ("The Ninth Circuit has held that the allegations of a complaint, considered along with a follow-up letter containing additional information about the dispute, were collectively sufficient to trigger an insurer's duty to defend under Arizona law. *Tri–Star Theme Builders, Inc. v. OneBeacon Ins. Co.*, 426 Fed. Appx. 506, 514 (9th Cir.2011)."); *Inscription Canyon Ranch Sanitary Dist. v. American Alternative Ins. Corp.*, No. 12–8019, 2013 U.S. Dist. LEXIS 131986 (D. Ariz. Sept. 16, 2013) (distinguishing *City of Glendale*) ("In that case, the underlying plaintiffs' notice of claim letter referenced the original complaint and specifically asserted that the plaintiffs had an additional claim for monetary damages as part of that same complaint. Then, the underlying plaintiffs filed an amended complaint adding those monetary damage claims. This is quite unlike the case here, where the underlying plaintiffs in the first suit asserted in their notice of claim letter only that one of the underlying plaintiffs threatened to bring a separate, additional lawsuit asserting monetary damages."); *Quihuis v. State Farm Mut. Auto. Ins. Co.*, 334 P.3d 719 (Ariz. 2014) ("Unlike in some states, in Arizona 'there is no absolute duty to defend,' especially when 'the alleged facts [in the complaint] ostensibly bring the case within the policy coverage but other facts which are not reflected in the complaint plainly take the case outside the policy coverage.'") (quoting *Kepner*); *Safety Dynamics, Inc. v. General Star Indemnity Co.*, No. 09-00695, 2015 U.S. Dist. LEXIS 177744 (D. Ariz. Feb. 6, 2015) ("Arizona imposes no duty to investigate facts outside the complaint except when the insured has come forward and made some factual showing that the suit is actually one for damages resulting from events which do fall into policy terms."); *Labertew v. Chartis Prop. Cas. Co.*, 363 F. Supp. 3d 1031 (D. Ariz. 2019) ("Under *Kepner*, when the allegations of a complaint suggest that a claim is covered, an insurer nonetheless may investigate the claim and determine, on the basis of facts outside the complaint, that there is no coverage. But when the claims stated in the complaint would not be covered, *Kepner* does not require the insurer to make such an investigation.") ("The Court concludes that Defendant properly considered the facts alleged in the complaint and determined there was no coverage. . . .Additional investigation was not required to deny coverage.").

Arkansas: The Supreme Court of Arkansas held that the determination of the duty to defend is not limited to the allegations in the complaint. *Commercial Union Ins. Co. of Am. v. Henshall*, 553 S.W.2d 274, 276 (Ark. 1977) ("[T]here may be situations where the insurance company's duty to defend cannot be determined simply from the allegations of the complaint. This is such a case. The insurance company may not close its eyes to facts it knew or should have known, because they were easily ascertainable. Information from the insured and a simple inspection of the property would have disclosed facts which would have raised questions."); *see also Watkins v. Southern Farm Bureau Cas. Ins. Co.*, 386 S.W.3d 6 (Ark. Ct. App. 2011) (citing *Henshall* and providing as an example of the permissible use of extrinsic evidence claims involving self-defense, in response to allegations of assault and battery, because plaintiffs cannot be expected to allege that they were assaulted by the insured while the insured was protecting life or property); *Silverball Amusement, Inc. v. Utah Home Fire Ins. Co.*, 842 F. Supp. 1151, 1156–57 (W.D. Ark. 1994) (recognizing that "[t]here are exceptions to the general rule that the complaint determines the duty to defend" and outlining a few of the "myriad cases on [the] subject"); *Kolbek v. Truck Ins. Exchange*, 431 S.W.3d 900 (Ark. 2014) ("Appellants also collectively argue that the circuit court erred in granting summary judgment because it improperly considered evidence outside the pleadings. Generally, insurers are not allowed to refuse to defend on the grounds that they are in possession of information establishing that the allegations in the complaint giving rise to coverage are untrue. (citation omitted). The evidence cited by [the insurer] in support of its summary-judgment motion did not provide facts to disprove the merits of the allegations; rather, they helped illustrate what the allegations lacked in order to assert injury or damages that would fall within policy coverage and how certain facts were not in dispute.").

California: The Supreme Court of California held that the determination of the duty to defend is not limited to the allegations in the complaint. *Scottsdale Ins. Co. v. MV Transp.*, 115 P.3d 460, 466 (Cal. 2005) ("Determination of the duty to defend depends, in the first instance, on a comparison between the allegations of the complaint and the terms of the policy. But the duty also exists where extrinsic facts known to the insurer suggest that the claim may be covered. Moreover, that the precise causes of action pled by the third party complaint may fall outside policy coverage does not excuse the duty to defend where, under the facts alleged, reasonably inferable, or otherwise known, the complaint could fairly be amended to state a covered liability."); *see also Golden Eagle Ins. Corp. v. Cen-Fed, Ltd.*, 56 Cal. Rptr. 3d 279, 284 (2007) ("If any facts stated or fairly inferable in the complaint, or otherwise known or discovered by the insurer, suggest a claim potentially covered by the policy, the insurer's duty to defend arises and is not extinguished until the insurer negates all facts suggesting potential coverage. On the other hand, if, as a matter of law, neither the complaint nor the known extrinsic facts indicate any basis for potential coverage, the duty to defend does not arise in the first instance."); *Ameron Intern. Corp. v. Ins. Co. of State of Pa.*, 242 P.3d 1020, 1028 (Cal. 2010) ("It is a settled rule that the insurer must look to the facts of the complaint and extrinsic evidence, if available, to determine whether there is a potential for coverage under the policy and a corresponding duty to defend.") (citation and internal quotes omitted); *Hartford Cas. Ins. Co. v. Swift Distribution, Inc.*, 326 P.3d 253 (Cal. 2014) ("Determination of the duty to defend depends, in the first instance, on a comparison between the allegations of the complaint and the terms of the policy. But the duty also exists where extrinsic facts known to the insurer suggest that the claim may be covered. This includes all facts, both disputed and undisputed, that the insurer knows or becomes aware of from any source if not at the inception of the third party lawsuit, then at the time of tender. Moreover, that the precise causes of action pled by the third party complaint may fall outside policy coverage does not excuse the duty to defend where, under the facts alleged, reasonably inferable, or otherwise known, the complaint could fairly be amended to state a covered liability. Thus, if any facts stated or fairly inferable in the complaint, or otherwise known or discovered by the insurer, suggest a claim potentially covered by the policy, the insurer's duty to defend arises and is not extinguished until the insurer negates all facts suggesting potential coverage.") (citations and internal quotes omitted); *Albert v. Mid-Century Ins. Co.*, 236 Cal. App. 4th 1281 (2015) ("Initially, the court compares the allegations of the complaint with the terms of the policy. The proper focus is on the facts alleged in the complaint, rather than the alleged theories for recovery. Nevertheless, the insured may not speculate about unpled third party claims to manufacture coverage and the insurer has no duty to defend where the potential for liability is tenuous and farfetched. The ultimate question is whether the facts alleged 'fairly apprise' the insurer that the suit is upon a covered claim."). (citations and internal quotation marks omitted).

However, Under California law, extrinsic evidence can also be used by an insurer to defeat a defense obligation: "The important issue to which [*Montrose Chemical Corp. v. Superior Court*, 861 P.2d 1153 (Cal. 1993)] then turned was the split of authority among several Courts of Appeal as to whether facts known to the insurer could, in spite of the allegations of the complaint in the underlying action, be used to *defeat* an insurer's duty to defend as well as to establish it. The Supreme Court endorsed the view set out in *State Farm Mut. Auto. Ins. Co.* v. *Flynt* (1971) 17 Cal. App. 3d 538, 548 [95 Cal. Rptr. 296], that an insurer could rely on facts known to it, which were extraneous to the allegations in the complaint, to defeat its duty to provide a defense. However, it required that such facts be *undisputed* and that they *conclusively* demonstrate that there was no *potential* for coverage. The court stated (quoting from the opinion of the Court of Appeal's decision in [*Montrose*]), 'neither logic, common sense, nor fair play supports a rule allowing only the insured to rely on extrinsic facts to determine the potential for coverage. It would be pointless, for example, to require an insurer to defend an action where undisputed facts developed early in the investigation conclusively showed, despite a contrary allegation in the complaint, that the underlying acts occurred on a date when the policy was not in effect or at a location concededly not covered by the policy.'" *Haskel, Inc. v. Superior Court*, 33 Cal. App. 4th 963 (1995) (emphasis in original). *See also Associated Indem. Corp. v. Argonaut Ins. Co.*, No. B254858, 2015 Cal. App. Unpub. LEXIS 4762

(Cal. Ct. App. July 7, 2015) ("Facts extrinsic to the complaint may also give rise to a duty to defend when they reveal a potential for coverage. Conversely, extrinsic facts may defeat the duty to defend when they conclusively negate the potential for coverage."); *Saarman Constr., Ltd. v. Ironshore Specialty Ins. Co.*, No. 15-03548, 2017 U.S. Dist. LEXIS 13633 (N.D. Calif. Jan. 31, 2017) ("To determine whether there was potential coverage, and thus a duty to defend, courts generally compare the allegations in the underlying complaint with the terms of the insurance policy. *See Montrose Chem. Corp. v. Superior Court*, 6 Cal. 4th 287, 295, 24 Cal. Rptr. 2d 467, 861 P.2d 1153 (1993). However, 'facts extrinsic to the complaint also give rise to a duty to defend when they reveal a possibility that the claim may be covered by the policy.' *Id.* By the same token, extrinsic evidence may defeat the duty to defend if 'such evidence presents undisputed facts which conclusively eliminate a potential for liability.'"); *Komin v. Travelers Prop. Cas. Ins. Co.*, No. F075381, 2019 Cal. App. Unpub. LEXIS 5713 (Cal. Ct. App. Aug. 27, 2019) (upholding insurer's use of extrinsic evidence to disclaim a duty to defend and rejecting insured's use of extrinsic evidence to trigger a defense obligation) (addressing whether assault and battery was an "occurrence"); *Berry v. State Farm Gen. Ins. Co.*, No. G055740, 2019 Cal. App. Unpub. LEXIS 4852 (Cal. Ct. App. July 22, 2019); ("Based upon this record, while it is true the arbitration complaint only pleaded failure to disclose claims, we liberally construe Ennen's testimony, and find a triable issue of material fact exists as to whether State Farm had knowledge of extrinsic evidence that created a bare potential of coverage which triggered a duty to defend the Berrys in the arbitration. State Farm's argument that the Policy's 'intentional conduct' exclusion entitled it to summary judgment fails.").

Colorado: Colorado has adopted several rules related to the determination of the duty to defend. "[I]f the insurer wishes to avoid the cost of a defense before the underlying litigation has concluded—either by simply refusing to defend or by bringing a declaratory judgment action while the litigation is proceeding—its duty to defend is determined under the complaint rule." *Pompa v. Am. Family Mut. Ins. Co.*, 520 F.3d 1139, 1146 (10th Cir. 2008) (applying Colorado law and citing *Cotter Corp. v. Am. Empire Surplus Lines Ins. Co.*, 90 P.3d 814, 828–29 (Colo. 2004)). However, the Tenth Circuit Court of Appeals in *Pompa* predicted that the Colorado Supreme Court would adopt an exception to the complaint rule, explaining that "[w]hen the extrinsic facts relied on by the insurer are relevant to the issue of coverage, but do not affect the third party's right of recovery, courts occasionally have held that the insurer may refuse to defend third-party actions, even though the allegations in the complaint suggest that coverage exists." *Id.* at 1147 (quotation and internal citation omitted). Lastly, if an insurer believes that it has no obligation to defend its insured, it may defend but reserve its rights to seek reimbursement should the facts at trial prove that the incident resulting in liability was not covered by the policy, or file a declaratory judgment action after the underlying case has been adjudicated. *Cotter*, 90 P. 3d at 827 (discussing *Hecla Mining v. N.H. Ins. Co.*, 811 P.2d 1083, 1089 (Colo. 1991)). Under these circumstances, the insurer may rely on facts outside of the complaint to determine whether it can recover its defense costs from the insured. *Id.* The Colorado Supreme Court was creating an incentive for insurers to defend by allowing them to subsequently seek reimbursement. *Id.* at 818; *see also Apartment Investment and Management Co. v. Nutmeg Ins. Co.*, 593 F.3d 1188, 1196 (10th Cir. 2010) (applying Colorado law) (discussing *Cotter*, *Hecla*, and *Pompa* and concluding that, for purposes of making a duty to defend determination, "an insurer cannot view the allegations contained in a single complaint in isolation when it is aware multiple complaints arising from a common core of operative facts have been filed against the insured."); *United Fire & Cas. Co. v. Boulder Plaza Residential, LLC*, 633 F.3d 951, 961 (10th Cir. 2011) (applying Colorado law) (declining to adopt an exception to the complaint rule "to include consideration of extrinsic evidence not necessarily contained in another complaint, as long as the insurer had knowledge of such evidence when it denied coverage") ("Neither the Colorado Supreme Court nor Colorado's lower courts has thus far recognized any exceptions to [the complaint] rule, nor has either ratified the two exceptions recognized by this Court in *Pompa* and [*Nutmeg*]. We are therefore wary of embracing a third, much broader exception to the plain language of Colorado's complaint rule absent clear authority from Colorado's highest court."); *Dish Network Corporation v. Arch Specialty Insurance Company*, 989 F. Supp. 2d 1137 (D. Colo. 2013) (noting that the *Pompa* court's prediction of the Colorado Supreme Court's holding – that a court can consider extrinsic evidence where it is unrelated to the merits of the underlying litigation – was binding on it) (*aff'd* 772 F.3d 856 (10th Cir. 2014)); *Continental Western Ins. Co. v. Colony Ins. Co.*, 69 F. Supp. 3d 1075 (D. Colo. 2014) (finding that the *Nutmeg* exception also applies to claim forms produced in the Claim Resolution Process to determine an insurer's duty to defend) ("In the context of the bankruptcy proceeding's Claim Resolution Process, the proofs of claim forms lay out each claimant's allegation against Pepper and serve as the functional equivalent to the complaint in the underlying action."); *Auto-Owners Ins. Co. v. High Country Coatings, Inc.*, No. 16-03196, 2017 U.S. Dist. LEXIS 90127 (D. Colo. June 12, 2017) (finding that the exception to the complaint rule in *Pompa* did not apply because the extrinsic fact that the insurer argued defeated its duty to defend was vigorously contested); *Landmark Am. Ins. Co. v. VO Remarketing Corp.*, 619 Fed. Appx. 705 (10th Cir. 2015) ("[T]he fact of VO's automobile use is 'an indisputable fact that is not an element of either the cause of action or a defense in the underlying litigation,' falling clearly within the *Pompa* exception. . . . Thus, although the underlying complaint did not allege the use of an automobile, the *Pompa* exception permitted the district court to look outside the four corners of the complaint."); *Auto-Owners Ins. Co. v. High Country Coatings, Inc.*, No. 16-03196, 2017 U.S. Dist. LEXIS 90127 (D. Colo. June 12, 2017) (concluding that the "*Pompa* exception" did not apply because, "by contrast, the 'extrinsic' fact that AOIC argues defeats its duty to defend—i.e., that HCC had prior knowledge of the damage at the project site before inception of its policy with AOIC—is vigorously contested by HCC"); *Am. Builders Ins. Co. v. Probuilders Specialty Ins. Co.*, No. 16-1832, 2017 U.S. Dist. LEXIS 218752 (D. Colo. June 30, 2017) (noting that, in *Cotter*, the Supreme Court left open the question whether allegations framed to trigger an insurance policy create a duty to defend); *Owners Ins. Co. v. Tipton*, No. 15-02638, 2017 U.S. Dist. LEXIS 231555 (D. Colo. Mar. 28, 2017) (under *Pompa*, allowing consideration of information in a letter, explicitly mentioned in the complaint, to trigger duty to defend); *Hecht v. Great N. Ins. Co.*, No. 17-02364, 2018 U.S. Dist. LEXIS 233191 (D. Colo. April 18, 2018); ("While both cases [*Pompa* and *Nutmeg*] address the propriety of an insurer's consideration of documents outside of the underlying complaint, Plaintiff's argument in this instance is a bridge too far; neither case contemplates an insurance company's review of the insured's answer or affirmative defenses asserted therein."); *Chavez v. Ariz. Auto. Ins. Co.*, 947 F.3d 642 (10th Cir. 2020) ("Chavez suggests that *Pompa* recognizes an actual knowledge exception to the complaint rule by which an insurer with actual knowledge of any claim not stated in a complaint must still provide a defense based on that extrinsic claim. But *Pompa* does not recognize such a broad exception to the complaint rule, and we doubt that the Colorado courts would do so."); *HT Servs., LLC v. Western Heritage Ins. Co.*, No. 19-02174, 2020 U.S. Dist. LEXIS 123661 (D. Colo. July 10, 2020) (court can consider extrinsic evidence, to determine under which policy a defense may be owed, where complaint is devoid of dates of negligent conduct or property damage).

Connecticut: The Supreme Court of Connecticut held that the determination of the duty to defend is not limited to the allegations in the complaint. *Hartford Cas. Ins. Co. v. Litchfield Mut. Fire Ins. Co.*, 876 A.2d 1139, 1144 (Conn. 2005)

("[I]t is well established … that a liability insurer has a duty to defend its insured in a pending lawsuit if the pleadings allege a covered occurrence, even though facts outside the four corners of those pleadings indicate that the claim may be meritless or not covered.") (citation and internal quotation omitted). "[I]t is irrelevant that the insurer may get information from the insured, or from anyone else, which indicates, or even demonstrates, that the injury is not in fact covered." *Id.* On the other hand, when it comes to the use of extrinsic evidence to establish the duty to defend, the Connecticut high court chose to follow New York's rule that " 'the sounder approach is to require the insurer to provide a defense when it has actual knowledge of facts establishing a reasonable possibility of coverage.'" *Id.* at 1146 (quoting *Fitzpatrick v. Am. Honda Motor Co., Inc.*, 575 N.E.2d 90, 93 (N.Y. 1991)); *see also Capstone Bldg. Corp. v. American Motorists Ins. Co.*, 67 A.3d 961 (Conn. 2013) (reiterating *Litchfield*'s rule that an insurer has a duty to defend even though facts outside the four corners of the complaint indicate that the claim may not be covered); *Travelers Cas. and Sur. Co. of America v. Netherlands Ins. Co.*, 95 A.3d 1031 (Conn. 2014) ("[A] liability insurer has a duty to defend its insured in a pending lawsuit if the pleadings allege a covered occurrence, even though facts outside the four corners of those pleadings indicate that the claim may be meritless or not covered.") (suggesting in a footnote that a court can go beyond the complaint to establish whether a person sued was actually an insured under the policy at issue); *New London County Mutual Ins. Co. v. Sielski*, 123 A.3d 925 (Conn. Ct. App. 2015) ("Although there are circumstances where facts beyond those alleged in the underlying complaint and which are known to the insurer can require the insurer to provide a defense, an insurer cannot rely on extrinsic facts to refuse to provide a defense."); *R.T. Vanderbilt Co. v. Hartford Accident & Indem. Co.*, 156 A.3d 539 (Conn. Ct. App. 2017) ("[W]e have recognized the necessary limits of this [duty to defend] rule, as we will not predicate the duty to defend on a reading of the complaint that is conceivable but tortured and unreasonable. Thus, although an insurer is not excused from its duty to defend merely because the underlying complaint does not specify the connection between the stated cause of action and the policy coverage[,] the insurer has a duty to defend only if the underlying complaint reasonably alleges an injury that is covered by the policy.") (internal quotes and ellipses omitted) (*aff'd* 216 A.3d 629 (Conn. 2019) but not addressing duty to defend); *Rodrigue v. Patrons Mut. Ins. Co.*, No. HHDCV176080235S, 2018 Conn. Super. LEXIS 5874 (Conn. Super. Ct. Dec. 28, 2018) (although "the court is instructed to take into consideration extrinsic evidence which tends to demonstrate a duty to defend exists," the evidence presented did not trigger a defense).

Delaware: The Supreme Court of Delaware held that the determination of the duty to defend is limited to the allegations in the complaint. *Pac. Ins. Co. v. Liberty Mut. Ins. Co.*, 956 A.2d 1246, 1254–55 (Del. 2008) ("In construing an insurer's duty to indemnify and/or defend a claim asserted against its insured, a court typically looks to the allegations of the complaint to decide whether the third party's action against the insured states a claim covered by the policy, thereby triggering the duty to defend. The test is whether the underlying complaint, read as a whole, alleges a risk within the coverage of the policy. Determining whether an insurer is bound to defend an action against its insured requires adherence to the following principles: (1) where there is some doubt as to whether the complaint against the insured alleges a risk insured against, that doubt should be resolved in favor of the insured; (2) any ambiguity in the pleadings should be resolved against the carrier; and (3) if even one count or theory alleged in the complaint lies within the policy coverage, the duty to defend arises.") (citations and internal quotation omitted). *See also CNH America, LLC v. American Casualty Company of Reading, PA.*, No. N12C–07–108, 2014 Del. Super. LEXIS 31 (Del. Super. Ct. Jan. 6, 2014) (quoting *Pacific Ins*). *But see Blue Hen Mech., Inc. v. Atl. States Ins. Co.*, No. N10C–04–078, 2011 Del. Super. LEXIS 176 (Del. Super. Ct. April 21, 2011), *affirmed* 29 A.3d 245 (Del. Supr. 2011) ("The complaint must allege some grounds for liability on the part of the insured, based upon a risk covered by the policy, for the duty to defend to arise. The Court is not bound by the narrow language in a complaint filed against an insured. The Court may review the complaint as a whole, considering all reasonable inferences that may be drawn from the alleged facts. An examination of the complaint is not limited to the plaintiff's unilateral characterization of the nature of the claims.") (citing no authority for a "reasonable inferences" standard for determining duty to defend); *Liberty Ins. Corp. v. Korn*, 210 F. Supp. 3d 612 (D. Del. 2016) (observing that the Delaware Supreme Court has adopted the "four corners" rule for purposes of determining an insurer's duty to defend, but adding that "while the four-corners guideline encourages definition of the parties' roles and responsibilities as early and efficiently as possible, it does not restrict a court from referring to the record when doing so would be *useful to its analysis*") (emphasis added); *Zurich Am. Ins. Co. v. Syngenta Crop Prot., LLC*, No. N19C-05-108, 2020 Del. Super. LEXIS 2867 (Del. Super. Ct. Aug. 3, 2020 ("The Court may review the complaint as a whole, considering all reasonable inferences that may be drawn from the alleged facts. An examination of the complaint is not limited to the plaintiff's unilateral characterization of the nature of the claims.") (citing *Blue Hen Mech.* and *United Westlabs, Inc. v. Greenwich Ins. Co.*, No. 09C-12-048, 2011 Del. Super. LEXIS 261 (Del. Super. Ct. June 13, 2011)).

District of Columbia: A District of Columbia District Court held that, to determine whether an insurer has a duty to defend, the court applies the "eight corners" rule, which considers only the four corners of the complaint to determine the scope of the allegations and the four corners of the policy to determine the scope of coverage. *Essex Ins. v. Café DuPont*, 674 F. Supp. 2d 166, 170 (D.D.C. 2009). In *Stevens v. United General Title Ins. Co.*, 801 A.2d 61, 71 (D.C. Cir. 2002), the District of Columbia Court of Appeals considered the adoption of a "factual exception" to the "eight corners" rule—following a close study of the New York Court of Appeals's decision in *Fitzpatrick* (discussed *supra*)—but concluded that it was a matter better considered by an en banc panel. "The fact that there was information in the public records (specifically the deed of trust which secured the promissory note held by Mr. Moy and his wife) which, with additional investigation, would have enabled United General to reconstruct details about Mr. Stevens' acquisition of the Third Street property is irrelevant to the application of an unmodified 'eight corners' rule. In short, under the application of the traditional 'eight corners' rule, Mr. Stevens cannot prevail on his assertion that United General had a duty to defend him against the 1438 E Street lawsuit." *Id.* at 70. *See also Navigators Ins. Co. v. Baylor & Jackson, PLLC*, 888 F. Supp. 2d 55 (D.D.C. 2012) ("When evaluating an insurer's obligation to cover a claim, D.C. courts apply what is known as 'the eight-corners' rule. Using this method, courts simply compare the scope of coverage in 'the four corners of the relevant policy' with the scope of the allegations in 'the four corners of the complaint.' As the D.C. Court of Appeals has explained, any facts outside of these documents 'are irrelevant.'") (citations omitted); *Fogg v. Fidelity Nat. Title Ins. Co.*, 89 A.3d 510 (D.C. Cir. 2014) (citing *Stevens* with approval) ("The obligation to defend is not affected by facts ascertained before suit, or developed in the process of litigation, or by the ultimate outcome of the suit."); *Burk & Reedy, LLP v. Am. Guar. & Liab. Ins. Co.*, 89 F. Supp. 3d 1 (D.D.C. 2015) (same); *Sec. Title Guar. Corp. v. 915 Decatur St. NW, LLC*, No. 18-11282019, U.S. Dist. LEXIS 213780 (D.D.C. 2019) ("Decatur repeatedly urges this Court to consider its arguments and evidence indicating that someone other than Decatur committed the alleged fraud. . . . In so doing, Decatur ignores the affirmation in *Stevens* and other cases of the District of Columbia's eight corners rule.").

Florida: The Supreme Court of Florida held that the determination of the duty to defend is limited to the allegations in the complaint. *Higgins v. State Farm Fire & Cas. Co.*, 894 So. 2d 5, 10 (Fla. 2004) ("[A]n insurer's obligation to defend is determined solely by the claimant's complaint if suit has been filed."). The *Higgins* Court also noted that, as a result of this, "there generally is no need for a declaratory action in respect to the insurer's obligation to defend." *Id.* However, the Florida high court also pointed out that an exception exists where the duty to defend is based on factual issues that would not normally be alleged in the underlying complaint, such as late notice. *Id.* at 10 n.2; *see also Transcon. Ins. Co. v. Jim Black & Assocs., Inc.*, 888 So. 2d 671, 675 (Fla. Dist. Ct. App. 2004) ("[A]n insurer's duty to defend a complaint depends solely on the allegations in the complaint filed by a third party against the insured. Even under the more liberal federal pleading requirements, a third-party plaintiff's claims against an insured should be sufficiently described to allow a determination of whether a duty to defend arises under the allegations of the complaint.") (citations and internal quotation omitted); *Essex Ins. Co. v. Big Top of Tampa, Inc.*, 53 So. 3d 1220, 1224 (Fla. Dist. Ct. App. 2011) ("We recognize that the supreme court has held that factual determinations may be made in a declaratory judgment action where it is necessary to resolve issues of fact in order to determine whether coverage exists under an insurance policy. *See Higgins*, 894 So. 2d at 9, 15. But here, there were no factual issues to determine because O'Fell's complaint clearly alleged that a battery occurred."); *Composite Structures, Inc. v. Continental Ins. Co.*, 560 Fed. App'x 861 (11th Cir. 2014) ("Under Florida law, Continental was permitted to consider the uncontroverted date of written notice when determining its duty to defend because the date of written notice to the insurance company is not a fact that would normally be alleged in the complaint.") (citing *Higgins*); *Diamond State Ins. Co. v. Boys' Home Association*, 172 F. Supp. 3d 1326 (M.D. Fla. 2016) ("Florida law does recognize some circumstances where a court may consider evidence extrinsic to the underlying complaint when determining the duty to defend. For example, in *Higgins v. State Farm Fire & Cas. Co.*, 894 So. 2d 5 (Fla. 2005), the Florida Supreme Court identified 'some natural exceptions' to the principal that the obligation to defend is determined solely by the claimant's complaint where an insurer's claim that there is no duty to defend is based on factual issues that would not normally be alleged in the complaint. In addition, Florida District Courts of Appeal have considered facts outside the underlying complaint to find no duty to defend where the insurer presented uncontroverted evidence of a fact placing a claim outside of coverage. However, the Eleventh Circuit has cautioned that this departure from the general practice in Florida appears only in exceptional cases in which courts have crafted an equitable remedy when it is manifestly obvious to all involved that the actual facts placed the claims outside the scope of coverage. Thus, in special circumstances, a court may consider extrinsic facts if those facts are undisputed, and, had they been pled in the complaint, they clearly would have placed the claims outside the scope of coverage. It appears that application of a prior knowledge exclusion may constitute a circumstance where consideration of extrinsic evidence is appropriate. Indeed, one would not necessarily expect the State Complaint to disclose the facts relevant to whether Boys' Home had knowledge of its alleged wrongful conduct prior to its execution of the insurance application.") (citations and internal quotes omitted); *Evanston Ins. Co. v. Dimucci Dev. Corp. of Ponce Inlet, Inc.*, No. 15-486, 2016 U.S. Dist. LEXIS 123678 (M.D. Fla. Sept. 13, 2016) (citing the *Composite Structures* exception to the eight corners rule and concluding that the case before it was "not exceptional as the parties do not dispute the material facts but, rather, only the interpretation of such facts"); *Voeller Constr., Inc. v. Southern-Owners Ins. Co.*, No. 13-3169, 2014 U.S. Dist. LEXIS 61862 (M.D. Fla. May 5, 2014) (limiting the *Composite Structures* exception to eliminating a duty to defend) ("The cases discussing this specific exception involve uncontroverted facts outside of the allegations in the underlying complaint that refer to facts that take the case outside of the policy coverage, not those that bring the case within coverage."); *Advanced Sys., Inc. v. Gotham Ins. Co.*, 272 So. 3d 523 (Fla. Ct. App. 2019) (*Composite Structures* exception did not apply; explaining that the "extrinsic evidence was not uncontroverted or manifestly obvious to all so as to preclude coverage"); *Evanston Ins. Co. v. Via Entm't*, No. 19-562, 2020 U.S. Dist. LEXIS 189385 (M.D. Fla. Oct. 6, 2020) ("As explained in detail above, the record evidence—specifically the police reports and the surveillance video—is undisputed that the subject accident and injuries occurred on March 10, 2018, at approximately 12:50 a.m. This is exactly the type of uncontroverted evidence that places any claim related to the accident outside of coverage because the Evanston Policy expired on March 10, 2018, at 12:01 a.m. Evanston has no duty to defend Ward or the Via Entities in the Underlying Action because the Evanston Policy does not apply to 'bodily injury' if that 'bodily injury' did not occur during the policy period."); *Atl. Cas. Ins. Co v. Legacy Roofing of FL/Ahead Gen. Contrs. & Restoration, LLC*, No. 19-22043, 2020 U.S. Dist. LEXIS 133700 (S.D. Fla. July 27, 2020) ("[W]hen there is an inconsistency between the facts and the complaint's allegations, the allegations control in determining the insurers' duty to defend. And when extrinsic evidence is not uncontroverted or manifestly obvious to all so as to preclude coverage, it should not be considered in determining whether there is a duty to defend.").

Georgia: The Supreme Court of Georgia held that the determination of the duty to defend is not limited to the allegations in the complaint. *Colonial Oil Indus. v. Underwriters Subscribing to Policy Nos. TO31504670 & TO31504671*, 491 S.E.2d 337, 338–39 (Ga. 1997) ("The generally accepted view is that in making a determination of whether to provide a defense, an insurer is entitled to base its decision on the complaint and the facts presented by its insured. The insurer is under no obligation to independently investigate the claims against its insured … . A different rule, however, applies when the complaint on its face shows no coverage, but the insured notifies the insurer of factual contentions that would place the claim within the policy coverage … . [I]n this situation the insurer has an obligation to give due consideration to its insured's factual contentions and to base its decision on 'true facts.' The requirement that an insurer base its decision on true facts will necessitate that the insurer conduct a reasonable investigation into its insured's contentions."); *see also Lawyers Title Ins. Corp. v. Stribling*, 670 S.E.2d 154, 157 (Ga. Ct. App. 2008) ("Placing a duty of investigation on insurers in these limited circumstances is not an unreasonable burden, especially in light of the availability of the procedurally safe course of providing a defense under a reservation of rights and filing a declaratory judgment action to determine its obligations.") (citation and internal quotations omitted); *Allstate Ins. Co. v. Harkleroad*, No. 409CV011, 2010 U.S. Dist. LEXIS 51240 (S.D. Ga. May 24, 2010) (following *Colonial Oil*); *Travelers Property Cas. Co. of America v. Kansas City Landsmen, L.L.C.*, No. 11–4401, 2014 U.S. Dist. LEXIS 19435 (N.D. Ga. Feb. 18, 2014) (following *Colonial Oil*); *Evanston Ins. Co. v. Sandersville R.R. Co.*, No. 15-247, 2016 U.S. Dist. LEXIS 134162 (M.D. Ga. Sept. 29, 2016) ("*Colonial Oil* merely establishes that an insurance company has no duty to investigate whether there are true facts outside of the complaint that might bring the action *within* coverage. It did not upset Georgia's longstanding rule that mere discovery of true facts showing a claim to be outside of coverage does not destroy the insurer's duty to defend against a complaint that is pled such that it could fall within the insured's coverage. … In short, the rule in Georgia is that: it is only where the complaint sets forth true factual allegations showing no coverage that the suit is one for which liability insurance coverage is not afforded and for which the insurer need not provide a defense.") (emphasis in original); *Capitol Specialty Ins. Corp. v. PTAV, Inc.*, 331 F. Supp. 3d 1329 (N.D. Ga. 2018) ("[T]he evidence presented by the parties indicates that Nautilus was made aware of certain limited factual contentions beyond what Manes included in her complaint in the underlying action. . . . As a result, in addressing this Motion for Summary Judgment, the Court considers not only the allegations in Manes's Superior Court complaint but also the assertions contained in her pre-litigation correspondence to which Nautilus was privy."); *Nautilus Ins. Co. v. Flor*, 801 Fed. Appx. 703 (11th Cir. 2020) (following *Colonial Oil*).

Hawaii: The Supreme Court of Hawaii overruled prior decisions to the "extent that they imply that an insurer may rely upon extrinsic facts that may be subject to dispute in the underlying lawsuit as a basis for disclaiming its duty to defend where the complaint in the underlying lawsuit alleges facts within coverage. Instead, we adopt the majority rule to the contrary [insurer cannot rely upon extrinsic evidence for the purpose of disclaiming the duty to defend] along with its limited exception -- that the insurer may only disclaim its duty to defend by showing that none of the facts upon which it relies might be resolved differently in the underlying lawsuit." *Dairy Road Partners v. Island Ins. Co., Ltd.*, 992 P.2d 93, 117 (Hawaii 2000). "One example of an extrinsic fact upon which an insurer might rely pursuant to the new rule arises when an insurer argues that an occurrence was outside of the effective period of the policy. In such a case, the factual issue regarding the parameters of the effective period of the policy would not normally be subject to dispute in the underlying action." *Id.*, n.14. In *Nautilus Ins. Co. v. Lexington Ins. Co.*, 321 P.3d 634 (Hawaii 2014), the Supreme Court of Hawaii addressed *Dairy Road Partners* at length and held that "a primary insurer may not look to another insurance policy in disclaiming its duty to defend. If a primary insurer is tendered a defense, and believes that it is actually an excess insurer or otherwise has no duty to defend by operation of its 'other insurance' clause, then that primary insurer must still defend in the action. This is the appropriate remedy, rather than leaving the defense up to other insurers or, potentially up to the insured, where the insured has contracted for primary insurance coverage." The court further explained its decision: "The extrinsic evidence considered in *Dairy Road Partners* included factual matters relevant to the outcome of the underlying litigation. Here, in contrast, the question is whether an insurer may take into account the operation of its policy in conjunction with other insurance policies, to determine if it must defend a particular suit. Thus, the insurer would be looking at the construction and operation of other insurance policies in disclaiming a duty to defend, which presents some different considerations than the 'extrinsic evidence' that was at issue in *Dairy Road Partners.*" *See also Hart v. Ticor Title Ins. Co.*, 272 P.3d 1215 (Hawaii 2012) (addressing the use of extrinsic evidence, beyond the complaint, to find a duty to defend) ("The insurer must employ a good-faith analysis of all information known to the insured or all information reasonably ascertainable by inquiry and investigation to determine whether the possibility of coverage under a policy exists."); *Gemini Ins. Co. v. ConstRX Ltd.*, 360 F. Supp. 3d 1055 (D. Hawaii 2018) ("Hawaii abides by the 'complaint allegation rule,' whereby the determination of whether an insurer has a duty to defend focuses on the claims and facts that are alleged."); *AIG Prop. Cas. Co. v. Anenberg*, No. 19-00679, 2020 U.S. Dist. LEXIS 143485 (D. Hawaii 2020) (noting that Hawaii courts apply the "complaint allegation rule" but also stating: "[A]n insurer must look beyond the effect of the pleadings and must consider any facts brought to its attention or any facts which it could reasonably discover in determining whether it has a duty to defend. . . . The possibility of coverage must be determined by a good-faith analysis of all information known to the insured or all information reasonably ascertainable by inquiry and investigation.").

Idaho: The Supreme Court of Idaho held that the determination of the duty to defend is limited to the allegations in the complaint. *Hoyle v. Utica Mut. Ins. Co.*, 48 P.3d 1256, 1264 (Idaho 2002) ("Despite [notice pleading], it makes little sense to require an insurer to defend a lawsuit simply because a complaint, with no covered claims, could potentially be amended to include covered claims. If this were true, an insurer would be required to defend every lawsuit regardless of the allegations. The better rule is that if there is a subsequent change in the pleadings, a duty to defend may arise and the issue of the duty to indemnify would likewise come before the court again."); *see also Amco Ins. Co. v. Tri-Spur Inv. Co.*, 101 P.3d 226, 231 (Idaho 2004) (quoting *Hoyle*, 48 P.3d at 1264); *County of Boise v. Idaho Counties Risk Management Program, Underwriters*, 265 P.3d 514 (Idaho 2011) ("The insurer need only look at the words of the complaint to determine if a possibility of coverage exists."); *Nautilus Ins. Co. v. Pro-Set Erectors, Inc.*, 928 F. Supp. 2d 1208 (D. Idaho 2013) (quoting *County of Boise*); *Scout, LLC v. Truck Ins. Exch.*, 434 P.3d 197 (Idaho 2019) ("[E]ven if we adopted Scout's interpretation of the Four Corners Rule [allowing extrinsic evidence] the district court also found that extrinsic facts, if considered, would still trigger the prior publication exclusion and relieve Truck Insurance's duty to defend.").

Illinois: The Supreme Court of Illinois held that the determination of the duty to defend is not limited to the allegations in the complaint. *Pekin Ins. Co. v. Wilson*, 930 N.E.2d 1011, 1020 (Ill. 2010) ("It is certainly true that the duty to defend flows in the first instance from the allegations in the underlying complaint; this is the concern at the initial stage of the proceedings when an insurance company encounters the primary decision of whether to defend its insured. However, if an insurer opts to file a declaratory proceeding, we believe that it may properly challenge the existence of such a duty by offering evidence to prove that the insured's actions fell within the limitations of one of the policy's exclusions. The only time such evidence should not be permitted is when it tends to determine an issue crucial to the determination of the underlying lawsuit … If a crucial issue will not be determined, we see no reason why the party seeking a declaration of rights should not have the prerogative to present evidence that is accorded generally to a party during a motion for summary judgment in a declaratory proceeding.") (quoting *Fidelity & Cas. Co. of New York v. Envirodyne Engineers, Inc.*, 461 N.E.2d 471, 473–74 (Ill. Ct. App. 1983)) (alteration in original). The Illinois high court also cited *American Economy Ins. Co. v. Holabird and Root*, 886 N.E.2d 1166 (Ill. App. Ct. 2008), *appeal allowed* 897 N.E.2d 249 (Ill. 2008), as setting forth a proper consideration for a circuit court's use of extrinsic evidence to determine the duty to defend: "[C]onsideration of a third-party complaint in determining a duty to defend is in line with the general rule that a trial court may consider evidence beyond the underlying complaint if in doing so the trial court does not determine an issue critical to the underlying action." *Wilson* at 1020–21 (quoting *Holabird and Root* at 1178) (alteration in original); *see also Konstant Products, Inc. v. Liberty Mut. Fire Ins. Co.*, No. 1–09–0080, 2010 Ill. App. LEXIS 378 (Ill. Ct. App. May 4, 2010) (decided two weeks prior to *Wilson* and interpreting *Holabird and Root* as limiting the consideration of extrinsic evidence to true but unpleaded facts about which the insurer is aware); *Amerisure Mut. Ins. Co. v. Microplastics, Inc.*, 622 F.3d 806 (7th Cir. 2010) (applying Illinois law) (declining to permit an insured from triggering a duty to defend a vaguely drafted complaint by hypothesizing situations which, if alleged or true, would bring the claim within the scope of coverage); *Pekin Ins. Co. v. Pulte Home Corp.*, 935 N.E.2d 1058, 1063 (Ill. App. Ct. 2010) (addressing *Wilson* and other Illinois duty to defense case law) ("Therefore, in determining whether Pekin has a duty to defend Pulte in the underlying litigation, we will compare the complaint to the terms of the insurance policy issued to Kunde Construction, but we will also look to other relevant pleadings and documents, including the contract between Pulte and Kunde Construction."); *Owners Ins. Co. v. Seamless Gutter Corp.*, 945 N.E.2d 1153 (Ill. 2011) (vacating judgment in *Owners Ins. Co. v. Westfield Homes of Illinois*, case no. 1–08–2924 (11/15/10) and directing appellate court to reconsider duty to defend in light of *Wilson*); *Pekin Ins. Co. v. United Contractors Midwest, Inc.*, 997 N.E.2d 235 (Ill. Ct. App. 2013) (declining consideration of a third-party complaint to determine an insurer's duty to defend because it was potentially self-serving); *Indiana Ins. Co. v. Philadelphia Indem. Ins. Co.*, No. 11–0830, 2013 Ill. App. Unpub. LEXIS 692 (Ill. Ct. App. Mar. 29, 2013) (*Pekin* is distinguishable from the instant case because our supreme court found that the trial court may look to other court pleadings to determine whether Pekin owed Wilson a duty to defend. Here, unlike *Pekin*, Philadelphia looked to the police report from the accident in the underlying complaint, not a pleading. We cannot say *Pekin* authorizes the court to consider a police report in determining a duty to defend."); *Pekin Ins. Co. v. Johnson-Downs Constr., Inc.*, No. 16-0601, 2017 Ill. App. LEXIS 453 (Ill. Ct. App. July 6, 2017) (court may not look to a putative additional insured's own third-party complaint, that it drafted, to determine a duty to defend it in the initial action); *Astor Plaza Condo. Ass'n v. Travelers Cas. & Sur. Co. of Am.*, No. 15-2546, 2017 Ill. App. Unpub. LEXIS 1364 (Ill. Ct. App. June 30, 2017) (not appropriate for court to fail to consider extrinsic evidence, to determine a duty to defend, as it involved a critical issue in the underlying action); *Pekin Ins. Co. v. AAA-1 Masonry & Tuckpointing, Inc.*, 81 N.E.3d 1040 (Ill. Ct. App. 2017) (allowing consideration of an insurer claim note, in conjunction with the allegations in the complaint, to trigger a defense); *State Auto Prop. & Cas. Ins. Co. v. Shores Builders, Inc.*, No. 19-773, 2020 U.S. Dist. LEXIS 71589 (S.D. Ill. April 23, 2020) (declining to consider extrinsic evidence to determine duty to defend as it was relevant to determining the insured's liability in the underlying action); *RLI Ins. Co. v. Acclaim Res. Partners, LLC*, No. 4-19-0757, 2020 Ill. App. Unpub. LEXIS 1554 (Ill. Ct. App. Sept. 16, 2020) ("Although we agree with Exchange that a vague or ambiguous situation would favor the insured, we do not agree that this is such a situation. Again, we analyze the underlying complaint for its substance, not for its mere labels. Accordingly, we conclude that while the Underlying Action may include claims that are described as negligence in performance of adjuster services, it is clear that the alleged conduct that forms the basis for Exchange's claim does not qualify as adjuster services. Because the substance of the claim carries the day, we conclude that RLI has no duty to defend."). In general, there are a substantial number of Illinois court decisions, often involving detailed analyses, that have addressed the permissibility of resort to extrinsic evidence to determine an insurer's duty to defend.

Indiana: The Supreme Court of Indiana held that the determination of the duty to defend is not limited to the allegations in the complaint. *Freidline v. Shelby Ins. Co.*, 774 N.E.2d 37, 43 n.6 (Ind. 2002) ("Where an insurer's independent investigation of the facts underlying a complaint against its insured reveals a claim is patently outside of the risk covered by the policy, the insurer may properly refuse to defend."). On the other hand, in *Transamerica Insurance Services v. Kopko*, 570 N.E.2d 1283, 1285 (Ind. 1991), the Supreme Court of Indiana stated that "[t]he duty to defend is determined solely by the nature of the complaint." However, numerous decisions from the Court of Appeals of Indiana and Indiana federal courts have either declined to follow *Kopko*, distinguished it or ignored it. *See, e.g., Monroe Guar. Ins. Co. v. Monroe*, 677 N.E.2d 620, 624 (Ind. Ct. App. 1997) ("[A]s a matter of law the Insurer has a duty to conduct a reasonable investigation into the facts underlying the complaint before it may refuse to defend the complaint."); *Ace Rent-A-Car, Inc. v. Empire Fire & Marine Ins. Co.*, 580 F. Supp. 2d 678, 689 (N.D. Ill. 2008) ("Several Indiana courts have questioned the validity of this statement of law [*Kopko's* statement that the duty to defend is determined solely by the nature of the complaint], or have simply ignored it and have continued to hold that the duty to defend is determined not only by the underlying complaint, but by a reasonable investigation on the part of the insurer."); *Property-Owners Ins. Co. v. Virk Boyz Liquor Stores, LLC*, 219 F. Supp. 3d 868 (N.D. Ind. 2016) ("Several Indiana appellate decisions have more recently declined to follow *Kopko* and found that in evaluating the factual basis of a claim and the insurer's concomitant duty to defend, this court may properly consider the evidentiary materials offered by the parties to show coverage."); *Fed. Ins. Co. v. Stroh Brewing Co.*, 127 F.3d 563, 566 (7th Cir. 1997) (applying Indiana law and finding that "[w]hile Indiana's courts may use differing language to describe the standard, we believe there is essentially only one standard—that the allegations of the complaint, including the facts alleged, give rise to a duty to defend whenever, if proved true, coverage would attach"); *Clark v. Ritter*, No. 1:08-cv-0710, 2010 U.S. Dist. LEXIS 49686 (S.D. Ind. May 17, 2010) ("If the insurer's independent investigation of the facts underlying the complaint against its insured reveals that the claim is patently outside the risk covered by the policy, the insurer may refuse to defend."); *City of Evansville v. U.S. Fidelity and Guar. Co.*, 965 N.E.2d 92 (Ind. Ct. App. 2012) ("[W]here an insurer's independent investigation of the facts underlying a complaint against its insured reveals a claim patently outside of the risks covered by the policy, the insurer may properly refuse to defend."); *5200 Keystone Ltd. Realty, LLC v. Netherlands Ins. Company*, 29 N.E.3d 156 (Ind. Ct. App. 2015) ("An insurer's duty to defend is examined based upon the allegations contained within the complaint against the insured, as well as upon those facts known or ascertainable by the insurer after reasonable investigation. . . . Additionally, an insurer may go beyond the face of the complaint and refuse to defend based upon the factual underpinnings of the claims contained within the complaint."); *Cont'l Ins. Co. v. George J. Beemsterboer, Inc.*, 148 F. Supp. 3d 770 (N.D. Ind. 2015) (declining to follow *Kopko*) ("Because the Indiana Supreme Court considered extrinsic evidence in assessing an insurer's duty to defend in *Harvey* [*Auto-Owners Ins. Co. v. Harvey*, 842 N.E.2d 1279 (Ind. 2006)], this Court finds it appropriate to consider extrinsic evidence here."); *State Farm Mut. Auto. Ins. Co. v. Sanders*, No. 17-137, 2017 U.S. Dist. LEXIS 173675 (N.D. Ind. Oct. 19, 2017) ("In this case, there is no underlying state court complaint to review. That is neither here nor there because in evaluating the factual basis of a claim and the insurer's concomitant duty to defend, this court may properly consider the evidentiary materials offered by the parties to show coverage.").

Iowa: The Supreme Court of Iowa held that the determination of the duty to defend is not limited to the allegations in the complaint. *Talen v. Employers Mut. Cas. Co.*, 703 N.W.2d 395, 406 (Iowa 2005) ("The scope of inquiry [for the duty to defend], however, must sometimes be expanded beyond the petition, especially under 'notice pleading' petitions which often give few facts upon which to assess an insurer's duty to defend. Quoting from an earlier case, we stated that an insurer has no duty to defend if after construing both the policy in question, the pleadings of the injured party and any other admissible and relevant facts in the record, it appears the claim made is not covered by the indemnity insurance contract. We find this principle to be especially relevant when the basis for withholding coverage is a policy exclusion the application of which is not readily ascertainable from the allegations of the petition and will not necessarily be determined in the tort litigation.") (citations and internal quotation omitted); *see also McNeilus Hog Farms v. Farm Bureau Mut. Ins. Co.*, No. 09-0699, 2010 Iowa App. LEXIS 193 (Iowa Ct. App. Feb. 4, 2010) ("Farm Bureau appears to argue that we should not consider any facts outside the petition in determining whether it has a duty to defend … *Talen* states otherwise."); *Gulf Underwriters Ins. Co. v. City of Council Bluffs*, 755 F. Supp. 2d 988 (S.D. Iowa 2010) (rejecting the argument that, when cases refer to consideration of facts "in the record," for purposes of determining a duty to defend, the record must be "fully developed"); *Decker Plastics, Inc. v. West Bend Mut. Ins. Co.*, No. 14-15, 2017 U.S. Dist. LEXIS 85103 (S.D. Iowa Jan. 12, 2017 ("The duty to defend arises when the petition contains any allegations that arguably or potentially bring the action within the policy coverage. (citations omitted) The insurer may also consider facts outside the petition when making its decision.").

Kansas: The Supreme Court of Kansas held that the determination of the duty to defend is not limited to the allegations in the complaint. *Miller v. Westport Ins.*

Corp., 200 P.3d 419, 424 (Kan. 2009) (quoting *Spivey v. Safeco Ins. Co.*, 865 P.2d 182, 188 (Kan. 1993)) ("Under Kansas law, lawsuit pleadings are merely a starting point for the duty to defend analysis. They are not dispositive. An insurer must additionally consider actual facts of which it is or should be aware when evaluating its duty to defend. The insurer 'must look beyond the effect of the pleadings and must consider any facts brought to its attention or any facts which it could reasonably discover in determining whether it has a duty to defend.' If these known or reasonably discoverable extrinsic facts give rise to potential liability on the insured's part, the insured (sic) has a duty to defend ... . This approach has become known as the 'extrinsic evidence' approach or rule. Under [this] approach, the insurer's duty to defend still hinges on the potential for coverage, but the universe of information from which that potential must be ascertained is much greater [than the universe used in an approach limited to the 'eight corners' of a pleading and the applicable insurance policy].") (alteration in original); *see also Allied Mut. Ins. Co. v. Moeder*, 48 P.3d 1, 4 (Kan. Ct. App. 2002) (quoting *Quality Painting, Inc. v. Truck Ins. Exch.*, 988 P.2d 749 (Kan. Ct. App. 1999)) (quoting *Spivey*, 865 P.2d at 188 (Kan. 1993)) ("The insurer determines if there is a potential of liability under the policy by examining the allegations in the complaint or petition and considering any facts brought to its attention or which it could reasonably discover."); *Hackman v. Western Agr. Ins. Co.*, No. 103,967, 2011 Kan. App. Unpub. LEXIS 334 (Kan. Ct. App. May 6, 2011) ("The ultimate showing test discussed in *South Central Kansas Health Ins. Group* was not abandoned or modified by the Kansas Supreme Court in *Westport*.") ("If an insurer erroneously takes the position that notwithstanding the allegations of the complaint it has no obligation to defend, and facts subsequently establish that such duty did exist, then we are confident that the law will allow the insured party an adequate remedy for breach by the insurer of its obligations under the policy. ... On the other hand, if the insurer's position is ultimately shown to be correct, then it should not be penalized by being forced to bear an expense which it did not contractually obligate itself to incur.") (citations and internal quotations omitted) (describing the "ultimate showing test"); *Hartford Fire Ins. Co. v. Vita Craft Corp.*, 911 F. Supp. 2d 1164 (D. Kan. 2012) ("The insurer must undertake a good-faith analysis of all information known to it or reasonably ascertainable by inquiry and investigation in order to determine the possibility of coverage."); *Certain Underwriters at Lloyd's London v. Garmin Intern. Inc.*, No. 11-2426, 2013 U.S. Dist. LEXIS 98186 (D. Kan. July 15, 2013) ("Before the general principle regarding the duty to defend applies, it must be shown that under the policy the defendant is in fact an insured, named or omnibus.

This must be so because the insurer's obligation is not to provide a defense for a stranger merely because the plaintiff alleges that the defendant is an insured or alleges facts which, if true, would make him an insured.") (describing the "ultimate showing test"); *Cincinnati Ins. Co. v. Gage Ctr. Dental Group, P.A.*, No. 12-2387, 2013 U.S. Dist. LEXIS 156844 (D. Kan. Nov. 1, 2013) ("[T]he duty to defend hinges on the potential for coverage, but the universe of information from which that potential must be ascertained is much greater than the universe used in an approach limited to the 'eight corners' of a pleading and the applicable insurance policy. On the other hand, where a petition alleges an act which the policy clearly does not cover, there is no potential of liability."); *Schlup v. Depositors Ins. Co.*, 426 F. Supp. 3d 831 (D. Kan. 2019) (extrinsic evidence used by insurer to provide a defense to insured served as a basis for court's conclusion that "plaintiff's theory of coverage is [not] frivolous as a matter of law").

Kentucky: The Supreme Court of Kentucky held that the determination of the duty to defend is limited to the allegations in the complaint. *James Graham Brown Foundation, Inc. v. St. Paul Fire & Marine Ins. Co.*, 814 S.W.2d 273, 279 (Ky. 1991) ("The insurer has a duty to defend if there is any allegation which potentially, possibly or might come within the coverage of the policy. The insurance company must defend any suit in which the language of the complaint would bring it within the policy coverage regardless of the merit of the action. The determination of whether a defense is required must be made at the outset of the litigation.") (citations omitted). *See also Cincinnati Ins. Co. v. Richie Enterprises LLC*, No. 12–00186, 2014 U.S. Dist. LEXIS 27306 (W.D. Ky. Mar. 4, 2014) ("Under Kentucky law, an insurer has the duty to defend the insured if there is any allegation which potentially, possibly or might come within the coverage of the policy.") (quoting *James Graham Brown*); *Liberty Corporate Capital Ltd. v. Sec. Safe Outlet*, 577 Fed. Appx. 399 (6th Cir. 2014) ("Kentucky courts determine whether an insurer has a duty to defend its insured by comparing the language of the underlying complaint to the terms of the policy. There is a duty to defend if there is any allegation which potentially, possibly or might come within the coverage of the policy."). Some Kentucky federal courts have stated that the determination of whether a defense is required must be made at the outset of the litigation by reference to the complaint *and known facts. E.g., Lenning v. Commer. Union Ins. Co.*, 260 F.3d 574, 581 (6th Cir. 2001); *Pizza Magia Int'l, LLC v. Assurance Co. of Am.*, 447 F. Supp. 2d 766, 778–79 (W.D. Ky. 2006); *Generali U.S. Branch v. Nat'l Trust Ins. Co.*, No. 5:07-CV-139, 2009 U.S. Dist. LEXIS 76890 (W.D. Ky. Aug. 27, 2009); *Auto Club Property-Casualty Ins. Co. v. Adler*, No. 14-46, 2015

U.S. Dist. LEXIS 108667 (W.D. Ky. Aug. 18, 2015). While these courts cite to *James Graham Brown* for this proposition, the "known facts" requirement is not contained in the Supreme Court of Kentucky's decision. In *KSPED LLC v. Va. Sur. Co.*, 567 Fed. Appx. 377 (6th Cir. 2014), the court stated that, "[u]nder Kentucky law, the decision whether to defend must be made at the outset of litigation by reference to the complaint and *known facts.*" (emphasis in original). The court concluded that the insurer failed to consider known facts at the time it made its decision not to defend, but that, if it had, the insurer still did not have a duty to defend. *But see Outdoor Venture Corp. v. Phila. Indem. Ins. Co.*, No. 20a0715n.06, 2020 U.S. App. LEXIS 40041 (6th Cir. Dec. 22, 2020) (duty to defend is determined "by comparing the allegations in the underlying complaint with the terms of the insurance policy" and not stating that known facts may also be considered, which the District Court did: 2018 U.S. Dist. LEXIS 167986 (E.D. Ky. Sept. 27, 2018)); *Liberty Mut. Ins. Co. v. Estate of Bobzien*, 377 F. Supp. 3d 723 (W.D. Ky. 2019) (same) (*aff'd* 798 Fed. Appx. 930 (6th Cir. 2020)).

Louisiana: The Supreme Court of Louisiana held that the determination of the duty to defend is limited to the allegations in the complaint. *Elliott v. Cont'l Cas. Co.*, 949 So. 2d 1247, 1250 (La. 2007) ("The insurer's duty to defend suits brought against its insured is determined by the allegations of the plaintiff's petition, with the insurer being obligated to furnish a defense unless the petition unambiguously excludes coverage. Accordingly, the insurer's obligation to defend suits against its insured is generally broader than its obligation to provide coverage for damage claims. Thus, if, assuming all of the allegations of the petition to be true, there would be both coverage under the policy and liability of the insured to the plaintiff, the insurer must defend the insured regardless of the outcome of the suit. An insured's (*sic*) duty to defend arises whenever the pleadings against the insured disclose even a possibility of liability under the policy.") (citations omitted); *see also Sibley v. Deer Valley Homebuilders, Inc.*, 32 So. 3d 1034 (La. Ct. App. 2010) (describing *Elliott*) ("This review of the petition and the policy has been referenced as the 'four corners' rule for the determination of the existence of the duty to defend."); *Looney Ricks Kiss Architects, Inc. v. Bryan*, No. 07-572, 2010 U.S. Dist. LEXIS 137561 (W.D. La. Dec. 30, 2010) ("The insurer's duty to defend is determined solely from the plaintiff's pleadings and the policy, without consideration of extraneous evidence.") (citation and internal quotations omitted); *Lodwick, L.L.C. v. Chevron U.S.A., Inc.*, 126 So. 3d 544 (La. Ct. App. 2013) ("The duty to defend is determined by the allegations of the injured plaintiff's petition, with the insurer being obligated to furnish a defense unless the petition unambiguously excludes coverage."); *Arceneaux v. Amstar Corp.*, 200 So. 3d 277 (La. 2016) (same); *Forrest v. Ville St. John Owners Ass'n*, 259 So. 3d 1063 (La. Ct. App. 2019) (restating rule that the determination of the duty to defend is limited to the allegations in the complaint).

Maine: The Supreme Judicial Court of Maine held that the determination of the duty to defend is limited to the allegations in the complaint. *York Ins. Group v. Lambert*, 740 A.2d 984, 985 (Me. 1999) ("The longstanding rule is that we determine the duty to defend by comparing the allegations in the underlying complaint with the provisions of the insurance policy. A duty to defend exists if a complaint reveals a *potential* that the facts ultimately proved may come within the coverage.") (citations and internal quotation omitted) (emphasis in original). The Maine high court explained the rationale for its rule as follows: "If we were to look beyond the complaint and engage in proof of actual facts, then the separate declaratory judgment actions … would become independent trials of the facts which the [insured] would have to carry on at his expense … . We see no reason why the insured, whose insurer is obligated by contract to defend him, should have to try the facts in a suit against his insurer in order to obtain a defense." *Id.* (quoting *Elliott v. Hanover Ins. Co.*, 711 A.2d 1310, 1312 (Me. 1998)); *see also Howe v. MMG Ins. Co.*, 95 A.3d 79 (Me. 2014) (holding that duty to defend owed because "facts could be developed at a trial on the . . . complaint, as currently drafted, that would support claims potentially falling within the coverage of the policy"); *Prime Tanning Co., Inc. v. Liberty Mut. Ins. Co.*, 750 F. Supp. 2d 198, 207 (D. Me. 2010) ("The pleading comparison test mandates that the Court compare the allegations in the underlying complaint with the provisions of the insurance policy.") (citation and internal quotations omitted). In *N.E. Ins. Co. v. Young*, 26 A.3d 794 (Me. 2011), the Supreme Judicial Court of Maine stated its rule that the duty to defend is determined by comparing the allegations in the underlying complaint with the provisions of the insurance policy and that, in most circumstances, "an insurer has a duty to defend and cannot avoid this duty by establishing, before the underlying action has concluded, that ultimately there will be no duty to indemnify." *Id.* at 799 (citations and internal quotes omitted). However, the court also acknowledged an exception: "We have, however, condoned earlier consideration of the duties to defend and indemnify when an insurer disputes those duties based on facts that are not related to the question of the insured's liability, such as 'nonpayment of a premium, cancellation of a policy, failure to cooperate or lack of timely notice.' *Garcia*, 1998 ME 38, ¶ 7, 707 A.2d at 386 (quotation marks omitted). A declaratory judgment action is appropriate in such circumstances because 'the coverage dispute depends entirely on the relationship between the insurer and the insured, not on facts to be determined in the underlying litigation.' *Id.*" *Id.; OneBeacon America Ins. Co. v. Johnny's Selected Seeds Inc.*, 12–00375, 2014 U.S. Dist. LEXIS 53098 (D. Me. Apr. 17, 2014) (noting that, outside narrowly construed exceptions, "the Law Court has consistently reinforced the 'policy comparison test' to the exclusion of extrinsic evidence") (citing *Young* as one exception and another being where a prior criminal conviction for murder, attempted murder or sexual abuse of a child would preclude litigation over the issue of the tortfeasor's intent, thereby precluding a duty to defend or indemnify where the policy excludes intentional torts); *Barnie's Bar & Grill, Inc. v. United States Liab. Ins. Co.*, 152 A.3d 613 (Me. 2016) ("In applying the comparison test, we examine the underlying complaint for *any potential* factual or legal basis that may obligate the insurer to defend the insured, even the mere intent to state a claim within the insurance coverage. . . . Except in rare circumstances, we will not consider facts extrinsic to the underlying complaint nor will we read allegations into the complaint in determining whether the insurer has a duty to defend.") (citations omitted and emphasis in original) ("Our body of case law should not, however, be misread as obliging courts to conjure the duty to defend from speculation or supposition."); *Harlor v. Amica Mut. Ins. Co.*, 150 A.3d 793 (Me. 2016) (describing the comparison test as a "low" threshold for triggering an insurer's duty to defend); *Medical Mut. Ins. Co. v. Burka*, 899 F.3d 61 (1st Cir. 2018) (no duty to defend) ("The duty to defend Burka thus requires a relationship of doctor to patient that is emphatically denied by the complaint's allegations and, hence, could only be 'conjure[d] . . . from speculation or supposition.'"); *Lewis v. Allstate Ins. Co.*, No. 18-272, 2019 Me. Super. LEXIS 41 (Me. Super. Ct. Mar. 8, 2019) (insurer precluded from considering extrinsic evidence, to determine that an assault was intentional, and that negligence allegation was artful pleading, because "resort to extrinsic evidence is foreclosed by Maine's well-settled rule that, for purposes of the duty to defend, the court's scrutiny is limited to a comparison of the complaint and the policy language").

Maryland: The Court of Appeals of Maryland has addressed the use of extrinsic evidence to determine an insurer's duty to defend and set forth rules for different circumstances. An insurer may not use extrinsic evidence to avoid a duty to defend if the underlying complaint establishes a potential for coverage. *Brohawn v. Transamerica Ins. Co.*, 347 A.2d 842, 850 (Md. 1975). However, an insured may use extrinsic evidence to establish that an insurer has a duty to defend a complaint that does not, on its face, give rise to the potential for coverage. *Aetna Cas. & Sur. Co. v. Cochran*, 651 A.2d 859, 864 (Md. 1995) ("*Brohawn* in no way intimates that reference to outside sources is prohibited if that reference is necessary to determine whether there is a potentiality of coverage under an insurance policy where the tort plaintiff's complaint neither conclusively establishes nor negates a potentiality of coverage."); *see also Moscarillo v. Prof'l Risk Mgmt. Servs.*, 921 A.2d 245, 252 (Md. 2007) (reaffirming the rules established by *Brohawn* and *Cochran* and addressing in detail the use of extrinsic evidence); *Marvin J. Perry, Inc. v. Hartford Cas. Ins. Co.*, No. 09–1639, 2011 U.S. App. LEXIS 4237 (4th Cir. Feb. 25, 2011) ("Maryland law permits the consideration of extrinsic evidence proffered by the insured when necessary to determine if there is a potentiality of coverage under an insurance policy."); *Capital City Real Estate, LLC v. Certain Underwriters at Lloyd's*, No. 13–1384, 2014 U.S. Dist. LEXIS 22756 (D. Md. Feb. 24, 2014) (allowing considering of extrinsic evidence to determine a duty to defend, but concluding that it did not do so) ("[T]he Court notes that coverage—and a duty to defend—may well be triggered by further developments in the Underlying Lawsuit. For example, should the underlying plaintiff be permitted to amend the complaint to assert vicarious liability, a duty to defend may arise. However, on the current record, the Court does not find a duty on the part of Underwriters to defend Capital City."); *Maryland Casualty Co. v. Blackstone Int'l Ltd.*, 114 A.3d 676 (Md. 2015) (finding the terms of the policy and allegations in the complaint to be conclusive so, therefore, not considering any extrinsic evidence) (dissent would have permitted extrinsic evidence based on an insurer being obligated to defend "if there is a *potentiality* that the claim could be covered by the policy") (emphasis in original); *Gemini Ins. Co. v. Earth Treks, Inc.*, No. 16-2520, 2017 U.S. Dist. LEXIS 72537 (D. Md. May 12, 2017) (noting that Maryland recognizes two limited exceptions to the general rule against an insurer's use of extrinsic evidence) ("First, when the underlying tort plaintiff has amended his allegations against the insured, the insurer may utilize the amendments as extrinsic evidence. If the amended allegations no longer raise a potentiality for coverage, the insurer no longer has a duty to defend. As a second exception to the general rule, a court is not obligated to 'turn a blind eye where [it is established] that an insured tortfeasor is excluded from coverage under [the] particular terms of the insurance policy.' In other words, an insurer may utilize uncontroverted extrinsic evidence from the underlying lawsuit if such evidence clearly establishes that the suit's allegations are beyond the scope of coverage.") (citations omitted) (*aff'd* 728 Fed. Appx. 182 (4th Cir. 2018)) (rejecting insured's argument that court could not consider deposition excerpts provided, but not highlighted by the insured, on the basis that such is "tantamount to considering extrinsic evidence provided by the insurer;" "To the contrary, the district court was not required to turn a blind eye to testimony that Earth Treks itself placed before the court.").

Massachusetts: The Supreme Judicial Court of Massachusetts held that the determination of the duty to defend is not limited to the allegations in the complaint. *Herbert A. Sullivan, Inc. v. Utica Mut. Ins. Co.*, 788 N.E.2d 522, 531 (Mass. 2003) ("The scope of an insurer's duty to defend is based on the facts alleged in the complaint and those facts which are known to the insurer. Specifically, the process is one of envisaging what kinds of losses may be proved as lying within the range of the allegations of the complaint, and then seeing whether any such loss fits the expectation of protective insurance reasonably generated by the terms of the policy.") (citations and internal quotation omitted); *see also Open Software Found., Inc. v. U.S. Fid. & Guar. Co.*, 307 F.3d 11, 16 (1st Cir. 2002) (discussing extrinsic facts as "an aid to interpreting" an underlying complaint and not serving as "independent grounds for a duty to defend"); *House of Clean Inc. v. St. Paul Fire & Marine Ins. Co.*, 705 F. Supp. 2d 102, 109 (D. Mass. 2010) ("Known or knowable extrinsic facts, such as those set forth in demand letters, therefore, serve to aid the interpretation of the underlying pleadings and can add substance and meaning to otherwise skeletal third-party claims. Extrinsic evidence cannot, however, provide independent grounds for a duty to defend.") (citing *Open Software*); *Clermont v. Cont'l Cas. Co.* 778 F. Supp. 2d 133, 144 (D. Mass. 2011) ("The duty to defend is determined by reference to the allegations in the complaint and 'facts known or readily knowable' by the insurer.") (citation omitted); *Metropolitan Property and Cas. Ins. Co. v. Morrison*, 951 N.E.2d 662, 664 (Mass. 2011) ("Even where the allegations in the complaint state or roughly sketch a claim covered by a liability policy, we have carved out narrow exceptions to the duty to defend: where there is undisputed, readily knowable, and publicly available information in court records that demonstrates that the insurer has no duty to defend, . . . and where there is an undisputed extrinsic fact that takes the case outside the coverage and that will not be litigated at the trial of the underlying action.") ("[A] guilty plea does not negate an insurer's duty to defend, even where the duty to defend would be negated by a criminal conviction after trial, because a guilty plea is not given preclusive effect and is simply evidence that the insured's acts were intentional and criminal.") (also addressing consequences for an insurer that denies a duty to defend and a default judgment is entered against the insured); *Deutsche Bank Nat. Ass'n v. First American Title Ins. Co.*,

991 N.E.2d 638 (Mass. 2013) (addressing Massachusetts duty to defend in detail and holding that "the broadly applied standard for determining whether a general liability insurer has a duty to defend is inapplicable in the context of title insurance."); *Nguyen v. Arbella Insurance Group*, 76 N.E.3d 1057 (Mass. Ct. App. 2017) ("An insurer has a duty to defend an insured when the allegations in a complaint are reasonably susceptible of an interpretation that states or roughly sketches a claim covered by the policy terms. The duty to defend is determined based on the facts alleged in the complaint, and on facts known or readily knowable by the insurer that may aid in its interpretation of the allegations in the complaint. In order for the duty of defense to arise, the underlying complaint need only show, through general allegations, a possibility that the liability claim falls within the insurance coverage. There is no requirement that the facts alleged in the complaint specifically and unequivocally make out a claim within the coverage. However, when the allegations in the underlying complaint lie expressly outside the policy coverage and its purpose, the insurer is relieved of the duty to investigate or defend the claimant."); *Mount Vernon Fire Insurance Company v. Visionaid, Inc.*, 76 N.E.3d 204 (Mass. 2017) ("[W]here an insurance policy provides that the insurer has the 'duty to defend any claim' initiated against the insured, the insurer's duty to defend does not require it to prosecute affirmative counterclaims on behalf of its insured."); *Consigli Constr. Co. v. Travelers Indem. Co.*, 256 F. Supp. 3d 62 (D. Mass. 2017) ("The pleadings filed in the underlying action establish the metes and bounds of the territory Travelers must survey in determining the duty to defend in this circumstance. The facts alleged in the underlying complaint do not support coverage here. That complaint has not been amended. I will not rely on belatedly developed extrinsic facts to find a duty to defend in these circumstances."); *Nagog Real Estate Consulting Corp. v. Nautilus Ins. Co.*, 474 F. Supp. 3d 459 (D. Mass. 2020) ("An insurer *may* use extrinsic evidence to deny a duty to defend based on facts irrelevant to the merits of the underlying litigation, such as whether the claim was first made during the policy period, whether the insured party reported the claim to the insurer as required by the policy, or whether the underlying wrongful acts were related to prior wrongful acts.") (emphasis in original); *Clarendon Nat'l Ins. Co. v. Phila. Indem. Ins. Co.*, 954 F.3d 397 (1st Cir. 2020) ("While Clarendon is correct that Massachusetts law does look to facts 'known or readily knowable by the insurer' as well as to the underlying complaint to determine whether a duty to defend has been triggered, information that is 'readily knowable' is distinct from the duty to investigate. . . . This Court has held that information known or readily knowable does not independently trigger

the duty to defend under Massachusetts law when the complaint does not 'adumbrate a claim.'").

Michigan: The Supreme Court of Michigan held that the determination of the duty to defend is not limited to the allegations in the complaint. *Am. Bumper & Mfg. Co. v. Hartford Fire Ins. Co.*, 550 N.W.2d 475 (Mich. 1996) ("An insurer has a duty to defend, despite theories of liability asserted against any insured which are not covered under the policy, if there are any theories of recovery that fall within the policy. The duty to defend cannot be limited by the precise language of the pleadings. The insurer has the duty to look behind the third party's allegations to analyze whether coverage is possible. In a case of doubt as to whether or not the complaint against the insured alleges a liability of the insurer under the policy, the doubt must be resolved in the insured's favor.") (citations and internal quotation omitted); *see also Dean v. Fid. Nat. Title Ins. Co.*, No. 295762, 2011 Mich. App. LEXIS 428 (Mich. Ct. App. Mar. 1, 2011) ("The duty to defend is not strictly limited to the language used in the third party's complaint; the insurer must look beyond the allegations to see if coverage is possible."); *Alticor, Inc. v. National Union Fire Ins. Co. of Pennsylvania*, 916 F. Supp. 2d 813 (W.D. Mich. 2013) ("Although the allegations in the *Nitro* Amended Complaint did not trigger coverage under the 98/99 policy, coverage was triggered under the 98/99 policy as the result of the answers produced by the *Nitro* plaintiffs during discovery."); *Livonia Public Schools v. Selective Ins. Co.*, No. 16-10324, 2017 U.S. Dist. LEXIS 31036 (E.D. Mich. Mar. 6, 2017) ("Michigan courts have repeatedly held that the duty to defend cannot be limited by the precise language of the pleadings [in the third party's action]. The insurer has a duty to look behind the third party's allegations to analyze whether coverage is possible. Thus the inquiry into whether an insurer has a duty to defend in a given case—whether undertaken by the insurer itself, or by a court after the fact—may take into account more than simply the insurance policy and the third-party allegations at issue. Plaintiffs have not shown that this Court's analysis of Defendant's duty to defend could not benefit from information turned up in discovery, and so the 'duty to defend' question does not justify a departure from this Court's regular practice of entertaining summary judgment motions only after the close of discovery."); *Livonia Public Schools v. Selective Ins. Co.*, No. 16-10324, 2020 U.S. Dist. LEXIS 25007 (E.D. Mich. Feb. 13, 2020) ("There are some situations . . . where, after some factual development, overwhelming evidence proves that coverage was never possible. This was the case with the Telerico plaintiff, who did not attend Webster during the 2010-2011 school year and therefore could not have been subjected to physical and verbal abuse that year. This type of evidence is distinguishable from a mere lack of evidence in support of a claim that is later proved groundless—once a defense has run its course, the duty to defend cannot be determined with the benefit of hindsight because that would eviscerate the duty.").

Minnesota: The Supreme Court of Minnesota held that the determination of the duty to defend is limited to the allegations in the complaint, unless the insurer is aware of facts indicating that there may be a covered claim. *Garvis v. Employers Mut. Cas. Co.*, 497 N.W.2d 254, 258 (Minn. 1993) ("This court has consistently stated that where the insurer has no knowledge to the contrary, it may make an initial determination of whether or not it is obligated to defend from the facts alleged in the complaint against its insured. Where the pleadings do not raise a claim arguably within the scope of coverage, the insurer has no duty to defend or investigate further to determine whether there are other facts present which trigger such a duty. Of course, if the insurer is aware of facts indicating that there may be a claim, either from what is said directly or inferentially in the complaint, or if the insured tells the insurer of such facts, or if the insurer has some independent knowledge of such facts, then the insurer must either accept tender of the defense or further investigate the potential claim.") (citations omitted); *see also Western Nat. Mut. Ins. Co. v. Structural Restoration, Inc.*, No. A09–1598, 2010 Minn. App. Unpub. LEXIS 406 (Minn. Ct. App. May 4, 2010) ("An insurance company may not rely on the allegations of the underlying complaint without investigating the facts, once the insured has come forward and made some factual showing that the suit is actually one for damages resulting from events which do fall into policy terms.") (citation and internal quotes omitted); *FACE, Festivals and Concert Events, Inc. v. Scottsdale Ins. Co.*, 632 F.3d 417, 420 (8th Cir. 2011) (applying Minnesota law) ("The insurer may not simply rely on the pleadings, however, if it has independent knowledge of facts that indicate there may be a covered claim, or if the insured tells the insurer of such facts.") (quoting *Garvis* at 258); *AMCO Ins. Co. v. Inspired Technologies, Inc.*, 648 F.3d 875 (8th Cir. 2011) (applying Minnesota law) (holding that insurer entitled to rely on answers to interrogatories as a source of actual facts outside the complaint to disclaim a duty to defend); *Nor-Son, Inc. v. Western Nat. Mut. Ins. Co.*, No. A11-2016, 2012 Minn. App. Unpub. LEXIS 411 (Minn. Ct. App. May 14, 2012) (noting that "the propriety of using a third-party complaint to establish a duty to defend has not been decided in Minnesota" and while none of the cases examined by the court involved extrinsic evidence submitted by means of a third-party complaint, none of them limited the use of such evidence); *Selective Ins. Co. of America v. Smart Candle, LLC*, No. 13–878,

2014 U.S. Dist. LECIS 4544 (D. Minn. Jan. 14, 2014) ("Smart Candle further argues that Selective should have examined uses of the term 'smart' as a slogan on its website. However, [w]here the pleadings do not raise a claim arguably within the scope of coverage, the insurer has no duty to ... investigate further to determine whether there are other facts present which trigger such a duty.") (*aff'd* 781 F.3d 983 (8th Cir. 2015); *Estate of Norby v. Waseca Mut. Ins. Co.*, No. A14-1146, 2015 Minn. App. Unpub. LEXIS 461 (Minn. Ct. App. May 18, 2015) ("Austin Mutual's letter informing Norby of its decision states that Norby did not provide Austin Mutual with a copy of the exhibits to the Minch complaint and invited Norby to provide additional information. We find nothing in the record suggesting that Norby did so. In sum, the 'readily available facts' that Norby relies on were not available to Austin Mutual when it determined that it did not have a duty to defend. To the extent that Norby suggests that Austin Mutual should have further investigated the Minch family's claims and discovered those 'readily available facts,' case law provides otherwise. The supreme court has consistently stated that where the insurer has no knowledge to the contrary, it may make an initial determination of whether or not it is obligated to defend from the facts alleged in the complaint against its insured."); *Kantrud v. Minn. Lawyers Mut. Ins. Co.*, No. A19-0628, 2019 Minn. App. Unpub. LEXIS 1105 (Minn. Ct. App. Nov. 25, 2019) (restating the rule from *Garvis*).

Mississippi: The Supreme Court of Mississippi held that the determination of the duty to defend is limited to the allegations in the complaint, but a true facts exception exists. *Farmland Mut. Ins. Co. v. Scruggs*, 886 So. 2d 714, 719 n.2 (Miss. 2004). "A liability insurance company has an absolute duty to defend a complaint which contains allegations covered by the language of the policy, but it has absolutely no duty to defend those claims which fall outside the coverage of the policy." *Id.* at 719. However, the *Scruggs* Court also acknowledged that "an insurer does have a duty to defend where a complaint fails to state a cause of action covered by policy but the insured informs the insurer that the true facts are inconsistent with the complaint, or where the insured learns from an independent investigation that the true facts present the potential liability of insured the insured (*sic*)." *Id.* at 719 n.2; *see also QBE Ins. Corp. v. Brown & Mitchell, Inc.*, 591 F.3d 439, 444–45 (5th Cir. 2009) (applying Miss. law) (concluding that the "true facts" raised by the insured did not trigger a duty to defend); *Architex Ass'n, Inc. v. Scottsdale Ins. Co.*, 27 So. 3d 1148, 1156 n.14 (Miss. 2010) ("Generally, [t]he obligation of the insurer to defend is to be determined by analyzing the allegations of the complaint or declaration in the underlying action. However, if the insured learns ... that the true facts, if established, present potential liability of insured, [the] insurer must defend until it appears that facts upon which liability is predicated exclude insurance coverage.") (citations and internal quotes omitted) (alteration in original); *Automobile Ins. Co. of Hartford v. Lipscomb*, 75 So. 3d 557 (Miss. 2011) (restating "true facts" exception to the duty to defend); *Carl E. Woodward, L.L.C. v. Acceptance Indem. Ins. Co.*, 749 F.3d 395 (5th Cir. 2014) ("We conclude simply that the identified passages in the Rimkus Report, even if the report should be considered in analyzing the duty to defend, do not reasonably and plausibly state that the damages occurred during DCM's ongoing operations."); *Nationwide Ins. Co. v. Lexington Relocation Services*, LLC, No. 12-181, 2014 U.S. Dist. LEXIS 38308 (N.D. Miss. Mar. 24, 2014) (discussing "true facts" exception and providing several examples of how it can and cannot be satisfied), *aff'd* 15 U.S. App. LEXIS 595 (5th Cir. Jan. 14, 2015) ("[P]laintiff's claim presents a case excluded from the coverage provided by the relevant policies. We do not interpret the 'true facts' rule to require an insurance company, when the claim is outside coverage, to consider the denials in an answer when deciding whether to defend or to review affidavits from the insured that support the denials. Such a rule would transform the narrow exception into a broad one. Mississippi case law does not support such a broad reading. Under our diversity jurisdiction, we will not extend this state-law doctrine to a place the state courts have not gone."); *Wesco Ins. Co. v. Archer Landscape Grp., LLC*, No. 16-165, 2018 U.S. Dist. LEXIS 198354 (N.D. Miss. Nov. 21, 2018) ("Brasfield also insists that the Court consider a proposed amended complaint in the state court action. However, Brasfield cites no authority which would support the proposition that the allegations of the complaint rule is inapplicable based on the existence of a proposed amended complaint which has not been filed.") (addressing whether "true facts" had been provided with respect to employment status).

Missouri: The Supreme Court of Missouri held that the determination of the duty to defend is not limited to the allegations in the complaint. *Marshall's U.S. Auto Supply v. Md. Cas. Co.*, 189 S.W.2d 529, 531 (Mo. 1945) ("We do not think that an insurance company can ignore actual facts (known to it or which could be known from reasonable investigation) in determining its liability to defend."); *Stark Liquidation Co. v. Florists' Mut. Ins. Co.*, 243 S.W.3d 385, 392 (Mo. Ct. App. 2007) (quoting *Truck Ins. Exch. v. Prairie Framing, LLC*, 162 S.W.3d 64, 83 (Mo. Ct. App. 2005)) ("The insurer has a duty to defend if the complaint merely alleges facts that give rise to a claim potentially within the policy's coverage. An insurer, however, may not merely rest upon the allegations contained within the petition. 'Rather it must also consider the petition in light of facts it knew or could have reasonably ascertained.'") (internal citations omitted); *Penn-Star Ins. Co. v. Griffey*, 306 S.W.3d 591, 597 (Mo. Ct. App. 2010) ("In addition to the allegations in the petition, the insurer must also consider other facts it knew or could reasonably have ascertained. If the allegations and ascertainable facts establish any *potential* or *possible* coverage, then the insurer has a duty to defend.") (emphasis in original); *Zeiser Motors, Inc. v. Sentry Select Ins. Co.*, No. 10-1261, 2011 U.S. Dist. LEXIS 44835 (E.D. Mo. Apr. 26, 2011 (following *Penn-Star*); *Allen v. Continental Western Ins. Co.*, 436 S.W.3d 548 (Mo. 2014) ("[T]he insurer's duty to defend arises only from potential coverage based on facts: (1) alleged in the petition; (2) the insurer knows at the outset of the case; or (3) that are reasonably apparent to the insurer at the outset of the case. *Zipkin*, 436 S.W.2d at 754; *see also McCormack Baron Mgmt. Servs., Inc.*, 989 S.W.2d at 170 (stating that facts adduced at trial that the insurer could not have known at the outset of the case do not give rise to a duty to defend); *Trainwreck W. Inc. v. Burlington Ins. Co.*, 235 S.W.3d 33, 39 (Mo. App. 2007) (holding that facts adduced solely from deposition testimony are not reasonably apparent at the outset of the case and do not give rise to a duty to defend). If there is no potential for coverage based on those facts, then the insurer has no duty to defend. *Marshall's U.S. Auto Supply*, 189 S.W.2d at 531 (holding that an insurer did not have a duty to defend based on facts that were reasonably apparent to the insurer at the outset of the case, although not alleged in the underlying petition, because regardless of those facts, there was no potential for coverage under the insurance policy."); *Piatt v. Indiana Lumbermen's Mut. Ins. Co.*, 461 S.W.3d 788 (Mo. 2015) ("Unless these facts [the three types listed in *Allen v. Continental Western*] support some reasonably apparent theory of recovery against the insured that would give rise to coverage, the insurer has no duty to defend."); *Allen v. Bryers*, 512 S.W.3d 17 (Mo. 2016) (restating *Allen v. Continental Western*).

Montana: The Supreme Court of Montana held that the determination of the duty to defend is not limited to the allegations in the complaint. *Burns v. Underwriters Adjusting Co.*, 765 P.2d 712, 713 (Mont. 1988) (upholding an insurer's disclaimer of a duty to defend a complaint that alleged negligence, based upon extrinsic evidence of an insured's guilty plea to felony aggravated assault). The *Burns* Court stated that "the proper focus of inquiry [for the duty to defend] is the acts giving rise to coverage, not the language of the complaint." *Id.* Then, in *Revelation Industries, Inc. v. St. Paul Fire & Marine Ins. Co.*, 206 P.3d 919 (Mont. 2009), the Montana high court—characterizing *Burns* as permitting an insurer to look beyond the allegations in the complaint to deny a duty to defend—held that the same rule applies when a complaint on its face does not trigger a duty to defend, but the insurer nonetheless has information that could give rise to a duty to defend and indemnify. *Id.* at 926. The court noted that, while an insurer need not seek out such information, it is not entitled to simply ignore factual information supplied to it by its insured, but not alleged in the complaint, which would trigger a duty to defend. *Id.* "[I]nsurers that look at facts beyond the allegations in the complaint do so at their own risk as they will be required to defend and/or indemnify based on the information discovered." *Id. See also Ames Const., Inc. v. Intermountain Indus., Inc.*, 712 F. Supp. 2d 1160, 1166 (D. Mont. 2010) (noting that an insurer cannot ignore knowledge of facts that may give rise to coverage under the policy simply because the complaint does not allege such facts); *Landa v. Assurance Co. of America*, 307 P.3d 284 (Mont. 2013) ("The facts alleged in Alsup's complaint were outside the policy's coverage, as Assurance correctly concluded. Landa's second tender of defense, with a statement of claim and our *Wagner–Ellsworth* case attached, did not provide facts sufficient to bring the claim within the policy's coverage, and Landa does not argue that Assurance possessed other information that would have triggered a duty to defend. Assurance therefore properly denied coverage based on the complaint and the information it possessed."); *Huckins v. United Servs. Auto. Ass'n.*, 396 P.3d 121 (Mont. 2017) ("[T]o determine whether [the insurer] had a duty to defend [the insured], we . . . look first to the terms of the policy, and next to the facts alleged [in the] complaint. . . . Further, an insurer's duty to defend may arise from an insurer's knowledge of facts obtained from outside the complaint. An insurer cannot ignore knowledge of facts that may give rise to coverage under the policy simply because the complaint . . . does not allege these facts of which the insurer has knowledge.") (quoting *Revelation Industries* and *Landa*); *Farmers Ins. Exch. v. Wessel*, 477 P.3d 1101 (Mont. 2020) ("[O]ur case law makes clear that the threshold question is whether the claim against the insured alleges facts that would trigger coverage. The Insureds cannot create coverage where it does not exist simply by denying the claims when the claims themselves do not trigger coverage."); *Emplrs Mut. Cas. Co. v. Hansen*, No. 19-114, 2021 U.S. Dist. LEXIS 48214 (D. Mont. March 15, 2021) (explaining in detail why insurer had no knowledge, outside of the complaint, that could trigger a defense).

Nebraska: The Supreme Court of Nebraska held that the determination of the duty to defend is not limited to the allegations in the complaint. *Peterson v. Ohio Cas. Group*, 724 N.W.2d 765, 773–74 (Neb. 2006) ("An insurer's duty to defend an action against the insured must, in the first instance, be measured by the allegations of the petition against the insured. In determining its duty to defend, an insurer must not only look to the petition or complaint filed against its insured, but must also investigate and ascertain the relevant facts from all available sources. An insurer is obligated to defend if (1) the allegations of the complaint, if true, would obligate the insurer to indemnify, or (2) a reasonable investigation of the actual facts by the insurer would or does disclose facts that would obligate the insurer to indemnify. An insurer, therefore, bears a duty to defend its insured whenever it ascertains facts which give rise to the potential of liability under the policy.") (also noting that "[i]f, according to the facts alleged in a pleading and ascertained by an insurer, the insurer has no potential liability to its insured under the insurance agreement, then the insurer may properly refuse to defend its insured"); *see also Mortgage Express, Inc. v. Tudor Ins. Co.*, 771 N.W.2d 137 (Neb. 2009) (reaffirming the standard set out in *Peterson*); *Behrens v. Arch Ins. Co.*, 631 F.3d 895, 898–99 (8th Cir. 2011) (applying Nebraska law) (following *Peterson* and *Mortgage Express*); *Federated Service Ins. Co. v. Alliance Const., LLC*, 805 N.W.2d 468 (Neb. 2011) (reaffirming the standard set out in *Peterson* with cite to *Mortgage Express*); *Rasmussen v. Global Indemnity Group, Inc.*, No. 16-92, 2016 U.S. Dist. LEXIS 187845 (D. Neb. Sept. 19, 2016) (while ultimately concluding that insurer had no duty to defend, court observed that, for duty to defend purposes, the insurer initially "ascertained sufficient facts" to establish the self-defense exception to the expected or intended exclusion); *Berkley Reg'l Specialty Ins. Co. v. Performance Roofing & Sheet Metal, Inc.*, No. 17-357, 2018 U.S. Dist. LEXIS 232548 (D. Neb. Feb. 12, 2108) (addressing the issue in the bad faith context) ("The information available to BRSIC at the time of denial [engineer's opinion] indicated the damage could have been caused by Performance's failure to maintain an adequate cover. Because this arguably implicates the open-roof exclusion, Lahood has failed in arguing that BRSIC had no basis to deny the claim."); *Merrick v. Fischer, Rounds & Assocs., Inc.*, 939 N.W.2d 795 (Neb. 2020) (setting out duty to defend rules from *Federated Service* and *Mortgage Express*).

Nevada: The Supreme Court of Nevada held that the determination of the duty to defend is not limited to the allegations in the complaint. *United Nat'l Ins. Co. v. Frontier Ins. Co.*, 99 P.3d 1153, 1158 (Nev. 2004) ("The duty to defend is broader than the duty to indemnify. There is no duty to defend where there is no potential for coverage. In other words, an insurer … bears a duty to defend its insured whenever it ascertains facts which give rise to the potential of liability under the policy. Once the duty to defend arises, this duty continues throughout the course of the litigation. If there is any doubt about whether the duty to defend arises, this doubt must be resolved in favor of the insured. The purpose behind construing the duty to defend so broadly is to prevent an insurer from evading its obligation to provide a defense for an insured without at least investigating the facts behind a complaint.") (citations and internal quotation omitted); *see also McClain v. Nat'l Fire & Marine Ins. Co.*, No. 2:05-cv-00706 (D. Nev. June 23, 2008) ("*United National Insurance* contemplates the consideration of facts outside of the complaint in order to compel an insurer to defend its insured. However, if an insurer seeks to avoid defending its insured, that insurer may only do so by demonstrating that the complaint shows there is no potential for coverage when compared with the insurer's policy.") (citation omitted); *Century Sur. Co. v. Casino West, Inc.*, No. 3:07-cv-00636, 2010 U.S. Dist. LEXIS 19807 (D. Nev. Mar. 4, 2010) ("An insured (sic) has a duty to defend an insured whenever it ascertains facts which give rise to the potential of liability under the policy.") (quoting *Frontier*). *But see Andrew v. Century Sur. Co.*, No. 12–00978, 2014 U.S. Dist. LEXIS 60972 (D. Nev. Apr. 29, 2014) (concluding that the Nevada Supreme Court's decision in *United National Insurance* is not clear and that the Nevada Supreme Court would adopt the four corners rule, and, as such, an insurer's duty to defend is determined by comparing the allegations of the complaint with the terms of the policy.) (addressing *United National Insurance's* reference to ascertaining facts which give rise to the potential of liability under the policy and concluding: "The most plausible reading is that the 'facts' an insurer must rely on are those alleged in the complaint, rather than facts derived from an insurance company's investigation."). That Nevada law may not be clear on the duty to defend test was recently discussed in *Nautilus Ins. Co. v. Access Med.*, LLC, No. 15-cv-00321, 2016 U.S. Dist. LEXIS 132300 (D. Nev. Sept. 27, 2016): "The Nevada Supreme Court has never explicitly adopted or rejected the 'four corners rule,' which limits the duty-to-defend inquiry to a comparison between the allegations in the complaint and the policy's terms. District Judge Andrew Gordon recently considered this issue in *Andrew v. Century Surety Company* and *Allstate Property and Casualty Insurance Company v. Yalda*. In *Andrew*, Judge Gordon acknowledged that the Nevada Supreme Court had never explicitly adopted the rule and concluded that the Nevada Supreme Court would likely apply the four-corners rule when the complaint raises the possibility of coverage but the insurer's own investigation suggests there is no possibility of coverage. He reasoned that, in this context, applying the four-corners rule appropriately errs on the side of resolving doubts about whether the duty to defend arises in favor of the insured. By contrast, he declined to apply the rule in *Yalda* because the extrinsic facts in that case raised—rather than discounted—the possibility of coverage. I find Judge Gordon's analysis in *Andrew* and *Yalda* persuasive. I predict that, where, as here, extrinsic facts known to the insurer may raise the possibility of coverage, the Nevada Supreme Court would likely not apply the four-corners rule to exclude those facts. I therefore conclude that the duty to defend may be triggered by facts known to the insurer through extrinsic sources or by the factual allegations in the complaint."

In *Zurich Am. Ins. Co. v. Ironshore Specialty Ins. Co.*, No. 18-16937, 2020 U.S. App. LEXIS 20815 (9th Cir. July 2, 2020), the Ninth Circuit concluded that the duty to defend issue is an open one under Nevada law and certified the following question to the Nevada Supreme Court: "Whether, under Nevada law, the burden of proving the applicability of an exception to an exclusion of coverage in an insurance policy falls on the insurer or the insured? Whichever party bears such a burden, may it rely on evidence extrinsic to the complaint to carry its burden, and if so, is it limited to extrinsic evidence available at the time the insured tendered the defense of the lawsuit to the insurer?"

New Hampshire: The Supreme Court of New Hampshire held that the determination of the duty to defend is not limited to the allegations in the complaint. *Webster v. Acadia Ins. Co.*, 934 A.2d 567, 570 (N.H. 2007) ("It is well-settled in New Hampshire that an insurer's obligation to defend its insured is determined by whether the cause of action against the insured alleges sufficient facts in the pleadings to bring it within the express terms of the policy. In considering whether a duty to defend exists based upon the sufficiency of the pleadings, we consider the reasonable expectations of the insured as to its rights under the policy. We have said, [a]n insurer's obligation is not merely to defend in cases of perfect declarations, but also in cases where by any reasonable intendment of the pleadings liability of the insured can be inferred, and neither ambiguity nor inconsistency in the underlying plaintiff's complaint can justify escape of the insurer from its obligation to defend.") (citations and internal quotation omitted); *see also N. Sec. Ins. Co. v. Connors*, 20 A.3d 912, 916 (N.H. 2011) (restating the standard set out in *Webster* and adding that, "[i]n cases of doubt as to whether the writ against the insured alleges a liability of the insurer under the policy, the doubt must be resolved in the insured's favor"); *Great American Dining, Inc. v. Philadelphia Indem. Ins. Co.*, 62 A.3d 843 (N.H. 2013) (restating the standard set out in *Webster* with cite to *Connors*); *Todd v. Vt. Mut. Ins. Co.*, 137 A.3d 1115 (N.H. 2016) (restating the standard set out in *Webster* with cite to *Connors*).

New Jersey: The Superior Court of New Jersey, Appellate Division, rejected the insured's argument that extrinsic evidence may only be considered to support coverage rather than to prove that the claims are not covered by the policy. *Polarome Intern., Inc. v. Greenwich Ins. Co.*, 961 A.2d 29, 48 (N.J. Super. Ct. App. Div. 2008). "If an insurer believes that the evidence indicates that the claim is not covered, the insurer is not always required to provide a defense." *Id.; Spartan Oil Co. v. New Jersey Property Liability Ins. Guar. Ass'n*, 2012 N.J. LEXIS 1177 (N.J. Super. Ct. App. Div. June 8, 2012) (noting that, "at times and in particular circumstances, the Supreme Court has condoned looking beyond a complaint to the underlying facts alleged by the claimant" and describing several cases where a duty to defend was determined in this manner); *EIC Group, LLC v. Travelers Indem. Co. of Am.*, No. A-2590-14T1, 2016 N.J. Super. Unpub. LEXIS 1683 (N.J. Super. Ct. App. Div. May 2, 2016) ("If an insurer believes that the evidence indicates that the claim is not covered, the insurer is not always required to provide a defense.") (quoting *Polarome*). *But see Kent Motor Cars, Inc. v. Reynolds and Reynolds, Co.*, 25 A.3d 1027, 1042 (N.J. 2011) (citing several cases for the rule that "[e]ssential to any evaluation of a claim that an insurer has a duty to defend is a comparison of the factual allegations in the complaint with the coverage language of the policy") (not addressing use of extrinsic evidence).

In *Abouzaid v. Mansard Gardens Associates*, 23 A.3d 338 (N.J. 2011), the New Jersey high court held that an insurer owed a duty to defend an insured for a complaint that, on its face, did not give rise to coverage. However, the court concluded that a defense was owed because of the possibility of facts being established in the underlying action. Because such facts, if established, would trigger coverage, the court held that a defense was owed from the outset of the action. *See also Carlin v. Cornell, Hegarty & Koch*, 2011 N.J. Super. Unpub. LEXIS 2155 (N.J. Super. Ct. App. Div. Aug. 11, 2011) ("Although courts generally look to the complaint to ascertain the duty to defend, the analysis is not necessarily limited to the facts asserted in the complaint. ... [A]n insurer's duty to provide a defense may also be triggered by 'facts indicating potential coverage that arise during the resolution of the underlying dispute.'" (quoting *Abouzaid*) (alteration in original); *Andrews v. Jerud*, No. A-6036-12T3, 2014 N.J. Super. Unpub. LEXIS 2417 (N.J. Super. Ct. App. Div. Oct. 8, 2014) (same) (quoting *Abouzaid*); *Sur. Mech. Servs., Inc. v. Phoenix Ins. Co.*, No. 12-3242, 2014 U.S. Dist. LEXIS 87665 (D.N.J. June 27, 2014) ("In determining whether a claim is potentially coverable, courts compare the complaint with the language of the insurance policy and resolve any doubts or ambiguities in favor of the insured. However, courts are not strictly limited to the complaint and may also consider facts that arise in the course of litigation") (citing *Abouzaid*); *Montville Twp. Bd. of Educ. v. Zurich Am. Ins. Co.*, No. 16-4466, 2018 U.S. Dist. LEXIS 8883 (D.N.J.

Jan. 19, 2018) ("[T]he duty to defend is not necessarily frozen by the complaint. The duty to defend may arise where facts extrinsic to the complaint in effect expand the claim, bringing the claim within the policy's coverage. (*Abouzaid*) That exception is to be distinguished, however, from the defendant insured's simply saying that it will prevail on the merits and thereby negate some exclusion or limitation on coverage. That does not change the nature of the claims being asserted."); *Albion Eng'g Co v. Hartford Fire Ins. Co.*, 779 Fed. Appx. 85 (3rd Cir. 2019) (concluding that the extrinsic evidence presented by the insured did not change the nature of the claims) (citing *Abouzaid*).

New Jersey's duty to defend analysis is also subject to the so-called *Burd* rule, but which is frequently not employed by insurers. The Supreme Court of New Jersey has held that, if the trial in the underlying action "will leave the question of coverage unresolved so that the insured may later be called upon to pay, or if the case may be so defended by a carrier as to prejudice the insured thereafter upon the issue of coverage, the carrier should not be permitted to control the defense." *Burd v. Sussex Mutual Insurance Co.*, 267 A.2d 7, 10 (N.J. 1970); *see also Flomerfelt v. Cardiello*, 997 A.2d 991, 999 (N.J. 2010) ("In short, in circumstances in which the underlying coverage question cannot be decided from the face of the complaint, the insurer is obligated to provide a defense until all potentially covered claims are resolved, but the resolution may be through adjudication of the complaint or in a separate proceeding between insured and insurer either before or after that decision is reached.") (discussing *Burd* at length). "[T]he practical effect of *Burd* is that an insured must initially assume the costs of defense itself, subject to reimbursement by the insurer if it prevails on the coverage question." *Trustees of Princeton University v. Aetna Cas. & Sur. Co.*, 680 A.2d 783, 787 (N.J. Super. Ct. App. Div. 1996) (quoting *Hartford Accident Indem. Co. v. Aetna Life & Cas. Ins. Co.*, 483 A.2d 402, 407 n.3 (N.J. 1984)). Further, such reimbursement obligation can be limited, when feasible, solely to those costs that were incurred to defend covered claims. *SL Indus. Inc. v. Am. Motorists Ins. Co.*, 607 A.2d 1266 (N.J. 1992). *See also Four Seasons at North Caldwell Condo. Assoc. v. K. Hovnanian at North Caldwell, III, LLC.*, No. ESX-L-7086-18 (N.J. Super. Ct. Law Div. Feb. 12, 2021) (rejecting the argument that *Burd* has been "effectively gutted" by *Abouzaid*) ("The court finds that *Burd* remains vital and was not expressly or impliedly overruled by *Abouzaid*."); *Passaic Valley Sewerage Commissioners v. St. Paul Fire & Marine Ins. Co.*, 21 A.3d 1151 (N.J. 2011) (holding that insurer did not breach its duty to defend by reimbursing its insured's defense costs for solely covered claims). *See also* Chapter 6 addressing the requirement, under

New Jersey law, for an insurer that wishes to retain counsel to defend its insured under a reservation of rights.

New Mexico: The Supreme Court of New Mexico held that the determination of the duty to defend is not limited to the allegations in the complaint. *Am. Gen. Fire & Cas. Co. v. Progressive Cas. Co.*, 799 P.2d 1113, 1116 (N.M. 1990) ("The duty of an insurer to defend arises from the allegations on the face of the complaint or from the known but unpleaded factual basis of the claim that brings it arguably within the scope of coverage. The duty may arise at the beginning of litigation or at some later stage if the issues are changed so as to bring the dispute within the scope of policy coverage.") (citations omitted); *see also G & G Servs., Inc. v. Agora Syndicate, Inc.*, 993 P.2d 751 (N.M. Ct. App. 1999) (discussing in detail the scope of an insurer's duty to investigate whether it is obligated to defend); *Western Heritage Bank v. Federal Ins. Co.*, 557 Fed. Appx. 807 (10th Cir. 2014) ("The duty to defend is determined by looking to the facts actually known by the insurer at the time of demand. Therefore, although the Fourth Amended Petition was the operative document at the time the Hawkins suit settled, the WHB parties filed their claims for defense based on the prior petitions. Because the Third Amended Petition has the most detailed facts, it is used to describe Hawkins' allegations against the WHB parties."); *Pulte Homes of N.M., Inc. v. Indiana Lumbermens Ins. Co.*, 367 P.3d 869 (N.M. Ct. App. 2015) ("[A]n insurance company must conduct such an investigation into the facts and circumstances underlying the complaint against its insured as is reasonable given the factual information provided by the insured or provided by the circumstances surrounding the claim in order to determine whether it has a duty to defend."); *Dove v. State Farm Fire & Cas. Co.*, No. 34,932, 2017 N.M. App. LEXIS 17 (N.M. Ct. App. Mar. 28, 2017) ("[T]here is a duty to defend when the facts in the complaint are not stated with sufficient clarity so that it can be determined from the face of the complaint whether the action falls within the coverage of the policy.") (*see* CoverageOpinions.info, Vol. 6, Iss. 5 (May 17, 2017), where Maniloff called *Dove* "maybe the best example ever of the breadth of the duty to defend"); *First Mercury Ins. Co. v. Cincinnati Ins. Co.*, 882 F.3d 1289 (10th Cir. 2018) (concluding that a party was an additional insured, despite being the only defendant named in the suit, because additional facts, as well as the defenses raised by the putative additional insured, implicated acts or omissions of the named insured or its employee, as required to satisfy the language of the additional insured endorsement).

New York: The Court of Appeals of New York held that the determination of the duty to defend is not limited to the allegations in the complaint. *Fitzpatrick v.*

Am. Honda Motor Co., Inc., 575 N.E.2d 90, 92 (N.Y. 1991) ("[T]he courts of this State have refused to permit insurers to look beyond the complaint's allegations to avoid their obligation to defend and have held that the duty to defend exists if the complaint contains any facts or allegations which bring the claim even potentially within the protection purchased. The holdings thus clearly establish that an insurer's duty to defend is at least broad enough to apply when the four corners of the complaint suggest the reasonable possibility of coverage. However, to say that the duty to defend is at least broad enough to apply to actions in which the complaint alleges a covered occurrence is a far cry from saying that the complaint allegations are the sole criteria for measuring the scope of that duty. Indeed, in these circumstances, where the insurer is attempting to shield itself from the responsibility to defend despite its actual knowledge that the lawsuit involves a covered event, wooden application of the 'four corners of the complaint' rule would render the duty to defend narrower than the duty to indemnify—clearly an unacceptable result. For that reason, courts and commentators have indicated that the insurer must provide a defense if it has knowledge of facts which potentially bring the claim within the policy's indemnity coverage."); *see also Fieldston Prop. Owners Ass'n, Inc. v. Hermitage Ins. Co., Inc.*, 945 N.E.2d 1013, 1018 (N.Y. 2011) (citing *Fitzpatrick* for New York's duty to defend standard); *United Parcel Service v. Lexington Ins. Group*, 983 F. Supp. 2d 258 (S.D.N.Y. 2013) ("The insurer must defend whenever the four corners of the complaint suggest—or the insurer has actual knowledge of facts establishing—a reasonable possibility of coverage under the policy. An insurer cannot ignore information supplied by the insured in assessing its duty to defend. An insurer may avoid its duty to defend only if it establishes, as a matter of law, that there is no possible factual or legal basis on which the insurer might eventually be obligated to indemnify the insured under any provision of the insurance policy."); *City of New York v. Wausau Underwriters Ins. Co.*, 45 N.Y.S.3d 3 (N.Y. App. Div. 2016) ("In this case, in order to determine whether Wausau had a duty to defend the City as an additional insured in any or all of five underlying actions, we must examine the allegations in each of the five underlying complaints, construing them liberally, for the suggestion of a reasonable possibility of coverage under the policy for the claims asserted. In addition, we must examine the record with respect to each case to determine whether Wausau had actual knowledge of facts establishing such a reasonable possibility. Among the facts we will examine to determine whether a reasonable possibility of recovery existed are the nature of the occurrence, the time and location of the occurrence and whether the trade contract and policy applicable to work performed at that location were in effect at the time of the alleged occurrence.") (discussing the extrinsic evidence that triggered the duty to defend); *City of New York v. Liberty Mut. Ins. Co.*, No. 15-8220, 2017 U.S. Dist. LEXIS 164134 (S.D.N.Y. Sept. 28, 2017) ("[T]he Court concludes that Liberty cannot defeat its duty to defend with extrinsic evidence here. That is because the three factual questions Liberty seeks to have this Court settle . . . are questions relevant to the merits of the underlying actions.") (detailed discussion of an insurer's permissible use of extrinsic evidence to defeat a duty to defend); *Quaco v. Liberty Ins. Underwriters Inc.*, No. 17-7980, 2018 U.S. Dist. LEXIS 162834 (S.D.N.Y. Sept. 23, 2018) ("Liberty is attempting to reach beyond the allegations in the underlying complaint — which clearly compel coverage — to dredge up facts that might help it escape coverage liability. Not surprisingly, courts applying New York law have rejected such attempts to convert *Fitzpatrick* from a shield for the insured into a sword for the insurer. *See, e.g., Cont'l Cas. Co.*, 2010 U.S. Dist. LEXIS 85467, 2010 WL 2834898, at *2 (collecting cases). As a result, Liberty cannot escape its duty to defend by relying on *Fitzpatrick* or extrinsic facts relating to its knowledge of the underlying lawsuit.").

North Carolina: The Supreme Court of North Carolina held that the determination of the duty to defend is not limited to the allegations in the complaint. *Waste Mgmt. of Carolinas, Inc. v. Peerless Ins. Co.*, 340 S.E.2d 374, 377–78 (N.C. 1986) ("Where the insurer knows or could reasonably ascertain facts that, if proven, would be covered by its policy, the duty to defend is not dismissed because the facts alleged in a third-party complaint appear to be outside coverage, or within a policy exception to coverage … . [Many] jurisdictions have recognized that the modern acceptance of notice pleading and of the plasticity of pleadings in general imposes upon the insurer a duty to investigate and evaluate facts expressed or implied in the third-party complaint as well as facts learned from the insured and from other sources. Even though the insurer is bound by the policy to defend 'groundless, false or fraudulent' lawsuits filed against the insured, if the facts are not even arguably covered by the policy, then the insurer has no duty to defend."); *see also Builders Mut. Ins. Co. v. Mitchell*, 709 S.E.2d 528, 534–35 (N.C. Ct. App. 2011) ("Although the insurer's duty to defend an action is generally determined by the pleadings, facts learned from the insured and facts discoverable by reasonable investigation may also be considered. There is a duty to defend [w]here the insurer knows or could reasonably ascertain facts that, if proven, would be covered by its policy. This is true even where the facts appear to be outside coverage or within a policy exception.") (citations and internal quotations omitted) (alteration in original); *Kubit v. MAG Mut. Ins. Co.*, 708

S.E.2d 138, 146 (N.C. Ct. App. 2011) (specifically holding that *Harleysville Mut. Ins. Co. v. Buzz Off Insect Shield, LLC*, 692 S.E.2d 605 (N.C. 2010) did not overrule the portion of *Waste Mgmt.* allowing consideration of extrinsic evidence to determine the duty to defend); *Economy Premier Assur. Co. v. Mitchell*, No. 12–326, 2013 U.S. Dist. LEXIS 75265 (W.D.N.C. May 29, 2013) (restating standard from *Waste Mgmt*); *Continental Casualty Co. v. Amerisure Ins. Co.*, No. 14-529, 2017 U.S. Dist. LEXIS 313 (W.D.N.C. Jan. 3, 2017) (noting that insurer could not rely on evidence outside the complaint to establish applicability of an exclusion to deny a duty to defend); *New NGC, Inc. v. ACE Am. Ins. Co.*, 105 F. Supp. 3d 552 (W.D.N.C. 2015) ("[W]here the complaint fails to assert claims falling within the coverage provided, an insurer's duty to defend may still be found where the insurer knows or could reasonably ascertain facts, that if proven, would be covered by [the] policy. However, the inverse of this inquiry has not been recognized by North Carolina courts and has been explicitly rejected by the Middle District of North Carolina in a decision affirmed by the Fourth Circuit Court of Appeals. *St. Paul Fire & Marine Ins. Co. v. Vigilant Ins. Co.*, 724 F. Supp. 1173, 1179 (M.D.N.C. 1989), *aff'd* 919 F.2d 235 (4th Cir. 1990) ('Once a complaint implicates the possibility of coverage, an insurer may not exonerate itself by preliminarily determining that no coverage actually exists despite the allegations of the complaint.'). *see also Peace Coll. of Raleigh, Inc. v. Am. Int'l Specialty Lines Ins. Co.*, 5:09-CV-479-FL, 2010 U.S. Dist. LEXIS 97282, 2010 WL 3743539 (E.D.N.C. Sept. 16, 2010). Permitting evidence outside the pleadings to negate allegations in the complaint is akin to a perfunctory review of the merits of the underlying claims against the insured. Such review is not consistent with the duty to defend as understood by the insured party and as explained by North Carolina law pertaining to the interpretation of contracts for insurance."); *Certain Underwriters at Lloyd's, London v. Medical Fusion, LLC*, No. 20-00041, 2020 U.S. Dist. LEXIS 189617 (W.D.N.C. Oct. 13, 2020) (court noting that it can "use the facts in the present lawsuit [coverage action], along with complaint from the underlying suit, to determine if there is a duty to defend").

North Dakota: The Supreme Court of North Dakota held that the determination of the duty to defend is not limited to the allegations in the complaint. *Ohio Cas. Ins. Co. v. Clark*, 583 N.W.2d 377, 380 (N.D. 1998). The North Dakota high court upheld the decision of an insurer to deny a defense for an underlying claim that alleged intentional conduct but plead it as negligence. *Id.* The court reasoned that "labeling Daniel Clark's conduct [conviction for manslaughter] as negligent does not alter its true nature." *Id.* (internal quotation omitted). *But see Bullis v. Minn.*

Lawyers Mut. Ins. Co., No. 3:06-cv-102, 2007 U.S. Dist. LEXIS 91457 (D.N.D. Dec. 10, 2007) ("Although [the insured] is correct that *Clark* allowed for a limited investigation beyond the pleadings by the trial court to determine whether the insured's acts were intentional or unintentional, generally, the Court is limited to the face of the complaint."); *First Nat'l Bank & Trust Co. v. St. Paul Fire & Marine Ins. Co.*, 971 F.2d 142, 144 (8th Cir. 1992) ("In the absence of other proceedings, it is presumed that information outside the complaint is not available to the insurer for the purposes of determining whether a duty to defend arises. This presumption should not, however, relieve St. Paul of an obligation to consider other information provided to it.") (citation omitted). *See also Ziegler v. Meadowbrook Ins. Group, Inc.*, 774 N.W.2d 782 (N.D. 2009) ("[I]t should be noted that there appear to be no North Dakota cases that explain how far beyond the complaint a court can look to determine whether or not an insurer should provide coverage. The North Dakota Supreme Court in *Clark* said the district court did not err in looking beyond the complaint to the underlying facts of the act. In *Farmers Union Mutual Ins. Co. [v]. Decker*, 2005 ND [173,] 704 N.W.2d 857, the Court said the allegations of the complaint should be reasonably interpreted in determining whether the claims are within the coverage and any doubt or ambiguity resolved in the insured's favor. So it appears that looking at the underlying transaction that is allegedly a 'sham' would be reasonable, considering that 'sham transaction' is a broad descriptive statement."); *Tibert v. Nodak Mut. Ins. Co.*, 816 N.W.2d 31 (N.D. 2012) ("[T]he district court and Nodak suggest that the jury's finding in the underlying civil suit somehow has a res judicata effect upon the insurer's duty to defend in that same civil case. However, if the allegations pleaded in the complaint viewed at the time of tender include any potential liability or possibility of coverage under the policy, there is a duty to defend, and the insurer cannot simply refuse to provide a defense in the hope that the facts as determined by the fact finder in the underlying lawsuit preclude coverage under a policy exclusion. The insurer is not free to refuse to provide a defense, wait until the case is tried, and then with the benefit of hindsight claim the jury's resolution of disputed factual allegations is res judicata on the issue of duty to defend. The insurer's duty to defend is set by the pleadings and must be determined as of the time the defense it tendered; it is not affected by 'the course and outcome of the litigation.'") (distinguishing *Clark* and another similar case on the basis that, "[i]n those cases, the relevant issues had been determined under the 'beyond a reasonable doubt' criminal standard *before* the civil action against the insured was commenced. Thus, the result of the criminal case was known and the relevant factual issues conclusively determined before the insurer's duty to defend in the civil action arose. Under those circumstances, there was no possibility of coverage and no duty to defend.") (emphasis in original); *Borsheim Builders Supply, Inc. v. Manger Ins., Inc.*, 917 N.W.2d 504 (N.D. 2018) (concluding that party entitled to a defense, as an additional insured, despite plaintiff's employer/named insured not being named as a defendant; putative additional insured alleged in its answer that employer/named insured would also be at fault) (discussing *Ramara*, *see* Pennsylvania).

Ohio: The Supreme Court of Ohio held that the determination of the duty to defend is not limited to the allegations in the complaint. *Willoughby Hills v. Cincinnati Ins. Co.*, 459 N.E.2d 555, 558 (Ohio 1984). The court held that "the pleadings alone may not provide sufficient factual information to determine whether the insurer has an obligation to defend the insured. It remains true that where the pleadings unequivocally bring the action within the coverage afforded by the policy, the duty to defend will attach. However, where the insurer's duty to defend is not apparent from the pleadings in the case against the insured, but the allegations do state a claim which is potentially or arguably within the policy coverage, or there is some doubt as to whether a theory of recovery within the policy coverage had been pleaded, the insurer must accept the defense of the claim. Thus, the 'scope of the allegations' may encompass matters well outside the four corners of the pleadings." *Id.* In *Ferro Corp. v. Cookson Group*, 561 F. Supp. 2d 888 (N.D. Ohio 2008), the Ohio District Court examined numerous decisions that have interpreted *Willoughby Hills*. The court concluded that "the inquiry into the insurer[']s duty to defend must naturally begin with a close scrutinization of the allegations of the disputed complaint. If such a review reveals claims which 'potentially' or 'arguably' fall within the purview of the policy, then, and only then, does *Willoughby Hills* dictate that a court look to extraneous matters to determine whether a defense is required of the insurer." *Id.* at 899 (alteration in original) (citations and internal quotation omitted). "Courts will not, … impose a duty to defend based on allegations outside the complaint, where the complaint does not state a claim that arguably triggers coverage." *Id.* at 900 (alteration in original) (citations and internal quotation omitted); *see also Ferro Corp. v. Cookson Group*, 585 F.3d 946 (6th Cir. 2009) ("[W]hether an insurer has a duty to defend an action against an insured is initially determined by the scope of the pleadings. If the underlying factual allegations in the complaint do not fall potentially or arguably within the policy coverage, then there is no need to look beyond the allegations in the complaint, and the duty to defend is not triggered."); *Motorists Mut. Ins. Co. v. Natl. Dairy Herd Improvement Assn., Inc.*, 750 N.E.2d 1169

(Ohio Ct. App. 2001) ("Because we have determined that the allegations in the *Agritronics* complaint do not state a claim that potentially or arguably falls within the purview of the insurance policy, we need not look at extraneous matter developed during the course of discovery."); *Cincinnati Specialty Underwriters Ins. Co. v. Larschied*, No. 1-14-01, 2014 Ohio App. LEXIS 4036 (Ohio Ct. App. Sept. 22, 2014) ("Even under the liberal notions of notice pleading it would be inherently unfair to require the insurer to provide a defense where the pleadings failed to notify, even arguably, that the insured is being sued on a claim covered by the policy."); *Mesa Underwriters Specialty Ins. Co. v. Myers*, No. 14-2201, 2016 U.S. Dist. LEXIS 108444 (N.D. Ohio Aug. 16, 2016) ("Sireco's claim for damages to its roof is not 'potentially or arguably' covered. The claim is for damages Sireco has incurred or will incur to fix Myers's negligent work on the roof itself, and thus outside the policy's coverage. Resort to extrinsic materials for purposes of fleshing out Sireco's claims is therefore unnecessary and impermissible under *City of Willoughby Hills* and *National Dairy Herd*."); *Maxum Indem. Co. v. Robbins Co.*, No. 17-1968, 2018 U.S. Dist. LEXIS 57729 (N.D. Ohio Mar. 22, 2018) ("*Willoughby Hills* stands for the proposition that the 'scope of the allegations may expand through discovery such that, while not apparent initially, the claims may become covered by the insurance.' *Ferro Corp. v. Cookson Grp.*, 561 F. Supp. 2d 888, 899 (N.D. Ohio 2008). However, *Willoughby Hills* 'does not stand for the proposition. . . . that coverage may arise after the filing of the complaint where the pleadings did not create even an arguable basis for coverage.'") (*aff'd* 784 Fed. Appx. 366 (6th Cir. 2019), but not substantively addressing duty to defend standard).

Oklahoma: The Supreme Court of Oklahoma held that the determination of the duty to defend is not limited to the allegations in the complaint. *First Bank of Turley v. Fid. & Deposit Ins. Co.*, 928 P.2d 298, 303 (Okla. 1996) ("The defense duty is measured by the nature and kinds of risks covered by the policy as well as by the reasonable expectations of the insured. An insurer has a duty to defend an insured whenever it ascertains the presence of facts that give rise to the potential of liability under the policy. The insurer's defense duty is determined on the basis of information gleaned from the petition (and other pleadings), from the insured and from other sources available to the insurer at the time the defense is demanded (or tendered) rather than by the outcome of the third-party action.") (citations omitted). The *Turley* Court stated: "The duty to defend cannot be limited by the precise language of the pleadings. The Insurer has the duty to look behind the third party's allegations to analyze whether coverage is possible." *Id.* at 303 n.15; *see also*

Fossil Creek Energy Corp. v. Cook's Oilfield Services, 242 P.3d 537, 544 n.14 (Ok. Ct. App. 2010) (quoting standard from *Turley*); *Colony Ins. Co. v. Bear Productions, Inc.*, No. 12-122, 2013 U.S. Dist. LEXIS 43716 (E.D. Okla. Mar 26, 2013) ("Colony has a duty to look beyond the precise language of the pleadings in the Underlying Action and look at the facts behind the third parties' allegations to analyze whether coverage is possible. More precisely stated, if the insurer knows the true facts concerning the subject of his insured's adversary's claim, and said facts make of it a claim, or action, against which the insurer is obliged, under the policy, to defend the insured, then the allegations of the adversary's pleadings are 'incidental', and not controlling as to the insured's obligation to defend.") (internal citations and quotations omitted); *Schwegman v. Continental Casualty Co.*, No. 16-0730, 2017 U.S. Dist. LEXIS 69129 (N.D. Ok. May 5, 2017) (discussing *Turley* and providing "several reasons to believe the Oklahoma Supreme Court would find that an insurer in this situation would have the duty to defend," including the use of extrinsic evidence); *Above It All Roofing & Constr., Inc. v. Sec. Nat'l Ins. Co.*, 285 F. Supp. 3d 1224 (N.D. Okla. 2018) (duty to defend triggered) ("[T]he court concludes that facts indicating that asbestos was not present at the Property, coupled with the original Petition's allegations of negligent workmanship, give rise to the potential for liability under the policy to which no exclusion would apparently apply."); *Schwegman v. Cont'l Cas. Co.*, No. 16-0730, 2017 U.S. Dist. LEXIS 69129 (N.D. Okla. May 5, 2017) (discussing *Turley* and holding that, while no claim was being asserted for professional negligence, a defense was owed, under a professional liability policy, where discovery showed that damages were being sought for professional negligence) ("This is not a case of the insured asserting that the insurer defend him against some nebulous claim that someone could assert against him. This is a case of a plaintiff filing pleadings that display the plaintiff's wish to bring a professional negligence claim against the insured, but going about it the wrong way.").

Oregon: The Supreme Court of Oregon held that the determination of the duty to defend is limited to the allegations in the complaint. *Ledford v. Gutoski*, 877 P.2d 80, 82 (Or. 1994) ("Whether an insurer has a duty to defend an action against its insured depends on two documents: the complaint and the insurance policy. An insurer has a duty to defend an action against its insured if the claim against the insured stated in the complaint could, without amendment, impose liability for conduct covered by the policy.") (citation omitted); *see also Isenhart v. Gen. Cas. Co.*, 377 P.2d 26, 28–29 (Or. 1962) ("If a contrary rule were adopted, requiring the insurer to take note of facts other than those alleged, the insurer frequently would be required to speculate upon whether the facts alleged could be proved. We do not think that this is a reasonable interpretation of the bargain to defend."); *see also Goritsan v. Nautilus Ins. Co.*, No. 10-433, 2010 U.S. Dist. LEXIS 141508 (D. Or. Nov. 16, 2010) (following *Ledford*); *Bresee Homes, Inc. v. Farmers Ins. Exchange*, 293 P.3d 1036 (Or. 2012) ("[N]either the failure to identify correctly the claims nor the failure to state them separately defeats the duty to defend. As long as the complaint contains allegations that, without amendment, state a basis for a claim covered by the policy, the duty to defend arises."); *Leach v. Scottsdale Indemn. Co.*, 323 P.3d 337 (Or. Ct. App. 2014) (finding that a duty to defend was owed after resolving, as it "must," an ambiguity in the complaint in favor of the insured). *But see Fred Shearer & Sons, Inc. v. Gemini Ins. Co.*, 240 P.3d 67 (Or. Ct. App. 2010) (distinguishing *Ledford* and concluding that, when the question is whether the insured is being held liable for conduct that falls within the scope of the policy, it makes sense to look exclusively to the complaint; but the same cannot be said with respect to whether a party seeking coverage is an "insured") (allowing a party to use extrinsic evidence to establish its status as an insured under a vendor's endorsement). More recently, in *West Hills Dev. Co. v. Chartis Claims, Inc.*, 385 P.3d 1053 (Or. 2016), the Supreme Court of Oregon discussed *Ledford* and *Bresee* and rejected the insurer's "assertion that there is no duty to defend unless the complaint 'rules in' coverage. Instead, as this court most recently held in *Bresee Homes*, the question is whether, '[r]egardless of the presence of ambiguity or unclarity in the complaint,. . . the court can reasonably interpret the allegations to include an incident or injury that falls within the coverage of the policy.'" The court's decision is demonstrated by its rationale for concluding that the insurer had a duty to defend: "The only remaining question is whether the allegations could result in West Hills being held liable for L&T's '*ongoing* operations.' As noted, Oregon Auto has argued that 'ongoing operations' requires that any covered damages must have occurred before L&T completed its work on the project. The Court of Appeals did not find it necessary to resolve that question . . . and neither do we. The complaint alleges that damages had occurred by the time the owners purchased their townhomes. It is possible that the damages occurred earlier. Reasonably interpreted, then, the complaint could result in West Hills being held liable for conduct covered by the policy. The court noted that it did "not see any need to resort to extrinsic evidence . . . or to modify [its] existing case law regarding when an insurer has a duty to defend." *See also PIH Beaverton LLC v. Red Shield Ins. Co.*, 412 P.3d 234 (Ore. Ct. App. 2018) (whether one party's liability is with respect to another party's ongoing operations does not relate to whether a party is an additional insured; therefore, the previously recognized four corners exception, for determining whether a party is an insured, does not apply); *Esurance Ins. Co. v. Hamm*, 387 F. Supp. 3d 1134 (D. Ore. 2019) ("In *Morgan* [*Allstate Ins. Co. v. Morgan*, 123 F. Supp. 3d 1266 (D. Ore. 2015)], the court identified the exceptions [to the four corners rule] as follows: (1) when extrinsic evidence provides the date an insurer was notified of a claim; (2) when the court needs to determine whether an organization or an individual was an insured under a policy; and (3) when a previous judicial decision precludes coverage, based on the doctrine of issue preclusion."); *Great Northern Ins. Co. v. Crown Pine Timber 4, L.P.*, No. 18-2104, 2021 U.S. Dist. LEXIS 1667 (D. Ore. Jan. 5, 2021) (declining to allow consideration of extrinsic evidence as it was undisputed that the party seeking a defense was an additional insured).

Pennsylvania: The Supreme Court of Pennsylvania held that the determination of the duty to defend is limited to the allegations in the complaint. *Kvaerner Metals Div. of Kvaerner U.S., Inc. v. Commercial Union Ins. Co.*, 908 A.2d 888, 896 (Pa. 2006) ("The Superior Court erred in looking beyond the allegations raised in Bethlehem's Complaint to determine whether National Union had a duty to defend Kvaerner and in finding that the Battery's damages may have been the result of an 'occurrence.' In doing so, it departed from the well-established precedent of this Court requiring that an insurer's duty to defend and indemnify be determined solely from the language of the complaint against the insured. We find no reason to expand upon the well-reasoned and long-standing rule that an insurer's duty to defend is triggered, if at all, by the factual averments contained in the complaint itself.") (citations omitted); *see also American & Foreign Ins. Co. v. Jerry's Sport Center, Inc.*, 2 A.3d 526, 541 (Pa. 2010) ("An insurer is obligated to defend its insured if the factual allegations of the complaint on its face encompass an injury that is actually or potentially within the scope of the policy."); *Allstate Prop. and Cas. Ins. Co. v. Filachek*, No. 10-3634, 2011 U.S. Dist. LEXIS 57336 (E.D. Pa. May 25, 2011) ("[I]n determining whether an insurer has a duty to defend, a court examines only the factual allegations made in the complaint, and cannot consider additional information which may come to light in discovery."); *Graziano Constr. & Develop. Co., Inc. v. Pa. Nat. Mut. Cas. Ins. Co.*, No. 1876 WDA 2009, 2011 Pa. Super. LEXIS 2680 (Pa. Super. Ct. May 26, 2011) (addressing in detail Pennsylvania's duty to defend standard and stating in clear terms that its determination is limited to consideration of the allegations in the complaint); *But see Lexington Ins. Co. v. Charter Oak Fire Ins. Co.*, 81 A.3d 903 (Pa. Super. Ct. 2013) ("[I]n the appropriate context, a court must be permitted to consider evidence that would absolve the insurer of its duty to defend.

Nevertheless, we conclude that the expert reports in this case are insufficient to confine the claims against CMX outside the scope of coverage afforded by the North River policy. This is because, while they support potential claims of professional negligence, they do not preclude the underlying plaintiffs from also pursuing general negligence claims."); *Selective Ins. Co. of S. Carolina v. Lower Providence Twp.*, No. 12-800, 2013 U.S. Dist. LEXIS 89592 (E.D. Pa. June 26, 2013) (noting that, under the facts at issue (involving employment status), the purpose of the four corners rule would not be well-served by "blindly following" it); *State Farm Fire & Cas. Co. v. Scalia*, No. 14-00049, 2014 U.S. Dist. LEXIS 170015 (M.D. Pa. Dec. 9, 2014) (finding it "far less than clear" that Pennsylvania's "four corners" rule has an exception "that where an insurer is on notice that the underlying complaint may be amended in a way that may bring it within the scope of the coverage of the insurance policy, the insurance company maintains a duty to defend"); *Unitrin Direct Ins. Co. v. Esposito*, 751 Fed. Appx. 213 (3rd Cir. 2018) (concluding that district court "erred by looking beyond the allegations of the underlying complaint to consider [insured's] claim that he acted in self-defense"); *Lupu v. Loan City, LLC*, 903 F.3d 382 (3rd Cir. 2018) (citing *Insurance Key Issues* as support for Pennsylvania being a four corners state) (concluding that H*effernan & Co. v. Hartford Ins. Co.*, 614 A.2d 295 (Pa. Super. Ct. 1992) -- where the court held that interrogatories triggered the duty to defend, even though the complaint had not yet been amended to include them – is not the law in Pennsylvania); *Foremost Ins. Co. v. Nosam, LLC*, 343 F. Supp. 3d 448 (E.D. Pa. 2018) ("If the language of the complaint alleges facts that would trigger an exclusion to coverage, but does not allege facts that would make applicable an exception to the exclusion, the insureds may introduce extrinsic evidence to prove an exception to a policy exclusion."); *Erie Ins. Exch. v. Moore*, 228 A.3d 258 (Pa. 2020) (discussing the role of artful pleadings in consideration of duty to defend). Pennsylvania courts will look beyond the four corners of the complaint to deny a defense for intentional conduct that is plead as negligence. *Erie Ins. Exch. v. Fidler*, 808 A.2d 587, 590 (Pa. Super. Ct. 2002) ("If we were to allow the manner in which the complainant frames the request for damages to control the coverage question, we would permit insureds to circumvent exclusions that are clearly part of the policy of insurance.").

In *Ramara, Inc. v. Westfield Ins. Co.*, 814 F.3d 660 (3d Cir. 2016), the Third Circuit Court of Appeals held that "[t]he four corners rule—even under Pennsylvania's strict construction—does not permit an insurer to make its coverage decision with blinders on, disclaiming any knowledge of coverage-triggering facts. Quite the opposite, knowledge that an injured employee has a claim under the Workers'

Compensation Act [which is why he did not name his employer in his complaint] must be factored into a determination of whether his allegations in an underlying tort complaint potentially trigger an obligation on an insurer to provide coverage for a defendant in the underlying case. If an insurer fails to account for the Act it may construe the factual allegations of an underlying complaint too narrowly, and the insurer who refuses to defend at the outset does so at its own peril." The *Ramara* court made the point that it was not deviating from Pennsylvania's "four corners" requirement – something it noted it could not do. Instead, the court characterized its decision as providing an "interpretive constraint" on insurers, when determining whether the allegations of a complaint fall outside of coverage under these circumstances. *See also Continental Casualty Co. v. Westfield Ins. Co.*, No. 16-5299, 2017 U.S. Dist. LEXIS 61889 (E.D. Pa. Apr. 24, 2017) ("*Ramara* applies specifically to cases in which a complaint omits a party because of its immunity under the Workers' Compensation Act."); *Liberty Mut. Fire Ins. Co. v. Harleysville Worcester Ins. Co.*, No. 20-5093, 2021 U.S. Dist. LEXIS 44652 (E.D. Pa. Mar. 10, 2021) (following *Ramara*).

Rhode Island: The Supreme Court of Rhode Island held that the determination of the duty to defend is limited to the allegations in the complaint. *Am. Commerce Ins. Co. v. Porto*, 811 A.2d 1185, 1191 (R.I. 2002). In *Am. Commerce Ins. Co. v. Porto*, the court noted that the duty to defend is determined by applying the "pleadings test," which it defined as requiring "the trial court to look at the allegations contained in the complaint, and if the pleadings recite facts bringing the injury complained of within the coverage of the insurance policy, the insurer must defend irrespective of the insured's ultimate liability to the plaintiff." *Id.* (internal quotation omitted). *See also Quality Concrete Corp. v. Travelers Property Cas. Co. of America*, 43 A.3d 16 (R.I. 2012) ("We have frequently articulated the principle that, in Rhode Island, whether an insurer is required to defend its insured is determined by applying the pleadings test."). However, the Supreme Court of Rhode Island carved out an exception in *Peerless Ins. Co. v. Viegas*, 667 A.2d 785 (R.I. 1995), where the court inferred an intent to cause harm and injury in cases involving the sexual molestation of a minor. *Id.* at 788–89. Thus, notwithstanding that the duty to defend is determined by the "pleadings test," the Supreme Court of Rhode Island held that, if the policy contains an intentional act exclusion, an insurer is not obligated to defend an insured that sexually abuses a minor, even if the allegations in the complaint are described in terms of negligence. *Id.*; *see also Narragansett Jewelry Co., Inc. v. St. Paul Fire & Marine Ins. Co.*, 555 F.3d 38, 41–42 (1st Cir. 2009) (applying R.I. law) (strictly applying the "pleadings test") (concluding that insured's post-hoc speculation, about what might be possible, did not create a duty to defend as it could not suffice to avoid the plain language of the complaint and the policy); *Allstate Ins. Co. v. Greloch*, No. 11-015, 2011 U.S. Dist. LEXIS 104238 (D.R.I. Sept. 14, 2011) (holding that duty to defend is determined by the pleadings test and declining insured's invitation to consider deposition testimony to establish duty to defend) (distinguishing *Scottsdale Ins. Co. v. Bitgood*, 10–430, 2011 U.S. Dist. LEXIS 100377 (D.R.I. Sept. 6, 2011), which looked beyond the allegations of a complaint to determine duty to defend, because the complaint there was devoid of any factual allegations); *Medical Malpractice Joint Underwriting Ass'n of R.I. v. Charlesgate Nursing Ctr., L.P.*, 115 A.3d 998 (R.I. 2015) ("[A]lthough the blind application of the 'pleadings test' may lead an insurer to defend an insured against groundless, false or fraudulent suits, the insurer is nevertheless bound to do so."); *Geovera Specialty Ins. Co. v. Poulton*, No. 16-432, 2017 U.S. Dist. LEXIS 165539 (D.R.I. Sept. 26, 2017) ("Extrinsic evidence obtained during discovery may reveal that the only occurrence(s) of property damage happened prior to October 2006, but the pleadings test focuses on the pleading allegations without consideration of extrinsic evidence; therefore, the duty to defend may arise even where known facts conflict with the facts alleged in the complaint."); *Textron, Inc. v. Travelers Cas. & Sur. Co.*, No. 2012-1371, 2017 R.I. Super. LEXIS 130 (D.R.I. Aug. 10, 2017) (using "pleadings test" to find duty to defend, for asbestos suits, as there were no allegations in complaints to show the injuries alleged occurred outside the policy periods); *Bacon Constr. Co. v. Arbella Prot. Ins. Co.*, 208 A.3d 595 (R.I. 2019) ("As discussed, the Arbella policy provides additional insured coverage only with respect to liability for injuries that were caused, at least in part, by U.S. Drywall's negligence, and there are no allegations in the Almeida complaint that U.S. Drywalls acts or omissions caused Almeidas injury. The fact that Bacon voluntarily dismissed, with prejudice, all claims against U.S. Drywall and reached a settlement agreement with Almeida is fatal because these actions extinguished any vicarious-liability claims that Bacon could have raised. As such, we conclude that the Almeida complaint is devoid of any allegations that bring the underlying case within or potentially within the risk coverage of the policy. It is our opinion, therefore, that Arbella has no duty to defend Bacon in the Almeida action.").

South Carolina: The Supreme Court of South Carolina held that the determination of the duty to defend is not limited to the allegations in the complaint. *See Allstate Indem. Co. v. Tilmon*, No. 13-00690, 2014 U.S. Dist. LEXIS 37160 (D.S.C. Mar. 21, 2014) ("[A]n insurer's duty to defend may also be determined by facts outside of the complaint that are known by the insurer.") (citing *USAA Property and Cas. Ins. Co. v. Clegg*, 661 S.E.2d 791 (S.C. 2008)); *See also City of Hartsville v. South Carolina Mun. Ins. & Risk Fin. Fund*, 677 S.E.2d 574, 579 (S.C. 2009) ("[W]e find Byrd's failure to plead the elements of the civil conspiracy did not negate the Insurer's duty to defend the City on this cause of action. Although a determination of an insurer's duty to defend is dependent upon the insured's complaint, an analysis of this duty involves the allegations of the complaint and not the specifically identified causes of action. Moreover, an insurer's duty to defend may arise from facts outside of the complaint that are known to the insurer."); *Jessco, Inc. v. Builders Mut. Ins. Co.*, 472 Fed. Appx. 225 (4th Cir. 2012) ("Although the duty to defend typically is determined by the allegations of the underlying complaint, an insurer's duty to defend is not strictly controlled by the allegations in the complaint. Instead, the duty to defend may also be determined by facts outside of the complaint that are known by the insurer.") (citing *Clegg*); *Allstate Ins. Co. v. Ingraham*, No. 15-3212, 2017 U.S. Dist. LEXIS 36129 (D.S.C. Mar. 14, 2017) ("In addition, the Supreme Court of South Carolina has indicated that orders issued by the underlying trial court may be considered when determining whether the underlying claims create a possibility of coverage under an insurer's liability policy. In *City of Hartsville*, the underlying trial court's orders recognized a cause of action that created a possibility of coverage, and authorized the claimant's pursuit of that claim, even though the claimant had failed to specifically plead the cause of action. The *City of Hartsville* court held that the insurer had an ongoing duty to defend based upon that cause of action, despite the fact that it was not specifically pled, because the underlying trial court recognized the existence of the claim at a hearing on a motion for summary judgment."); *State Farm Fire & Cas. Co. v. Mitchell*, No. 15-1673, 2016 U.S. Dist. LEXIS 135603 (D.S.C. Sept. 30, 2016) ("As Mitchell asserts he was acting in self-defense . . . the Court concludes that the allegations in the underlying state court pleadings and filings, along with the facts known to the insurer, create a possibility of coverage under the Policy in the state court proceeding."). In *Collins Holding Corp. v. Wausau Underwriters Ins. Co.*, 666 S.E.2d 897, 899 (S.C. 2008), the South Carolina Supreme Court reiterated South Carolina law that the obligation of a liability insurer to defend is determined by the allegations in the complaint and if the facts alleged in the complaint fail to bring a claim within the policy's coverage, the insurer has no duty to defend. *Id.* However, the *Collins Holding* Court also adopted the rule that if "a complaint mischaracterizes intentional conduct as negligent conduct, a court may find no duty to defend despite the label of negligence in the complaint." *Id.* at

900. *See also Gibbs Int'l, Inc. v. ACE Am. Ins. Co.*, No. 15-4568, 2018 U.S. Dist. LEXIS 54420 (D.S.C. Mar. 30, 2018) (noting that, in *City of Hartsville v. S.C. Mun. Ins. & Risk Fin. Fund*, 677 S.E.2d 574 (S.C. 2009), the Supreme Court of South Carolina, when determining duty to defend, indicated that orders issued by the underlying trial court may be considered).

South Dakota: The Supreme Court of South Dakota held that the determination of the duty to defend is not limited to the allegations in the complaint. *State Farm Fire & Cas. Co. v. Harbert*, 741 N.W.2d 228, 234 (S.D. 2007) ("Under South Dakota law, a liability insurer's duty to defend extends to any third party claim asserted against an insured that arguably falls within the policy's coverages. If disputed, the issue of whether an insurer has a duty to defend is determined by the third party's complaint and 'other evidence of record.'"); *see also De Smet Farm Mut. Ins. Co. of South Dakota v. Gulbranson Dev. Co., Inc.*, 779 N.W.2d 148, 158 (S.D. 2010) ("The trial court did not err when it considered facts outside the record of the underlying action in determining whether coverage under a theory of estoppel existed."); *Demaray v. De Smet Farm Mut. Ins. Co.*, 801 N.W.2d 284 (S.D. 2011) ("To ascertain whether a duty to defend exists we look to the complaint and other evidence of record); *Swenson v. Auto Owners Ins. Co.*, 831 N.W.2d 402 (S.D. 2013) (same); *Lowery Constr. & Concrete, LLC v. Owners Ins. Co.*, 901 N.W.2d 481 (S.D. 2017) ("[T]he duty to defend an insured against a third-party complaint is to be determined by examining the pleadings and the terms of the policy, not extrinsic evidence of trade customs.") (citing *Hawkeye-Security Ins. Co. v. Clifford*, 366 N.W.2d 489 (S.D. 1985), where the court stated that, since the duty to defend was triggered based on the pleadings, it did "not reach the issue whether the trial court can resolve the ambiguity by considering depositions and other evidence outside the pleadings").

Tennessee: In 2018, Tennessee passed a law to mandate a "four corners" test for the duty to defend: "An insurance company's duty to defend depends solely on the allegations contained in the underlying complaint describing acts or events covered by the policy of insurance. This subsection (e) does not impose a duty to defend on an insurance company that has no duty to defend pursuant to this title or that has an express exclusion of the duty to defend in the policy of insurance." Tenn. Code Ann. § 56-7-102(e). Prior case law has been the same. The Supreme Court of Tennessee held that the determination of the duty to defend is limited to the allegations in the complaint. *Travelers Indem. Co. of Am. v. Moore & Assocs., Inc.*, 216 S.W.3d 302, 305 (Tenn. 2007) (citing *St. Paul Fire & Marine Ins. Co. v. Torpoco*, 879 S.W.2d 831,

835 (Tenn. 1994)) ("We previously have held that whether a duty to defend arises depends solely on the allegations contained in the underlying complaint. Accordingly, the insurer has a duty to defend when the underlying complaint alleges damages that are within the risk covered by the insurance contract and for which there is a potential basis for recovery.") (internal citation omitted); *see also Phoenix Ins. Co. v. Estate of Gainer*, No. M2007-01446, 2008 Tenn. App. LEXIS 748 (Tenn. Ct. App. Dec. 19, 2008) ("[W]hether a duty to defend arises depends solely on the allegations contained in the underlying complaint.") (citing *Moore* and *Torpoco*); *Forrest Const., Inc. v. Cincinnati Ins. Co.*, 703 F.3d 359 (6th Cir. 2013) (same); *Interstate Packaging Co. v. Century Indem. Co.*, No. 11-00589, 2013 U.S. Dist. LEXIS 45459 (M.D. Tenn. Mar. 29, 2013) ("Plaintiff admits that, under the 'four-corners rule' of Tennessee law that the Court followed in its Order, a duty to defend is determined solely by the allegations contained in the underlying complaint. However, Plaintiff argues that the Court should have followed decisions of the Tennessee Court of Appeals propounding circumstances where additional facts may be considered. The Court finds that its application of the four-corners rule was not a clear error. The two cases that Plaintiff cites are not particularly persuasive, as one is over forty years old and the other is an unpublished opinion. (citations omitted) Most importantly, the Tennessee Supreme Court has more recently, repeatedly, and clearly, stated the rule that the duty to defend 'is to be determined *solely* by the allegations contained in the complaint.'") (emphasis in original and quoting *Torpoco*); *Auto-Owners Ins. Co. v. Southeastern Car Wash Sys.*, 184 F. Supp. 3d 625 (E.D. Tenn. May 25, 2016) ("Under Tennessee law, the existence of an insurer's duty to defend is a legal question that depends solely on the allegations of the complaint in the underlying action.") (citing *Moore*); *Starr Indem. & Liab. Co. v. i3 Verticals, LLC*, No. 16-2832, 2018 U.S. Dist. LEXIS 231906 (M.D. Tenn. Mar. 12, 2018) ("The merchants' underlying complaint alleges that i3 Verticals is a successor-in-interest to Payment Systems. It alleges with specificity the fraudulent conduct undertaken by Payment Systems. Under Tennessee law, the court need only determine whether those allegations describe circumstances that, if true, would fall into the Policy's contract and professional services exclusions. No more is required to conclude if Starr has a duty to defend.").

Texas: Whether Texas's duty to defend rule is four corners (eight corners, as called in Texas) or allows for extrinsic evidence has long been in flux. A definitive answer to question is seemingly on its way. The Texas Supreme Court agreed to address the issue shortly before publication of this book. What follows is the discussion of the duty to defend standard that has appeared in the prior edition of this book. At the conclusion is a discussion of the forthcoming Texas Supreme Court decision.

The Texas Supreme Court held that, "[u]nder the eight-corners rule, the duty to defend is determined by the claims alleged in the petition and the coverage provided in the policy." *Pine Oak Builders, Inc. v. Great American Lloyds Ins. Co.*, 279 S.W.3d 650, 654 (Tex. 2009). "[I]n deciding the duty to defend, the court should not consider extrinsic evidence from either the insurer or the insured that contradicts the allegations of the underlying petition. The duty to defend depends on the language of the policy setting out the contractual agreement between insurer and insured." *Id.* at 655. In *GuideOne Elite Ins. Co. v. Fielder Road Baptist Church*, 197 S.W.3d 305 (Tex. 2005), the Supreme Court of Texas declined to adopt a narrow exception to the "eight-corners" rule, as some courts have, that allows for the consideration of extrinsic evidence that "goes solely to a fundamental issue of coverage which does not overlap with the merits of or engage the truth or falsity of any facts alleged in the underlying case." *Id.* at 308–09. The court likewise rejected, as an exception to the eight-corners rule, extrinsic evidence that is relevant both to coverage and the merits of the underlying action—so-called overlapping evidence. *Id.* at 309; *see also Energy Resources, LLC v. Petroleum Solutions Intern., LLC*, No. H:08–656, 2011 U.S. Dist. LEXIS 91829 (S.D. Tex. Aug. 17, 2011) ("Although PSI is correct that the Texas Supreme Court has not explicitly rejected an exception to the eight-corners rule when the extrinsic evidence in question does not contradict the allegations in the underlying complaint or touch on the merits of the underlying complaint, Lexington is also correct that the Texas Supreme Court has never recognized or applied any such exception. Neither the *GuideOne Elite* decision nor the *Pine Oak Builders* decision expressly recognized an exception, even in dicta, and neither offers convincing support for PSI's argument that an exception is permitted under Texas law. This court thus finds it relatively clear that, at this point, no applicable exception exists under Texas law."). *But see Weingarten Realty Mgmt. Co. v. Liberty Mut. Fire Ins. Co.*, 343 S.W.3d 859, 865 (Tex. Ct. App. 2011) (addressing *GuideOne* in detail and adopting an exception to the "eight corners" rule) ("In light of the facts of this case, we are persuaded of the need for a very narrow exception to the eight-corners rule. The exception applies only when an insurer establishes by extrinsic evidence that a party seeking a defense is a stranger to the policy and could not be entitled to a defense under any set of facts. Under this exception, the extrinsic evidence must go strictly to an issue of coverage without contradicting any allegation in the third-party claimant's pleadings material to the merits of that underlying claim.");

Star-Tex Resources, L.L.C. v. Granite State Ins. Co., 553 Fed. Appx. 366 (5th Cir. 2014) (making an "*Erie* guess," based on earlier Fifth Circuit case law, that "the Texas Supreme Court would recognize an exception to the eight-corners rule when it is initially impossible to discern whether coverage is potentially implicated and when the extrinsic evidence goes solely to a fundamental issue of coverage which does not overlap with the merits of or engage the truth or falsity of any facts alleged in the underlying case").

In *Allstate Cnty. Mut. Ins. Co. v. Wootton*, 494 S.W.3d 825 (Tex. Ct. App. 2016), *pet. for review denied* 2016 Tex. LEXIS 1121 (Tex. Dec. 16, 2016) the Court of Appeals of Texas described the state of Texas duty to defend law as follows: "According to the United States Court of Appeals for the Fifth Circuit, the teaching of *GuideOne* is that, though the Supreme Court of Texas may never recognize an exception to the eight-corners rule, if it were to recognize an exception, it would do so only in the narrow circumstance in which it is 'impossible to discern whether coverage is potentially implicated *and* when the extrinsic evidence goes solely to a fundamental issue of coverage which does not overlap with the merits of or engage the truth or falsity of any facts alleged in the underlying case.' After the Fifth Circuit decided *Graham*, the Supreme Court of Texas, in the *Nokia* case, embraced this characterization of *GuideOne*. See *Nokia, Inc.*, 268 S.W.3d at 497-98. The *Nokia* court described the foregoing narrow situation in which an exception to the eight-corners rule might be recognized. The *Nokia* court then concluded that, even if the extrinsic evidence in *Nokia* pertained solely to coverage, the circumstances in *Nokia* did not fit within the narrow scenario in which an exception might be granted because it was not 'initially impossible to discern whether coverage is potentially implicated.' Under current law, if the Supreme Court of Texas were to allow any exception to the eight-corners rule, it would be the Narrow Exception." (citations omitted). The court declined to recognize an exception to the eight-corners rule because the circumstances of the "narrow exception" were not present.

In *D.R. Horton-Texas, Ltd. v. Markel International Ins. Co., Ltd.*, 300 S.W.3d 740 (Tex. 2009), the Supreme Court of Texas held that "the duty to indemnify is not dependent on the duty to defend and that an insurer may have a duty to indemnify its insured even if the duty to defend never arises." *Id.* at 741; *see also Burlington Northern and Santa Fe Ry. Co. v. Nat'l Union Fire Ins. Co.*, 334 S.W.3d 217, 220 (Tex. 2011) (reaffirming *D.R. Horton*) ("Assuming, without deciding, that the court of appeals correctly determined that National Union owed no duty to defend, the court nevertheless erred by not considering all the evidence presented by the parties when it determined the question of National Union's duty to indemnify BNSF."); *Colony Ins. Co. v. Peachtree Constr., Ltd.*, 647 F.3d 248 (5th Cir. 2011) (holding that the District Court's grant of summary judgment for the insurer was premature and incorrect based on the rule adopted in *D.R. Horton*).

In *Loya Ins. Co. v. Avalos*, 610 S.W.3d 878 (Tex. 2020), the Texas Supreme Court held that an exception to the eight-corners rule exists "where the parties to the underlying suit collude to make false allegations that would invoke the insurer's duty to defend." *Id.* at 881-82. In *Richards v. State Farm Lloyds*, 597 S.W.3d 492 (Tex. 2020), the Texas Supreme Court held that "the 'policy-language exception' to the eight-corners rule articulated by the federal district court in *B. Hall Contracting [v. Evanston Ins. Co.*, 447 F. Supp. 2d 634 (N.D. Tex. 2006)] -- under which the eight-corners rule does not apply unless the policy contains a groundless-claims clause -- is not a permissible exception under Texas law." *Id.* at 500.

In *Bitco Gen. Ins. Corp. v. Monroe Guar. Ins. Co.*, 846 Fed. Appx. 248 (5th Cir. 2021), the federal appeals court certified the following questions to the Texas Supreme Court, which agreed to answer them: "1. Is the exception to the eight-corners rule articulated in *Northfield Ins. Co. v. Loving Home Care, Inc.*, 363 F.3d 523 (5th Cir. 2004), permissible under Texas law? 2. When applying such an exception, may a court consider extrinsic evidence of the date of an occurrence when (1) it is initially impossible to discern whether a duty to defend potentially exists from the eight-corners of the policy and pleadings alone; (2) the date goes solely to the issue of coverage and does not overlap with the merits of liability; and (3) the date does not engage the truth or falsity of any facts alleged in the third party pleadings?"). *Id.* at 252. Given the time that it may take for the court to rule, the debate will surely continue.

Utah: The Supreme Court of Utah held that "whether extrinsic evidence is admissible to determine whether an insurer has a duty to defend an insured turns on the parties' contractual terms. If the parties make the duty to defend dependent on the *allegations* against the insured, extrinsic evidence is irrelevant to a determination of whether a duty to defend exists. However, if, for example, the parties make the duty to defend dependent on whether there is actually a 'covered claim or suit,' extrinsic evidence would be relevant to a determination of whether a duty to defend exists." *Fire Ins. Exch. v. Estate of Therkelsen*, 27 P.3d 555, 561 (Utah 2001) (emphasis in original); *see also Mid-America Pipeline Co., LLC v. Mountain States Mut. Cas. Co.*, No. 2:05-CV-153, 2006 U.S. Dist. LEXIS 30245 (D. Utah May 8, 2006) (recognizing that "the Utah Supreme Court identified two categories of insurance provisions creating a duty to defend": first, where "an insurance contract requires an insurer to defend an insured against a suit 'alleging liability within the coverage afforded by the policy,'" extrinsic evidence is irrelevant and inadmissible, and second, where "an insurance contract provides that an insurer will defend a 'covered suit,'" it requires a court to "examine extrinsic evidence to determine if a particular suit is covered"); *Equine Assisted Growth and Learning Ass'n v. Carolina Cas. Ins. Co.*, 216 P.3d 971, 973 (Utah Ct. App. 2009) (following *Therkelsen* and holding that, in the context of an "insured versus insured" exclusion, the duty to defend consideration was not limited to the allegations in the complaint) (observing that the circumstances triggering the clause constitute objective facts, the truth or falsity of which are not determined solely by the allegations in the complaint) ("To paraphrase *Therkelsen*, the parties' contract has made Carolina Casualty's duty to defend dependent on whether the Kersten complaint 'is actually' a claim 'by, on behalf of, or in the right of' EAGALA, and extrinsic evidence is therefore relevant to a determination of whether a duty to defend exists.") (*see* 266 P.3d 733 (Utah 2011) for further discussion in Utah Supreme Court's decision affirming Court of Appeals); *Hamlet Homes Corp. v. Mid-Continent Cas. Co.*, No. 12-305, 2013 U.S. Dist. LEXIS 3616 (D. Utah Jan. 9, 2013) (explaining rules from *Therkelsen* and concluding that the policy language at issue – insurer "will have the right and duty to defend the insured against any 'suit' seeking [damages because of bodily injury or property damage]. However, we will have no duty to defend the insured against any 'suit' seeking damages for 'bodily injury' or 'property damage' to which this insurance does not apply" -- allowed the duty to defend to be determined based on extrinsic evidence."); *Travelers Prop. Cas. Co. of Am. v. Fed. Recovery Servs.*, 156 F. Supp. 3d 1330 (D. Utah 2016) (explaining rules from *Therkelsen* and concluding that consideration of extrinsic evidence was irrelevant in determining duty to defend in a policy that conditioned it on "any claim or 'suit' seeking damages for loss to which the insurance provided . . . applies."); *Church Mut. Ins. Co. v. Ma'Afu*, 657 Fed. Appx. 747 (10th Cir. 2016) ("Church Mutual promised to defend . . . 'against any 'suit' seeking payment for 'loss.' The term 'suit' is defined in the policy as 'a civil proceeding' in which a covered loss 'is alleged.' . . Given the language in [the policy], we apply the eight corners rule and compare each policy's terms to the Free Wesleyans' allegations in the state-court proceedings."); *Hartford Cas. Ins. v. Swapp Law, PLLC*, No. 17-01130, 2019 U.S. Dist. LEXIS 129664 (D. Utah Aug. 1, 2019) ("[T]he terms of the Policy state that '[Hartford] will have the right and duty to defend [Swapp Law] against any 'suit' [to which this insurance applies]. However, [Hartford] will have no duty to defend [Swapp Law] against any 'suit' seeking damages for . . . 'personal and advertising injury' to which this insurance does not apply.' Thus, Hartford's duty to defend Swapp Law, and thus its duty to compensate Swapp Law for any legal costs and fees incurred by Swapp Law, hinged exclusively on whether the claims asserted in the Underlying Action fell under the plain language of the Policy.").

Vermont: The Supreme Court of Vermont held that a court "determine[s] whether the insurer has a duty to defend by comparing the allegations in the underlying claim to the policy's coverage terms." *Hardwick Recycling & Salvage, Inc. v. Acadia Ins. Co.*, 869 A.2d 82, 87 (Vt. 2004) (citing *City of Burlington v. Nat'l Union Fire Ins. Co.*, 655 A.2d 719, 721 (Vt. 1994)). However, "[o]ccasionally, [Vermont courts] have looked to the known facts underlying a plaintiff's complaint to understand the application of policy provisions or exclusions." *Garneau v. Curtis & Bedell, Inc.*, 610 A.2d 132, 134 (Vt. 1992); *see also Fine Paints of Europe, Inc. v. Acadia Ins. Co.*, No. 2:08-CV-81, 2009 U.S. Dist. LEXIS 24188 (D. Vt. Mar. 24, 2009) ("The insurer's duty to defend is determined by comparing the allegations in the underlying complaint to the terms of the policy. If necessary, a court may examine the known facts underlying a plaintiff's complaint to understand the application of policy provisions or exclusions.") (citation and internal quotes omitted); *Murphy v. Acceptance Indem. Ins. Co.*, 472 Fed. Appx. 5 (2nd Cir. 2012) ("[T]he Vermont Supreme Court has regularly found no duty to defend, notwithstanding a complaint's negligence claim, where that claim is inconsistent with the facts alleged in the underlying complaint."); *Sharon Acad., Inc. v. Wieczorek Ins., Inc.*, No. 442-7-13, 2015 Vt. Super. LEXIS 76 (Vt. Super. Ct. Feb. 25, 2015) ("[I]n considering whether Ms. Koren is an insured, it is appropriate to pierce the allegations of the underlying complaint and evaluate extrinsic evidence. There are exceptions to the rule that the duty to defend must be triggered by the underlying allegations. One is as follows: 'an insurer should not have a duty to defend an insured when the facts alleged in the complaint ostensibly bring the case within the policy's coverage, but other facts that are not reflected in the complaint and are unrelated to the merits of the plaintiff's action plainly take the case outside the policy coverage.' 1 Allan D. Windt, Insurance Claims and Disputes § 4:4 (6th ed.) (WL updated Mar. 2014). Windt cites *Blake v. Nationwide Ins. Co.*, 180 Vt. 14, 904 A.2d 1071 (2006) in support. A related exception applies 'when the company determines that, even assuming that the insured is liable based on the allegations in the complaint, there can, in fact, be no coverage because of the falsity of some extraneous fact alleged in the complaint.' Insurance Claims and Disputes § 4:4. The exception applies with even more vigor when the question is whether the tort defendant is an insured at all."); *Citizens Ins. Co. of Am. v. Vt. Sch. Bd. Ins. Trust, Inc.*, No. 333-6-19, 2020 Vt. Super. LEXIS 28 (Vt. Feb. 6, 2020) ("The only reasonable interpretation of the 'actual complaint, not some hypothetical version' reveals no allegation of bodily injury occurring during the Catlin coverage period. Citizens' argument that the Court should allow the parties to engage in discovery to determine whether Catlin's coverage is triggered is out of step with Vermont law. That determination is made based on the factual allegations of the tort complaint.").

Virginia: The Supreme Court of Virginia acknowledged that, in several prior decisions, it applied the rule that only the allegations in the complaint and the terms of the policy can be considered in deciding if there is a duty to defend. *Copp v. Nationwide Mut. Ins. Co.*, 692 S.E.2d 220, 224 (Va. 2010) (quoting several cases including *Brenner v. Lawyers Title Ins. Corp.*, 397 S.E. 2d 100 (Va. 1990)). However, the court noted that none of the prior decisions involved the situation before it— applicability of an exception to the "expected or intended" exclusion if the insured acted in self-defense. *Id.* at 225. Despite allowing the consideration of self-defense evidence in its duty to defend determination, it does not appear that the court created an exception to the four corners rule. Rather, the court's decision appears to be that the self-defense evidence must be considered in order to give effect to the "expected or intended" exception, which "is found in one of the four corners of the insurance contract and stands on an equal footing with other provisions thereof." *Id.*; *see also CACI Intern., Inc. v. St. Paul Fire and Marine Ins. Co.*, 566 F.3d 150, 156 (4th Cir. 2009) (applying Va. law) ("[B]ecause Virginia courts have not signaled a readiness to look beyond the underlying complaint, we will decline to consider those documents attached to the complaints or on which the complaints in the underlying action rely."); *Global Title, LLC v. St. Paul Fire & Marine Ins. Co.*, 788 F. Supp. 2d 453, 461 (E.D. Va. 2011) ("As the Supreme Court of Virginia has repeatedly stated, 'only the allegations in the complaint and the provisions of the insurance policy are to be considered in deciding whether there is a duty on the part of the insurer to defend and indemnify the insured.'") (quoting *Copp*) (limiting *Copp's* allowance of extrinsic evidence to its "unique" situation); *The AES Corp. v. Steadfast Ins. Co.*, 725 S.E.2d 532 (Va. 2012) ("Both AES and Steadfast agree that it is a well-established principle, consistently applied in this Commonwealth, that only the allegations in the complaint and the provisions of the insurance policy are to be considered in deciding whether there is a duty on the part of the insurer to defend and indemnify the insured."); *Nautilus Ins. Co. v. Strongwell Corp.*, 968 F. Supp. 2d 807 (W.D. Va. 2013) ("[A]s Nautilus specifically acknowledges in its initial brief, the circumstances justifying the basis for an exception to the eight corners rule in *Copp* are not present in the instant case. While Nautilus contends that an exception to the rule should nonetheless apply, the court finds its arguments unpersuasive.") ("Nautilus's argument is also unsupported by the plain language of the policies[.] . . . [T]he policies obligate Nautilus to defend an insured against any 'suit' *seeking* damages. The term 'suit,' in turn, refers to 'a civil proceeding in which damages because of 'bodily injury' [or] 'personal property' ... to which this insurance applies are *alleged*.") (emphasis in original); *Travelers Cas. & Sur. Co. v. Schur*, 146 F. Supp. 3d 795 (E.D. Va. 2015) ("In Virginia, it is a well-established principle that only the allegations in the complaint and the provisions of the insurance policy are to be considered in deciding whether there is a duty on the part of the insurer to defend the insured."); *Marks v. Scottsdale Ins. Co.*, 791 F.3d 448 (4th Cir. 2015) ("In analyzing Scottsdale's duty to defend, the magistrate judge referred not only to the allegations of the Marks Suit complaint but also to undisputed facts adduced during discovery. To the extent the magistrate judge relied on materials outside the complaint, it appears to have erred under Virginia law."); *Panel Sys. v. Selective Ins. Co. of Am.*, No. 18-687, 2019 U.S. Dist. LEXIS 29769 (E.D. Va. Feb. 25, 2019) ("The Court agrees with Panel Systems that it must consider only the MCV Complaint and the Endorsement in determining whether any of the exclusions relieved Selective of its duty to defend."); *W. World Ins. Co. v. Air Tech, Inc.*, No. 17-518, 2019 U.S. Dist. LEXIS 53683 (W.D. Va. Mar. 29, 2019) (court cannot looking beyond the allegations in the complaint to determine duty to defend in an occurrence-defective work situation).

Washington: The Supreme Court of Washington held that the determination of the duty to defend is not limited to the allegations in the complaint. *Woo v. Fireman's Fund Ins. Co.*, 164 P.3d 454, 459 (Wash. 2007) ("There are two exceptions to the rule that the duty to defend must be determined only from the complaint, and both the exceptions favor the insured. First, if it is not clear from the face of the complaint that the policy provides coverage, but coverage could exist, the insurer must investigate and give the insured the benefit of the doubt that the insurer has a duty to defend ... . Second, if the allegations in the complaint conflict with facts known to or readily ascertainable by the insurer, or if the allegations ... are ambiguous or inadequate, facts outside the complaint may be considered. The insurer may not rely on facts extrinsic to the complaint to deny the duty to defend— it may do so only to trigger the duty.") (citations and internal quotations omitted); *see also Campbell v. Ticor Title Ins. Co.*, 209 P.3d 859 (Wash. 2009) (same) (quoting *Woo*);

N. Seattle Cmty. Coll. Found. v. Great Am. E & S, No. C09-635, 2010 U.S. Dist. LEXIS 17905 (W.D. Wash. Mar. 1, 2010) (determining that insurer undertook investigation and it did not reveal a duty to defend) ("The record reflects that Great American conducted further investigation, including several discussions with Foundation officials and the Foundation's counsel. Nothing in the record, however, shows that the Foundation discovered anything in its investigation that would have overcome the complaint's failure to raise a covered claim."); *Hartford Fire Ins. Co. v. Leahy*, No. C10-0262, 2011 U.S. Dist. LEXIS 20186 (W.D. Wash. Mar. 1, 2011) (allowing insurer to consider extrinsic evidence to establish that a person was not entitled to a defense because he was not an insured); *Western Nat. Assur. Co. v. Maxcare of Washington, Inc.*, No. 67952-0-I, 2012 Wash. App. LEXIS 2933 (Wash. Ct. App. Dec. 24, 2012) ("Where it is clear from the face of the complaint that the allegations are not covered by the insurance policy, there is no obligation to consider extrinsic facts."); *Grange Ins. Ass'n v. Roberts*, 320 P.3d 77 (Wash. Ct. App. 2013) ("Notice pleading rules, which require only a short and plain statement of the claim showing that the pleader is entitled to relief, impose a significant burden on the insurer to determine if there are *any* facts in the pleadings that could conceivably give rise to a duty to defend.") (emphasis in original); *United Services. Auto. Ass'n v. Speed*, 317 P.3d 532 (Wash. Ct. App. 2014) (applying Washington's duty to defend rules to the allegations in a demand letter, when a policy obligated an insurer to defend, in addition to a "suit," a "claim" made for damages). In *State Farm Fire & Cas. Co. v. Doucette*, No. 16-5169, 2016 U.S. Dist. LEXIS 125211 (W.D. Wash. Sept. 14, 2016) a Washington federal court allowed extrinsic evidence to preclude an insurer's duty to defend: "[T]he Estate argues that, as a matter of law, State Farm may not look outside the four corners of the complaint in challenging its duty to defend. While State Farm may not rely on facts outside the complaint in order to deny its duty to defend, neither the Estate nor the Doucette have submitted any authority for the proposition that the Court is precluded from relying on facts outside the complaint in declaring that State Farm owes no duty to defend. If the declaratory judgment court was precluded from considering facts outside the complaint, then these actions would be reduced to the simple task of construing the underlying complaint. For example, assume that an underlying complaint alleges that a particular person committed some negligent act triggering coverage. Also assume that, after the complaint was filed, the insurer discovers evidence that conclusively proves that the person was jailed in a foreign country at the time of the alleged incident and directly contradict a necessary allegation in the complaint. Under the Estate's rationale, the Court would be precluded from using that evidence to enter a declaration that the underlying claim is clearly not covered by the policy. Although Washington law prevents State Farm from using that extrinsic evidence to initially deny the duty to defend, it is preposterous to argue that the Court is precluded from relying on additional evidence to support a declaration of no duty to defend." *Id.* at *9-10. *See also Developers Sur. & Indem. Co. v. Alis Homes, LLC*, No. C17-0707, 2018 U.S. Dist. LEXIS 63741 (W.D. Wash. Apr. 16, 2018) (not needing to address whether an endorsement, allowing insurer to "rely on extrinsic evidence to deny the defense and/or indemnity of a 'suit'" is permissible under Washington law); *2FL Enters., LLC v. Houston Specialty Ins. Co.*, No. 17-676, 2018 U.S. Dist. LEXIS 18605 (W.D. Wash. Feb. 15, 2018) ("In looking up the property in question on the Assessor's website, Tristar found the 'present use' listed as 'Condominium: Residential.' Plaintiff's policy had an exclusion for condominiums and Defendant used this information as one of its justifications (many months later) for finding no coverage and no duty to defend. There are several problems with this rationale. . . .The second problem is that, under Washington law, an insurer is not permitted to utilize information extrinsic to (a) the complaint or (b) the insurance policy to arrive at a decision regarding denial of a tender of defense."); *Cincinnati Ins. Co. v. Zaycon Foods LLC*, No. 17-0014, 2018 U.S. Dist. LEXIS 23526 (E.D. Wash. Feb. 13, 2018) (explaining why, even considering extrinsic facts, a duty to defend was not triggered).

West Virginia: The Supreme Court of Appeals of West Virginia held that the determination of the duty to defend is limited to the allegations in the complaint. *Bowyer v. Hi-Lad, Inc.*, 609 S.E.2d 895, 912 (W. Va. 2004) ("An insurance company has a duty to defend an action against its insured if the claim stated in the underlying complaint could, without amendment, impose liability for risks the policy covers. If, however, the causes of action alleged in the plaintiff's complaint are entirely foreign to the risks covered by the insurance policy, then the insurance company is relieved of its duties under the policy. Included in the consideration of whether an insurer has a duty to defend is whether the allegations in the complaint are reasonably susceptible of an interpretation that the claim may be covered by the terms of the insurance policy.") (citation and internal quotation omitted). In *Bruceton Bank v. United States Fidelity & Guaranty Insurance Co.*, 486 S.E.2d 19 (W. Va. 1997), the Supreme Court of Appeals of West Virginia stated that the court's mandate in *Farmers & Mechanics Mutual Fire Insurance Co. v. Hutzler*, 447 S.E.2d 22 (W. Va. 1994), to conduct a reasonable inquiry into the facts behind the allegations of the complaint, was clarified to the extent that it differed from the aforementioned duty to defend standard. *Bruceton Bank*, 486 S.E.2d at 23; *see also Erie Ins. Prop. & Cas. Co., Inc. v. Edmond*, 785 F. Supp. 2d 561 (N.D.W.Va. 2011) (same) (citing *Bowyer* and *Bruceton Bank*). *But see Wilson Works, Inc. v. Great American Ins. Group*, 495 Fed. Appx. 378 (4th Cir. 2012) ("[T]he district court applied the appropriate standard and correctly concluded that the insurers have no duty to defend Wilson Works in the Walhonde Tools action. First, the district court properly looked beyond Walhonde Tools' bare allegations and determined that its claims could not reasonably be interpreted as falling within the scope of coverage. The court's opinion specifically cites to materials in the record other than Walhonde Tools' complaint, and includes the very same standard that Wilson Works proposes.") (however, relying on *State Auto. Mutual Ins. Co. v. Alpha Engineering Services, Inc.*, 542 S.E.2d 876 (W.Va. 2000), which relied on *Hutzler's* reasonable inquiry requirement as its duty to defend standard, which was clarified in *Bruceton Bank*); *State ex rel. Nationwide Mut. Ins. Co. v. Wilson*, 778 S.E.2d 677 (W. Va. 2015) ("Allegations in a complaint against an insured trigger the duty to defend if they are reasonably susceptible of an interpretation that the claim may be covered by the terms of the insurance policies."); *Westfield Ins. Co. v. Matulis*, 421 F. Supp. 3d 331 (S.D.W.Va. 2019) ("An insurer must look beyond the bare allegations contained in the pleadings and conduct a reasonable inquiry into the facts in order to ascertain whether the claims asserted may come within the scope of the coverage that the insurer is obligated to provide.") (citing to *Farmers & Mechs. Mut. Ins. Co. v. Cook*, 557 S.E.2d 801 (W.Va. 2001), which relied on *Hutzler's* reasonable inquiry requirement as its duty to defend standard, which was clarified in *Bruceton Bank*).

Wisconsin: The Supreme Court of Wisconsin held that the determination of the duty to defend is limited to the allegations in the complaint. *Fireman's Fund Ins. Co. v. Bradley Corp.*, 660 N.W.2d 666, 673 (Wis. 2003) ("An insurer's duty to defend an insured is determined by comparing the allegations of the complaint to the terms of the insurance policy. An insurer's duty to defend the insured in a third-party suit is predicated on allegations in a complaint which, if proven, would give rise to the possibility of recovery that falls under the terms and conditions of the insurance policy. The duty to defend is based solely on the allegations contained within the four corners of the complaint, without resort to extrinsic facts or evidence.") (citations and internal quotation omitted); *see also Lakeside Foods, Inc. v. Liberty Mut. Fire Ins. Co.*, No. 2009AP1428, 2010 Wisc. App. LEXIS 562 (Wis. Ct. App. July 21, 2010) ("[T]he duty of an insurer to provide a defense to its insured is determined by the complaint and not by extrinsic evidence."); *Camelot Dev. Group, LLC v. Jim Karrels Trucking Sand & Gravel, Inc.*, No. 2009AP592, 2009 Wisc. App. LEXIS 871 (Wis. Ct. App. Nov. 11, 2009) ("That coverage exists under the facts in the complaint need only be fairly debatable for there to be a duty to defend."); *Johnson v. Wood County*, No. 2008AP424, 2009 Wisc. App. LEXIS 139 (Wis. Ct. App. Feb. 26, 2009) (acknowledging general rule, but concluding that simply comparing the complaint to the policy was not adequate to determine duty to defend when it turned on late notice); *Air Engineering, Inc. v. Industrial Air Power, LLC*, 828 N.W.2d 565 (Wis. Ct. App. 2013) ("The duty to defend is basely solely on the four corners of the complaint; no extrinsic facts or evidence are considered."). In *Water Well Solutions Serv. Group Inc. v. Consol. Ins. Co.*, 881 N.W.2d 285 (Wis. 2016), the Supreme Court of Wisconsin "unequivocally [held] that there is no exception to the four-corners rule in duty to defend cases in Wisconsin.") (a strong dissent, noting that 31 states have exceptions to the four corners rule, argued that when a complaint is factually incomplete or ambiguous, Wisconsin should adopt the narrow known fact exception to the four-corners rule). *See also Country World Media Group, Inc. v. Erie Ins. Co.*, No. 2016AP1343, 2017 Wisc. App. LEXIS 312 (Wis. Ct. App. May 2, 2017) ("We use a three-step process when comparing the underlying complaint to the terms of the policy in duty to defend cases. First, we determine whether the policy provides an initial grant of coverage for the allegations set forth in the plaintiff's complaint. If so, we next consider whether any of the policy's exclusions preclude coverage. If an exclusion applies, we then consider whether an exception to that exclusion reinstates coverage. If coverage is not restored by an exception to an exclusion, then there is no duty to defend.") (quoting *Water Well Solutions*); *Paustian Med. & Surgical Ctr. v. IMT Ins. Co.*, 942 N.W.2d 494 (Wis. Ct. App. 2020) ("Paustian points to discovery to support its assertions of physical damage to its property, specifically relating to 'the removal of drywall, ceiling, piping, lighting, and fixtures, as well as the addition of protective lining to the floors and walls,' and the addition of 'required components such as doors, air handling units, and walls in new locations.' This argument fails because the asserted physical damage was not alleged in the complaint, and under the controlling law cited above, our analysis must be limited to the four corners of the complaint. There was no amendment to the complaint making these allegations.") (citing *Water Well Solutions*).

Wyoming: The Supreme Court of Wyoming held that the determination of the duty to defend is limited to the allegations in the complaint. *First Wyo. Bank, N.A. v. Cont'l Ins. Co.*, 860 P.2d 1094, 1097 (Wyo. 1993) ("[T]he duty of an insurer to defend a claim is broader than the duty of the insurer to indemnify. Analysis of the duty to defend is not made based on the ultimate liability of the insurer to indemnify the insured or on the basis of whether the underlying action is groundless or unsuccessful. Instead, we analyze the duty to defend by examining the facts alleged in the complaint that the claim is based upon.") (citations omitted); *see also Reisig v. Union Ins. Co.*, 870 P.2d 1066, 1071 (Wyo. 1994) (declining to adopt a duty to defend standard based on extrinsic evidence); *Employers Mut. Cas. Co. v. Bartile Roofs, Inc.*, 618 F.3d 1153, 1171 (10th Cir. 2010) (addressing Wyoming and Utah law) ("[W]e look only to the allegations of the Complaint filed by [the third-party complainant] to see if there is alleged a loss caused by an occurrence as required by the CGL policy.") (alteration in original) (quoting *Reisig*); *Medlock v. State Farm Mut. Auto. Ins. Co.*, No. 14-143, 2015 U.S. Dist. LEXIS 179394 (D. Wyo. July 17, 2015) ("State Farm's duty to defend did not arise and could not be triggered until the lawsuits were filed and, therefore, could not be breached before State Farm had the opportunity to examine the allegations in the complaints. The duty to defend is 'litigation insurance,' and its existence is governed by the allegations in the litigation."); *Carolina Cas. Ins. Co. v. Burlington Ins. Co.*, 951 F.3d 1199 (10th Cir. 2020) ("The district court abused its discretion by granting Burlington's Rule 59(e) motion to impose on Carolina a duty to defend. As we read its cases, the Wyoming Supreme Court has not allowed consideration of extrinsic evidence in evaluating the duty to defend.").

CHAPTER

6

Insured's Right to Independent Counsel

The question whether an insurer is obligated to provide a defense to its insured, for a suit filed against it, turns on whether the claim is potentially covered under the terms of the policy. It is a substantive question and one that can sometimes be the subject of significant analysis and dispute over the answer. Once the insurer determines that it has a defense obligation, the focus shifts to a seemingly easier task and, indeed, one that sounds ministerial—picking up the phone and hiring a lawyer. But it is sometimes far from it. Just as the question whether a defense was owed in the first place can be complex, and a source of great dispute between insurer and insured, so too can be the question of which lawyer to hire to represent the insured.

After an insured has been sued and served with the complaint, the clock begins to tick on the time available under the applicable court rules for the insured to file an answer or other type of responsive pleading. Since time is of the essence, it makes sense that insurance companies maintain lists of law firms that have been pre-screened as acceptable to represent their insureds in the various type of legal proceeding in which they find themselves. By maintaining lawyers at the ready—often referred to as "panel counsel"—the insurer can act quickly to protect its insured's interests. Much time is saved because the insurer knows that the law firm it is hiring is qualified to handle the type of case at issue, at a previously agreed upon hourly rate or other payment arrangement, and has familiarity concerning the insurer's various guidelines on billing, reporting, and litigation management.

While the use of panel counsel makes sense in a lot of ways, not all insureds are content being represented by the defense counsel selected by the insurer. This is particularly the case when the defense is being provided by the insurer under a reservation of rights. In this situation, the insurer has agreed to hire counsel to represent its insured, but, at the same time, has informed the insured that some or all of any damages that may be awarded against it may not be covered under the terms of the policy.

This situation is created by the so-called tripartite relationship:

In the usual tripartite insurer-attorney-insured relationship, the insurer has a duty to defend the insured, and hires counsel to provide the defense. So long as the interests of the insurer and the insured coincide, they are both the clients of the defense attorney and the defense attorney's fiduciary duty runs to both the insurer and the insured. The insurance defense attorney is placed in a position of conflict, however, when issues of coverage are asserted by the insurer through a reservation of rights.

Kroll & Tract v. Paris & Paris, 72 Cal. App. 4th 1537, 1542 (Cal. App. Ct. 1999).

Facing the prospect of uninsured liability for some or all of the damages at issue, some insureds conclude that they would prefer to have a say in choosing the lawyer whose job will be to prevent or minimize their exposure—with the cost of such defense being borne by the insurer, just as if the insurer had hired panel counsel. In other words, while a liability insurer usually has the right to control the defense, some insureds argue that a different rule should apply when it is the insured's own money that is on the line. Under these circumstances, insureds sometimes demand the right to choose defense counsel, usually referred to as "independent counsel," based on the insured's belief that the lawyer, because it was selected by the insurance company, is not independent.

The motivation for insureds to demand that they be allowed to hire independent counsel is that they look at the relationship between insurers and their panel counsel with a jaundiced eye. As they see it, the law firm is in a position to receive future assignments from the insurer when other insureds are named as defendants in the jurisdictions in which the firm practices. Indeed, some law firms have served as panel counsel for certain insurers for years, receiving hundreds, if not thousands, of case assignments. Insureds may conclude that, because of this arrangement, the lawyer hired to represent it is not truly independent because it has, as its principal concern, making sure that it does nothing to jeopardize the steady stream of work that comes from serving as panel counsel. Since the defense is being provided under a reservation of rights, the possibility exists that, when the case is over, some or all of any damages awarded may not be covered by the insurer, and, hence, would become the personal responsibility of the insured. Under this scenario, the concern for insureds may be that, in handling the case, the lawyer's objective will be to minimize the extent to which any damage award is covered by the terms of the insurer's policy.

This risk was explained—without any sugar coating and with support from, some might say, a higher authority than any court—by the Eighth Circuit Court of

Appeals in *U.S. Fid. & Guar. Co. v. Louis A. Roser Co.*, 585 F.2d 932, 938 n.5 (8th Cir. 1978) (applying Utah law):

> Even the most optimistic view of human nature requires us to realize that an attorney employed by an insurance company will slant his efforts, perhaps unconsciously, in the interests of his real client the one who is paying his fee and from whom he hopes to receive future business the insurance company. Although it has perhaps become trite, the biblical injunction found in Matthew 6:24 retains a particular relevancy in circumstances such as these, "No man can serve two masters ... ."

The classic example of an asserted conflict of interest, giving rise to a demand by an insured for independent counsel, is a suit alleging that the insured's liability is based on intentional or negligent conduct (or some other alternative causes of action where one is covered and one is not):

> Under a typical liability insurance policy, coverage is available for negligent acts but not for intentional acts. The insurer therefore would benefit from either a defense verdict or a finding of intentional wrongdoing. The insured, on the other hand, would benefit from either a defense verdict or a finding of negligence. Absent informed consent of both the insurer and the insured, an attorney trying to represent both the insured and the insurer would face an insurmountable conflict of interest.

Armstrong Cleaners, Inc. v. Erie Ins. Exch., 364 F. Supp. 2d 797, 806 (S.D. Ind. 2005).

In this situation, an insured may fear that its counsel, wanting to please the insurer, in hopes of continuing to benefit from its status as panel counsel, will handle the case in such a way that any damage award is based on intentional, rather than negligent, conduct. This is the so-called "steering" argument: "the insurer may steer result to judgment under an uninsured theory of recovery." *CHI of Alaska, Inc. v. Employers Reinsurance Corp.*, 844 P.2d 1113, 1118 (Alaska 1993). "[I]f a plaintiff alleged both negligence and an intentional tort as alternative theories of recovery, an insurer operating under a reservation of rights might covertly frame its defense to achieve a verdict based upon commission of the intentional tort, so that it could later assert that the defendant was not covered, since the policy provided no coverage for intentional torts. In the absence of a reservation of rights agreement, however, the insurer would be liable for indemnification regardless of whether the verdict established negligence or an intentional tort, and thus would be more likely to defend vigorously on both grounds." *Continental Ins. Co. v. Bayless and Roberts, Inc.*, 608 P.2d 281, 289–90 (Alaska 1980).

Another possible conflict of interest arises if "the insurer knows it can later assert non-coverage, it … may offer only a token defense of its insured. If the insurer does not think that the loss on which it is defending will be covered under the policy, it may not be motivated to achieve the lowest possible settlement or in other ways treat the interests of its insured as its own." *Id.* at 289.

There is nothing new about this conundrum. To the contrary, the potential conflict of interest among the liability insurance company, the insured, and the insurance defense attorney has been referred to as the law's "eternal triangle." *Id.* at 801. "[T]he ethical dilemma thus imposed upon the carrier-employed defense attorney would tax Socrates, and no decision or authority we have studied furnishes a completely satisfactory answer." *Hartford Accdent. & Indem. Co. v. Foster*, 528 So. 2d 255, 273 (Miss. 1988).

There is no consensus solution for resolving asserted conflicts of interest under these circumstances, and reasonable minds can differ on the best approach. *See Finley v. The Home Ins. Co.*, 975 P.2d 1145, 1151 (Haw. 1998) ("The magnitude of the difficulty in resolving the issue is reflected in the volume of litigation nationwide, and, in the instant case, the number of amicus curiae briefs representing divergent views."). As the following fifty-state survey reveals, courts have responded with several methods for addressing conflicts of interest, and they vary widely. In addition, some states have turned to their legislatures for the solution.

In addition to the perceived conflict of interest, insureds sometimes object to the insurer's selection of counsel for other reasons, such as a belief that the insurer's selected counsel is not qualified, lacks sufficient knowledge of the insured's business, or, when the dispute has a lengthy pre-suit history, the insurer's chosen counsel lacks the necessary background knowledge. In general, when a defense is provided under a reservation of rights, causing an insured to have skin in the game, insureds may assert a host of reasons why they object to being defended by counsel selected by the insurance company. But perhaps the insured's motivation for demanding choice of counsel actually comes down to something as simple as this: "[W]hatever his estimate of lawyers in general, a man usually has faith in 'my lawyer.' This intangible is a valuable right." *Merchants Indem. Corp. v. Eggleston*, 179 A.2d 505, 511 (N.J. 1962).

The simplest solution to an insured's demand for independent counsel is for the court to adopt a blanket rule. Some have done so by concluding that a defense provided under a reservation of rights creates a per se conflict of interest—no questions asked—thereby entitling the insured to independent counsel at the insurer's expense. *Moeller v. Am. Guarantee & Liab. Ins. Co.*, 707 So. 2d 1062, 1071 (Miss. 1996) (quoting *State Farm Mut. Auto. Ins. Co. v. Commercial Union Ins. Co.*, 394 So.2d 890, 894 (Miss. 1981)) ("A law firm which cannot be one hundred percent faithful to the interests of its clients offers no defense at all. 'There is no higher ethical duty in the legal profession than complete absolute fidelity to the interest of the client.'").

Some courts have adopted a blanket rule in the other direction—a reservation of rights does not create a conflict of interest in any case. In *Finley v. Home Ins. Co.*, 975 P.2d 1145 (Haw. 1998), the Supreme Court of Hawaii concluded that, because of the safeguards inherent in the Rules of Professional Conduct, as well as alternate remedies existing in the case of attorney misconduct, an attorney retained by an insurer can represent the insured without the insured's informed consent. *Id.* at 1154. Using a different method, but achieving the same result, the Supreme Court of South Dakota in *St. Paul Fire & Marine Ins. Co. v. Engelmann*, 639 N.W.2d 192 (S.D. 2002) concluded that, because the insurer and insured are not estopped to litigate in a subsequent coverage action facts that were determined in the underlying action, no conflict was created by the insurer's choice of defense counsel. *Id.* at 200.

As the following fifty-state survey of the issue reveals, the majority of courts confronted with the conflict of interest issue have declined to adopt a black-and-white rule one way or the other. Rather, they conclude that the circumstances of each case must be examined to determine whether a conflict exists:

> Whether the potential conflict of interest is sufficient to require the insured's consent is a question of degree that requires some predictions about the course of the representation. If there is a reasonable possibility that the manner in which the insured is defended could affect the outcome of the insurer's coverage dispute, then the conflict may be sufficient to require the insurer to pay for counsel of the insured's choice. Evaluating that risk requires close attention to the details of the underlying litigation. The court must then make a reasonable judgment about whether there is a significant risk that the attorney selected by the insurance company will have the representation of the insureds significantly impaired by the attorney's relationship with the insurer.

Armstrong Cleaners, 364 F. Supp. 2d at 808.

When determining if the manner in which the insured is defended could affect the outcome of the insurer's coverage dispute, thereby requiring the insurer to pay for counsel of the insured's choice, courts look to various possibilities:

> First, if the insurer knows that it can later assert non-coverage, or if it thinks that the loss which it is defending will not be covered under the policy, it may only go through the motions of defending: "it may offer only a token defense … . [I]t may not be motivated to achieve the lowest possible settlement or in other ways treat the interests of the insured as its own." Second, if there are several theories of recovery, at least one of which is not covered under the policy, the insurer might conduct the defense in such a manner as to make the likelihood of a plaintiff's verdict greater under the uninsured theory. Third, the insurer might gain access to confidential or privileged information in the process of the defense which it might later use to its advantage in litigation concerning coverage.

CHI of Alaska, Inc. v. Employers Reinsurance Corp., 844 P.2d 1113, 1116 (Alaska 1993) (alteration in original) (citations omitted).

Once the determination has been made that the insured is entitled to select its own counsel, to be paid for by the insurer, it is not uncommon for a dispute to arise over the hourly rates to be paid to counsel. The source of such dispute is almost always that the hourly rates charged by the insurer's panel counsel are less than— and sometimes significantly so—the rates charged by independent counsel retained by the insurer.

The insurer usually maintains that it will pay independent counsel reasonable rates, which it asserts are the same rates it would have paid panel counsel, if there had been no need to retain independent counsel. The typical insured response is that panel counsel's hourly rates are lower than market rates (i.e., the rates sought to be charged by independent counsel) because panel counsel is willing to work at a discount—in exchange for the volume of work that is receives on account of serving as panel counsel.

While California and Alaska statutorily permit an insurer to pay independent counsel the same rates as panel counsel, discussed *infra*, most of the time clear-cut answers to the rate issue do not exist. The case law on the subject is relatively sparse and that which does exist is fact specific and does not make general pronouncements. For guidance on the rate issue, *see PhotoMedex, Inc. v. St. Paul Fire & Marine*

Ins. Co., No. 07–0025, 2008 U.S. Dist. LEXIS 8526 (E.D. Pa. Feb. 6, 2008) ("The determination of a reasonable fee is a fact-intensive inquiry, requiring competent evidence.") (scheduling a trial to determine whether the insured's counsel's fees were reasonable) (rate disparity of $685 and $360 per hour for insured's counsel versus $175 per hour for insurer's selected counsel); *HK Systems, Inc. v. Admiral Ins. Co.*, No. 03 C 0795, 2005 U.S. Dist. LEXIS 39939 (D. Wis. June 27, 2005) (simply because the insured was paying its counsel's rates does not establish that it would have done so if there were no hope of recovering such payments) (rate disparity of $495 per hour for insured's counsel versus $105 to $145 per hour for insurer's selected counsel); *Watts Water Techs. v. Fireman's Fund Ins. Co.*, No. 05–2604-BLS2, 2007 Mass. Super. LEXIS 266 (Mass. Super. Ct. July 11, 2007) (noting that there are many factors for determining the reasonableness of legal fees incurred by the insured, one of which is " 'the usual price charged for similar services by other attorneys in the same area,' *not* the usual price paid *by insurance companies* to other attorneys for similar services in the same area") (citation omitted) (emphasis in original); *Employers Ins. Co. of Wausau v. Harleysville Ins. Co. of N.J.*, No. 05–4900, 2008 U.S. Dist. LEXIS 95003 (D.N.J. Nov. 20, 2008) (agreeing with insurer that basic legal services should have been delegated by senior attorneys to associates or paralegals) ("Michelangelo should not charge Sistine Chapel rates for painting a farmer's barn.") (citation omitted).

50-State Survey: Insured's Right to Independent Counsel

Alabama: The Supreme Court of Alabama specifically adopted the Supreme Court of Washington's test, set forth in *Tank v. State Farm Fire & Cas. Co.*, 715 P.2d 1133 (Wash. 1986), discussed *infra*, for determining whether an insured being defended under a reservation of rights is entitled to independent counsel at the insurer's expense. *L & S Roofing Supply Co. v. St. Paul Fire & Marine Ins. Co.*, 521 So. 2d 1298, 1304 (Ala. 1987). "The standard set forth in *Tank, supra*, requiring an *enhanced obligation of good faith* coupled with the specific criteria that must be met by both the insurer as well as the defense counsel retained by the insurer, provides an adequate means for safeguarding the interests of the insured without, at the same time, engaging in the presumption that any and all defense counsel retained by the insurance industry to represent its insureds under a reservation of rights are conclusively unable to do so without consciously or unconsciously compromising the interests of the insureds." *Id.* at 1304 (emphasis added); *see also Aetna Cas. & Sur. Co. v. Mitchell*

Brothers, Inc., 814 So. 2d 191, 193 (Ala. 2001) (addressing whether an insurer has met its "enhanced obligation of good faith" required under *L & S Supply*); *State Farm and Cas. Co. v. Myrick*, 611 F. Supp. 2d 1287, 1295–99 (M.D. Ala. 2009) (same); *Lifestar Response, Inc. v. Admiral Ins. Co.*, 17 So. 3d 200, 219 (Ala. 2009) (addressing *L & S Supply* and holding that insurer is not vicariously liable for the conduct of counsel retained to defend insured); *Ibrahim Sabbah v. Nationwide Mut. Ins. Co.*, No. 15-1772, 2017 U.S. Dist. LEXIS 71726 (N.D. Ala. May 11, 2017) ("Where, as in the instant case, an insured accepts the defense of an action under reservation of rights, but never relinquishes control of the lawsuit, including settlement negotiations, to the insured (sic), the insurer does not have an 'enhanced obligation of good faith' to its insureds."). *L & S Roofing's* "enhanced obligation of good faith" is made up of numerous factors and the cases addressing whether the test has been met are quite fact specific. Resort to the cases is critical. *See MetLife Auto & Home Ins. Co. v. Reid*, No. 09–01762, 2013 U.S. Dist. LEXIS 179424 (N.D. Ala. Dec. 23, 2013); *Scottsdale Ins. Co. v. Alabama Municipal Ins. Corp.*, No. 11–668, 2013 U.S. Dist. LEXIS 131779 (M.D. Ala. Sep. 16, 2013); *Sellers v. Nationwide Mut. Fire Ins. Co.*, No. 15-957, 2018 U.S. Dist. LEXIS 36223 (N.D. Ala. Mar. 6, 2018) (court struck the use of depositions, taken in underlying action, from coverage action) (insurer's enhanced duty to its insured – citing *L & S Roofing* -- prevented insurer from examining the deponents for its own interests regarding coverage).

Alaska: "If an insurer has a duty to defend an insured under a policy of insurance and a conflict of interest arises that imposes a duty on the insurer to provide independent counsel to the insured, the insurer shall provide independent counsel to the insured unless the insured in writing waives the right to independent counsel." ALASKA STAT. § 21.96.100(a) (2009). The statute sets forth certain scenarios that do not constitute a conflict of interest, requires that independent counsel have certain experience and malpractice insurance, and provides that the fee charged by independent counsel is limited to the rate paid by the insurer for similar actions in the community in which the claim arose or is being defended. The statute also contains an allocation provision: "In providing independent counsel, the insurer is not responsible for the fees and costs of defending an allegation for which coverage is properly denied and shall be responsible only for the fees and costs to defend those allegations for which the insurer either reserves its position as to coverage or accepts coverage. The independent counsel shall keep detailed records allocating fees and costs accordingly." *Id.* at § 21.96.100(d). In general the statute shares several similarities with California's *Cumis* statute. *See Great Divide Ins. Co. v. Carpenter*,

79 P.3d 599, 617 (Alaska 2003) (discussing statute); *CHI of Alaska v. Employers Rein-surance Corp.*, 844 P.2d 1113, 1116 (Alaska 1993) (discussing insured's right to counsel pre-statute); *Attorneys Liability Protection Society, Inc. v. Ingaldson Fitzgerald, P.C.*, 370 P.3d 1101 (Alaska 2016) (addressing § 21.96.100(a) in detail in the context of an insurer's right to seek reimbursement of defense costs) (see discussion of *Ingaldson Fitzgerald* in chapter 7).

Arizona: Arizona addresses the independent counsel issue in conjunction with its "Morris Agreement" case law. The Supreme Court of Arizona held that an insurer with a good faith coverage defense may appropriately comply with its contractual duty to defend while simultaneously reserving the right to later assert the defense. *Parking Concepts, Inc. v. Tenney*, 83 P.3d 19, 22 (Ariz. 2004). However, an insurer that chooses this course of action faces the prospect of its insured entering into a *Morris* agreement [*United Servs. Auto Ass'n v. Morris*, 741 P.2d 246 (Ariz. 1987)]. *Tenney*, 83 P.3d at 22. A *Morris* agreement is a reasonable and prudent settlement that is entered into by an insured that is being defended under a reservation of rights. *Id.* Specifically, the insured stipulates to a judgment, assigns his policy rights to the claimant and, in return, receives a covenant that the claimant will not execute against it. *Id.* at 20, n.1. Under these circumstances, the insured will not be deemed to have violated the cooperation clause's prohibition against the insured settling a case without the insurer's consent. *Id.* at 21–22. A *Morris* agreement must be preceded by notice to the insurer to provide it with the opportunity to withdraw the reservation of rights and unconditionally assume liability under the policy. *Id.* at 22; *see also Leflet v. Redwood Fire and Cas. Ins. Co.*, 247 P.3d 180, 185 (Ariz. Ct. App. 2011) ("[T]he mere threat of *Morris* in the course of settlement negotiations does not constitute sufficient notice. Instead, the insurer must be made aware that it may waive its reservation of rights and provide an unqualified defense, or defend solely on coverage and reasonableness grounds against the judgment resulting from the *Morris* agreement."); *Lennar Corp. v. Transamerica Ins. Co.*, No. 1 CA–CV 10–0686, 2011 Ariz. App. Unpub. LEXIS 1386 (Ariz. Ct. App. Nov. 8, 2011) ("[E]ven if the reservation of rights gave rise to a conflict between Gerling and Lennar, such a conflict would not justify the role that Fennemore [insured's personal counsel] actually played in Lennar's defense. Given the potential for conflict that existed between Gerling and Lennar because of the reservation of rights, Lennar could reasonably have reshaped Fennemore's role to that of an independent guardian of its rights concerning coverage. But Lennar chose instead to have two lead defense attorneys equally participating in the decision-making and workload. Because such an arrangement was not justified by a conflict of interest—actual or potential—we find no legal authority upon which Lennar was entitled to reimbursement for Fennemore's continued service as co-counsel after it accepted Lorber's [insurer retained counsel] representation."); *Nucor Corp. v. Emplrs Ins. Co.*, 975 F. Supp. 2d 1048 (D. Ariz. 2013) ("Typically, when a defense is provided by a liability insurer, as part of the insurer's obligation to provide for the insured's defense, the policy grants the insurer the right to control that defense — which includes the power to select the lawyer that will defend the claim. However, where an insurer accepts the duty to defend under a reservation of rights, it relinquishes to the insured control of the litigation. (*Morris*) An insured that is notified of its insurer's reservation of rights is on notice of the conflict of interest and is free, upon proper notice to the insurer, to act to protect its rights in the litigation with the claimant.") ("The Court agrees with Wausau that there is no support in Arizona case for the blanket proposition that an insurer defending under a reservation of rights loses its right to appoint defense counsel for its insured.").

Arkansas: An Arkansas District Court held that a reservation of rights creates a per se conflict that allows the insured to choose its own counsel to be paid for by the insurer. *Union Ins. Co. v. The Knife Co.*, 902 F. Supp. 877, 880 (W.D. Ark. 1995). *The Knife Company* Court concluded that a conflict cannot be eliminated so long as the insurer chooses defense counsel. *Id.* at 881. "It is simply a matter of human nature." *Id.* The court called the insurer's suggestion for addressing any conflict—the insured can always sue the insurer's chosen counsel for malpractice if he engages in misconduct—"cavalier." *Id.; Northland Ins. Co. v. Heck's Service Co., Inc.*, 620 F. Supp. 107 (D. Ark. 1985) ("In order to effectuate Northland's duty to defend Heck's, Heck's must be allowed to select its own legal counsel for defense of the Eckler suit."); *Hortica-Florists' Mut. Ins. Co. v. Pittman Nursery Corp.*, 729 F.3d 846 (8th Cir. 2013) (applying Arkansas law) ("PNC [insured] argues Hortica [insurer] *assigned* Cross Gunter to represent PNC, despite PNC's 'absolute right' to choose its own counsel. Hortica counters it had no prior relationship with Cross Gunter and the firm was well qualified to represent PNC. Arkansas law does not directly address this question, but two federal courts have held the insured has a right to select its own counsel in cases where an insurer-appointed counsel would face a conflict of interest. [citing *The Knife Company* and *Heck's Service*] But even assuming Arkansas law provides PNC the right to choose its own counsel, PNC presents no evidence Hortica chose Cross Gunter out of malice or dishonesty. Nor does PNC explain how its inability to choose proximately caused its harm. We are not anxious to infer bad faith or negligence in such speculative circumstances.") (emphasis in original); *Bull v. Federated Mut. Ins. Co.*, 338 F. Supp. 3d 958 (E.D. Ark. 2018) (citing *The Knife Company, Heck's* and *Hortica-Florists*,' but noting that there are no Arkansas precedents holding that an insured is entitled to select his own independent counsel paid for at an insurer's expense) (concluding that insurer had no obligation to pay the insured's counsel as there was no evidence that counsel retained by the insurer was inadequate nor that he acted contrary to the insured's best interest) ("[T]he Policy contains no promise by Federated to pay for Mr. Bull's independent counsel. The Court declines to read a provision into the Policy for which the parties could otherwise have bargained.").

California: The California legislature adopted Cal. Civ. Code Ann. § 2860 to address an insured's right to independent counsel. The statute is a codification of the Court of Appeal of California's decision in *San Diego Navy Fed. Credit Union v. Cumis Ins. Soc'y*, 208 Cal. Rptr. 494 (Cal. Ct. App. 1984). California's answer to the conflict issue is well known, so much so that "independent counsel" is sometimes referred to colloquially as "*Cumis* counsel"—even when describing independent counsel outside of California.

Section 2860(b) provides that "when an insurer reserves its rights on a given issue and the outcome of that coverage issue can be controlled by counsel first retained by the insurer for the defense of the claim, a conflict of interest may exist." If a conflict does exist, the insurer must provide independent counsel to the insured, unless the insured waives its right. Cal. Civ. Code Ann. § 2860 (a), (f). Section 2860 does not answer whether a disqualifying conflict exists. That determination is left to the courts. Substantial litigation has been brought in California on that subject, and it has produced no simple answers. *See Gulf Ins. Co. v. Berger*, 93 Cal. Rptr. 2d 534, 79 Cal. App. 4th 114 (Cal. Ct. App. 2000) ("There is no talismanic rule that allows a facile determination of whether a disqualifying conflict of interest exists. Instead, [t]he potential for conflict requires a careful analysis of the parties respective interests to determine whether they can be reconciled … or whether an actual conflict of interest precludes insurer-appointed defense counsel from presenting a quality defense for the insured.") (citations and internal quotations omitted). The issue must be addressed on a case-by-case basis, in conjunction with an examination of how other conflict situations have been addressed by California courts and whether they were determined to be disqualifying.

Whether a disqualifying conflict exists is extremely fact intensive and numerous California state and federal courts have addressed the issue. Resort to the cases for guidance is critical. Some examples include *James 3 Corp. v. Truck Ins. Exch.*, 111 Cal. Rptr. 2d 181 (Cal. Ct. App. 2001); *Dynamic Concepts, Inc. v. Truck Ins. Exch.*, 71 Cal. Rptr. 2d 882 (Cal. Ct. App. 1998); *Blanchard v. State Farm*, 2 Cal. Rptr. 2d 884 (Cal. Ct. App. 1991); *Native Sun Inv. Group v. Ticor Title Ins. Co.*, 235 Cal. Rptr. 34 (Cal. Ct. App. 1987); *Extradition Transp. of Am., LLC v. Houston Cas. Co.*, 2014 U.S. Dist. LEXIS 188668, No. 12-1646 (C.D. Cal. Mar. 7, 2014); *Hollyway Cleaners & Laundry Co. v. Ctr. Nat'l Ins. Co. of Omaha, Inc.*, 219 F. Supp. 3d 996 (C.D. Cal. 2016); *Travelers Prop. v. Centex Homes*, No. C 10-02757, 2011 U.S. Dist. LEXIS 36128 (N.D. Cal. Apr. 1, 2011) (determining that conflict of interest did not exist between insured– general contractor and attorney selected by insurer due to a question of timing of damages) (explaining that potential for attorney to "be in a position to focus liability outside the policy periods through manipulation of the pre-trial investigation and presentation at trial" is merely a potential conflict, and "whether the damages occurred before, during, or after the policy period is a factual issue outside of counsel's control"); *Endurance Am. Specialty Ins. Co. v. Lance-Kashian & Co.*, No. CV F 10-1284, 2010 U.S. Dist. LEXIS 100467 (E.D. Cal. Sept. 13, 2010) (determining that reservation of insurer's right to exclude coverage based on intentional acts did not create conflict of interest, as "a court or jury, not defense counsel, will determine if the insureds engaged in intentional acts not subject to coverage" even though the court noted that "the most common situation in which a conflict of interest exists and independent or *Cumis* counsel is required occurs when the insured's allegedly wrongful conduct could be found to be intentional, with coverage thus depending on the ultimate characterization of the insured's actions"); *Carter v. Entercom Sacramento, LLC*, 161 Cal. Rptr. 3d 782 (Cal. Ct. App. 2013) ("[Insured] has failed to show that the mere prospect of punitive damages prevented the attorney retained by [insurer] from providing [him] with a complete defense or created a conflict of interest that made it necessary for him to retain independent counsel."); *Federal Ins. Co. v. MBL, Inc.*, 160 Cal. Rptr. 3d 910 (Cal. Ct. App. 2013) (examining numerous coverage issues, including pollution exclusion, number of occurrences and damages outside policy period, and concluding that none gave rise to a right to independent counsel); *Swanson v. State Farm General Insurance Company*, 162 Cal. Rptr. 3d 477 (Cal. Ct. App. 2013) ("[A]n insurer has a duty to provide *Cumis* counsel to its insured only while the insurer maintains a *Cumis*-triggering reservation of rights. Thus, when State Farm withdrew its *Cumis*-triggering reservation of rights, it no longer had an obligation to allow Swanson to control the litigation or an obligation to pay the attorneys' fees of Swanson's *Cumis* counsel."); *W. World Ins. Co. v. Prof'l Collection Consultants*, No. 15-2342, 2018 U.S. Dist. LEXIS 242917 (C.D. Calif. July 13, 2018) ("The coverage dispute centered on whether PCC knowingly (or with a reasonable belief) failed to disclose the potential for a 'future claim' against it in light of the federal investigation. The underlying Hudson and Pole lawsuits centered on whether PCC acted with retaliatory motivation when it terminated those employees. Since these issues are separate from one another, Western's reservation of rights in this case did not endow PCC with a right to hire Garen or any other attorney of its choosing under *Cumis* and its progeny."); *Pac. Intercultural Exch. v. Scottsdale Ins. Co.*, No. D071478, 2018 Cal. App. Unpub. LEXIS 6432 (Cal. Ct. App. Sept. 20, 2018) (lengthy discussion of § 2860 and whether independent counsel owed); *Centex Homes v. St. Paul Fire & Marine Ins. Co.*, 19 Cal. App. 5th 789 (2018) ("To the extent *Cumis* (various page citations omitted) suggests 'potential' conflicts or whenever the insurer has reserved its rights to deny coverage are sufficient to require appointment of independent counsel, we emphasize that section 2860 clarifies and limits the *Cumis* decision."); *Evanston Ins. Co. v. Versa Cardio, LLC*, No. 17-180, 2018 U.S. Dist. LEXIS 222874 (C.D. Calif. March 21, 2018) ("[T]he Court concludes that the Policy covers negligent TCPA violations with statutory damages of $500 but not willful TCPA violations with statutory damages of $1,500. Therefore, the Court agrees with Versa that it is in Evanston's interest for insurance-appointed defense counsel not to dispute that any violations were intentional, and thus not covered under the Policy, which creates a conflict of interest requiring independent counsel."); *Aspen Am. Ins. Co. v. William*, No. 18-2312, 2019 U.S. Dist. LEXIS 77822 (C.D. Calif. Mar. 14, 2019) (lengthy discussion of § 2860 and whether independent counsel owed) ("[B]ecause the Parties do not dispute that Aspen's claims turn on what Ou 'knew regarding the incident or claim and when he knew it,' there is an actual conflict of interest and Ou has met his burden to show that, as a matter of law, he has a right independent counsel at Aspen's expense."); *L.A. Terminals, Inc. v. United Nat'l Ins. Co.*, No. 19-00286, 2020 U.S. Dist. LEXIS 180268 (C.D. Calif. Sept. 30, 2020) (addressing § 2860 and a conflict created when an insurer is defending two parties in the same litigation) ("[W]hen an insure[r] is obligated to provide defenses for two or more insureds with adverse interests, there is a sufficient conflict of interest that the insurer must provide independent counsel for each insured at its own expense."); *Sempra Energy v. Associated Elec. & Gas Ins. Servs.*, 473 F. Supp. 3d 1052 (C.D. Calif. 2020) (no conflict of interest) ("Continental reserves rights unrelated to the Underlying Lawsuits. Continental reserves the rights to assert that no individual raises a claim for personal or property damages from an occurrence within the period of the Harbor Policies. However, this is immaterial to the Underlying Lawsuits, because the pleadings in the Underlying Lawsuits do not succeed or fail based on the time period of the claim."); *Travelers Indem. Co. v. Newlin*, No. 20-765, 2021 U.S. Dist. LEXIS 65019 (S.D. Calif. Apr. 2, 2021) (lengthy discussion of § 2860 and types of conflicts that give rise to independent counsel).

California Civil Code § 2860 also addresses other facets of the independent counsel issue, such as: a conflict does not exist with respect to allegations for which an insurer denies coverage or punitive damages or because the insured is sued for an amount in excess of its policy limits, § 2860(b); the insurer can require that independent counsel have errors and omissions insurance and at least five years of civil litigation experience, including substantial relevant experience, § 2860(c); the fees to be paid to independent counsel shall be limited to the rates paid by the insurer to its panel counsel to defend similar claims in the community where the claim arose or is being defended, § 2860(c); independent counsel must timely report to the insurer and disclose all information concerning the action except privileged materials relevant to coverage disputes, § 2860(d); and counsel selected by the insurer and independent counsel shall both be allowed to participate in all aspects of the litigation and they shall exchange information subject to each counsel's ethical and legal obligations to the insured, § 2860(f). *See City Art, Inc. v. Superior Court*, No. B256132, 2014 Cal. App. Unpub. LEXIS 8741 (Cal. Ct. App. Dec. 9, 2014) (holding that § 2860 rate limitation did not apply retroactively to attorney's fees incurred prior to the time insurer began paying defense costs); *Signal Products Inc. v. American Zurich Ins. Co.*, No. 13-04581 (C.D. Cal. Aug. 4, 2014) ("Having accepted that multiple attorneys may serve as Cumis counsel, there does not appear to be any principled grounds for requiring as a matter of law that all of those attorneys need to be employed at the same law firm.") (second firm's involvement must be established to be reasonable and necessary); *Hartford Casualty Ins. Co. v. J.R. Marketing, LLC*, 353 P.3d 319 (Cal. 2015) (concluding that insurer may seek recovery of overbilled amounts directly from *Cumis* counsel); *Travelers Indem. Co. v. Walking U. Ranch, LLC*, No. 18-024822018, U.S. Dist. LEXIS 132968 (C.D. Cal. Aug. 6, 2018) (denying insurer's request for arbitration on rate issue on account of other issues being litigated in the underlying action) ("Because the threshold issues of whether Travelers breached its duty to defend and breach the implied covenant of good faith and fair dealing remain unresolved at this juncture, the Court will resolve these claims first to avoid the potentially prejudicial effect of an arbitrator's factual findings on these counterclaims.").

Colorado: No instructive authority. *See Hecla Mining Company v. N.H. Ins. Co.*, 811 P.2d 1083, 1098 n.7 (Colo. 1991) (Mullarkey, J., dissenting) ("The issue of whether the insurers would be involved in a conflict of interest requiring them to provide independent counsel, possibly of [the insured's] choosing, or to obtain [the insured's] consent to allow the insurers to conduct the defense is not before us. I would therefore leave this issue to the trial court to resolve."). More recently the Colorado Court of Appeals addressed the issue by concluding, as an apparent matter of first impression in Colorado, "that issue preclusion will not bar an insurer from later denying coverage to its insured when the insurer defended the insured under a reservation of rights and the insurer had an interest in establishing a different set of facts than its insured advanced in the underlying litigation." *Shelter Mutual Ins. Co. v. Vaughn*, 300 P.3d 998 (Colo. Ct. App. 2013) (noting that, under the Colorado Rules of Professional Conduct, the attorney that the insurer hired for the insured owed a duty only to the insured).

Connecticut: No instructive authority.

Delaware: A Delaware trial court held that "[i]f an insurer has a conflict of interest, either real or potential, it is not relieved of its duty to defend. The insurer must either provide independent counsel to represent its insured, or pay the cost of defense incurred by the insured." *Int'l Underwriters, Inc. v. Stevenson Enters., Inc.*, No. 80C-SE-82, 1983 Del. Super. LEXIS 649, at *7 (Del. Super. Ct. Oct. 4, 1983). The *Stevenson Enterprises* Court provided no explanation of its decision. However, the court characterized the counsel retained by the insurer as "independent." *Id.* The court also cited to *U.S. Fidelity & Guaranty Co. v. Louis A. Roser Co.*, 585 F.2d 932 (8th Cir. 1978) and *Brohawn v. Transamerica Insurance Co.*, 347 A.2d 842 (Md. 1975) as support for its decision. *Id.* (both discussed *infra*.).

District of Columbia: A District of Columbia District Court, while not addressing the issue in detail, suggested that an insured, being defended under a reservation of rights, is entitled to independent counsel if it can prove a conflict of interest. In *Athridge v. Aetna Cas. and Sur. Co.*, No. CIV.A. 96-2708, 2001 U.S. Dist. LEXIS 26148 (D.D.C. Mar. 2, 2001), the court rejected the argument that an insured was entitled to independent counsel. However, the court's reason for doing so was that a conflict did not exist between the insurer and the insured. The court distinguished *Village Management, Inc. v. Hartford Accident Indem. Co.*, 662 F. Supp. 1366 (N.D. Ill. 1987), which involved a direct conflict because the insured's conduct was potentially excluded from coverage because it might have involved an intentional act, thereby giving the insurer an interest in establishing intent, while the insured had an interest in asserting negligent conduct, which is covered by the policy. The *Athridge* Court stated: "The conflict of interest situation described in *Village Management* is easily distinguishable from the present case. Aetna was not obliged to appoint independent counsel for Jorge in the lawsuit brought against Jorge by Tommy and his parents. Jorge had no interest in coverage since he was judgment proof. Further, the insurer had no interest in whether or not Jorge was found liable to the Athridges. It already had secured a declaratory judgment denying coverage. Thus, neither Jorge nor Aetna had any interest, let alone conflicting ones, in the resolution of the Athridges' suit against Jorge." On appeal, the District of Columbia Court of Appeals found no "basis for supposing that District law imposes a requirement that an insurer provide an already represented insured with additional counsel in a declaratory judgment action on the scope of the policy." 351 F.3d 1166 (D.C. Cir. 2003) (also addressing choice of counsel in the context of a malpractice action). *See also Wallace v. AMTRAK*, 5 F. Supp. 3d 452 (S.D.N.Y. 2014) ("It is well established in the District of Columbia (and elsewhere) that an insurer who accepts an insured's tender of a defense without reserving the right to contest its coverage under the insurance policy is estopped from later denying coverage. (citations omitted) That is because an insurer's reservation of rights suggests that its representation may not be as robust as if the insurer expected to bear the insured's losses, or that exclusions from policy coverage may result in a preference between the plaintiffs theories of recovery.") (citing *Athridge*); *Feld v. Fireman's Fund Ins. Co.*, 263 F. Supp. 3d 74 (D.D.C. 2017) ("Unlike the parties in *Brohawn* [*see* Maryland], then, there is no situation where Feld would prefer to win on one theory of liability and lose on another, while FFIC would prefer the opposite. There was no actual conflict of interest between FFIC and Feld that required FFIC to provide him with an independent attorney, and therefore FFIC's willingness to do so was consideration for agreement on rates.").

Florida: A Florida District Court held that there was no conclusive presumption that defense counsel chosen by the insurer was unable to fully represent its client, the insured, without consciously or unconsciously compromising the insured's interests. The court concluded that the rules governing the Florida bar were sufficient to protect the insured's interests. *Travelers Indem. Co. v. Royal Oak Enters., Inc.*, 344 F. Supp. 2d 1358, 1373 (M.D. Fla. 2004). The *Royal Oak* Court stated that "[m]embers of the Florida bar are charged with the responsibility of properly determining whether an actual conflict of interest exists, and if so, whether withdrawal from the representation is required. If counsel fails to do so and violates his or her duty of loyalty, he or she may face disciplinary actions and malpractice liability." *Id.* at 1375; *see also Ernie Haire Ford, Inc. v. Universal Underwriters Ins. Co.*, Nos. 07-288-Orl-28DAB, 07-595-Orl-28DAB, 2008 U.S. Dist. LEXIS 38963 (M.D. Fla. May 13, 2008) (following *Royal Oak*); *BellSouth Telecommunications, Inc. v. Church & Tower of Florida, Inc.*, 930 So. 2d 668, 670–71 (Fla. App. Ct. 2006) ("It is well-settled law that, when an insurer agrees to defend under a reservation of rights or refuses to defend, the insurer transfers to the insured the power to conduct its own defense, and if it is later determined that the insured was entitled to coverage, the insured will be entitled to full reimbursement of the insured's litigation costs."); *Mid-Continent Cas. Co. v. Am. Pride Bldg. Co.*, 601 F.3d 1143, 1149 (11th Cir. 2010) (applying Florida law) (following *BellSouth* but noting that insured "by accepting and not rejecting [insurer's] full-funded defense … was required to cooperate with [insurer] throughout the … litigation") (noting that, if insured properly rejects insurer's defense, insured is free to enter into a settlement); *Doe v. OneBeacon America Ins. Co.*, No. 11–275, 2012 U.S. Dist. LEXIS 166388 (N.D. Fla. Nov. 21, 2012) ("[B]ecause a defense provided under a reservation of rights is conditional, and requires the insured to risk the possibility that the insurer will not pay the judgment, Florida law does not require an insured to accept such a defense."); *Regions Bank v. Commonwealth Land Title Ins. Co.*, 977 F. Supp. 2d 1237 (S.D. Fla. 2013) (citing rules from *BellSouth*); *EmbroidMe.com, Inc. v. Travelers Prop. Cas. Co. of Am.*, 845 F.3d 1099 (11th Cir. 2017) ("An insurer does not breach its duty to defend by offering to defend under a reservation of rights. Yet, because an insured might be concerned that an insurer who defends under a reservation of rights will be half-hearted in its defense of the case, Florida law does not require an insured to accept such a defense. Instead, the decision by the insurer to defend under a reservation of rights constructively transfers to the insured the power to defend the case. In short, 'if the insurer offers to defend under a reservation of rights, the insured has the right to reject the defense and hire its own attorneys and control the defense, without jeopardizing its right to later seek indemnification from the insurer for liability.") (quoting, in part, *BellSouth*); *Foremost Signature Ins., M.I. v. Silverboys, LLC*, 793 Fed. Appx. 962 (11th Cir. 2019) (insured, being defended under a reservation of rights, would have been entitled to a full reimbursement of its litigation costs, but it had none) (citing *BellSouth*).

In addition, FLA. STAT. ANN. § 627.426(2)(b)(3) provides: "A liability insurer shall not be permitted to deny coverage based on a particular coverage defense unless: (a) Within 30 days after the liability insurer knew or should have known of the coverage defense, written notice of reservation of rights to assert a coverage defense is given to the named insured by registered or certified mail sent to the last known address of the insured or by hand delivery; and (b) Within 60 days of compliance with paragraph (a) or receipt of a summons and complaint naming the insured as a defendant, whichever is later, but in no case later than 30 days before trial, the insurer: 1. Gives written notice to the named insured by registered or certified mail of its refusal to defend the insured; 2. Obtains from the insured a nonwaiver agreement following full disclosure of the specific facts and policy provisions upon which the coverage defense is asserted and the duties, obligations, and liabilities of the insurer during and following the pendency of the subject litigation; or 3. Retains independent counsel which is mutually agreeable to the parties. Reasonable fees for the counsel may be agreed upon between the parties or, if no agreement is reached, shall be set by the court." *See AIU Ins. Co. v. Block Marina Invest., Inc.*, 544 So. 2d 998 (Fla. 1989) and its progeny for the impact of an insurer's breach of this statutory obligation.

Georgia: The Eleventh Circuit Court of Appeals concluded that "'where a conflict of interest exists between the insurer and the insured in the conduct of the defense of the action brought against the insured, the insured has the right to refuse to accept an offer of the counsel appointed by the insurer[.] In such circumstances, [the insurer] would have been obligated to pay for [the insured's] defense.'" *Am. Family Life Assurance Co. v. U.S. Fire Co.*, 885 F.2d 826, 831 (11th Cir. 1989) (citations omitted); *see also Utility Serv. Co., v. St. Paul Travelers Ins. Co.*, No. 5:06-CV-207, 2007 U.S. Dist. LEXIS 4634 (M.D. Ga. Jan. 22, 2007) ("*Am. Family Life* held that the presence of a conflict of interest may enable the insured to retain independent counsel at the expense of the insurer.").

Hawaii: The Supreme Court of Hawaii concluded that if an attorney retained by an insurer follows the Hawaii Rules of Professional Conduct, he or she will be sufficiently independent. The court declined to accept an assumption that the attorney will slant its representation to the determine of the insured. *Finley v. Home Ins. Co.*, 975 P.2d 1145, 1154 (Haw. 1998). The *Finley* Court explained its decision as follows: "Although it is incontrovertible that the insurer and the insured have divergent economic interests in the outcome of the litigation, HRPC Rule 1.7 bars the attorney's representation only if this conflict will 'materially [limit]' the lawyer's representation of the insured. Because of the safeguards inherent in the HRPC, as well as alternate remedies existing in the case of misconduct, we disagree … that HRPC Rule 1.7 bars an attorney retained by the insurer from representing the insured under these circumstances without the informed consent of the insured." *Id.* at 1154. *See also Anastasi v. Fid. National Title Ins. Co.*, 366 P.3d 160 (Haw. 2016) ("When any insurer, including a title insurer, defends an insured under a reservation of rights, the insurer maintains the right to evaluate and disclaim coverage. Therefore, there is inherently a potential for conflict between the insurer and the insured in such a situation, and there is nothing distinctive about title insurance that would eliminate such potential."); *Aloha Petroleum, Ltd. v. National Union Fire Ins. Co.*, No. 13-0296, 2014 U.S. Dist. LEXIS 92660 (D. Haw. July 8, 2014) (noting that *Finley* adopted an "enhanced" standard of good faith when an insurer defends subject to a reservation of rights).

Idaho: No instructive authority.

Illinois: The Appellate Court of Illinois refused to adopt a rule that a defense provided by an insurer, under a reservation of rights, creates a per se conflict that automatically entitles the insured to retain independent counsel at the insurer's expense. *Nandorf, Inc. v. CNA Ins. Cos.*, 479 N.E. 2d 988, 992 (Ill. App. Ct. 1985). The court explained its decision concerning the potential right to independent counsel as follows: "In determining whether a conflict of interest exists, Illinois courts have considered whether, in comparing the allegations of the complaint to the policy terms, the interest of the insurer would be furthered by providing a less-than-vigorous defense to those allegations. An insurer's interest in negating policy coverage does not, in and of itself, create sufficient conflict of interest to preclude the insurer from assuming the defense of its insured. However, a conflict of interest has been found where the underlying action asserts claims that are covered by the insurance policy and other causes which the insurer is required to defend but asserts are not covered by the policy." *Id.* at 992. (citations omitted); *see also Maryland Cas. Co. v. Peppers*, 355 N.E.2d 24, 31 (Ill. 1976) (recognizing that the insured is entitled to have independent counsel in a conflict situation and that the insurer is entitled to have an attorney of its choosing participate in all phases of the litigation subjection to the control of the case by the insured's attorney); *Stoneridge Dev. Co. v. Essex Ins. Co.*, 888 N.E.2d 633, 645 (Ill. App. Ct. 2008) (providing examples of cases in which Illinois courts have found the existence of a conflict of interest); *Indiana Insurance Company v. CE Design Ltd.*, 6 F. Supp. 3d. 858 (N.D. Ill. 2013) ("[A]n insurer is not estopped from raising coverage defenses unless the insured … has been prejudiced by the conflict of interest or appointed counsel."); *National Cas. Co. v. Forge Indus. Staffing Inc.*, 567 F.3d 871, 878 (7th Cir. 2009) (applying Illinois law) (holding that the requirements for the appointment of independent counsel were not met because the case did not present mutually exclusive theories of liability or factual allegations which, when resolved, would preclude coverage); *Fox v. American Alternative Ins. Co.*, 757 F.3d 680 (7th Cir. 2014) (applying Illinois law) ("A conflict does not arise simply because a plaintiff seeks both punitive and compensatory damages. Rather, only when the plaintiff seeks punitive damages vastly in excess of compensatory damages does the potential conflict of interest arise."); *Perma-Pipe, Inc. v. Liberty Surplus Ins. Corp.*, 38 F. Supp. 3d 890 (N.D. Ill. 2014) (insured being sued for more than $40 million and policy had a $1 million per occurrence limit; conflict existed because there was a "nontrivial probability" that there would be an excess judgment); *Nautilus Ins. Co. v. Dubin & Associates, Inc.*, No. 11-1251, 2012 U.S. Dist. LEXIS 89066 (N.D. Ill. June 27, 2012) ("[T]he Seventh Circuit has not been steadfast in its requirement that an insurer face an either/or outcome for a conflict to be serious."); *Std. Mut. Ins. Co. v. Lay*, 989 N.E.2d 591 (Ill. 2013) ("In the case at bar, Standard's reservation-of-rights letter specifically referred to the coverage defense and conflict of interest regarding violations of penal statutes. Also, the 12-page letter included an extensive list of policy defenses Standard planned to assert. Thus, Lay knowingly and intelligently chose to accept defense counsel provided by Standard."); *DHR Int'l, Inc. v. Travelers Cas. & Sur. Co. of Am.*, No. 15-4880, 2016 U.S. Dist. LEXIS 17719 (N.D. Ill. Feb. 12, 2016) (finding that covered and uncovered claims did not "present mutually exclusive theories of liability, thereby creating a serious conflict necessitating appointment of independent counsel"); *DePasquale Steel Erectors Inc. v. Gemini Ins. Co.*, 249 F. Supp. 3d 899 (N.D. Ill. 2017) (insured entitled to independent counsel, despite defense without reservation of rights, based on possibility of verdict in excess of limits); *Prof'l Sols. Ins. Co. v. Giolas*, 297 F. Supp. 3d 805 (N.D. Ill. 2017) ("[T]he sexual misconduct exception [to a sexual misconduct exclusion] may place the insured and the insurer in conflict where a factual finding of sexual misconduct may relieve the insurer of its duty to indemnify."); *Xtreme Prot. Servs., LLC v. Steadfast Ins. Co.*, 143 N.E.3d 128 (Ill. App. Ct. May 3, 2019) (holding that the insured was entitled to obtain independent counsel because "[w]here punitive damages form a substantial portion of the potential liability in the underlying action and Steadfast disclaims liability for punitive damages, Xtreme is left with the greater interest and risk in the litigation") (in the context of an underlying lawsuit seeking no less than $800,000 in compensatory damages and no less than $4 million in punitive damages); *Bean Prods. Inc. v. Scottsdale Ins. Co.*, No. 17-0421, 2018 Ill. App. Unpub. LEXIS 89 (Ill. App. Ct. Jan. 22, 2018) ("[N]o actual conflict of interest existed to entitle Bean to independent counsel based simply on the fact that the complaint sought punitive damages. We decline to extend the holding in *Nandorf* beyond the particular facts of that case."); *Joseph T. Ryerson & Son, Inc. v. Travelers Indem. Co. of Am.*, No. 18-2491, 2020 IL App (1st) 182491 (Ill. App. Ct. Apr. 7, 2020) (disagreeing that *Perma-Pipe* mandated the finding that a conflict of interest existed) ("The fact that Travelers had an interest in creating favorable precedent that would be useful in other cases involving its insureds does not negate the fact that Ryerson fully shared its interests in prevailing on appeal."); *Builders Concrete Servs., LLC v. Westfield Nat'l Ins. Co.*, 486 F. Supp. 3d 1225 (N.D. Ill. 2020) (rejecting an insured's argument that it was entitled to independent counsel in a construction defect action because the insurer's chosen counsel could emphasize the damage to the insured's own work product and downplay the damage to the other parts of the building, on the basis that at least some of the alleged damage would fall within the policy's coverage, and pursuant to *Forge*, "if different results in the underlying litigation affect only the relative responsibility of the insurer and the insured for the judgment without eliminating coverage completely and irreparably, the insurer retains the right to control the defense"); *Consol Chassis Mgmt. LLC v. Northland Ins. Co.*, No. 19-05287, 2020 U.S. Dist. LEXIS 197520 (N.D. Ill. Oct. 23, 2020) (finding that an insured was not entitled to independent counsel after asserting cross-claims against other co-insureds on the basis that "seeking contribution and making alternative allegations against other insureds does not mean that the parties are 'diametrically opposed' nor does it mean that they are 'enem[ies] in the litigation,'" because if any insured were found liable, the insurer would be obligated to provide coverage up to its policy limit) (additionally rejecting insureds' argument that they were entitled to independent counsel on the basis that the underlying plaintiff may recover damages exceeding the insurer's policy limit because independent counsel is limited to those circumstances in which an "insurer fails to notify the insured of a known likelihood that the jury verdict will be significantly above the policy limit").

Indiana: An Indiana District Court declined to hold that a reservation of rights presents a per se conflict of interest for defense counsel. *Armstrong Cleaners, Inc. v. Erie Ins. Exch.*, 364 F. Supp. 2d 797, 816 (S.D. Ind. 2005). Instead, the court concluded that the determination must be made on a case-by-case basis and requires that some predictions be made about the course of the representation. *Id.* "If there is a reasonable possibility that the manner in which the insured is defended could affect the outcome of the insurer's coverage dispute, then the conflict may be sufficient to require the insurer to pay for counsel of the insured's choice. Evaluating that risk requires close attention to the details of the underlying litigation. The court must then make a reasonable judgment about whether there is a significant risk that the attorney selected by the insurance company will have the representation of the insureds significantly impaired by the attorney's relationship with the insurer." *Id.* at 808; *see also American Family Mut. Ins. Co. v. C.M.A. Mortg., Inc.*, 682 F. Supp. 2d 879, 890–91 (S.D. Ind. 2010) ("This position taken by [the insurer] created an immediate conflict of interest between it and [the insured] insofar as a finding of intentional conduct would benefit [the insurer] but not [the insured][.] … An insurer faced with such a conflict is required to reimburse its insured's independent counsel as part of its duty to defend."); *Harleysville Lake States Ins. Co. v. Granite Ridge Builders, Inc.*, No. 1:06-CV-00397, 2008 U.S. Dist. LEXIS 93786 (N.D. Ind. Nov. 17, 2008) (holding that oral communication and nondetailed e-mail reservation of rights constituted only "bare notice," which inhibited insured's capacity to properly assess whether to retain independent counsel, and, thus, obliges insurer to control defense without ability of "asserting any coverage defenses against [insured]"); *Auto-Owners Ins. Co. v. Lake Erie Land Co.*, No. 12–184, 2013 U.S. Dist. LEXIS 114481 (N.D. Ind. Aug. 13, 2013) ("Simply put, the Court believes that, on the facts of this case, the significant risk that the dispositive coverage issue of intent will be decided in the underlying lawsuit creates a conflict of interest under the governing rule and necessitates the appointment of independent defense counsel at the Plaintiff Insurer's expense. *See* Ind. R. Prof. Cond. 1.7(a)(2)."); *Ranburn Corp. v. Argonaut Ins. Co.*, No. 16-00088, 2018 U.S. Dist. LEXIS 51658 (N.D. Ind. Mar. 28, 2018) (addressing *Armstrong* and concluding that an insurer that defended under a reservation of rights, and allowed the insured to select its defense team, did not intentionally relinquish its right to control the defense once it accepted coverage) (quoting *Armstrong* and stating that "courts applying Indiana law have noted that 'not every reservation of rights poses a conflict' that would entitle an insured to select its own defense counsel"); *Smarte Carte v. Simon Prop. Group*, No. 20A-CT-975, 2020 Ind. App. Unpub. LEXIS 1463 (Ind. Ct. App. Dec. 21, 2020) (addressing *Armstrong Cleaners* and Rule 1.7(b) of the Indiana Rules of Professional Conduct and concluding, in a contractual indemnity scenario, that a party was entitled to independent counsel).

Iowa: The Court of Appeals for the Eighth Circuit, applying Iowa law, addressed whether an insurer that defended its insured for several months, without issuing a reservation of rights, was estopped to deny coverage. *City of Carter Lake v. Aetna*

Casualty & Surety Company, 604 F.2d 1052, 1059 (8th Cir. 1979). The decision did not address the independent counsel issue. However, among the court's various reasons why the insured was prejudiced by the insurer's defense was the possibility of a conflict of interest. *Id.* at 1062. "During the time [insurer] had control of the city's defense against the [insureds'] claim, its attorneys could have simultaneously prepared a defense for [insurer] against the city on policy coverage." *Id.*

Kansas: The Supreme Court of Kansas held that if there is a conflict of interest between the insured and the insurer, the proper procedure to protect the rights of both parties is for the insurer to hire independent counsel to defend the insured and notify the insured that it is reserving all rights under the policy. *Patrons Mut. Ins. Ass'n v. Harmon*, 732 P.2d 741, 745 (Kan. 1987). Such procedure eliminates the necessity of multiple suits to determine the same issues. *Id.* The *Harmon* Court did not discuss what qualifies as a conflict. However, by way of the example, the underlying action involved liability that could have been based on either negligent or intentional conduct and the court concluded that, under such circumstances, the interest of the insurer and the insured were adverse. *Id.* The *Harmon* Court provided no guidance on how counsel qualifies as "independent." *See also Hackman v. Western Agr. Ins. Co.*, 275 P.3d 73 (Kan. Ct. App. 2012) ("When an insurer hires an attorney to defend an insured in a lawsuit under a reservation of rights, the attorney's client is the insured and not the insurer. When there are facts to demonstrate that the attorney violated these rules and allowed the insurer to direct or control the attorney's actions in defending the insured, the attorney likely will be considered the agent of the insured (sic) and, in turn, the insurer may be held vicariously liable for the attorney's negligent conduct."); *Eye Style Optics, LLC v. State Farm Fire and Cas. Co.*, No. 14–2118, 2014 U.S. Dist. LEXIS 75031 (D. Kan. June 3, 2014) ("Eye Style's argument appears to boil down to a claim that under the facts alleged in this case where the underlying lawsuit involves covered and uncovered claims of negligent and intentional misconduct, any counsel selected by defendant cannot be considered 'independent.' This is not how this court reads the Kansas cases cited in the previous paragraph [*Harmon*, *Hackman* and others]. As Eye Style has not alleged any other facts from which a court could find that defendant's appointed counsel was not 'independent' or able to defend all claims asserted against Eye Style showing loyalty to Eye Style as the insured, the court finds that Eye Style has not alleged a plausible claim that defendant has violated its duty to defend under the insurance contract."); *Progressive Northwestern Ins. Co. v. Gant*, No. 15-9267, 2018 U.S. Dist. LEXIS 163624 (D. Kan. Sep. 24, 2018) (addressing possible conflict of interest – non-reservation of rights-based -- by counsel representing four insureds) (predicting that the Kansas Supreme Court would not require an insurer to determine a conflict of interest prior to or at the same time as the appointment of counsel), *aff'd* 957 F.3d 1144 (10th Cir. 2020) (addressing insurer's possible liability, including with a discussion of the ALI Restatement of Liability Insurance, for negligent hiring of defense counsel).

Kentucky: No instructive authority. *But see Am. Ins. Ass'n v. Ky. Bar Ass'n*, 917 S.W.2d 568, 573 (Ky. 1996) (prohibiting a lawyer from defending an insured under a flat fee arrangement). The Supreme Court of Kentucky rejected the insurer's argument that the potential for conflict is very often lacking in a flat fee arrangement. *Id.* After examining some of the potential conflicts, the court held that the "mere appearance of impropriety is just as egregious as any actual or real conflict." *Id.* "Inherent in all of these potential conflicts is the fear that the entity paying the attorney, the insurer, and not the one to whom the attorney is obligated to defend, the insured, is controlling the legal representation." *Id. See also Auto-Owners Ins. Co. v. Egnew*, No. 13-222, 152 F. Supp. 3d 868 (E.D. Ky. Jan. 25, 2016) (noting, in a jurisdictional dispute, that "the right to independent counsel when an insurance company defends under a reservation of rights . . . is a novel question[] of state law); *Twin City Fire Ins. Co. v. Chewning*, No. 18-124, 2019 U.S. Dist. LEXIS 80773 (W.D. Ky. May 14, 2019) ("Because this case involves the interpretation of Kentucky's insurance law and the regulation of Kentucky's attorneys, the final sub-factor weighs heavily in favor of declining jurisdiction. To determine whether an insured is entitled to independent representation when he is being provided a defense under a reservation of rights, which is a novel issue of Kentucky law, will necessarily implicate important state policies. These same important policies will be implicated by the determination of whether an insurer must notify the insured of this right in its reservation of rights letter. The Sixth Circuit has recognized that Kentucky state courts are more familiar and better situated to resolve issues implicating important state policies. Therefore, the third sub-factor weighs heavily in favor of declining jurisdiction at this time."); *Outdoor Venture Corp. v. Phila. Indem. Ins. Co.*, No. 20-5306, 2020 U.S. App. LEXIS 40041 (6th Cir. Dec. 22, 2020) ("[T]he plaintiffs' appellate brief claims to identify 'examples of how counsel appointed by Scottsdale could manipulate the proof . . . in a way that would have a real impact on the coverage determination.' But before the district court, the plaintiffs admitted that they 'are certainly not suggesting that appointed counsel did anything wrong in these cases[.]' So the plaintiffs essentially argue that Scottsdale's reservation of rights alone created the prospect of a conflict of interest, entitling them to select their own counsel at the expense of Scottsdale. Of course, some jurisdictions hold that a reservation of rights issued on certain bases creates a conflict of interest such that the Insured is entitled to 'independent counsel' paid for by the Insurer. Ky. Bar Ass'n Ethics Op. KBA E-410 (1999). But that stance is based on the notion that the attorney has as clients both the Insured and the Insurer, a view to which Kentucky does not adhere.").

Louisiana: The Court of Appeal of Louisiana held that, because the insurer asserted at least six grounds of noncoverage, a conflict of interest existed that entitled the insured to select independent counsel at the insurer's expense. *Belanger v. Gabriel Chemicals, Inc.*, 787 So. 2d 559, 566 (La. Ct. App. 2001). The *Belanger* Court stated that, to determine whether the insurer and the insured have a conflict, the question is whether the interests of the insurer would be furthered by providing a less than vigorous defense to the allegations in the complaint. *Id.* However, the court provided no explanation why a conflict existed that was sufficient to justify the insured's retention of independent counsel at the insurer's expense. *See also Emery v. Progressive Cas. Ins. Co.*, 49 So. 3d 17, 21 (La. Ct. App. 2010) ("As waiver principles are to be applied stringently to uphold the prohibition against conflicts of interest between the insurer and the insured that could potentially affect legal representation in order to reinforce the role of the lawyer as the loyal advocate of the client's interest, we must find that Progressive waived its coverage defenses by assigning only one attorney to represent itself and its insured for seventeen months despite having knowledge of facts indicating noncoverage under the policy."); *Maister Assoc. v. State Farm Fire & Cas. Co.*, 350 Fed. App'x 978, 979 (5th Cir. 2009) (applying Louisiana law) (following *Belanger* and holding that insurer acted appropriately in employing the lawyer selected by the insured).

Maine: The Supreme Judicial Court of Maine sought guidance from the Supreme Court of Arizona's decision in *United Services Auto Ass'n v. Morris*, 741 P.2d 246 (Ariz. 1987) and held that "an insured being defended under a reservation of rights is entitled to enter into a reasonable, noncollusive, nonfraudulent settlement with a claimant, after notice to, but without the consent of, the insurer. The insurer is not bound by any factual stipulations entered as part of the underlying settlement, and is free to litigate the facts of coverage in a declaratory judgment action brought after the settlement is entered. If the insurer prevails on the coverage issue, it is not liable on the settlement. If the insurer does not prevail as to coverage, it may be bound by the settlement, provided the settlement, including the amount of damages, is shown to be fair and reasonable, and free from fraud and collusion." *Patrons Oxford Insurance Company v. Harris*, 905 A.2d 819, 828 (Me. 2006); *see also Colony Ins. Co. v. Danly, Inc.*, 755 F. Supp. 2d 219, 225 (D. Me. 2010) (following *Patrons* in determining that insurer has right to intervene after settlement has been entered between plaintiff and insured in order "to determine whether the settlement … is reasonable, in good faith and not the product of collusion"); *Metro. Prop. & Cas. Ins. Co. v. Googins*, No. 13-102, 2014 Me. Super. LEXIS 228 (Me. Sup. Ct. Oct. 31, 2014) ("[W]hen an insurer has either denied coverage or reserved its right to deny coverage, an insured has the right to control the defense of the case and may enter into a settlement that shields him from personal liability while allowing recovery from the insurer -- if coverage exists.") (citing *Patrons*).

Maryland: The Court of Appeals for the Fourth Circuit, applying Maryland law, relied on the Maryland high court's decision in *Brohawn v. Transamerica Insurance Co.*, 347 A.2d 842 (Md. 1975) to conclude that "Maryland has rejected a per se rule whereby the insurer is required to pay for the insured's independent counsel any time that the insured's objectives might differ from the objectives of the insurer. However, when an actual conflict of interest does exist, an insurer's duty to defend necessarily involves the duty to pay for the insured's independent counsel." *Driggs Corp. v. Pa. Mfrs.' Ass'n Ins. Co.*, No. 98–2140, 1999 U.S. App. LEXIS 9182 (4th Cir. May 14, 1999) (citation omitted) (concluding that an actual conflict of interest did not exist when counsel retained by the insurer was specifically instructed to defend the insured without consideration of the insurer's interest and rejecting the insured's argument that appointed counsel could "steer" the case toward uncovered claims). "[U]nder the Canons of Professional Responsibility, the attorney selected by the insurer to represent the insured, although employed by the insurer, still has the duty to represent the insured with complete fidelity and may not advance the interests of the insurer to the prejudice of the rights of the insured." *Brohawn* at 852. "When such a conflict of interest arises, the insured must be informed of the nature of the conflict and given the right either to accept an independent attorney selected by the insurer or to select an attorney himself to conduct his defense. If the insured elects to choose his own attorney, the insurer must assume the reasonable costs of the defense provided." *Id.* at 854.

Massachusetts: The Supreme Judicial Court of Massachusetts held that a reservation of rights creates a per se conflict that allows the insured to choose its own counsel to be paid for by the insurer. *Sullivan, Inc. v. Utica Mut. Ins. Co.*, 788 N.E.2d 522, 539 (Mass. 2003). The *Sullivan* Court stated that "[w]hen an insurer seeks to defend its insured under a reservation of rights, and the insured is unwilling that the insurer do so, the insured may require the insurer either to relinquish its reservation of rights or relinquish its defense of the insured and reimburse the insured for its defense costs." *Id.*; *see also Watts Water Techs. v. Fireman's Fund Ins. Co.*, No. 05–2604-BLS2, 2007 Mass. Super. LEXIS 266 (Mass. Super. Ct. July 11, 2007) ("The insurer cannot reserve its rights to disclaim liability in a case and at the same time insist on retaining control of its defense.") (internal quotation and citation omitted); *N. Sec. Ins. Co., Inc. v. R.H. Realty Trust*, 941 N.E.2d 688, 692 (Mass. App. Ct. 2011) (affirming trial court decision that hourly rate of $225 for independent counsel was extremely reasonable even though insurer's highest panel rate was $140 per hour because, among other reasons, independent counsel was experienced and respected and usually worked for $385 per hour and insurer could have addressed the cost of defense in its policy) ("[T]he insured was entitled to have a reasonable fee paid, based on market rather than panel rates. Panel rates ... often reflect ... what [insurer] was able to bargain for as a large insurance company handling various cases involving many attorneys, who presumably wish to continue receiving referrals ..."); *Graphic Arts Mut. Ins. Co. v. D.N. Lukens, Inc.*, No. 11–10460, 2013 U.S. Dist. LEXIS 75201 (D. Mass. May 29, 2013) (insurer not responsible to assume insured's uninsured periods simply because insured was not given control of the defense of the underlying cases); *Rass Corporation v. The Travelers Companies, Inc.*, 63 N.E.3d 40 (Mass. Ct. App. 2016) (addressing fees to be paid to independent counsel and upholding reductions for several reasons: case generally did not raise complex legal issues; submissions outside the procedural rules and frivolous; and excessive and duplicative time billed for certain pleadings and motions) (noting that the judge was "well warranted in reducing the fees requested by a large percentage" and "was not required to provide an hour-by-hour accounting of the result reached"); *OneBeacon American Insurance Company v. Celanese Corporation*, No. 16-P-203, 2017 Mass. App. LEXIS 140 (Mass. App. Ct. Oct. 16, 2017) (rejecting numerous arguments of the insured that it was entitled to be paid for its independent counsel despite insurer defending it without a reservation of rights); *Mount Vernon Fire Ins. Co. v. VisionAid, Inc.*, 875 F.3d 716 (1st Cir. 2017) ("Given the particulars of the current controversy, we believe the SJC would agree that the presence of the embezzlement counterclaim — which Mount Vernon neither has to prosecute nor pay for — does not generate a conflict of interest entitling VisionAid to separate counsel to defend against Sullivan's suit at Mount Vernon's expense.").

Michigan: The Court of Appeals of Michigan held that "[a]n insurance company may tender a defense under a reservation of rights and retain independent counsel to represent its insured. No attorney-client relationship exists between an insurance company and the attorney representing the insurance company's insured. The attorney's sole loyalty and duty is owed to the client, not the insurer. In the absence of any record showing by Bronson that the law firm acted in fact against the interests of Bronson, we will not presume that the firm had or would fail to carry out its responsibilities to its client." *Michigan Millers Mutual Insurance Company v. Bronson Plating Co.*, 496 NW 2d 373 (Mich. Ct. App. 1992), *aff'd* 445 Mich 558 (1994), overruled in part on other grounds in *Wilkie v Auto-Owners Insurance Company*, 664 NW 2d 776 (2003) (citations omitted). A Michigan District Court declined to hold that a conflict of interest is presumed because the insurer selects defense counsel. *Cent. Mich. Bd. of Trs. v. Employers Reinsurance Corp.*, 117 F. Supp. 2d 627, 636 (E.D. Mich. 2000). The court held that "under Michigan law an insurer complies with its duty to defend when, after it has reserved its rights to contest its obligation to indemnify, it fully informs the insured of the nature of the conflict and selects independent counsel to represent the insured in the underlying litigation. The insured has no absolute right to select the attorney himself, as long as the insurer exercises good faith in its selection and the attorney selected is truly independent." *Id.* at 634–35. The court based its decision on the attorney's fiduciary obligation owed to its client. "[F]or the very reason that the interest of the insured and the insurer are not always congruent, 'courts have consistently held that the defense attorney's primary duty of loyalty lies with the insured, and not the insurer.'" *Id.* at 636 (quoting *Atlanta Int'l Ins. Co. v. Bell*, 475 N.W.2d 294, 297 (Mich. 1991)); *see also Lapham v. Jacobs Technology, Inc.*, Nos. 295482, 295489, 2011 Mich. App. LEXIS 1318 (Mich. Ct. App. July 19, 2011) (holding that insured did not submit evidence that the law firm hired by its insurer acted against its interests or failed to carry out its responsibilities to the insured) (addressing whether various communications between insurer and law firm were inappropriate); *Stanton v. Auto Owners Ins. Co.*, 2016 Mich. App. LEXIS 1981, No. 327007 (Mich. Ct. App. Oct. 25, 2016) (quoting *Bronson Plating*).

Minnesota: The Supreme Court of Minnesota held in *Prahm v. Rupp Const. Co.*, 277 N.W.2d 389 (Minn. 1979): "We recognize that requiring Great American to defend the suit against Rupp creates a conflict of interest for Great American because it would be required to take opposing positions at trial to defend Rupp against plaintiffs' claim and, at the same time, to defend itself on the coverage question. This conflict of interest does not relieve Great American of its duty to defend, but rather transforms that duty into the duty to reimburse Rupp for reasonable attorneys' fees incurred in defending the lawsuit. Rupp should retain its own counsel to defend against plaintiffs' claim. Great American is required to reimburse Rupp for this expense and should have its own counsel present at trial to establish the facts necessary to determine the coverage question." The Court of Appeals of Minnesota declined to adopt the rule that a reservation of rights by itself creates a conflict of interest that justifies the insured retaining independent counsel. *Mut. Serv. Cas. Ins. Co. v. Luetmer*, 474 N.W.2d 365, 368 (Minn. Ct. App. 1991). "We believe the more reasoned approach to be that before an insured will be entitled to counsel of its own choice, an actual conflict of interest, rather than an appearance of a conflict of interest, must be established." *Id.*; *see also C.H. Robinson Co. v. Zurich Am. Ins. Co.*, No. 02–4794, 2004 U.S. Dist. LEXIS 22797 (D. Minn. Nov. 5, 2004) ("When an insurer reserves its right to deny coverage for punitive damages, a risk exists that the insurer will be less motivated to achieve the best possible result if it believes that the loss will result from punitive damages. Furthermore, it may be tempted to devote more effort into the non-coverage issue than into defending the insured.") (holding that conflict under *Luetmer* avoided because insurer tendered its limits, making its reservation of rights moot); *Hawkins, Inc. v. Am. Intl. Specialty Lines Ins. Co.*, No. A07–1529, 2008 Minn. App. Unpub. LEXIS 1218 (Minn. Ct. App. Oct. 14, 2008) (discussing *Luetmer* in the context of two insureds' right to separate counsel on account of conflicting interests); *Continental Cas. Co. v. National Union Fire Ins. Co.*, 940 F. Supp. 2d 898 (D. Minn. 2013) ("Generally, in the absence of an actual conflict of interest between the insured and the insurer, the insured has no right to choose independent defense counsel to provide the insured with a defense. When a conflict of interest exists—such as when an insurer accepts the tender of defense but also disputes coverage—the insurer's duty to defend is transformed into a 'duty to reimburse [the insured] for reasonable attorneys' fees.'") (quoting *Rupp*); *Select Comfort Corp. v. Arrowood Indem. Co.*, No. 13–2975. 2014 U.S. Dist. LEXIS 118494 (D. Minn. Aug. 26, 2014) (holding that reservation of rights gave rise to right to independent counsel as insurer's "communications show a cautious attempt to preserve the right to challenge coverage based on the intentionality question along with the ability to argue that it was not reserved") ("Although parts of the communications may be characterized as ambiguous, the same principle behind the rule that ambiguities in insurance contracts are construed against the insurer counsels in favor of resolving the ambiguity in its reservation of rights communications against it."); *Select Comfort Corp. v. Arrowood Indemnity Co.*, 13-2975, 2015 U.S. Dist. LEXIS

111070 (D. Minn. Aug. 20, 2015) ("The Court has no duty to Arrowood to pore over the hundreds of pages of records Select Comfort has submitted, searching for potentially objectionable billing. The award Select Comfort requests is not facially unreasonable, is supported by detailed documentation, and seems commensurate with the rate of compensation that the jury found to be the reasonable cost of litigating the *Stearns* action."); *Nat'l Union Fire Ins. Co. v. Donaldson Co.*, 272 F. Supp. 3d 1099 (D. Minn. Aug. 23, 2017) (citing *C.H. Robinson* for the proposition that "Minnesota courts have 'declined to adopt a rule that assumes a conflict of interest arises when an insurer defends under a general reservation of rights'"); *Johnson v. West Bend Mut. Ins. Co.*, No. A17-1957, 2018 Minn. App. Unpub. LEXIS 1037 (Minn. Ct. App. Dec. 17, 2018) (rejecting insured's argument that the insurer is "required to hire—not just pay reasonable fees and costs" for independent counsel once the duty to appoint independent counsel is triggered because the Minnesota Supreme Court has clearly stated that "[w]hen an insurer is obligated to defend its insured and contests coverage in the same suit, the insurer must pay reasonable attorneys' fees for its insured rather than conduct the defense itself"); *Cont'l Ins. Co. v. Daikin Applied Americas. Inc.*, No. 17-552, 2018 U.S. Dist. LEXIS 14327 (D. Minn. Jan. 30, 2018) ("While a reservation of rights cannot, by itself, constitute a conflict of interest, the reservation of rights coupled with the nearly two-year delay raises the claim beyond the speculative.").

Mississippi: The Supreme Court of Mississippi adopted a per se rule that a reservation of rights requires the insurer to pay for the insured's independent counsel. *Moeller v. Am. Guarantee & Liab. Ins. Co.*, 707 So. 2d 1062, 1071 (Miss. 1996). "A law firm which cannot be one hundred percent faithful to the interests of its clients offers no defense at all. 'There is no higher ethical duty in the legal profession than complete absolute fidelity to the interest of the client.'" *Id.* (quoting *State Farm. Mut. Auto. Ins. Co. v. Commercial Union Ins. Co.*, 394 So.2d 890, 894 (Miss. 1981)). The *Moeller* Court also concluded—while recognizing the inconvenience—that the insurer could have retained counsel to defend solely the one covered claim against the insured. *Id.* at 1070; *see also Liberty Mut. Ins. Co. v. Tedford*, 658 F. Supp. 2d 786, 797–98 (N.D. Miss. 2009) (insured presented genuine issues of material fact whether insurer should be equitably estopped from denying coverage, because of prejudice sustained by the insured, on account of the insurer failing to advise it of its rights under *Moeller*); *Hartford Underwriters Inc. Co. v. Found. Health Serv. Inc.*, 524 F.3d 588, 592–99 (Miss. Ct. App. 2008) (determining that Mississippi law applied because "Mississippi law requires an insurer defending an insured under a reservation of rights to provide the insured with independent counsel because of the 'built-in' conflict that is created" and applying Louisiana law, which requires a concurrent conflict of interest to trigger the right to independent counsel, would infringe upon Mississippi's interest "to enforce its conflict of interest rules in litigation in order to protect parties and the judicial process"); *Maryland Cas. Co. v. Nestle*, No. 1:09cv644, 2010 U.S. Dist. LEXIS 98053 (S.D. Miss. Sept. 17, 2010) (following *Moeller* and noting that insurer should afford the insured ample opportunity to select his own independent counsel to look after his interest) (citations omitted); *PIC Group, Inc. v. LandCoast Insulation, Inc.*, 795 F. Supp. 2d 459, 464 (S.D. Miss. 2011) ("*Moeller* has been the law in Mississippi for almost fifteen years. It is reasonable for a party being defended by an insurance company under a reservation of rights to retain *Moeller* counsel. Indeed, the Mississippi Supreme Court noted that a law firm chosen and hired by an insurer to defend claims against an insured under a reservation of rights 'offers no defense at all.'") (quoting *Moeller*) (addressing reasonableness of *Moeller* counsel fees); *Deviney Construction Co. v. Ace Utility Boring & Trenching, LLC*, No. 11-468, 2014 U.S. Dist. LEXIS 88658 (S.D. Miss. June 30, 2014) (noting that an additional insured is entitled to *Moeller* counsel); *Fed. Ins. Co. v. Singing River Health Sys.*, 850 F.3d 187 (5th Cir. 2017) ("At bottom, the Mississippi Supreme Court in *Southern Healthcare* [*Services v. Lloyd's of London*, 110 So. 3d 735 (Miss. 2013)] determined that the general duty to provide independent counsel set forth in *Moeller* is subject to the terms of the applicable policy. Applying this rationale, Federal's duty to pay Defense Costs is subject to the terms of the 2014-2015 Policy, which states in multiple locations that Defense Costs erode policy limits. Indeed, SRHS specifically declined to purchase separate coverage for Defense Costs."); *Grain Dealers Mut. Ins. Co. v. Cooley*, 734 Fed. Appx. 223 (5th Cir. 2018) (rejecting the argument that *Moeller* does not apply when insurer defends but also disclaims coverage for any liability, *i.e.*, defense not under a reservation of rights) ("We see no relevant distinction between Grain Dealers' outright denial of coverage from the start versus a reservation to later deny coverage. Grain Dealers' refusal to ultimately cover the claim creates the same conflict of interest addressed in *Moeller*.").

Missouri: The Eighth Circuit Court of Appeals, interpreting Missouri law, concluded that when a complaint alleged alternative grounds for relief, one covered by the policy and one not, the insurer "must either provide an independent attorney to represent the insured or pay the costs incurred by the insured in hiring counsel of its own choice." *Howard v. Russell Stover Candies, Inc.*, 649 F.2d 620, 625 (8th Cir. 1981) (quoting *U.S. Fidelity & Guar. Co. v. Louis A. Roser Co.*, 585 F.2d 932, 939 n.6

(8th Cir. 1978)). *See also Heubel Materials Handling Co., Inc. v. Universal Underwriters Ins. Co.*, 704 F. 3d 558 (8th Cir. 2013) (applying Missouri law) (looking to *Russell Stover* and noting that "where an underlying suit presents some circumstance that potentially could reward the insurer for failing to provide a full and vigorous defense to its insured, the insurer cannot be permitted to exercise its right to control the defense in the underlying suit"; but holding that "no reservation of rights or conflict of interest entitled [insured] to select its own counsel while continuing to enjoy the coverage benefits of the Universal policy."); *Western Heritage Ins. Co. v. Love*, 24 F. Supp. 3d 866 (W.D. Mo. 2014) (stating, without explanation, that one of ten things in an effective reservation of rights letter is advis[ing] the insured of its right to independent defense counsel); *Nautilus Ins. Co. v. RDB Universal Servs., LLC*, No. 16-120, 2017 U.S. Dist. LEXIS 63300 (E.D. Mo. Apr. 26, 2017) ("If the insurer decides to defend the insured subject to a reservation of rights, the insured may elect to allow the insurer to defend it, or it may refuse to allow a defense under a reservation of rights, instead retaining its own attorney to defend it and perhaps sue the insurer later."); *Am Family Mut. Ins. Co. v. St. Louis Heart Ctr., Inc.*, No. 15-1544, 2017 U.S. Dist. LEXIS 149025 (E.D. Mo. Aug. 14, 2017) ("The insured may reject an insurer's offer to defend with a reservation of rights, and if the insurer refuses to withdraw the reservation of rights, the insured is then free to hire independent counsel to defend the underlying suit and obtain compensation from the insurer if the underlying suit later is held to be covered by the policy.") (quoting *Heubel Materials*) ("[T]he Court finds that with its reservation of rights correspondence, American Family satisfied its obligations under Missouri law. American Family informed Vein Centers of specific policy provisions that might preclude coverage, and encouraged Vein Centers to consider employing its own attorney to protect its interests. Finally, while American Family stated that any attorney so retained would be at Vein Centers' expense, as noted above such expense would have been subject to reimbursement from American Family if the underlying suit was found to be covered by the policy").

Montana: A Montana trial court concluded that the Montana Supreme Court "would hold that when an insurer has a duty to defend but sends a reservation of rights letter to its insured on a coverage issue, the inherent conflict of interest between the insurer and the insured affords the insured the opportunity to choose counsel of his or her own choice at the insurer's expense." *Safeco Ins. Co. v. Liss*, No. DV 29–99–12, 2005 Mont. Dist. LEXIS 1073, at *40–41 (Mont. Dist. Ct. Mar. 11, 2005). *See also State Farm Fire and Cas. Co. v. Schwan*, 308 P.3d 48

(Mont. 2013) (following the rule of other jurisdictions that "it is not necessary for co-insurers to provide duplicative counsel for the insured, as long as the insured is fully defended"); *Mid-Century Ins. Co. v. Windfall, Inc.*, No. 15-146, 2016 U.S. Dist. LEXIS 67482 (D. Mont. May 23, 2016) (addressing an insurer's potential obligation to provide separate counsel when defending multiple insureds).

Nebraska: The Supreme Court of Nebraska addressed whether an insurer that defended its insured for over twelve months, without issuing a reservation of rights, was estopped to deny coverage. *First United Bank of Bellevue v. First Am. Title Ins. Co.*, 496 N.W.2d 474, 480–81 (Neb. 1993). The decision did not address the independent counsel issue. However, among the court's various reasons why the insurer was estopped was the possibility of a conflict of interest. *Id.* at 481. The court reasoned: "Moreover, the record indicates that, while American Title was controlling First United's defense, American Title was collecting data which would only be relevant in litigation against its insured … . Such conduct on the part of American Title at least raises the inference of divided loyalties." *Id.*

Nevada: The Supreme Court of Nevada held in *State Farm Mut. Auto. Ins. Co. v. Hansen*, 357 P.3d 338 (Nev. 2015) that "Nevada law requires an insurer to provide independent counsel for its insured when a conflict of interest arises between the insurer and the insured. … We further conclude that an insurer is only obligated to provide independent counsel when the insured's and the insurer's legal interests actually conflict. A reservation of rights letter does not create a per se conflict of interest." The Nevada high court was guided by California's *Cumis* rule: "Nevada, like California, recognizes that the insurer and the insured are dual clients of insurer-appointed counsel. Where the clients' interests conflict, the rules of professional conduct prevent the same lawyer from representing both clients. California's *Cumis* rule is well-adapted to this scenario. It requires insurers to fulfill their duty to defend by allowing insureds to select their own counsel and paying the reasonable costs for the independent counsel's representation. We find this approach more workable than the alternatives presented by amici. Therefore, we answer the first certified question in the affirmative: When a conflict of interest exists between an insurer and its insured, Nevada law requires the insurer to satisfy its contractual duty to provide representation by permitting the insured to select independent counsel and by paying the reasonable costs of such counsel." *See also Andrew v. Century Surety Co.*, 134 F. Supp. 3d 1249 (D. Nev. 2015) (discussing *Hansen* and concluding that no conflict of interest existed between the insurer and insured); *USF Ins. Co. v. Smith's Food and Drug Center, Inc.*, 921 F. Supp. 2d 1082 (D. Nev. 2013) (rejecting insurers argument that it was not obligated to retain independent counsel because of a policy provision prohibiting insured from selecting its own counsel) ("[Such provision] cannot swallow the principle that the insurer's duty to defend its insured recognizes its obligation to pay for independent counsel when a conflict emerges.") (basing its decision on *Hansen v. State Farm Mut. Auto. Ins. Co.*, No. 10-01434, 2012 U.S. Dist. LEXIS 176057 (D. Nev. Dec. 12, 2012) which is consistent with the Nevada Supreme Court's decision in *Hansen*); *Starr Indem. & Liab. Co. v. Young*, 379 F. Supp. 3d 1103 (D. Nev. 2019) (discussing *Hansen*) ("The Court finds that under Nevada law in order for an insurer to demonstrate that it has fulfilled its contractual duty to defend in a case where there is continued dual representation after the emergence of an actual conflict, the insurer must demonstrate that the insured waived their right to independent counsel. Without the requirement of an explicit waiver as opposed to simply notice, the insured's right to independent counsel would be unavailing.") (noting that the reservation of rights letter failed to explain the nature of the conflict that arose between insurer and insured and that the insured "would have right to 'independent' counsel who would have no duty to report to or protect the interests of [the insurer]"); *Hall CA-NV LLC v. Old Republic Nat'l Title Ins. Co.*, No. 20-10268, 2021 U.S. App. LEXIS 7053 (5th Cir. March 10, 2021) (finding that, under Nevada law, vague testimony from a corporate representative that the insured spent "[m]aybe a couple hundred thousand dollars" "[d]oing things" that the title insurer would have done but for its dual obligations to another insured was insufficient to allege a conflict of interest entitling the insured to independent counsel).

New Hampshire: The Supreme Court of New Hampshire, responding to an insurer's argument that a conflict precluded it from defending its insured, addressed the insured's right to independent counsel. *White Mountain Cable Constr. Corp. v. Transamerica Ins. Co.*, 631 A.2d 907, 912–13 (N.H. 1993). While the court did not provide any analysis of the issue, it suggested that a conflict gives rise to an insured's right to independent counsel, stating "[t]his conflict, argues the [insurer], both prevented it from controlling the [insured's] defense and destroyed the privity between the [insured] and [insurer]. The [insurer] is correct to the extent that if there was a conflict of interest, it could not control the plaintiff's defense. Controlling the defense, however, is not synonymous with providing a defense. Having a duty to defend, and faced with a conflict of interest, the [insurer] could have hired independent counsel to defend the [insured] while intervening on its own behalf. In the alternative, the [insurer] could have provided the defense but reserved its right to later deny coverage." *Id.*

New Jersey: The Supreme Court of New Jersey held that an insurer that wishes to control its insured's defense, and simultaneously reserve the right to deny coverage, can do so only with the insured's consent. *Merchants Indem. Corp. v. Eggleston*, 179 A.2d 505, 512 (N.J. 1962). If the insured does not consent, it is free to defend itself, but the insurer's potential obligation to reimburse defense costs is subject to the applicability of *SL Indus. Inc. v. Am. Motorists Ins. Co.*, 607 A.2d 1266 (N.J. 1992) and its progeny (permitting allocation of defense costs between covered and uncovered claims when feasible). *Id.*; *see also Nazario v. Lobster House*, Nos. A-3025-07T1, A-3043-07T1, 2009 N.J. Super. Unpub. LEXIS 1069 (N.J. Super. Ct. App. Div. 2009) ("We find nothing in *Eggleston* or its progeny which suggests that the insured must prove actual prejudice to create coverage, or that the carrier may prove lack of prejudice to avoid coverage by estoppel, when a fully informed written consent is lacking. The control of the litigation without proper consent equates to creating the coverage without qualification under *Eggleston*."); *Petersen v. New Jersey Mfrs. Ins. Co.*, 2014 N.J. Super. Unpub. LEXIS 995 (N.J. Super. Ct. App. Div. May 2, 2014) ("In order to properly reserve its rights, so as to control the defense while avoiding estoppel, an insurer must advise its insureds of the potential of disclaimer, fairly inform the insureds of their right to reject the insurer's defense on those terms, and secure the insureds' explicit or implicit consent.") (noting that, under *Eggleston*, "an agreement may be inferred from an insured's failure to reject an offer to defend upon those terms, but to spell out acquiescence by silence, the letter must fairly inform the insured that the offer may be accepted or rejected").

New Mexico: The Supreme Court of New Mexico cited the Supreme Court of Rhode Island's decision in *Employers' Fire Ins. Co. v. Beals*, 240 A.2d 397 (R.I. 1968), *overruled on other grounds by Peerless Ins. Co. v. Viegas*, 667 A.2d 785 (R.I. 1995), for its solution to a conflict of interest between the insurer and the insured. *Am. Employers' Ins. Co. v. Crawford*, 533 P.2d 1203, 1209 (N.M 1975). In *Beals*, the court held that the insurer could insist that the insured hire independent counsel or the insurer could hire two attorneys—one to represent the insured and the other to represent the insurer. *Id.*

New York: The Court of Appeals of New York held that, because the insurer was liable only for some, but not all, of the claims at issue, the insurer's interest in defending the lawsuit was in conflict with the insured's interest. Thus, the insured was entitled to a defense by an attorney of its own choosing, whose reasonable fee was to be paid by the insurer. *Pub. Serv. Mut. Ins. v. Goldfarb*, 425 N.E.2d 810, 815 (N.Y. 1981). But the New York high court was also clear to point out that independent counsel was not required in every case involving multiple claims, stating that "[i]ndependent counsel is only necessary in cases where the defense attorney's duty to the insured would require that he defeat liability on any ground and his duty to the insurer would require that he defeat liability only upon grounds which would render the insurer liable." *Id.* The Appellate Division of New York expanded upon *Goldfarb* in *Elacqua v. Physicians' Reciprocal Insurers*, 800 N.Y.S.2d 469 (A.D. 2005), holding that, in a situation in which *Goldfarb* applies, the insurer has an affirmative obligation to advise the insured of its right to independent counsel. Then, in a subsequent decision in *Elacqua*, the Appellate Division held that an insurer commits a deceptive business practice, under N.Y. GEN. BUS. LAW § 349 (Consol.), if it fails to advise its insured that it is entitled to retain independent counsel. *Elacqua v. Physicians' Reciprocal Insurers*, 860 N.Y.S.2d 229, 231–32 (N.Y. App. Div. 2008); *see also N.Y. Marine & Gen. Ins. Co. v. Lafarge N. Am. Inc.*, 599 F.3d 102, 125 (2nd Cir. 2010) (applying N.Y. law) (rejecting insured's argument that a conflict is created under *Goldfarb* on the basis of a substantial difference between the amount at stake in the litigation and the limits of liability under the policy); *Executive Risk Indem. Inc. v. Icon Title Agency, LLC, 739 F. Supp. 2d 446 (S.D.N.Y. 2010)* (noting that New York's Appellate Departments are split on whether an insurer's failure to inform its insured, of the insured's right to retain its own counsel, at the insurer's expense, can constitute a "deceptive act or practice" within N.Y. GEN. BUS. LAW § 349); *Hytko v. Hennessey*, 879 N.Y.S.2d 595 (N.Y. App. Div. 2009) (following *Elacqua* and holding that medical malpractice insurer could not invoke indemnification through subrogation against nurse practitioner because "[b]oth subrogation and implied indemnification are equitable causes of action," which are excluded to parties with "unclean hands" resulting from "some unconscionable act," and insurer "was guilty of deceptive business practices" after insurer failed to notify insureds that insurer's "interests were adverse to those of its insureds in the litigation" and allow them to seek independent counsel); *Carrucci v. Argonaut Ins. Co.*, No. 06-CV-862A, 2009 U.S. Dist. LEXIS 75290 (W.D.N.Y. Aug. 24, 2009) (determining that conflict of interest and need for independent counsel did not exist once insurer withdrew reservation of rights); *QBE Ins. Corp. v. Jinx-Proof Inc.*, 6 N.E.3d 583 (N.Y. 2014) ("QBE was required to advise Jinx-Proof that, under the *Goldfarb* rule, it was entitled to defense by an attorney of its own choosing, whose fees were to be paid by QBE. . . . Moreover, it is beyond debate that, in such situations, the insurer has an affirmative obligation to advise the insured of his right to independent counsel paid for by the insurer. Indeed, the Third Department has gone so far as to hold that an insurer commits a deceptive business practice, under General Business Law § 349, if it fails to advise its insured that it is entitled to retain independent counsel (*Elacqua v Physicians' Reciprocal Insurers*, 52 AD3d 886, 888-889, 860 NYS2d 229 [3d Dept 2008]).")*; Med-Plus, Inc. v. Am. Cas. Co. of Reading*, No. 16-2985, 2017 U.S. Dist. LEXIS 123553 (E.D.N.Y. Aug. 4, 2017) (claim for punitive damages entitled insured to independent counsel, despite being defended by insurer without a reservation of rights); *Liberty Mut. Fire Ins. Co. v. Hamilton Ins. Co.*, 356 F. Supp. 3d 326 (S.D.N.Y. 2018) (citing *Goldfarb*) ("Here, the specter of conflict from the cross-claims and third-party action loomed larger due to Hamilton's repeated, and unsuccessful, attempts to persuade Gilbane to drop those claims. Under these circumstances, the apparent conflict of interest between Hamilton and Gilbane entitled Gilbane to counsel of its own choosing. Thus, Gilbane's refusal to accept Hamilton's offer of defense under the condition of a change of counsel did not absolve Hamilton of its duty to defend."); *Great Am. Ins. Co. v. Houlihan Lawrence, Inc.*, No. 19-1055, 2020 U.S. Dist. LEXIS 54406 (S.D.N.Y. Mar. 27, 2020) ("Here, the remaining claims in the Underlying Action are those for breach of fiduciary duty and violation of GBL § 349. As explained, both claims involve allegations that Defendant acted intentionally, but also may result in a finding that Defendant acted negligently. . . . [Defendant] has alleged a potential conflict of interest sufficient to trigger a right to independent counsel.").

North Carolina: No instructive authority.

North Dakota: No instructive authority. *But see Extradition Transportation of America, LLC v. Houston Casualty Co.*, No. 14-125, 2015 U.S. Dist. LEXIS 185304 (D.N.D. June 12, 2015) (addressing when a malpractice plaintiff should have been on notice that a possible claim exists in the context of the scope of representation of a law firm retained by an insurer to defend an insured).

Ohio: An Ohio Appeals Court declined to adopt a rule that a reservation of rights automatically requires the insurer to pay for the insured's private counsel. *Red Head Brass, Inc. v. Buckeye Union Ins.*, 735 N.E.2d 48, 55 (Ohio Ct. App. 1999). The *Red Head Brass* Court instead held that "an insurer in Ohio may proceed to defend the insured so long as the situation does not arise that the insurer's defense of the insured and its defense of its own interests are mutually exclusive. In such a case, the insurer, still bound in its duty to defend the insured, would have to pay the cost of the insured's private counsel." *Id. See also Wegrzyn v. American Family Ins. Co.*, No. 2004-2807, 2012 Ohio Misc. LEXIS 19851 (Ohio Ct. Com. Pl. June 26, 2012) ("It is not unprecedented for an insurer to take steps to avoid any conflict of interest by hiring separate counsel, once that insurer has indicated it was reserving its rights under the policy and questioning coverage. *See e.g. Britton v. Smythe* (2000), 139 Ohio App.3d 337, 345, 743 N.E.2d 960 ('An insurer's reservation of rights is important because insurers often find themselves in positions that might create a conflict of interest. In some circumstances, an insurer might believe that its insured's conduct constitutes excluded conduct under an insurance policy. Hence, it may be to the insurer's financial advantage to see that the conduct is excluded, thus precluding indemnification. This constitutes a potential (though not necessarily actual) conflict of interest.'") (with no discussion of whether this is legally required).

Oklahoma: The Court of Appeals of Oklahoma concluded, after examining cases nationally on the issue, that "not every perceived or potential conflict of interest automatically gives rise to a duty on the part of the insurer to pay for the insured's choice of independent counsel." *Nisson v. Am. Home Assurance Co.*, 917 P.2d 488, 490 (Okla. Civ. App. 1996). "Independent counsel is only necessary in cases where the defense attorney's duty to the insured would require that he defeat liability on any ground and his duty to the insurer would require that he defeat liability only upon grounds that would render the insurer liable." *Id.* (quoting *Pub. Serv. Mut. Ins. Co. v. Goldfarb*, 425 N.E.2d 810, 815 (N.Y. 1981).

Oregon: The Supreme Court of Oregon addressed the conflict issue by concluding that the judgment in the underlying action is not binding on the insurer or insured in a subsequent coverage action. *Ferguson v. Birmingham Fire Ins. Co.*, 460 P.2d 342, 349 (Or. 1969). As such, "there would be no conflict of interests between the insurer and the insured in the sense that the insurer could gain any advantage in the original action which would accrue to it in a subsequent action in which coverage is in issue." *Id.* The Oregon high court also declared minimal the risk of an insurer offering only a "token defense" in the action against its insured if it knows that it can later assert noncoverage. *Id.* "The insurer knows that when it is the defendant in a lawsuit brought by one of its policy holders the jury's sympathy for the insured frequently produces a plaintiff verdict even when the insurer's case is strong. Knowing this, the insurer is not likely to relax its efforts in defending the action against the insured." *Id.* An Oregon statute addresses the issue in the context of environmental claims: "If the provisions of a general liability insurance policy impose a duty to defend upon an insurer, and the insurer has undertaken the defense of an environmental claim on behalf of an insured under a reservation of rights, or if the insured has potential liability for the environmental claim in excess of the limits of the general liability insurance policy, the insurer shall provide independent counsel to defend the insured who shall represent only the insured and not the insurer." ORS § 465.483(1). Refer to the statute for additional provisions. *See also Carr Chevrolet v. Am. Hardware*, No. Civ. 01-1508-AA, 2004 U.S. Dist. LEXIS 21056 (D. Or. Oct. 13, 2004) (citing *Ferguson* for proposition that "when an insurer defends a lawsuit against its insured under a reservation of rights … a conflict of interest exists between the insurer and the insured, and therefore the doctrine of estoppel by judgment should not be applied to a judgment rendered in an action against the insured"); *FountainCourt Homeowners' Association v. FountainCourt Development*, 380 P.3d 916 (Or. 2016) (discussing *Ferguson* in detail and noting that the judgment in the underlying case does not have any "preclusive effect as to factual issues and legal issues relating to insurance coverage" and addressing "how such determinations are to be made in subsequent proceedings concerning insurance coverage"); *Siltronic Corp. v. Employers Ins. Co. of Wausau*, No. 11-1493, 2018 U.S. Dist. LEXIS 92443 (D. Or. Jan. 3, 2018) (addressing ORS § 465.483(1) and the meaning of "independent counsel" and concluding that it refers to "Cumis counsel" and not "independent defense counsel," which is "defense counsel who represents both the insurer and the insured, but who operates independently of the insurer and is directed and controlled by the insured").

Pennsylvania: A Pennsylvania District Court stated that it is settled law that "where conflicts of interest between an insurer and its insured arise, such that a question as to the loyalty of the insurer's counsel to that insured is raised, the insured is entitled to select its counsel, whose reasonable fee is to be paid by the insurer." *Rector, Wardens & Vestryman of Saint Peter's Church v. Am. Nat'l Fire Ins. Co.*, No. 00–2806, 2002 U.S. Dist. LEXIS 625 (E.D. Pa. Jan. 14, 2002) (internal quotation marks and citations omitted). The *Rector* Court concluded that an actual conflict, and not merely a theoretical one, existed because the underlying liability could rest on either of two causes of action, one covered and one not. "In this situation, an insurer would be tempted to construct a defense which would place any damage award outside policy coverage." (internal quotation marks and citations omitted). *See also PhotoMedex, Inc. v. St. Paul Fire & Marine Ins. Co.*, No. 09–00896, 2009 U.S. Dist. LEXIS 65335 (E.D. Pa. July 28, 2009) (same, quoting *Rector*); *St. Paul Fire & Marine Ins. Co. v. Roach Brothers*, 639 F. Supp. 134, 139 (E.D. Pa. 1986) ("With respect to the existence of both covered and uncovered claims or theories of liability, the potential for conflict is much greater, but actual conflict is not inevitable."); *Eckman v. Erie Ins. Exchange*, 21 A.3d 1203, 1209 (Pa. Super. Ct. 2011) (rejecting insured's argument that any attorney selected by insurer to represent insureds under a reservation of rights has a conflict) ("The categorical supposition that all attorneys compensated by a third party will breach their ethical duties is undeveloped, unsupported, and not cognizable under established principles of law. The trial court properly rejected it. Furthermore, numerous references in the Rules of Professional Conduct to circumstances in which a lawyer may represent a client and be paid by a third party … belie [insureds'] supposition that the Rules contemplate, let alone require, any such *per se* disqualification.") (not addressing the insured's right to independent counsel if insured can establish that a conflict exists); *Yaron v. Darwin National Insurance Co.*, No. 502, 2011 Phila. Ct. Com. Pl. LEXIS 167 (Phila. Ct. Com. Pl. July 5, 2011) ("This court is unwilling to adopt a *per se* rule that a reservation of rights letter creates a conflict of interest between the insurer and insured. Actual proof that attorneys have disregarded their ethical duties to their clients as set forth in the professional rules of conduct is necessary to establish the conflict of interest. To hold otherwise would require this court to recognize a conclusive presumption, based on nothing more than the existence of a potential conflict between the insured and the insurer, that counsel is unable to provide independent representation. This court is not willing to implant such an unwarranted presumption into the law. Instead, there must be some evidence to suggest that the conflict between the insurer and the insured actually affected counsel's representation so that it may be said that counsel's actions elevated the interests of the insurer over those of his client, the insured."); *Transp. Ins. Co. v. Motorists Mut. Ins. Co.*, No. 14-01438, 2017 U.S. Dist. LEXIS 2486 (M.D. Pa. Jan. 9, 2017) (holding that insurer, that breached the duty to defend, had no right to conduct discovery on the reasonableness of the defense fees incurred by the insured) (rejecting cases cited by the insurer, addressing reasonableness of fees, as they involved ones where a "reservation of rights clause created a conflict of interest between the insurer and insured, necessitating the appointment of independent counsel to represent the insured"). In *Babcock & Wilcox v. American Nuclear Insurers*, 131 A.3d 445 (Pa. 2015), the Supreme Court of Pennsylvania adopted a variation of the Arizona Supreme Court's decision in *United States Auto Ass'n. v. Morris*, 741 P.2d 246 (Ariz. 1987), discussed above, and the Pennsylvania high court suggested that, on account of the protection afforded to insureds under *Morris*, they may have a more difficult time arguing that, by being provided with a defense under a reservation of rights, they are entitled to retain independent counsel at the insurer's expense.

Rhode Island: The Supreme Court of Rhode Island held that, because of the existence of a conflict of interest (both negligent and intentional injuries were alleged), the insured should be entitled to select its own counsel at the expense of the insurer *or* the insurer and the insured should each be represented by separate counsel. *Employers' Fire Ins. Co. v. Beals*, 240 A.2d 397, 404 (R.I. 1968), *overruled on other grounds by Peerless Ins. Co. v. Viegas*, 667 A.2d 785 (R.I. 1995). The *Beals* Court expressed its belief that insurers should approve of either method "[b]ecause the insurer has a legitimate interest in seeing that any recovery based on finding of negligence on the part of its insured is kept within reasonable bounds[.]" *Id. See also Quality Concrete Corp. v. Travelers Property Cas. Co. of America*, 43 A.3d 16 (R.I. 2012) (declining to extend *Beals*, except in "rare circumstances," to entitle insured to independent counsel "whenever there is an 'adversarial communication' [pre-suit] from a potential plaintiff with respect to an incident involving potential liability on the part of the insured"); *Andromeda Real Estate Partners, LLC v. Commonwealth Land Title Ins. Co.*, No. 15-224, 2016 U.S. Dist. LEXIS 20667 (D.R.I. Feb. 19, 2016) (citing *Beals*) ("Because certain of the allegations in the Sedona Action, such as those relating to a conspiracy, if proven, could have triggered a policy coverage exclusion for intentional conduct, the Court finds that there was an inherent conflict here and Commonwealth was obligated to pay for non-conflicted representation of Andromeda's choosing.").

South Carolina: The Fourth Circuit Court of Appeals, interpreting South Carolina law, declined to hold that a reservation of rights letter per se allowed an insured to hire counsel of its choosing at the insurer's expense. *Twin City Fire Ins. Co. v. Ben Arnold-Sunbelt Beverage Co. of S.C., LP*, 433 F.3d 365, 373 (4th Cir. 2005). Addressing whether a conclusive presumption exists that counsel hired by an insurer is unable to fully represent the insured without consciously or unconsciously compromising the insured's interests, the court stated that is was "unable to conclude that the Supreme Court of South Carolina would profess so little confidence in the integrity of the members of the South Carolina Bar." *Id.* Instead, the Fourth Circuit looked to various provisions of the South Carolina Rules of Professional Conduct which provide rigorous ethical standards governing a lawyer's independence and duty of loyalty owed to its client, the insured, despite having been retained by the insurer. *Id.* The court concluded that these rules, various sanctions imposed for their violation and the threat of malpractice actions "provide strong external incentives for attorneys to comply with their ethical obligations." *Id. See also State Nat'l Ins. Co. v. Eastwood Constr. LLC*, No. 16-02607, 2018 U.S. Dist. LEXIS 232022 (D.S.C. Sept. 5, 2018) (discussing *Ben Arnold-Sunbelt* in detail) ("Eastwood certainly has the right not to consent to the attorneys selected by State National and to use RTT.

However, those rights do not nullify the terms of the insurance contract. Eastwood is not entitled to have State National pay for an attorney of Eastwood's own choosing per the terms of the State National Policies."); *Flexi-Van Leasing, Inc. v. Travelers Indem. Co.*, No. 19-1847, 2020 U.S. App. LEXIS 36859 (4th Cir. Nov. 23, 2020) ("The district court rightly found 'the refusal to initiate a third-party action against Interstar arose from Travelers's refusal to pay Wall [counsel retained by Travelers] to file a third-party action, not from any independent decision-making on the part of Wall.' In fact, '[f]inding a conflict of interest in this scenario would destroy the ability of an insurer to hire counsel to defend its insured solely within the scope of an insurance policy.' The existence of a coverage issue alone does not give rise to an actual conflict.").

South Dakota: The Supreme Court of South Dakota concluded that a conflict of interest is avoided when an insurer defends its insured under a reservation of rights because the parties will not be estopped from litigating coverage issues in a later proceeding. *St. Paul Fire & Marine Ins. Co. v. Engelmann*, 639 N.W.2d 192, 200 (S.D. 2002). Under this arrangement, "the interests of the insured and the insurer in defending against the injured claimant will be identical." *Id.* Under *Engelmann*, because the insurer and insured will litigate in a subsequent coverage action whether the jury's verdict in the underlying action was based on uncovered intentional acts or covered negligence, no conflict was created by the insurer's choice of defense counsel. *Id. See also American Family Ins. Group v. Robnik*, 787 N.W.2d 768 (S.D. 2010) ("[T]he preclusive effects of res judicata do not apply in this type of situation where the insurer participated under its duty to defend. As we have previously noted, when the insurer participates under its duty to defend, the insurer must defend the insured without regard to the insurer's interest. This creates a conflict of interest for the insurer. Hence the usual rule that an [insurer] is precluded by the determination of issues which he litigates on behalf of an [insured] stated in [Restatement (Second) of Judgments] § 57, should not apply to an [insurer] who defends, under the compulsion of an independent duty to defend, an [insured] with whom he has a conflict of interest. Therefore, claim preclusion did not bar consideration of the expected damage issue in American Family's declaratory action.") (citations and internal quotes omitted); *State Farm Mutual Automobile Ins. Co. v. Deerfield Hutterian Brethren Inc.*, No. 16-1016, 2017 U.S. Dist. LEXIS 47682 (D.S.D. Mar. 30, 2017) ("In the plaintiff's complaint, it asserts that Janos Stahl did not have the consent of Deerfield Colony to drive the 2000 GMC Jimmy off its property on February 9, 2014. There is a conflict of interest because the jury in the wrongful death action will decide the issue of whether Janos had implied permission to drive the 2000 GMC Jimmy on public roads that night. The answer to such question will be helpful in determining whether the automobile accident is covered by the insurance policy. By reserving the noncoverage issue, a conflict of interest will be avoided and the interests of the insured and the insurer in defending against the injured claimant will be identical. Therefore, the Court finds the issue of coverage is not yet fit for adjudication, and that there will be little hardship to the parties in withholding court consideration, as this matter lacks ripeness.").

Tennessee: A Tennessee District Court concluded that the mere existence of a relationship between an insurer and defense counsel was not sufficient to create a conflict of interest. *Tyson v. Equity Title & Escrow Co. of Memphis, LLC*, 282 F. Supp. 2d 829, 832 (W.D. Tenn. 2003). The court seemed persuaded that the Tennessee Rules of Professional Conduct were sufficient to safeguard the insured, stating that "[t]ypically, the relationship between an insurance company and the attorney that it hires to defend an insured is that of principal and independent contractor. An insurance company clearly possesses no right to control the methods or means by which an attorney defends its insured. The employment of an attorney by an insurance company to represent its insured does not impose upon that attorney any duty or loyalty to the insurance company that could impair the attorney-client relationship between the attorney and the insured." *Id.* at 831–32 (citations omitted); *see also In re Petition of Youngblood*, 895 S.W.2d 322, 328–29 (Tenn. 1995) (rejecting a per se rule that an insurer cannot use staff counsel to defend its insureds and instead finding that whether there is a conflict in such arrangement must be determined on a case-by-case basis under the Tennessee Code of Professional Conduct); *Developers Diversified of Tenn., Inc. v. Tokio Marine & Fire Ins. Co.*, No. 04-00015, 2019 U.S. Dist. LEXIS 70184 (M.D. Tenn. Apr. 25, 2019) (looking to *Tyson* for guidance in determining whether a law firm had a conflict of interest to warrant disqualification) ("As an insurance company, '[t]he employment of an attorney . . . to represent its insured does not impose upon that attorney any duty or loyalty to the insurance company that could impair the attorney-client relationship between the attorney and the insured.'") (quoting *Tyson*).

Texas: The Supreme Court of Texas held that, when defending an insured under a reservation of rights, if "the facts to be adjudicated in the liability lawsuit are the same facts upon which coverage depends, the conflict of interest will prevent the insurer from conducting the defense." *N. County Mut. Ins. Co. v. Davalos*, 140 S.W.3d 685, 689 (Tex. 2004). If so, the insurer loses the right to conduct the defense, but remains obligated to pay for it. *Id.* at 686. The *Davalos* court also listed other types of conflicts that may justify an insured's refusal of an offered defense: "(1) when the defense tendered 'is not a complete defense under circumstances in which it should have been,' (2) when 'the attorney hired by the carrier acts unethically and, at the insurer's direction, advances the insurer's interests at the expense of the insured's,' (3) when 'the defense would not, under the governing law, satisfy the insurer's duty to defend,' and (4) when, though the defense is otherwise proper, 'the insurer attempts to obtain some type of concession from the insured before it will defend.'" *Davalos*, 140 S.W.3d at 689 (quoting 1 ALLAN D. WINDT, INSURANCE CLAIMS & DISPUTES § 4.25 at 393 (4th ed. 2001)); *see also Rx.com, Inc. v. Hartford Fire Ins. Co.*, 426 F. Supp. 2d 546, 561 (S.D. Tex. 2006) ("Hartford's reservation of rights letter did not invoke a coverage exclusion that would be established by proof of the same facts to be decided in the underlying lawsuit."); *In re CES Envtl. Serv. Inc.*, No. H-11-560, 2011 (S.D. Tex. Mar. 31, 2011) (holding that trustee in estate in bankruptcy proceeding, as fiduciary of the estate, should choose defense counsel because insurer had issued several reservation of rights letters and insurer's "only interest [was] showing that the harm [was] not covered under the policies") (citing *Davalos*); *Taylor v. Allstate Ins. Co.*, 356 S.W.3d 92 (Tex. Ct. App. 2011) (citing rule from *Davalos* in addressing whether Texas law recognizes a cause of action by an insured against its insurer for tortious interference with the insured's relationship with his attorney); *Partain v. Mid-Continent Specialty Ins. Services, Inc.*, 838 F. Supp. 2d 547 (S.D. Tex. 2012) (examining five issues presented in a reservation of rights letter to determine if facts upon which coverage clearly depends will be adjudicated in the underlying action); *Downhole Navigator, L.L.C. v. Nautilus Ins. Co.*, 686 F.3d 325 (5th Cir. 2012) (applying Texas law) (concluding that "the facts to be adjudicated" in the underlying litigation were not the same "facts upon which coverage depends") ("[A]lthough the policy excludes coverage for 'testing' or 'consulting' services, the facts about whether Downhole breached a duty to Sedona by failing to act as a reasonably prudent provider of deviation-correction services are not equivalent to the facts that could determine whether Downhole was 'testing' or 'consulting' for Sedona."); *Graper v. Mid-Continent Cas. Co.*, 756 F.3d 388 (5th Cir. 2014) (applying Texas law) ("An adjudication of the accrual date (the fact to be adjudicated in the underlying lawsuit) need not be a judicial ruling necessarily deciding the date of when the infringing conduct occurred (the fact upon which coverage depends). Thus, under the *Davalos* same facts test, there is no disqualifiable conflict of interest between the Insureds and Mid–Continent in litigating the statute of limitations defense.") ("[W]e hold that an application of the *Davalos* 'same facts' standard evidences no conflict here. The underlying trial court's determination that there was a willful violation of KFA's copyright under § 504(c)(2) would not settle the issue of whether that violation was knowing; a violation can amount to reckless conduct and still be willful under the statute. Because the infringement could be willful conduct under § 504(c)(2), entitling KFA to enhanced damages, without a finding of knowing infringement thereby excluding coverage, there is no disqualifying conflict of interest under *Davalos*."); *Allstate Cnty. Mut. Ins. Co. v. Wootton*, 494 S.W.3d 825 (Tex. Ct. App. 2016) (addressing *Davalos* and whether the facts at issue gave rise to the right to independent counsel); *Stadium Motorcars, LLC v. Fed. Ins. Co.*, No. H-18-1920, 2019 U.S. Dist. LEXIS 82251 (S.D. Tex. May 15, 2019) (reviewing issues in a reservation of rights letter and concluding that there was no disqualifying conflict of interest under *Davalos*); *Amerisure Ins. Co. v. Thermacor Process, Inc.*, No. 20-01089, 2021 U.S. Dist. LEXIS 51896 (N.D. Tex. Mar. 19, 2020) (finding that the insured was entitled to independent counsel because the insurer "did not simply send a reservation-of-rights letter upon providing a defense" but "took the additional step" of filing a declaratory judgment action against the insured while the underlying lawsuit was pending, and attempted to communicate with the underlying plaintiff "in an attempt to include [it] in this coverage lawsuit").

Utah: The Eight Circuit Court of Appeals, applying Utah law, left little doubt about what it thought of the risk for conflict when an insurer undertakes to defend its insured under a reservation of rights, stating "we cannot escape the conclusion that it is impossible for one attorney to adequately and fairly represent two parties in litigation in the face of the real conflict of interest which existed here. Even the most optimistic view of human nature requires us to realize that an attorney employed by an insurance company will slant his efforts, perhaps unconsciously, in the interests of his real client the one who is paying his fee and from whom he hopes to receive future business the insurance company." *U.S. Fidelity & Guar. Co. v. Louis A. Roser Co.*, 585 F.2d 932, 938 n.5 (8th Cir. 1978). Nonetheless, the court did not adopt the rule that a reservation of rights creates a *per se* conflict of interest. Rather, the court concluded that a conflict existed based on the specific facts at hand. *Id.* at 939. Among others, one of the three theories of recovery alleged in the underlying action was not covered by the policy. *Id.* at 938. In addition, the insurer filed a declaratory judgment action seeking a determination of no coverage. *Id.* at 940. *See also State Farm Fire & Cas. Co. v. Inevat, LLC*, No. 17-00901, 2018 U.S. Dist. LEXIS 97075 (D. Utah June 8, 2018) (concluding that no right to independent counsel existed in the context of some sort of alleged postponement of the litigation to the insured's detriment) ("Defendants contend a conflict of interest has arisen between themselves and State Farm appointed counsel, requiring State Farm to pay for independent counsel selected by the Defendants. State Farm counters, arguing no conflict exists because under a 'dual-client' paradigm the attorney's allegiance is always to the insured because of an insurer's duty to provide a defense in good faith. The parties agree that Utah courts have not directly addressed the conflict of interest issue, but decline the court's invitation for certification.").

Vermont: The Supreme Court of Vermont held that a unilateral reservation of rights by an insurer is ineffective. *Am. Fidelity Co. v. Kerr*, 416 A.2d 163, 165 (Vt. 1980). "Control of the defense, with knowledge of the facts and without consent of the insured, constitutes an election to stand by the terms of the policy." *Id.*; *see also Beatty v. Employers' Liab. Assurance Corp., Ltd.*, 168 A. 919, 923 (Vt. 1933) (emphasis added) ("The insurer may, if it is in doubt as to its liability, refuse to assume the defense, and await the result, thus leaving the insured free to defend or compromise in his own way through his own counsel; or it may obtain some agreement with the insured, under which, by proceeding to defend, it shall not be considered to have enlarged its obligation under the policy, thus reserving its rights under that instrument."); *Northern Security Insurance Co. v. Claudia & David Pratt & Greystone Estates Residents Ass'n*, No. 838-11-10, 2011 Vt. Super. LEXIS 36 (Vt. Super. Ct. May 19, 2011) (addressing the rules concerning an insurer's handling of a defense in some detail and applying them to a specific factual scenario).

Virginia: The Supreme Court of Virginia addressed the conflict issue in the context of its decision that an insurer that defends its insured under a reservation of rights is not estopped from relitigating a fact issue that bears on coverage—specifically, whether its insured fired a gun negligently or intentionally. *State Farm Fire & Cas. Co. v. Mabry*, 497 S.E.2d 844 (Va. 1998). In *Mabry*, the court held that, in the underlying tort action, the insurer could not assert its position on the nature of the insured's conduct as the insurer was not a party. *Id.* at 846. The insurer also could not do so in conjunction with providing a defense to its insured because of the duty owed by the attorney retained by the insurer to the insured. *Id.* Thus, the court concluded that the declaratory judgment proceeding was the insurer's first opportunity to try its coverage defense on the merits. *Id.* at 847. By permitting the insurer to relitigate in a subsequent coverage forum an issue that was resolved in the underlying tort action, the Virginia high court's decision avoids the need for independent counsel. *Id. See also Nationwide Prop. & Cas. Ins. Co. v. Fraraccio*,

No. 16-1485, 2017 U.S. Dist. LEXIS 65401 (E.D. Va. Apr. 24, 2017) (addressing the impact of *Mabry* in the context of the timing for a declaratory judgment action vis-à-vis an underlying wrongful death action).

Washington: The Court of Appeals of Washington held that there is no presumption that a reservation of rights creates an automatic conflict of interest. *Johnson v. Cont'l Cas. Co.*, 788 P.2d 598, 601 (Wash. Ct. App. 1990). Instead, an insurer providing a defense under a reservation of rights must fulfill an "enhanced obligation of fairness." *Id.* at 600 (citing *Tank v. State Farm Fire & Cas. Co.*, 715 P.2d 1133, 1137 (Wash. 1986)). This enhanced obligation has been explained by the Supreme Court of Washington as follows: "First, the [insurer] must thoroughly investigate the cause of the insured's accident and the nature and severity of the plaintiff's injuries. Second, it must retain competent defense counsel for the insured. Both retained defense counsel and the insurer must understand that only the *insured* is the client. Third, the company has the responsibility for fully informing the insured not only of the reservation of rights defense itself, but of *all* developments relevant to his policy coverage and the progress of his lawsuit. Information regarding progress of the lawsuit includes disclosure of all settlement offers made by the company. Finally, an insurance company must refrain from engaging in any action which would demonstrate a greater concern for the insurer's monetary interest than for the insured's financial risk." *Tank*, 715 P.2d at 1137.

In addition to the criteria that must be satisfied by the insurer, the *Tank* Court also set out a list of obligations that must be satisfied by counsel who has been retained by the insurer to provide a defense under a reservation of rights. Counsel must understand that he or she represents only the insured, not the company. *Id.* at 1137. Defense counsel owes a duty of full and ongoing disclosure to the insured. *Id.* "This duty of disclosure has three aspects. First, potential conflicts of interest between insurer and insured must be fully disclosed and resolved in favor of the insured … . Second, all information relevant to the insured's defense, including a realistic and periodic assessment of the insured's chances to win or lose the pending lawsuit, must be communicated to the insured. Finally, *all* offers of settlement must be disclosed to the insured as those offers are presented." *Id.* at 1137–38 (emphasis in original); *see also Carolina Cas. Ins. Co. v. Ott*, No. C09-5540, 2010 U.S. Dist. LEXIS 44933 (W.D. Wash. May 7, 2010) (discussing *Tank* factors); *Jaco Environmental, Inc. v. Am. Intern. Specialty Lines Ins. Co.*, No. 2:09-cv-0145, 2009 U.S. Dist. LEXIS 51785 (W.D. Wash. May 19, 2009) (discussing *Johnson* and explaining why Washington's independent counsel rules differ from California's); *Weinstein & Riley*,

P.S. v. Westport Ins. Corp., No. C08-1694JLR, 2011 U.S. Dist. LEXIS 26369 (W.D. Wash. Mar. 14, 2011) (addressing issue in the context of a policy containing a provision that allows for independent counsel if the insurer reserves its rights on grounds that create a conflict) ("Washington does not recognize entitlement to 'independent counsel' as it is understood under the *Cumis* model. In Washington, an insured is not entitled by law to choose independent counsel to represent it where there is a potential conflict with the insurer in a reservation of rights situation ... Instead, the insured is entitled to a defense provided by a lawyer selected by the insurer, and the appointed lawyer owes an enhanced obligation of fairness to the insured."); *Evanston Ins. Co. v. Clartre, Inc.*, No. 14-00085, 2016 U.S. Dist. LEXIS 37248 (W.D. Wash. Mar. 22, 2016) ("Evanston acted reasonably in refusing to reimburse a small portion of Defendants' attorney's fees (some amount less than $50,000 out of $1,472,487.13) based upon Defendants' failure to comply with Evanston's Litigation Management Guidelines. Defendants may now disagree with those Guidelines, but they agreed to abide by them when choosing to be defended by attorneys of their own choice.") (discussing specific guidelines that were violated); *National Union Fire Ins. Co. v. Coinstar, Inc.*, No. C13-1014, 2014 U.S. Dist. LEXIS 94578 (W.D. Wash. July 10, 2014) (addressing permissible discovery in connection with a dispute over the rates to pay defense counsel); *Arden v. Forsberg & Umlauf, PS*, 402 P.3d 245 (Wash. 2017) ("We reject the suggestion advanced that wherever a previous relationship between the insurer and retained counsel exists, a per se disqualification rule is supported. We have no concerns recognizing the rule requiring disclosure of conflicts, potential or actual, in the context of attorneys hired by insurance companies to represent insureds' interests in civil litigation, whether such representation is provided under an ROR or not. These same responsibilities exist in the context of dual representation."); *Zurich Am. Ins. Co. v. Ledcor Indus. (USA) Inc.*, No. 76490, 2019 Wash. App. LEXIS 645 (Wash. Ct. App. Jun. 7, 2018) (concluding that *Tank* factors were satisfied and rejecting argument that insurer engaged "in any action which would demonstrate a greater concern for the insurer's monetary interest than for the insured's financial risk during the course of its defense . . . and in making its later coverage decision").

West Virginia: The Supreme Court of Appeals of West Virginia addressed whether an insurer can be held liable under the West Virginia Unfair Trade Practices Act for the actions of a defense attorney retained to defend an insured (the simple answer is no). *Barefield v. DPIC Cos., Inc.*, 600 S.E.2d 256 (W. Va. 2004). The decision did not address the independent counsel issue. However, in arriving at its decision, the West Virginia high court addressed the tri-partite relationship in some detail, including citing to *U.S. Fidelity & Guar. Co. v. Louis A. Roser Co.*, 585 F.2d 932 (8th Cir. 1978) (see Utah). *Id.* at 557. *See also West Virginia Mut. Ins. Co. v. Vargas*, 933 F. Supp. 2d 847 (N.D.W.Va. 2013) ("[A] defense attorney hired by insurance company to represent insured does not represent insurer.") (citing *Barefield*). More recently, in *State ex rel. Universal Underwriters Ins. Co. v. Wilson*, No. 17-0004, 2017 W. Va. LEXIS 417 (W. Va. June 1, 2017), the Supreme Court of Appeals of West Virginia addressed the specific question of independent counsel: "[U]nder the terms of most liability insurance policies, the insured agrees to permit the insurer to choose counsel to defend the insured against claims by third parties. Generally, the insurer and insured have compatible interests and goals in responding to a tort claim. However, their interests may diverge at times, creating a potential or actual conflict of interest. This case presents the common situation where the conflict of interest between Zurich and the Cava defendants concerns the amount of coverage available under the policy. On this issue, the Cava defendants' interests are more in line with the plaintiff's interest, as they want to establish that the umbrella policy covers her claims against Salvatore Cava. This evident conflict of interest made it necessary for Zurich to retain independent counsel for the Cava defendants and itself.").

Wisconsin: A Wisconsin District Court held that the Wisconsin Supreme Court would not conclude that a mere reservation of rights automatically creates a conflict of interest between insured and insurer, which divests the insurer of control of the defense. *HK Systems, Inc. v. Admiral Ins. Co.*, No. 03 C 0795, 2005 U.S. Dist. LEXIS 39939 (D. Wis. June 27, 2005). Rather, for the insurer to be required to relinquish control of the defense, a real conflict of interest based on opposing defenses of insured and insurer must exist. The *HK Systems* Court concluded that a real conflict of interest did exist because the insurer may benefit if HK Systems were found liable on certain claims, such as breach of contract or warranty, but not on others, such as negligence.; *see also Lakeside Foods, Inc. v. Liberty Mut. Fire. Ins. Co.*, 789 N.W.2d 754 (Table) (Wis. Ct. App. 2010) (citing *HK Systems* and noting that "even in those jurisdictions where the insurer is permitted to select counsel, the appointed counsel must be truly independent and the insurer may not delay in disapproving the insured's choice of counsel"); *Haley v. Kolbe & Kolbe Millwork Co.*, No. 13-CV-278-J, 2015 U.S. Dist. LEXIS 148023 (W.D. Wis. Nov. 2, 2105) and 97 F. Supp. 3d 1047 (W.D. Wis. 2015) (protracted litigation involving an insurer's delay in making decisions regarding counsel and its attempt to impose its own choice of counsel on the insured rather than accept the insured's choice).

Wyoming: No instructive authority.

CHAPTER
7

Insurer's Right to Reimbursement of Defense Costs

Many coverage issues develop over time, in response to new exposures for which insurance is sought. Such issues then sometimes fracture into various schools of thought as nuances emerge and more courts consider the issue. The duty to defend is not one of these issues. Rather, it is static and has been that way for a long time. Clearly no citation is needed for the principle that, in virtually all states, the duty to defend is broader than the duty to indemnify. And it has been that way for a very long time. *See Greer-Robbins Co. v. Pac. Sur. Co.*, 174 P. 110, 111 (Cal. Ct. App. 1918) (holding that the duty to defend is based on the allegations of the complaint and rejecting the insurer's argument that such duty depends upon the outcome of the action against the insured).

It is perhaps because the breadth of the duty to defend has achieved such taken-for-granted status that insureds do not take it lightly anytime they perceive an insurer straying from what they believe to be such a sacrosanct principle. One such circumstance is when an insurer, following a judicial determination that its duty to defend did not in fact exist, then attempts to recover the defense costs from the insured to whom it nonetheless provided a defense.

Insureds typically respond that reimbursement of defense costs must be impermissible because it would amount to the insurer achieving, at the conclusion of the case, that which it was not permitted to do at the inception of the case, namely, treating the duty to defend as other than broader than the duty to indemnify. *See Perdue Farms v. Travelers Cas. & Sur. Co.*, 448 F.3d 252, 258 (4th Cir. 2006) ("Under Maryland's comprehensive duty to defend, if an insurance policy potentially covers any claim in an underlying complaint, the insurer, as Travelers did here, must typically defend the entire suit, including non-covered claims. Properly considered, a partial right of reimbursement would thus serve only as a backdoor narrowing of the duty to defend, and would appreciably erode Maryland's long-held view that the duty to defend is broader than the duty to indemnify.") (citation omitted); *see also id.* at 259 ("In the absence of any contrary indication from the Maryland courts, we are unwilling to grant insurers a substantial rebate on their duty to defend.").

Nonetheless, despite this perceived challenge, litigation surrounding an insurer's right to reimbursement of defense costs has been active for the past twenty-plus years. As the following 50 state survey reveals, both sides can claim many victories.

Any discussion of an insurer's right to reimbursement of defense costs must begin with the best known case on the subject— *Jerry Buss v. Superior Court of Los Angeles County (Transamerica Ins. Co.)*, 939 P.2d 766 (Cal. 1997). Buss owned the Los Angeles Lakers basketball team as well as other sports teams in Los Angeles, the Great Western Forum indoor arena, and various cable television broadcasting networks. *Id.* at 769. A dispute arose between Buss and H&H Sports over the provision of advertising for Buss. *Id.* H&H filed a twenty-seven-count complaint against Buss. *Id.* Buss sought coverage from Transamerica under commercial general liability policies. *Id.* Transamerica agreed to defend Buss on the basis of a defamation cause of action—the only cause of action out of twenty-seven that Transamerica believed was potentially covered. *Id.* at 770.

Transamerica reserved all of its rights, "including to deny that any cause of action was actually covered, and, '[w]ith respect to defense costs incurred or to be incurred in the future, … to be reimbursed and/or [to obtain] an allocation of attorney's fees and expenses in this action if it is determined that there is no coverage.'" *Buss*, 939 P.2d at 770 (alteration in original).

Buss paid H&H Sports $8.5 million to settle the dispute. *Id.* Transamerica paid Buss's defense counsel approximately $1 million, and a Transamerica expert concluded that the amount to defend the defamation cause of action was between $21,000 and $55,000. *Id.*

Addressing a dispute over coverage for defense costs, the Supreme Court of California held that, in a so-called "mixed" action, in which some claims are potentially covered and others are not—thereby triggering a duty to defend the action in its entirety—an insurer may thereafter seek reimbursement of defense costs for claims that are not potentially covered. *Id.* at 776–77. The *Buss* court rested its decision on the following rationale:

> Under the policy, the insurer does not have a duty to defend the insured as to the claims that are not even potentially covered. With regard to defense costs for these claims, the insurer has not been paid premiums by the insured. It did not bargain to bear these costs. To attempt to shift them would not upset the arrangement. The insurer therefore has a right of reimbursement that is implied in law as quasi-contractual, whether or not it has one

that is implied in fact in the policy as contractual. As stated, under the law of restitution such a right runs against the person who benefits from "unjust enrichment" and in favor of the person who suffers loss thereby. The "enrichment" of the insured by the insurer through the insurer's bearing of unbargained-for defense costs is inconsistent with the insurer's freedom under the policy and therefore must be deemed "unjust."

Id. (citations omitted).

Other courts have permitted an insurer to recoup defense costs, but based on a rationale that differs from the one offered by *Buss*. Instead of concluding that the right to reimbursement is one that is implied in law to prevent unjust enrichment, as *Buss* did, some courts have reasoned that the insured's acceptance of the insurer's defense, with an express reservation of the insurer's right to recover defense costs, creates an implied in fact contract.

In *Colony Insurance Co. v. G & E Tires & Service, Inc.*, 777 So. 2d 1034 (Fla. Dist. Ct. App. 2000), the insurer was requested to provide a defense to its insured for claims by an employee for battery, sexual harassment, invasion of privacy, and intentional infliction of emotional distress. The insurer was adamant that no defense was owed because the claims were intentional torts and for injuries to employees in the workplace. *Id.* at 1035–36. Nonetheless, after initially sending three disclaimer letters, the insurer finally agreed to defend, but subject to a reservation of its right to be reimbursed for "defense costs incurred or to be incurred in the future." *Id.* at 1036. It was ultimately determined that the insurer was correct in its determination—the policy unequivocally excluded coverage for liability arising from the injuries. *Id.* at 1039. The insurer sought reimbursement of the defense costs incurred. *Id.* at 1038.

While the Florida appeals court in *G & E Tires* cited favorably to *Buss* in finding for the insurer, including quoting *Buss's* restitution analysis, the court did not expressly rely upon this rationale for its decision. *Id.* Instead, the *G & E Tires* court rested its decision on contract principles—although not flowing from the insurance contract, but, rather, the reservation of rights. *G&E Tires*, 777 So. 2d at 1038. The *G & E Tires* court held:

Colony timely and expressly reserved the right to seek reimbursement of the costs of defending clearly uncovered claims, which it consistently identified as such. Having accepted Colony's offer of a defense with a reservation of the right to seek reimbursement, G & E ought in fairness make Colony

whole, now that it has been judicially determined that no duty to defend
ever existed.

A party cannot accept tendered performance while unilaterally altering
the material terms on which it is offered. See generally *Restatement (Second)
of Contracts* § 69 (1981). *** G & E's acceptance of the defense Colony offered to finance manifested acceptance of the terms on which Colony's offer
to pay for the defense was tendered.

Id. at 1039; *see also Travelers Cas. & Sur. Co. v. Ribi Immunochem Research*, 108 P.3d
469, 480 (Mont. 2005) ("Travelers expressly reserved its right to recoup defense
costs if a court determined that it had no duty to provide such costs. Travelers also
provided specific and adequate notice of the possibility of reimbursement. Ribi
implicitly accepted Traveler's defense under a reservation of rights when it posed no
objections. Under these circumstances, the District Court appropriately concluded
that Travelers may recoup its defense costs.")

But not all courts have been convinced that an insured's acceptance of a defense,
with the insurer's express reservation of rights to recoup defense costs if it is determined that no duty to defend was owed, converts the reservation of rights letter into
an implied in fact contract. Indeed, some courts see it the exact opposite.

In *Westchester Fire Insurance Co. v. Wallerich*, 563 F.3d 707, 719 (8th Cir. 2009), the
Eighth Circuit Court of Appeals, interpreting Minnesota law, held that the insurer
was not entitled to reimbursement of defense costs, despite asserting such right in
its reservation of rights letter. Following an extensive survey of the law nationally
on the issue, the court concluded that the insurer could have included a right to
reimbursement in its policy. *Id.* As it did not, the insurer could not now unilaterally amend the policy through a reservation of rights letter. *Id.* Further, the court
observed that the insureds explicitly rejected the terms of the reservation of rights,
but accepted the defense nonetheless. *Id.* In this situation, because the insurer still
tendered a defense, despite the insureds' rejection of the terms of the reservation of
rights, the court concluded that the insurer was impliedly agreeing to proceed on
the insureds' terms. *Id.*

Another rationale used by courts to reject an insurer's right to reimbursement of
defense costs has its origin in *Terra Nova Insurance Company, Ltd. v. 900 Bar, Inc.*, 887
F.2d 1213 (3d Cir. 1989) (applying Pennsylvania law). Decided at a time when there
was very little law on the issue, as evidenced by the fact that the *Terra Nova* court
cited none (either controlling or persuasive), the court rested its decision on its view
of certain practicalities of insurance and litigation. The *Terra Nova* court stated:

> Faced with uncertainty as to its duty to indemnify, an insurer offers a de-
> fense under reservation of rights to avoid the risks that an inept or lackadai-
> sical defense of the underlying action may expose it to if it turns out there
> is a duty to indemnify. At the same time, the insurer wishes to preserve its
> right to contest the duty to indemnify if the defense is unsuccessful. Thus,
> such an offer is made at least as much for the insurer's own benefit as for
> the insured's. If the insurer could recover defense costs, the insured would
> be required to pay for the insurer's action in protecting itself against the
> estoppel to deny coverage that would be implied if it undertook the defense
> without reservation.

Terra Nova, 887 F.2d at 1219–20. The *Terra Nova* court's rationale for rejecting the
insurer's right to reimbursement of defense costs was simple. Since an insurer that is
faced with uncertainty about its duty to indemnify receives a benefit from providing
a defense, the insured is not unjustly enriched, even if it is ultimately determined
that no duty to defend arose. *Id.*

   It is not uncommon for courts that reject an insurer's right to reimbursement of
defense costs to conclude that the insurer could have included such right in its policy. *See General Agents Ins. Co. of Am., Inc. v. Midwest Sporting Goods Co.*, 828 N.E.2d
1092, 1102 (Ill. 2005) ("Certainly, if an insurer wishes to retain its right to seek
reimbursement of defense costs in the event it later is determined that the underlying claim is not covered by the policy, the insurer is free to include such a term
in its insurance contract. Absent such a provision in the policy, however, an insurer
cannot later attempt to amend the policy by including the right to reimbursement
in its reservation of rights letter.").

   While there is no shortage of states that allow an insurer to recover its defense
costs following a determination that no duty to defend was owed, insurers sometimes
find that practical problems associated with the implementation of this right dimin-
ish its actual value. As *Buss* itself noted: "An insurer is only entitled to recover those
defense expenses which can be fairly and reasonably allocated *solely* to non-covered
claims for which there never was any potential for coverage." *Buss*, 939 P.2d at 778
n.15 (quoting the Court of Appeal's decision in the case) (emphasis in original).
Further, the court acknowledged that the task of allocating defense costs solely to
claims that are not even potentially covered is at best extremely difficult and may
never be feasible. *Id.* at 781 (discussing *Hogan v. Midland Nat'l Ins. Co.*, 476 P.2d 825
(Cal. 1970)). Thus, defense costs incurred to defend both actually or potentially
covered claims, as well as noncovered claims, cannot be recovered. *Id.*

Since the majority of defense costs are incurred for claims that are both potentially covered and not covered, in many cases an insurer's right to reimbursement of defense costs has more bark than bite. This reality likely prevents some insurers from pursuing reimbursement of defense costs—either in an attempt to create the right or enforce it. For this reason, the real benefit for insurers when it comes to reimbursement of defense costs is likely limited to those cases that are not "mixed" actions, but, rather, where an insurer has undertaken a defense and can then establish that there were in fact no claims whatsoever that triggered such duty.

50-State Survey: Insurer's Right to Reimbursement of Defense Costs

Alabama: The Supreme Court of Alabama held that an insurer was not entitled to reimbursement of a payment made to settle a third-party claim against its insured if it were determined in a subsequent action that the policy did not provide coverage. *Mount Airy Ins. Co. v. The Doe Law Firm*, 668 So. 2d 534, 539 (Ala. 1995). Relying on the state's long history of disallowing recovery of voluntary payments, the court concluded, despite the insurer providing notice to the insured, that it would seek to recover the settlement payment, "such a protest by itself was insufficient to make the payment 'involuntary.'" *Id.* at 538. The court suggested that, to preserve a right to reimbursement of monies paid to settle a claim, an insurer must obtain a written nonwaiver agreement or a court order granting it the right to participate in a settlement without waiving the right to reimbursement. *Id.* (citations omitted). While the decision involved reimbursement of a settlement payment, the court's rationale would likely apply equally to defense costs. *See Amerisure Mut. Ins. Co. v. QBE Ins. Corp.*, No. 11–J–1751, 2012 U.S. Dist. LEXIS 125811 (N.D. Ala. Sept. 5, 2012) (not involving pre-tender defense costs but noting that "[i]t has been the law in Alabama for over 150 years that where one party, with full knowledge of all the facts, voluntarily pays money to satisfy the colorable legal demand of another, no action will lie to recover such a voluntary payment, in the absence of fraud, duress, or extortion."). *James River Ins. Co. v. Arlington Pebble Creek, LLC*, 188 F. Supp. 3d 1246 (N.D. Fla. 2016) (predicting that Alabama Supreme Court's decision in *Mt. Airy* could also be applied to cases involving defense costs).

    Alaska: The Supreme Court of Alaska held that "When an insurer has a duty to defend, Alaska law prohibits enforcement of a policy provision entitling that insurer to reimbursement of fees and costs incurred during the defense of claims under a reservation of rights…even in cases where…(1) the insurer explicitly reserved the right to seek reimbursement in its offer to tender a defense provided by independent counsel, (2) the insured accepted the defense subject to the reservation of rights, and (3) the claims are later determined to be excluded from coverage under the policy." *Attorneys Liability Protection Society, Inc. v. Ingaldson Fitzgerald, P.C.*, 370 P.3d 1101 (Alaska 2016). In addition, the court held that "Alaska law prohibits reimbursement of fees and costs incurred by the insurer defending claims under a reservation of rights, even in circumstances where it is later discovered that there was 'no possibility of coverage' under the policy."

Arizona: An Arizona District Court held that liability insurers were permitted to send unilateral reservation of rights letters to insureds in order to recover defense costs and settlement paid by the insurer in defending and settling a malpractice claim against the insureds. *Phillips & Assoc. v. Navigators Ins. Co.*, 764 F. Supp. 2d 1174, 1175–77 (D. Ariz. 2011). The court declined to decide whether to apply Arizona or California law to the case because, as the court noted, "[b]oth Arizona and California recognize that an insurer's unilateral reservation of rights is proper, absent bad faith and provided notice is given to the insured." *Id.* at 1175. In justifying its decision and determining that the insurer "satisfied all prerequisites to seeking reimbursement under a reservation of rights," the court found that the insurers sent the reservation of rights letter to the insurer "upon initially accepting the defense, which was seven months prior to the settlement date," and "[t]he insureds were aware of this reservation well before settlement and did not disagree with Navigators on whether to accept settlement." *Id.* at 1177. "If an insurer waived its coverage position simply by settling a claim for the insured, the insurer would be forced either to refuse to settle and face a bad faith claim, or to settle the lawsuit and lose its coverage defenses." *Id.* at 1176. However, an Arizona District Court predicted that the Arizona Supreme Court would follow the *Jerry's Sport* approach [See Pa.] in determining if an insurer is entitled to reimbursement of defense costs. *Great Am. Assur. Co. v. PCR Venture of Phoenix LLC*, 161 F. Supp. 3d 778 (D. Ariz. 2015): "The Arizona Supreme Court is also likely to hold 1) courts should not insert provisions into contracts that the parties did not; 2) one party cannot unilaterally alter the terms of a contract by issuing a reservation of rights letter with new terms; and 3) unjust enrichment is not an available remedy when a contract exists."

Arkansas: The Supreme Court of Arkansas held that an insurer was not entitled to reimbursement of defense costs because attorney's fees are not recoverable except where expressly provided for by statute or rule—and none existed. *Med. Liab. Mut. Ins. Co. v. Alan Curtis Enters. Inc.*, 285 S.W.3d 233, 235 (Ark. 2008). By relying on the so-called "American Rule," which provides that, absent a statute or agreement to the contrary, litigants bear their own attorney's fees, the court concluded that it did not need to consider the approaches taken by courts around the country that have addressed an insurer's right to reimbursement of defense costs. *Id.* A vigorous dissent maintained that the majority misapplied the American Rule, which applies to claims for attorney's fees by prevailing litigants. *Id.* at 238 (Brown, J., dissenting). "Whether an implied contract was formed to reimburse costs advanced in defense of a third-party claim is a far cry from the issue of payment of costs to a prevailing litigant, which is the subject of the American Rule. Simply put, that rule has no relevancy to the certified question before us." *Id.* "Our research has disclosed that no state court or federal court has based its reservation-of-rights [reimbursement of defense costs] decision on the American Rule, or even discussed it." *Id.* at 237.

California: The Supreme Court of California held that an insurer had a right to reimbursement of defense costs for claims that are not covered under the policy. *Jerry Buss v. Superior Court of Los Angeles County (Transamerica Ins. Co.)*, 939 P.2d 766, 775–78 (Cal. 1997). The court concluded that the insurer's right of reimbursement is one that is implied in law, to prevent unjust enrichment by the insured of defense costs for claims that were not covered by the policy, and, hence, for which the insured paid no premium. *Id.* at 776–77. Because such right is implied in law as quasi contractual, the insurer must specifically reserve it. *Id.* at 784 n.27. Further, the *Buss* court's decision applied to a so-called "mixed action," in which some claims were potentially covered and others were not. *Id.* at 775–77. However, the *Buss* court noted that, as a practical matter, the task of allocating defense costs solely to claims that are not potentially covered is at best extremely difficult and may never be feasible. *Id.* at 780 n.16; *see also Scottsdale Ins. Co. v. MV Trans.*, 115 P.3d 460, 471 (Cal. 2005) (holding that *Buss* also applies outside the context of a "mixed action," i.e., where no claim was potentially covered); *State Farm Gen. Ins. Co. v. Mintarsih*, 175 Cal. App.4th 274, 286 (2009) (applying *Buss* to hold that the insurer was not obligated to provide coverage for prevailing party attorney's fees, as costs, that could be allocated solely to claims that are not potentially covered); *Griffin Dewatering Corp. v. N. Ins. Co. of N.Y.*, 97 Cal. Rptr. 3d 568, 598–605 (Cal. Ct. App. 2009) (discussing *Buss* and related issues at length); *Burlington Ins. Co. v. Devdhara*, No. C 09-00421, 2010 U.S. Dist. LEXIS 99955 (N.D. Cal. Sept. 23, 2010) (applying principles of reimbursement of defense costs and a settlement to a multi-count complaint); *Toll Bros., Inc. v. OneBeacon Ins. Co.*, No. G042196, 2011 Cal. App. Unpub. LEXIS 1947 (Cal. Ct. App. Mar. 15, 2011) (following *Buss* and affirming trial court decision to allow insurer to recover defense costs where no duty to defend ever existed and insurer defended insured under a reservation of rights); *Axis Surplus Ins. Co. v. Reinoso*, 208 Cal. App.4th 181 (2012) ("The insurer seeking recovery against the insured for expenditures in settling a case when the claims were not covered should allocate those expenditures among the insureds. . . . The right to reimbursement may run against the person who benefits from 'unjust enrichment', but it should do so only to the extent the person actually benefits. That benefit, at least here, is the benefit of eliminating potential liability and not the time or costs expended on any particular person or entity being defended.") (citations and internal quotes omitted); *Hanes v. Armed Forces Insurance Exchange*, No. 12–05410, 2014 U.S. Dist. LEXIS 106036 (N.D. Cal. July 31, 2014) ("An insurer must carry the burden of proof for reimbursement by a preponderance of the evidence that the defense expenses are solely allocable to claims not potentially covered."); *Hanover Ins. Co. v. Poway Acad. of Hair Design, Inc.*, No. 15-536, 2016 U.S. Dist. LEXIS 158041 (S.D. Cal. Nov. 14, 2016) (insurer could not provide evidence that the defense costs for which it sought reimbursement were allocated solely to the claims that were not even potentially covered); *State Farm Fire & Cas. Co. v. Pyorre*, No. A147302, 2017 Cal. App. Unpub. LEXIS 212 (Cal. Ct. App. Jan. 10, 2017) (insurer entitled to reimbursement of defense costs, after issuing a supplemental recoupment reservation of rights, on account of a possible change in the law that could affect its duty to defend); *Phila. Indem. Ins. Co. v. Hollycal Prod.*, No. 18-768, 2018 U.S. Dist. LEXIS 211289 (C.D. Cal. Dec. 7, 2018) (reiterating *Buss* and permitting reimbursement); *Adir Int'l, LLC v. Starr Indem. & Liab. Co.*, No. 19-04352, 2019 U.S. Dist. LEXIS 155321 (C.D. Cal. Sep. 10, 2019) ("implied" right of reimbursement, under *Buss*, must be explicitly reserved, but, here, reservation of the right to reimbursement was not necessary as right was explicitly stated in policy); *Evanston Ins. Co. v. Winstar Props.*, No. 18-07740, 2019 U.S. Dist. LEXIS 189602 (C.D. Cal. Oct. 24, 2019) (right to reimbursement is the insurer's; deeming it irrelevant whether the insured knew of the insurer's reservation); *Atain Specialty Ins. Co. v. JKT Assocs.*, No. 19-07588, 2020 U.S. Dist. LEXIS 247934 (N.D. Cal. Aug. 3, 2020) (noting that it is unclear whether an insurer is "automatically entitled to recover all of its expenses or only those that were reasonable and necessary"); *Northfield Ins. Co. v. Sandy's Place, LLC*, No. 19-00897, 2021 U.S. Dist. LEXIS 64352 (E.D. Cal. Mar. 31, 2021) (finding that, where an insurer tenders a defense and timely and adequately reserves its rights, it may seek reimbursement of defense costs for any uncovered claims). In general, there is a substantial amount of California state and federal case law addressing a variety of reimbursement of defense costs scenarios.

Colorado: The Supreme Court of Colorado held that "[t]he appropriate course of action for an insurer who believes that it is under no obligation to defend, is to provide a defense to the insured under a reservation of its rights to seek reimbursement should the facts at trial prove that the incident resulting in liability was not covered by the policy, or to file a declaratory judgment action after the underlying case has been adjudicated." *Hecla Mining Co. v. N.H. Ins. Co.*, 811 P.2d 1083, 1089 (Colo. 1991); *see also Valley Forge Ins. Co. v. Health Care Mgmt. Partners*, 616 F.3d 1086 (10th Cir. 2010) (applying Colorado law) (predicting, based on *Hecla Mining* and *Cotter Corp. v. Am. Empire Surplus Lines Ins. Co.*, 90 P.3d 814 (Colo. 2004), that the Colorado Supreme Court would allow an insurer to recover defense costs from its insured, where it reserved the right to do so by letter, regardless whether the insurer also reserved that right in the underlying insurance policy); *Am. Family Mut. Ins. Co. v. St. Paul Fire & Marine Ins. Co.*, No. 13-1162, 2015 U.S. Dist. LEXIS 27708 (D. Colo. March 6, 2015) (interpreting *Cotter* to also include cases that do not go to trial) ("The reasoning turns on an insurer's response to its duty to defend, not on whether the underlying case goes to trial. Surely it makes no sense to tell an insurer who honors its duty to defend that it must force the case to trial (thereby increasing the defense costs and the risk to its insured) if it wishes fully to develop its reserved position that there was no coverage. Whether the insurer is entitled to reimbursement of defense costs paid turn on whether there was coverage under the policy, however that might be determined."); *Colony Ins. Co. v. Expert Group Int'l Inc.*, No. 15-02499, 2017 U.S. Dist. LEXIS 75073 (D. Colo. May 17, 2017) (reiterating *Hecla Mining*, *Valley Forge* and *Cotter*).

Connecticut: A Connecticut District Court described the Supreme Court of California's decision in *Buss* as "very logical and compelling" and predicted that, "given the right case and analogous set of facts," the Supreme Court of Connecticut would adopt a similar legal doctrine. *Ranger Ins. Co. v. Kovach*, No. 3:96CV02421, 1999 U.S. Dist. LEXIS 18937 (D. Conn. Dec. 3, 1999). Albeit in a different context, the Supreme Court of Connecticut also relied upon *Buss* in support of its conclusion that, for purposes of multiple-triggered policies, the appropriate method for allocation is pro rata and the insured must reimburse its insurer for defense costs attributed to periods of self-insurance. *Ins. Co. of Hartford v. Lumbermens Mut. Cas. Co.*, 826 A.2d 107, 125 (Conn. 2003). "A cause of action for reimbursement is cognizable to the extent required to ensure that the insured not reap a benefit for which it has not paid and thus be unjustly enriched. Where the insurer defends the insured against an action that includes claims not even potentially covered by the insurance policy, a court will order reimbursement for the cost of defending the uncovered claims in order to prevent the insured from receiving a windfall." *Id.; see also Nationwide Mut. Ins. Co. v. Mortensen*, No. 3:00-CV-1180, 2011 U.S. Dist. LEXIS 77356 (D. Conn. July 18, 2011) (holding that, although it was ultimately determined that insurer did not have a duty to defend, because there was at least the potential that the claims would be covered, insurer was not entitled to recoup its defense costs); *Scottsdale Ins. Co. v. R.I. Pools, Inc.*, 710 F.3d 488 (2nd Cir. 2013) (applying Connecticut law) ("Because this duty [to defend] exists up until the point at which it is legally determined that there is no possibility for coverage under the policies, Scottsdale has not shown entitlement to any reimbursement for defense costs it previously expended."); *New London Cty. Mut. Ins. Co. v. Cardillo*, No. CV-1760671125S, 2018 Conn. Super. LEXIS 6214 (Conn. Sup. Ct. Oct. 3, 2018) ("[E]ven though the plaintiff has at this stage of the proceedings established that it has no duty to defend the Cardillos pursuant to the first and second counts of its complaint, it has not met its burden of establishing that it is entitled to judgment as a matter of law on its claim for reimbursement in the third count of its complaint, as no binding authority in this jurisdiction has recognized such a claim in analogous circumstances.").

Delaware: The Superior Court of Delaware, without analysis, held that the insurer had a duty to defend on all claims, "but it may seek reimbursement from [insured] of those expenses, costs or fees incurred by providing his defense on those claims which may be proven later to fall outside the policy coverage." *Nationwide Mut. Ins. Co. v. Flagg*, 789 A.2d 586 (Del. Super. Ct. 2001).

District of Columbia: No instructive authority. *But see Armada de la Republica Argentina v. Yorkington Limited Partnership*, No. 92-0285, 1995 U.S. Dist. LEXIS 1317 (D.D.C. Jan. 27, 1995) ("[W]hen it is impossible or infeasible to allocate defense expenses between covered and noncovered claims, it is often reasonable to require the insurance company, which is obligated to defend some of the claims, to defend the entire lawsuit. However, there are some circumstances where this rationale does not apply. For example, when costs may practicably be apportioned between covered and noncovered claims, there is no compelling reason to require the insurance company to assume the costs of defending the noncovered claims.").

Florida: The Court of Appeal of Florida, relying on *Buss*, held that an insurer is entitled to reimbursement of the costs of defending "clearly uncovered claims." *Colony Ins. Co. v. G & E Tries & Serv., Inc.*, 777 So. 2d 1034, 1039 (Fla. Dist. Ct. App. 2000). "[The insurer] timely and expressly reserved the right to seek reimbursement of the costs of defending clearly uncovered claims, which it consistently identified as such. Having accepted Colony's offer of a defense with a reservation of the right to seek reimbursement, [the insured] ought in fairness make [the insurer] whole, now that it has been judicially determined that no duty to defend ever existed." *Id.*; *accord Black & Assocs. v. Transcon. Ins. Co.*, 932 So. 2d 516, 518 (Fla. Dist. Ct. App. 2006) (relying on *Colony*). *But see Nationwide Mut. Fire Ins. Co. v. Hardin J. Royall, Jr.*, 588 F. Supp. 2d 1306, 1318 (M.D. Fla. 2008) (discussing *Colony Insurance* and *Jim Black* and predicting that the Supreme Court of Florida would require that some reasonable time elapse before an insured's acquiescence of a defense constitutes acceptance) ("[T]he insurer should be required to give the insured a specific, reasonable time (*e.g.*, fifteen days) within which to accept or reject a written offer of a defense conditioned upon the reimbursement of fees and costs. Where this written offer clearly and expressly states that the failure to reject the offered defense within the stated period will constitute an acceptance, the insurer will be entitled to reimbursement in the event the insured fails to object and it is later determined that there is no coverage under the policy."); *James River Ins. Co v. Arlington Pebble Creek, LLC*, 188 F. Supp. 3d 1246, (N.D. Fla. 2016) (respectfully disagreeing with the court in *Royall* in predicting the Supreme Court of Florida's interpretation of *Colony Insurance* and *Jim Black*) ("Both *Colony* and *Jim Black* are directly on point and do not suggest that a reservation of rights is ineffective if it does not provide a date-certain by which the insured can reject the offer. There is no indication, other than the *Royall* court's speculation, that the Florida Supreme Court would disagree."); *Pennsylvania Lumbermens Mut. Ins. Co. v. Indiana Lumbermens Mut. Ins. Co.*, 43 So. 3d 182, 188 (Fla. Dist. Ct. App. 2010) (distinguishing present case from *Colony Insurance* and *Jim Black* by determining that those cases concerned insurers that did not possess a duty to defend whereas the present case involved an insurer that had a duty to defend which barred insurer from recouping defense costs) ("If *Colony Insurance* and *Jim Black* recognized that an insurer could seek reimbursement for defense costs, even when a duty to defend existed, as long as the insured signed a reservation of rights agreement, then insurance companies could avoid their contractual obligations to provide a defense by simply having the insured sign a reservation of rights. This is contrary to case law and public policy."); *Certain Interested Underwriters at Lloyd's, London v. Halikoytakis*, 556 Fed. Appx. 9530 (11th Cir. 2014) (citing *Colony Insurance* and *Jim Black* in support of insurer's entitlement to reimbursement) ("Underwriters defended Hali Plaza for over two years. When Hali Plaza accepted the defense, it necessarily agreed to the terms on which Underwriters extended the offer, including the reservation of rights."); *Covington Specialty*

Ins. Co. v. Hillsborough, LLC, No. 18-1299, 2019 U.S. Dist. LEXIS 26681 (M.D. Fla. Feb. 20, 2019) (denying reimbursement where insurer had duty to defend); *Travelers Indem. Co. v. Figg Bridge Eng'rs, Inc.*, 389 F. Supp. 3d 1060 (S.D. Fla. 2019) (permitting reimbursement and joining *James River* in respectfully disagreeing with *Royall* that a reservation of rights is ineffective if it does not provide a date-certain by which the insured can reject the offer); *Alt. Cas. Ins. Co. v. Legacy Roofing of Fl/Ahead Gen. Contrs. & Restoration*, No. 19-22043, 2020 U.S. Dist. LEXIS 215906 (S.D. Fla. Nov. 16, 2020) (citing *James River* and *Colony* for the proposition that where "an insurer reserves its right to seek reimbursement and the insured accepts the defense — an insurer 'is entitled to reimbursement'" once it has been determined that there was never a duty to defend).

Georgia: A Georgia District Court held that, in the absence of a provision in the reservation of rights letter requiring reimbursement of defense costs for uncovered claims, or case law instructing the court otherwise, the court was unwilling to allow reimbursement. *Transp. Ins. Co. v. Freedom Elecs., Inc.*, 264 F. Supp. 2d 1214, 1221 (N.D. Ga. 2003). The court reasoned that, since the bilateral reservation of rights and defense agreement did not specifically permit reimbursement, it would not recognize such right. *Id.* Moreover, the court concluded that, by its express terms, the reservation of rights precluded reimbursement. The agreement stated in pertinent part, "Carrier hereby agrees to assume defense of the claims presented by the underlying litigation from the date such claims were originally tendered … *unless and until such time* as it is established in a court of law that no duty to defend exists under the subject policy." *Id.* (emphasis added). However, more recently, in *Illinois Union Ins. Co. v. NRI Const. Inc.*, 846 F. Supp. 2d 1366 (N.D. Ga. 2012), a Georgia District Court, calling it a case of first impression in Georgia, reviewed the issue nationally, noted the two schools of thought and held that an insurer was entitled to reimbursement of defense costs: "NRI of Georgia accepted its insurer's defense without objection and enjoyed free legal defense of claims Illinois Union had no duty to defend. The court finds the majority view more persuasive and supported by Georgia case law. A right of reimbursement is justified under either an unjust enrichment or implied in fact contract theory. Therefore, the court concludes that under the circumstances as presented here, the Supreme Court of Georgia would adopt the majority approach, and that Illinois Union is entitled to recoupment of its legal costs expended defending NRI of Georgia in the Underlying Action." *See also Ga. Interlocal Risk Mgmt. Agency v. City of Sandy Springs*, 788 S.E.2d 74 (Ga. Ct. App. 2016) ("In *Illinois Union*, the Northern District found the majority view among the nation's courts to be the most persuasive based on theories of implied-in-fact contract and unjust enrichment. That view holds that where no contractual provision exists, a right to recoup defense costs still exists where the insurer timely and explicitly reserved that right.") (court does not adopt a rule because insurer did not timely reserve its rights.); *Evanston Ins. Co. v. Sandersville R.R. Co.*, No. 15-247, 2017 U.S. Dist. LEXIS 115686 (M.D. Ga. July 25, 2017) (discussing *Illinois Union* and *Ga. Interlocal* (which it characterized as stating that this question remains unresolved in Georgia) and concluding that "[t]he Court need not predict whether Georgia will follow the majority rule or the minority rule because Evanston has not demonstrated that it has properly reserved its rights as required by the majority rule."); *Fairbanks Co. v. Nat'l Union Fire Ins. Co. (In re Fairbanks Co.)*, No. 18-41768, 2020 Bankr. LEXIS 2385 (Bankr. N.D. Ga. Sep. 9, 2020) (finding that an insurer, that failed to explicitly reserve its right to seek reimbursement for defense costs until 10 years after the insurer began its defense under a reservation of rights, was not entitled to reimbursement) (noting that the insurer was also not entitled to defense costs incurred after it reserved its right to seek reimbursement, as it was not timely). In *Am. Family Ins. Co. v. Almassud*, No. 16-4023, 2021 U.S. Dist. LEXIS 58620 (Feb. 17, 2021), the court noted that the reimbursement question is an open one in Georgia. The court acknowledged that the "'majority' approach allows for recoupment under a reservation of rights, applying either an implied contract or unjust enrichment theory." *Id.* at *10. However, the court adopted the minority approach: "[A]bsent a provision in the insurance policy—or some other express agreement—an insurer who issued an otherwise valid, unilateral reservation of rights cannot recoup its costs of defense." *Id.* at *12. *See also Cont'l Cas. Co. v. Winder Labs.*, No. 19-00016, 2021 U.S. Dist. LEXIS 103013 (N.D. Ga. April 20, 2021) (*Almassud* applies with "equal force") ("This Court adopts the 'minority' approach. Along with the court in [*Ill. Union Ins. Co. v. William C. Meredith Co.*, No. 07-1840, 2009 U.S. Dist. LEXIS 140145 (N.D. Ga. June 5, 2009)], and the Restatement of the Law of Liability Insurance § 21 (2019), the Court finds that the rationale underlying a no-recoupment default rule makes more sense and believes that a Georgia court deciding the issue would agree. Simply put, the insurer should not be able to unilaterally alter the terms of an insurance policy.") ("Of course, there is nothing wrong with the concept of recoupment. But if a right to recoupment is a benefit that the insurer deems sufficiently important, it can easily secure that right by including it in the policy agreement.").

Hawaii: A Hawaii District Court, relying on the Supreme Court of California's decisions in *Buss* and *MV Transportation*, and other decisions nationally, held that an insurer that expressly reserved the right to seek reimbursement of defense costs was entitled to such recovery if the insured accepted the defense and it was determined that the insurer did not have a duty to defend. *Scottsdale Ins. Co. v. Sullivan Props., Inc.*, No. 04–00550, 2007 U.S. Dist. LEXIS 57021 (D. Hawaii Feb. 27, 2006). *But see Executive Risk Indem. Inc. v. Pac. Educ. Servs., Inc.*, 451 F. Supp. 2d 1147, 1163–64 (D. Hawaii 2006) (expressing no opinion on whether Hawaii law recognizes a right to reimbursement of defense costs, the court was unwilling to decide the issue—which could "overhaul insurance litigation in Hawaii"—because it had not been the subject of adversarial briefing and the insurer provided no description of the costs and expenses it sought to recover); *GGA, Inc. v. Kiewit Infrastructure West Co.*, No. 18-00110, 2020 U.S. Dist. LEXIS 10151 (D. Hawaii Jan. 22, 2020) (declining to answer whether Hawaii law permits an insurer, defending under a reservation of rights, to seek reimbursement of defense costs, as the action's complex procedural history provided a poor vehicle to do so).

Idaho: An Idaho District Court held that an insurer was not entitled to reimbursement of defense costs, despite the fact that it asserted such right in its reservation of rights letter. *St. Paul Fire & Marine Ins. Co. v. Holland Realty, Inc.*, No. CV07–390, 2008 U.S. Dist. LEXIS 59431 (D. Idaho Aug. 6, 2008). Relying on the Supreme Court of Illinois's decision in *General Agents Ins. Co. of Am., Inc. v. Midwest Sporting Goods Co.*, 828 N.E.2d 1092 (Ill. 2005), the court concluded that a reservation of rights letter can preserve only those rights that are listed in the policy. Since the policy did not include a provision for reimbursement of defense costs, the insurer had no such right. *Id.*; *see also Blue Cross of Idaho v. Atlantic Mut. Ins. Co.*, 734 F. Supp. 2d 1107 (D. Idaho 2010) (addressing the reimbursement issue at length and following the "well reasoned" opinion in *Holland*); *Huntsman Advanced Materials LLC v. OneBeacon America Ins. Co.*, No. 08–00229, 2012 U.S. Dist. LEXIS 19053 (D. Idaho Feb. 13, 2012) ("Consistent with the views expressed by Judge Lodge in [*Holland*], the Court finds that the Idaho appellate courts would conclude that where the terms of an insurance contract dictate the obligations of the parties, reimbursement is not allowed unless it is spelled out in the contract. The Court has already explained that Idaho draws a distinction between a duty to defend and a duty to indemnify. A natural extension of this distinction is that an insurer may only recoup its defense costs, if it has included an express provision for reimbursement in the terms of the policy. Moreover, as pointed out in [*Holland*], a reservation of rights letter can only preserve rights already agreed to by the parties.") (citations and internal quotes omitted); *Evanston Ins. Co v. Bosski, Inc.*, No. 14-00227, 2017 U.S. Dist. LEXIS 48177 (D. Idaho March 28, 2017) (reiterating holdings from *Holland*, *Atlantic Mutual* and *Huntsman* that "an insurer cannot seek reimbursement for the defense costs provided under a reservation of rights unless the insurance policy at issue provides for insurer reimbursement.").

Illinois: The Supreme Court of Illinois held that an insurer was not entitled to reimbursement of defense costs, despite the fact that it asserted such right in its reservation of rights letter. *General Agents Ins. Co. of Am., Inc. v. Midwest Sporting Goods Co.*, 828 N.E.2d 1092, 1104 (Ill. 2005). While the court acknowledged that other jurisdictions allow an insurer to recover defense costs from its insured, where the insurer provides a defense subject to this condition, the court declined to adopt such rule. *Id.* The court reasoned that the insured is not unjustly enriched when its insurer tenders a defense, even if it is later determined that the insurer did not owe such defense, because the insurer is protecting itself at least as much as it is protecting the insured. *Id.* at 1103. However, the court also stated that an insurer is free to include a provision in its policy that entitles it to seek reimbursement of defense costs if it were later determined that the underlying claim was not covered. *Id.* at 1104; *see also Zurich Specialties London Ltd. v. Village of Bellwood, Ill.*, No. 07 CV 2171, 2011 U.S. Dist. LEXIS 7271 (N.D. Ill. Jan 26, 2011) (determining that insurer would not be entitled to recover costs it had already incurred in defending insured under a reservation of rights even if the court determined that insurer had no duty to defend) (following *General Agents*); *Scottsdale Ins. Co. v. Walsh Const. Co.*, No. 10 C 1565, 2011 U.S. Dist. LEXIS 111413 (N.D. Ill. Sept. 29, 2011) (following *General Agents* and holding that, because policy did not contain an express provision, granting insurer the right to reimbursement of defense costs, no such right existed, despite insurer reserving the right when accepting defense); *Liberty Mut. Fire Ins. Co. v. Ferrara Candy Co.*, No. 1-18-1385, 2019 IL App (1st) 181385-U (Ill. App. Ct. Dec. 11, 2019) (following *General Agents* and holding that, because the policy contained a defense cost endorsement, the insurer was permitted to recoup defense costs for uncovered claims); *State Auto Prop. & Cas. Ins. Co. v. Bell & Arthur Condo. Ass'n*, No. 18-5927, 2020 U.S. Dist. LEXIS 190922 (N.D. Ill. Oct. 15, 2020) (allowing an insurer to recover defense costs expended on uncovered claims where the policy included a clear and unambiguous defense cost reimbursement endorsement).

Indiana: An Indiana District Court was skeptical about permitting reimbursement of defense costs to insurers, stating "while there do not appear to be any reported cases applying Indiana law to this issue, other courts have found that an insurer does not have a right to recoup fees it pays under a duty to defend after resolution of the underlying litigation absent a policy provision allowing it to do so." *Selective Ins. Co. of Am. v. Smiley Body Shop, Inc.*, No.16-00062, 2017 U.S. Dist. LEXIS 81007 (S.D. Ind. May 26, 2017).

Iowa: An Iowa District Court, following a comprehensive study of the issue, acknowledged that the majority of courts nationally permit an insurer to recover defense costs, based on an implied contract or unjust enrichment, but predicted that the Supreme Court of Iowa would not adopt such rule. *Pekin Ins. Co. v. TYSA, Inc.*, No. 3:05-cv-00030-JEG, 2006 U.S. Dist. LEXIS 93525 (S.D. Iowa Dec. 27, 2006). The court was persuaded to follow those courts nationally that have found "that using a reservation of rights to permit recovery of defense costs amounts to a unilateral modification of the policy terms and that, because the duty to defend is broader than the duty to indemnify, the insured is not unjustly enriched when the insurer provides a defense for claims that are at least possibly within the coverage terms, although such claims may later be found to be outside the policy."

Kansas: No instructive authority. *But see AKH Co., Inc. v. Universal Underwriters Ins. Co.*, No. 13–2003, 2013 U.S. Dist. LEXIS 95281 (D. Kan. July 9, 2013) ("The conflict of law with respect to an insurer's reimbursement right is that California recognizes the right, and to date Kansas does not.") (without citation to asserted Kansas rule) (court unable to determine whether the insurer was entitled to pursue a right of reimbursement because it was not yet able to determine which state's law applied).

Kentucky: The Sixth Circuit Court of Appeals, applying Kentucky law, held that, where the insurer asserted a timely reservation of rights, notified the insured of its intent to seek reimbursement and where the insured had meaningful control of the defense and settlement negotiations, Kentucky courts would permit an insurer to seek reimbursement of an amount paid in settlement. *Travelers Property Casualty Co. of America v. Hillerich & Bradsby Co.*, 598 F.3d 257, 268 (6th Cir. 2010). The court based its decision on an implied-in-law contract theory. *Id.* The court also relied on a fairness rationale in reaching its decision: "Here the insured was arguing that coverage was afforded for both defense and settlement costs, but refused to allow the insurer to seek reimbursement if a court later determined that the insured's position was incorrect. It would seem to be an unjust outcome for the insurer if this Court were to sanction that position." *Id.* at 269; *see also Employers Reinsurance Corp. v. Mut. Ins. Co.*, No. 05-556-S, 2007 U.S. Dist. LEXIS 10399 (W.D. Ky. Feb. 9, 2007) (holding that an insurer was entitled to reimbursement of defense costs, if it were later determined that no coverage existed under the policy, as the insurer asserted such right in its reservation of rights letter) (insured could have declined to agree to the reservation of rights but it did not do so); *Nat'l Trust Ins. Co. v. Heaven Hill Distilleries, Inc.*, No. 14-394, 2018 U.S. Dist. LEXIS 52569 (W.D. Ky. Mar. 29, 2018) ("The Court concludes pursuant to *Employers Reinsurance* and *SST Fitness*, and in light of applicable Kentucky contract law as applied in *Travelers*, that Kentucky would allow an insurer to seek reimbursement of defense costs pursuant to an explicit, timely reservation of its right to do so.") (holding that insurer could not establish that it provided an explicit reservation of its right to seek reimbursement); *Appalachian Reg'l Healthcare, Inc. v. U.S. Nursing Corp.*, No. 14-122, 2018 U.S. Dist. LEXIS 86548 (E.D. Ky. May 23, 2018) (permitting reimbursement and citing *Travelers, SST* and just-decided *Heaven Hill Distilleries*); *Darwin Select Ins. Co v. Ashland Hosp. Corp.*, No. 2016-000372, 2020 Ky. App. Unpub. LEXIS 104 (Ky. Ct. App. Feb. 14, 2020) (stating that "when there is a clear statement from an insurer -- and there is in these cases -- to the effect that it is reserving its right to seek recoupment of any defense expenses advanced under a reservation of rights -- as there was below from Darwin and Homeland -- Kentucky law permits an insurer the right to recoup those defense expenses if it is later judicially determined that the terms of the insurance policy never required the insurer to provide a defense").

Louisiana: No instructive authority. In *Bridger Lake, LLC v. Seneca Ins. Co., Inc.*, No. 11–0342, 2014 U.S. Dist. LEXIS 27703 (W.D. La. Mar. 4, 2014) the court held that an insurer who advanced funds to its insured, following an event appearing to be covered under the policy, should be allowed to seek reimbursement of those funds if it is subsequently determined the event is not covered. In reaching this decision the court stated that case law denying an insurer the right of reimbursement of defense costs was "easily distinguishable."

Maine: No instructive authority. In *Marcus v. Allied World Ins. Co.*, 384 F. Supp. 3d 115 (D. Maine 2019), the court did not rule whether an insurer's right to reimbursement of defense costs exists, but concluded that the insurer did not act in bad faith by sending a reservation of rights letter, that included a recoupment provision that the insured did not reject, and then attempting to enforce it. The court cited with approval the Restatement of the Law, Liability Insurance § 21, cmt. a, which states: "When an insurer's claim to recoupment is based on a contractual right to reimbursement—whether because of a provision of the insurance policy or a subsequent agreement with the insured—it presents no legal difficulty." The court then noted: "Here, Allied World's reservation-of-rights letter had a recoupment provision and the plaintiffs did not reject it."

Maryland: The Court of Appeals for the Fourth Circuit, applying Maryland law, held that an insurer did not have a right to partial reimbursement of defense costs if it were later determined that there was no duty to defend certain claims. *Perdue Farms Inc. v. Travelers Cas. & Sur. Co.*, 448 F.3d 252, 254 (4th Cir. 2006). The court concluded that a partial right to reimbursement would be tantamount to a "backdoor narrowing" of the duty to defend and appreciably erode Maryland's long-held view that the duty to defend is broader than the duty to indemnify. *Id.* at 258. "In the absence of any contrary indication from the Maryland courts, we are unwilling to grant insurers a substantial rebate on their duty to defend." *Id.* at 259. The court also recognized that, even if Maryland looked favorably on a right of partial reimbursement, in this case the defense costs for covered and noncovered claims may have significantly overlapped. *Id. See also Selective Way Ins. Co. v. Nationwide Prop. & Cas. Ins. Co.*, 219 A.3d 20 (Md. App. Ct. 2019) ("[A] rule limiting the insured to a 'partial right of reimbursement' for defense costs would 'serve only as a backdoor narrowing of the duty to defend,' which would 'erode Maryland's long-held view that the duty to defend is broader than the duty to indemnify' and 'undermine the bargain that Maryland courts describe insurers reaching with their insureds.'") (quoting from *Perdue Farms*).

Massachusetts: The Supreme Judicial Court of Massachusetts held that "[w]here an insurer defends under a reservation of rights to later disclaim coverage ... it may later seek reimbursement for an amount paid to settle the underlying tort action only if the insured has agreed that the insurer may commit the insured's own funds to a reasonable settlement with the right later to seek reimbursement from the insured, or if the insurer secures specific authority to reach a particular settlement which the insured agrees to pay. The insurer may also notify the insured of a reasonable settlement offer and give the insured an opportunity to accept the offer or assume its own defense." *Med. Malpractice Joint Underwriting Ass'n of Mass. v. Goldberg*, 680 N.E.2d 1121, 1129 (Mass. 1997); *see also Dash v. Chi. Ins. Co.*, No. 00–11911, 2004 U.S. Dist. LEXIS 17309 (D. Mass. Aug. 23, 2004) (discussing *Buss* but declining to reach the issue because the insurer had breached its duty to defend); *Welch Foods Inc. v. Nat. Union Fire Ins. Co.*, No. 09-12087, 2011 U.S. Dist. LEXIS 17134 (D. Mass. Feb. 9, 2011) (noting that Massachusetts has not decided "whether an insurer is entitled to reimbursement of defense costs paid prior to a court's determination that the insurer had no duty to defend the insured," but ultimately declaring that the Supreme Court of Pennsylvania's decision in "*Jerry's Sport* achieves an appropriate allocation of responsibilities and, therefore, that the insurer bears the responsibility for making this determination, and the concomitant risk if its decision to advance fees is wrong") (affirmed without discussion of reimbursement of defense costs, 659 F.3d 191 (1st Cir. 2011)); *Lexington Ins. Co. v. CareCore Nat'l, LLC*, No. 2012-01782, 2014 Mass. Super. LEXIS 200 (Mass. Super. Ct. July 17, 2014) ("Although some jurisdictions outside of Massachusetts have concluded that an insurer may recoup those costs, they have so held only where the insurer in (sic) made it clear to the insured, either in the policy itself or in its reservation of rights, that it retains the right to seek reimbursement of those costs if a court later determines there was no duty to defend.") ("Moreover, this Court has considerable doubt that the SJC would recognize as enforceable even an express reservation of rights regarding defense costs, given its holding in *Cotter* [*Metro. Life Ins. Co. v. Cotter*, 984 N.E.2d 835 (Mass. 2013)] with respect to indemnification."); *Holyoke Mut. Ins. Co. v. Vibram USA, Inc.*, No. 2015-2321, 2017 Mass. Super. LEXIS 12 (Mass. Super. Ct. Mar. 20, 2017) (applying the Supreme Court of Pennsylvania's decision in *Jerry's Sport* and holding that an insurer was not entitled to recoupment of defense costs incurred prior to a declaratory judgment that a lawsuit was not covered under the policy, because the right to recoupment was not included in the insurer's policies).

Michigan: A Michigan District Court, looking to *Buss* for guidance, held that an insurer may recoup defense costs incurred for those claims which "clearly and unequivocally do not give rise to a duty to defend." *Travelers Prop. Cas. Co. v. R.L. Polk & Co.*, No. 06–12895, 2008 U.S. Dist. LEXIS 22676 (E.D. Mich. Mar. 24, 2008). "Under the policy, the insurer does not have a duty to defend the insured as to the claims that are not even potentially covered. With regard to defense costs for these claims, the insurer has not been paid premiums by the insured. It did not bargain to bear these costs. To attempt to shift them would not upset the arrangement." (quoting *Buss*, 939 P.2d at 776) (internal quotations omitted); *see also Lumbermens Mut. Cas. Co. v. RGIS Inventory Specialists, LLC*, No. 08 Civ. 1316, 2010 U.S. Dist. LEXIS 50022 (S.D.N.Y. May 20, 2010) (applying Michigan law) ("Although the Michigan Supreme Court has not addressed this question, decisions of other courts in Michigan support a prediction that Michigan would allow an insurer to recoup a contribution to a settlement, where it is ultimately determined that the insured was not entitled to coverage under the insurance policy.") (finding instructive *Travelers Property Casualty Co. of America v. Hillerich & Bradsby Co.*, 598 F.3d 257 (6th Cir.

2010) (applying Ky. law)); *Cont'l Cas. Co. v. Indian Head Indus.*, 666 Fed. Appx. 456 (6th Cir. 2016) (holding that insurer was entitled to reimbursement because insurer's sending of a reservation of rights letter met the standard of implied contract) ("In order to have the right under an implied-in-law contract, the insurer must: 1) timely assert its rights to reimbursement; 2) provide notice of the intent to seek reimburseent; and 3) allow the insured to have meaningful control of the defense and negotiation process."); *Peerless Ins. Co. v. Conifer Holdings, Inc.*, No. 17-10223, 2018 U.S. Dist. LEXIS 11261 (E.D. Mich. Jan. 24, 2018) (declining to rule on reimbursement as premature) (insurer cited *R.L. Polk & Co.* to support reimbursement and insured cited *Hastings Mut. Ins. Co. v. Mosher Dolan Cataldo & Kelly, Inc.*, 856 N.W.2d 550 (Mich. 2014) in support of its argument that where a duty to defend exists as to any claim, the insurer is not entitled to any reimbursement).

Minnesota: The Eighth Circuit Court of Appeals, applying Minnesota law, held that an insurer was not entitled to reimbursement of defense costs, despite asserting such right in its reservation of rights letter. *Westchester Fire Ins. Co. v. Wallerich*, 563 F.3d 707, 719 (8th Cir. 2009). Following an extensive survey of the law nationally on the issue, the court concluded that the insurer could have included a right to reimbursement in its policy. *Id.* As it did not, the insurer could not now unilaterally amend the policy through a reservation of rights letter. *Id.* Further, the court observed that the insureds explicitly rejected the terms of the reservation of rights, but accepted the defense nonetheless. In this situation, because the insurer still tendered a defense, despite the insureds' rejection of the terms of the reservation of rights, the court concluded that the insurer was impliedly agreeing to proceed on the insureds' terms. *Id. See also Northstar Educ. Finance, Inc. v. St. Paul Mercury Ins. Co.*, No. A12-0959, 2013 Minn. App. Unpub. LEXIS 32 (Minn. Ct. App. Jan 14, 2013) (discussing *Wallerich* and concluding that the policy language "to the extent that it is finally established that any such Defense Costs are not covered under this Policy, the Insureds ... agree to repay the Insurer such Defense Costs" "unambiguously provides that the defense costs are subject to recovery by [the insurer]."); *Select Comfort Corp. v. Arrowood Indem. Co.*, No. 13-2975, 2014 U.S. Dist. LEXIS 173551 (D. Minn. Dec. 12, 2014) (analyzing *Wallerich* and stating that "the Eighth Circuit has determined that an insured may not be made to reimburse the insurer for defense costs where the insured did not agree to such a condition on the insurer's contractual duty to defend"); *Continental Ins. Co. v. Daikin Applied Americas, Inc.*, No. 17-552, 2019 U.S. Dist. LEXIS 216639 (D. Minn. Dec. 17, 2019) (addressing reimbursement in the context of pleading the claim).

Mississippi: A Mississippi District Court held that the insurer was not entitled to reimbursement of defense costs incurred prior to the court's determination that the insurer had no duty to defend. *Certain Underwriters at Lloyd's London v. Magnolia Mgmt. Corp.*, No. 04CV540TSL, 2009 U.S. Dist. LEXIS 60083 (S.D. Miss. June 26, 2009). The court's reasoning was minimal and related to the specifics of the case. However, addressing the right to reimbursement in general, the court set forth the test from *United Nat'l. Ins. Co. v. SST Fitness Corp.*, 309 F.3d 914, 921 (6th Cir. 2002) (applying Ohio law), and concluded that no right to reimbursement existed because the policy did not provide such a right and the reservation of rights letter was not specific or clear enough to have afforded notice of such right.; *see also Liberty Mut. Ins. Co. v. Tedford*, 658 F. Supp. 2d 786, 801 (N.D. Miss. 2009) ("Without holding that Mississippi recognizes or should recognize a right of reimbursement, under the facts of this case, namely Liberty Mutual's duty to defend the underlying complaint, even jurisdictions that authorize a right of reimbursement would not find reimbursement proper here."); *Mississippi Farm Bureau Cas. Ins. Co. v. Amerisure Ins. Co.*, No. 11–706, 2013 U.S. Dist. LEXIS 9592 (S.D. Miss. Jan. 24, 2013) (addressing issue in the context of insurer vs. insurer) ("Because Farm Bureau had no contractual obligation to defend Conlan against counts two and four, but chose to do so without exercising the legal remedies available to it to resist Conlan's and Amerisure's demands for Conlan's full defense, Mississippi's volunteer payment doctrine bars Farm Bureau from recovering costs from Amerisure in this action.").

Missouri: The Eighth Circuit Court of Appeals, applying Missouri law, held that the insurer was not entitled to reimbursement of defense costs following a determination that it had no duty to defend. *Liberty Mut. Ins. Co. v. FAG Bearings Corp.*, 153 F.3d 919, 924 (8th Cir. 1998). The court did not address the various arguments often raised for and against the right to reimbursement. Instead, the court rested its decision on the insurer's obligation to defend its insured so long as there remained any question whether the underlying claims were covered by the policy. *Id*

Montana: The Supreme Court of Montana held that an insurer was entitled to reimbursement of defense costs when it was determined that the insurer had no duty to defend. *Travelers Cas. and Sur. Co. v. Ribi Immunochem Research, Inc.*, 108 P.3d 469, 480 (Mont. 2005). The court concluded that reimbursement was permissible because the insurer had timely and explicitly reserved such right and the insured implicitly accepted the defense under the reservation of rights when it posed no objections. *Id.* at 479–80 (citing, among other authorities, *Grinnell Mut. Reinsurance Co. v. Shierk*, 996 F. Supp. 836 (S.D. Ill. 1998) in support of its decision).

But see Gen. Agents Ins. Co. of Am. v. Midwest Sporting Goods Co., 828 N.E.2d 1092, 1104 (Ill. 2005) (repudiating *Shierk*). In *Horace Mann Ins. Co. v. Hanke*, 312 P.3d 429 (Mont. 2013), the Montana Supreme Court applied *Ribi* to reimbursement of an insurer's settlement payment: "The correspondence between Horace Mann and the Hankes and their counsel establishes that Horace Mann reserved its right to recover the additional $34,000.00 that it paid to the settlement with Warner. Horace Mann protected the Hankes' $54,000.00 settlement in furtherance of Horace Mann's agreement with the Hankes. Horace Mann adhered to the procedure that this Court has established to contest the boundaries of coverage and to recoup expenses. *Ribi Immunochem.* We affirm the District Court's award of $34,000.00 to reimburse Horace Mann for its advancement of the Hankes' share of the settlement." *See also Johnson v. Federated Rural Elec. Ins. Exch.*, No. 13-18, 2016 U.S. Dist. LEXIS 173037 (D. Mont. Dec. 14, 2016) ("Federated's first reservation of rights letter, dated May 4, 2012, does not explicitly state that it reserved its right to recoup defense costs. Therefore, the Court concludes that Federated is not entitled to seek reimbursement of defense costs related to Johnson's conversion of $14,264.17. Even if the Court was to allow reimbursement, it would be impossible to distinguish between defense costs advanced to defend that claim as opposed to the other claims."); *Am. Econ. Ins. Co. v. Hartford Fire Ins. Co.*, 695 Fed. Appx. 194 (9th Cir. 2017) ("Under Montana law, Liberty Mutual and Hartford were entitled to recoup defense costs because Aspen Way 'implicitly accepted' their defenses under a reservation of rights. [citing *Ribi* and *Horace Mann*] Aspen Way's untimely objection to Liberty Mutual's reservation of rights three years after the defense commenced does not sufficiently distinguish this case from *Ribi* and *Horace Mann*."); *Capitol Specialty Ins. Corp. v. Big Sky Diagnostic Imaging, LLC*, No. 17-54, 2019 U.S. Dist. LEXIS 45234 (D. Mont. Jan. 30, 2019) (reiterating *Ribi* and *Horace Mann*); *West Am. Ins. Co. v. MVP Holdings, LLC*, No. 20-59, 2020 U.S. Dist. LEXIS 217037 (D. Mont. Nov. 19, 2020) (finding that an insurer that issued a timely letter, explicitly reserving the right to seek reimbursement, and who provided the insured with notice of the potential for reimbursement, met the requirements of *Ribi*); *Safeco Ins. Co. v. Grieshop*, No. 20-24, 2021 U.S. Dist. LEXIS 62084 (D. Mont. Mar. 31, 2021) (allowing for reimbursement when, "within approximately 6 weeks of tendering the claim to Safeco, Grieshop was given explicit notice of Safeco's reservation of rights, which included notice of the right to seek reimbursement").

Nebraska: No instructive authority.

Nevada: In *Nautilus Ins. Co. v. Access Med. LLC*, 482 P.3d 683, 2021 Nev. LEXIS 11 (Nev. 2021), the Nevada Supreme Court addressed the following question certified from the Ninth Circuit Court of Appeals: "Is an insurer entitled to reimbursement of costs already expended in defense of its insureds where a determination has been made that the insurer owed no duty to defend and the insurer expressly reserved its right to seek reimbursement in writing after defense has been tendered but where the insurance policy contains no reservation of rights?" *Id.* at *2. The Nevada high court answered yes: "When a court determines that an insurer never owed a duty to defend, the insurer expressly reserved its right to seek reimbursement in writing after defense was tendered, and the policyholder accepted the defense from the insurer, then the insurer is entitled to that reimbursement. Under generally applicable principles of unjust enrichment and restitution, the insurer has conferred a benefit on the policyholder; the policyholder appreciated the benefit; and, because it is reasonable for the insurer to accede to the policyholder's demand, it is equitable to require the policyholder to pay. This result gives effect to the parties' agreement, as well as the court's judgment, by recognizing that the insurer was never contractually obligated to furnish a defense." *Id.* at *18-19.

New Hampshire: No instructive authority.

New Jersey: A New Jersey District Court, in granting a motion to stay a declaratory judgment action, held that, upon completion of the underlying litigation, the insurer may recommence the coverage action to recoup defense expenses. *Transcon. Ins. Co. v. Jocama Constr. Corp.*, No. 06-cv-03358, 2007 U.S. Dist. LEXIS 54901 (D.N.J. July 27, 2007). The court did not provide any analysis of the right of reimbursement of defense costs. However, the court reasoned that the insurer was not unduly prejudiced by defending its insured under a reservation of rights because the insurer could subsequently seek reimbursement for defense costs incurred. *See also Electric Ins. Co. v. Marcantonis ex rel. Marcantonis*, No. 09–5076, 2011 U.S. Dist. LEXIS 24817 (D.N.J. Mar. 11, 2011) ("EIC is entitled to reimbursement for the money it paid for the defense of the Martorana Litigation. EIC expressed the view that its position on coverage would prevent it from assuming defense of the matter. However, subject to certain limitations, it agreed to fund the costs of defense. Counsel was selected by Defendant, and it does not appear that EIC sought to be informed about the progress of the case or otherwise exert control over the defense. As a disclaiming carrier, EIC declined to exercise the 'contractual right of control' it would have had if it had conceded coverage. Although EIC paid legal fees and costs, it did not get any benefit from doing so. Since Defendant benefitted by selecting the attorney and controlling the defense, it should bear the corresponding burden of assuming the costs for what this Court has determined are claims not covered by the Policy."); *United Specialty Ins. Co. v. Sussex Airport, Inc.*, No. 14-5494, 2016 U.S. Dist. LEXIS 60770 (D.N.J. May 9, 2016) ("The right of reimbursement exists in cases where an insurer honored its duty to defend but sought reimbursement from an insured for fees incurred in defending a non-covered claim 'because the insured would be unjustly enriched in benefitting by, without paying for, the defense of a non-covered claim.'") (quoting *Hebela v. Healthcare Ins. Co.*, 851 A.2d 75 (N.J. Super. Ct. App. Div. 2004)); *Canopius U.S. Ins., Inc. v. Graham Trucking, LLC*, No. 17-4616, 2018 U.S. Dist. LEXIS 61855 (D.N.J. Apr. 12, 2018) ("Having found that Plaintiff has no duty to defend the Graham Defendants in the Montero Action, the Court also finds that Plaintiff is entitled to reimbursement for the fees and costs incurred in defending the Graham Defendants in that case.") (*citing U.S. Specialty Ins. Co. v. Sussex Airport, Inc.*, No. 14-5494, 2016 U.S. Dist. LEXIS 60770 (D.N.J. May 9, 2016)). Any consideration of an insurer's right to reimbursement of defense costs under New Jersey law would also likely be affected by the manner in which the defense is being handled vis-à-vis *Burd v. Sussex Mutual Insurance Co.*, 267 A.2d 7 (N.J. 1970). *See* Chapter 5.

New Mexico: A Louisiana District Court, applying New Mexico law, held that an insurer was entitled to reimbursement of defense costs for uncovered claims. *Resure, Inc. v. Chemical Distribs., Inc.*, 927 F. Supp. 190, 194 (M.D. La. 1996). Without citing another case, the court concluded that such right existed because the insurer issued a timely reservation of rights that specifically referred to the possibility that it might seek reimbursement for any and all costs of defense. *Id.* Further, there was nothing in the record to suggest that the insured objected to such reservation. *Id.*

New York: Historically, numerous New York federal courts have addressed the reimbursement question, with the great majority concluding that insurers had such right. However, in *Am. W. Home Ins. Co. v. Gjonaj Realty & Mgt.*, 138 N.Y.S.3d 626 (N.Y. App. Div. 2020), the Appellate Division, following a lengthy discussion of the issue, including some of the federal decisions, concluded that the insurer was not entitled to reimbursement: "[E]ven if an unjust enrichment claim were available, there is no unjust enrichment here. Given New York's policy imposing upon insurers a broad duty to defend, there could be no finding that the insureds were unjustly enriched as a result of the defense provided by the insurance company for claims that were later found to be outside of the policy. Indeed, the policies of equity and fairness weigh against allowing the insurance company to obtain reimbursement of its defense costs because an insurer benefits unfairly if it can hedge on its defense obligations by reserving its right to reimbursement while potentially controlling the defense and avoiding a bad faith claim from its insured." *Id.* at 636. For pre-*Gjonaj* decisions, see the following: A New York District Court held that an insurer was entitled to reimbursement of defense costs. *Gotham Ins. Co. v. GLNX, Inc.,* No. 92 Civ. 6415, 1993 U.S. Dist. LEXIS 10891 (S.D.N.Y. Aug. 6, 1993). The court reasoned that the insurer was so entitled because it explicitly reserved its right to seek reimbursement if it were determined that no duty to defend existed. Further, the insured offered no evidence that it expressly refused to consent to the insurer's reservation of rights as to reimbursement or that the defense costs related to a certain claim that was in fact covered. *See also Max Specialty Ins. Co. v. WSG Investors, LLC,* No. 09–5237, 2012 U.S. Dist. LEXIS 108601 (E.D.N.Y. Apr. 20, 2012) ("Here, as in *Gotham,* Max Specialty made an explicit reservation of the right to pursue recoupment in its letter to WSG disclaiming coverage. Suben Decl., Ex. 8 at 8 ('Max reserves the right to seek recovery of defense expenses incurred in connection with the lawsuit.'). Mand has put forth no evidence that WSG objected to this reservation. Therefore, because Max Specialty specifically reserved this right and is entitled to it under New York law, Max Specialty is entitled to a declaration that it may recoup the legal fees it expended in defense of WSG in the underlying action."); *Federal Ins. Co. v. Marlyn Nutraceuticals, Inc.,* No. 13-0137, 2013 U.S. Dist. LEXIS 178565 (E.D.N.Y. Dec 19, 2013) (citing *Gotham* and *Max Specialty* favorably but denying reimbursement because "[t]he Reservation Letter, however, contained no such explicit reservation"); *Maxum Indem. Co. v. VLK Constr., Inc.,* No. 14-1616, 2016 U.S. Dist. LEXIS 121476 (E.D.N.Y. Sept. 8, 2016) ("In order to be entitled to reimbursement of defense costs, the insurer must explicitly advise the named insured that it was reserving its right to seek reimbursement against the named insured in the event it is determined the insurer had no defense obligation, and the insured must not object to the reservation."); *Am. Home Assur. Co. v. Allan Window Techs., Ltd.,* No. 15-5138, 2016 U.S. Dist. LEXIS 101118 (S.D.N.Y. Aug. 2, 2016) ("Insurers are entitled to reimbursement of defense costs upon a determination of non-coverage so long as the reservation was communicated to the insured and the insured did not object to the reservation.") (citing numerous cases); *United Specialty Ins. Co. v. CDC Hous., Inc.,* No. 16-406, 2017 U.S. Dist. LEXIS 20731 (S.D.N.Y. Feb. 9, 2017) ("Courts have consistently determined that insurers are entitled to reimbursement of defense costs upon a determination of non-coverage so long as the reservation was communicated to the insured, who did not expressly refuse to consent to the reservation."); *American Home Assur. Co. v. Port. Auth. of N.Y. & N.J.*, No. 651096/2012, 2017 N.Y. Misc. LEXIS 4589 (N.Y. Sup. Ct. Nov. 28, 2017) (insurer entitled to reimbursement unless the policy expressly prohibits it); *Maxum Indem. Co. v. Happy Garden Constr. Corp.*, No. 17-02961, 2018 U.S. Dist. LEXIS 76776 (E.D.N.Y. May 7, 2018) (citing *Gotham* and permitting reimbursement); *Crescent Beach Club LLC v. Indian Harbor Ins. Co.*, No. 18-5951, 2020 U.S. Dist. LEXIS 108862 (E.D.N.Y. June 22, 2020) ("[S]ince the duty to defend existed until it was legally determined that there is no possibility for coverage under the Policy, defendant is not entitled to any reimbursement for defense costs it previously expended in the underlying action."). *But see General Star Indem. Co. v. Driven Sports, Inc.*, 80 F. Supp. 3d 442 (E.D.N.Y. 2015) ("[E]ven if plaintiff's claim of unjust enrichment is not precluded by the Policy, the Court holds that defendant was not unjustly enriched by plaintiff's coverage of legal representation. Under these circumstances, the Court finds that the New York Court of Appeals would find recoupment to be an inappropriate remedy.") (reaching decision following a lengthy analysis of the issue).

North Carolina: A North Carolina District Court, observing that the North Carolina Supreme Court and Court of Appeals have not addressed the issue, concluded that the insurer was not entitled to reimbursement of its defense costs if it were determined that it had no duty to defend. *Hanover Ins. Co. v. Blue Ridge Property Management*, No. 18-1018, 2020 U.S. Dist. LEXIS 177325 (M.D.N.C. Sept. 28, 2020). The court examined case law nationally and chose to follow the Fourth Circuit's decision in *Perdue Farms Inc. v. Travelers Cas. & Sur. Co.*, 448 F.3d 252 (4th Cir. 2006) (applying Maryland law). As in *Perdue Farms*, the court noted that permitting reimbursement would be a "back door" narrowing of the duty to defend.

North Dakota: In *Alps Prop. & Cas. Ins. Co. v. Bredahl & Assocs., P.C.*, No. 19-00195, 2020 U.S. Dist. LEXIS 197186 (D.N.D. Oct. 23, 2020), the court permitted reimbursement where a policy contained an express provision allowing for it, the insured reserved its rights to seek reimbursement and the insured accepted the defense: "The North Dakota Supreme Court has not addressed an insurer's right to reimbursement of defense costs when the reimbursement provision is contained in the policy and the insurer has reserved its right under the policy. As a source of persuasive authority, the Defendants rely on *Westchester Fire Insurance Company v. Wallerich*, 563 F.3d 707 (8th Cir. 2009), for their argument that the Eighth Circuit Court of Appeals has rejected an insurer's right to reimbursement in these circumstances. But *Westcheseter* confirms the opposite. In that case, the Eighth Circuit held that the insurer did not have a right to reimbursement because there was no such right in the insurance policy and the insurer only mentioned reimbursement in a reservation of rights letter. Still, the court indicated that the outcome would have been different if the insurer had included in the policy an express provision for such reimbursement." *Id.* at *21-22.

Ohio: The Sixth Circuit Court of Appeals, applying Ohio law, following a review of decisions nationally, held that an insurer had a right to reimbursement of defense costs for uncovered claims. *United Nat'l Ins. Co. v. SST Fitness Corp.*, 309 F.3d 914, 921 (6th Cir. 2002). The court adopted the rationale that, by accepting the defense subject to the insurer's right to reimbursement, the insured entered into an implied in fact contract. *Id.* at 917–21 (citing, among other authorities, *Grinnell Mut. Reinsurance Co. v. Shierk*, 996 F. Supp. 836 (S.D. Ill. 1998) in support of its decision). *But see Gen. Agents Ins. Co. of Am. v. Midwest Sporting Goods Co.*, 828 N.E.2d 1092, 1104 (Ill. 2005) (repudiating *Shierk*); *Columbia Cas. Co. v. City of St. Clairsville, OH*, No. 05 CV 898, 2007 U.S. Dist. LEXIS 16797 (S.D. Ohio 2007) (holding that insurer was entitled to recover costs incurred to defend insured-city under a reservation of rights, for counts that the court ultimately found no duty to defend was owed); *Chiquita Brands Int'l, Inc. v. Nat'l Union Fire Ins. Co.*, 57 N.E.3d 97 (Ohio Ct. App. 2015) ("[W]here (1) an insurer does not provide a defense until after a court has entered judgment declaring that the insurer has a duty to defend, (2) the insured demands that the insurer provide a defense, (3) the insurer provides the defense under a reservation-of-rights stating that it may seek to be reimbursed, and later (4) an appellate court determines that a duty-to-defend never existed, then (5) the insurer is entitled to be reimbursed for its defense-cost expenditures under a theory of restitution.").

Oklahoma: An Oklahoma District Court held that an insurer was entitled to reimbursement of a settlement payment if it were subsequently determined that no coverage was owed. *Melton Truck Lines, Inc. v. Indem. Ins. Co. of N. Am.*, No. 04-CV-263-JHP-SAJ, 2006 U.S. Dist. LEXIS 43179 (N.D. Okla. June 26, 2006). The court relied on the fact that, under Oklahoma law, an insurer who settles an underlying claim does not waive any coverage defenses vis-à-vis its insured. Cautionary Note: The *Melton Truck* court also relied on the Supreme Court of Texas's 2005 decision in *Excess Underwriters at Lloyd's v. Franks Casing Crew & Rental Tools*, No. 02–0730, 2005 Tex. LEXIS 418 (Tex. May 27, 2005), and its reasoning that an insured is not prejudiced by a requirement that it reimburse its insurer for settlement payments if there is no coverage because, in such case, the insured is in the same position, or at least no worse position, than it would have been if there had been no insurance policy. However, at the time of the Oklahoma District Court's decision in *Melton Truck*, *Franks Casing* had been withdrawn by the Supreme Court of Texas by a January 6, 2006 grant of rehearing and was substituted with a decision in 2008. *See* Texas.

Oregon: No instructive authority.

Pennsylvania: The Supreme Court of Pennsylvania held that an insurer was not entitled to reimbursement of defense costs when it was determined that the insurer had no duty to defend. *American & Foreign Ins. Co. v. Jerry's Sport Center, Inc.*, 2 A.3d 526, 546 (Pa. 2010). "[P]ermitting reimbursement by reservation of rights, absent an insurance policy provision authorizing the right in the first place, is tantamount to allowing the insurer to extract a unilateral amendment to the insurance contract." *Id.* at 544. "Insured was not unjustly enriched by [insurer's] payment of defense costs. [The insurer] had not only the duty to defend, but the right to defend under the insurance contract. This arrangement benefited both parties. The duty to defend benefited Insured to protect it from the cost of defense, while the right to defend allowed [the insurer] to control the defense to protect itself against potential indemnity exposure." *Id.* at 545; *see also Axis Specialty Ins. Co. v. Brickman Group, LTD*, 756 F. Supp. 2d 644, 655 (E.D. Pa. 2010) ("[W]e conclude that, under Pennsylvania law, an insurer who makes a settlement payment on its insured's behalf may assert an unjust enrichment claim for reimbursement if it is determined after the payment is made that the insurer was not obligated to make the payment under the terms of the insurance policy. The insurer may not, however, proceed on a pure breach of contract theory if there is no specific provision in the insurance policy that provides for reimbursement claims. Moreover, in order to prevail on an unjust enrichment claim for reimbursement, the insurer must establish that (1) it did not make the payment due to a mistake of law; (2) the insured was on notice at the time of the payment that the insurer disputed its obligation to pay; (3) it did not make the payment primarily to protect its own interest; and (4) permitting reimbursement under the circumstances presented would not upset the delicate incentive structure inherent in the insurer/insured relationship.") (discussing *Jerry's Sport* and reaching decision despite it); *Rachell II, Inc. v. State Nat'l Ins. Co.*, No. 15-01096, 2016 U.S. Dist. LEXIS 44432 (E.D. Pa. Mar. 31, 2016) (reiterating *Jerry's Sport* and holding "[b]ut if it turns out that the insurer's duty to defend did not apply, the insurer may be unable to recover the costs of the defense from its insured because, under Pennsylvania law, 'an insurer is not entitled to be reimbursed for defense costs absent an express provision in the written insurance contract.'"); *Zurich Am. Ins. Co. v. Century Steel Erectors Co. L.P.*, No. 19-998, 2020 U.S. Dist. LEXIS 65724 (W.D. Pa. Apr. 14, 2020) (distinguishing *Jerry's Sport* because the policy expressly provided for reimbursement).

Rhode Island: No instructive authority.

South Carolina: No instructive authority.

South Dakota: No instructive authority.

Tennessee: A Tennessee District Court, fully incorporating a magistrate judge's report and recommendation, predicted that the Supreme Court of Tennessee would recognize a right to reimbursement of defense costs. *Cincinnati Ins. Co. v. Grand Pointe, LLC*, 501 F. Supp. 2d 1145, 1168 (E.D. Tenn. 2007). The court examined case law nationally on both sides of the issue and concluded that an insurer has a right to reimbursement, even if the policy does not contain an express provision to such effect, so long as the insurer provided timely, specific, and adequate notice to the insured of the insurer's right to seek reimbursement if it were determined there was no duty to defend. *Id. See also Catlin Specialty Ins. Co. v. CBL & Assocs. Props.*, C.A. No. N16C-07-166, 2018 Del. Super. LEXIS 342 (Del. Super. Ct. Aug. 9, 2018) (applying Tennessee law) ("Under *Grand Pointe* and applicable Tennessee law, [insurer's offer of a defense, with reservation of the right to seek reimbursement and insured's acceptance without objection] formed a quasi-contract or a contract implied in law based on unjust enrichment. Catlin conferred the benefit of a defense subject to a reservation of rights; CBL Defendants accepted such a defense; and it would be inequitable for CBL Defendants to retain the benefit of the defense without payment of its value.").

Texas: The Supreme Court of Texas held that "when coverage is disputed and the insurer is presented with a reasonable settlement demand within policy limits, the insurer may fund the settlement and seek reimbursement only if it obtains the insured's clear and unequivocal consent to the settlement and the insurer's right to seek reimbursement." *Texas Ass'n of Counties County Government Risk Management Pool v. Matagorda County*, 52 S.W.3d 128, 135 (Tex. 2000). The court recognized that insurers faced with a reasonable settlement offer within policy limits, where coverage is in question, are in an untenable position. *Id.* at 135. However, the court concluded that an insurer in such a position can seek prompt resolution of the coverage dispute in a declaratory judgment action, a step that the court noted it has encouraged insurers to take. *Id.* The court was also persuaded that "[o]n balance, insurers are better positioned to handle this risk, either by drafting policies to specifically provide for reimbursement or by accounting for the possibility that they may occasionally pay uncovered claims in their rate structure." *Id.* at 136. *See also Excess Underwriters at Lloyd's London v. Frank's Casing Crew and Rental Tools, Inc.*, 246 S.W.3d 42, 43 (Tex. 2008) (refusing to recognize an exception to *Matagorda County* and a reimbursement obligation when the policy involves excess coverage, the insurer has no duty to defend under the policy, and the insured acknowledges that the claimant's settlement offer is reasonable and demands that the insurer accept it). [These cases suggest that Texas would not allow reimbursement of defense costs following a determination of no duty to defend.]; *Aldous v. Darwin Nat'l Assur. Co.*, 851 F.3d 473 (5th Cir. 2017) (reiterating *Matagorda County*) ("Under Texas law, if an insurance company disputes coverage with its insured but nonetheless settles the action on the insured's behalf, there is no right to equitable reimbursement if the third party's claims are later determined to be uncovered by the policy. This is true even where the insurer has provided coverage under a reservation of rights. But nothing stops insurers from including a right to reimbursement in its Policy or obtaining 'the insured's clear and unequivocal consent to the settlement and the insurer's right to seek reimbursement.'"); *Columbia Lloyds Ins. Co. v. Liberty Ins. Underwriters, Inc.*, No. 17-005, 2019 U.S. Dist. LEXIS 44231 (S.D. Tex. Jan. 30, 2019) (holding that a Fraud Exclusion included the insurer's right to reimbursement of defense costs and *Frank's Casing* did not dictate a different result) (accepting and adopting magistrate's recommendation, 2019 U.S. Dist. LEXIS 44000 (S.D. Tex. Mar. 5, 2019)).

Utah: A Utah District Court denied an insurer's request for reimbursement of defense costs pending the Supreme Court of Utah's ruling on whether such request is permissible under Utah law. *Westport Ins. Corp. v. Ong*, No. 1:07CV10 DAK, 2008 U.S. Dist. LEXIS 26683 (D. Utah Mar. 28, 2008). The court certified the question to the Utah high court because the issue had never been addressed by Utah courts, was controlling in the case and there was significant split among courts across the country. However, the parties subsequently filed a stipulated dismissal with prejudice of all claims and counterclaims. *Westport Ins. Corp. v. Ong*, No. 1:07CV10 DAK, Docket Entry No. 47 (D. Utah Sept. 30, 2008). In *U.S. Fidelity v. U.S. Sports Specialty*, 270 P.3d 464 (Utah 2012) the Supreme Court of Utah answered a certified question and held that "[u]nder Utah law, an insurer may not seek restitution based on the extracontractual theory of unjust enrichment where there is an express contract governing the 'subject matter' of the dispute." *Id.* at 471. "[T]here can be no extracontractual right to restitution between the insurer and its insured, and only the express terms of a policy create an enforceable right to reimbursement." *Id.* At issue was an insurer's claim for reimbursement of a judgment paid in excess of limits. *See also Colony Nat. Ins. Co. v. Sorenson Medical, Inc.*, No. 2010–74, 2013 U.S. Dist. LEXIS 104172 (E.D. Ky. July 25, 2013) (following *U.S. Sports Specialty*); *Hartford Cas. Ins. v. Swapp Law, PLLC*, No. 17-01130, 2019 U.S. Dist. LEXIS 129664 (D. Utah Aug. 1, 2019) ("[W]hile *U.S. Fidelity* supports Hartford's argument that, under Utah law, its duty to defend cannot be enlarged beyond that explicitly provided under the Policy, it also casts serious doubt on the validity of Hartford's extracontractual, unilateral reservation of rights to seek reimbursement of attorneys' fees it has already paid.").

Vermont: No instructive authority.

Virginia: The Fourth Circuit Court of Appeals, applying Virginia law, held that certain coverage issues were not ripe for appellate review. *Penn-America Ins. Co. v. Mapp*, 521 F.3d 290, 298 (4th Cir. 2008). However, the court also concluded, without analysis, that once the issues became ripe, the insurer, pursuant to its reservation of rights, could seek reimbursement of its defense costs if it were determined that the insurer did not have a duty to defend. *Id. See also Protection Strategies, Inc. v. Starr Indemnity & Liability Co.*, No. 13–00763, 2014 U.S. Dist. LEXIS 56652 (E.D. Va. Apr. 23, 2014) ("[A]lthough there is a split among courts regarding whether a reservation of rights *letter* is sufficient to reserve a right to recoupment not found within the insurance contract, the cases uniformly suggest that recoupment is an available remedy when it is expressly written into the policy. While express recoupment provisions may be uncommon in duty to defend policies, ultimately '[a]n insurance company's duty to defend is part of its contractual obligation and is defined by the language of the insurance policy.'") (emphasis in original) (addressing D&O policy) (*affirmed* 611 Fed. Appx. 775 (4th Cir. 2015)).

Washington: The Supreme Court of Washington, following a detailed review of the issue nationally, held that an insurer was not entitled to reimbursement of defense costs. *National Surety Corp. v. Immunex Corp.*, 297 P.3d 688 (Wash. 2013). The court explained the rationale for its decision as follows: "It is the insurer that decides whether to defend (with or without a reservation of rights) *before* any judicial determination of coverage. Providing a defense benefits the insurer by giving it the ability to monitor the defense and better limit its exposure. When an insurer defends under a reservation of rights, it insulates itself from potential claims of breach and bad faith, which can lead to significant damages, including coverage by estoppel. In turn, the insured receives the benefit of a defense until a court declares none is owed. Conversely, when an insurer declines to defend altogether, it saves money on legal fees but assumes the risk it may have breached its duty to defend or committed bad faith. We reject National Surety's view that an insurer can have the best of both options: protection from claims of bad faith or breach without any responsibility for the costs of defense if a court later determines there is no duty to defend. This 'all reward, no risk' proposition renders the *defense* portion of a reservation of rights defense illusory. The insured receives no greater benefit than if its insurer had refused to defend outright." (emphasis added). *Id.* at 693-94. *See also Mass. Bay Ins. Co. v. Walflor Indus., Inc.*, 383 F. Supp. 3d 1148 (W.D. Wash. 2019) (permitting reimbursement, despite *Immunex*, as the policy expressly entitled insurer to such right and finding no public policy basis for invalidating the reimbursement provision); *Mid-Century Ins. Co. v. Hunt's Plumbing & Mech. LLC*, No. C19-0285, 2019 U.S. Dist. LEXIS 160098 (W.D. Wash. Sept. 17, 2019) (same as *Walflor Indus.*); *United Fin. Cas. Co. v. Christensen, Inc.*, No. 19-05658, 2020 U.S. Dist. LEXIS 128651 (W.D. Wash. Jul. 21, 2020) (noting that an "insurer cannot recover money spent on a defense prior to a judicial declaration of non-coverage" unless the policy provides for reimbursement of defense costs).

West Virginia: No instructive authority.

Wisconsin: A Wisconsin District Court addressed the issue of reimbursement of defense costs for uncovered claims, following a reservation of such right by the insurer, in the context of deciding the insurer's motion to file an amended counterclaim seeking reimbursement. *Kreuger Int'l, Inc. v. Fed. Ins. Co.*, 637 F. Supp. 2d 604 (E.D. Wis. 2008). While the court did not resolve the question, it concluded, following a review of case law nationally on both sides of the issue, that the insurer's claim for reimbursement of defense costs was not frivolous. *Id.* at 624. As such, the court granted the motion to amend because it would not be futile to do so. *Id.* at 620; *see also Appleton Papers, Inc. v. George A. Whiting Paper Co.*, 2009 U.S. Dist. LEXIS 4344 (E.D. Wis. Jan. 8, 2009) (citing *Kreuger* and noting the possibility that an insurer could attempt to recoup costs incurred in defending insured if court determines that insurer owed no coverage to insured) ("Although the viability of that remedy under Wisconsin law is far from certain, it is not clear that General Casualty would necessarily be deprived of its expenses forever in the event there is no coverage."); *Sentry Ins. v. Regal Ware, Inc.*, No. 10–168, 2012 U.S. Dist. LEXIS 45277 (W.D. Wis. Mar. 30, 2012) (denying insurer's attempt to recover the portion of its defense costs attributable to non-covered claims) ("[T]here is Sentry's policy argument: that refusing to allow reimbursement will frustrate the contractual expectations of the parties. . . . But Sentry does not offer any evidence that it entered into the contract expecting to pay only for the cost of defending covered claims. Indeed, given the state of Wisconsin law, which is at best undecided on the issue, if Sentry had this expectation is was not a particularly reasonable one, especially in light of Wisconsin's broad duty to defend and the presumption that ambiguities in insurance policies will be construed in favor of insureds. Moreover, there is no evidence that the parties attempted to contract around Wisconsin's default duty to defend rule. It seems likely, therefore, that a Wisconsin rule allowing for reimbursement would *defeat*, rather than the preserve, the parties' legitimate expectations.") (emphasis in original); *WRR Envtl. Servs. v. Admiral Ins. Co.*, No. 10-843, 2015 U.S. Dist. LEXIS 26984 (E.D. Wis. Mar. 4, 2015) (citing *Appleton Papers* and stating that "Wisconsin law is unsettled with regard to whether nonbreaching insurers may attempt to recoup their defense payments made under the duty to defend while maintaining the right to later contest coverage.") ("Because there has been 'no final determination' of the nonbreaching insurers' legal obligations, there can be no determination, in this case, of 'who owes what.'"); *Hanover Ins. Co. v. BMOC, Inc.*, No. 18-325, 2019 U.S. Dist. LEXIS 30764 (W.D. Wis. Feb. 27, 2019) ("While admittedly Wisconsin law functions to coerce insurance companies into defending until a court adjudicates the duty to defend, that is generally a cost of doing business. If [insurer] had wanted to ensure that it could recoup preliminary defense costs, it should have written the policy to provide that option.") (acknowledging that the issue is unsettled under Wisconsin law); *Hayes v. Wis. & S.R.R., LLC*, No. 18-923, 2021 U.S. Dist. LEXIS 10175 (E.D. Wis. Jan. 20, 2021) ("If an insurer wishes to obtain reimbursement of costs expended defending uncovered claims, then it must include such a provision in the policy.") ("[I]f presented with the question, the Wisconsin Supreme Court would likely hold that under Wisconsin law an insurer may not, by way of a claim of unjust enrichment, seek to recover from its insured the costs it expended defending a claim for which the insurance policy did not provide coverage.").

Wyoming: The Supreme Court of Wyoming held that allocation of defense costs between covered and uncovered claims, followed by requiring reimbursement by the insured of defense costs for uncovered claims, was not permitted, even if such right is asserted by the insured in its reservation of rights letter. *Shoshone First Bank v. Pac. Employers Ins. Co.*, 2 P.3d 510, 515–16 (Wyo. 2000). The court based its decision on the recognition that an insurer is charged with the duty of defending the entire suit and the insurer could have included an allocation provision in its policy, but failed to do so. *Id.* Further, the court observed that "[t]he question as to whether there is a duty to defend an insured is a difficult one, but because that is the business of an insurance carrier, it is the insurance carrier's duty to make that decision. If an insurance carrier believes that no coverage exists, then it should deny its insured a defense at the beginning instead of defending and later attempting to recoup from its insured the costs of defending the underlying action." *Id.* at 516 (quoting *Am. States Ins. Co. v. Ridco, Inc.*, No. 95CV158D (D. Wyo. Feb. 8, 1996)); *see also Employers Mut. Cas. Co. v. Bartile Roofs, Inc.*, 618 F.3d 1153, 1175–76 (10th Cir. 2010) (applying Wyoming law) (holding that Wyoming law prevented insurer from recovering defense costs from insured-subcontractor under commercial general liability policies because the "CGL policies contain[ed] no provisions reserving [insurer's] right to recoup defense costs" and insurer's reservation of rights letter "constituted a unilateral attempt either to modify the existing CGL policies or to create a new contract authorizing recoupment") (rejecting insurer's attempt to distinguish *Shoshone* on the basis that it involved the recovery of defense costs in a case involving covered and uncovered claims, while case at hand involved only noncovered claims).

CHAPTER
8

Prevailing Insured's Right to Recover Attorney's Fees in Coverage Litigation

When an insurance company is evaluating whether to file a declaratory judgment action or defend one filed against it, the principal issues under consideration are likely to be the insurer's chance of success and the amount of attorney's fees that will be incurred to achieve the desired result. Of course, those are the paramount considerations of *any* party that is contemplating litigation over *any* issue—not just insurance coverage.

On one hand, insurers are like all others parties that undertake the deliberative process when deciding to enter the litigation arena. On the other hand, insurers must often weigh an additional factor in the litigation equation that most others need not: If the insurer does not prevail, will it be obligated to pay its insured's attorney's fees? To be clear, these are attorney's fees that are *in addition to* any attorney's fees that the insurer may be obligated to pay to its insured, for the defense of an underlying action, if the insurer did not provide a defense and it was now determined in the coverage litigation that a defense was in fact owed.

As a general rule, in almost all litigation, the losing party is not obligated to pay the prevailing party's attorney's fees. This is often referred to as the "American Rule." *ACMAT Corp. v. Greater N.Y. Mut. Ins. Co.*, 923 A.2d 697, 702 (Conn. 2007) ("The general rule of law known as the American rule is that attorney's fees and ordinary expenses and burdens of litigation are not allowed to the successful party absent a contractual or statutory exception.") (citations and internal quotation omitted); *see also Barnes v. Okla. Farm Bureau Mut. Ins. Co.*, 11 P.3d 162, 185 n.11 (Okla. 2000) ("In contrast to the American Rule, the English Rule calls for an across-the-board *postdecisional* cost- and counsel-fee shifting in favor of the victorious party.") (emphasis in original).

Therefore, the possibility of an unsuccessful insurer in coverage litigation being obligated to pay its insured's attorney's fees hinges on the existence of an exception to the American Rule in the relevant state. And such exceptions are not granted lightly. *Monahan v. GMAC Mortgage Corp.*, 893 A.2d 298, 322 (Vt. 2005) ("We have recognized that courts may invoke their equity powers to deviate from [the American] rule, but only in exceptional cases and for dominating reasons of justice.") (citation and internal quotation omitted).

Notwithstanding this demanding standard, most states have carved out an exception of some type to the American Rule when it is judicially determined that an insurer is obligated to provide coverage to an insured. One commonly cited rationale for this exception is that, if the insured must bear the expense of obtaining coverage from its insurer, it may be no better off financially than if it did not have the insurance policy in the first place. *See Mountain W. Farm Bureau Mut. Ins. Co. v. Brewer*, 69 P.3d 652, 657–58 (Mont. 2003) (citing 7C John Alan Appleman et al., *Insurance Law and Practice* § 4691, at 282–83 (1979)); *see also Olympic Steamship Co., Inc. v. Centennial Ins. Co.*, 811 P.2d 673, 681 (Wash. 1991) ("When an insured purchases a contract of insurance, it seeks protection from expenses arising from litigation, not vexatious, time-consuming, expensive litigation with its insurer.") (citation and internal quotation omitted).

While an unsuccessful insurer in coverage litigation likely faces an exception to the American Rule, requiring it to pay for its insured's attorney's fees, the specific approaches vary widely and can have a significant impact on the likelihood of the insurer in fact incurring such obligation. *Crist v. Ins. Co. of N. Am.*, 529 F. Supp. 601, 606 (D. Utah 1982) ("There are innumerable cases dealing with this specific issue [recovery of attorney's fees in bringing a declaratory judgment action against an insurer], and the courts have resolved the issue in practically every conceivable way.").

In general, some states have enacted statutes that provide for a prevailing insured's recovery of attorney's fees in an action to secure coverage. Other states achieve similar results, but do so through common law. But whichever approach applies, the most important factor is the same: whether the prevailing insured's right to recover attorney's fees is automatic or must the insured prove that the insurer's conduct was unreasonable or egregious in some way.

For example, a Hawaii statute mandates an award of attorney's fees without regard to the insurer's conduct in denying the claim. In other words, it imposes strict liability for attorney's fees on an insurer that is ordered to pay a claim. HAW. REV. STAT. ANN. § 431:10–242 ("Where an insurer has contested its liability under a policy and is ordered by the courts to pay benefits under the policy, the policyholder, the beneficiary under a policy, or the person who has acquired the rights of the policyholder or beneficiary under the policy shall be awarded reasonable attorney's fees and the costs of suit, in addition to the benefits under the policy.").

Maryland also takes a strict liability approach, but it is the result of a decision from its highest court. *Bausch & Lomb, Inc. v. Utica Mut. Ins. Co.*, 735 A.2d 1081, 1094–95 (Md. 1999) ("[I]n the absence of a statute, rule or contract expressly allowing the recovery of attorneys' fees, a prevailing party in a lawsuit may not ordinarily recover attorneys' fees. There is one nonstatutory exception to the American rule in actions involving insurance policies. Where an action is brought to enforce an insurer's obligations under the third party liability provisions of a policy, and it is determined that there is coverage under the policy, the insurer is liable for the prevailing party's attorneys' fees.") (citations and internal quotation omitted).

Alternatively, a Virginia statute departs from strict liability and permits an award of attorney's fees, but only if there was a finding that the insurer's denial of coverage was not in good faith. VA. CODE ANN. § 38.2-209 ("[I]n any civil case in which an insured individual [defined to include a company or organization] sues his insurer to determine what coverage, if any, exists under his present policy … or the extent to which his insurer is liable for compensating a covered loss, the individual insured shall be entitled to recover from the insurer costs and such reasonable attorney fees as the court may award. However, these costs and attorney's fees shall not be awarded unless the court determines that the insurer, not acting in good faith, has either denied coverage or failed or refused to make payment to the insured under the policy.").

Connecticut also rejects a strict liability rule, but it was established judicially and not legislatively. *ACMAT Corp.*, 923 A.2d at 708 ("[E]ven without an authorizing contractual or statutory provision, a trial court may award attorney's fees to a policyholder that has prevailed in a declaratory judgment action against its insurance company only if the policyholder can prove that the insurer has engaged in bad faith conduct prior to or in the course of the litigation.").

A handful of states use a combination of legislative and judicial avenues to address whether attorney's fees are to be awarded to a prevailing insured. Under this hybrid approach, consideration is first given to the state's general statute that allows for an award of attorney's fees in an action on a contract. The court then interprets this statute, covering contracts in general, to include an insurance contract dispute. For example, ARIZ. STAT. ANN. § 12-341.01(A) provides that "[i]n any contested action arising out of a contract, express or implied, the court may award the successful party reasonable attorney fees."). The Arizona Court of Appeals in *Lennar*

Corp. v. Auto-Owners Ins. Co., 151 P.3d 538, 553 (Ariz. Ct. App. 2007) then held that "[w]e have the discretion to award reasonable attorneys' fees to a prevailing party in an insurance contract dispute pursuant to [ARIZ. STAT. ANN. § 12–341.01(A)].").

And some states address the issue by applying their general statutes permitting an award of attorney's fees against a party that engages in frivolous or vexatious litigation. For example, a Colorado statute provides that a court may award attorney's fees "when the bringing or defense of an action, or part thereof … is determined to have been substantially frivolous, substantially groundless, or substantially vexatious." COLO. REV. STAT. ANN. § 13–17–101.

While the vast majority of states provide a mechanism of some sort for a prevailing insured in a coverage action to recover its attorney's fees, a few states maintain strict adherence to the American Rule and do not allow such recovery. *See Clark v. Exch. Ins. Ass'n*, 161 So. 2d 817, 819–20 (Ala. 1964) (holding that the insurer was not liable for attorney's fees in a declaratory judgment action, regardless of who brings the action or whether it is successful or unsuccessful from the complainant's view); *see also AIK Selective Self-Insurance Fund v. Minton*, 192 S.W.3d 415, 420 (Ky. 2006) (quoting *Aetna Cas. & Sur. Co. v. Commonwealth*, 179 S.W.3d 830, 842 (Ky. 2005)) ("[W]ith the exception of a specific contractual provision allowing for recovery of attorneys' fees or a fee-shifting statute … each party assumes responsibility for his or her own attorneys' fees.").

While the mechanisms vary, in almost all cases an insurer that is unsuccessful in coverage litigation will either be automatically obligated to pay for its insured's attorney's fees or may be litigating post-trial whether such obligation exists. Whichever the case, the potential for being saddled with the attorney's fees incurred by its prevailing insured in a declaratory judgment action is a consideration that insurers will usually not be able to avoid.

50-State Survey: Prevailing Insured's Right to Recover Attorney's Fees in Coverage Litigation

Alabama: The Supreme Court of Alabama held that "Alabama has long recognized that, absent a pertinent statute or contractual provision, an insured may not recover from his insurer attorney fees incurred in a declaratory judgment action to determine the existence of coverage under a liability policy." *Alliance Ins. Co. v. Reynolds*, 504 So. 2d 1215, 1216 (Ala. Civ. App. 1987); *see also Clark v. Exch. Ins. Ass'n*, 161 So. 2d 817, 819–20 (Ala. 1964) (holding that the insurer was not liable for attorney's fees in a declaratory judgment action, regardless of who brings the action or whether it is successful or unsuccessful from the complainant's view); *Miller v. Nationwide Ret. Solutions, Inc.*, No. 15-01574, 2017 U.S. Dist. LEXIS 224414 (N.D. Ala. Jan. 17, 2017) (non-insurance context but citing *Reynolds* and discussing Alabama's adherence to the American Rule) ("Jacquetta has not pled, nor does the court's review of record otherwise reveal, any statute, contract provision, or special equitable circumstances by which she might be entitled to recover her attorney's fees in this action from NRS, even if she were to establish a right to some or all of the proceeds of the Plan Account.").

Alaska: An Alaska statute provides that "[e]xcept as otherwise provided by law or agreed to by the parties, the prevailing party in a civil case shall be awarded attorney's fees calculated under this rule." ALASKA R. CIV. P. 82 (stating that a percentage of attorney's fees is awarded and it varies depending on the amount of the judgment, whether the case was contested, and whether the case went to trial, with the maximum award being 20 percent); *see also State v. Native of Nunapitchuk*, 156 P.3d 389, 394 (Alaska 2007) (noting that "Alaska is the only state with a general "loser pays" rule for attorney's fees in most civil litigation"); *Ryan v. Sea Air, Inc.*, 902 F. Supp. 1064, 1070 (D. Alaska 1995) (noting that Alaska follows the English Rule in upholding an award of attorney's fees an insurer incurred in bringing a declaratory judgment action against its insured); *Williams v. Geico Cas. Co.*, 301 P.3d 1220 (Alaska 2013) ("Although there may be cases in which the award of attorney's fees to an insurance company that filed a declaratory action against its insured would be unreasonable, this is not such a case."); *Evanston Ins. Co. v. Matanuska-Susitna Borough*, No. 14-00049, 2016 U.S. Dist. LEXIS 44971 (D. Alaska Mar. 31, 2016) ("[W]hen litigation is dismissed as a result of the delay or intransigence of one of the litigants, the trial court may deem the other litigant the prevailing party for purposes of Rule 82. That is clearly not the situation presented here. This is also not a case where the plaintiff voluntarily dismissed the case or where dismissal was based on *forum non conveniens*. The case or controversy went away because the underlying litigation went away for reasons that were unrelated to Evanston's actions and unrelated to any decision in this matter. No party can be said to have prevailed, particularly given that the court did not finally resolve the rights of the parties in this court.").

Arizona: An Arizona statute gives a court discretion to award attorney's fees in an action on a contract. ARIZ. STAT. ANN. § 12–341.01(A). "In any contested action arising out of a contract, express or implied, the court may award the successful party reasonable attorney fees. If a written settlement offer is rejected and the judgment finally obtained is equal to or more favorable to the offeror than an offer made in writing to settle any contested action arising out of a contract, the offeror is deemed to be the successful party from the date of the offer and the court may award the successful party reasonable attorney fees." *Id.* The Supreme Court of Arizona in *Associated Indemnity Corp. v. Warner*, 694 P.2d 1181 (Ariz. 1985) listed the following factors for a trial court to consider when determining if an award of attorney's fees is appropriate: merits of the claim or defense presented by the unsuccessful party; litigation could have been avoided or settled and the successful party's efforts were completely superfluous in achieving the result; assessing fees against the unsuccessful party would cause an extreme hardship; successful party did not prevail with respect to all of the relief sought; novelty of the legal question presented; whether the claim or defense had previously been adjudicated in this jurisdiction; and whether the award in any particular case would discourage other parties with tenable claims or defenses from litigating or defending legitimate contract issues for fear of incurring liability for substantial amounts of attorney's fees. The statute has been interpreted to apply to the prevailing party, including an insurer, in an insurance coverage dispute. *See Lennar Corp. v. Auto-Owners Ins. Co.*, 151 P.3d 538, 553 (Ariz. Ct. App. 2007) ("We have the discretion to award reasonable attorneys' fees to a prevailing party in an insurance contract dispute pursuant to [Ariz. Stat. Ann. § 12-341.01(A)]."); *Irvin v. Lexington Ins. Co.*, No. 1 CA-CV 09-0270, 2010 Ariz. App. Unpub. LEXIS 53 (Ariz. Ct. App. Sept. 2, 2010) (determining that former government official was entitled to recover attorney's fees because official was "the successful party for purposes of A.R.S. § 12-341.01(A)" where he "brought action against State's excess insurer for breach of contract and bad faith after [insurer] refused to provide [official] with excess coverage to continue litigating federal case against him"); *Interstate Fire & Cas. Co., Inc. v. Roman Catholic Church of Diocese of Phoenix*, No. CV-09-01405, 2012 U.S. Dist. LEXIS 146747 (D. Ariz. Oct. 11, 2012) (holding that insured was "net winner," winning three out of four coverage claims, and therefore was the "successful party") (Insured was awarded attorney's fees for three successful claims, but not for unsuccessful claim); *Farmers Ins. Exch. v. Brewer*, No. 16-0478, 2017 Ariz. App. Unpub. LEXIS 750 (Ariz. Ct. App. June 15, 2017) ("It is well-established that a successful party on a contract claim may recover not only attorneys' fees expended on the contract claim, but also fees expended in litigating an 'interwoven' tort claim."); *Preciado v. Young Am. Ins. Co.*, No. 16-0082, 2017 Ariz. App. Unpub. LEXIS 842 (Ariz. Ct. App. June 29, 2017) ("Because the fee award does not allocate separate amounts for each of Preciado's claims, we conclude that implicit in the trial court's fee award was the determination that Preciado's bad faith claim was 'intrinsically related' to his breach of contract claim. Accordingly, as the prevailing party on a breach of contract claim and an 'intrinsically related' bad faith tort claim, Preciado is entitled to reasonable attorneys' fees, and the trial court's fee award was not an abuse of discretion."); *Lexington Ins. Co. v. Scott Homes Multifamily Inc.*, No. 12-02119, 2016 U.S. Dist. LEXIS 128806 (D. Ariz. Sept. 21, 2016) (lengthy opinion addressing six factors that a court should consider to determine whether to exercise its discretion to award attorney's fees and then twelve factors to determine if the fees sought are reasonable); *Admiral Ins. Co. v. Community Ins. Group SPC Ltd.*, No. 14-08152, 2017 U.S. Dist. LEXIS 25440 (D. Ariz. Feb. 23, 2017) (addressing whether to award attorney's fees and the reasonableness of fees sought); *Guzman v. Liberty Mut. Ins. Co.*, No. 16-00530, 2018 U.S. Dist. LEXIS 77209 (D. Ariz. May 8, 2018) (requiring insured to pay insurer's attorney's fees) ("It is not necessary to find unreasonableness to award fees under the statute, but actual unreasonableness in bringing or continuing the litigation is a powerful factor in favor of an award of fees. Just as an insurer's unreasonable denial of coverage strongly favors assessment of fees, an insured's unreasonable persistence in a claim strongly favors assessment of fees.").

Arkansas: An Arkansas statute permits the recovery of attorney's fees in an action for coverage under an insurance policy. ARK. CODE ANN. § 23-79-209. "In all suits in which the judgment or decree of a court is against a life, property, accident and health, or liability insurance company, either in a suit by it to cancel or lapse a policy or to change or alter the terms or conditions thereof in any way that may have the effect of depriving the holder of the policy of any of his or her rights thereunder, or in a suit for a declaratory judgment under the policy, or in a suit by the holder of the policy to require the company to reinstate the policy, the company shall also be liable to pay the holder of the policy all reasonable attorney's fees for the defense or prosecution of the suit, as the case may be." *Id.*; *see also* ARK. CODE ANN. § 23-79-208 (allowing attorney's fees and 12 percent penalty under certain circumstances); *Med. Liab. Mut. Ins. Co. v. Alan Curtis Enters.*, 285 S.W.3d 233 (Ark. 2008) (addressing statutes); *Shelter Mut. Ins. Co. v. Smith*, 779 S.W.2d 149 (Ark. 1989) (addressing statutes); *Lexicon, Inc. v. Ace Am. Ins. Co.*, No. 4:09CV00067, 2009 U.S. Dist. LEXIS 121530 (E.D. Ark. Dec. 31, 2009) (following § 23-79-209 and noting that insured would be entitled to attorney's fees and 12 percent statutory penalty if successful); *S. Farm Bureau Cas. Ins. Co. v. Watkins*, 386 S.W.3d 6 (Ark. Ct. App. 2011) (affirming circuit court's decision that "section 23-79-208 is not more specific than section 23-79-209" as both statutes "provide[] alternative, complementary provisions for the award of attorney's fees in different situations"); *Southern Farm Bureau Cas. Ins. Co. v. Krouse*, 375 S.W.3d 763 (Ark. Ct. App. 2010) (determining that section 23-79-209 applied in case where insured "successfully defended against [insurer's] suit for declaratory judgment, even if presented as [insurer's] counterclaim") (noting that application of section 208 does not preclude application of section 209); *Hortica-Florists' Mut. Ins. Co. v. Pittman Nursery Corp.*, 729 F.3d 846 (8th Cir. 2013) (following § 23-79-209 and concluding that insurer was required to pay insured attorneys' fees because payment did not depend on success with respect to insured's declaratory counter-claims) (on remand the court examined several factors to determine the amount of attorney's fees to which the insured was entitled. 2014 U.S. Dist. LEXIS 64293 (W.D. Ark. May 9, 2014)); *Scottsdale Ins. Co. v. Morrowland Valley Co., LLC*, 411 S.W.3d 184 (Ark. 2012) (concluding that insured could not recover attorney's fees for in-house counsel, but could recover other attorneys' fees); *Simmons Foods, Inc. v. Indus. Risk Insurers*, 863 F.3d 792 (8th Cir. 2017) (addressing in detail whether the insured recovered an amount within 20% of the amount demanded or which was sought in the suit, to warrant an award of attorney's fees and 12 percent penalty under § 23-79-208(d)(1)).

California: The Supreme Court of California held that "[w]hen an insurer's tortious conduct [failing to deal fairly and in good faith with its insured by refusing, without proper cause, to compensate its insured for a loss covered by the policy] reasonably compels the insured to retain an attorney to obtain the benefits due under a policy, it follows that the insurer should be liable in a tort action for that expense. The attorney's fees are an economic loss—damages—proximately caused by the tort. These fees must be distinguished from recovery of attorney's fees *qua* attorney's fees, such as those attributable to the bringing of the bad faith action itself." *Brandt v. Superior Court*, 693 P.2d 796, 798 (Cal. 1985) (citation omitted); *see also Essex Ins. Co. v. Five Star Dye House, Inc.*, 137 P.3d 192, 194 (Cal. 2006) (holding that an assignee of a bad faith claim has the right to recover *Brandt* fees); *Decena v. Pac. Specialty Ins. Co.*, No. B208401, 2010 Cal. App. Unpub. LEXIS 4080 (Cal. Ct. App. May 28, 2010) (explaining *Brandt* and holding that *Brandt* fees were not appropriate because "there was no finding of bad faith"); *Griffin Dewatering Corp. v. Northern Ins. Co.*, 97 Cal. Rptr. 3d 568, 605 (Cal. Ct. App. 2009) (explaining that insured may receive tort damages in the form of *Brandt* fees when insurer unreasonably denies coverage, but noting that only contract damages may be recovered when insurer "acts reasonably, though incorrectly"); *Metro. Bus. Mgmt. v. Allstate Ins. Co.*, 448 Fed. Appx. 677 (9th Cir. Aug. 18, 2011) (determining that, despite declaratory judgment that insurer had duty to defend, insureds were not entitled to *Brandt* fees because they may be awarded only by the trier of fact, unless the parties stipulate otherwise, and no such stipulation was entered into); *Amor Ministries v. Century Sur. Co.*, No. 13-02517, 2016 U.S. Dist. LEXIS 47965 (S.D. Cal. Apr. 7, 2016) ("*Brandt* fees are unique, in that they are viewed as economic loss damages—proximately caused by the tort. *Brandt* fees are thus governed by their own standard, and a recover (sic) of *Brandt* fees requires more than fair proximations.") (holding that insured "failed to prove, by a preponderance of the evidence, the time their counsel spent working on recovering the benefits owed under the policy that proximately resulted from the insurer's tortious, bad faith conduct"); *Olsen v. Std. Fire Ins. Co.*, No. H042250, 2017 Cal. App. Unpub. LEXIS 948 (Cal. Ct. App. Feb. 9, 2017) ("This court has determined that *Brandt* attorney's fees are recoverable on appeal. We agree with the Ninth Circuit in *McGregor* [*v. Paul Revere Life Ins. Co.*, 369 F.3d 1099 (9th Cir. 2004)] that attorney fees the insured has incurred to defend a judgment against the insurer's appeal are a logical extension of the fees incurred in pursuing the recovery in the trial court. The collection of the benefits due is not complete when the insurer resists the judgment by challenging the judgment on appeal. Thus, to the extent that appellate attorney fees reflect the continuation of services performed to obtain the rejected payment of policy benefits, they should be recoverable under the rationale of *Brandt*."); *Saddleback Inn v. Certain Underwriters at Lloyd's London*, No. G051121, 2017 Cal. App. Unpub. LEXIS 2297 (Cal. Ct. App. Mar. 30, 2017) ("*Brandt* established an insured's right to recover attorney fees in a bad faith action against the insurer. The fees recovered may not exceed the amount attributable to the attorney's efforts to obtain the rejected payment due on the insurance contract. Fees attributable to obtaining any portion of the plaintiff's award which exceeds the amount due under the policy are not recoverable. The policy behind *Brandt* is to compensate the insured for the cost of hiring an attorney to recover policy benefits, and cannot include the cost of obtaining a compensatory damages award that exceeds the amount due under the policy. The amount of fees incurred to obtain an award of compensatory damages for bad faith or punitive damages cannot be included in a *Brandt* fee award. The determination of the reasonableness of the fees is made by the trier of fact."); *MJC Supply, LLC v. Scottsdale Ins. Co.*, No. 18-01265, 2019 U.S. Dist. LEXIS 94570 (C.D. Cal. Jun. 4, 2019) ("[S]ince *Brandt* fees are an element of damages to be proved at trial, the burden rests with Plaintiffs to produce such evidence. . . . Because Plaintiffs have failed to identify, produce evidence of, or segregate its fees, Defendant is unable to answer the 'key question' involved in ascertaining Brandt damages, how much did it cost the insured—how much were her damages—to hire an attorney when her insurer acted in bad faith and denied the benefits due her under her policy. Without this information, Plaintiffs have failed to provide evidence establishing their entitlement to Brandt damages as a matter of law."); *Sahadi v. Liberty Mut. Ins.*, No. 18-04061, 2019 U.S. Dist. LEXIS 162262 (N.D. Cal. Sep. 16, 2019) (declining to award *Brandt* fees because, on account of a contingency fee agreement, insurer's alleged bad faith did not serve as a 'necessary antecedent' of any portion of the attorney's fees that Plaintiff incurred); *Draeger v. Transamerica Life Ins. Co.*, No. 19-10478, 2020 U.S. Dist. LEXIS 88019 (C.D. Cal. May 18, 2020) ("*Brandt* fees assignable, such that assignee may recover attorneys' fees incurred in recovering the benefits originally due to the insured) (citing *Essex Ins. Co. v. Five Star Dye House, Inc.*, 137 P.3d 192 (Cal. 2006)).

Colorado: A Colorado statute provides that a court may award attorney's fees "when the bringing or defense of an action, or part thereof … is determined to have been substantially frivolous, substantially groundless, or substantially vexatious." Colo. Rev. Stat. Ann. § 13-17-101. The statute further provides that "[a]ll courts shall liberally construe the provisions of this article to effectuate substantial justice." *Id.*; *see also Allstate Ins. Co. v. Huizar*, 52 P.3d 816, 821–22 (Colo. 2002) (citing Section 13-17-101 as providing for the award of attorney's fees incurred in a declaratory judgment action, but holding that the facts before it lacked substantial frivolity or vexatiousness to warrant such an award, despite an insured prevailing in an action to establish that an insurance policy was void as against public policy); *Gustafson v. Am. Family Mut. Ins. Co.*, No. 11-01303, 2012 U.S. Dist. LEXIS 167292 (D. Colo. Nov. 26, 2012) (holding that insured was entitled to attorneys' fees incurred in defense of insurer's declaratory judgment action, and fees were not limited only to reasonable ones); *MacKiney v. Allstate Fire & Cas. Ins. Co.*, No. 16-01447, 2016 U.S. Dist. LEXIS 166738 (D. Colo. Dec. 1, 2016) ("[T]rial courts have observed that 'a claim or defense is frivolous if the proponent can present no rational argument based on the evidence or law in support of that claim or defense.' Moreover, a claim is frivolous if the plaintiff cannot support it with any credible evidence at trial, even if the allegations in the complaint are sufficient to survive a motion to dismiss."). Colo. Rev. Stat. Ann. § 10-3-1116 also provides "(1) A first-party claimant as defined in section 10-3-1115 whose claim for payment of benefits has been unreasonably delayed or denied may bring an action in a district court to recover reasonable attorney fees and court costs and two times the covered benefit." *See also Home Loan Inv. Co. v. St. Paul Mercury Ins. Co.*, 78 F. Supp. 3d 1307 (D. Colo. 2014) (providing a detailed discussion of the calculation of fees under § 10-3-1116).

Connecticut: The Supreme Court of Connecticut held that "even without an authorizing contractual or statutory provision, a trial court may award attorney's fees to a policyholder that has prevailed in a declaratory judgment action against its insurance company only if the policyholder can prove that the insurer has engaged in bad faith conduct prior to or in the course of the litigation. This limited exception reflects an appropriate accommodation between the policy underlying the American rule of permitting parties, including insurance companies, to litigate claims in good faith, but still provides protection to those policyholders that might confront 'stubbornly litigious' insurance companies that take specious positions in order to attempt to avoid paying legitimate claims." *ACMAT Corp. v. Greater N.Y. Mut. Ins. Co.*, 923 A.2d 697, 708 (Conn. 2007). *But see Middlesex Ins. Co. v. Mara*, 699 F. Supp. 2d 439, 461 (D. Conn. 2010) ("Connecticut courts in insurance cases have declined to award attorney's fees when rendering declaratory judgment absent a showing of statutory or contractual entitlement."). *See also Lincoln Gen. Ins. Co. v. Rodriguez*, No. CV085007513, 2010 Conn. Super. LEXIS 3009 (Conn. Super. Ct. Nov. 17, 2010) (discussing *ACMAT* as a bad faith exception to the American Rule and allowing prayer for relief for attorney's fees to stand); *Opin v. Ohio Cas. Ins. Co.*, No. NNHCV106011625, 2013 Conn. Super. LEXIS 1784 (Conn. Super. Ct. Aug. 8, 2013) (citing *ACMAT* and holding that insureds were not entitled to attorney's fees because they did not allege a statutory or contractual exception to the American Rule or a claim for bad faith); *Chi. Title Ins. Co. v. Accurate Title Searches, Inc.*, 164 A.3d 682 (Conn Ct. App. 2017) (addressing ACMAT, and the purpose of the American Rule, in determining whether attorney's fees were owed).

Delaware: A Delaware statute permits the recovery of attorney's fees in an action for coverage under a property insurance policy: "The court upon rendering judgment against any insurer upon any policy of property insurance, as 'property' insurance is defined in § 904 of this title, shall allow the plaintiff a reasonable sum as attorney's fees to be taxed as part of the costs." DEL. CODE ANN. tit. 18, § 4102; *see also Galiotti v. Travelers Indem. Co.*, 333 A.2d 176, 180 (Del. Super. Ct. 1975) ("Nothing in the statute indicates a legislative intent to confine such award to instances where an insurer has taken an unreasonable position."); *Nassau Gallery, Inc. v. Nationwide Mut. Fire Ins. Co.*, No. 00C-05–034, 2003 Del. Super. LEXIS 401 (Del. Super. Ct.

Nov. 18, 2003) (addressing what constitutes reasonable attorney's fees). It does not appear that attorney's fees are recoverable in an action for coverage under a liability insurance policy. *See Bellanca v. Ins. Co. of North America*, No. 80C-DE-122, 1983 Del. Super. LEXIS 738, at *9–10 (Del. Super. Ct. July 20, 1983) ("[P]laintiff's claim for attorney's fee would appear to hinge upon his success in establishing INA's duty to defend. In the absence of such success his entitlement cannot be recognized. In any event, recovery of attorney's fees is not permitted in the absence of a specific statutory authorization which is lacking here."); *American General Life Ins. v. Goldstein*, 741 F. Supp. 2d 604, 617 (D. Del. 2010) ("Delaware follows the American rule where, absent a statute or contract to the contrary, prevailing litigants are responsible for the payment of their own attorney fees.") ("The decision to award attorney fees under special circumstances such as fraud is a discretionary one left to the court. As such, the court will only make this determination after all the facts have been determined through discovery and will not deny plaintiff's request for attorney fees at this stage of the proceedings.") (citation omitted); *National Grange Mut. Ins. Co. v. Elegant Slumming, Inc.*, 59 A.3d 928 (Del. Supr. Ct. 2013) (finding that fee-shifting statute (DEL. CODE ANN. tit. 18, § 4102) applied in the context of a property policy dispute and award of attorney's fees was reasonable).

District of Columbia: A District of Columbia District Court declared that an insured may be able to recover attorney's fees incurred in coverage litigation. *Nugent v. Unum Life Ins. Co.*, 752 F. Supp. 2d 46, 57 (D.D.C. 2010). The court acknowledged that the District of Columbia "follows the 'American Rule' where, unless modified by statute or contract, generally, each litigant must bear his or her own attorney's fees and litigation costs," but recognized an exception to the "American Rule" where "attorney fees could be awarded due to the oppressive or vexatious conduct of the defendant." *Id.* It was not disputed that there was no contractual or statutory basis for an award of attorney's fees. *Id. See also D.C. Hartford Mut. Ins. Co. v. New Ledroit Park Bldg. Co., LLC*, 313 F. Supp. 3d 40 (D.D.C. 2018) ("Defendants apparently seek to invoke the bad faith exception to the 'American Rule' that parties generally bear their own attorney's fees, as is evidenced by the cases they cite in support of their claim. This exception is a general principle of equity that allows one party to recover attorney's fees based on the opposing party's especially vexatious conduct. Such fees must be sought by motion.") (citing *Hundley v. Johnston*, 18 A.3d 802 (D.C. 2011), which addresses the attorney's fees issue in detail).

Florida: A Florida statute permits the recovery of attorney's fees in an action for coverage under an insurance policy. FLA. STAT. ANN. § 627.428(1). "Upon the rendition of a judgment or decree by any of the courts of this state against an insurer and in favor of any named or omnibus insured or the named beneficiary under a policy or contract executed by the insurer, the trial court or, in the event of an appeal in which the insured or beneficiary prevails, the appellate court shall adjudge or decree against the insurer and in favor of the insured or beneficiary a reasonable sum as fees or compensation for the insured's or beneficiary's attorney prosecuting the suit in which the recovery is had." *Id.*; *see also Lewis v. Universal Prop. & Cas. Ins. Co.*, 13 So. 3d 1079, 1081 (Fla. Dist. Ct. App. 2009) ("The purpose behind section 627.428 is to place the insured in the place she would have been if the carrier had seasonably paid the claim or benefits without causing the payee to engage counsel and incur obligations for attorney's fees.") (citation and internal quotation marks omitted); *First Floridian Auto & Home Ins. Co. v. Myrick*, 969 So. 2d 1121, 1123–24 (Fla. Dist. Ct. App. 2007) ("The legislature enacted section 627.428 to discourage an insurer from contesting a valid claim and to level the playing field so that the insurer's economic power does not overwhelm the insured."); *Kopp v. Meritplan Ins. Co.*, No. 8:09-cv-1109-T-23, 2011 U.S. Dist. LEXIS 10181 (M.D. Fla. Jan. 14, 2011) (noting that "Florida courts have consistently held that the purpose of [Section 627.428] is to discourage insurance companies from contesting valid claims or engaging in dilatory conduct in processing claims and therefore forcing insureds to engage in unnecessary litigation to enforce the terms of an insurance policy"); *Underwood Anderson & Associates, Inc. v. Lilo's Italian Restaurant, Inc.*, 36 So. 3d 885, 888 (Fla. Dist. Ct. App. 2010) (holding that "a strict construction of section 627.428 excludes the [insurance] agent from liability for attorney's fees" where "[a]n agent who is not a party to an insurance contract has no authority to pay on the policy" because "the purpose of the statute is not served by making agents liable for fees incurred in enforcing the policy"); *Beverly v. State Farm Ins. Co.*, 50 So. 3d 628, 633 (Fla. Dist. Ct. App. 2010) ("[A]n insurer's post-suit payment of additional policy proceeds entitles the insured to section 627.428 attorney's fees where the insurer wrongfully caused its insured to resort to litigation in order to resolve a conflict with its insurer when it was within the company's power to resolve it.") (property policy) (citation and internal quotes omitted); *Barreto v. United Services Auto. Ass'n*, 82 So. 3d 159 (Fla. Dist. Ct. App. 2012) (holding that "because the insurer paid the full amounts claimed only after suit was filed, it essentially confessed judgment," which supported insured's award of attorneys' fees); *Blakely v. Safeco Ins. Co. of Illinois*, No. 13-796-Orl-37, 2014 U.S. Dist. LEXIS 36720 (M.D. Fla. Apr. 1, 2014) (finding that insured was entitled to attorney's fees incurred in response to insurer's motion);

Nat'l Union Fire Ins. Co. v. Fla. Crystals Corp., No. 14-81134, 2016 U.S. Dist. LEXIS 7898 (S.D. Fla. Jan. 19, 2016) ("But where, as here, the Court has established a duty to defend and a claim for a declaration that there is no duty to indemnify remains unresolved, a motion for attorneys' fees and costs under section 627.428 is not yet ripe for decision."); *Maiden Specialty Ins. Co. v. Three Chefs & A Chicken, Inc.*, No. 12-22724, 2016 U.S. Dist. LEXIS 116552 (S.D. Fla. July 7, 2016) ("While a plaintiff is entitled to fees for successfully defending a judgment, he is not entitled to fees associated with an unrelated and unsuccessful cross-appeal.") (setting forth detailed discussion of allocation between recoverable and non-recoverable fees). The Supreme Court of Florida recently addressed the standard for the recovery of fees under section 627.428. *See Johnson v. Omega Ins. Co.*, 200 So. 3d 1207 (Fla. 2016) ("[T]here is confusion in the Fifth District as to whether a recovery of attorney's fees under section 627.428, Florida Statutes, requires bad faith or malicious conduct on the part of the insurance carrier as a prerequisite for such an award. Because the precedent in this area of law clearly rejects a bad faith or maliciousness requirement and the court below relied on distinguishable jurisprudence, we decline to construct an additional hurdle of bad faith for insureds to overcome. Therefore, consistent with the opinions of this Court and others, we make abundantly clear today that in the context of section 627.428, a denial of benefits simply means an incorrect denial."); *Starling v. Geovera Specialty Ins. Co.*, No. 18-60988, 2019 U.S. Dist. LEXIS 111511 (S.D. Fla. July 2, 2019) (fee award is not warranted) (insurer never denied benefits and was willing to further investigate the claim even before it learned of the suit and insured's counsel failed to reach out to insurer before filing suit); *Sos v. State Farm Mut. Auto. Ins. Co.*, No. 17-890, 2020 U.S. Dist. LEXIS 127688 (M.D. Fla. July 8, 2020) ("[T]o the extent that State Farm's remediation program constitutes a settlement, § 627.428 continues to apply with equal force. The statutory obligation for attorney's fees cannot be avoided simply by paying the policy proceeds after suit is filed but before a judgment is actually entered. When the insurance company has agreed to settle a disputed case, it has, in effect, declined to defend its position in the pending suit. Thus, the payment of the claim is, indeed, the functional equivalent of a confession of judgment or a verdict in favor of the insured.").

Georgia: A Georgia statute permits the recovery of attorney's fees in an action for coverage under an insurance policy. GA. CODE ANN. § 33–7-15 (b.1). "In the event the insurer denies coverage and it is determined by declaratory judgment or other civil process that there is in fact coverage, the insurer shall be liable to the insured for legal cost and attorney's fees as may be awarded by the court." *Id.*

However, the Court of Appeals of Georgia held that the statute is limited to those situations involving noncooperation by an insured with his insurance company. *Stedman v. Cotton States Ins. Co.*, 562 S.E.2d 256, 259 (Ga. Ct. App. 2002). "Although the language of subsection (b.1) does not expressly limit recovery of attorney fees only to situations of non-cooperation by the insured, placement of the subsection in the context of GA. CODE ANN. § 33–7-15 [titled "Cooperation by insured with insurer in connection with defense of action or threatened action under policy"] leads to the conclusion that the legislature did intend to so limit the application of the subsection." *Id.*

Hawaii: A Hawaii statute permits the recovery of attorney's fees in an action for coverage under an insurance policy: "Where an insurer has contested its liability under a policy and is ordered by the courts to pay benefits under the policy, the policyholder, the beneficiary under a policy, or the person who has acquired the rights of the policyholder or beneficiary under the policy shall be awarded reasonable attorney's fees and the costs of suit, in addition to the benefits under the policy." HAW. REV. STAT. ANN. § 431: 10–242; *see also Allstate Ins. Co. v. Pruett*, 186 P.3d 609, 621 (Haw. 2008) ("[T]he fundamental question with respect to the issue of awarding attorney's fees and the costs of suit is whether the insurer has in fact been ordered to pay benefits within the meaning of … § 431:10–242.") (citation and internal quotation omitted); *Weight v. USAA Cas. Ins. Co.*, 782 F. Supp. 2d 1114 (D. Hawaii 2011) (citing section 431:10-242 and holding that insurer was required to provide reasonable attorney's fees and costs incurred by insured in challenging insurer's obligation to defend insured after court ruled in favor of insured).

Idaho: An Idaho statute provides that "[a]ny insurer … [that] fail[s] for a period of thirty (30) days after proof of loss has been furnished as provided in [its] policy … to pay to the person entitled thereto…the amount that person is justly due under such policy … shall in any action thereafter commenced against the insurer in any court in this state… for recovery under the terms of the policy … pay such further amount as the court shall adjudge reasonable as attorney's fees in such action." IDAHO CODE ANN. § 41–1839. This section and Section 12–123 (allowing attorney's fees to be awarded to any party adversely affected by another party's frivolous conduct) "provide the exclusive remedy for the award of statutory attorney's fees in all actions…between insured and insurers involving disputes arising under policies of insurance. Provided, attorney's fees may be awarded … when … a case was brought, pursued or defended frivolously, unreasonably or without foundation." *Id.*; *see also Allstate Ins. Co. v. Mocaby*, 990 P.2d 1204, 1213 (Idaho 1999) (holding that the insured was not entitled to attorney's fees under Section 41–1839 because the insurer reasonably believed it had a basis for noncoverage and therefore could not be said to have acted unreasonably or frivolously); *Northland Ins. Co. v. Boise's Best Autos & Repairs*, 958 P.2d 589, 591 (Idaho 1998) (holding that the insured was not entitled to collect attorney's fees under Section 41–1839 because, having provided a defense to its insured, there was no evidence that the insurer failed to pay an amount "justly due" under the policy); *Hill v. Am. Family Mut. Ins. Co.*, 249 P.3d 812, 823–24 (Idaho 2011) (holding that insured could not recover attorney's fees from insurer because insured had "not yet established that an amount, if any, is justly due under the policy" even though court ruled that underinsured motorist exhaustion clause barring insured's recovery violated public policy and was, therefore, invalid); *Bank of Idaho v. First Am. Title Ins. Co.*, 329 P.3d 1066 (Idaho 2014) (remanded case to district court for determination whether insured was entitled to attorney's fees as prevailing party on appeal); *Parks v. Safeco Ins. Co.*, 376 P.3d 760 (Idaho 2016) ("Here, the Parks' arguments were unreasonable and lacked foundation. The language in the Policy was unambiguous. Moreover, Safeco, on numerous occasions, informed the Parks' of their options. Therefore, we award Safeco attorney fees according to Idaho Code section 41-1839(4). Additionally, Safeco, as the prevailing party, is entitled to costs pursuant to Idaho Appellate Rule 40.").

Illinois: An Illinois statute provides that when an insurer's denial of coverage is "vexatious and unreasonable," the imposition of attorney's fees is proper, subject to certain statutory maximums. 215 ILL. COMP. STAT. ANN. 5/155. Based on this statute, the Illinois Court of Appeal held that "[a]bsent vexatious behavior by the insurer, an insured cannot recover attorney fees incurred in bringing a declaratory judgment action against the insurer to establish coverage. Nor can an insured recover attorney fees and costs for defending a declaratory judgment action brought by an insurer absent vexatiousness." *Westchester Fire Ins. Co. v. G. Heileman Brewing Co.*, 747 N.E.2d 955, 968 (Ill. App. Ct. 2001); *see also Am. Alliance Ins. Co. v. 1212 Restaurant Group, L.L.C.*, 794 N.E.2d 892, 901 (Ill. App. Ct. 2003) (finding that, given the facts of the case, the insurer did not act vexatiously or unreasonably in denying coverage); *W. Bend Mut. Ins. v. Norton*, 940 N.E.2d 1176, 1179–80 (Ill. App. Ct. 2010) (explaining that insurer's actions could not be deemed "unreasonable or vexatious" where insurer had *bona fide* basis for defending claim and "any delay in resolution of this matter was attributable to [insured's] rejection of the arbitration award and not to any action on the part of [insurer]"); *Am. States Ins. Co. v. CFM Const. Co.*, 923 N.E.2d 299, 308–09 (Ill. App. Ct. 2010) (determining that one insurer was not inherently vexatious or unreasonable in dispute with another insurer because the parties had a *bona fide* dispute regarding the effects of an "other insurance" clause); *Rhone v. First Am. Title Ins. Co.*, 928 N.E.2d 1185, 1204 (Ill. App. Ct. 2010) ("The question of whether the insurer's acts are unreasonable and vexatious is one of fact. A court may award reasonable attorney fees and other costs for a vexatious and unreasonable action by a company where there is an issue of the liability of a company on an insurance policy or the amount of the loss payable thereunder, or for an unreasonable delay in settling a claim. A court should consider the totality of the circumstances when deciding whether an insurer's conduct is vexatious and unreasonable, including the insurer's attitude, whether the insured was forced to sue to recover, and whether the insured was deprived of the use of his property. If a *bona fide* coverage dispute exists, an insurer's delay in settling a claim will not be deemed vexatious or unreasonable for purposes of section 155 sanctions."); *Auto-Owners Ins. Co. v. Yocum*, 987 N.E.2d 494 (Ill. App. Ct. 2013) ("An insurer will not be liable for attorney fees and costs under section 155 of the [Insurance] Code merely because it litigated and lost the issue of insurance coverage. [W]here a *bona fide* dispute concerning coverage exists, costs and sanctions [under section 155] are inappropriate. In determining whether an insurer's conduct is vexatious and unreasonable, a trial court must consider the totality of the circumstances, including the insurer's attitude, whether the insured was forced to sue to recover, and whether the insured was deprived of the use of his property."); *Harleysville Lake States Ins. Co. v. Lancor Equities, Ltd.*, No. 13-6391, 2014 U.S. Dist. LEXIS 154685 (N.D. Ill. Oct. 31, 2014) (court addressed permissible scope of discovery in a dispute whether insurer's conduct was vexatious or unreasonable to satisfy 215 ILL. COMP. STAT. ANN. 5/155); *State Farm Fire & Cas. Co. v. Hutchins*, No. 14-0028, 2015 Ill. App. Unpub. LEXIS 768 (Ill. App. Ct. Apr. 8, 2015) (detailed examination of the facts at issue to determine whether insurer's conduct was vexatious or unreasonable); *Hartford Fire Ins. Co. v. Thermos LLC*, 146 F. Supp. 3d 1005 (N.D. Ill. 2015) (detailed examination of the facts at issue to determine whether insurer's conduct was vexatious or unreasonable); *Cooke v. Jackson Nat'l Life Ins. Co.*, No. 15-817, 2017 U.S. Dist. LEXIS 40413 (N.D. Ill. Mar. 20, 2017) (detailed examination of the facts at issue to determine whether insurer's conduct was vexatious or unreasonable); *Nat'l Cas. Co. v. South Shore Iron Works, Inc.*, 341 F. Supp. 3d 884 (N.D. Ill. 2018) ("Notwithstanding that National Casualty has not prevailed on its arguments regarding whether South Shore's qualifies as an insured, its arguments were 'presented with reasoned support,' and therefore raised a bona fide dispute as to coverage."); *Rogers Cartage Co. v. Travelers Indem. Co.*, 103 N.E.3d 504 (Ill. App. Ct. 2018) (addressing whether a settlement already included attorney's fees and its impact on the recovery of attorney's fees for insurer's vexatious and unreasonable conduct within the meaning of section 155); *Ill. Farmers Ins. Co. v. Modory*, No. 18-0721, 2019 Ill. App. Unpub. LEXIS 418 (Ill. App. Ct. Mar. 15, 2019) (detailed examination of the facts at issue to determine whether insurer's conduct was vexatious or unreasonable).

Indiana: The Court of Appeals of Indiana held that an insured's entitlement to attorney's fees incurred in a declaratory judgment action depends on "whether [the insurer] acted in bad faith in denying the coverage to [the insured]." *Learman v. Auto-Owners Ins. Co.*, 769 N.E.2d 1171, 1178 (Ind. Ct. App. 2002); *see also Mikel v. Am. Ambassador Cas. Co.*, 644 N.E.2d 168, 172 (Ind. Ct. App. 1994) ("We hold that when the insured brings an action for a declaration of coverage and prevails, absent a bad faith denial of coverage by the insurer, attorney's fees incurred by the insured in the prosecution of that action are not incurred at the 'request' of the insurer. Our holding is consistent with the long-standing rule in Indiana that the insurer may dispute claims in good faith."). *But see Pearman v. Stewart Title Guar. Co.*, No. 73A05-1708, 2018 Ind. App. Unpub. LEXIS 741 (Ind. Ct. App. Jun. 27, 2018) ("Indiana follows the American Rule, whereby each party pays his or her own attorney fees. Thus, an award of attorney fees is not permissible in the absence of a statute or some agreement or stipulation authorizing such an award.") (citing *Liberty Mut. Ins. Co. v. OSI Indus., Inc.*, 831 N.E.2d 192 (Ind. Ct. App. 2005)).

Iowa: The Supreme Court of Iowa held that, when an insurer seeks a declaratory judgment to determine its obligation to provide coverage, the insurer is liable for attorney's fees incurred by the insured to defend the lawsuit only where "there is a showing … that the insurance company … acted in 'bad faith or fraudulently or was stubbornly litigious.'" *Clark-Peterson Co. v. Indep. Ins. Assocs.*, 514 N.W.2d 914, 915–16 (Iowa 1994) (quoting *N.H. Ins. Co. v. Christy*, 200 N.W.2d 834, 845 (Iowa 1972)). The *Clark-Petersen* Court concluded that the insurer was not overly litigious, but merely believed that no coverage existed under the policy. *Id.* at 916. Further, the insurer did not act fraudulently in initially denying the claim because coverage was reasonably debatable. *Id. See also Thornton v. Am. Interstate Ins. Co.*, No. 15-1032, 2017 Iowa Sup. LEXIS 52 (Iowa May 19, 2017) ("*Christy* allows Thornton to recover his attorneys fees incurred *in the workers compensation proceedings* as consequential damages caused by American Interstate's bad faith. These fees are akin to attorney fees incurred to 'establish insurance coverage.' . . . But *Christy* does not support awarding additional fees incurred in prosecuting the bad-faith action. The American rule controls.") (emphasis in original).

Kansas: A Kansas statute provides "[t]hat in all actions hereafter commenced, in which judgment is rendered against any insurance company as defined in *K.S.A.* 40–201, and including in addition thereto any fraternal benefit society and any reciprocal or interinsurance exchange on any policy or certificate of any type or kind of insurance, if it appear from the evidence that such company, society or exchange has refused without just cause or excuse to pay the full amount of such loss, the court in rendering such judgment shall allow the plaintiff a reasonable sum as an attorney's fee for services in such action, including proceeding upon appeal, to be recovered and collected as a part of the costs: Provided, however, That when a tender is made by such insurance company, society or exchange before the commencement of the action in which judgment is rendered and the amount recovered is not in excess of such tender no such costs shall be allowed." KAN. STAT. ANN. § 40–256; *see also Farm Bureau Mut. Ins. Co. v. Kurtenbach by & Through Kurtenbach*, 961 P.2d 53, 64 (Kan. 1998) ("[W]here an insurer denies coverage and the duty to defend and brings a declaratory judgment action against the insured to determine that issue, the insured may recover his or her attorney fees incurred in the defense of the declaratory judgment action if it is determined as a result of that action that there is coverage. The same rule is applicable where an insurer agrees to assume the duty to defend under a reservation of rights, but before the underlying matter is resolved brings a declaratory judgment action seeking a determination that no duty to defend or coverage exists.") (citation omitted); *Snider v. Am. Family Mut. Ins. Co.*, 298 P.3d 1120 (Kan. 2013) (holding that trial court's determination to limit insured's recovery of reasonable attorney's fees to $5,000 was abuse of discretion after insured prevailed on coverage claim because insured's attorney could not have appropriately handled the case for $5,000); *Hartford Fire Ins. Co. v. Vita Craft Corp.*, 911 F. Supp. 2d 1164 (D. Kan. 2012) (concluding that insured was entitled to award of attorney's fees because insurer's reasons for refusing to defend the insured were "without just cause or excuse"); *Boardwalk Apts., L.C. v. State Auto Prop. & Cas. Ins. Co.*, No. 11-2714, 2015 U.S. Dist. LEXIS 24590 (D. Kan. Mar. 2, 2015) (award of attorneys' fees not permissible under § 40–256) (lengthy decision addressing the potential award of attorney's fees under several claim scenarios) ("The Court finds that State Auto advanced legitimate, albeit unsuccessful, grounds for refusing to pay the claims asserted in this action. On the property damage claim, State Auto asserted and continues to assert that coinsurance should have applied to reduce Boardwalk's recovery. The application of coinsurance in this case involved difficult and highly contentious issues. The Court was required to interpret the terms of the Policy in light of previous rulings in the Missouri litigation. The Court cannot find that it was unreasonable for State Auto to take the position that coinsurance applied, nor that its position was arbitrary, capricious, or made in bad faith.") (*vacated by* 2016 U.S. App. 4644 (10th Cir. Mar. 14, 2016), but not addressing attorney's fees aspects of the District Court's decision); *State Auto Prop. & Cas. Ins. Co. v. Ward Kraft*, No. 18-2671, 2020 U.S. Dist. LEXIS 11059 (D. Kan. Jan. 23, 2020) (rejecting insurer's argument that "fees are not available under *Kurtenbach* unless and until it is shown that it also has a duty to indemnify") ("State Auto has cited no authority supporting that position, however, and *Kurtenbach* itself says otherwise. That case makes clear that if an insurer unsuccessfully seeks a declaratory judgment with respect to the duty to defend, it must pay the costs incurred by the insured to enforce that duty.").

Kentucky: The Supreme Court of Kentucky held that, "with the exception of a specific contractual provision allowing for recovery of attorneys' fees or a fee-shifting statute … each party assumes responsibility for his or her own attorneys' fees." *AIK Selective Self-Insurance Fund v. Minton*, 192 S.W.3d 415, 420 (Ky. 2006) (quoting *Aetna Cas. & Sur. Co. v. Commonwealth*, 179 S.W.3d 830, 842 (Ky. 2005)). *See also Asher v. Unarco Material Handling, Inc.*, 862 F. Supp. 2d 551 (E.D. Ky. 2012) (holding that insured was not entitled to recover attorneys' fees incurred in pursing coverage litigation because such a result would eliminate the American Rule) ("Kentucky … is one of seven states that follow the American rule strictly and have not yet adopted any common-law exceptions allowing for the payment of attorney's fees to policyholders that are successful in coverage actions against their insurance companies. Unsurprisingly, Unarco does not cite a single case in which Kentucky courts have allowed an insured to recover the costs and attorney's fees of a coverage action against his insurer.") (calling into question whether Kentucky courts retain equitable discretion to award attorney's fees); *Secura Ins. Co. v. Gray Const., Inc.*, 717 F. Supp. 2d 710, 721–22 (W.D. Ky. 2010) (distinguishing *Aetna* and holding that insured was entitled to attorney's fees resulting from insurer's declaratory judgment based on language in an indemnity agreement).

Louisiana: The Supreme Court of Louisiana held that, because the insurance policy did not impose a duty on the insurer to pay attorney's fees in connection with the insured's pursuit of coverage, and nor was there any statute providing for such, the insured was not entitled to recover its attorney's fees. *Steptore v. Masco Construction Co.*, 643 So. 2d 1213, 1218 (La. 1994). *See also Shaffer v. Stewart*

Construction Co., 865 So. 2d 213 (La. Ct. App. 2004) (same); *Weaver v. CCA Industries, Inc.*, No. 01–2096, 2009 U.S. Dist. LEXIS 40095 (W.D. La. May 12, 2009) ("Under Louisiana law, attorney's fees are recoverable only when authorized by contract or statute."); *Homestead Ins. Co. v. Guarantee Mut. Life Co.*, 459 Fed. Appx. 398 (5th Cir. 2012) (finding that insured could not recover attorneys' fees in defending declaratory judgment action because there was not contractual or statutory authorization for the award); *Black Stallion Enter. v. Bay & Ocean Marine, LLC*, Nos. 09-4504, 09-6656, 2011 U.S. Dist. LEXIS 44884 (E.D. La. Apr. 25, 2011) (following *Shaffer* and noting that "insureds may recover attorneys' fees incurred in coverage disputes, provided that the insurers' reasons for denying coverage are arbitrary and capricious or unreasonable or without probable cause") ("When an insurer files a declaratory judgment action claiming that it has not duty to defend its insured, it is initiating a coverage dispute. While Louisiana law clearly states that the insured is responsible for paying his own legal fees in such coverage disputes, there is an exception for attorneys' fees incurred in coverage disputes that are unreasonable or without probable cause.") (rejecting insurer's argument that *Shaffer* was distinguishable because, unlike in *Shaffer*, the insurer "did not refuse to defend its insured, but merely filed a declaratory action to determine if it was required to defend its insured"); *Bourbon Heat, LLC v. Liberty Surplus Ins. Co.*, No. 13-2623, 2014 U.S. Dist. LEXIS 85051 (E.D. La. June 23, 2014) (holding that insurer may be liable for attorney's fees if its refusal to defend insured was arbitrary or capricious) (acknowledging that LA. REV. STAT. 22:1892 authorizes an award of reasonable attorneys' fees when an insurer declines coverage "unreasonabl[y] or without probable cause").

Maine: A Maine statute provides that when an insurer seeks a declaratory judgment "to determine [its] contractual duty to defend an insured under an insurance policy, if the insured prevails on such action, the insurer shall pay court costs and reasonable attorney's fees." ME. REV. STAT. ANN. tit. 24-A, § 2436-B. With this statute the Maine Legislature codified Maine common law which held an insurer liable for its insured's attorney's fees when an insured prevails in a declaratory judgment to establish the insurer's duty to defend. *See Foremost Ins. Co. v. Leversque*, 926 A.2d 1185, 1188 (Me. 2007) (addressing *Gibson v. Farm Family Mut. Ins. Co.*, 673 A.2d 1350 (Me. 1996)). In *Leversque*, the Supreme Judicial Court of Maine concluded that the statute was limited to the duty to defend and did not include the duty to indemnify. *Id.* Faced with that, the court determined to extend its common law rules, allowing for the recovery of attorney's fees to establish the duty to defend, to the duty to indemnify: "Unsuccessful litigation filed by an insurer against its insured subjects the insured to significant costs that may render victory for the insured on the indemnification issue meaningless. In that case, the insured will be in no better position than he would be without having purchased insurance." *Id.* at 1190; *see also Centennial Ins. Co. v. Patterson*, No. 07-63-B-H, 2009 U.S. Dist. LEXIS 62754 (D. Me. July 21, 2009) (following *Levesque* but rejecting insured's argument that expenses resulting from telephone calls, online legal research, and travel can be recovered by insured as "court costs" because, even though "such costs are typically billed by lawyers to their clients," the statutory language controls the determination); *OneBeacon Am. Ins. Co. v. Johnny's Selected Seeds Inc.*, No. 1:12-00375, 2014 U.S. Dist. LEXIS 53098 (D. Me. Apr. 17, 2014) (noting that statute applies only to a natural person and excludes corporations) (holding that, based on pre-statutory case law, because duty to defend was clear from outset of the declaratory judgment action, insured was entitled to attorney's fees); *Pinkham v. Liberty Ins. Corp.*, No. 18-222, 2018 U.S. Dist. LEXIS 128923 (D. Me. Aug. 1, 2018) (noting that *Leversque* only allows for attorney's fees in declaratory judgment actions brought by an insurer and declining to extend *Leversque* to a declaratory judgment actions brought by an insured) ("As the plaintiff suggests, some of the [*Levesque*] reasoning might support an extension of the *Gibson* rule to coverage claims brought by plaintiffs. . . . But the Law Court has not yet said so, and federal court is not the place to make new state law."); *Metro Prop. & Cas. Ins. Co. v. McCarthy*, No. 15-0263, 2018 Me. Super. LEXIS 80 (Me. Super. Ct. May 16, 2018) (discussing *Levesque* and concluding that prevailing party not entitled to attorney's fees as the court did not determine "the central issue that supports an award of attorney's fees: whether Metropolitan indeed has a duty to indemnify").

Maryland: The Court of Appeals of Maryland held that "Maryland follows the American rule which stands as a barrier to the recovery, as consequential damages, of foreseeable counsel fees incurred in enforcing remedies for breach of contract. Therefore, in the absence of a statute, rule or contract expressly allowing the recovery of attorneys' fees, a prevailing party in a lawsuit may not ordinarily recover attorneys' fees. There is one nonstatutory exception to the American rule in actions involving insurance policies. Where an action is brought to enforce an insurer's obligations under the third party liability provisions of a policy, and it is determined that there is coverage under the policy, the insurer is liable for the prevailing party's attorneys' fees." *Bausch & Lomb, Inc. v. Utica Mut. Ins. Co.*, 735 A.2d 1081, 1094–95 (Md. 1999) (citations and internal quotation omitted). *See also Young v. Travelers Ins. Co.*, No. 13-02092, 2013 U.S. Dist. LEXIS 133934 (D. Md. Sept. 19, 2013) (citing

Bausch & Lomb and holding that "Maryland law does not permit an award of attorney's fees in an action against an insurer to enforce first party coverage"); *Gao v. Progressive Max. Ins. Co.*, No. 278, 2019 Md. App. LEXIS 321 (Md. Ct. App. Apr. 16, 2019) (claimant not an "insured person" under tortfeasor's policy, and, therefore, not entitled to attorneys' fees under the exception to the American Rule); *Selective Way Ins. Co. v. Nationwide Prop. & Cas. Ins. Co.*, 219 A.3d 20 (Md. Ct. App. 2019) (addressing Maryland law in detail and concluding that insurer had the right to a jury trial to determine amount of attorney's fees owed); *Feld v. Fireman's Fund Ins. Co.*, No. 12-1789, 2020 U.S. Dist. LEXIS 139049 (D.D.C. Aug. 5, 2020 (insured entitled to attorney's fees under Maryland exception to the American Rule and addressing whether fees were "incurred" in the context of a contingency fee agreement between insured and its counsel).

Massachusetts: The Supreme Judicial Court of Massachusetts adopted an exception to its traditional rule disallowing attorney's fees and expenses and held that an insured is entitled to the reasonable attorney's fees and expenses incurred in successfully establishing the insurer's duty to defend. *Preferred Mut. Ins. Co. v. Gamache*, 686 N.E.2d 989, 993 (Mass. 1997). *See also John T. Callahan & Sons, Inc. v. Worcester Ins. Co.*, 902 N.E.2d 923, 926–27 (Mass. 2009) (declining to extend *Gamache* to allow one insurer to recovery attorney's fees incurred to establish another insurer's duty to defend); *Wilkinson v. Citation Ins. Co.*, 856 N.E.2d 829, 837 (Mass. 2006) (declining to extend *Gamache* to the duty to indemnify); *Global Investors Agent Corp. v. Nat. Fire Ins. Co. of Hartford*, 927 N.E.2d 480, 495–96 (Mass. Ct. App. 2010) (addressing *Gamache* and permitting the insured to recover attorney's fees and costs only for the time period necessary to establish the insurer's duty to defend, as well as significantly reducing the amount of recoverable fees based on an assessment of reasonableness factors); *House of Clean, Inc. v. St. Paul Fire and Marine Ins. Co., Inc.*, No. 07-10839, 2011 U.S. Dist. LEXIS 57281 (D. Mass. May 27, 2011) (citing *Gamache* for insurance exception to the American Rule); *Peabody Essex Museum v. United States Fire Ins. Co.*, No. 6-11209, 2013 U.S. Dist. LEXIS 21291 (D. Mass. Feb. 15, 2013) (citing *Gamache* and *Wilkinson* and holding that "the *Gamache* rule is to be narrowly construed and does not apply broadly to indemnity disputes or other controversies between policy holders and their insurers," and, therefore, insured was not entitled to recover attorney's fees incurred that were not related to efforts to obtain declaration of insurer's duty to defend); *Preferred Mut. Ins. Co. v. Lodigiani*, No. 13-30138, 2015 U.S. Dist. LEXIS 89262 (D. Mass. July 8, 2015) ("PMIC sought a judgment that would end its duty to defend prior to any liability of the insured having been established, bringing it within the universe of duty to defend cases and entitling Lodigiani to attorney's fees once the jury ruled in his favor."); *Innovative Mold Sols., Inc. v. Cent. Mut. Ins. Co.*, 227 F. Supp. 3d 222 (D. Mass. 2017) (discussing rationale for an awarded of attorney's fees to insured that prevails in action to establish insurer's duty to defend and the method for determining amount of fees owed); *Duane v. Vt. Mut. Ins. Co.*, No. 17-11982, 2020 U.S. Dist. LEXIS 30590 (D. Mass. Feb. 21, 2020) (declining to award attorney's fees) ("Vermont Mutual, despite some huffing and puffing, never walked away from its obligation to defend Duane, and unlike the insureds in those two cases, Duane was never forced to dig into his own pocket to fund any aspect of the litigation.").

Michigan: The Court of Appeals of Michigan held that "[a]lthough actual attorneys' fees for the insured's defense of an action by a third party are recoverable from the insurer which breaches its duty to defend, the established rule in Michigan is that the insured may not be allowed attorneys' fees in excess of taxable costs for the declaratory action to enforce insurance coverage." *Shepard Marine Constr. Co. v. Maryland Cas. Co.*, 250 N.W.2d 541, 543 (Mich. Ct. App. 1976); *accord Iacobelli Constr. Co. v. W. Cas. & Sur. Co.*, 343 N.W.2d 517, 523 (Mich. Ct. App. 1983); *see also Aladdin's Carpet Cleaning v. Farm Bureau Gen. Ins. Co.*, No. 278605, 2009 Mich. App. LEXIS 423 (Mich. Ct. App. Feb. 26, 2009) ("We note that while plaintiff is entitled to damages consisting of its costs, expenses, and fees incurred in defending the underlying Earns litigation, it is not entitled to attorney fees incurred in the present suit against defendant Farm Bureau."); *Auto-Owners Ins. Co. v. Ferwerda Enterprises, Inc.*, No. 277574, 2010 Mich. App. LEXIS 213 (Mich. App. Ct. Jan. 28, 2010) (holding that, because the insurer's declaratory judgment action was not frivolous, attorney's fees were not proper under MCR 2.625); *Graham v. Hall*, No. 346734, 2020 Mich. App. LEXIS 3897 (Mich. Ct. App. Jun. 18, 2020) (addressing entitlement to attorney's fees, under MCLS § 500.3148, which concerns motor vehicle policies: "[A]n attorney is entitled to a reasonable fee for advising and representing a claimant in an action for personal or property protection insurance benefits that are overdue. The attorney's fee is a charge against the insurer in addition to the benefits recovered, if the court finds that the insurer unreasonably refused to pay the claim or unreasonably delayed in making proper payment.").

Minnesota: The Supreme Court of Minnesota held that "[t]he insured is not entitled to recover attorney fees incurred in maintaining or defending a declaratory action to determine the question of coverage unless the insurer has breached the insurance contract in some respect—usually by wrongfully refusing to defend the insured." *American Standard Ins. Co. v. Le*, 551 N.W.2d 923, 927 (Minn. 1996). *See also Jarvis & Sons, Inc. v. Int'l Marine Underwriters*, 768 N.W.2d 385, 371 (Minn. Ct. App. 2009) ("Where an insurer has breached a duty to defend an insured, the insured is entitled to recover reasonable attorney fees expended in maintaining a declaratory judgment action to determine coverage."); *Milwaukee Mut. Ins. Co. v. Val Pro, Inc.*, No. 12-1658, 2013 U.S. Dist. LEXIS 172198 (D. Minn. Dec. 6, 2013) (holding that policy provision that insurer will pay "all reasonable expenses incurred by the insured at our request to assist us in the investigation or defense of the claim or 'suit'" obligated insurer to pay insured's costs in successfully defending a declaratory judgment action).

Mississippi: The Supreme Court of Mississippi held that "[i]n the absence of a showing of gross negligence or willful wrong entitling the [m]ovant to punitive damages," a successful litigant is not entitled to attorney's fees. *Miller v. Allstate Ins. Co.*, 631 So. 2d 789, 795 (Miss. 1994) (citing *Cent. Bank v. Butler*, 517 So. 2d 507, 512 (Miss. 1988) and *Aetna Cas. & Sur. Co. v. Steele*, 373 So. 2d 797, 801 (Miss. 1979)). *See also Barden Mississippi Gaming, LLC v. Great Northern Ins. Co.*, 638 F.3d 476 (5th Cir. 2011) (holding that, although it was determined that the insurer's decision not to provide a defense was incorrect, there existed a legitimate, arguable reason for the decision and it was not wrongful or tortious, thereby precluding recovery of attorney's fees); *Abel v. Allstate Prop. & Cas. Ins. Co.*, No. 14-00064, 2015 U.S. Dist. LEXIS 35852 (N.D. Miss. Mar. 23, 2015) ("Mississippi has long followed the rule that, with the sole exception of punitive damages cases, attorneys' fees cannot be awarded absent some contractual or statutory authority. The Mississippi uninsured motorists statutory scheme does not authorize the award of attorneys' fees. Nor has Allstate alleged that any contractual authority under the insurance policy authorizes an award of attorneys' fees in this action. Thus, because Abel is unlikely to recover punitive damages, she is similarly unlikely to recover attorneys' fees under Mississippi law.").

Missouri: A Missouri statute provides a court discretion to award attorney's fees in a declaratory judgment action. Mo. Rev. Stat. § 527.100. "In any proceeding under sections 527.010 to 527.130 [declaratory judgments] the court may make such award of costs as may seem equitable and just." *Id.*; *see also Am. Econ. Ins. Co. v. Ledbetter*, 903 S.W.2d 272, 276 (Mo. Ct. App. 1995) ("While the absence of 'bad faith' in filing suit is a factor in arriving at equity and justice in assessing costs, such absence does not compel denial of attorney fees."); *Windsor Ins. Co. v. Lucas*, 24 S.W.3d 151, 156 (Mo. Ct. App. 2000) ("[C]osts under section 527.100 does not necessarily include attorney's fees. Rather, the American Rule applies to declaratory judgment actions. Under the American Rule, absent statutory authorization or contractual agreement, with few exceptions, each litigant must bear his own attorney's fee.") (citations and internal quotation omitted); *Westchester Surplus Lines Ins. Co. v. Maverick Tube Corp.*, 722 F. Supp. 2d 787, 799 (S.D. Tex. 2010) (applying Missouri law) ("Although Missouri courts have held that 'costs' may include attorneys' fees, subsequent cases have clarified that attorneys' fees may be awarded as costs under § 527.100 only under 'very unusual circumstances.'") (citation omitted); *State Auto Pro. & Cas. Ins. Co. v. Larkin*, No. 4:12-1853, 2015 U.S. Dist. LEXIS 79540 (E.D. Mo. June 18, 2015) ("The special circumstances exception is narrow, strictly applied, and does not apply every time two litigants maintain inconsistent positions.") (holding that insurer was entitled to award of attorney's fees on the basis that jurors specifically found intentional misconduct by insureds with regard to their claim).

Montana: The Supreme Court of Montana held that "an insured is entitled to recover attorney fees, pursuant to the insurance exception to the American Rule, when the insurer forces the insured to assume the burden of legal action to obtain the full benefit of the insurance contract, regardless of whether the insurer's duty to defend is at issue." *Mountain W. Farm Bureau Mut. Ins. Co. v. Brewer*, 69 P.3d 652, 660 (Mont. 2003); *see also Jacobsen v. Allstate Ins. Co.*, 215 P.3d 649, 656 (Mont. 2009) (discussing *Brewer* and declining to extend the insurance exception to a third-party claimant, even one that proves tortious conduct by the insurer, because the insurer did not owe a fiduciary duty to the claimant—a nonparty to the insurance contract) (*affirmed* by 310 P.3d 452 (Mont. 2013)); *Riordan v. State Farm Mut. Auto. Ins. Co.*, 589 F.3d 999, 1007 (9th Cir. 2009) (applying Montana law) (holding that insured was entitled to attorney's fees under the insurance exception to the American Rule recognized in *Brewer* after insured "was forced to litigate to obtain the full benefit of his contract with [insurer]"); *In re Conservatorship of Adair*, 242 P.3d 1287 (Mont. 2010) (recognizing Montana's adoption of the insurance exception but holding that it did not apply where insurer agreed to paid full amount under the policy before insured hired counsel and before any court action); *Gotham Ins. Co. v. Allegiance Ben. Plan Management, Inc.*, No. CV-11–39, 2011 U.S. Dist. LEXIS 88159 (D. Mont. Aug. 9, 2011) (holding that *Brewer* is not limited to situations in which the insurer outright refuses to defend, but that the right of recovery of attorney's fees applies even if the insurer was defending the insured); *Winter v. State Farm Mut. Auto. Ins. Co.*, 328 P.3d 665 (Mont. 2014) (citing *Brewer* and holding that insured was "entitled to attorney fees as a matter of law under the insurance exception because he was forced to pursue legal action in order to obtain the full benefit of the insurance contract"); *Newman v. Scottsdale Ins. Co.*, 301 P.3d 348 (Mont. 2013) (concluding that third-party assignee who had been assigned insured's first-party rights was entitled to award of attorney's fees for "the attorney's time and expenses incurred in pursuing insurance coverage," but could not recover attorney's fees on assignee's contingency agreement in wrongful death action); *Winter v. State Farm Mut. Auto. Ins. Co.*, 328 P.3d 665 (Mont. 2014) (an award of attorney fees, pursuant to the insurance exception to the American Rule, is not discretionary); *Estate of Gleason v. Cent. United Life Ins. Co.*, 360 P.3d 349 (Mont. 2015) (discussing attorney's fees under the insurance exception to the American Rule compared to attorneys' fees as damages under the Unfair Trade Practices Act); *Mlekush v. Farmers Ins. Exch.*, 358 P.3d 913 (Mont. 2015) ("The determination of whether an insured is entitled to attorney fees under the insurance exception, though a matter of law, necessitates factual findings that take into consideration both parties' actions during the entire process leading up to the ultimate resolution of the claim. The District Court's conclusion as to whether the exception applies must then be based on these factual findings."); *Johnson v. Federated Rural Elec. Ins. Exch.*, No. 13-18, 2017 U.S. Dist. LEXIS 63253 (D. Mont. Apr. 26, 2017) (addressing whether fees owed under Uniform Declaratory Judgment Act, § 27-8-313 MCA, which allows supplemental relief when equitable considerations support the award); *Mlekush v. Farmers Ins. Exch.*, 404 P.3d 704 (Mont. 2017) ("[W]hen a first-party insured is compelled to pursue litigation and a jury returns a verdict in excess of the insurer's last offer to settle an underinsured motorist claim, the insurer must pay the first-party insured's attorney fees in an amount subsequently determined by the district court to be reasonable."); *Cramer v. Farmers Ins. Exch.*, 423 P.3d 1067 (Mont. 2018) (rejecting insurer's argument that a party must prevail on all claims to be awarded fees and discussing that only reasonable fees may be considered) ("[A]ctions by the plaintiff, such as unreasonably multiplying the litigation, may be considered.") ("[R]easonable fees may not include efforts undertaken to pursue positions on which [insured] did not ultimately prevail."); *Abbey/Land v. Glacier Constr. Partners, LLC*, 433 P.3d 1230 (Mont. 2018) (declining to award attorney's fees under the *Brewer* exception to the American Rule, but awarding them under Uniform Declaratory Judgment Act, § 27-8-313 MCA, where court determined that a stipulated judgment, between plaintiff and defendant-insured, was unreasonable and collusive); *United States Fire Ins. Co. v. Greater Missoula Family YMCA*, No. 19-21, 2020 U.S. Dist. LEXIS

62879 (D. Mont. Apr. 9, 2020) (giving insurer opportunity to address whether fees can or should be awarded where it was the insurer that originally brought the action to determine coverage and application of certain exclusions raised "close questions under Montana insurance law").

Nebraska: A Nebraska statute permits the recovery of attorney's fees in an action for coverage under an insurance policy. NEB. REV. STAT. ANN. § 44-359. "In all cases when the beneficiary or other person entitled thereto brings an action upon any type of insurance policy, except workers' compensation insurance, or upon any certificate issued by a fraternal benefit society, against any company, person, or association doing business in this state, the court, upon rendering judgment against such company, person, or association, shall allow the plaintiff a reasonable sum as an attorney's fee in addition to the amount of his or her recovery, to be taxed as part of the costs. If such cause is appealed, the appellate court shall likewise allow a reasonable sum as an attorney's fee for the appellate proceedings, except that if the plaintiff fails to obtain judgment for more than may have been offered by such company, person, or association in accordance with section 25–901, then the plaintiff shall not recover the attorney's fee provided by this section." *Id. See also Esch v. State Farm Mut. Auto. Ins. Co.*, No. A-08–199, 2009 Neb. App. LEXIS 4 (Neb. Ct. App. Jan. 6, 2009) (addressing § 44-359 and noting that attorney's fees and expenses may be recovered only where provided for by statute or pursuant to a recognized and accepted uniform course of procedure); *Oriental Trading Co. v. Am. Safety Indem. Co.*, No. 8:08CV327, 2011 U.S. Dist. LEXIS 1443 (D. Neb. Jan 5, 2011) ("The Nebraska Supreme Court has construed [section 44-359] to permit an award of attorneys' fees to an insured who prevails in a disputed coverage action brought by an insurer.") (denying recovery of expert fees, despite being reasonable and contributing to the success in the litigation, because they are not allowable under the statute); *Kaapa Ethanol, LLC v. Affiliated FM Ins. Co.*, No. 7:05CV5010, 2010 U.S. Dist. LEXIS 57712 (D. Neb. Jun. 11, 2010), *rev'd on other grounds*, 2011 U.S. App. LEXIS 22158 (8th Cir. Nov. 3, 2011) (examining what constitutes a reasonable sum for attorney's fees under section 44-359 and also noting that insured's fees/expenses related to claims for bad faith, punitive damages, and nonpolicy claims against third parties are not recoverable under the statute) ("An attorney fee awarded under the provisions of § 44-359 must be solely and only for services actually rendered in the preparation and trial of the litigation on the policy in question.") (citation omitted); *Dutton-Lainson Co. v. Cont'l Ins. Co.*, 778 N.W.2d 433, 446 (Neb. 2010) (holding that insurers had no obligation to pay attorney's fees to insured after insured refused insurers' confessions of judgment before trial began and such amounts exceeded the final judgment awarded to insured); *Tierone Bank v. Hartford Cas. Ins. Co.*, No. 4:08CV3156, 2009 U.S. Dist. LEXIS 114010 (D. Neb. Dec. 8, 2009) (addressing in detail the calculation of reasonable attorney's fees under the statute); *Bowen v. Allied Prop. and Cas. Ins. Co.*, No. 11-3163, 2013 U.S. Dist. LEXIS 33174 (D. Neb. Mar. 11, 2013) (holding that insured was entitled to "total attorneys' fees, costs, and expenses" pursuant to NEB. REV. STAT. ANN. § 44–359) (calculating in detail the determination of reasonable attorney's fees under the statute); *Patterson v. Mut. Omaha Ins. Co.*, No. 10-26, 2014 U.S. Dist. LEXIS 168812 (D. Neb. Dec. 4, 2014) ("Nebraska courts—both state and federal—consider nine factors in evaluating a claim for attorney's fees under NEB. REV. STAT. § 44-359 (citations omitted). The nine factors are: (1) The amount involved, (2) the nature of the litigation, (3) the time and labor required, (4) the novelty and difficulty of the questions raised and the skill required to properly conduct the case, (5) the responsibility assumed, (6) the care and diligence exhibited, (7) the result of the suit, (8) the character and standing of the attorney, and (9) the customary charges of the bar for similar services.").

Nevada: A Nevada statute provides that "[i]n addition to the cases where an allowance is authorized by specific statute, the court may make an allowance of attorney's fees to a prevailing party: (a) When he has not recovered more than $20,000; or (b) Without regard to the recovery sought, when the court finds that the claim, counterclaim, cross-claim or third-party complaint or defense of the opposing party was brought or maintained without reasonable ground or to harass the prevailing party. The court shall liberally construe the provisions of this paragraph in favor of awarding attorney's fees in all appropriate situations." NEV. REV. STAT. ANN. § 18.010. *See also Am. Excess Ins. Co. v. MGM Grand Hotels, Inc.*, 729 P.2d 1352, 1355 (Nev. 1986) (holding that the district court improperly awarded attorney's fees to the insured under section 18.010 because there was no evidence that the insurer brought the declaratory judgment action "without reasonable ground or to harass" the insured given that the issue was one of first impression); *Tracey v. Am. Family Mut. Ins. Co.*, No. 2:09-CV-1257, 2010 U.S. Dist. LEXIS 139323 (D. Nev. Dec. 30, 2010) (holding that insured was not entitled to attorney's fees under section 18.010 because defendant-insurer had reasonable grounds for disputing coverage and award was more than $20,000); *Liberty Mut. Ins. Group v. Panelized Structures, Inc.*, No. 10-01951, 2013 U.S. Dist. LEXIS 84090 (D. Nev. June 14, 2013) (finding that insurer's actions had not risen to a level necessary to award insured attorney's fees); *Nationwide Ins. Co. of Am. v. Walter*, No. 2:14-00743, 2015 U.S. Dist. LEXIS

121633 (D. Nev. Sept. 10, 2015) ("Although Nationwide's case was dismissed, this litigant put forward a detailed, non-frivolous argument for an extension of the law to cover its claim. Nationwide supported its contentions with persuasive authority and spent considerable time factually distinguishing the cases Walter cited in his motion to dismiss. Nationwide's arguments were not patently frivolous, and there is no evidence in the record that it filed suit to harass Walter. Accordingly, Walter is not entitled to fees under NRS 18.010(2)(a) or (b)."); *Young v. Mercury Cas. Co.*, No. 12-00091, 2016 U.S. Dist. LEXIS 100227 (D. Nev. July 29, 2016) ("Based on its review of the applicable law, the Court finds that if Young prevails on any of his claims, he may seek attorney's fees in a post-trial motion as set forth in N.R.S. 18.010. However, Young has not shown, and the Court does not find, that Nevada's UCPA [Unfair Claims Practice Act] itself provides for attorney's fees. Although the statute authorizes recovery for 'any damages sustained by the insured as a result of the commission of any act set forth in subsection 1 as an unfair practice,' N.R.S. 686A.310(2), the statute does not authorize recovery for fees, costs, penalties, or any other categories that would suggest that attorney's fees are recoverable."); *Fire Ins. Exch. v. Efficient Enters.*, No. 60555, 2017 Nev. Unpub. LEXIS 545 (Nev. June 27, 2017) (discussing various cases that examine whether the statutory requirement of a frivolous or groundless claim has been met) (subsequent Supreme Court opinion not altering outcome (2019 Nev. Unpub. LEXIS 688 (Nev. Jun. 26, 2019))).

New Hampshire: A New Hampshire statute permits the recovery of attorney's fees in an action for coverage under an insurance policy. N.H. Rev. Stat. Ann. § 491:22-b. "In any action to determine coverage of an insurance policy pursuant to RSA 491:22 [regarding declaratory judgments], if the insured prevails in such action, he shall receive court costs and reasonable attorneys' fees from the insurer." *Id. See also EnergyNorth Natural Gas, Inc. v. Certain Underwriters at Lloyd's*, 934 A.2d 517, 528 (N.H. 2007) ("Recovery of these fees and costs [under RSA 491:22-b] does not depend upon whether, after all is said and done, the excess insurer actually has to pay any indemnification. The insured becomes entitled to the fees and costs once it obtains rulings that demonstrate that there is coverage under the excess insurance policy."); *Desjardins v. Fidelity Nat. Title Ins. Co.*, No. 12-272, 2013 U.S. Dist. LEXIS 84892 (D.N.H. June 14, 2013) (holding that insureds were "entitled to an award of costs and attorney's fees reasonably incurred in successfully prosecuting this declaratory judgment suit").

New Jersey: A New Jersey court rule permits the recovery of attorney's fees in an action for coverage under an insurance policy. N.J. Ct. R. Ann. 4:42–9.

"No fee for legal services shall be allowed in the taxed costs or otherwise, except (6) In an action upon a liability or indemnity policy of insurance, in favor of a successful claimant." *Id.; see also Shore Orthopaedic Group, LLC v. Equitable Life Assur. Soc'y*, 938 A.2d 962 (N.J. Super. Ct. App. Div. 2008), *affirmed* 972 A.2d 381 (N.J. 2009) (addressing applicability of the rule to liability policies); *Myron Corp. v. Atlantic Mut. Ins. Corp.*, 970 A.2d 1083 (N.J. Super. Ct. App. Div. 2009), *affirmed* 4 A.3d 999 (N.J. 2010) (addressing applicability of the rule to coverage litigation taking place outside of New Jersey in conjunction with New Jersey–venued coverage litigation); *Illinois Nat. Ins. Co. v. Wyndham Worldwide Operations, Inc.*, No. 09-1724, 2011 U.S. Dist. LEXIS 28593 (D.N.J. Mar. 21, 2011) (holding that it did not matter, for purposes of the applicability of 4:42–9(a)(6), that the prevailing party-insured was the defendant in an action brought by the insurer; nor did it matter that the insured did not fund its own defense); *Passaic Valley Sewerage Comm'rs v. St. Paul Fire and Marine Ins. Co.*, 21 A.3d 1151, 1164 (N.J. 2011) (award of counsel fees to a prevailing party is not mandatory and is in the discretion of the trial judge); *Baskay v. Franklin Mut. Ins. Co.*, No. A-0441-11T2, 2014 N.J. Super. Unpub. LEXIS 910 (N.J. Super. Ct. App. Div. Apr. 23, 2014) (dispute under property policy) (holding that "Rule 4:42-9(a) (6)…has not been extended beyond its express terms to encompass counsel fee awards sought by an insured who commences a direct suit against the insurer to enforce direct coverage"); *Travelers Prop. Cas. Co. of Am. v. USA Container Co., Inc.*, No. 09-1612, 2014 U.S. Dist. LEXIS 99635 (D.N.J. July 21, 2014) (rejecting insurer's argument that the policy rationale supporting attorney's fees was inapplicable because its disclaimer of coverage was not groundless; while insurer bad faith is a factor for an award of attorney's fees, it is not a requirement) (*aff'd* 2017 U.S. App. LEXIS 6602 (3d Cir. Apr. 18, 2017)) ("Under New Jersey law, fee determinations by trial courts will be disturbed only on the rarest occasions, and then only because of a clear abuse of discretion."); *Am. Southern Home Ins. Co. v. Unity Bank*, No. 16-3046, 2017 U.S. Dist. LEXIS 62381 (D.N.J. Apr. 25, 2017) ("[W]hile Unity argues that it is entitled to attorneys' fees because it was required to bring its counterclaims in response to American Southern's declaratory judgment action, that argument is misplaced. The simple fact that Unity has filed a counterclaim against American Southern does not automatically bring it within the purview of N.J. Ct. R. 4:42-9(a)(6). Rather, courts look to the substance of the claim to determine whether the Rule is applicable. Here, it is clear that Unity is not attempting to require American Southern to defend or indemnify Unity against liability for claims made against it by a third party. Instead, Unity's counterclaims involve claims for direct first-party coverage. Specifically, Unity seek a declaration that its loss at the Property was caused by vandalism, and that American Southern wrongfully denied Unity's claim for coverage under the terms of the Policy. Thus, attorneys' fees are not available under N.J. Ct. R. 4:42-9(a)(6)."). In *Occhifinto v. Olivo Construction Co., LLC*, 114 A.3d 333 (N.J. 2015), the New Jersey Supreme Court held that a plaintiff in a negligence action can be a "successful claimant," under Rule 4:42-9(a) (6), when it obtains a favorable adjudication of a coverage question under the defendant-insured's policy. The court observed that "[the insurer's] attempt to disclaim coverage by filing a declaratory judgment action forced Occhifinto -- a third-party beneficiary of Keppler's liability insurance policy -- to defend so that, if successful in the underlying liability action, he would be able to recover damages awarded against Keppler." *Id.* at 339. *See also C.M.S. Inv. Ventures, Inc. v. Am. European Ins. Co.*, No. A-2056-17T3, 2019 N.J. Super. Unpub. LEXIS 1215 (N.J. Super. Ct. App. Div. Feb. 7, 2019) ("[E]ven if successful, CMS's negligence claims against AEIC did not bear on whether, under the policy, AEIC was obligated to defend CMS against A.G.'s claim. Therefore, it was proper for the trial judge to exclude any fees incurred litigating those claims because both fell outside the gambit of Rule 4:42-9(a)(6).") (addressing factors relevant to determining the amount of fees to be awarded); *Kurz v. State Farm Fire & Cas. Co.*, No. 16-8681, 2017 U.S. Dist. LEXIS 152540 (D.N.J. Sep. 19, 2017) (premature to address whether attorney's fees can be awarded in a first party property claim).

New Mexico: The Court of Appeals of New Mexico held that "[f]ees for counsel representing the insured in disputes with the insurer are ordinarily not recoverable in the absence of statute or contract." *Lujan v. Gonzales*, 501 P.2d 673, 682 (N.M. Ct. App. 1972) (citations omitted); *see also Rodeo, Inc. v. Columbia Cas. Ins. Co.*, Nos. 28,384, 28,445, 2009 N.M. App. Unpub. LEXIS 332 (N.M. Ct. App. Aug. 20, 2009) (reversing trial court decision to award attorney's fees to insured pursuant to N.M. Stat. § 39-2-1, which states that "[i]n any action where an insured prevails against an insurer who has not paid a claim on any type of first party coverage, the insured person may be awarded reasonable attorney's fees and cost of the action upon a finding by the court that the insurer acted unreasonably in failing to pay the claim," because court determined that insurer had not acted unreasonably in denying insured's claim) (court concluded that, based on its decision, it did not need to address insurer's argument whether the claim—involving duty to defend—involved first party coverage); *Romero v. Progressive Northwestern Ins. Co.*, No. 31,549, 2013 N.M. App. Unpub. LEXIS 189 (N.M. Ct. App. June 4, 2013) (holding that insured was entitled to award of attorney's fees because insurer's denial of coverage was unreasonable) (stating that section 39-2-1, which "provides for attorney fees when the insured prevails in an action based on any type of first party coverage against an insurer … encompasses three analyses: whether the insured prevailed in an action against an insurer, whether the insurer acted unreasonably, and what amount of attorney fees is reasonable"); *Torpy v. Unum Life Ins. Co. of Am.*, No. 16-410, 2017 U.S. Dist. LEXIS 186611 (M.D. Fla. Aug. 11, 2017) (applying New Mexico law and addressing N.M. Stat. § 39-2-1) ("[I]t could be said that Defendant was unreasonable in failing to at least acknowledge coverage to [Plaintiff] due to [Defendant]'s mistaken interpretation of the policy, but it does not necessarily follow that, on that basis alone, Defendant acted unreasonably in failing to pay the claim. . . . Defendant made reasonable and non-frivolous arguments in defending this case.").

New York: The Court of Appeals of New York held that an insured who is "cast in a defensive posture by the legal steps an insurer takes in an effort to free itself from its policy obligations," and who prevails on the merits, may recover attorneys' fees incurred in defending against the insurer's action. *Mighty Midgets v. Centennial Ins. Co.*, 389 N.E.2d 1080, 1085 (N.Y. 1979). In other words, "such a recovery may not be had in an affirmative action brought by an assured to settle its rights." *Id.*; *see also U.S. Underwriters Ins. Co. v. City Club Hotel, LLC*, 822 N.E.2d 777, 780 (N.Y. 2004) ("We hold that under *Mighty Midgets*, an insured who prevails in an action brought by an insurance company seeking a declaratory judgment that it has no duty to defend or indemnify the insured may recover attorneys' fees regardless of whether the insurer provided a defense to the insured."); *RLI Ins. Co. v. Smiedala*, No. CA 09-02296, 2010 N.Y. App. Div. LEXIS 6927 (N.Y. App. Div. Oct. 1, 2010) (holding that insured may recover attorney's fees from an excess insurer, even if its duty to defend had not been triggered because primary insurance had not been exhausted, because insured was "cast in a defensive posture") (quoting *Mighty Midgets*); *Ins. Co. of Greater New York v. Clermont Armory, LLC*, 923 N.Y.S.2d 661, 663–64 (N.Y. App. Div. 2011) (determining that insured was not entitled to recovery of attorney's fees under a property policy because, since insurer had no duty to defend, insured could not be placed "in a defensive posture"); *Westport Ins. Corp. v. Hamilton Wharton Group, Inc.*, No. 10 Civ. 2188, 2011 U.S. Dist. LEXIS 20535 (S.D.N.Y. Feb. 23, 2011) (holding that successful insured was entitled to recover attorney's fees incurred in defending against insurer's declaratory judgment action, which sought to free insurer from its policy obligation to defend and indemnify, because such action placed insured in a defensive position); *Suffolk Federal Credit Union v. CUMIS Ins. Soc., Inc.*, 910 F.

Supp. 2d 446 (E.D.N.Y. 2012) (holding that insured could not recover attorney's fees because insured brought suit against insurer, and, therefore, was not in defensive position); *MIC Gen. Ins. Co. v. Chambers*, No. 15-3324, 2016 U.S. Dist. LEXIS 75018 (S.D.N.Y. June 8, 2016) (declining to expand *Mighty Midgets* to "cover parties who merely litigate on the same side of the 'v.' as an insured"); *United Specialty Ins. Co. v. Lux. Maint. & Ren. Corp.*, No. 18-3083, 2019 U.S. Dist. LEXIS 201805 (S.D.N.Y. Nov. 20, 2019) (addressing New York law in detail and rejecting argument that "insured may recover his legal expenses in a controversy with a carrier over coverage only when there was a showing of such bad faith in denying coverage that no reasonable carrier would, under the given facts, be expected to assert it.") ("While that may be a true statement of law [insurer relied on *Sukup v. State*, 227 N.E.2d 842 (N.Y. 1967)], the instant action plainly falls under the narrow exception to that general rule carved out by the New York courts in *Mighty Midgets* and *City Club Hotel*. Accordingly, the Hospital Defendants' request for their legal expenses in the instant action is granted."); *American Empire Surplus Lines Ins. Co. v. L&G Masonry Corp.*, No. 652695/2018, 2020 N.Y. Misc. LEXIS 1970 (N.Y. Sup. Ct. May 7, 2020) ("A judgment obtained by a plaintiff as against a defaulting defendant does not entitle the plaintiff to collateral estoppel against the non-defaulting defendants who would otherwise be denied a full and fair opportunity to litigate issues of liability. As such, the answering defendants were not 'put in a defensive posture' such that the recovery of attorneys' fees is warranted."); *Great Am. Ins. Co. v. Zelik*, No. 19-1805, 2020 U.S. Dist. LEXIS 5229 (S.D.N.Y. Jan. 3, 2020) (because merits of claim unresolved, court could not determine whether attorney's fees were warranted).

North Carolina: The North Carolina Court of Appeals held that "attorney's fees incurred by the insured … are not recoverable as damages where those fees are incurred in the course of litigation to determine coverage and compel the insurer to perform its duties. Our decision today does not hold that an insured's attorney's fees can never be recovered in coverage litigation. Attorney's fees clearly can be recovered in situations, for example, where an insurer acts in bad faith in denying coverage or where recovery of fees is otherwise authorized by contract or statute." *Collins & Aikman Prods. Co. v. Hartford Accident & Indem. Co.*, 481 S.E.2d 96, 97–98 (N.C. Ct. App. 1997); *see also Hubbard Tel. Contractors Inc. v. Mich. Mut. Ins. Co.*, No. COA02–1090, 2003 N.C. App. LEXIS 767 (N.C. Ct. App. May 6, 2003) (citing *Collins* for the proposition that attorney's fees are recoverable in a declaratory action against an insurer where it is shown that the insurer acted in bad faith in denying coverage); *Crescent Univ. City Venture, LLC v. AP Atl., Inc.*, No. 15-14745,

2019 NCBC LEXIS 46 (N.C. Super. Ct. Aug. 8, 2019) (in non-insurance context, discussing North Carolina law, including *Collins*, concerning an insured's right to recover attorney's fees, from insurer, incurred to establish coverage).

North Dakota: A North Dakota statute provides that "[f]urther relief based on a declaratory judgment or decree may be granted whenever necessary or proper." N.D. CENT. CODE § 32–23–08. North Dakota courts utilize this statute in awarding attorney's fees incurred by an insured in bringing or defending a declaratory judgment action. *See, e.g.*, *State Farm Fire and Cas. Co. v. Sigman*, 508 N.W.2d 323, 326–27 (N.D. 1993) (awarding attorney's fees based on language of the insurance policy, by which the insurer agreed to pay "reasonable expenses an insured incurs at [the insurer's] request," and on Section 32–23–08, reasoning that "[w]hen the insured gets that policy protection only by court order after litigating coverage, it is both 'necessary' and 'proper' to award attorney fees and costs to give the insured the full benefit of his insurance contract … . If an insured is not awarded attorney fees as supplemental relief, he is effectively denied the benefit he bargained for in the insurance policy"); *see also R.D. Offutt Co. v. Lexington Ins. Co.*, 494 F.3d 668, 675–76 (8th Cir. 2007) (applying North Dakota law) (upholding an award of attorney's fees based on section 32–23–08 and *Sigman*, and establishing that an award of attorney's fees under section 32–23–08 is appropriate "even if an insurer denies coverage in good faith," regardless of which party initiates the litigation and even absent a contractual provision providing for the award of such fees); *SW Design Build, Inc. v. Auto-Owners Ins.*, No. 16-82, 2017 U.S. Dist. LEXIS 215504 (D.N.D. Sept. 29, 2017) (explaining that *Sigman* is based on the principle that when "an insured purchases a contract of insurance, it seeks protection from expenses arising from litigation, not vexatious, time-consuming, expensive litigation with his insurer") (because insurer had a duty to defend and indemnify, insured was entitled to the payment of attorney's fees).

Ohio: An Ohio statute provides that "[a] court of record shall not award attorney's fees to any party on a claim or proceeding for declaratory relief under this chapter unless: (a) A section of the Revised Code explicitly authorizes a court of record to award attorney's fees on a claim for declaratory relief under this chapter." OHIO REV. CODE ANN. § 2721.16. Notwithstanding that Ohio has expressed its adherence to the American Rule via statute, the Court of Appeals of Ohio has recognized certain exceptions. *See Westfield Cos. v. O.K.L. Can Line*, 804 N.E.2d 45, 53–54 (Ohio Ct. App. 2003) (attorney's fees awarded upon a finding that the "losing party has acted in bad faith, vexatiously, wantonly, obdurately, or for oppressive reasons") (quoting *Sorin v. Bd. of Educ. of Warrensville Heights Sch. Dist.*, 347 N.E.2d 527, 530 (Ohio 1976)); *see also id.* at 56 (upholding an award of attorney's fees due to the insurer's "stubborn propensity for needless litigation," and finding such propensity evidenced by the insurer "filing a declaratory-judgment action under an old insurance policy not at issue, using a reversed case as legal authority for an argument before the court, and blaming [the insured] for its confusion"); *Canady v. Ohio Cas. Ins. Co.*, No. CT2013-0020, 2014 Ohio App. LEXIS 574 (Ohio Ct. App. Feb. 18, 2014) (holding that insured could recover attorney's fees because insurer breached its duty to defend); *Weitz Co., LLC v. Acuity*, No. 12-855, 2016 U.S. Dist. LEXIS 150433 (S.D. Ohio Oct. 31, 2016) ("Ohio has long adhered to the 'American Rule' with respect to the recovery of attorney fees: a prevailing party in a civil action may not recover attorney fees as part of the costs of litigation. Exceptions to the rule allow for recovery when a statute or an enforceable contract specifically provides for the losing party to pay the prevailing party's attorney fees, or when the prevailing party demonstrates bad faith on the part of the unsuccessful litigant.").

Oklahoma: An Oklahoma statute provides that "[i]t shall be the duty of the insurer, receiving a proof of loss, to submit a written offer of settlement or rejection of the claim to the insured within ninety (90) days of receipt of that proof of loss. Upon a judgment rendered to either party, costs and attorney fees shall be allowable to the prevailing party. For purposes of this section, the prevailing party is the insurer in those cases where judgment does not exceed written offer of settlement. In all other judgments the insured shall be the prevailing party." OKLA. ST. ANN. tit. 36, § 3629(B); *see also An-son Corp. v. Holland-America Ins. Co.*, 767 F.2d 700, 703–04 (10th Cir. 1985) (applying Oklahoma law) (rejecting the insurer's argument that Oklahoma courts only apply section 3629(B) to "first party" cases); *Stauth v. Nat'l Union Fire Ins. Co. of Pittsburgh*, 236 F.3d 1260, 1264 (10th Cir. 2001) (applying Oklahoma law) (holding that an insured was entitled to an award of attorney's fees under section 3629(B) when it prevailed in a declaratory judgment action against its insurer, whether such action is to determine the insurer's duty to defend or duty to indemnify); *Reg'l Air, Inc. v. Canal Ins. Co.*, 639 F.3d 1229 (10th Cir. 2011) (applying Oklahoma law) (addressing various aspects of how to apply the statute); *McCrary v. Country Mut. Ins. Co.*, No. 13-507, 2016 U.S. Dist. LEXIS 183563 (N.D. Okla. June 22, 2016) ("The Court's determination that no fees would be awarded under Fed. R. Civ. P. 37 does not control its analysis of the fee issue presented under § 3629(B). The statute provides that once a judgment is rendered for a party, 'costs and attorney fees shall be allowable to the prevailing party.' The fees sought were reasonably incurred in defense of Defendant's Motion to Compel and are allowable under the statute, even where the Court in its discretion did not award them under Rule 37. In essence, in this instance, the Oklahoma statute 'trumps' Rule 37."); *Thomas v. Farmers Ins. Co.*, No. 16-17, 2019 U.S. Dist. LEXIS 51185 (N.D. Okla. Mar. 27, 2019) (insurer was "prevailing party" and entitled to recover attorney fees because it rejected the claim and no judgment was awarded to Plaintiffs; insured's inability to pay fees not relevant as an award is mandatory under § 3629). In *JP Energy Mktg., LLC v. Commerce & Indus. Ins. Co.*, 419 P.3d 215 (Okla. 2018), the Supreme Court of Oklahoma noted that it had never addressed the attorney's fees issue, but found "the federal court decisions persuasive." *Id.* at 217. The court remanded for an adversarial hearing to determine the amount of attorney's fees to be awarded the insured under § 3629.

Oregon: An Oregon statute provides that "[e]xcept as otherwise provided in subsections (2) and (3) of this section [relating to certain automobile claims], if settlement is not made within six months from the date proof of loss is filed with an insurer and an action is brought in any court of this state upon any policy of insurance of any kind or nature, and the plaintiff's recovery exceeds the amount of any tender made by the defendant in such action, a reasonable amount to be fixed by the court as attorney fees shall be taxed as part of the costs of the action and any appeal thereon." OR. REV. STAT. ANN. § 742.061 (formerly cited as section 743.114); *see also McGraw v. Gwinner*, 578 P.2d 1250, 1253 (Or. 1978) ("We adhere to the proposition that in order to secure attorney fees pursuant to [section 742.061], the insured must recover a money judgment against the insurer; it is not sufficient that the insured establish coverage which may in turn lead to a subsequent recovery of money."); *Knowledge Learning Corp. v. Nat. Union Fire Ins. Co.*, No. CV-10-188, 2011 U.S. Dist. LEXIS 57174 (D. Or. Apr. 19, 2011) (determining that statute applied because insurer refused to defend, which differs from situation where insurer defends, under a reservation of rights, and files a declaratory judgment action to determine whether it is required to continue to defend) (addressing in detail whether attorney's fees were reasonable); *Stuart v. Pittman*, 255 P.3d 482, 488 (Or. 2011) (acknowledging that "a recovery under an enforceable insurance binder can support an award of attorney fees pursuant to ORS 742.061"); *ZRZ Realty Co. v. Beneficial Fire & Cas. Ins. Co.*, 266 P.3d 61 (Or. 2011) ("We note that our decision today does not preclude Zidell from recovering attorney fees in the future for the work that its attorneys have done both at trial and on appeal to establish London's duty to indemnify if London did not settle with Zidell within six months of Zidell's filing a proof of loss and if Zidell recovers on remand more indemnification costs than London tendered.") (also addressing surplus lines exception to ORS 742.061); *Hoffman v. Foremost Signature Ins. Co.*, No.12-01534, 2014 U.S. Dist. LEXIS 30349 (D. Or. Mar. 10, 2014) (discussing in detail the determination of reasonable attorney's fees under OR. REV. STAT. ANN. § 742.061); *Schnitzer Steel Industries, Inc. v. Continental Cas. Corp.*, No. 10–01174, 2014 U.S. Dist. LEXIS 160032 (D. Or. Nov. 12, 2014) (discussing in detail the factors the Court must consider, under ORS § 20.075, in determining the amount of an award of attorney fees) (*aff'd* 2016 U.S. App. LEXIS 9854 (9th Cir. May 31, 2016)); *Precision Seed Cleaners v. Country Mut. Ins. Co.*, 976 F. Supp. 2d 1228 (D. Or. 2013) (concluding that insured met statutory requirements for award of attorney's fees, but because insurer and insured both engaged in conduct that needlessly prolonged litigation, the court would not adjust otherwise reasonable attorney's fees) (providing in-depth analysis of statutory elements for award of attorney's fees and determination of their reasonableness); *Beck v. Metro. Prop. & Cas. Ins. Co.*, No. 13-00879, 2016 U.S. Dist. LEXIS 126335 (D. Or. Sept. 16, 2016) (discussing in detail the factors the court must consider, under ORS § 20.075, in determining the amount of an award of attorney's fees). In *Long v. Farmers Ins. Co.*, 388 P. 3d 312 (Or. 2017) the Oregon Supreme Court held that "when an insured files an action against an insurer to recover sums owing on an insurance policy and the insurer subsequently pays the insured more than the amount of any tender made within six months from the insured's proof of loss, the insured obtains a 'recovery' that entitles the insured to an award of reasonable attorney fees." In other words, as the court put it: "A declaration of *coverage* is not sufficient to make ORS 742.061 applicable; an insured must obtain a *monetary* recovery after filing an action, although that recovery need not be memorialized in a judgment." (emphasis in original).

Pennsylvania: A Pennsylvania statute provides that "[i]n an action arising under an insurance policy, if the court finds that the insurer has acted in bad faith toward the insured, the court may … (3) [a]ssess court costs and attorney fees against the insurer." 42 PA. CONS. STAT. ANN. § 8371; *see also Regis Ins. Co. v. Wood*, 852 A.2d 347, 350–51 (Pa. Super. Ct. 2004) (noting that, in addition to being recoverable generally in any action arising under an insurance policy where the insurer acted in bad faith, attorney's fees are also recoverable under the Declaratory Judgment Act, 42 PA. CONS. STAT. ANN. §§ 7531–7541. Like attorney's fees awarded under Section 8371, attorney's fees awarded under the Declaratory Judgment Act require a showing that the "'insurance company has acted in bad faith or fraudulently or was stubbornly litigious,'" with this bad faith standard "being [no] less stringent than it [is] in the

Section 8371 context." *Regis*, 852 A.2d at 350–51 (citing *Kelmo Enterprises, Inc. v. Commercial Union Ins. Co.*, 426 A.2d 680, 685 (Pa. Super. Ct. 1981)); *Craker v. State Farm Mut. Auto. Ins. Co.*, CA No. 11-0225, 2011 U.S. Dist. LEXIS 47342 (W.D. Pa. May 3, 2011) (explaining that insured cannot recover attorney's fees through breach of contract claim, but may be able to recover such fees through a bad faith claim). *See also UPS Freight v. Nat'l Union Fire Ins. Co.*, No. 06-137, 2012 U.S. Dist. LEXIS 19505 (W.D. Pa. Feb. 14, 2012) (finding that insured was not entitled to recover its attorney's fees because it had failed to show insurer acted in bad faith in breaching its duty to defend); *Villalta v. State Farm Mut. Ins. Co.*, No. 13-00832, 2013 U.S. Dist. LEXIS 195973 (W.D. Pa. Sept. 27, 2013) ("Under Pennsylvania law, absent a fee-shifting statutory or contract provision to the contrary, parties are not entitled to attorneys' fees. As Plaintiff has identified no statutory or contractual provision entitling her to attorney's fees for breach of contract, such demand will be stricken from the pleadings. Plaintiff may recover attorney's fees for her bad faith claim under 42 Pa. C.S.A. § 8371(3)."); *Transp. Ins. Co. v. Motorists Mut. Ins. Co.*, No. 14-01438, 2017 U.S. Dist. LEXIS 2486 (M.D. Pa. Jan. 9, 2017) (noting that, in *Kelmo Enterprises*, the Superior Court "eschewed the traditional American rule mandating a litigant pay their own expenses. Instead, the Court found such a position 'unfair,' and stated that an insurer who guessed wrong as to its duty[] should be compelled to bear the consequences thereof.") ("Under the doctrine of subrogation, the excess carrier stepping into the shoes of the insured is afforded the same right.").

Rhode Island: A Rhode Island statute provides that "an insured … may bring an action against [its] insurer … when it is alleged the insurer wrongfully and in bad faith refused to pay or settle a claim made pursuant to the provisions of the policy, or otherwise wrongfully and in bad faith refused to timely perform its obligations under the contract of insurance. In any action brought pursuant to this section, an insured may also make claim for compensatory damages, punitive damages, and reasonable attorney fees." R.I. GEN. LAWS § 9–1-33; *see also Skaling v. Aetna Ins. Co.*, 799 A.2d 997, 1010 (R.I. 2002) (holding that "bad faith is established when the proof demonstrates that the insurer denied coverage or refused payment without a reasonable basis in fact or law for the denial"); R.I. GEN. LAWS § 9–1-45 ("The court may award a reasonable attorney's fee to the prevailing party in any civil action arising from a breach of contract in which the court: (1) Finds that there was a complete absence of a justiciable issue of either law or fact raised by the losing party[.]"); *Ins. Co. of N. Am. v. Kayser-Roth Corp.*, 770 A.2d 403, 419 (R.I. 2001) (noting that attorney's fees may only be awarded when there exists a contractual or statutory authorization and citing both Sections 9–1-33 and 9–1-45 as providing such statutory authorization). *But see Furey Roofing and Const. Co. v. Employers Mut. Cas. Co.*, No. KC-2009-0685, 2010 R.I. Super. LEXIS 24 (R.I. Super. Ct. Feb. 1, 2010) ("[E]ven without an authorizing contractual or statutory provision, a trial court may award attorney's fees to a policyholder that has prevailed in a declaratory judgment action against its insurance company only if the policyholder can prove that the insurer has engaged in bad faith conduct prior to or in the course of litigation. This limited exception reflects an appropriate accommodation between the policy underlying the American rule of permitting parties, including insurance companies, to litigate claims in good faith, but still provides protection to those policyholders that might confront 'stubbornly litigious' insurance companies that take specious positions in order to attempt to avoid paying legitimate claims.").

South Carolina: The Supreme Court of South Carolina held that the legal fees incurred by an insured, in successfully asserting its rights against its insurer's attempt, by way of a declaratory judgment action, to avoid its obligation to defend, were recoverable as damages arising directly as a result of the breach of the contract. *Hegler v. Gulf Ins. Co.*, 243 S.E.2d 443, 444–45 (S.C. 1978). The South Carolina high court reasoned that "the insured has a contract right to have actions against him defended by the insurer, at its expense. If the insurer can force him into a declaratory judgment proceeding and, even though it loses in such action, compel him to bear the expense of such litigation, the insured is actually no better off financially than if he had never had the contract right mentioned above." *Id.* (internal citation and quotation omitted); *see also State Auto Prop. & Cas. Ins. Co. v. Raynolds*, 592 S.E.2d 633, 637 (S.C. 2004) ("It is well-settled in South Carolina that when a defendant insured prevails in a declaratory judgment action, the insured is entitled to recover attorney's fees."); *NGM Ins. Co. v. Carolina's Power Wash & Painting, LLC*, No. 2:08-CV-3378, 2010 U.S. Dist. LEXIS 113565 (D.S.C. Oct. 25, 2010) ("[A] successful insured in a declaratory judgment action is entitled to recover attorney's fees, regardless of whether the insured specifically pled attorney's fees as special damages. Nowhere in [the *Hegler*] opinion did the Supreme Court of South Carolina articulate a requirement that attorney's fees must be specifically pled in that particular context, even though the plaintiff in *Hegler* happened to include attorney's fees in his complaint."); *Berenyi, Inc. v. Landmark Am. Ins. Co.*, No. 2:09-CV-01556, 2010 U.S. Dist. LEXIS 3018 (D.S.C. Jan. 14, 2010) (following *Hegler* and holding that insured "is entitled to recover attorney fees incurred in bringing … action to establish [insurer's] duty to defend"); *Baiden & Assocs. v. Crum & Forster*

Specialty Ins. Co., No. 11-00267, 2012 U.S. Dist. LEXIS 23053 (D.S.C. Feb. 23, 2012) (noting that *Hegler* does not limit award of attorney's fees to insured to only cases where insurer brought suit) (the central question of whether attorney's fees are appropriate in these types of cases depends on whether suit involves dispute with insurer as to insurer's duty to defend, and "not whether the declaratory judgment action was brought by the insurer or the insured"); *Allstate Fire & Cas. Co. v. Simpson*, No. 15-1908, 2016 U.S. Dist. LEXIS 171034 (D.S.C. Mar. 7, 2016) ("The court finds that *Hegler* is analogous to the case at bar. . . . The Defendants were successful in their defense of this lawsuit and the court reformed the policy to include UIM coverage for Joseph equal to the liability limits of the Policy. Absent the actions of Allstate, the Defendants would not have been forced to expend attorney's fees to obtain UIM coverage. Based on the foregoing, the court finds that the Defendants are entitled to attorney's fees."); *Owners Ins. Co. v. Warren Mech., LLC*, 324 F. Supp. 3d 650 (D.S.C. 2018) (declining to apply *Hegler* because there was no request by insurer for a declaration that it did not have a duty to indemnify an insured in an underlying action; insurer sought to determine if policy was void ab initio because of material misrepresentations in the application); *GuideOne Nat'l Ins. Co. v. Western World Ins. Grp., Inc.*, No. 17-1361, 2020 U.S. Dist. LEXIS 3655 (D.S.C. Jan. 9, 2020) ("[T]he court declines to find that the same considerations of unfairness that concerned the *Hegler* court should be extended to a mortgagee under a policy of insurance. In that situation, the mortgagee has bargained with the insured, not the insurer, to provide coverage, and may enforce its contractual remedies under the mortgage should the insured default in its obligation to maintain insurance.").

South Dakota: A South Dakota statute provides that "[i]n all actions or proceedings hereafter commenced against [an] ... insurance company ... on any policy ... of insurance, if it appears from the evidence that such company ... has refused to pay the full amount of such loss, and that such refusal is vexatious or without reasonable cause, the ... court, shall, if judgment or an award is rendered for [the insured], allow the [insured] a reasonable sum as an attorney's fee to be recovered ... provided, however, that when a tender is made by such insurance company ... before the commencement of the action or proceeding in which judgment or an award is rendered and the amount recovered is not in excess of such tender, no such cost shall be allowed." S.D. CODIFIED LAWS § 58–12–3. Despite the express language of the statute ("in all actions ... commenced *against* [an] ... insurance company," *id.* (emphasis added)), the Supreme Court of South Dakota held that "whether the insurer is the named plaintiff and the insured named the defendant is not dispositive of attorney fee liability." *All Nation Ins. Co. v. Brown*, 344 N.W.2d 493, 494 (S.D. 1984) (holding that if the insurer's refusal to pay was vexatious or unreasonable the insured would be entitled to recover attorney's fees incurred when insurer brought declaratory judgment action against insured to determine liability). *See also Bjornestad v. Progressive N. Ins. Co.*, No. 08-4105, 2010 U.S. Dist. LEXIS 120034 (D.S.D. Nov. 10, 2010) (determining insurer's actions to be "vexatious") ("[T]he evidence shows that Progressive had knowledge of facts indicating that Bjornestad was entitled to more than $25,000 under her insurance contract, yet Mr. Sedevie and Progressive repeatedly offered only $25,000 while requesting a full and final release of all claims. Progressive intentionally represented to Bjornestad that her claim was worth less than $25,000 when its own records show that her claim was actually valued at no less than $25,350. Finally, there is evidence that Progressive provided false information to Dr. Cederberg about when Bjornestad's low back pain began.") (*affirmed by* 664 F.3d 1195 (8th Cir. 2011) (adding that jury's rejection of insured's bad faith claim did not preclude an award of attorney's fees)); *Tripp v. W. Nat. Mut. Ins. Co.*, 664 F.3d 1200 (8th Cir. 2011) (explaining that attorney's fees may be recovered by insured under SDCL 58-12-3 even if insurer was not found to have acted in bad faith) (addressing whether insured's attorney's fees were reasonable); *Hot Stuff Foods, LLC v. Houston Cas. Co.*, 771 F.3d 1071 (8th Cir. 2014) ("At the end of a hard-fought damage trial, HCC argued to the jury that only fifty-five percent of the claimed recall expenses were reasonable and necessary, and none of the claimed lost gross profits should be awarded. We agree with the district court this did not turn HCC's failure to offer to pay the 'uncontested' amount into a vexatious 'refus[al] to pay the full amount of such loss' within the meaning of § 58–12–3. This was not a case where the insurer valued the insured's claim 'much higher than its offer,' or engaged in long delay and then 'tendered a settlement offer far below the amount due.'"); *Kern v. Progressive N. Ins. Co.*, 883 N.W.2d 511 (S.D. 2016) (noting that the court's decision whether the insurer's conduct was vexatious or without reasonable cause is a finding of fact and will not be reversed unless clearly erroneous) ("The facts of this case are complicated, and the trial judge had the benefit of observing the trial's many subtleties. In light of this, and upon looking at the entire record, it cannot be said that the trial judge's finding that Progressive did not act without reason was clearly erroneous.").

Tennessee: The Supreme Court of Tennessee held that "[i]n the absence of contract, statute, or recognized ground of equity, there is no inherent right to have attorneys' fees paid by opposing side." *Carter v. Virginia Surety Co.*, 216 S.W.2d 324, 328 (Tenn. 1948); *see also State v. Thomas*, 585 S.W.2d 606, 607 (Tenn. 1979) ("The rule is well established in this state that in the absence of a contract, statute or recognized ground of equity so providing there is no right to have attorneys' fees paid by an opposing party in civil litigation.") (non-insurance context); *Forrest Construction, Inc. v. The Cincinnati Ins. Co.*, 728 F. Supp. 2d. 955 (M.D. Tenn. 2010) (interpreting *Carter* to be in accord with the rule of those jurisdictions that only award attorney's fees to the insured in the case of bad faith on the part of the insurer); *N. Am. Specialty Ins. Co. v. Heritage Glass, LLC*, No. 16-263, 2017 U.S. Dist. LEXIS 13035 (E.D. Tenn. Jan. 9, 2017) ("Generally, Tennessee follows the American Rule that in absence of a contract, statute, or recognized ground of equity so providing there is no right to have attorney's fees paid by an opposing party in civil litigation. However, where a contract expressly provides for attorney's fees, the parties are entitled to have their contract enforced according to its express terms.") (non-insurance context).

Texas: The Texas Declaratory Judgment Act provides that "[i]n any proceeding under this chapter, the court may award costs and reasonable and necessary attorney's fees as are equitable and just." TEX. CIV. PRAC. & REM. CODE § 37.009. "[T]he Declaratory Judgments Act entrusts attorney fee awards to the trial court's sound discretion, subject to the requirements that any fees awarded be reasonable and necessary, which are matters of fact, and to the additional requirements that fees be equitable and just, which are matters of law." *Bocquet v. Herring*, 972 S.W.2d 19, 21 (Tex. 1998); *see also Stevens Transport, Inc. v. Nat'l Cont'l Ins. Co.*, No. 05–98–00244-CV, 2000 Tex. App. LEXIS 3070 (Tex. Ct. App. May 11, 2000) (overturning an award of attorney's fees under the Declaratory Judgment Act by reasoning that the insurer's counterclaim for declaratory relief "did not present any new disputes that were not already pending before the trial court"); *Elliott Appraisers, LLC v. JM Ins. Services, LLC*, No. H-10-2231, 2011 U.S. Dist. LEXIS 16975 (S.D. Tex. Feb. 22, 2011) (holding that insurer breached its duty to defend because there was a potentially covered claim, and therefore, insured was entitled to attorney's fees) (award made pursuant to TEX. CIV. PRAC. & REM. CODE § 38.001(7) which states that a party, in a breach of contract action, "may recover reasonable attorney's fees from an individual or corporation, in addition to the amount of a valid claim and costs"); *Tex. Trailer Corp. v. Nat'l Union Fire Ins. Co.*, No. 15-02453, 2016 U.S. Dist. LEXIS 84074 (N.D. Tex. June 28, 2016) (noting that Texas's Uniform Declaratory Judgment Act -- Tex. Civ. Prac. & Rem. Code § 37.009 -- permits a court to award "necessary attorney's fees as are equitable and just" in a declaratory judgment action and a prevailing party may also recover attorney's fees in a breach of contract action under Tex. Civ. Prac. & Rem. Code § 38.001(8)).

Utah: The Supreme Court of Utah held that an insured may recover attorney's fees incurred in a declaratory judgment action. *Farmers Ins. Exch. v. Call*, 712 P.2d 231, 237 (Utah 1985). However, "'[b]efore an award of attorney's fees [can] be made in the declaratory judgment action, it must appear that the insurance company acted in bad faith or fraudulently or was stubbornly litigious.'" *Id.* (alteration in the original) (quoting *Am. States Ins. Co. v. Walker*, 486 P.2d 1042, 1044 (Utah 1971)). The *Farmers* Court observed that attorney's fees are not warranted where an insurer merely states its position and initiates an action of what appears to be a judiciable controversy. *Id.* at 237–38; *see also W. Am. Ins. Co. v. AV & S, Inc.*, 145 F.3d 1224, 1231 (10th Cir. 1998) (interpreting Utah law and citing *Farmers* in affirming the district court's award of attorney's fees); *Beach House Club v. Travelers Prop. Cas. Co. of Am.*, No. 2:08CV287, 2009 U.S. Dist. LEXIS 102875 (D. Utah Oct. 30, 2009) (citing *Walker* and holding that insured was not entitled to attorney's fees because there was "no evidence in the record suggesting bad faith or stubbornly litigious behavior on the part of [the insurer]" and "[the insurer] had a fair basis for disputing the claim") (also concluding that attorney's fees are only recoverable as consequential damages for breach of an insurance contract when there is a breach of the implied covenant of good faith and fair dealing); *Doctors' Co. v. Drezga*, 218 P.3d 598, 608–09 (Utah 2009) ("[W]here an insurer files a complaint for declaratory relief against its own insured, who is absent and unaware of the litigation, and where such relief would adversely affect the interests of an innocent third party, it is within the inherent equitable authority of the court to both appoint counsel for the insured and to order that the insurer pay attorney fees for appointed counsel, if and when the insured prevails in the action."); *Chapman Constr., LC v. United Fire & Cas. Co.*, No. 15-00172, 2015 U.S. Dist. LEXIS 163068 (D. Utah Dec. 4, 2015) ("Utah Courts have permitted an award of attorney's fees in a declaratory judgment action if it appears that the insurance company acted in bad faith or fraudulently or was stubbornly litigious. However, when an insured's claim is fairly debatable, the insurer is entitled to debate it and cannot be held to have breached the implied covenant if it chooses to do so.") (concluding that attorney's fees not owed because, while the court disagreed with the insurer, the claim for coverage was fairly debatable); *Fire Ins. Exch. v. Oltmanns*, 416 P.3d 1148 (Utah 2018) (declining to award attorney's fees, as insurer was within its rights to file a declaratory judgment action, and noting that insureds "face a very high bar in proving that an insurer filed a declaratory judgment in bad faith or to be stubbornly litigious").

Vermont: The Supreme Court of Vermont generally follows the American Rule, requiring litigants to bear their own attorney's fees and deviates from this rule "only in exceptional cases and for dominating reasons of justice." *D.J. Painting, Inc. v. Baraw Enters.*, 776 A.2d 413, 419 (Vt. 2001) (quoting *Sprague v. Ticonic Nat'l Bank*, 307 U.S. 161, 167 (1939)). The Vermont Supreme Court suggested that bad faith may be one such "exceptional case." *Id.* at 419–20; *see also Concord Gen. Mut. Ins. Co. v. Woods*, 824 A.2d 572, 579 (Vt. 2003) ("In the absence of a finding of bad faith on the part of the insurance company, or outrageous conduct … [which] we have held to be necessary to justify a departure from the American Rule … [insureds] are not entitled to attorneys' fees incurred in defending against a declaratory judgment action."). However, the Vermont high court has since indicated that the language from *Woods* was merely *dicta*, the status of the rule in Vermont is in fact unclear and the court declined to settle the issue. *Monahan v. GMAC Mortgage Corp.*, 893 A.2d 298, 323–34 (Vt. 2005); *Southwick v. City of Rutland*, 30 A.3d 1298 (Vt. 2011) (stating that bad faith conduct—but in the context of breach of an indemnification cause—was the intended target of the exception to the American Rule for "exceptional cases and for dominating reasons of justice").

Virginia: A Virginia statute provides that "in any civil case in which an insured individual [defined to include a company or organization] sues his insurer to determine what coverage, if any, exists under his present policy … or the extent to which his insurer is liable for compensating a covered loss, the individual insured shall be entitled to recover from the insurer costs and such reasonable attorney fees as the court may award. However, these costs and attorney's fees shall not be awarded unless the court determines that the insurer, not acting in good faith, has either denied coverage or failed or refused to make payment to the insured under the policy." Va. Code Ann. § 38.2–209. Whether an insurer acted in bad faith, so as to warrant the award of attorney's fees under this section, requires a determination of "whether reasonable minds could differ in the interpretation of policy provisions defining coverage and exclusions; whether the insurer had made a reasonable investigation of the facts and circumstances underlying the insured's claim; whether the evidence discovered reasonably supports a denial of liability; whether it appears that the insurer's refusal to pay was used merely as a tool in settlement negotiations; and whether the defense the insurer asserts at trial raises an issue of first impression or a reasonably debatable question of law or fact." *Nationwide Mut. Ins. Co. v. St. John*, 524 S.E.2d 649, 651 (Va. 2000) (citing *CUNA Mut. Ins. Soc'y v. Norman*, 375 S.E.2d 724, 727 (1989)); *see also Yorktowne Shopping Center, LLC v. Nat. Sur. Corp.*, No. 1:10-cv-1333, 2011U.S. Dist. LEXIS 63880 (E.D. Va. June 15, 2011) (citing section 38.2-209 but determining that insurer was not obligated to reimburse insured for attorney's fees incurred in coverage dispute because insurer won summary judgment on bad faith claim as "reasonable minds could differ in interpreting the Policy"); *Botkin v. Donegal Mut. Ins. Co.*, No. 5:10CV00077, 2011 U.S. Dist. LEXIS 33668 (W.D. Va. Mar. 29, 2011) (asserting that "Virginia law does not recognize a separate cause of action for bad faith in the context of insurance disputes," but noting that "[t]here is … a statutorily created remedy [section 38.2-209] that allows a court to award attorney's fees and costs to the insured if the insurer acted in bad faith"); *TRAX, LLC v. Cont'l Cas. Co.*, No. 10-CV-6901, 2013 U.S. Dist. LEXIS 28130 (N.D. Ill. Feb. 28, 2013) (applying Virginia law) (holding that insured was not entitled to attorney's fees because insurer did not act in bad faith and providing detailed analysis for determining whether insurer acted in bad faith, warranting attorney's fees); *REVI, LLC v. Chi. Title Ins. Co.*, 776 S.E.2d 808 (Va. 2015) ("[T]he word 'court,' as used in Code § 38.2-209(A), means 'judge.' A judge, not a jury, must determine whether an insurer 'has either denied coverage or failed or refused to make payment to the insured under the policy' in bad faith. We also conclude that Code § 38.2-209(A) does not implicate the right to a jury trial under Article I, Section 11 of the Constitution of Virginia.") (citing test for bad faith under *Norman* and holding that attorney's fees were not warranted because insurer put forth a colorable and good faith basis for denying coverage); *S. Boston Energy LLC v. Hartford Steam Boiler Specialty Ins. Co.*, No. 18-596, 2019 U.S. Dist. LEXIS 138847 (E.D. Va. Aug. 15, 2019) (concluding that insurer acted in bad faith, awarding attorney's fees under § 38.2–209 and discussing in detail the amount of such fees to be awarded; addressing several factors, including rates and documentation).

Washington: The Supreme Court of Washington held that an insured may "recoup attorney fees that it incurs because an insurer refuses to defend or pay the justified action or claim of the insured, regardless of whether a lawsuit is filed against the insured … . When an insured purchases a contract of insurance, it seeks protection from expenses arising from litigation, not 'vexatious, time-consuming expensive litigation with its insurer.' Whether the insured must defend a suit filed by third parties, appear in a declaratory action, or … file a suit for damages to obtain the benefit of its insurance contract is irrelevant. In every case, the conduct of the insurer imposes upon the insured the cost of compelling the insurer to honor its commitment and, thus, is equally burdensome to the insured." *Olympic Steamship Co. v. Centennial Ins. Co.*, 811 P.2d 673, 681 (Wash. 1991) (internal citations omitted). The Supreme Court of Washington held that *Olympic Steamship* fees are not awarded when an insurer simply disputes the value of a claim. *Dayton v. Farmers Ins. Group*, 876 P.2d 896, 898 (Wash. 1994); *see also Colo. Structures, Inc. v. Ins. Co. of the W.*, 167 P.3d 1125, 1141 (Wash. 2007) (en banc) (stating that while "[g]enerally, when an insured must bring a suit against its own insurer to obtain a legal determination interpreting the meaning or application of an insurance policy, it is a coverage dispute," when the dispute involves a question of liability in tort or extent of the damages it is not a coverage dispute and the *Olympic Steamship* rule does not apply to allow the award of attorney's fees); *Peterson v. Big Bend Ins. Agency, Inc.*, 202 P.3d 372, 382 (Wash. Ct. App. 2009) (rejecting insured's argument that *Olympic Steamship* required court to award attorney's fees incurred in coverage dispute where the dispute arose from insurance agent's negligence and misrepresentation and insurer was vicariously liable, as opposed to an action to compel the insurer to provide benefits under the policy); *Muse Apartments, LLC v. Travelers Cas. and Sur. Co. of Am.*, No. C12-2021, 2014 U.S. Dist. LEXIS 82525 (W.D. Wa. June 17, 2014) (following *Peterson* and holding that insured was not entitled to award of attorney's fees in action that arose from claim of insurer's negligence); *Unigard Ins. Co. v. Mut. of Enumclaw Ins. Co.*, 250 P.3d 121, 130 (Wash. Ct. App. 2011) (holding that insurer was entitled to recover attorney's fees from another insurer for refusing to defend); *Vision One, LLC v. Philadelphia Indem. Ins. Co.*, 276 P.3d 300 (Wash. 2012) (citing *Olympic Steamship* and holding that insured was entitled to attorney's fees on appeal because insurer owed insured coverage under the policy); *Ainsworth v. Progressive Cas. Ins. Co.*, 322 P.3d 6 (Wash. Ct. App. 2014) (concluding that, because case involved coverage, and was rejected as a valuation dispute, award of attorney's fees pursuant to *Olympic Steamship* were appropriate) (insured also entitled to reasonable appellate costs and fees because he prevailed in coverage dispute); *Lains v. Am. Family Mut. Ins. Co.*, No. C14-1982, 2015 U.S. Dist. LEXIS 180832 (W.D. Wash. July 9, 2015) ("The law does not require the entire dispute, the majority of the dispute, or even a significant portion of the dispute to be over coverage for *Olympic Steamship* attorney fees to be awarded. All the law requires is that the dispute is not merely one of valuation and some small part of it concerns coverage."); *Port of Longview v. Arrowood Indem. Co.*, No. 46654-62016, Wash. App. LEXIS 3100 (Wash. Ct. App. Dec. 21, 2016) (insured entitled to recover attorney fees for its claims under excess policies but not primary policies because insured breached the primary policy's notice provision – despite a finding of no prejudice); *King County v. Vinci Constr. Grands Projets/ Parsons RCI/Frontier-Kemper, JV*, 398 P.3d 1093 (Wash. 2017) ("This court has previously held that the rule in *Olympic Steamship* applies to performance bonds in the surety context. Although a statutory fee provision exists for public works contracts under RCW 39.04.240, we hold that it is not the exclusive fee remedy available."); *Collazo v. Balboa Ins. Co.*, No. C13-0892, 2014 U.S. Dist. LEXIS 189870 (W.D. Wash. Oct. 22, 2014) (rejecting insurer's argument that the dispute was only about value) ("However, coverage disputes include both cases in which the issue of any coverage is disputed and cases in which the extent of the benefit provided by an insurance contract is at issue. Here, Balboa did not dispute the existence of coverage, but it did dispute the extent of the ordinance or law coverage, and the availability of overhead and profit expenses, and it erred in assessing the amount of the deducible. There was, therefore, a coverage dispute. Collazo is entitled to reasonable attorney fees under *Olympic Steamship*."); *Eagle West Ins. Co. v. SAT, 2400, LLC*, No. C15-1098, 2017 U.S. Dist. LEXIS 214446 (W.D. Wash. Jan. 12, 2017) (apportioning *Olympic Steamship* fees owed for a successful claim for coverage versus those not owed for an unsuccessful claim under the Insurance Fair Conduct Act); *Costco Wholesale Corp. v. Arrowood Indem. Co.*, 387 F. Supp. 3d 1165 (W.D. Wash. 2019) ("If Arrowood had denied coverage or if, upon presentation of invoices for payment, it had refused to act and effectively denied coverage, the argument for an award of attorney's fees under *Olympic Steamship* would be much stronger. As it is, however, Costco sued while Arrowood was still investigating the claim and nine months before the underlying policy limits were exhausted. There may be instances where an insurer effectively refuses to provide the benefits of the insurance contract without expressly denying a claim for coverage, but this is not one of them."); *City of Olympia v. Travelers Cas. & Sur. Co.*, No. 19-5562, 2020 U.S. Dist. LEXIS 928 (W.D. Wash. Jan. 3, 2020) ("Olympia correctly argues that it was forced to bring this declaratory judgment action to force Travelers to honor its commitment under the Bond. It is a coverage dispute because Travelers's refusal to pay is based on its interpretation of the Bond and Contract, not a factual dispute over the amount of a claim. Consequently, Olympia is entitled to attorney fees in this matter under Olympic Steamship and Colorado Construction.").

West Virginia: The Supreme Court of Appeals of West Virginia held that "where an insurer has violated its contractual obligation to defend its insured, the insured should be fully compensated for all expenses incurred as a result of the insurer's breach of contract, including those expenses incurred in a declaratory judgment action. To hold otherwise would be unfair to the insured, who originally purchased the insurance policy to be protected from incurring attorney's fees and expenses arising from litigation." *Aetna Cas. & Sur. Co. v. Pitrolo*, 342 S.E.2d 156, 160 (W. Va. 1986); *see also Hayseeds, Inc. v. State Farm Fire & Cas.*, 352 S.E.2d 73, 79–80 (W. Va. 1986) (quoting *Pitrolo* and holding "that whenever a policyholder must sue his own insurance company over any property damage claim, and the policyholder substantially prevails in the action, the company is liable for the payment of the policyholder's reasonable attorneys' fees"); *Lemasters v. Nationwide Mut. Ins. Co.*, 751 S.E.2d 735 (W.Va. 2013) (holding that *Hayseeds'* damages do not continue through the duration of a bad faith action) ("The insurer is liable for the insured's reasonable attorneys' fees in vindicating its claim, the insured's damages for net economic loss caused by the delay in settlement, and damages for aggravation and inconvenience."); *Admiral Ins. Co. v. Fisher*, No. 17-0671, 2018 W. Va. LEXIS 467 (W. Va. June 5, 2018) (stating, in guidance to trial court on remand, that no court had ever awarded *Pitrolo* or *Hayseeds* damages in the content of a coverage dispute over an insured's misrepresentation in an application for insurance).

Wisconsin: The Supreme Court of Wisconsin held that "the supplemental relief under sec. 806.04(8) [Declaratory Judgment Act] may include a recovery of attorney fees incurred by the insured in successfully establishing coverage under an insurance policy. Therefore, we need not fashion an exception to the American Rule because the statute permits an award of attorney fees." *Elliott v. Donahue*, 485 N.W.2d 403, 409 (Wis. 1992). *But see Reid v. Benz*, 629 N.W.2d 262, 273–74 (Wis. 2001), where the Wisconsin high court held that an insurer was not liable for its insured's attorney's fees when the insurer obtained a stay in the underlying liability case to have a "fairly debatable question of coverage determined." *Id.* The court distinguished the situation from *Elliott*, where the insured was awarded its attorney's fees. The *Reid* Court reasoned that equities compelled the award of attorney's fees in *Elliott* due to the insurer's indirect breach of its duty to defend in failing to comply with the dictates of *Mowry v. Badger State Mut. Cas. Co.*, 385 N.W.2d 171 (Wis. 1986), which required the insurer to bifurcate the coverage and liability issues and obtain a stay of the liability case until coverage has been decided. *Benz*, 629 N.W.2d at 272–73. In *Benz*, in contrast, "[t]here [was] no contention that [the insurer] … breached its duty to defend … nor … that [the insurer's] challenge to coverage was unfair or unreasonable, or in bad faith." *Id.* at 273; *see also Chicago Title Ins. Co. v. Voss*, 791 N.W.2d 404 (Wis. Ct. App. 2010) ("We conclude that *Elliott* and its progeny do not authorize an award of attorney fees under WIS. STAT. § 806.04(8) under the facts and circumstances presented here, where there has been no breach of the duty to defend. Despite the fact that Voss had to expend money to establish coverage that fell within the ambit of the insurance policy, the basis for the attorney fees award in *Elliott* is absent here.") (citation and internal quotes omitted) (also allowing an award of costs under WIS. STAT. § 806.04(10)); *Ryder Truck Rental, Inc. v. Nat'l Fire Ins. Co.*, 246 F. Supp. 3d 1231 (E.D. Wis. 2017) (citing *Elliott* and holding that, because insurer breached its duty to defend, it was obligated to pay the costs and attorney's fees that its insured incurred in establishing its right to coverage); *Steadfast Ins. Co. v. Greenwich Ins. Co.*, 922 N.W.2d 71 (Wis. 2019) (permitting subrogating insurer to recover attorney fees for establishing that another insurer breached co-insured's duty to defend) ("[N]either the principles of contractual subrogation, nor the rationale behind attorney fee awards for breach of a duty to defend, foreclose this result."); *Choinsky v. Emplrs. Ins. Co.*, 938 N.W.2d 548 (Wis. 2020) ("When the circuit court denied the Insurer's motion to stay the liability proceedings, the Insurer provided a full defense, retroactive to the date of tender. By doing so, the Insurer complied with its contractual responsibilities to its Insured and therefore is not responsible for the School District's coverage attorney fees.").

Wyoming: A Wyoming statute provides that "[i]n any actions or proceedings commenced against any insurance company on any insurance policy or certificate of any type or kind of insurance, or in any case where an insurer is obligated by a liability insurance policy to defend any suit or claim or pay any judgment on behalf of a named insured, if it is determined that the company refuses to pay the full amount of a loss covered by the policy and that the refusal is unreasonable or without cause, any court in which judgment is rendered for a claimant may also award a reasonable sum as an attorney's fee and interest at ten percent (10%) per year." WYO. STAT. ANN. § 26–15–124; *see also Stewart Title Guar. Co. v. Tilden*, 110 P.3d 865, 874 (Wyo. 2005) (upholding the award of attorney's fees under Section 26–15–124; finding the insurer's failure to cure a title defect in a timely manner unreasonable); *Schofield v. Argon*, No. 14-103, 2015 U.S. Dist. LEXIS 179004 (D. Wyo. Mar. 24, 2015) (noting that awarding attorney's fees under the statute is discretionary). In *Cornhusker Cas. Co. v. Skaj*, 786 F.3d 842 (10th Cir. 2015) the court explained that "[i]t is well-settled Wyoming law that the policy behind the attorneys' fees statute is not to penalize insurance companies, but, rather, to chill any tendencies upon the part of insurance companies to unreasonably reject claims. And, according to the Wyoming Supreme Court, establishing one's entitlement to statutory attorneys' fees '*requires*' proving that a determination was made in [the relevant] action or proceeding that the [insurer's] refusal was unreasonable or without cause." *Id.* at 865 (citations omitted and emphasis in original). Further, in addressing the application of the statute, the court explained: "[T]hough we do not expressly hold that one claim necessarily resolves the other, we believe the district court properly looked to the bad-faith standard for guidance in addressing the Skajs' attorneys' fees claim. This approach is appropriate, given Wyoming's position that its attorneys' fees statute complements and enforces the duty of good faith and fair dealing that an insurer owes to its insured. Cornhusker had a reasonable basis for its chosen course of conduct in these proceedings. Having so concluded, we will not reverse course here and find that the Skajs are nonetheless entitled to attorneys' fees based on unreasonableness." *Id.*

CHAPTER

9

Number of Occurrences

Most disputes under general liability policies center around the fundamental question whether an insurer is obligated to defend and/or indemnify its insured for certain "bodily injury" or "property damage." But, in some cases, after it is determined that indemnity is owed, a dispute ensues over the extent of the insurer's obligation. In particular, a significant issue bearing on the amount of the insurer's obligation may be the number of "occurrences" that caused the covered "bodily injury" or "property damage."

This issue arises because the Insuring Agreement of virtually all commercial general liability policies states that coverage is owed for "bodily injury" or "property damage" that is caused by an "occurrence." *See, e.g.*, INS. SERVS. OFFICE, INC., COMMERCIAL GENERAL LIABILITY COVERAGE FORM, No. CG 00010413, § I1b(1) (2012). In addition, the commercial general liability (CGL) policy's Limits of Liability section typically states that the policy's Each Occurrence Limit is the most that the insurer will pay for the sum of damages because of all "bodily injury" and "property damage" arising out of any one "occurrence." ISO FORM, CG 000110413 at § III5. Lastly, most policies define "occurrence" as "an accident, including continuous or repeated exposure to substantially the same general harmful conditions." ISO FORM, CG 00010413 at § V13. The combination of these policy provisions, when applied to certain facts, leads to what is commonly referred to the "number of occurrences" issue.

Consider a commercial general liability policy that is subject to a $1 million Each Occurrence Limit and a $2 million General Aggregate Limit (being the most that will be paid under the policy for *all* damages—perhaps with an exception for those damages included in the "products-completed operations hazard," which may have its own Aggregate Limit). Under this relatively common limits of liability scenario, if all "bodily injury" and "property damage," even if there are multiple persons injured and multiple properties damaged, arises out of one "occurrence," then the insurer's maximum liability for *all* such damage will be capped at the policy's $1 million Each Occurrence Limit. On the other hand, if the same injury to persons and properties damaged is determined to have been caused by separate "occurrences," then *each* injured person or damaged property (or some combination of persons or property) will be covered up to the policy's $1 million Each Occurrence Limit. Because there is now more than one "occurrence," with each having a $1 million limit, the insured is in a position to collect up to the policy's $2 million General Aggregate Limit for all such damages.

As this simple, but not unrealistic, illustration demonstrates, the determination of "number of occurrences" can have a significant impact on the amount of an insured's recovery and, hence, an insurer's exposure for a claim. It can oftentimes double, or more, the limits of liability at issue. For this reason, it is not surprising that so much litigation has arisen over determining the number of occurrences.

One example of number of occurrences litigation with a lot at stake—and, because of that, it even drew the attention of the mainstream media—was over the amount payable by numerous insurers for the September 11, 2001, collapse of the World Trade Center. The property was collectively insured by multiple insurers for approximately $3.5 billion. However, the property owners sought to collect $7 billion on the basis that each plane attack qualified as a separate occurrence. Following protracted litigation, including a lengthy decision from the Second Circuit Court of Appeals, the court largely upheld a single occurrence determination. *World Trade Ctr. Props., LLC v. Hartford Fire Ins. Co.*, 345 F.3d 154, 190 (2d Cir. 2003). A subsequent jury trial led to certain insurers being obligated to pay based on two occurrences. In the end, the potential recovery under the policy was $4.6 billion. In essence, number of occurrences had the potential to be a $3.5 billion issue.

As with many coverage issues, courts confronted with a "number of occurrences" dispute usually examine the various tests that courts coming before them have adopted to resolve the issue and then decide which of the approaches to follow. In general, courts nationally have adopted two approaches for determining number of occurrences. Under the "effect" test, number of occurrences is determined by examining the effect that an event had, i.e., how many individual claims or injuries resulted from it. Conversely, under the "cause" test, number of occurrences is determined by examining the cause or causes of the damage. The "cause" test is the majority rule nationwide. *Liberty Mut. Ins. Co. v. Pella Corp.*, 631 F. Supp. 2d 1125, 1135 (S.D. Iowa 2009).

A typical example of a court adopting the "cause" test, and holding that, despite the existence of multiple injuries, all such injuries were caused by a single occurrence, and, hence subject to a single limit of liability, is *Donegal Mutual Insurance Co. v. Baumhammers*, 938 A.2d 286 (Pa. 2007). Here, the Supreme Court of Pennsylvania adopted the "cause" test and held that, where the insured's son, over a two-hour period, shot and killed a neighbor and then drove to three townships where he shot and killed four people and wounded another, all such "bodily injury" was caused by a single "occurrence." *Id.* at 295–96. Based on the "cause" approach, the court concluded that the insured-parents' negligence—failing to confiscate their son's weapon and/or notify law enforcement or his mental health providers of his unstable condition—constituted a single occurrence. *Id.* The court reasoned that "[s]ince the policy was intended to insure Parents for their liabilities, the occurrence should be an event over which Parents had some control." *Id.* at 296.

Compare *Baumhammers* to *Lombard v. Sewerage and Water Board of New Orleans*, 284 So. 2d 905 (La. 1973), where the Supreme Court of Louisiana applied the "effects" test and held that, where 119 plaintiffs were damaged as a consequence of the construction of an underground drainage canal, there were multiple occurrences. *Id.* at 915–16. The court concluded that the word "occurrence" must be construed from the point of view of the persons whose property was damaged and, therefore, the damage to each plaintiff was a separate occurrence. *Id.* at 915.

While most courts resolve number of occurrences disputes by deciding whether to adopt the "cause" test or the "effect" test, one court specifically declined to adopt a one-size-fits-all approach. In *Owners Insurance Co. v. Salmonsen*, 622 S.E.2d 525 (S.C. 2005), the Supreme Court of South Carolina addressed number of occurrences for multiple claims against a distributor for property damage allegedly caused by defective stucco. The court noted that "[t]he discussion of a majority-versus-minority view summarizes an amalgam of cases, including vehicle accidents, flooding, fist-fights, and so on, and is not limited to product liability cases. Notably, there is no prevailing view in the specific context of product liability cases involving the distribution of a defective product. In light of the diverse contexts in which the meaning of 'occurrence' may arise, we decline the district court's invitation to simply choose the majority or minority view and instead focus narrowly on the issue at hand." *Id.* at 526.

In general, a court's adoption of the "cause" test frequently leads to a single "occurrence" determination—on the basis that, despite multiple injuries or damaged properties, it all has a common cause. That the "cause" test frequently leads to a single "occurrence" determination, despite multiple injuries or damaged properties, is also tied to the fact that the definition of "occurrence" in many policies includes "continuous or repeated exposure to substantially the same general harmful conditions," or some language to that effect.

But despite the "cause" test frequently leading to a single "occurrence" determination, it would be unwise to reach a number of occurrences conclusion based solely on the label of the test that a state applies. For example, in *Koikos v. Travelers Insurance Co.*, 849 So. 2d 263 (Fla. 2003), the Supreme Court of Florida, despite specifically adopting the "cause" test, held that injuries sustained by two individuals who were shot in a restaurant lobby constituted separate occurrences. The policy defined "occurrence" as "an accident, including continuous or repeated exposure to substantially the same general harmful conditions." *Id.* at 266. The court concluded that, notwithstanding that the insured–restaurant owner was sued for negligent failure to provide security [akin to the single cause of the multiple injuries in *Baumhammers*, 938 A.2d 286], "occurrence" was defined by the immediate injury-producing act and not by the underlying tortious omission. *Id.* at 272. Florida's high court stated: "[I]n this case, the immediate causes of the injuries were the intervening intentional acts of the third-party—the intruder's gunshots." *Id.*

Another example of "don't judge number of occurrences solely on the applicable test" is the Supreme Court of Illinois's recent decisions on the issue. In both cases, the court applied the "cause" test, yet concluded that the injuries or damages were separate occurrences. *See Addison Ins. Co. v. Fay*, 905 N.E.2d 747, 756 (Ill. 2009) (holding that only "if cause and result are simultaneous or so closely linked in time and space as to be considered by the average person as one event, then the injuries will be deemed the result of one occurrence") and *Nicor Inc. v. Associated Elec. & Gas Ins. Servs., Ltd.*, 860 N.E.2d 280, 294 (Ill. 2006) (adopting the "cause" test, but concluding that "where each asserted loss is the result of a separate and intervening human act, whether negligent or intentional, or each act increased the insured's exposure to liability, Illinois law will deem each such loss to have arisen from a separate occurrence").

The Supreme Court of South Carolina would likely point to these Illinois decisions as an example of why, in *Salmonsen, supra*, it declined to be pigeon-holed into a majority or minority view on the "number of occurrences" issue and instead adopted an approach that requires resort to each case individually.

In addition to number of occurrences determinations having a direct affect on the limits of liability available for certain injuries or damages, the same analysis can also dictate the number of deductibles or self-insured retentions that must be satisfied by an insured. This is so because, just as with limits of liability, deductibles and self-insured retentions are often applicable on a "per occurrence" or similar basis.

When number of occurrences arises for purposes of determining the number of deductibles or self-insured retentions that an insured must satisfy, as opposed to the number of limits of liability that an insurer must pay, some insureds and insurers may sometimes find themselves making what appear to be atypical arguments.

For example, when a number of occurrences dispute is over the number of limits of liability that an insurer must pay, insureds can be expected to argue for a multiple occurrences determination. Here, more occurrences means more coverage under the policy for the insured. But when number of deductibles or self-insured retentions are at issue, some insureds may find themselves arguing for a single occurrence determination, so that they need only satisfy a single deductible or self-insured retention. Now, more occurrences means more personal exposure under the policy for the insured.

Likewise, insurers that argue for a single occurrence, when the issue arises in the context of determining its limits of liability, may argue for multiple occurrences, when number of deductibles or self-insured retentions are at issue. *See CSX Transp., Inc. v. Cont'l Ins. Co.*, 680 A.2d 1082 (Md. 1996) (involving the insurers' argument that each of 20,000-plus noise-induced hearing loss claims arose from a separate occurrence for purposes of policies that contained self-insured retentions that ranged from $100,000 to $3 million for each occurrence); *see also Washoe County v. Transcon. Ins. Co.*, 878 P.2d 306 (Nev. 1994) (involving the insurers' argument that each child sexually abused by a daycare center worker constituted a separate occurrence for purposes of settlements between $2,000 and $25,000 per child under policies that contained a $50,000 self-insured retention). Despite this, as an Illinois appeals court observed, the context for the issue should not matter: "[I]f an insured's conduct is a single occurrence for purposes of establishing the applicable deductible, it should be the same for purposes of setting the limits of the insurer's liability." *United Conveyor Corp. v. Allstate Ins. Co.*, 92 N.E.3d 561, 569-70 (Ill. Ct. App. 2017).

In a similar vein, a primary insurer that argues for a single occurrence may now advocate for multiple occurrences when it is operating in the capacity as an excess insurer. Excess insurers typically benefit from a multiple occurrence determination as it may serve to increase the amount of primary limits that must be exhausted before the excess policy attaches.

Nobody disputes that courts' number of occurrences determinations can have a dramatic impact on the amount of coverage owed for certain claims. As a result, for claims involving significant injuries or damages, a multiple occurrences determination can serve as a basis for providing the amount of coverage that, in hindsight, needed to be purchased by the insured. As a result, there may a temptation for some courts to make number of occurrences decisions that are outcome determinative. At least one court has recognized this possibility and cautioned against it. *Unigard Ins. Co. v. U.S. Fid. & Guar. Co.*, 728 P.2d 780, 782 (Idaho Ct. App. 1986) ("A determination of the number of occurrences cannot be result-oriented. It must rest on a principled analysis that is not predisposed to favor insureds or insurers.").

50-State Survey: Number of Occurrences

Alabama: The Supreme Court of Alabama adopted the "cause" test and held that, where a roofing crew failed to adequately cover the exposed portion of a roof under repair, causing additional damage, the two events, because they were easily distinguishable in time and space, and because one event did not cause the other, each constituted a separate occurrence. *U.S. Fire Ins. Co. v. Safeco Ins. Co.*, 444 So. 2d 844, 846–47 (Ala. 1983). The policy defined "one occurrence" "[f]or the purpose of determining the limit of the company's liability" as "all bodily injury and property damage arising out of continuous or repeated exposure to substantially the same general conditions shall be considered as arising out of one occurrence." *Id.* at 845–46. The court held that "[a]s long as the injuries stem from one proximate cause there is a single occurrence." *Id.* at 846 (quoting *Appalachian Ins. Co. v. Liberty Mut. Ins. Co.*, 676 F.2d 56, 61 (3rd Cir. 1982)). The court viewed the negligent act of the roofing crew as a separate, intervening cause and not a proximate cause. *Id.* at 847; *see also St. Paul Fire & Marine Ins. Co. v. Christiansen Marine, Inc.*, 893 So. 2d 1124, 1137 (Ala. 2004) (holding that, for purposes of calculating the deductible owed, in the absence of evidence of more than one proximate cause, the breakup of several barges constituted a single occurrence); *Certain Underwriters at Lloyd's, London v. Southern Natural Gas Co.*, 142 So. 3d 436 (Ala. 2013) (discussing *Safeco* and *Christiansen Marine* and finding a single occurrence) ("Based on the arguments before us, we cannot say that there was a separate intervening cause. Sonat had cleanup areas at each site where Pydraul (and the PCBs in that lubricant) had contaminated the groundwater; that contamination was caused by the use of Pydraul through a unitary pipeline, and the manner of operating each compressor station was the same."); *Am. Cas. Co. of Reading v. Allen*, No. 12-2414, 2015 U.S. Dist. LEXIS 130979 (N.D. Ala. Sept. 29, 2015) (involving professional liability policy and discussing *Christiansen Marine*) ("[T]he state-court plaintiffs and their decedents were injured at different time periods, at different hospitals, and, perhaps, by different strains of bacteria. These claims may be related if the alleged injuries arise from the same cause — a single act, error, or omission or related acts, errors, or omission connected by a common fact, circumstance, situation, transaction, event, advice, or decision.").

Alaska: The Supreme Court of Alaska held that injuries sustained by six people, on account of a teenager firing a single shot from a gun, killing one friend and injuring another, were caused by a single occurrence. *United Services Auto. Ass'n v. Neary*, 307 P.3d 907 (Alaska 2013). The shooter's parents' homeowner's policy defined "occurrence" as "an accident, including continuous or repeated exposure to substantially the same general harmful conditions, which results ... in ... bodily injury." The court explained: "[I]t was not the Michauds' alleged failure to secure their firearms, nor their alleged failure to supervise their son, that constituted the event that was 'unforeseen and unexpected' from their standpoint as insureds; rather, it was 'the shooting that gave rise to the injuries' that was 'unforeseen and unexpected' and therefore, from their perspective, was the accident. The analysis is the same as it was in *Koikos* [*see* Florida], though the mathematics are different. Here there may have been multiple acts of negligence, but it was a single gunshot that caused the plaintiffs' damages. The single gunshot was the one occurrence for purposes of liability coverage." The court specifically rejected the shooter's parents call to adopt the "effects" test and find that, because there were six discrete injuries (the single bullet struck two individuals which in turn caused emotional distress to both sets of their parents) there were six occurrences. "Courts have correctly observed that the [effects] test renders insurers' liability both unpredictable and limitless, since any one event can cause many injuries to many people."

Arizona: The Supreme Court of Arizona held that embezzlement, committed over a five-year period by an employee of the insured, by forging company checks, constituted a single occurrence under an employee fidelity policy. *Employers Mut. Cas. Co. v. DGG & CAR, Inc.*, 183 P.3d 513, 518–19 (Ariz. 2008). The policy defined "occurrence" as "all loss caused by, or involving, one or more 'employees,' whether the result of a single act or series of acts." *Id.* at 515. The court held that, based on this definition, the employee's embezzlement, although including a number of thefts, was a "series of acts," each one following the other. *Id.* "The policy plainly considers the loss resulting from the embezzlement of a single employee an occurrence, with an attendant $50,000 policy limit." *Id.* at 516. The Supreme Court of Arizona also concluded that its decision was consistent with the majority of courts interpreting similar policy language in corresponding factual situations. *Id.*; *see also Superstition Crushing, LLC v. Travelers Cas. and Sur. Co. of Am.*, 360 Fed. Appx. 844, 846 (9th Cir.

2009) ("The fact that one employee was guilty of multiple embezzlements does not mean that there were multiple occurrences, because all of her embezzlements were part of a single 'series of acts.' Here, there was only one occurrence, a series of embezzlements by one employee. Thus, this interpretation is supported by the policy language as a whole, as well as by Arizona case law.") (following *Employers*) (finding guidance in the public policy rationale discussed by *Employers*—that if an "occurrence" happens each time there is an individual theft, it actually hurts insureds who suffer small losses because they would be less than the deductible); *Austin Mut. Ins. Co. v. Aldecoa*, No. 2 CA–CV 2011–0040, 2011 Ariz. App. Unpub. LEXIS 1265 (Ariz. Ct. App. Oct. 11, 2011) (holding that the meaning of "occurrence" centers on whether there was but one proximate, uninterrupted and continuing cause which resulted in all of the injuries and damage) ("In this case, the actions of each grandparent—leaving the pool gate unlocked and failing to supervise the children properly—constituted two causative acts and, therefore, two 'occurrences' under the policy. As conceded by Austin, each act was necessary to produce an injury that otherwise would not have occurred. The actions were taken by separate actors on separate days, each presumably acting without actual knowledge of the other's act. We cannot conclude that these separate acts constituted one uninterrupted 'natural and continuous sequence.'") (citations omitted); *Grain Dealers Mut. Ins. Co. v. Sharbono*, No. 12–02607, 2013 U.S. Dist. LEXIS 170939 (D. Ariz. Dec. 4, 2013) ("[T]he definition of 'occurrence' in *Helme* [*Arizona Property and Cas. Ins. Guar. Fund v. Helme*, 735 P.2d 451 (Ariz. 1987)] is significantly different from that in the present case. In *Helme*, 'occurrence' was defined as 'any incident, act or omission, or series of related incidents, acts or omissions resulting in injury.' Because the policy defined an occurrence as something 'resulting in' injury, the *Helme* court analyzed the number of causative acts that resulted in the injury. The Flores policy at issue here, however, does not define 'occurrence' in causal language, rather it defines 'occurrence' as an 'accident' with no reference to the causes of injury in the accident. The plain language of the Flores policy contemplates coverage for each accident, i.e., the collision between the pickup truck and tractor trailer, not the individual acts of negligence of the policy holder that might have led to the accident."); *Am. Strategic Ins. Corp. v. Clark*, No. 1 CA-CV 12-0881, 2013 Ariz. App. Unpub. LEXIS 1398 (Ariz. Ct. App. Dec. 19, 2013) ("Ordinarily, courts addressing causation surrounding an 'occurrence' under an insurance contract will examine whether 'there was but one proximate, uninterrupted, and continuing cause which resulted in all of the injuries and damages.' Thus, 'even though there have been multiple causative acts, there will be a single 'occurrence' if the acts are causally *related to each other* as well as to the final result.'") (quoting *Helme* and emphasis in original); *Cincinnati Indem. Co. v. Southwestern Line Constructors Joint Apprenticeship & Training Program*, 422 P.3d 1086 (Ariz. Ct. App. 2018) (rejecting the argument that, under *Helme*, the number of independent acts that caused a pole to break (five), determines the number of occurrences) ("The policy at issue in *Helme* defined 'occurrence' in relation to incidents, acts, or omissions that result in injury. Cincinnati Indemnity's Policy, in contrast, defines an 'occurrence' as an 'accident,' not the precipitating causes of the accident. This difference in policy language renders *Helme* inapplicable here."); *Landmark Am. Ins. Co. v. Shurwest LLC*, No. 19-04743, 2020 U.S. Dist. LEXIS 167774 (D. Ariz. July 23, 2020) (involving professional liability policy and discussing *Helme*) ("For the eleven lawsuits to be related or part of the same series of omissions, there would have to be some indication that the acts alleged in one lawsuit 'caused' the other. There is no such indication here.").

Arkansas: The Supreme Court of Arkansas applied the "cause" test and held that, where a man purchased a pistol and a shotgun at a sporting goods store, shot a policeman, killed and wounded several other persons, and then committed suicide, the insured's sale of the weapons constituted a single occurrence within the meaning of the policy. *Travelers Indem. Co. v. Olive's Sporting Goods, Inc.*, 764 S.W.2d 596, 599 (Ark. 1989). The policy defined "occurrence," in pertinent part as, "an accident including continuance [of] or repeated exposure to conditions." *Id.* (alteration in original). The policy also provided that "the limit stated in the declarations as applicable to 'each occurrence' is the total limit of liability … for all damages … arising out of bodily injury … sustained by one or more persons … as a result of any one occurrence." *Id.* The court based its decision on the terms of the policy and its conclusion that, following a review of decisions from other jurisdictions, the "cause" test, rather than the "effect" test, holds the better view. *Id.*; *see also Fireman's Fund Ins. Co. v. Scottsdale Ins. Co.*, 968 F. Supp. 444, 448 (E.D. Ark. 1997) (applying the cause test and predicting that the Supreme Court of Arkansas would hold that, in the absence of evidence of two or more independent events/causes, multiple sales of contaminated food at a restaurant to several customers constitute a single occurrence within the meaning of a commercial general liability policy); *Hortica-Florists' Mut. Ins. Co. v. Pittman Nursery Corp.*, No. 07–1119, 2011 U.S. Dist. LEXIS 93263 (W.D. Ark. Aug. 22, 2011) ("The Policy states: 'All loss or damage: (1) Caused by one or more persons; or (2) Involving a single act or series of related acts; is considered one occurrence'. In attempting to interpret this language, it is not clear to the

Court whether an 'occurrence' is defined as all acts committed by a single individual, a number of 'related acts' committed by an individual, or a single act committed by an individual. In the case at bar, PNC alleges that Mr. Aydani committed multiple acts of theft or embezzlement spanning multiple years, using multiple sources of funding. Considering the complex nature of the counterclaim for recovery for Mr. Aydani's acts of theft and the ambiguity of the contractual language on this subject, summary judgment is inappropriate.").

California: The Court of Appeal of California adopted the "cause" test and held that damage to downhill property caused by a landslide constituted one "occurrence." *Safeco Ins. Co. of America v. Fireman's Fund Ins. Co.*, 148 Cal. App. 4th 620, 633–34 (Cal. Ct. App. 2007). The policies at issue defined "occurrence," in relevant part, as "[a]n accident, including continuous or repeated exposure to the same or similar harmful conditions, which results, during the policy period, in 'bodily injury' or 'property damage.'" *Id.* at 631 (alteration in original). "When all injuries emanate from a common source … , there is only a single occurrence for purposes of policy coverage. It is irrelevant that there are multiple injuries or injuries of different magnitudes, or that the injuries *extend over a period of time*. Conversely, when a cause is interrupted, or when there are several autonomous causes, there are multiple 'occurrences' for purposes of determining policy limits and assessing deductibles." *Id.* at 633–34 (quotation omitted) (emphasis and alteration in original). The court concluded that there was one uninterrupted cause or event, the landslide, that resulted in all of the damage. *Id.* at 634; *see also Evanston Ins. Co. v. Ghillie Suits. com, Inc.*, No. C 08–2099, 2009 U.S. Dist. LEXIS 22256 (N.D. Cal. Mar. 19, 2009) (recognizing *Safeco* as the appropriate law but holding that two Marines injured by fire constituted separate occurrences because the proximate cause of the first Marine's injuries was the ignition of his camouflage suit, while the other Marine's suit ignited after he decided to rescue the first Marine and came into contact with the fire) ("Allowing the insurer to limit the number of occurrences to a particular remote cause would effectively eviscerate the purpose of having a per-occurrence limitation as opposed to an aggregate limit."); *Pennsylvania Gen. Ins. Co. v. Am. Safety Indem. Co.*, 185 Cal.App. 4th 1515 (2010) (citing various California cases holding that "occurrence" refers to the underlying cause of injury, rather than the injury or claim itself, when determining how to apply per occurrence limits or per occurrence deductibles); *Budway Enters., Inc. v. Fed. Ins. Co.*, No. EDCV 09-448, 2009 U.S. Dist. LEXIS 31584 (C.D. Cal. Apr. 14, 2009) (examining several California cases, holding that the cause test applied and that there were insufficient factual allegations to show multiple occurrences as the cause of injury) (cargo insurance); *D.R. Horton Los Angeles Holding Co., Inc. v. American Safety Indem. Co.*, No. 10CV443, 2012 U.S. Dist. LEXIS 1881 (S.D.Cal. Jan. 5, 2012) ("With regard to whether there is a single or multiple occurrences, the court looks to the underlying proximate cause."); *Landmark American Insurance Company v. Liberty Surplus Insurance Corporation*, No. 12-10728, 2014 U.S. Dist. LEXIS 190535 (C.D. Cal. Apr. 9, 2014) ("Like the other leading cases discussing the definition of 'occurrence' in standard general liability policies under California law, the resolution of the present case depends heavily on the specific facts. If, for example, the defects were each caused by failure to apply sealant, the case may have come out differently. On the facts as presented in the record, it appears that distinct causal conditions caused water intrusion damage in these two distinct areas of the project. Under California law, the fact that the damage resulted from two distinct causes means that there were two 'occurrences' within the meaning of the Landmark Policy and the Liberty Policy."); *St. Paul Fire & Marine Ins. Co. v. Ins. Co. of the State of Pa.*, No. 15-02744, 2017 U.S. Dist. LEXIS 32551 (N.D. Cal. March 7, 2017) ("Here, the exterior and interior damage allegedly caused by Devcon's 'negligent supervision' is more like the separate 'police harassment' and 'excessive force' allegations in *Mead Reinsurance [v. Granite State Ins. Co.*, 873 F.2d 1185 (9th Cir. 1998)] than a single policy of excessive force. The harms to the interior and exterior of the Housing Project were caused by different people, different events, and different acts of negligence. There has been no showing that the 'negligent supervision' that allegedly caused the interior damage is the same as the 'negligent supervision' that caused the exterior damage. Thus, Travelers and Zurich have failed to show that Devcon's negligent supervision caused the Regents to be exposed to 'continuous or repeated exposure to substantially the same general harmful conditions,' which is required to show a single occurrence under the Travelers and Zurich policies."); *Ins. Co. of the State of Pa. v. Cty. of San Bernardino*, No. 16-0128, 2017 U.S. Dist. LEXIS 185541 (C.D. Cal. July 24, 2017) ("If ICSOP can demonstrate that the leaks were continuous or repeated (through, for example, the same contaminants leaking through the same crack in the landfill's infrastructure) and for substantially the same reasons, then ICSOP will have established that it is appropriate to assess all of the County's damage under the 'continuous or repeated exposure' standard. However, if the County can demonstrate that the leaks resulted at distinct moments in time and for different reasons, then it will be up to the jury to decide how many 'events' the ICSOP Policies must cover."); *Liberty Mut. Fire Ins. Co. v. Bosa Dev. Cal. II, Inc.*, No. 17-0666, 2020 U.S. Dist. LEXIS

65243 (S.D. Cal. Apr. 13, 2020) (addressing California and case law nationally and rejecting condominium developer-insured's "one occurrence" argument – negligent supervision -- for purposes of number of deductibles) ("[T]here is no showing that the 'negligent supervision' of the waterproofing that allegedly caused the water damage is the same as the 'negligent supervision' that caused the improper installation of plumbing, or the improper selection of materials. In fact, Bosa fails to produce any evidence that it was negligent as a developer of the project at all.").

Colorado: No instructive authority.

Connecticut: The Supreme Court of Connecticut held that hundreds of thousands of asbestos bodily injury claims, filed against an insurer of employee healthcare plans, alleging that the insurer failed to adequately publicize the health risks of exposure to asbestos, constituted multiple occurrences (but each claimant was not automatically a separate occurrence). *Metro. Life Ins. Co. v. Aetna Cas. & Sur. Co.*, 765 A.2d 891, 896 (Conn. 2001). The policies did not define the term "occurrence." *Id.* at 897. However, the policies contained "continuous exposure" language that combined claims arising from each claimant's exposure to asbestos at the same place, at approximately the same time, into one occurrence. *Id.* at 898. The court concluded that "the language of the defendants' insurance policies is not ambiguous. A plain reading of the policies indicates that the occurrence in this case was the exposure of the claimants to asbestos, not [the insurer's] alleged failure to warn. Moreover, the proper interpretation of the continuous exposure clause is that it combines exposures to asbestos that occurred at the same place, at approximately the same time, resulting *still*, in multiple occurrences under the policy. The clause cannot be read plausibly, as Metropolitan contends, to combine hundreds of thousands of exposures that occurred under different circumstances throughout the country over a period of sixty years, into one occurrence." *Id.* at 900 (emphasis in original); *see also Progressive Cas. Ins. Co. v. Farkas*, No. CV095015726S, 2010 Conn. Super. LEXIS 1625 (Conn. Super. Ct. June 24, 2010) (the single "event" that triggered liability on the insured's part was not her singular act of negligent driving, but, rather, the two collisions that it caused) ("The 'event' is the point in the causal chain at which time the liability is triggered. *See Metropolitan Life Ins. Co. v. Aetna Casualty & Surety Co., supra*, 255 Conn. at 322. It is not determined by reference to any point earlier in causal chain, even if, at such point, there was potential for future injury."); *Harleysville Worcester Ins. Co. v. Paramount Concrete, Inc.*, No. 11-578, 2014 U.S. Dist. LEXIS 43889 (D. Conn. Mar. 31, 2014) (following *Metropolitan*) ("All of Paramount's prior mistakes; its bad formula, reckless management, and disregard for industry standards, were just steps in a chain of events that ended in the company's defective product destroying swimming pools. There were nineteen separate occurrences here[.]"). The Supreme Court of Connecticut addressed the issue in the context of a professional liability policy in *Lexington Ins. Co. v. Lexington Healthcare Group, Inc.*, 84 A.3d 1167 (Conn. 2014) (interpreting "All claims arising from continuous, related, or repeated medical incidents shall be treated as arising out of one medical incident") ("[W]e conclude that the phrase related medical incidents does not clearly and unambiguously encompass incidents in which multiple losses are suffered by multiple people, when each loss has been caused by a unique set of negligent acts, errors or omissions by the insured, even though there may be a common precipitating factor.").

Delaware: The Supreme Court of Delaware adopted the "cause" test and held that thousands of claims for property damage, on account of defective resin material used in polybutylene plumbing systems, constituted a single occurrence. *Stonewall Ins. Co. v. E.I. DuPont De Nemours & Co.*, 996 A.2d 1254, 1257–58 (Del. 2010). The policies at issue defined "occurrence" as "an accident or a happening or event or a continuous or repeated exposure to conditions which unexpectedly and unintentionally results in personal injury, property damage or advertising liability during the policy period. All such exposure to substantially the same general conditions existing at or emanating from one premises location shall be deemed one occurrence." *Id.* at 1257. The supreme court concluded that the lower court correctly identified and applied the "cause" test and affirmed the court's decision that, when determining the number of occurrences in a products liability case, the proper focus is on production and dispersal—not on the location of injury or the specific means by which injury occurred. *Id.* at 1258. "Therefore, DuPont's production of an unsuitable product triggered only one single occurrence under the policies." *Id.* The court observed that, if the excess insurer's multiple occurrence position were adopted, DuPont would have to incur almost $24 trillion in damages before being entitled to reach its excess insurers. *Id.*; *see also ConAgra Foods, Inc. v. Lexington Ins. Co.*, 21 A.3d 62 (Del. 2011) (holding that a Lot or Batch Provision in an umbrella policy issued to a peanut butter manufacturer was ambiguous because it was susceptible to two reasonable and competing interpretations—one that limits coverage and one that expands coverage) ("The Lot or Batch Provision defines a 'lot or batch' as 'a single production run at a single facility not to exceed a 7 day period.' The Lot or Batch Provision provides that 'all Bodily Injury or Property Damages arising out of one lot or batch of products … shall be considered one Occurrence.'") (Because

Lot or Batch Provision was negotiated, the court remanded to the trial court to consider extrinsic evidence of what the parties intended); *Valley Forge Ins. Co. v. National Union Fire Ins. Co.*, No. N10C–07–135, 2012 Del. Super. LEXIS 130 (Del. Super. Ct. Mar. 15, 2012) ("[T]he alleged burn injuries and deaths covered by the Valley Forge Policy all allegedly occurred when a 100% chenille Robe, spec'd and sold by Blair, made contact with either a candle, cigarette lighter or stove. Each claimant has alleged that the Robe's poor design and/or inherent flammability, without appropriate warnings of its dangerousness, caused the plaintiff's or plaintiff's decedent's alleged burn injuries or deaths. Given the consistent factual and legal predicates of each of these claims, the Court is satisfied that the 'cause' of the losses for which Blair and Orchard seek coverage is Blair's alleged negligence and/or strict liability in connection with the production and distribution of an unreasonably dangerous product. This single 'cause' constitutes a single 'occurrence' i.e. 'continuous or repeated exposure to substantially the same harmful conditions,' under the Valley Forge Policy."); *Motors Liquidation Co. v. Allianz Ins. Co.*, No. N11C-12-022, 2013 Del. Super. LEXIS 605 (Del. Super. Ct. Dec. 31, 2013) ("In Delaware, *Stonewall* similarly held that producing a product that caused plumbing leaks in thousands of homes triggered only one occurrence. *Stonewall* affirmed the holding that the 'proper focus is ... on production and dispersal-not on the location of injury or the specific means by which injury occurred.'"); *Rite Aid Corp. v. ACE Am. Ins. Co.*, No. N19C-04-150, 2020 Del. Super. LEXIS 2797 (Del. Super. Ct. Sept. 22, 2020) (citing *Valley Forge v. National Union* for the proposition that Delaware applies the "substantially the same 'cause' test" to determine number of occurrences).

District of Columbia: A District of Columbia District Court held that numerous asbestos bodily injury claims, caused by the insured's manufacture of a thermal insulation product, constituted a single occurrence. *Owens-Illinois, Inc. v. Aetna Cas. & Sur. Co.*, 597 F. Supp. 1515, 1528 (D.D.C. 1984). The policies at issue generally defined "occurrence" as "an accident, including continuous or repeated exposure to conditions, which results in personal injury ... which is neither expected nor intended from the standpoint of the insured." *Id.* at 1525 (alteration in original). "Given the policies' definition of 'occurrence' and the policies' unifying definitional provisions, the calculation of the number of occurrences must focus on the underlying *circumstances* which resulted in the personal injury and claims for damage rather than each individual claimant's *injury*." *Id.* (emphasis in original). The court concluded that "the underlying circumstance that gave rise to the claims for damages was O-I's manufacture and sale of a hazardous asbestos containing product." *Id.* at 1527. The court's decision resulted in the insured's obligation being limited to a single deductible.

Florida: The Supreme Court of Florida held that injuries sustained by two individuals who were shot in a restaurant lobby constituted separate occurrences. *Koikos v. Travelers Ins. Co.*, 849 So. 2d 263, 273 (Fla. 2003). The policy defined "occurrence" as "an accident, including continuous or repeated exposure to substantially the same general harmful conditions." *Id.* at 266. The court concluded that, notwithstanding that the insured restaurant owner was sued for negligent failure to provide security, "occurrence" is defined by the immediate injury-producing act and not by the underlying tortious omission. *Id.* at 272. Despite this multiple occurrence holding, the court specifically emphasized that it was adopting the "cause," and not the "effect," test. *Id.* at 273. "[I]n this case, the immediate causes of the injuries were the intervening intentional acts of the third-party—the intruder's gunshots." *Id.* at 272; *see also GuideOne Elite Ins. Co. v. Old Cutler Presbyterian Church, Inc.*, 420 F.3d 1317, 1332 (11th Cir. 2005) (applying *Koikos* and holding that the rape, robbery, kidnapping, and each act of assault and battery upon a victim, and each of her children, were each separate occurrences since the various acts committed by the perpetrator were separated by sufficient "time and space"); *State Nat. Ins. Co. v. Lamberti*, 362 Fed. Appx. 76, 82 (11th Cir. 2010) (applying Florida law) ("[T]he immediate cause of the FTAA Claims plaintiffs' injuries is not the single, coordinated police action, as BSO argues. Instead, each interaction with the individual officers is the cause of the claim, and is distinguishable in time and space. Thus, each interaction could be a separate occurrence. The number of occurrences is not immediately clear, but this court is only called upon to determine whether there is one occurrence or more than one occurrence. It is clear that it is the latter."); *Mid-Continent Cas. Co. v. Basdeo*, 742 F. Supp. 2d 1293, 1347–48 (S.D. Fla. 2010) ("Upon review of the relevant cases, the Court concludes that three occurrences transpired: (1) damages caused in connection with First State's tarping work; (2) damages caused in connection with First State's work on the roofs; and (3) damages caused in connection with First State's work on the mansards. Each of these categories of damages resulted from a separate force, distinguishable in time and space.") (affirmed with further discussion at 477 Fed. Appx. 702 (11th Cir. 2012)); *Citizens Property Ins. Corp. v. Cook*, 93 So. 3d 479 (Fla. Ct. App. 2012) (rejecting trial court's conclusion that each drink provided to each deceased minor constituted a separate occurrence and instead held that there was only one occurrence causing the deaths, i.e., the car crash); *Maddox v. Florida Farm Bureau General*, 129 So. 3d

1179 (Fla. Ct. App. 2014) ("[I]n this case, it is reasonable to construe the occurrence as the entire dog attack or as each separate dog bite. Because ambiguous provisions must be construed against the insurer, the occurrence language in the instant policy must be construed as meaning each separate dog bite that resulted in a separate injury to a separate victim was a separate occurrence."); *Port Consol., Inc. v. Int'l Ins. Co. of Hannover, PLC*, 826 Fed. Appx. 822 (11th Cir. 2020) ("[U]nder Florida law, an 'occurrence' under the Policy is defined by the 'immediate injury-producing act.' Here, the immediate injury-producing acts consist of numerous alleged fuel thefts by several of Allied's affiliated drivers from different fuel dispensers at the Garden Road Facility on different days over the course of a year. Because each alleged fuel theft was an act separated and distinguishable in 'time and space,' we find that each alleged act of fuel theft constituted a separate 'occurrence' under the Policy.") (citing *Koikos* and *GuideOne*); *Travelers Indem. Co. v. Garcia*, No. 19-2911, 2020 U.S. Dist. LEXIS 203339 (M.D. Fla. Oct. 28, 2020) (analyzing *Koikos* in the context of a vehicle collision); *Belt v. USAA Cas. Ins. Co.*, No. 4D20-339, 2021 Fla. App. LEXIS 3522 (Fla. Ct. App. Mar. 10, 2021) ("The trial court employed the *Matty* [*see* Georgia] definition in its instruction: '[m]ultiple impacts will be considered one accident if there is but one proximate, uninterrupted, and continuing cause of injury.' It also provided the jury with factors to consider in that determination, gleaned from *Matty* and other cases. We agree with *Matty* as to the policy construction and the court's instruction was consistent with the cause theory and the policy language.").

Georgia: The Supreme Court of Georgia adopted the "cause" test for purposes of determining how many accidents occurred when a motorist struck two bicyclists, perhaps just over one second apart. *State Auto Prop. & Cas. Co. v. Matty*, 690 S.E.2d 614, 618 (Ga. 2010). "[T]he term 'each accident' appears in the limitation of liability section of the State Auto policy, which clearly contemplates that there can be a single 'accident' in which there are multiple vehicles, injured parties, and claims and provides that for that type of single accident, there will be a liability limit of $100,000." *Id.* at 618–19. The court rejected the "effect" theory (number of impacts), as it would mean that there would never be a single limit of liability in a multiple vehicle collision, because it is virtually impossible for multiple vehicles to collide simultaneously. *Id.* at 617. The Supreme Court remanded to the trial court to determine whether, applying the "cause" theory, there was "but one proximate, uninterrupted, and continuing cause which resulted in all of the injuries and damage." *Id.* at 619 (citation omitted). *See also Travelers Prop. Cas. Co. of Am. v. Cont'l Cas. Co.*, No. 14-2207, 2017 U.S. Dist. LEXIS 41796 (N.D. Ga. Jan. 4, 2017) ("Here, the

Underlying Cases undeniably involve multiple plaintiffs who suffered multiple injuries on multiple dates whose claims are set forth in multiple and varied complaints prepared by multiple attorneys. These facts, however, are irrelevant to the determination of what caused those injuries under the cause test. CKS bottle remains the 'constant, uninterrupted cause' that led to the injuries. The basis for CKS's alleged liability in each of the Underlying Cases was the decision to use the CKS bottle to package gel fuel for use in firepots."); *Grange Mut. Cas. Co. v. Slaughter*, 958 F.3d 1050 (11th Cir. 2020)

Hawaii: A Hawaii District Court held that an employee's discharge, in retaliation for objecting to sexual harassment, constituted one "occurrence" under a liability policy. *CIM Ins. Corp. v. Masamitsu*, 74 F. Supp. 2d 975, 988 (D. Haw. 1999). The policy defined "occurrence" as "continuous or repeated exposure to substantially the same general harmful conditions." *Id.* at 979 n.2. The court noted that most courts determine number of occurrences by looking to the cause of the damage and not the number of claims or injuries. *Id.* The court concluded that the retaliation claim constituted a single occurrence—a pattern and practice of tolerating harassment. *Id.*

Idaho: The Court of Appeals of Idaho applied the "continuous process test" and held that a snow plow that damaged ninety-eight doors of a mini-storage rental facility, in a four-hour period, constituted one "occurrence," and, hence, only one deductible applied. *Unigard Ins. Co. v. U.S. Fid. & Guar. Co.*, 728 P.2d 780, 783 (Idaho Ct. App. 1986). The policy did not define the term "occurrence." *Id.* at 782. The court determined that the cause of the damage was the negligence of the snow plow operator, which was continuous and repetitive. *Id.* at 783.

Illinois: The Supreme Court of Illinois adopted the "cause" test and held that damage caused by mercury, which spilled from gas meters while being replaced in numerous residences, constituted multiple occurrences. *Nicor Inc. v. Associated Elec. & Gas Ins. Servs., Ltd.*, 860 N.E.2d 280, 299 (Ill. 2006). The policies at issue defined "occurrence" as "one happening or series of happenings arising out of or due to one event taking place during the term of this contract" and "(1) an accident, or (2) event or continuous or repeated exposure to conditions which result in bodily injury, personal injury, death or physical damage to or destruction of tangible property, including the loss of use. All damages arising out of such exposure to substantially the same general conditions shall be considered as arising out of one occurrence." *Id.* at 284. The supreme court adopted the appellate court's view that each mercury spill constituted a separate occurrence as each asserted loss was the result of a separate and intervening human act or each act increased the insured's exposure to liability. *Id.* at 295. As the spills had no common cause and occurred at different times over a seventeen-year period, "[t]o say that each of the 195 spills emanated from a single cause would, under these circumstances, be completely untenable." *Id.* In *Addison Insurance Co. v. Fay*, 905 N.E.2d 747 (Ill. 2009), the Supreme Court of Illinois expanded upon *Nicor's* "cause" test and adopted a "time and space" test—"if cause and result are simultaneous or so closely linked in time and space as to be considered by the average person as one event, then the injuries will be deemed the result of one occurrence." *Id.* at 756 (quoting *Doria v. Ins. Co. of N. Am.*, 509 A.2d 220, 224 (N.J. Super. App. Div. 1986)). Then, once the insured provides the necessary facts to establish coverage and the value of the loss, the burden shifts to the insurer to prove that the event or events giving rise to the damage constituted a single occurrence. *Id.* at 753; *see also Auto-Owners Ins. Co. v. Munroe*, 614 F.3d. 322 (7th Cir. 2010) (applying Illinois law) (discussing *Nicor* and *Fay* and holding that, even if causes could properly be called separate, none were intervening, but, rather, came together at the same time to produce a single set of circumstances that caused a single accident) (addressing an uninterrupted chain reaction involving several vehicles); *Chicago Hosp. Risk Pooling Program v. Illinois State Med. Inter-Insurance Exch.*, 925 N.E.2d 1216, 1230 (Ill. Ct. App. 2010) ("As our supreme court recently reiterated in [*Fay*], once an insured establishes a right to coverage, it is an insurer's duty to establish that a limitation in the policy applies. Thus, if CHRPP maintained that its primary limits were exhausted in settlement by its $1 million per occurrence limit of liability rather than its $3 million aggregate limit, it bore the burden to establish that the deaths of the twins constituted one occurrence."); *Travelers Property Cas. Co. of America v. RSUI Indem. Co.*, 844 F. Supp. 2d 933 (N.D. Ill. 2012) ("[T]he negligence asserted against Valley Meats is a discreet act—the production of a single batch of tainted meat. There were no intervening acts of negligence by Valley Meats that occurred between the time Strike and Fenstermaker became ill. Because the damages for which coverage is sought result from the manufacture and sale of a defective product, 'the loss emanates from a single cause and there is but one occurrence.'"); *Ware v. First Specialty Ins. Corp.*, 983 N.E.2d 1115 (Ill. Ct. App. 2013) ("[E]ven if we were to apply the time and space test to the case at bar, we would still reach the same result. . . . [T]here is no dispute regarding the causes or circumstances surrounding plaintiffs' injuries and deaths. As the trial court correctly noted, 'much was unknown as to the cause of the boys' deaths [in *Addison*]. That mystery, however, is not present in this case. All of the Plaintiffs' deaths and injuries can be directly traced to one cause: the porch collapse.'"); *United Conveyor*

Corp. v. Allstate Ins. Co., 92 N.E.3d 561 (Ill. Ct. App. 2017) (finding single occurrence and per-occurrence limit applied) ("[I]f an insured's conduct is a single occurrence for purposes of establishing the applicable deductible, it should be the same for purposes of setting the limits of the insurer's liability.") ("The single, unitary cause of claims against United is the fact that it incorporated asbestos-containing components or products into each of its systems designed for high-heat operations. Contrary to United's position, the cause of its loss was not attributable to the installation and maintenance by United's customers of each conveyor system that contained asbestos products. Likewise, unlike *Nicor*, no separate human intervening event attributable to the conveyor system's installation and maintenance is involved. Specifically, the installation and maintenance by United's customers did not give rise to United's liability; its manufacturing activities did.").

Indiana: An Indiana District Court held that property damage, caused by defective concrete supplied by the insured to contractors, constituted multiple occurrences. *Irving Materials, Inc. v. Zurich Am. Ins. Co.*, No. 1:03-CV-361, 2007 U.S. Dist. LEXIS 98914 (S.D. Ind. Mar. 30, 2007). The policy defined "occurrence" as "an accident including continuous or repeated exposure to substantially the same general harmful conditions." The court held that each contract between the insured and a third party, requiring the insured to deliver a specific formulation of concrete, was a separate occurrence. The court reasoned that the event for which the insured was liable under its contract was the distribution of defective concrete, and not some other event in the causal chain, such as its receipt of faulty aggregate from a supplier. *See also State Farm Fire & Cas. Co. v. C.W.*, No. 4:08-CV-51, 2010 U.S. Dist. LEXIS 14069 (N.D. Ind. Feb. 17, 2010) ("The molestations occurred over a six-year period in which State Farm issued six different policies. If any of the policies covered an event occurring within the policy period, each policy did; nothing in any policy allows a construction that excludes from coverage a failure to supervise that mirrors a failure to supervise covered by a predecessor policy. Subject to the W. family's ultimate proof in the underlying case, there may have been as many as six occurrences."); *Ports of Indiana v. Lexington Ins. Co.*, No. 09–0854, 2011 U.S. Dist. LEXIS 130979 (S.D. Ind. Nov. 14, 2011) ("The essence of Ports' case has always been that the unusually low water level of Lake Michigan over the course of weeks or months during the winter of 2007–2008 was the key factor which, in concert with other natural events, caused the damage to the dock wall. The low lake level was a continuous or ongoing event. The level did not rise and fall dramatically on a daily basis, but lowered over the course of a lengthy time period before rising over a similarly lengthy period of time. Damage incurred over the course of time as a result of the same event or chain of events has been interpreted by the courts to be the result of a single occurrence."); *Thomson Inc. v. Insurance Co. of North America*, 11 N.E.3d 982 (Ind. Ct. App. 2014) (finding two occurrences and rejecting argument that each bodily injury must be a separate occurrence) ("[P]laintiffs' alleged injuries have two causes: (1) exposure to organic solvents while working in the factory (through inhalation, dermal contact, and ingestion of contaminated water); and (2) exposure to organic solvents while using contaminated groundwater in the dormitories (through drinking, bathing, and clothes washing). The specific means and timing of exposure and the resulting injuries may differ with respect to each plaintiff, but it is undeniable that the alleged injuries were caused by 'continuous or repeated exposure to *substantially* the same *general* harmful conditions' in the factory and in the dormitories.") (emphasis in original); *TIG Ins. Co. v. City of Elkhart*, 122 F. Supp. 3d 795 (N.D. Ind. 2015) ("Because an 'occurrence' under the TIG policies includes 'continuous or repeated exposure to substantially the same general harmful conditions,' a series of related acts of police misconduct (which would include perjured trial testimony or other misconduct after the false charges are brought) constitutes a single occurrence. This 'restrictive' policy definition sweeps into a single occurrence all injuries and damage resulting from one 'proximate, uninterrupted and continuing cause,' such as here with the malfeasance of Elkhart law enforcement."); *Auto-Owners Ins. Co. v. Long*, 112 N.E.3d 1165 (Ind. Ct. App. 2018) ("While the Insured failed to both properly label and package the box [violating U.S. Postal shipping requirements], there was only one accident that resulted from the Insured's failure to take appropriate preventative measures to avoid a spill. Stated differently, although the Insured did two things wrong in shipping the package, the wrongdoing resulted in one spill, i.e., 'one proximate, uninterrupted, and continuing cause which resulted in' Long's injury."); *First Specialty Ins. Corp. v. Supreme Corp.*, No. 12-1862018, U.S. Dist. LEXIS 167613 (N.D. Ind. Sept. 28, 2018) ("[T]he timing and nature of the drivers' illnesses may differ as to each driver, and the buses may have suffered from a multitude of defects that caused noxious fumes to seep into the cabin, but the bodily injury resulted from substantially the same general conditions: exposure to noxious fumes caused by defective bus parts. That exposure was continuous for at least as long as it took to render the drivers ill.").

Iowa: An Iowa District Court adopted the "cause" test and held that, defective windows manufactured and sold by the insured, that resulted in water damage, constituted a single "occurrence." *Liberty Mut. Ins. Co. v. Pella Corp.*, 631 F. Supp. 2d

1125, 1135–36 (S.D. Iowa 2009), *aff'd in part and rev'd in part on other grounds*, 650 F.3d 1161 (8th Cir. 2011). The policy defined "occurrence" as "an accident, including continuous or repeated exposure to substantially the same general harmful conditions." *Id.* at 1136. After acknowledging a lack of guidance under Iowa law, the court adopted the majority view—the "cause" test—and held that "the damages alleged by each of the plaintiffs in the Underlying Lawsuits arise from the 'the continuous or repeated exposure to the same general harmful conditions'—that is, to the design, manufacture, and allegedly fraudulent sale of a product containing the same latent defect." *Id. See also Pella Corp. v. Liberty Mut. Ins. Co.*, 246 F. Supp. 3d 1247 (S.D. Iowa 2017) ("The parties agree that the Court should determine the number of occurrences with reference to the underlying cause(s) of covered property damage but disagree regarding the level of generality at which that concept should be applied.") (court undertook a detailed factual analysis).In *Just v. Farmers Auto. Ins. Ass'n*, 877 N.W.2d 467 (Iowa 2016), the Iowa Supreme Court, following a lengthy and nationwide review, adopted the cause test in the context of automobile accident: "[W]e think the policy language 'regardless of the number of . . . [v]ehicles involved in the auto accident' provides sufficient clarification for purposes of this case. As we have already noted, in common vernacular a multi-vehicle accident took place. Furthermore, we believe the prevailing cause theory should apply here. That theory is consistent with Iowa's existing approach to insurance policy interpretation. Under that theory, no cause intervened between the truck—SUV collision, in which Crivaro was killed and his SUV was wrecked, and the motorcycle—SUV collision seconds later. Additionally, only a minimal span of time elapsed. Therefore, we find that the single accident limit on bodily injury liability in the Farmers policy unambiguously applies under the facts of this case."

Kansas: The Supreme Court of Kansas adopted the "cause" test and held that, where the cause of a patient's injuries were a physician's failure to diagnose a malignant lesion, followed by continuing failure to diagnose, there was one proximate, uninterrupted, and continuing cause that resulted in all of the injuries and damages. *Wilson v. Ramirez*, 2 P.3d 778, 785 (Kan. 2000); *see also American Family Mutual Insurance Co. v. Wilkins*, 179 P.3d 1104, 1114 (Kan. 2008) (adopting the "cause" test and holding that number of occurrences, in the context of an automobile accident, was based on the time-space continuum between the collisions and the drivers' level of control over the vehicle) ("Collisions with multiple vehicles constitute one occurrence when the collisions are nearly simultaneous or separated by a very short period of time and the insured does not maintain or regain control over his or her vehicle between collisions. When collisions between multiple vehicles are separated by a period of time or the insured maintains or regains control of the vehicle before a subsequent collision, there are multiple occurrences."); *Health Midwest Ins. Co., Ltd. v. Cont'l Cas. Co.*, No. 96–661, 2008 Kan. App. Unpub. LEXIS 250 (Kan. Ct. App. Mar. 28, 2008) (holding that the lower court correctly distinguished *Wilson* on the basis that intervening medical mistakes created a situation where there were two separate causes instead of one) (also considering certain relevant Kansas statutory language in reaching its decision).

Kentucky: The Court of Appeals of Kentucky held that injuries sustained by three patrons of a nightclub, in an altercation with employees of the club, constituted one "occurrence." *Cont'l Ins. Cos. v. Hancock*, 507 S.W.2d 146, 152 (Ky. Ct. App. 1973). The court held, without explanation, that all of the injuries arose out of "continuous exposure to substantially the same general conditions." *Id.*; *see also Meridian Citizens Mut. Ins. Co. v. Horton*, No. 5:08-CV-302, 2010 U.S. Dist. LEXIS 28797 (E.D. Ky. Mar. 25, 2010) (citing non-Kentucky cases in discussion of number of deductibles) (concluding that court lacked insufficient factual evidence to determine whether the insured's former employees concocted one scheme to steal the insured's cattle, or whether they formed multiple independent schemes to steal) (property policy); *Piles Chevrolet Pontiac Buick, Inc. v. Auto Owners Ins. Co.*, No. 2011–002317, 2013 Ky. App. Unpub. LEXIS 397 (Ky. Ct. App. May 17, 2013) (following the majority of courts and holding that an embezzlement scheme carried out by a single employee was one occurrence because it constitutes a series of acts, each one following the other) (occurrence defined as "all loss caused by, or involving one or more 'employees', whether the result of a single act or series of acts"); *Davis v. Kentucky Farm Bureau Mutual Ins. Co.*, 495 S.W.3d 159 (Ky. Ct. App. 2016) (adopting the cause test) ("[M]erely because there were multiple negligent acts that combined to cause a single injury or multiple causes of action may be asserted does not mean there were multiple occurrences as that term is unambiguously defined in the Kentucky Farm Bureau policy ["an accident, including continuous or repeated exposure to substantially the same general harmful conditions"]. There are frequently multiple acts of negligence that cause a single injury. For instance, a negligent driver in a car accident may have been inattentive because he was intoxicated and distracted by his texting and speeding. As a result of the driver's negligence, a collision occurs injuring another person. Under those circumstances, although there were multiple acts of negligence, it cannot be reasonably argued there was more than one accident caused by the driver's negligence."); *Evanston Ins. Co. v. Hous. Auth. of Somerset*, 867

F.3d 653 (6th Cir. 2017) ("The individuals cannot solve this problem by claiming that different branches of the same tree caused the different injuries, creating three accidents, not one. That slices things too finely. You can't 'cut a plank so many times that it ha[s] just one side.' The individuals separately argue that the deaths arose from multiple causes—cardiac arrest in one case, blunt force in another—and thus that each qualifies as an occurrence under the cause approach. But that is a variation on a defeated theme, defeated indeed by the Kentucky Supreme Court in *Hancock*."); *W. Heritage Ins. Co. v. Coffman Welding & Metal Work*, No. 2018-CA-001186, 2020 Ky. App. Unpub. LEXIS 256 (Ky. Ct. App. Apr. 10, 2020) (discussing *Davis*) ("If we held a policy was unambiguous so that a child's estate could not recover for two claims resulting from the same occurrence, then we should not allow Western Heritage to charge a deductible per claim when the claims result from the same occurrence, especially when 'occurrence' is defined in Coffman's policy but 'claim' or 'per claim' is not and no explanation is provided in the policy for how the deductible provision applies.").

Louisiana: The Supreme Court of Louisiana held that damage to 119 properties, caused by the construction of an underground drainage canal, constituted multiple occurrences. *Lombard v. Sewerage & Water Bd. of New Orleans*, 284 So. 2d 905, 915–16 (La. 1973). The policy defined "occurrence" as "an accident or a continuous or repeated exposure to conditions which results during the policy period in injury to person or real or tangible property which is accidentally caused. All damages arising out of such exposure to substantially the same general conditions shall be considered as arising out of one occurrence." *Id.* at 915. The court reasoned that the word "occurrence" "must be construed from the point of view of the many persons whose property was damaged." *Id.* "As to each of these plaintiffs, the cumulated activities causing damage should be considered as one occurrence, though the circumstances causing damage consist of a continuous or repeated exposure to conditions resulting in damage arising out of such exposure." *Id.* at 915–16; *see also Liberty Mut. Ins. Co. v. Jotun Paints, Inc.*, 555 F. Supp. 2d 686, 695–96 (E.D. La. 2008) (surveying Louisiana case law addressing number of occurrences) ("The property damage in the DuroSeal petitions allegedly arose because of several negligent and fraudulent acts on the part of [the insured] and others. Each of these acts does not constitute a separate occurrence, but rather the acts combined constitute one occurrence for each party injured, *i.e.*, a separate occurrence for each plaintiff."); *Washington v. McCauley*, 62 So. 3d 173 (La. Ct. App. 2011) (addressing numerous Louisiana decisions on number of accidents and occurrences) (holding that an automobile collision was a single accident because the two collisions were almost simultaneous and not distinct nor separated by time and distance); *Marshall v. Air Liquide-Big Three, Inc.*, 107 So. 3d 13 (La. Ct. App. 2012) (removal of carbide lime from facility caused airborne carbide lime dust and resulting injuries to nearby inhabitants) ("We find the trial court accurately applied *Lombard* and its progeny and appropriately found an occurrence to each class member involving continuous or repeated exposure to carbide lime over a period of time. It is longstanding Louisiana law that when the separate property of each plaintiff was damaged by a series of events, one occurrence was involved insofar as each property owner was concerned. *See Lombard, supra.* This principle must be applied in this case."). In *Thebault v. Am. Home Assur. Co.*, 195 So. 3d 113 (La. Ct. App. 2016), the court distinguished *Lombard* because it "involved damages caused by a series of events over a significant period of time, whereas the present case involves a single uninterrupted loss of power." The court explained: "The loss of power (or failure of the generator) in this case constituted a single occurrence, not a series of events occurring over time. Thus, the term occurrence is not determined from the perspective of each plaintiff's individual damages, but rather, from the manner in which it is defined in the policy." The court also found the *Lombard* line of cases distinguishable because "they addressed the application of the term 'occurrence' within a limits of liability clause rather than a retained limit endorsement, as in this case." *See also Gibbs Constr., L.L.C. v. Nat'l Rice Mill, L.L.C.*, 294 So. 3d 552 (La. Ct. App. 2020) (addressing Louisiana law in detail and finding a single occurrence) ("[U]nlike *Lombard*, there was a single plaintiff and a single 'Occurrence,' as defined by the Westchester CGL policy, which was the continuous or repeated exposure [two storms fourteen months apart] to the alleged defective masonry restoration that resulted in property damage to the apartment complex.").

Maine: A Maine District Court adopted the "cause" test and held that damage to a large dryer, manufactured by the insured for use by paper manufacturers, constituted separate "occurrences." *Honeycomb Sys., Inc. v. Admiral Ins. Co.*, 567 F. Supp. 1400, 1406 (D. Me. 1983). The policy defined "occurrence" as "an accident, including continuous or repeated exposure to conditions." *Id.* at 1404. The court concluded that there was not one proximate, uninterrupted, and continuing cause which resulted in all of the injuries and damage. *Id.* at 1405–06. "The 1977 failure was not a recurrence of the 1975 failure, but rather a crack in the back head caused by a failure to follow the design in boring out the hub and affixing the hub plate. It had nothing to do with welding [1975 failure]. Thus in no meaningful sense can the failures be said to have the same proximate cause." *Id.* at 1406. *See also Me.*

Woods Pellet Co., LLC v. Western World Ins. Co., 401 F. Supp. 3d 194 (D. Me. 2019) (lengthy discussion of case law nationally on number of occurrences – but none in Maine, including *Honeycomb* -- addressing whether a cogeneration plant suffered three shutdowns or a single shutdown) ("While the cause theory might be useful when interpreting 'accident' and 'occurrence' in a liability policy, the approach is not particularly helpful in a property loss policy. Standard liability policies, from which the cause test derives, ordinarily do not specifically define 'accident' and usually define an 'occurrence' broadly as including 'continuous or repeated exposure to substantially the same general harmful conditions.' In this equipment breakdown policy, the term 'accident' is more narrowly defined. In the relevant provision of this contract, 'accident' means a 'fortuitous event,' and that 'event,' in this case, 'must be' a 'mechanical breakdown' to be covered. The question is whether three mechanical breakdowns or a single prolonged mechanical breakdown occurred.").

Maryland: The Court of Appeals of Maryland held that, for purposes of determining the number of applicable self-insured retentions, each of thousands of noise-induced hearing loss claims constituted a separate "occurrence." *CSX Trans., Inc. v. Cont'l Ins. Co.*, 680 A.2d 1082, 1097 (Md. 1996). Many of the 246 excess liability policies at issue defined "occurrence," and most did so as "an accident, including continuous or repeated exposure to conditions, which result in personal injury or property damage neither expected or [*sic*] intended from the standpoint of the insured." *Id.* at 1086. The court rejected the insured's argument that each claim had a common cause—the insured's failure to prevent the exposure by mandating the use of hearing protection. *Id.* at 1097. The court concluded that, to have "arisen out of one occurrence, the exposure of each claimant must have some commonality with the exposure of the other claimant; each exposure must have occurred at the same place or been caused by the same source." *Id.* at 1097; *see also Commercial Union Ins. Co. v. Porter Hayden Co.*, 698 A.2d 1167, 1211 (Md. 1997) (holding that each claimant's exposure to asbestos must be viewed as a separate "occurrence" because each individual claimant had a unique work history); *Griffith Energy Servs. v. Nat'l Union Fire Ins. Co.*, 120 A.3d 808 (Md. Ct. App. 2015) ("The majority of courts construing this language in insurance policies adopt a 'cause' approach, by referring to the cause or causes of the damage or injury and not to the number of injuries or claims.") (citing *CSX*) ("[T]he act of the insured that caused the property damage was the erroneous pumping of heating oil into the basement of 1135. That pumping was accomplished by using a fuel hose attached to a fuel delivery truck, a covered auto. Once the oil had been pumped into 1135, all three houses in the triplex were continuously exposed to the same conditions — oil seepage — and all of the resulting property damage was caused by that exposure."); *Board of County Commissioners of St. Mary's County v. Marcas, LLC*, 4 A.3d 946 (Md. 2010) (citing "number of occurrences" decisions and holding that multiple injuries to property, resulting from migration of toxic substances from a county landfill, constituted the "same occurrence" for purposes of the monetary caps on the county's liability under the Maryland Local Government Tort Claims Act); *Rutherford v. Nationwide Affinity Ins. Co.*, 424 F. Supp. 3d 393 (D. Md. 2019) ("[T]his Court agrees that the driver of the phantom vehicle, if identified, would be liable for his/her negligence in causing the accident, but disagrees that the involvement of the phantom vehicle constitutes a separate occurrence causing injury to the Decedent. This case involves a single accident and a single injury to the Decedent, proximately caused by the race and the resulting impact between Hayes's Mustang and the Decedent's car. The phantom vehicle's action participating in the race contributed to the injury the Decedent sustained in that occurrence, but did not cause a separate occurrence.").

Massachusetts: The Appeals Court of Massachusetts applied the "cause" test and held that a shooting spree by a college student that lasted eighteen minutes, spanned approximately a quarter of a mile and resulted in two deaths and injuries to four people, arose from a single "occurrence." *RLI Ins. Co. v. Simon's Rock Early College*, 765 N.E.2d 247, 255 (Mass. App. Ct. 2002). The policy defined "occurrence" as an "accident, including continuous or repeated exposure to substantially the same general harmful conditions." *Id.* at 251. The court held that the insured college's negligent acts or omissions in failing to prevent the student from using his gun constituted the "occurrence" for purposes of determining general liability coverage. *Id. But see Worcester Ins. Co. v. Fells Acres Day Sch., Inc.*, 558 N.E.2d 958, 973–74 (Mass. 1990) ("The tort plaintiffs allege numerous discrete acts of abuse, negligence, and breach of duty by several different defendants, some individual and one corporate, at different locations. These allegations preclude the possibility that there was but a 'single, ongoing cause' of the injuries alleged. Further, we have rejected attempts by insurers to characterize seemingly discrete events as emanating from a single, ongoing cause."). *See also Keyspan New England, LLC v. Hanover Ins. Co.*, Nos. 93–01458, 04–01855, 2008 Mass. Super. LEXIS 326 (Mass. Super. Ct. Aug. 14, 2008) (reconciling *Fells Acres* and *Simon's Rock*) ("[T]he conduct of the insured giving rise to the underlying claims is its ownership of the complex, and its conduct of operations there in such a manner as to permit (or fail to prevent) discharges of toxic materials into the environment, combined with its failure to remedy the contamination resulting from such discharges. The discharges, of course, happened repeatedly over a period of decades; indeed, the parties agree that it would be impossible to identify discrete discharges or to trace the contamination resulting from any particular discharge. Here, as in *Simons Rock*, the policy language 'clearly contemplates the possibility that multiple acts taking place over a space of time may contribute to a single occurrence for purposes of coverage.' (citation omitted) It follows that the contamination on the site, arising from multiple discharges over time, constitutes one occurrence.") ("The allegations involved in *Fells Acres* bear little similarity to those presented here. The insurer's effort to characterize repeated acts of sexual abuse as merely continuous exposure to abuse conditions was clearly a stretch of reasoning, and the Court treated it as such."); *Massachusetts Homeland Ins. Co. v. Walsh*, 944 N.E.2d 1095 (Mass. App. Ct. 2011) ("On the record before us, Leisher's injuries arose from a single, continuous episode of ramming of his vehicle that occurred in a short spatial and temporal span so as to render his injuries the result of a single occurrence with a single cause.") (citing *Simon's Rock*); *Tig Ins. Co. v. Old Republic Ins. Co.*, No. 18-12548, 2021 U.S. Dist. LEXIS 104844 (D. Mass. May 5, 2021) ("[T]he Court is required to look to the 'conduct of the insured' when determining the number of occurrences, *Simon's Rock*, and these two events arose from separate types of negligent conduct on the part of Dimeo/RMT, which also indicates separate occurrences. It is undisputed that McNulty's fall from a ladder was caused by a wheelbarrow striking a steel door frame that Dimeo/RMT ought to have secured, and that her fall into a hole was caused by Dimeo/RMT's failure to provide adequate covering and warning around floor holes. These are two distinct and specifically identified safety failures on the part of Dimeo/RMT. McNulty was injured by these distinct safety failures, and not by 'repeated exposure to substantially the same general harmful conditions.'").

Michigan: A Michigan District Court applied the "cause" test and held that pipe leaks, caused by defective resin manufactured by the insured, constituted a single occurrence. *Associated Indem. Corp. v. Dow Chem. Co.*, 814 F. Supp. 613, 623 (E.D. Mich. 1993). The policy defined "occurrence" as "an event, including continuous or repeated exposure to conditions which results, during the policy period, in personal injury or property damage not intended from the standpoint of the insured." *Id.* at 617. The court determined that the "production of defective resin was the sole, proximate, uninterrupted, and continuing cause of all of the property damage in the case for which Dow Canada could be responsible." *Id.* at 623. The court distinguished its decision from others involving Dow and its insurers which concluded that damage to building facades, caused by the use of Dow's mortar, constituted separate occurrences. *Id.* at 620. *See also Motors Liquidation Co. DIP Lenders Trust v. Allianz Ins. Co.*, No. N11C-12-022, 2017 Del. Super. LEXIS 279 (Del. Super. Ct. June 8, 2017) (applying Michigan law) (finding single occurrence in the context of numerous asbestos products claims) ("GM sold certain inherently defective products that caused injuries. There is no additional, independent link in the causal chain that had to be forged subsequent to the products' production and sale in order for them to become harmful.") (*aff'd on other grounds* 191 A.3d 1109 (Del. 2018)); *Alticor Global Holdings, Inc. v. Am. Int'l Specialty Lines Ins. Co.*, No. 17-388, 2019 U.S. Dist. LEXIS 195302 (W.D. Mich. Mar. 22, 2019) (not citing any case law, Michigan or otherwise) ("Amway contends that it is 'beyond dispute' that all the infringements alleged in the Internet Video Claim amount to a single Occurrence under the policy. The Court disagrees. The more than 1,000 alleged infringements took place over a period of more than ten years and involved more than 300 uploads by multiple different parties. Whether all these alleged infringements, or clusters of the alleged infringements, 'arise from the same, related or repeated injurious material or act' is in genuine dispute and requires factual determinations, precluding judgment as a matter of law."); *Livonia Pub. Sch. v. Selective Ins. Co.*, No. 16-10324, 2020 U.S. Dist. LEXIS 25007 (E.D. Mich. Feb. 13, 2020) ("The reasoning of courts that have found that multiple related acts of abuse against multiple victims constitute one occurrence per victim is persuasive. The allegations of sexual abuse and related allegations of negligent supervision in those cases are more analogous to the allegations of physical abuse and related allegations of deliberate indifference, failure to report, and failure to adequately investigate in the underlying lawsuits than are the allegations of a policy of condoning excessive force by the police in *Mead* [*Reinsurance v. Granite State Ins. Co.*, 873 F.2d 1185 (9th.Cir. 1988)].").

Minnesota: The Supreme Court of Minnesota held that an employee's embezzlement scheme constituted two "occurrences" under an employee dishonesty policy. *Am. Commerce Ins. Brokers, Inc. v. Minn. Mut. Fire & Cas. Co.*, 551 N.W.2d 224, 231 (Minn. 1996). The court declined to adopt the "cause" test, but, rather, held that "a court may consider several factors in concluding whether dishonest acts are part of a 'series of related acts,' including whether the acts are connected by time, place, opportunity, pattern, and, most importantly, method or modus operandi." *Id.* The court examined the nature of the embezzlement scheme and concluded that it involved two distinct "series of related acts." *Id.; see also Farmers Ins. Exchange v. Hallaway*, 564 F. Supp. 2d 1047, 1053–54 (D. Minn. 2008) (following *Am.*

Commerce and concluding that a defamatory e-mail campaign, occurring over a two-year period, constituted one "occurrence" under a homeowner's policy that provided "[r]epeated or continuous exposure to the same general conditions is considered to be one occurrence"); *Diocese of Duluth v. Liberty Mut. Group*, 565 B.R. 914 (D. Minn. Bkcy. Ct. 2017) (addressing trigger of coverage) ("[T]here are specific occurrences that are discrete and identifiable events; the priests' sexual abuse of the victims. Each victim suffered an injury and has readily identifiable damage on each separate occasion of sexual abuse. The sexual abuse is what caused the damages to the victims. Therefore under the actual-injury rule, the occurrence is the time when the victims were sexually abused by the priests. (citation omitted). There are separate occurrences for each separate sexual abuse for each victim and each priest. The victims each suffered separate abuse and it is this occurrence that triggers an insurance policy that is at risk at that time."); *Nat'l Union Fire Ins. Co. v. Donaldson Co.*, 926 F.3d 1014 (8th Cir. 2019) (discussing number of occurrences in the context of interpreting a batch clause).

Mississippi: The Court of Appeals of Mississippi held that a claim against the perpetrator of an assault, for failure to seek medical assistance for his victim, constituted only one occurrence. *Cooper v. Missey*, 881 So. 2d 889, 895 (Miss. Ct. App. 2004). The policy defined "occurrence" as "continuous and repeated exposure to the same general conditions." *Id.* at 894. The court reasoned that "[e]ven if we assume that [the victim's] condition was such that [the insured-perpetrator] knew or should have known that [the victim] needed medical assistance, that knowledge and the resulting failure to seek medical assistance continued unbroken until the time that [the insured-perpetrator] ultimately called for an ambulance … . [T]here is no evidence that would break the chain of negligence once [the victim's] condition rose to a level that demanded medical assistance. If we follow [the victim's] argument, every minute could constitute a separate occurrence under the policy." *Id.* The *Cooper* Court addressed *Crum v. Johnson*, 809 So. 2d 663 (Miss. 2002) and *Universal Underwriters Insurance Co. v. Ford*, 734 So. 2d 173 (Miss. 1999), both Supreme Court of Mississippi decisions finding multiple occurrences because the policies at issue did not unambiguously state that multiple injuries may not result in multiple occurrences. *Id.* at 894. *Crum* was used as support in a trigger of coverage decision. *See Travelers Indem. Co. v. Forrest County*, No. 14-22, 2016 U.S. Dist. LEXIS 85399 (S.D. Miss. June 30, 2016) ("Indeed, the Mississippi Supreme Court's prior treatment of multiple actions forming a single occurrence suggests that the Court's plain, direct approach is correct: '[A] factual issue of whether multiple acts are sufficiently related to constitute one occurrence of loss only arises where the applicable policy language unambiguously states that multiple acts may be so treated.' *Crum v. Johnson*, 809 So. 2d 663, 667 (Miss. 2002). Therefore, absent a policy provision explicitly stating that multiple actions and/or omissions over a course of time must be treated as a single action and/or omission, the Court will treat multiple actions/omissions as multiple triggers.") (*See* later decision at 2017 U.S. Dist. LEXIS 217767 (S.D. Miss. Mar. 30, 2017) reiterating reference to *Crum* for purposes of addressing trigger of coverage).

Missouri: A Missouri District Court held that a claim for injuries sustained by two joggers that were attacked by the insured's dog constituted one occurrence. *Allstate Prop. & Cas. Co. v. McBee*, No. 08–0534, 2009 U.S. Dist. LEXIS 35158 (W.D. Mo. Apr. 27, 2009). The policy defined "occurrence" as "an accident, including continuous or repeated exposure to substantially the same general harmful conditions during the policy period, resulting in bodily injury or property damage." The court declined to follow the Supreme Court of Florida's decision in *Koikos v. Travelers Ins. Co.*, 849 So. 2d 263 (Fla. 2003). Instead, the court adopted the "cause" test and concluded that the injuries sustained by each of the McBees were the result of continuous exposure to substantially the same harmful condition—the insured's failure to prevent the dog's escape. *See also Kansas Fire & Cas. Co. v. Koelling*, 729 S.W.2d 251, 252–53 (Mo. Ct. App. 1987) (adopting the "cause" test in the context of an automobile policy and concluding that a near simultaneous collision with two automobiles constituted only one accident); *Westchester Surplus Lines Ins. Co. v. Maverick Tube Corp.*, 722 F. Supp. 2d 787, 796 (S.D. Tex. 2010) (applying Missouri law) (distinguishing *McBee* and *Koelling* but nonetheless adopting the cause test and finding a single occurrence) ("The liability-causing event was Maverick's defective manufacturing of the drill casing. All of the damage flowed proximately from the manufacturing defect. Neither the sale of the casing nor its installation, as Westchester suggests, were necessary to make Maverick liable. Nor did those later events interrupt the causal chain. The 'cause' analysis supports a conclusion that Maverick's defective manufacturing was a single 'occurrence.'"); *Munroe v. Continental Western Ins. Co.*, 735 F.3d 783 (8th Cir. 2013) ("Under the cause approach in *Haulers* [*Ins. Co., Inc. v. Wyatt*], 170 S.W.3d 541 (Mo. Ct. App. 2005) and *Kansas Fire*, Munroe's injuries resulted from continuous or repeated exposure to the same conditions (collision) and constitute a single accident."); *Doe Run Res. Corp. v. Certain Underwriters at Lloyd's London*, 400 S.W.3d 463 (Mo. Ct. App. 2013) ("The active contamination, tailings ponds, and chat piles, however, constitute separate and distinct causes of contamination that resulted in separate occurrences at each of the six sites at issue.

When determining the number of occurrences, Missouri typically applies a 'cause' approach which examines the cause or causes of the accident or occurrence to determine whether there is a single or multiple occurrence. (citing *Koelling*) The chat piles and tailings ponds were physically distinct with different migration profiles to constitute separate causes of contamination."); *Fellowship of Christian Athletes v. Axis Ins. Co.*, 758 F.3d 982 (8th Cir. 2014) (following *Kansas Fire* and declining to apply the time and space test set forth in *Fay* (*see* Illinois)) ("The underlying litigation alleges that the FCA was negligent in allowing Nehmson and Gael to attend the pool party while knowing that the boys could not swim and in failing to properly train and supervise the camp counselors. Moreover, it is undisputed that the boys arrived at the Pella Aquatic Center at the same time, swam in the pool during the same one-hour period, and were discovered at the bottom of the pool at the same time. Accordingly, the FCA's alleged negligent conduct constituted one occurrence under the Axis policy because the underlying lawsuit alleges that the drownings were caused by 'exposure to substantially the same general harmful conditions.'").

Montana: The Supreme Court of Montana adopted the "cause" test and held that the death of a thirteen-month-old girl, from a toxic dose of diphenhydramine administered at a daycare facility, constituted one "occurrence." *Heggem v. Capitol Indem. Corp.*, 154 P.3d 1189 (Mont. 2007). The policy defined "occurrence" as "an accident, including continuous or repeated exposure to substantially the same general harmful conditions." *Id.* at 1193–94. The court determined that the only cause of the child's death was the lethal dose of diphenhydramine. *Id.* at 1197. "In interpreting the term 'occurrence' as used in liability policies which limit the insurer's liability to a specified amount per 'occurrence' the vast majority of courts view it from the perspective of causation—referring to the cause or causes of the damage or injury—and not the number of injuries or claims. (citations omitted). We adopt this 'cause' theory for interpreting the term 'occurrence' in an insurance liability policy that limits the insurer's liability to a specified amount per 'occurrence.'" *See also Crow v. Safeco Ins. Co. of Illinois*, No. 12–71, 2013 U.S. Dist. LEXIS 36233 (D. Mont. Mar. 13, 2013) ("The Montana Supreme Court's reasoning for adopting the cause theory in *Heggem* applies equally in this case even though the policies are not identical. The only link between the first and second accidents is Crow's contention that his injuries from the first accident caused the second accident."); *Progressive Northwestern Ins. Co. v. Jensen*, No. 16-29, 2017 U.S. Dist. LEXIS 25673 (D. Mont. Feb. 23, 2017) ("Neither *Crow* nor *Heggem* is factually analogous. Here, the parties disagree whether it was inevitable that Jensen would eventually strike James when she initially crossed over into the lane of oncoming traffic. Unlike the unsuccessful parties in *Heggem* and *Crow*, Respondents have not alleged that all injuries were caused by a single event. Remaining factual disputes are relevant to the question of whether the two collisions constituted a single accident or two separate accidents.").

Nebraska: The Supreme Court of Nebraska adopted the "cause" test and held that contamination by an insured, at four different sites, over the course of several decades, constituted one occurrence. *See Dutton-Lainson Co. v. Continental Ins. Co.*, 778 N.W.2d 433, 443 (Neb. 2010). The policy defined "occurrence" as "an accident, including continuous or repeated exposure to conditions, which results in bodily injury or property damage neither expected nor intended from the standpoint of the insured." *Id.* "Contamination occurred at four different sites, but all of the contamination was caused by the actions of [the insured]. The underlying cause of the damage was the use of TCE and TCA in the manufacturing operation. This action was continuous and repeated over a number of years." *Id.*

Nevada: The Supreme Court of Nevada applied the "cause" test and held that, for purposes of determining the number of applicable self-insured retentions, the sexual abuse of numerous children at a daycare center, over a three-year period, constituted one "occurrence." *Washoe County v. Transcon. Ins. Co.*, 878 P.2d 306, 310 (Nev. 1994). The policy defined "occurrence" as "an accident, or event, including injurious exposure to conditions, which results, during the policy period, in personal injury, property damage, or public officials errors and omissions." *Id.* at 307. The court concluded that the term "occurrence" should be defined in a way to give meaning to the insured's connection to liability. *Id.* at 310. On that basis, because the county "caused" the children's injuries, through its failure to act with the requisite care in the process of licensing the daycare center, such failure constituted a single "occurrence." *Id. See also APMC Hotel Management, LLC v. Fidelity and Deposit Co. of Maryland*, No. 09–2100, 2011 U.S. Dist. LEXIS 131638 (D. Nev. Nov. 10, 2011) (crime policy defined "occurrence" as "all loss caused by, or involving, one or more 'employees', whether the result of a single act or series of acts") (rejecting the argument that there were three separate occurrences because an employee used three general methods to commit a number of thefts) ("Although 'series' does impose a relatedness condition between the multiple acts upon which an 'occurrence' is based, those 'acts' are related in that they were committed by an employee (or employees) and that they caused loss, not that they caused loss in any particular way."); *Century Sur. Co. v. Casino West, Inc.*, 99 F. Supp. 3d 1262 (D. Nev. 2015) ("Finally, as Century points out, the language in the Policy states that a single 'occurrence' arises if the bodily injury is caused by exposure to 'substantially the same general harmful conditions.' Even if the various defects identified by Admiral are considered individual 'causes' of the victims' deaths, there can be no question that these causes taken together still constitute the same general harmful conditions. Each 'cause' had a role in producing, trapping, and channeling a lethal amount of carbon monoxide into the victims' room. Thus, although the defects may have individually contributed, the proximate cause of the deaths in this case was Casino West's negligence in failing to properly maintain the heater and equipment room. Under the Policy and Nevada law, this constitutes a single 'occurrence.'") (citing *Washoe County*); *United Nat'l Ins. Co. v. Assurance Co. of Am.*, No. 10-1086, 2015 U.S. Dist. LEXIS 153822 (D. Nev. Nov. 12, 2015) (finding multiple occurrences) ("[T]he damages to the homes constructed within the Seneca Falls development flowed from four independent causes—the grading and paving work that R.B. Petersen performed in each of the four units of that development."); *AIG Specialty Ins. Co. v. Liberty Mut. Fire Ins. Co.*, No. 17-01260, 2018 U.S. Dist. LEXIS 65198 (D. Nev. April 18, 2018) ("While the parties have submitted two reports identifying numerous negligent acts in selection of materials, faulty installation of various aspects of the pool system, and failure to clean up, there is no opinion expressed about whether all of these defects together are the single proximate cause of the humid environment leading to the rusting, or whether there are multiple independent causes.") (addressing *Washoe County* and *Casino West*).

New Hampshire: The Supreme Court of New Hampshire held that damage to several properties caused by a fire constituted one "accident" under a liability policy. *Travelers Indem. Co. v. New England Box Co.*, 157 A.2d 765, 768–69 (N.H. 1960). The policy provided that the "each accident" limit was the total limit for all damages for injury of all property of one or more persons as a result of any one accident. *Id.* at 768–69. The court held that such policy language was an indication that, in interpreting the limit of property damage liability for "each accident," the word "accident" was intended to be construed from the standpoint of cause rather than effect. *Id.* at 769.

New Jersey: The New Jersey Superior Court, Appellate Division, held that claims arising out of an insured's adult son firing a shotgun and hitting two police officers multiple times constituted a single occurrence. *Bomba v. State Farm Fire & Cas. Co.*, 879 A.2d 1252, 1256 (N.J. Super. Ct. App. Div. 2005). The policy defined "occurrence" as "an accident, including exposure to conditions, which results in: a. bodily injury." *Id.* at 1253. Relying on the court's adoption of the "cause" test in

Doria v. Insurance Co. of North America, 509 A.2d 220, 221 (N.J. Super. Ct. App. Div. 1986), the court held that the cause of the injuries was the negligence of the gunman's parents in permitting him to have access to firearms in their home. *Id.* at 1255. In *Doria*, the Appellate Division of the New Jersey Superior Court held that injury to two boys that fell into a swimming pool were one occurrence because the cause of the injuries was the insured's failure to properly fence in and cover an abandoned pool. *Id.* at 224; *see also Pine Belt Auto., Inc. v. Royal Indem. Co.*, No. 06-5995, 2008 U.S. Dist. LEXIS 84393 (D.N.J. Oct. 28, 2008) ("In applying this test [from *Bomba*], the Court finds that the injury sustained from the conversion of money orders stems from a common cause-the ongoing embezzlement by Thomson. The Court finds it irrelevant whether or not Thomson may have batched and cashed the checks several times. [E]ven if there were multiple instances, each instance was related to the overall scheme to embezzle money from Pine Belt.") (policy defined "occurrence" as "all loss caused by, or involving, one or more 'employees' whether the result of a single act or series of acts.") (*aff'd* 400 Fed. Appx. 621 (3rd Cir. 2010)); *Cooper Indus., LLC v. Emplrs Ins. of Wausau*, No. L-9284-11, 2017 N.J. Super. Unpub. LEXIS 3239 (N.J. Super. Ct. Law Div. Oct. 16, 2017) (discussing *Bomba* and rejecting a single occurrence for pollution discharge from two geographically distinct plants) ("The Certain Insurers have not identified any link or continuity between these plants that would justify treating them as a single cause. The two plants were notably never operating at the same time as one another; Glen Ridge closed in 1910, while West Orange opened in 1912."); *Penn Nat'l Ins. Co. v. North River Ins. Co.*, 783 Fed. Appx. 195 (3rd Cir. 2019) (addressing *Doria* and number of occurrences in the context of a statute of limitations dispute).

New Mexico: No instructive authority.

New York: The New York Court of Appeals applied the "unfortunate events" test and held that each individual exposed to asbestos insulation in turbines, at work sites across the country, constituted a separate occurrence. *Appalachian Ins. Co. v. Gen. Elec. Co.*, 863 N.E.2d 994, 1000 (N.Y. 2007). The policies defined occurrence as "an accident, event, happening or continuous or repeated exposure to conditions which unintentionally results in injury or damage during the policy period." *Id.* at 996. Relying on its prior decisions in *Arthur A. Johnson Corp. v. Indem. Ins. Co. of N. Am.*, 164 N.E.2d 704 (N.Y. 1959) and *Hartford Acc. & Indem. Co. v. Wesolowski*, 305 N.E.2d 907 (N.Y. 1973) for guidance, New York's highest court analyzed the policy language, the "temporal and spatial relationships between the incidents and the extent to which they were part of an undisputed continuum" and concluded that, since the policy language did not reflect an intent to group incidents, and there was no spatial or temporal relationship, "there were unquestionably multiple occurrences." *Id.* at 1000–01. The court concluded that each individual plaintiff's "continuous or repeated exposure" to asbestos gave rise to liability. *Id.* at 1000; *see also Nesmith v. Allstate Ins. Co.*, 25 N.E.3d 924 (N.Y. 2014) (finding that injuries to subsequent tenants of apartment, on account of exposure to lead paint, were part of a single "accidental loss" and only one policy limit was available to the two families) ("Young's children and Nesmith's grandchildren were exposed to the same hazard, lead paint, in the same apartment. Perhaps they were not exposed to *exactly* the same conditions; but to say that the 'general conditions' were not the same would deprive the word 'general' of all meaning.") (emphasis in original); *ExxonMobil Corp. v. Certain Underwriters at Lloyd's, London*, 855 N.Y.S. 2d 484, 485 (N.Y. App. Div. 2008) ("Each installation of ExxonMobil's polybutylene resin into a municipal utility water system, and each introduction of AV-1 lubricant into an aircraft engine, created 'exposure' to a condition that resulted in property damage, to multiple claimants on different dates over many years. Under the circumstances, the underlying product liability claims 'share few, if any, commonalities.'") (quoting *Appalachian*); *Bausch & Lomb Inc. v. Lexington Ins. Co.*, 679 F. Supp. 2d 345, 353–54 (W.D.N.Y. 2009) (addressing *Appalachian* in detail) ("[T]here is no dispute that the incidents giving rise to liability: i.e., exposure to the plaintiff's contact lens solutions, occurred in thousands of different locations, at thousands of different times, as a result of different solutions manufactured at different times and in different locations. The record reveals that claimants come from several different states and countries, allege different types of injuries, and allege that the exposure to the plaintiff's products took place in various locations at various times over the course of several years. As a result, there is no close temporal and spatial relationship between the incidents giving rise to the alleged injuries, and there is no basis for holding that the incidents can be viewed as part of the same causal continuum, without intervening agents or factors."), *aff'd* 414 Fed. Appx. 366, 370 (2d Cir. 2011) ("Like the district court, we conclude that the MoistureLoc incidents share few commonalities, differing in 'when and where exposure occurred,' how long or how often plaintiffs used MoistureLoc, and what intervening agents or factors existed.") ("To determine if multiple incidents arise from a single occurrence or multiple occurrences, the unfortunate events test analyzes 'whether there is a close temporal and spatial relationship between' or 'the same causal continuum' for the incidents giving rise to the injuries.") (quoting *Appalachian*); *Mt. McKinley Ins. Co. v. Corning Inc.*, 903 N.Y.S.2d 709

(N.Y. Sup. Ct. 2010) (lengthy discussion of New York law concerning number of occurrences); *Roman Catholic Diocese of Brooklyn v. National Union Fire Ins. Co. of Pittsburgh, Pa.*, 991 N.E.2d 666 (N.Y. 2013) (in the context of number of applicable self-insured retentions, finding multiple occurrences where a priest sexually abused an individual, on several occasions, over a six year period, in several locations) (addressing New York's number of occurrences law in detail and holding that where "each incident involved a distinct act of sexual abuse perpetrated in unique locations and interspersed over an extended period of time, it cannot be said, like the uninterrupted, instantaneous collisions in *Wesolowski*, that these incidents were precipitated by a single causal continuum and should be grouped into one occurrence"); *Nat'l Liab. & Fire Ins. Co. v. Itzkowitz*, No. 14-3651, 2015 U.S. App. LEXIS 16763 (2nd Cir. Sept. 22, 2015) (analyzing the unfortunate event test in detail) ("Applying the unfortunate event test, we hold that three separate accidents occurred for purposes of the National policy. The damage to the overpass was not temporally or spatially proximate to the Itzkowitz vehicle's collision with the dump box, and the events were part of distinct causal chains. Additionally, even though there was spatial proximity between the second and third incidents, they too were distinct accidents, both because the second incident did not play a role in causing the third and because the relative timing between the two incidents played no role in the third incident's occurrence."); *Verlus v. Liberty Mut. Ins. Co.*, No. 14-2493, 2015 U.S. Dist. LEXIS 153908 (S.D.N.Y. Nov. 12, 2015) (concluding that a multi-dog, multi-victim attack constituted one occurrence) ("The unfortunate event test will not apply, however, when an insurance policy indicates 'an intent to aggregate separate incidents into a single occurrence.' In *Roman Catholic Diocese of Brooklyn*, the New York Court of Appeals provided the following as an example of such aggregating language: '(a)ll such exposure to or events resulting from substantially the same general conditions during the policy period shall be deemed one occurrence.'") ("The Policy includes unambiguous language that 'bodily injury' . . . resulting from any one accident or from continuous or repeated exposure to substantially the same general harmful conditions shall be considered to be the result of one occurrence.' The Court therefore declines to apply the unfortunate event test to determine the number of occurrences under the Policy."); *National Union Fire Ins. Co. of Pittsburgh, PA v Roman Catholic Diocese of Brooklyn*, No. 653575/2014, 2017 N.Y. Misc. LEXIS 687 (N.Y. Sup. Ct. Feb. 27, 2017) ("Because the policies do not contain any provision that allows for the 'grouping' of the underlying injuries, New York's 'unfortunate event' test applies to determine the number of occurrences.. . . Applying the unfortunate event test, the court finds that the abuse suffered by each of the claimants in the underlying lawsuit do not share the 'requisite temporal and spatial closeness to join the incidents' into a single occurrence under New York's unfortunate event test."); *American Home Assur. Co. v Port Auth. of N.Y. & N.J.*, No. 651096/2012, 2017 N.Y. Misc. LEXIS 4589 (N.Y. Sup. Ct. Nov. 28, 2017) ("[E]ven if the claimants were exposed to a common source of 'spray-on fireproofing' (analogous to the single rainfall in *Johnson*), it is the exposure and injury of each claimant (analogous to the collapses of the walls) that constitutes the unfortunate event. Moreover, unlike the car accident in *Wesolowski*, Mario & DiBono's operations were protracted and intermittent, and thus, each alleged exposure to 'spray-on fireproofing' could not be part of an 'unbroken continuum.' In sum, the WTC Fireproofing Claims do not arise from a single occurrence, because they lack the temporal and spatial relationship required to be a single unfortunate event.") (*aff'd* 2018 N.Y. App. Div. LEXIS 7793); *Dan Tait, Inc. v Farm Family Cas. Ins. Co.*, No. 7910-17, 2018 N.Y. Misc. LEXIS 2686 (N.Y. Sup. Ct. July 2, 2018) ("[T]he unfortunate-event test applies only in the absence of policy language that speaks to the issue of the aggregation of separate incidents into one 'occurrence' or 'accident.'"); *Humphries v Metropolitan Prop. & Cas. Ins. Co.*, No. 152521/2015, 2020 N.Y. Misc. LEXIS 2663 (N.Y. Sup. Ct. May 26, 2020) ("[T]he two fires are separate occurrences within the meaning of the policy. As stated, the second fire, although a rekindling, took place a day after the first. Further, the original fire was 'confined and extinguished' on March 17. In addition, the fires did not occur in the same space, but on different floors of the building. Therefore, there was not the sort of undisrupted continuum the Court of Appeals contemplated in *Appalachian*.").

North Carolina: The Supreme Court of North Carolina held that the leakage of a contaminant from pressure vessels into sixty tons of a dye product constituted a single "occurrence." *Gaston County Dyeing Machine Co. v. Northfield Ins. Co.*, 524 S.E.2d 558, 564 (N.C. 2000). The policy defined "occurrence" as "an accident, including continuous or repeated exposure to substantially the same general harmful conditions." *Id.* The court concluded that "all the damage occurred as a result of exposure to the same harmful condition—continued leakage of the contaminant into the dye product." *Id.*; *see also W. World Ins. Co. v. Wilkie*, No. 5:06-CV-64-H, 2007 U.S. Dist. LEXIS 81677 (E.D.N.C. Nov. 2, 2007) (following *Gaston County* and predicting that the Supreme Court of North Carolina would conclude that the contracting of *E. coli* by several minors during visits to a petting zoo constituted a single occurrence); *Gen. Cas. Co. of Wisconsin v. Image Builders, Inc.*, No. 1:09cv159,

2010 U.S. Dist. LEXIS 115631 (W.D.N.C. Oct. 29, 2010) ("In determining whether there was a single occurrence or multiple occurrences, we look to the cause of the property damage rather than to the effect.") (quoting *Gaston County*); *Mitsui Sumitomo Ins. Co. of Am. v. Automatic Elevator Co., Inc.*, No. 1:09–CV–00480, 2011 U.S. Dist. LEXIS 103165 (M.D.N.C. Sept. 13, 2011) ("On the instant facts, a proper application of the cause approach (which the North Carolina Supreme Court would adopt) requires asking which negligent act, or continuum of negligent acts, on the part of the insured gave rise to liability. From the facts stipulated in the instant case, liability arose on the part of Automatic Elevator from the allegedly negligent handling of the plastic barrels containing used hydraulic fluid in the Duke Health parking deck. This act led to the hydraulic fluid's mistaken use as surgical cleanser on surgical instruments which were subsequently employed in a series of operations. A finding that each of the 127 surgeries constitutes a separate occurrence would blur the line between the cause approach and the effect approach. Such a ruling thus would effectively ignore the North Carolina courts' explicit adoption of a cause rather than an effects standard, something this Court declines to do."). In affirming *Automatic Elevator*, the Fourth Circuit held: "[L]ooking to the number of surgeries or instances of using hydraulic fluid to wash surgical instruments to determine the number of occurrences would turn the focus in this case from Automatic Elevator's alleged negligence to Duke's actions. Because Automatic Elevator is the insured party, calculating the number of occurrences based on Duke's conduct would contradict other courts' conclusions that it is more appropriate to 'focus on the act of the insured that gave rise to their liability.'. . . The only action that Automatic Elevator took in this case was placing the barrels of hydraulic fluid in its designated storage area at DHRH. Consequently, although we recognize that these out-of-state holdings are not binding precedent in North Carolina, the consensus among these courts suggests that the Supreme Court of North Carolina would find that the hydraulic fluid mistake involved one occurrence because it would similarly look to Automatic Elevator's single act of negligence rather than Duke's intervening actions." *Mitsui Sumitomo Ins. Co. of America v. Duke University Health System, Inc.*, 509 Fed. Appx. 233 (4th Cir. 2013).

North Dakota: No instructive authority. *But see Williston Basin Interstate Pipeline Co. v. Factory Mut. Ins. Co.*, 270 F.R.D. 456, 462 (D.N.D. 2010) (examining cases nationally and holding that insurer did not demonstrate that the term "occurrence" is so clearly unambiguous that the court should deny discovery of possibly relevant extrinsic evidence to address number of occurrences) ("Considering only this policy language ['The Company's maximum limit of liability in a single occurrence regardless of the number of Locations or coverages involved will not exceed the Policy limit of liability. …' as well as other language] and the dictionary definition of 'occurrence,' is an 'occurrence' simply an event or incident of property damage or loss, regardless of cause and cause being relevant only when there might be an applicable exclusion? Or, is an occurrence an event or incident that *causes* the property damage or loss? And, if the focus is upon the latter, how far back in the chain of causation does one go? For example, in this case, is the production from each of the individual wells a cause of loss, such that an argument can be made there were multiple occurrences—particularly if there was some separation in time and space with respect to the production from the wells? Or, is the production from all of the wells one event or incident because, among other things, they were drilled pursuant to a common scheme or plan?") (emphasis in original).

Ohio: The Court of Appeals of Ohio held that numerous asbestos bodily injury claims, caused by the manufacture and sale of defective protective masks, each constituted a separate occurrence. *Cincinnati Ins. Co. v. ACE INA Holdings, Inc.*, 886 N.E.2d 876, 887 (Ohio Ct. App. 2007). The policy defined "occurrence" as "an accident, including injurious exposure to conditions, which results, during the policy period, in bodily injury." *Id.* at 885. The court reasoned that "[the insured's] masks were not intrinsically harmful; they failed to protect, and that failure to protect led to a multitude of physically and temporally distinct injuries under a multitude of differing factual scenarios that did not constitute the 'same general conditions' contemplated under the plain language of the [policy]." *Id.* at 887. The court concluded with a cautionary note that "blanket judicial application of any one test could frustrate the contracting parties' intent." *Id.* at 888; *see also Libbey v. Factory Mut. Ins. Co.*, No. 06 CV-2412, 2007 U.S. Dist. LEXIS 45160 (N.D. Ohio June 21, 2007) (adopting the cause test and holding that multiple claims for misformulated oil that was injected into certain machines constituted a single occurrence); *Dutch Maid Logistics, Inc. v. Acuity*, Nos. 91932 and 92002, 2009 Ohio App. LEXIS 1512 (Ohio Ct. App. Apr. 16, 2009) (adopting the cause test) ("A plain reading of the policy language establishes that the policy defines an 'accident' as one encompassing as many vehicles and injuries as caused by the same tortfeasor. The trial court, in rendering its decision, correctly concluded that there was but one continuous accident that caused all the bodily injury claims that flowed from it."); *LuK Clutch Systems, LLC v. Century Indem. Co.*, 805 F. Supp. 2d 370 (N.D. Ohio 2011) ("Looking to the language of the Policies, the facts of this case and applying the cause test, the Court finds that the underlying cause that resulted in the claimants' personal injuries is each individual claimants' continued and repeated exposure to LuK Clutch's asbestos-containing product. Thus, each claimant's exposure is a separate occurrence. Under the Policies' terms, however, each individual exposure, *i.e.*, the continuous and repeated exposure, to LuK Clutch's asbestos-containing product by any one claimant is considered a single occurrence."); *Westfield Ins. Co. v. Cont'l Ins. Co.*, No. 13-02367, 2015 U.S. Dist. LEXIS 45437 (N.D. Ohio Apr. 7, 2015) ("Continental ignores that the claims filed against MVS, while certainly related to its role as a distributor, are caused by exposure to the asbestos fibers within different products with different distributions to different customers and sites at different times over many years. There is simply_no way to logically conclude that a single decision to distribute asbestos-containing products is the cause of claimants' injuries under these facts. Rather, claimants' injuries were proximately caused by exposure to asbestos fibers under unique conditions and circumstances. For this reason, and because Continental's preferred definition of 'occurrence' is not consistent with the Policies' definition of that term, the Court finds that the MVS claimants' claims arose from multiple occurrences."); *William Powell Co. v. OneBeacon Ins. Co.*, No. C-160291, 2016 Ohio App. LEXIS 4982 (Ohio Ct. App. Dec. 14, 2016) ("Thus, we conclude that *Cincinnati Ins.* controls. An occurrence constitutes each individual claimant's exposure to asbestos."); *Big Lots Stores, Inc. v. Am. Guar. & Liab. Ins. Co.*, No. 14-02635, 2017 U.S. Dist. LEXIS 29675 (S.D. Ohio Mar. 2, 2017) (addressing number of self-insured retentions) ("Like the *Pincoffs* court [*see* Texas], this Court concludes that the occurrence to which the [Arch and American Guarantee Policies] must refer is the occurrence of the events or incidents for which [Big Lots] is liable, and it was the sale of the torches for which Big Lots is liable. And for each sale of a torch, there was a new exposure and another occurrence. The Court notes that it is focusing on each sale as the act from which liability arose, *not* creating a rule in products liability cases that each sale constitutes an 'occurrence' under an insurance policy.") (emphasis in original); *Scott Fetzer Co. v. Zurich Am. Ins. Co.*, 769 Fed. Appx. 322 (6th Cir. 2019) ("If the relevant 'occurrence' is negligent supervision, there is only one occurrence. This conclusion is buttressed by Ohio law, which follows the cause test. Under the cause test, the number of occurrences is determined by reference to the cause or causes of the damage or injury, rather than by the number of individual claims.") (citing *Cincinnati Ins. Co. v. ACE INA Holdings*).

Oklahoma: The Tenth Circuit Court of Appeals, applying Oklahoma law, held that embezzlement by an employee, who wrote forty fraudulent checks, constituted one loss under a property policy. *Bus. Interiors, Inc. v. Aetna Cas. & Sur. Co.*, 751 F.2d 361, 363 (10th Cir. 1984) The court adopted the "cause" test and held that the insured's loss was the continued dishonesty of one employee. *Id.*; *see also Republic Underwriters Ins. Co. v. Moore*, 493 Fed. Appx. 907 (10th Cir. 2012) ("[T]he proper test for ascertaining the number of occurrences is whether there was one or more causes of the injuries. *See Business Interiors* . . . Applying the causation rule here leads to the inescapable conclusion that there was only one occurrence. All the injuries were caused by the restaurant's ongoing preparation of contaminated food. That the contaminated food was prepared and served at another location is irrelevant."); *Nat'l Cas. Co. v. Western Express*, 356 F. Supp. 3d 128 (W.D. Okla. 2018) (addressing *Moore* and concluding that an automobile collision qualifies as two accidents) ("Mr. Schneider was in control at the time he impacted the BMW, and at best maintained control until he was hit from behind by Mr. Crittenden. After the impact between Mr. Schneider's semi-truck and the Crittenden vehicle, his ability to avoid additional impacts was not dependent on his ability to maintain control of his vehicle; his vehicle was at that time relocated into the westbound lanes of traffic by the collisions. Although he may have had the ability to control his vehicle until he was hit by Crittenden, he never gained control of the situation.").

Oregon: An Oregon District Court held that numerous claims against an insured, for damage caused by the failure of its siding product, constituted one occurrence. *Cal. Ins. Co. v. Stimson Lumber Co.*, No. 01–514, 2005 U.S. Dist. LEXIS 4621 (D. Ore. Mar. 17, 2005). The policy defined "occurrence" as "an accident, including continuous or repeated exposure to substantially the same general harmful conditions." The court held that the "occurrence" was the continuous exposure to the siding manufactured and sold by the insured, which allegedly resulted in similar kinds of property damage to the plaintiffs' homes and buildings. *See also Knowledge Learning Corp. v. Nat'l Union Fire Ins. Co. of Pittsburgh, Pa.*, No. 10-188, 2010 U.S. Dist. LEXIS 127506 (D. Ore. Nov. 30, 2010) (addressing whether the physical and mental abuse at a daycare center, alleged in six separate lawsuits, constitutes one "occurrence") (policy defined "occurrence" as "an act or threatened act of abuse or molestation. All 'bodily injury' and 'personal and advertising injury' arising out of the acts of abuse or molestation by one person or two or more persons acting together toward any one person will be deemed a single 'occurrence'. A series of related acts of abuse or molestation will be treated as a single 'occurrence.'") (holding that the only plausible interpretation of the definition of "occurrence" treats all six actions as one "occurrence"; finding it notable that the second sentence specifically limits coverage for "bodily injury" caused by actions made "toward any one person" whereas the third sentence grants broad coverage without limitation to the number of victims affected by the abusive acts) (*affirmed at* 475 Fed. Appx. 137 (9th Cir. 2012)) (addressing the definition of "occurrence" in some detail and holding that "'series of related acts of abuse' refers to related acts of abuse whether involving one or multiple victims"); *Wright v. Turner*, 322 P.3d 476 (Ore. 2013) (addressing the issue in the context of the state's UM and UIM statute); *Flores-Haro v. Slade*, No. 12-01616, 2019 U.S. Dist. LEXIS 1513 (D. Ore. Jan. 1, 2019) (addressing the issue in the context of the state's tort claims act).

Pennsylvania: The Supreme Court of Pennsylvania adopted the "cause" test and held that there was a single "occurrence" where the insured's son, over a two-hour period, shot and killed a neighbor and then drove to three townships where he shot and killed four people and wounded another. *Donegal Mut. Ins. Co. v. Baumhammers*, 938 A.2d 286, 296 (Pa. 2007). The homeowner's policy at issue defined "occurrence" as an "accident, including continuous or repeated exposure to substantially the same general harmful conditions, which results during the policy period in ... bodily injury or property damage." *Id.* at 289 (alteration in original). Adopting the "cause" test, the court held that the insured-parents' negligence—failing to confiscate their son's weapon and/or notify law enforcement or his mental health providers of his unstable condition—constituted a single occurrence. *Id.* at 295–96. "Determining the number of occurrences by looking to the underlying negligence of the insured recognizes that the question of the extent of coverage rests upon the contractual obligation of the insurer to the insured. Since the policy was intended to insure Parents for their liabilities, the occurrence should be an event over which Parents had some control." *Id.* at 298; *see also Liberty Mut. Ins. Co. v. Treesdale, Inc.*, 418 F.3d 330, 339 (3d Cir. 2005) (applying Pennsylvania law) (holding that several thousand asbestos products claims arose from a single occurrence); *Kinney-Lindstrom v. Medical Care Availability and Reduction of Error Fund*, 73 A.3d 543 (Pa. 2013) (addressing *Baumhammers* in detail) ("[W]e hold that the number of occurrences under Section 715 is determined by examining whether there is one or multiple instances of professional negligence that caused the harm alleged; the number of victims of the medical malpractice is not controlling when considering the MCARE Fund's liability limit. Additionally, each instance of negligence must be associated with a distinct injury."); *Cincinnati Ins. Co. v. Devon Intern., Inc.*, 924 F. Supp. 2d 587 (E.D. Pa. 2013) ("[A]ll the injuries to the underlying plaintiffs and claims against Devon originate from a common source: Devon's single purchase and shipment of defective drywall from Shandong. Moreover, Devon 'had some control' over the cause of the injuries, in that it chose to purchase and distribute the defective drywall. Therefore, the Court finds that there is only one 'occurrence' for purposes of insurance coverage."); *Hollis v. Lexington Ins. Co.*, No. 16-1533, 2017 U.S. App. LEXIS 5088 (4th Cir. March 22, 2017) (applying Pennsylvania law) ("[R]egardless of the number of alleged negligent acts or victims, the injuries have a single proximate cause — the misfired firework that exploded near Kathryn and her sons. Because the injuries only have one cause, only one occurrence took place.") (addressing *Baumhammers*); *Giant Eagle, Inc. v. Am. Guar. & Liab. Ins. Co.*, No. 19-00904, 2020 U.S. Dist. LEXIS 208951 (W.D. Pa. Nov. 9, 2020) ("It is certainly possible, given the facts alleged in the complaints in the underlying lawsuits, that a court could find that a single occurrence, i.e. Giant Eagle's comprehensive failure to maintain effective controls over its opioid distribution and sales, resulted in the injuries suffered by the plaintiffs in the underlying lawsuits. As such, the Court finds that the underlying lawsuits allege facts that would potentially support a finding of a single occurrence.") (addressing *Baumhammers*); *Busby v. Steadfast Ins. Co.*, No. 19-2225, 420 F. Supp. 3d 289 (E.D. Pa. Oct. 31, 2019) (addressing Pennsylvania law in detail and concluding that its Supreme Court would find two accidents in the context of a motor vehicle crash that did not involve a chain reaction "where the last car hits the car in front of it which then hits the car in front of it as a result of the first impact").

Rhode Island: A Rhode Island District Court adopted the "cause" test and held that a claim against the manufacturer of car-washing equipment, whose defective equipment resulted in the shutdown of a carwash, constituted a single "occurrence." *Bartholomew v. Ins. Co. of N. Am.*, 502 F. Supp. 246, 252 (D.R.I. 1980). The policy defined "occurrence" as "an accident, including continuous or repeated exposure to conditions." *Id.* at 251. The court concluded that, while the damage sustained from the shutdown of the entire operation may have differed from the damage caused by the intermittent operation of the machine, the source of all of the injury was a single event—the sale of a defectively designed and constructed carwash unit. *Id.* at 252.; *see also Avco Corp. v. Aetna Cas. & Sur. Co.*, 679 A.2d 323, 328 (R.I. 1996) (stating in the context of a notice issue that "the dissemination of contaminants from [the insured's] Williamsport plant site into area ground water resulting in the contamination of the Williamsport municipal water supply and in the various claims made against [the insured] as a result thereof must be classified as *an* occurrence, and more specifically as one occurrence") (emphasis in original); *see also Allstate Ins. Co. v. Bonn*, No. 09–171ML, 2010 U.S. Dist. LEXIS 43178 (D.R.I. May 3, 2010) (relying on *Bartholomew* and finding a single occurrence in the context of exposure to lead paint in a residential setting) ("[T]he allegations of the underlying complaint all point to the same uninterrupted cause for the injuries suffered by D. and B.: the continuing, unabated presence of lead in the residence throughout the Jessups' tenancy. Although the children may have ingested the lead at different times and their blood tests showed different levels of exposure, the injuries all flowed from the same conditions in their immediate environment."); *Rhode Island Res. Recovery Corp. v. Travelers Cas. and Sur. Co.*, No. 10–294, 2011 U.S. Dist. LEXIS 58007 (D.R.I. May 25, 2011) ("[T]he Policies provide for two competing interpretations: one prohibiting the aggregation of unrelated thefts committed by two or more distinct sets of employees, and one aggregating those thefts based solely on the common participation of 'other persons' in the thefts. Of these competing interpretations, the former is more favorable to the Insured, as it provides for broader coverage.") (refraining from holding that the facts presented constituted either a Single Loss or more than one Single Loss as such a determination would be premature as discovery was ongoing).

In *Employers Mut. Cas. Co. v. Arbella Prot. Ins. Co.*, 24 A.3d 544 (R.I. 2011) the Supreme Court of Rhode Island addressed number of occurrences in the context of a dispute between insurers over the timing of an occurrence. The court held that the determination was fact intensive. "[I]t could rationally be concluded that flooding events alleged to have taken place '[o]n numerous occasion[s]' over the course of five years, or that were 'continual,' could be the result of multiple, discrete occurrences *rather than* one occurrence—which occurrence, Employers alleged, was constituted of an uninterrupted pattern and practice on the part of Viking Stone. The facts as alleged do not permit an unequivocal conclusion that the flooding constituted 'continuous or repeated exposure to substantially the same general harmful conditions'—because, again, there is an issue of material fact with respect to whether the flooding, even if it was caused by one or more of the defendants in the underlying civil action, was the result of separate and distinct acts by one or more of those defendants, rather than being the result of a single pattern and practice that resulted in the requisite 'continuous or repeated exposure.'" *Id.* at 556 (emphasis in original).

South Carolina: The Supreme Court of South Carolina declined to adopt either the majority or minority view on number of occurrences because it is based on a summary of numerous types of cases. *Owners Ins. Co. v. Salmonsen*, 622 S.E.2d 525, 526 (S.C. 2005). Instead, the court chose to focus narrowly on the issue at hand—distribution of a defective product. The policy defined "occurrence" as "an accident, including continuous or repeated exposure to substantially the same general harmful conditions." *Id.* at 525. The court held that, because the distributor took no distinct action giving rise to liability for each sale—the case did not involve defective distribution—the placing of a defective product into the stream of commerce was one occurrence under the policy. *See also Med. Protective Co. of Fort Wayne, Ind. v. S.C. Malpractice Liab. Ins. Joint Underwriting Assoc.*, 648 F. Supp. 2d 753, 759 (D.S.C. 2009) (holding that a doctor's course of treatment provided to a patient and her resulting damages constituted a single "occurrence" under the occurrence-based policies); *Beaufort County School Dist. v. United Nat. Ins. Co.*, 709 S.E.2d 85 (S.C. Ct. App. 2011) (holding that seven students that were sexually molested by an elementary school teacher gave rise to seven claims for purposes of sexual abuse and sexual harassment endorsements in a CGL policy) (discussion of case law nationally and interpretation of various policy provisions) ($150,000 SIR applicable to each claim).

South Dakota: No instructive authority.

Tennessee: A Tennessee District Court held that the sexual abuse of several minors at a childcare facility, by a facility employee, constituted a single "sexual abuse occurrence." *TIG Ins. Co. v. Merryland Childcare & Dev. Ctr., Inc.*, No. 04–2666, 2007 U.S. Dist. LEXIS 8190 (W.D. Tenn. Jan. 31, 2007). The policy defined "sexual abuse occurrence," in pertinent part, as "[a] single act, or multiple, continuous, sporadic, or related acts of sexual abuse or molestation caused by one perpetrator, or by two or more perpetrators acting together … . All acts of 'sexual abuse occurrence' by an actual or alleged perpetrator or perpetrators, including 'negligent employment' of such perpetrator or perpetrators, shall be deemed and construed as one occurrence which takes place when the first act of sexual abuse or molestation occurs, regardless of the number of persons involved, or the number of incidents or locations involved, or the period of time during which the acts of sexual abuse or molestation took place." The court concluded that the abuse perpetrated by the facility's employee upon the students constituted one occurrence. *See also American Modern Select Ins. Co. v. Humphrey*, No. 11–129, 2012 U.S. Dist. LEXIS 20800 (E.D. Tenn. Feb. 17, 2012) (rejecting argument that a policy provision limiting liability coverage to $10,000.00 per occurrence (an accident, including continuous or repeated exposure to substantially the same general harmful conditions) requires payment of up to $10,000.00 for each of plaintiff's 147 dog bites as separate, multiple occurrences or up to $10,000.00 for each of the seven dogs involved in an attack) (noting that "Tennessee courts look not to the cause of an incident when construing a 'per occurrence' or 'per accident' provision, but to the result or effect of the attack on the victim or victims" and concluding that "looking at the effect of the dog attack—that McCoy was severely injured—the Policy's per 'occurrence' provision does not focus on the number of wounds inflicted on McCoy, but rather, the fact that she was injured") ("The amount of time elapsing between the various bites inflicted on McCoy, assuming those time intervals are even ascertainable, would be closely linked in time and space. Further, the twenty-minute dog attack that ranged from 15 to 20 yards down a street constitutes a sufficiently close connection of cause—the attack—and effect—McCoy's wounds—for the attack to be considered one occurrence."); *CHS/Community Health Systems, Inc. v. Lexington Ins. Co.*, No. 11–00449, 2013 U.S. Dist. LEXIS 175788 (M.D. Tenn. Dec. 9, 2013) (addressing number of self-insured retentions that must be satisfied under an errors and omissions policy containing non-standard language).

Texas: The Court of Appeals of Texas held that, under the "cause" test, each claim against a builder, for water damage to homes that it built using synthetic stucco (EIFS), constituted a separate "occurrence." *Lennar Corp. v. Great American Ins. Co.*, 200 S.W.3d 651, 683 (Tex. Ct. App. 2006). The policies defined "occurrence" as "an accident, including continuous or repeated exposure to substantially the same general harmful conditions." *Id.* at 663. "Lennar was not the designer or the manufacturer of EIFS. Rather, Lennar's liability stemmed from the fact that it built and sold homes with EIFS. Thus, Lennar's liability to a particular homeowner stemmed from the application of EIFS, and the resulting damage, if any, to his or her particular home. Further, there was not one entrapment of water that caused damage to all the homes. Instead, the EIFS's entrapment of water on a particular home caused the damage to that home only. Therefore, Lennar was exposed to a new and separate liability for each home on which EIFS was applied." *Id.* at 682–83; *see also National Union Fire Ins. Co. v. Puget Plastics Corp.*, 649 F. Supp. 2d 613, 627–29 (S.D. Tex. 2009) (surveying Texas case law addressing number of occurrences); *Pennzoil-Quaker State Co. v. American Intern. Specialty Lines Ins. Co.*, 653 F. Supp. 2d 690, 707 (S.D. Tex. 2009) (rejecting insured's single occurrence argument) ("The petitions in the underlying suits allege distinct kinds of emissions and releases, with distinct causes … . The petitions also allege that releases of different types of contaminants into two distinct areas—air and subsurface water—have occurred continuously for years."); *LSG Techs., Inc. v. U.S. Fire Ins. Co.*, No. 2:07-CV-399 (E.D. Tex. Sept. 10, 2010) ("After review of the policy language, the Court finds that claimants exposed to the gaskets at the same time and location were exposed to substantially the same general condition[.] … Put another way, the repeated exposure to the gaskets caused the claimants' bodily injury. The policy language regarding continuance exposure supports this conclusion. The claimants who were exposed to the gaskets at the same time and location were subjected to 'continuous or repeated exposure to conditions' as defined in the Trinity policies or 'exposure to substantially the same general conditions' under the U.S. Fire policies."); *Axis Ins. Co. v. Buffalo Marine Services, Inc.*, No. 12–0178, 2013 U.S. Dist. LEXIS 132333 (S.D.Tex. Sept. 12, 2013) ("[T]here was not a single happening that resulted in damage to customers' bunkers; the four separate barges were loaded with the contaminated cutter stock on different dates, and their residue subsequently contaminated later loaded bunkers at varying times, and they delivered the contaminated bunkers to different customers at divergent times. The claims arising from the deliveries of each barge where they are not causally related should be seen as separate occurrences. Each instance of loading, transporting, and delivering a customer's bunkers was a separate event, with new loadings between jobs. Each of the four barges in the instant action operated the way the Maurice Pincoffs Company in *Pincoffs* did.") (*see Maurice Pincoffs Co. v. St. Paul Fire & Marine Ins. Co.*, 447 F.2d 204 (5th Cir. 1971) holding that insured did not contaminate bird seed but received it in contaminated condition, thus each of the eight subsequent sales and deliveries was a new exposure and another occurrence); *Trammell Crow Residential Co. v. St. Paul Fire & Marine Ins. Co.*, No. 11-2853, 2014 U.S. Dist. LEXIS 184876 (N.D. Tex. Jan. 21, 2014) (describing its decision as consistent with *Maurice Pincoffs*) ("[T]he Court did not hold that there was a separate occurrence each time a canary met its demise. By analogy, here there was not a separate occurrence each time a building sprang a leak. The sole occurrence for which the insureds are liable was the sale of the property."); *Evanston Ins. Co. v. Mid-Continent Cas. Co.*, 909 F.3d 143 (5th Cir. 2018) (addressing Texas law in detail in the context of a motor vehicle collision) ("[T]he appropriate inquiry is whether there was one proximate, uninterrupted, and continuing cause which resulted in all of the injuries and damage. If so, then there was a single occurrence. If the chain of proximate causation was broken by a pause in the negligent conduct or by some intervening cause, then there were multiple occurrences, even if the insured's negligent conduct which caused each of the injuries was the same kind of negligent conduct."); *Liberty Ins. Underwriters Inc. v. First Mercury Ins. Co.*, No. 17-3029, 2019 U.S. Dist. LEXIS 227200 (N.D. Tex. Aug. 2, 2019) (finding single occurrence) ("Although, here there are various types of construction defects, leading to different types of property damage, all of the property damage in this case was caused by a single event at a single facility — the defective construction by JWCC, or its subcontractors, of the performing arts center.”); *Travelers Cas. Ins. Co. of Am. v. Mediterranean Grill & Kabob Inc.*, No. 20-CA-0040, 2020 U.S. Dist. LEXIS 210212 (W.D. Tex. Nov. 4, 2020) (addressing Texas law in detail and concluding that nearly 200 cases of food poisoning, from salmonella bacteria at a restaurant, constituted a single occurrence, as the suits arose from the restaurant's own preparation of a contaminated product which was then sold to the claimants) (“[A]fter Pasha's alleged negligence allowed the food to become contaminated, there is no allegation or evidence that Pasha returned to preparing food safely, allowed the food to become contaminated again, and then, because of Pasha's negligence, exposed more patrons to contaminated food. Thus, Pasha's purported negligence is alleged to have caused one uninterrupted chain of events, meaning there was but one proximate, uninterrupted and continuing cause of the contamination for which it may be liable.”).

Utah: No instructive authority.

Vermont: No instructive authority.

Virginia: The Supreme Court of Virginia held that the sexual assault of several minors, by the resident manager of an apartment complex owned by the insured, constituted separate occurrences. *S.F. v. W. Am. Ins. Co.*, 463 S.E.2d 450, 452 (Va. 1995). The policy defined “occurrence” as “an accident, including continuous or repeated exposure to conditions, which results in bodily injury or property damage neither expected nor intended from the standpoint of the insured.” *Id.* The court concluded that, because the occurrence could have been one of several things, the term was ambiguous and must be construed against the insurer. *Id.* However, the policy also stated that “[f]or the purpose of determining the limit of the Company's liability, all bodily injury and property damage arising out of a continuous or repeated exposure to substantially the same general conditions shall be considered as arising out of one occurrence.” *Id.* Based on this language, the court held that, even though each minor was subjected to several acts of sexual molestation, such acts constituted only one occurrence per minor. *Id.*; *see also Norfolk & W. Ry. Co. v. Accident & Cas. Ins. Co. of Winterthur*, 796 F. Supp. 929, 937 (W.D. Va. 1992) (finding multiple occurrences for hearing-loss claims); *Dragas Mgmt. Corp. v. Hanover Ins. Co.*, 798 F. Supp. 2d 758 (E.D. Va. 2011) (holding that, based on *S.F.* and *Lennar Corp. v. Great American Ins. Co.* (*see* Texas), each installation of defective drywall constituted a separate occurrence) (“Under the ‘cause’ analysis, the proper focus in interpreting ‘occurrence’ under a liability policy is on the number of events that cause the injuries and give rise to the insured's liability. By focusing only on the initial purchase of the drywall, Citizens' and Hanover's causation argument begins too early in the process and limits 'occurrence' to this one action. While it is true that the initial purchase of the Chinese drywall was certainly a but-for cause of the damage, it was the act of installing the drywall in each home which set the chain of events culminating in the damage to that home. Thus, there were seventy-four (74) occurrences in this case, one for each affected home.") (citation and internal quotations omitted); *CSB, LLC v. Middlesex Mut. Assur. Co.*, No. 16-105, 2016 U.S. Dist. LEXIS 189746 (E.D. Va. Dec. 8, 2016) (addressing Virginia law in detail) ("The failure to put the student tenants on notice of a known and concealed dangerous condition was the basis of the fraudulent concealment claim. In light of the fact that a duty to disclose would necessarily have been owed to each student tenant of the apartment separately, then each fraudulent concealment must constitute a separate occurrence. This conclusion is consistent with the Virginia Supreme Court's holding in *S.F.*").

Washington: The Supreme Court of Washington applied the "cause" test and held that, "if each accident, collision, or injury has its own proximate cause then each will be deemed a separate 'accident' for insurance policy purposes even if the two accidents occurred coincident, or nearly coincident, in time." *Greengo v. Pub. Employees Mut. Ins. Co.*, 959 P.2d 657, 664 (Wash. 1998); *see also Transcon. Ins. Co. v. Wash. Pub. Utils. Dists.' Util. Sys.*, 760 P.2d 337, 346 (Wash. 1988) (holding that claims against a public utility for bond defaults "may exist on the basis of the bondholders' allegations of multiple separate causes, continuing causes, or longstanding causes resulting in injury during the policy period"); *Spokane County v. Am. Re-Insurance Co.*, No. CS-90-256, 1993 U.S. Dist. LEXIS 21038 (E.D. Wash. May 12, 1993) (citing *Washington Public Utilities* for the proposition that Washington is a "cause" state and holding that, because there was only one cause of injury—pollutants leaking into groundwater—all injury resulting from the contamination of groundwater, on- and off-site, is one occurrence); *Certain Underwriters at Lloyd's London v. Valiant Ins. Co.*, 229 P.3d 930, 932 (Wash. Ct. App. 2010) (characterizing *Transcon.* and other Washington decisions as providing a general rule that the number of occurrences equals the number of causes of liability) ("The key to the present case is the Zurich policy definition of 'occurrence' as an 'accident, including continuous and repeated exposure to substantially the same general harmful conditions.' The continuous and repeated exposure of Chateau Pacific to harmful moisture that gradually intruded through the building envelope over a five year period from different sources fits this definition."); *Navigators Ins. Co. v. National Union Fire Ins. Co.*, No. C12–13, 2013

U.S. Dist. LEXIS 109903 (W.D. Wash. Aug. 5, 2013) (noting that, even if multiple inter-related factors contributed to the construction-related property damage, it may constitute a single occurrence).

West Virginia: The Supreme Court of Appeals of West Virginia held that a physician's failure to diagnose a patient with cancer, during several examinations over a lengthy period of time, constituted one "incident" under a physician's professional liability policy. *Auber v. Jellen*, 469 S.E.2d 104, 108 (W. Va. 1996). The court reached its conclusion on the basis that the policy language "'all injury resulting from a series of acts or omissions in providing medical services to one person' will be *considered one incident*" was clear and unambiguous and would be given its plain, ordinary meaning. *Id.* (emphasis in original); *see also Beckley Mech., Inc. v. Erie Ins. Co.*, 374 Fed. Appx. 381, 383–84 (4th Cir. 2010) (applying W. Va. law) (holding that embezzlement by a bookkeeper, who drafted approximately 293 checks to herself, was a "series of acts" and therefore considered one occurrence); *Smallwood-Small Insurance, Inc. v. American Automobile Ins. Co.*, No. 3:06-CV-107, 2007 U.S. Dist. LEXIS 93592 (N.D. W.Va. Dec. 20, 2007) (holding that failure by an insurance agency to obtain insurance for three clients constituted separate occurrences); *Kosnoski v. Rogers*, No. 13–0494, 2014 W. Va. LEXIS 151 (W.Va. Feb. 18, 2014) ("It is clear from the record that there was a leak of carbon monoxide from a single source, the gas boiler furnace. While the gas undoubtedly traveled to different rooms within the single building at different times over several hours, the injuries to petitioners and the decedent were from continuous or repeated exposure to substantially the same general harmful conditions. As in *Shamblin*, we find that the definition of occurrence at issue in the instant case is not ambiguous, at least not in the sense meant by petitioners in this case. Therefore, we find that under the facts presented in this case, there was a single occurrence under the policy at issue."); *Brotherhood Mut. Ins. Co. v. Bible Baptist Church*, No. 16-00341, 2017 U.S. Dist. LEXIS 201429 (S.D. W.Va. Dec. 7, 2017) (holding that sexual abuse, physical abuse, malnutrition and educational neglect constitute separate occurrences for purposes of claims by students against a boarding school).

Wisconsin: The Supreme Court of Wisconsin applied the "cause" test and held that, where individuals were exposed to asbestos at different times and different geographical locations, each individual's repeated and continuous exposure to asbestos-containing products constituted a separate "occurrence." *Plastics Eng'g Co. v. Liberty Mut. Ins. Co.*, 759 N.W.2d 613, 623 (Wis. 2009). The policies defined "occurrence" similarly, including as "an accident, including continuous or repeated exposure to conditions, which results in bodily injury or property damage neither expected nor intended form the standpoint of the insured." *Id.* at 617. The court rejected the insurer's argument that it was the sale of asbestos-containing products without warning that was the occurrence. "The exposure must, quite obviously, be exposure to the injured person and not exposure to [the insured–Plastics Engineering Company]." *Id.* at 623; *see also Basler Turbo Conversions, LLC v. HCC Ins. Co.*, 601 F. Supp. 2d 1082, 1091 (E.D. Wis. 2009) (holding that a series of thefts over a six-month period by the same individual did not constitute a single "occurrence" and the insured was subject to a separate deductible for each theft); *Wilson Mut. Ins. Co. v. Falk*, 857 N.W.2d 156 (Wis. 2014) ("Similar to *Plastics*, where we rejected the argument that the manufacture, sale, and installation of asbestos containing products, without warning, constituted one occurrence, and concluded each individual's repeated exposure to asbestos constituted a unique occurrence, we likewise reject the argument that the spreading of manure constituted one occurrence, and conclude each well's exposure to manure constituted a unique occurrence."); *Secura Ins. v. Lyme St. Croix Forest Co., LLC*, 918 N.W.2d 885 (Wis. 2018) (addressing Wisconsin law in detail concerning a fire that burned 7,000-plus acres, over the course of three days, damaging real and personal property belonging to many individuals and businesses) ("Rather than being analogous to *Falk*, this case is more akin to *Welter* [*v. Singer*, 376 N.W.2d 84 (Wis. 1985)]. In *Welter* [bicyclist struck by a car and suffered injuries from repeated contact with the car] there may have been 'multiple injuries' that were of 'different magnitudes' over a short period of time, but that fact did not alter the court's conclusion that there was a single occurrence.") ("If it is an occurrence each time a fire refuels and expands [as Court of Appeals concluded], then a fire, which is constantly refueling and expanding, will necessarily result in an unfathomably large number of occurrences regardless of how many property lines it crosses. A court's interpretation of an insurance policy should avoid unreasonable results.").

Wyoming: The Supreme Court of Wyoming adopted the "cause" test in the context of determining the amount owed under an uninsured motorist policy, with an "each accident" limit of liability, where two insureds, while riding separate bicycles, were struck by an uninsured motorist. *Hurst v. Metropolitan Prop. & Cas. Co.*, 401 P.3d 891 (Wyo. 2017). The court undertook a review of case law nationally that has addressed the three legal theories or analytical approaches to interpret the term "one accident" – cause theory, effect theory and event theory. The court noted that "[s]everal of the seminal cases that adopted the cause theory for construing the term 'accident' employ this reasoning: 'The insured and the insurer intended by this contract to indemnify the insured's tort liability to third persons. Such liability arises from a negligent act on the part of the insured which is the proximate cause of an injury. The absence of proximate cause precludes tort liability. Proximate cause is an integral part of any interpretation of the words 'accident' or 'occurrence,' as used in a contract for liability insurance which indemnifies the insured for his tortious acts." *Id.* at 899. The court held that, under the scenario at hand, the possibility of two accidents existed: "Here, the stipulated facts reveal that the collisions with Larry Hurst and Sara Hurst could be separate incidents, each arising out of Terry's independent collision with each of the Hursts, riding his/her own, separate bicycle. There was no chain reaction or causal connection between the impact with Larry Hurst's bicycle and Sara Hurst's bicycle; nothing that necessitated an impact of the latter by virtue of the impact with the former, *so long as* Terry was in control of her vehicle at the time. The events occurred approximately thirty (30) feet away from each other and approximately one (1) second apart from each other." *Id.* at 900 (emphasis in original). The court focused on the element of "control" that the driver had over the vehicle, noting that it "has a significant, if not overriding, impact on the determination of whether there is more than one accident, for without which there can be no single proximate, uninterrupted, and continuing cause." *Id.* "The record is void of any evidence such as debris in the road, brake marks, skid marks, swerving, obstacles that impacted Terry's ability to have control of the minivan. An inference could well be made, then, that Terry was in control of the vehicle enough to make deliberate decisions about how and where to drive it, and maintained control over her vehicle throughout these consecutive events. However, this Court is not permitted to make such inferences in a grant of summary judgment in favor of the Hursts." The court remanded the case to the trial court for factual development of the "control" element required of the cause theory.

CHAPTER

10

Coverage for Innocent Co-Insureds: "Any" Insured vs. "The" Insured and the Severability of Interests Clause

It is routine for a court, setting out to resolve an insurance coverage dispute, to begin its opinion by laying out the rules that will determine its decision. And it is likely that somewhere in the court's recitation will be a statement that its most important consideration is to be the language of the policy. This is the case today. *See James River Ins. Co. v. Ground Down Engineering, Inc.*, 540 F.3d 1270, 1274 (11th Cir. 2008) (quoting *Taurus Holdings, Inc. v. U.S. Fid. & Guar. Co.*, 913 So.2d 528, 537 (Fla. 2005) ("In interpreting insurance contracts … 'the language of the policy is the most important factor.'"). And that was also the case when Teddy Roosevelt was president. *See White v. Standard Life & Accident Ins. Co.*, 103 N.W. 735, 736 (Minn. 1905) ("While the rule is thoroughly settled that policies of this and like character are to be construed liberally, and that ambiguous provisions or those capable of two constructions should be construed favorably to the insured and most strongly against the insurer, plain, explicit language cannot be disregarded, nor an interpretation given the policy at variance with the clearly disclosed intent of the parties.").

Then, at the conclusion of the opinion resolving the coverage dispute, it is likely that one party will believe that the court was true to its word and made its decision by applying solely the plain language of the policy. The other party is likely to see it otherwise.

But there is one situation where both parties can likely agree that the court's decision was, at least up to a point, completely faithful to the policy language. Consider a suit filed by the victim of an attack at the hands of a teenager neighbor living in his parents' home. The teenager, as an "insured" under his parents' homeowners policy, will likely seek coverage for the suit under the liability section of such policy. In many instances, the policy will contain an exclusion for, among other things, bodily injury which results from "the criminal acts of any [or an] insured." And not surprisingly, if the teenage perpetrator–insured was convicted of a crime, the criminal act exclusion will usually preclude coverage for him.

It is likely that the plaintiff's attorney in the underlying case is well aware that coverage for the perpetrator may be hard to come by because of the possible existence of a "criminal act" exclusion. For that reason, the plaintiff may allege that the teen's parents bear responsibility for the victim's injuries, by *failing to prevent* their son from causing them. What's at work here is, in all likelihood, an effort by the plaintiff to secure insurance dollars by arguing that, *because the parents did not themselves commit a criminal act*, they are not bound by the policy exclusion. *See L.C.S., Inc. v. Lexington Ins. Co.*, 853 A.2d 974, 980 (N.J. App. Div. 2004) (discussing the possibility that a "failure to prevent" claim against an employer, for assault and battery committed by an employee, is a "bogus or thinly veiled attempt by a plaintiff designed only to reach the pot of gold at the end of the rainbow of an employer general liability policy").

While it is true that the parents themselves did not commit a criminal act, insurers frequently argue that coverage nonetheless remains unavailable to them. The insurer's expected argument will be that the exclusion at issue applies to injury that results from the "criminal acts of *any insured*"—and "any insured" (the parents' son) in fact committed a criminal act. In other words, in such a situation, expect insurers to maintain that the applicability of the criminal act exclusion is not limited solely to *the insured* that actually committed the criminal act. Rather, so the argument goes, it applies to all insureds, including so-called "innocent co-insureds." Insurers frequently make this argument for good reason—because many courts accept it.

But despite concluding that no coverage is owed to the innocent co-insured, courts sometimes point out that their decision would have been different if the exclusion at issue had applied to "criminal acts of *the insured.*" If so, the exclusion's applicability would have been limited solely to *the insured* that committed the criminal act (the teenage son) and coverage for his parents would have remained available. Likewise, when an exclusion uses the phrase "the insured," and, as a result, does not preclude coverage for an innocent co-insured, courts sometimes point out that the insurer could have used different policy language to achieve a different result. *See, e.g., Travelers Indem. Co. v. Bloomington Steel & Supply Co.*, 718 N.W.2d 888, 895 (Minn. 2006) ("Instead of excluding coverage for bodily injury expected or intended from the standpoint of '*the*' insured, the Travelers' policies could have excluded coverage for bodily injury expected or intended from the standpoint of '*an*' or '*any*' insured.") (emphasis in original).

Numerous decisions abound following this pattern when addressing the scope of various general liability, homeowners, and auto policy exclusions under a host of circumstances. *See, e.g., Am. Family Mut. Ins. Co. v. Corrigan*, 697 N.W.2d 108, 109 (Iowa 2005) (addressing coverage for a parent-insured, for abuse committed by his son, during the operation of a daycare business in the parent's home, in the context of a policy exclusion for bodily injury arising out of violation of any criminal law for which *any* insured is convicted); *Litz v. State Farm Fire & Cas. Co.*, 695 A.2d 566, 572 (Md. 1997) (addressing coverage under the liability section of a homeowner's policy for an insured-husband, for injury to a child being cared for by his insured-wife, in the context of a policy exclusion for bodily injury arising out of business pursuits of *an insured*); *Am. Family Mut. Ins. Co. v. Copeland-Williams*, 941 S.W.2d 625, 629–30 (Mo. Ct. App. 1997) (addressing coverage under the liability section of a home-owner's policy for an insured-wife, for failing to prevent her insured-husband from molesting his step-granddaughter, in the context of a policy exclusion for bodily injury which is either expected or intended from the standpoint of *any insured*); *Hayner Hoyt Corp. v. Utica First Ins. Co.*, 760 N.Y.S.2d 706, 706 (N.Y. App. Div. 2003) (addressing coverage under a commercial general liability policy for an additional insured, for bodily injury to employees of the named insured, in the context of a policy exclusion for bodily injury to an employee of *an insured* if it occurs in the course of employment); *BP Am. Inc. v. State Auto Prop. & Cas. Co.*, 148 P.3d 832, 836–42 (Okla. 2005) (addressing coverage under a commercial general liability policy for an additional insured, for bodily injury caused by a motor vehicle in which the named insured's employee was allegedly at fault, in the context of a policy exclusion for bodily injury arising out of the ownership, maintenance, use, or entrustment to others of any auto owned or operated by or rented or loaned to *any insured*).

Insureds that are denied coverage, and perhaps for a very significant claim, based on the difference between "any" or "an" and "the" may find themselves in disbelief that such seemingly innocuous words could have so much import. Their response may be that the insurer is simply hiding behind a technicality. But courts that uphold the distinction do not see it that way. *See, e.g., Vanguard Ins. Co. v. McKinney*, 459 N.W.2d 316, 319–20 (Mich. Ct. App. 1990) (dismissing the insured's argument that the distinction between "an" insured and "the" insured is "irrelevant semantics").

Perhaps the starkest evidence that a court determining the availability of coverage between the words "any" or "an" and "the" is not just hiding behind a technicality, comes from the highest court of Maine. In *Johnson v. Allstate*, 687 A.2d 642, 644 (Me. 1997), the Supreme Judicial Court of Maine held that no coverage was owed under the liability section of a homeowner's policy to a grandmother for failing to prevent her husband from sexually abusing their granddaughter. A policy exclusion applied to bodily injury intentionally caused by *an insured person*. *Id.* The court held that an exclusion for damages intentionally caused by "an insured person" excludes coverage for damages intentionally caused by *any* insured person. *Id.*

However, *less than one month later*, Maine's Supreme Judicial Court held in *Hanover Insurance Co. v. Crocker*, 688 A.2d 928, 932 (Me. 1997) that coverage was owed under the liability section of a homeowner's policy to an insured-mother for her failure to take steps to prevent an insured-father's sexual abuse of their daughter. A policy exclusion applied to "bodily injury … which is either expected or intended from the standpoint of *the insured*." *Id.* at 931 (emphasis added). The court held that coverage was owed to the mother because the injury was not expected or intended from her standpoint. *Id.* "Our conclusion is consistent with the majority of other jurisdictions that have held that provisions excluding from coverage injuries intentionally caused by 'the insured' refer to a definite, specific insured, who is directly involved in the occurrence that causes the injury." *Id.*

It would appear that, when a court concludes that "any" means any, thereby precluding coverage for an innocent co-insured, it is being completely faithful to the policy language. But policyholders often say, not so fast. Even if forced to concede that, at least on its face, "any" does mean any, policyholders are likely to argue that coverage nonetheless remains available for innocent co-insureds, because any other outcome would be inconsistent with the policy's "Separation of Insureds" provision.

Most commercial general liability policies and, to a lesser extent, homeowners policies, contain a Separation of Insureds provision—sometimes referred to interchangeably as a "Severability of Interests" provision. A typical Separation of Insureds clause, contained in a commercial general liability policy, provides as follows:

7. Separation of Insureds
    Except with respect to the Limits of Insurance, and any rights or duties specifically assigned in this Coverage Part to the first Named Insured, this insurance applies:
        a. As if each Named Insured were the only Named Insured; and
        b. Separately to each insured against whom claim is made or "suit" is brought.

See, e.g., Ins. Servs. Office Props., Inc., Commercial General Liability Coverage Form, No. CG 00010413, § IV7 (2012).

"The intent of the severability clause is to provide each insured with separate coverage, as if each were separately insured with a distinct policy, subject to the liability limits of the policy." *Bituminous Cas. Corp. v. Maxey*, 110 S.W.3d 203, 210 (Tex. Ct. App. 2003) (citation omitted).

Not surprisingly, innocent co-insureds, facing the prospect of no coverage because of an exclusion that applies to the conduct of "any insured," point to the Separation of Insureds clause in an effort to prevent such outcome. Their argument is that, to determine the availability of coverage for one insured, based on the conduct of another insured, would not be treating each insured as if they were separately insured with a distinct policy.

There is certainly support for this position. *See Litz v. State Farm Fire & Cas. Co.*, 695 A.2d 566, 572 (Md. 1997) ("This provision [severability clause] is a clear reflection that the parties intended the insurance policy to provide coverage for each named insureds separately. In light of this express severability clause, we construe the business pursuits exception in the Litzes' policy to mean that the business pursuits of 'an' insured disqualify only that insured from coverage in the event of property damage or bodily injury resulting from the business pursuit; other insureds, i.e., those not engaging in a business pursuit, remain covered under the policy."); *see also Premier Ins. Co. v. Adams*, 632 So. 2d 1054, 1057 (Fla. Dist. Ct. App. 1994) ("In accordance with the rules of construction of a contract, the most plausible interpretation is that the exclusionary clause [intentional acts of any insured] is to exclude coverage for the separate insurable interest of that insured who intentionally causes the injury. With this interpretation, all provisions in the policy are given meaning and one provision is not rendered meaningless by the other.").

However, the majority of courts have concluded that the presence of a Separation of Insureds provision does not serve as a basis to afford coverage to an innocent co-insured when the exclusion at issue applies to the conduct of "any insured." *Minkler v. Safeco Ins. Co.*, 232 P.3d. 612, 623 (Cal. 2010); *Argent v. Brady*, 901 A.2d 419, 425 (N.J. Super. Ct. App. Div. 2006). Courts rely on various rationales for this conclusion.

For example, if a Separation of Insureds clause is given effect, then the language of an exclusion, as it relates to "an insured" or "any insured" is "robbed of any meaning." *Argent v. Brady*, 901 A.2d at 426. "[T]he purpose of a severability clause … is designed solely to render the coverage actually provided by the insuring provisions of the policy applicable to all insureds equally, up to coverage limits. The severability clause is not denominated a 'coverage provision,' and it would be unreasonable to find that it operated independently in that capacity to increase the insurance afforded under the insuring provisions of the policy, or to partially nullify existing coverage exclusions." *Id.* at 426–27.

On one hand, "any" meaning any, as used in a policy exclusion, may be one situation where both insurers and policyholders can agree that the court's interpretation was completely faithful to the policy language. On the other hand, any such agreement is likely to be short-lived. Expect a dispute to quickly ensue whether the existence of a Separation of Insureds provision means that "any" really means "the."

50-State Survey: Coverage for Innocent Co-Insureds: "Any" Insured vs. "The" Insured and the Severability of Interests Clause

Alabama: The Supreme Court of Alabama held that coverage was owed under a fleet policy, to insured-supervisors of an employee, who was fatally injured while driving a vehicle within the scope of his employment for a board of education. *Wilson v. State Farm Mut. Auto. Ins. Co.*, 540 So. 2d 749, 752 (Ala. 1989). The fleet policy, issued to the board of education, contained an exclusion that applied to "any bodily injury to: … any employee of *an insured* arising out of his or her employment." *Id.* at 751 (emphasis added). The court reasoned that the exclusion did not apply to the supervisors because they did not employ the victim. *Id.* at 752. The court also concluded that the addition of a severability of interests clause did "not eliminate the ambiguity that exits in the exclusion where there are multiple insureds and the injured party is an employee of one or some, but not all." Id.; *see also State Farm Fire & Casualty Co. v. Davis*, 612 So. 2d 458 (Ala. 1993) ("In this case, the relevant provisions exclude coverage for bodily injury or property damage 'which is either expected or intended by *an* insured; or to any person or property which is the result of willful and malicious acts of *an* insured.' We hold that this policy provision excludes coverage for Delores Davis for harm directly attributable to the intentional conduct of her husband, Jerry Davis."); *Essex Ins. Co. v. Avondale Mills, Inc.*, 639 So. 2d 1339, 1342 (Ala. 1994) (following *Wilson* and holding that the employee exclusion only applied if the insured were sued by its own employees, rather than by those of another insured); *Safeco Ins. Co. of America v. Golden*, 984 F. Supp. 2d 1162 (M.D. Ala. 2013) ("Unlike the exclusions for intentional acts and criminal acts, this exclusion ['arising out of … sexual molestation or sexual harassment'] is unconditional and does not require that the molestation be committed by 'any insured.' As this exclusion does not require that Golden herself molested the Bences' daughter, it is unaffected by the severability clause; the exclusion applies regardless as to who committed the molestation."); *James River Ins. Co. v. Ultratec Special Effects, Inc.*, No. 16-00949, 2020 U.S. Dist. LEXIS 53628 (N.D. Ala. Mar. 27, 2020) ("[B]ased on Alabama law and the Separation of Insureds Provision's express terms, the court must read the Policy, including its exclusions, as if coverage is only for Ultratec, or only for Thouin, or only for MST. As a result, the court finds that when the [Employer's Liability] Exclusion Endorsement ['bodily injury' to any employee of any Insured] is read in conjunction with the Separation of Insureds Provision, the Endorsement does not preclude coverage for the Employees' claims against Ultratec, Thouin, or MST because those insureds are not the Employees' employer.").

Alaska: The Supreme Court of Alaska held that no coverage was owed to the Department of Transportation, as an additional insured on a liability policy issued to an airline, for the death of an airline employee who was struck and killed while driving a snow machine across a runway. *State Dep't of Transp. & Pub. Facilities v. Houston Cas. Co.*, 797 P.2d 1200, 1204 (Alaska 1990). The policy contained an exclusion for "bodily injury … caused by … Aircraft owned, chartered, used, or operated by or on account of *the Insured*." *Id.* at 1203 (emphasis added). The court held that, "in the absence of a severability of interest clause or other 'clearly stated condition[]' excluding the named insured [airline] from the term 'insured,' we conclude that the parties intended DOT's coverage to be co-extensive with, rather than independent from, [the airline's]." *Id.* at 1204. *See also Colonial Ins. Co. of California v. Tumbleson*, 889 F. Supp. 1136, 1141 (D. Alaska 1995) ("Ordinary usage of the words 'the' and 'an,' combined with the reasoning provided by *Houston*," "leads to the conclusion that 'an insured' means any person insured under the policy."); *United Services Auto. Ass'n v. Neary*, 307 P.3d 907, 912, n.14 (Alaska 2013) (recognizing that some exclusions are specifically worded such that their application to any insured excludes coverage for all insureds; noting that courts disagree on the effect of severability clauses in such circumstances; and concluding that the court did not need to decide that issue); *Barba v. Allianz Global Risks US Ins. Co.*, No. 16 Civ. 2673, 2016 U.S. Dist. LEXIS 147179 (S.D.N.Y. Oct. 24, 2016) (applying Alaska law) (reviewing case law nationally after noting that there is "no case law in Alaska squarely addressing the interplay between a Separation of Insureds clause and an exclusion along the lines of that here, which excludes claims against one insured in the event that claims against 'any insured' are excluded") ("The text of the exclusion here, however, is different and clearer than in *Minkler* and in the above line of cases. Its phrase 'any insured'—as opposed to 'an insured'—specifically and unavoidably highlights that the application of the exclusion to either insured (Pollux or Larrivee) precludes coverage under the Policy for the other. It is hard to imagine a clearer way to capture this concept. Unsurprisingly, the overwhelming majority of courts to consider such an exclusion have held it unambiguous, and binding, even in the presence of a Separation of Insureds clause.").

Arizona: The Court of Appeals of Arizona held that no coverage was owed under the liability section of a homeowner's policy to insured-parents, for negligent supervision of their insured-son, who struck a male in the head with a pipe and was later convicted of aggravated assault. *Am. Family Mut. Ins. Co. v. White*, 65 P.3d 449, 457 (Ariz. Ct. App. 2003). The policy contained a "violation of law" exclusion which stated that "[w]e will not cover bodily injury or property damage arising out of … violation of any criminal law for which *any insured* is convicted." *Id.* at 452 (emphasis added) (alteration in original). "Courts have consistently interpreted the language 'any insured' as expressing a contractual intent to prohibit recovery by innocent co-insureds. Thus, if any one of the insureds [violates the exclusion], no other insureds can recover." *Id.* (quotation omitted) (alteration in original). Of note, the court concluded that "the phrase 'any insured' in an exclusionary clause means something more than the phrase 'an insured,'" with the distinction being that "an" refers to one object and "any" refers to one or more objects of a certain type. *Id.* (quotation omitted). The presence of a severability clause in the policy did not dictate a different result.

In *Interstate Fire and Cas. Co. v. Roman Catholic Church of the Diocese of Phoenix*, 761 F.3d 953 (9th Cir. 2014), the court rejected the insured's argument that "any Assured" and "such Assured" should be presumed to have different meanings and held that an exclusion for "liability of any Assured for assault and battery committed by or at the direction of such Assured . . . ." applied to innocent co-insureds. Addressing the term "such Assured," the court explained that "such" "is defined as 'of a kind or character about to be indicated, suggested, or exemplified' or 'having a quality already or just specified—used to avoid repetition of a descriptive term.' This definition indicates that 'such Assured' in the exclusion carries the precise meaning as the assured 'just specified.'" Following that, the court held that "[r]eading the policy in context, the ordinary meaning provides that 'such' refers back to 'any,' thus indicating that the exclusion applies to 'any official, trustee or employee' of the Diocese." *See also Chartis Property Cas. Co. v. Alpert*, No. 11–2067, 2013 U.S. Dist. LEXIS 116966 (D. Ariz. Aug. 16, 2013) (relying on *White* and holding that the "or others" language in an exclusion for "Personal injury […] arising out of an insured person's business [...] pursuits, investment activity or any activity intended to realize a profit for either an insured person or others" operated to exclude coverage for insured's spouse) (alteration in original).

Arkansas: The Supreme Court of Arkansas held that no coverage was owed under a homeowner's policy to an insured-spouse whose insured-wife committed arson. *Noland v. Farmers Ins. Co.*, 892 S.W.2d 271, 273 (Ark. 1995). The policy contained an exclusion that provided: "[i]f *any insured* directly causes or arranges for a loss of covered property in order to obtain insurance benefits, this policy is void. We will not pay you or *any other insured* for this loss." *Id.* (emphasis added); *see also Bryan v. Employers Nat'l Ins. Corp.*, 742 S.W.2d 557, 557–58 (Ark. 1988) (holding that no coverage was available under a property policy to an innocent business partner-insured whose co-partner-insured committed arson) (policy language excluded coverage for any criminal act by "any insured"); *Brawner v. Allstate Indem. Co.*, No. 4:07-CV-00482 (E.D. Ark. Jan. 11, 2008) (following *Noland*); *Atl. Cas. Ins. Co. v. CM Sellers, LLC*, No. 16-1002, 2017 U.S. Dist. LEXIS 159736 (W.D. Ark. Sept. 28, 2017) (distinguishing between the phrase "any insured," which is unambiguous and "the insured" which was found ambiguous in *Employers Mut. Liab. Ins. Co. of Wisconsin v. Farm Bureau Mut. Ins. Co. of Arkansas*, 549 S.W.2d 267 (Ark. 1977)); *Shelter Mut. Ins. Co. v. Lovelace*, 594 S.W.3d 84 (Ark. 2020) ("The homeowners' policy terms here are clear and unambiguous. The policy explicitly excludes coverage for losses caused by an intentional act by 'any insured.' Lovelace and Williams contracted with Shelter Mutual upon these terms. Williams was 'any insured' and allegedly engaged in an intentional act when he set fire to the home. Under the clear terms of the policy, and under our precedent, Lovelace would be precluded from recovery if Williams intentionally caused the fire."). In none of the cases did the court discuss a severability of interests clause.

California: The Supreme Court of California held that coverage was owed under the liability section of homeowner's policies to an insured-mother for failing to take reasonable steps to prevent her insured-son from sexually molesting a minor over the course of several years. *Minkler v. Safeco Ins. Co.*, 232 P.3d. 612, 624 (Cal. 2010). The policies contained exclusions for "Personal Liability [coverage] ... do[es] not apply to bodily injury or property damage: (a) which is expected or intended by *an insured* or which is the foreseeable result of an act or omission intended by *an insured*." *Id.* at 617 (emphasis added and alteration in original). The court held "that, in light of the severability clause, Betty would reasonably have expected Safeco's policies, whose general purpose was to provide coverage for each insured's 'legal[] liab[ility]' for 'injury or … damage' to others, to cover her *separately* for her *independent* acts or omissions causing such injury or damage, so long as *her* conduct did not fall within the policies' intentional acts exclusion, even if the acts of *another* insured contributing to the same injury or damage *were* intentional. Especially when informed by the policies that '[t]his insurance applies separately to each insured,' it is unlikely Betty understood that by allowing David to reside in her home, and thus to become an additional insured on her homeowners policies, [she was] *narrowing* [*her*] *own coverage* for claims arising from his [intentional] torts. In light of the severability provision, Safeco's intent to achieve that result was not clearly expressed, and the ambiguity must be resolved in the [insured's] favor." *Id.* at 618 (alteration and emphasis in original) (internal quotes omitted). In reaching its decision, the California high court observed that courts nationally are "split on the general issue whether a severability-of-interests provision in a policy covering multiple insureds alters the otherwise collective effect of an exclusion for the acts of 'an' or 'any' insured." *Id.* at 614. The court acknowledged that it was adopting the minority view. *Id.* at 623. More recently, some courts have declined to apply *Minkler*, noting that the Supreme Court stated that its decision was limited to the specific facts at issue. *See also Century Nat. Ins. Co. v. Garcia*, 246 P.3d 621, 627 (Cal. 2011) (expanding *Minkler* in area of fire insurance coverage and holding that homeowner's policy did not preclude coverage to insured parents, whose son damaged house in fire, even though policy excluded coverage for the intentional or criminal conduct of "any Insured," because California legislature, as evidenced by the state legislature's standard form, intended fire insurance policies to provide protection to innocent co-insureds). In *Wawanesa Gen. Ins. Co. v. A.M.*, No. B242128, 2013 Cal. App. Unpub. LEXIS 1727 (Cal. Ct. App. Mar. 7, 2013) the court held that an exclusion for bodily injury "[a]rising out of sexual molestation, corporal punishment, or physical or mental abuse" was not limited to an insured person's conduct and also served to preclude coverage for negligent supervision. The court determined that *Minkler* was inapposite because the exclusion there applied only to the intentional act of an insured and the exclusion before it contained no such limitation. *See also Safeco Ins. Co. of Am. v. Thomas*, 13-0170, 2013 U.S. Dist. LEXIS 194482 (S.D. Cal. Nov. 26, 2013) ("The holding in *Minkler* involved the narrow interplay between a severability clause and an exclusion for intentional acts based on 'an insured.' *Minkler* is inapposite in the instant case, the exclusion there only applied to the intentional act of an insured, where as this case deals with an exclusion that contains no such limitation.) (exclusion for "bodily injury arising out of … sexual molestation or sexual harassment"); *Liberty*

Mut. Fire Ins. Co. v. Shaibaz S., 15-03943, 2017 U.S. Dist. LEXIS 74535 (N.D. Cal. May 16, 2017) ("[T]he Liberty Mutual policies have a clear sexual molestation provision, without reference to 'an insured,' and *Minkler* is inapposite."); *Burlington Ins. Co. v. Minadora Holdings, LLC*, No. 15-55702, 2017 U.S. App. LEXIS 8 (9th Cir. May 9, 2017) ("Generally, in a policy with multiple insureds, exclusions from coverage described with reference to the acts of 'an' or 'any,' as opposed to 'the,' insured are deemed under California law to apply collectively, so that if one insured has committed acts for which coverage is excluded, the exclusion applies to all insured with respect to the same occurrence. However, a 'separate insurance' clause providing that '[t]his insurance applies separately to each insured' means that each insured 'would be treated, for all policy purposes, as if he or she were the sole person covered.'") (quoting from *Minkler*); *Praetorian Ins. Co. v. Western Milling, LLC*, No. 15-00557, 2017 U.S. Dist. LEXIS 159181 (E.D. Calif. Sept. 27, 2017) ("[T]he exclusion Praetorian argues applies so as to prevent coverage in this case is one which excludes coverage for property damage to '[p]ersonal property in the care, custody or control of *the* insured.' Thus, California law requires that each insured's actions in caring for the property, or exercising care, custody, or control of it, must be considered separately, not collectively in this case.") (noting that, in fact, the separation of insureds clause would have only come into play if the exclusionary language applied to "an" or "any" insured, then California law (*see Minkler*) would have required the court to interpret the exclusion as pertaining to the actions of the insureds separately); *Bayes v. State Farm Gen. Ins. Co.*, 776 Fed. Appx. 403 (9th Cir. 2018) (exclusion for injury or damage "arising out of or resulting from the actual, alleged or threatened sexual molestation of a minor by [] any insured" applied to an innocent co-insured (sued for negligent supervision)) (declining to apply *Minkler* because the California Supreme Court noted that the policy there did not contain a specific exclusion for claims arising from sexual molestation); *J & J Realty Holdings v. Great Am. E & S Ins. Co.*, No. 19-56172, 2020 U.S. App. LEXIS 38835 (9th Cir. Dec. 11, 2020) ("Although *Minkler* does contain an ostensibly broad direction to treat each insured as if they were the 'sole person covered' for all policy purposes, the California Supreme Court was also careful to limit *Minkler's* holding to its facts. Specifically, the court made clear that the 'reasoning and conclusion' in *Minkler* were only meant to apply to 'the specific circumstances of this case, which involves the interplay between a severability clause and an exclusion for the intentional acts of 'an' insured,' and that *Minkler* should not be read to 'mean a severability clause necessarily affects all exclusions framed in terms of 'an' or 'any' insured.' What is more, *Minkler* explicitly acknowledged that there could be 'some cases' where 'the collective application of an exclusion that refers to 'an' or 'any' insured may be so clear in context that the presence of a severability clause could neither create, nor resolve, an ambiguity.' This is one of those clear cases, and *Minkler* is readily distinguishable."); *Dunbar v. USAA Cas. Ins. Co.*, No. 20-08176, 2021 U.S. Dist. LEXIS 92631 (C.D. Cal. May 14, 2021) ("Under California law, in a policy with multiple insureds like the one here, exclusions from coverage referencing the acts of 'an' or 'any' insured generally apply collectively, so that if the conduct of one insured triggers an exclusion, coverage is excluded for all insureds regarding that occurrence. However, where a policy also includes a severability clause providing that coverage 'applies separately to each insured,' the exclusion applies only to the insured who performed the excluded act.").

Colorado: The Supreme Court of Colorado held that no coverage was owed under the liability section of a homeowner's policy to insured-parents whose insured-son vandalized an elementary school. *Chacon v. Am. Family Mut. Ins.*, 788 P.2d 748, 752 (Colo. 1990). A policy exclusion stated that the insurer would "not pay for property damage … caused intentionally by *any insured* who has attained the age of 13." *Id.* at 750 (emphasis added). "The inclusion of a severability clause within the contract is not inconsistent with the creation of a blanket exclusion for intentional acts. Instead, the inquiry is whether the contract indicates that the parties intended such a result." *Id.* at 752 n.6; *see also Swentkowski By and Through Reed v. Dawson*, 881 P.2d 437, 439 (Colo. App. Ct. 1994) ("Dawson contends that *Chacon v. American Family Mutual Insurance Co.*, *supra*, is distinguishable because there the parents were vicariously liable under a statute. This argument is without merit. The supreme court analysis did not turn on the statute's imposition of vicarious liability, but rather, on its interpretation of the phrase 'any insured' in the exclusionary clause to preclude coverage for all insureds when one insured had acted intentionally."); *Government Employees Ins. Co. v. Brown*, 739 F. Supp. 2d 1317 (D. Colo. 2010) ("GEICO's exclusion for damage caused intentionally by or at the direction of 'an insured' has a similar meaning as 'any insured' and so the rule established in *Chacon* would apply here."); *Safeco Ins. Co. of Am. v. Henri*, No. 19-01825, 2020 U.S. Dist. LEXIS 169275 (D. Colo. July 23, 2020) (finding Intentional Acts and Criminal Acts exclusions which contained the phrase "any insured" applied to preclude coverage for all insureds) (citing *Chacon*).

Connecticut: The Appellate Court of Connecticut held that coverage was owed under a liability policy, to an additional insured property owner, for a bodily

injury claim brought by an employee of a named insured restaurant tenant, alleging that the property owner failed to properly maintain the grounds. *Sacharko v.
Ctr. Ltd. P'ship*, 479 A.2d 1219, 1223 (Conn. App. Ct. 1984). The policy contained
an exclusion for "[p]ersonal injury to any employee of the Insured arising out of
and in the course of his employment by the insured." *Id.* at 1222 n.4 (alteration in
original). "Where a policy contains a severability of interests clause, it is a recognition by the insurer that it has a separate and distinct obligation to each insured
under the policy, and that the exclusion under the policy as to employees of the
insured is confined to the employee of the insured who seeks protection under the
policy." *Id.* at 1222; *see also Nationwide Mut. v. Mazur*, No. CV98–0489231S, 1999
Conn. Super. LEXIS 1533 (Conn. Super. Ct. June 3, 1999) ("The policy's specific
use of the words, 'each' and 'an,' as opposed to the determiner 'any,' demonstrates
an intent to provide coverage to the insureds separately."); *Nationwide Mut. Fire Ins.
Co. v. Pahl*, No. CV106007423, 2013 Conn. Super. LEXIS 2262 (Conn. Super. Ct.
Oct. 3, 2013) ("Because Nationwide undertook, via the severability clause it placed
in both the elite policy and the homeowners policy, to provide individual coverage
to each insured under the policy, Mrs. Pahl had a right to expect such coverage
regardless of the conduct of other insureds. Nationwide's attempt to limit its exposure by excluding coverage for certain acts committed by '*an* insured' created an
ambiguity which must be resolved in favor of Mrs. Pahl.") (emphasis in original)
(distinguishing an appeals court decision that did not involve a severability clause).

Delaware: A Delaware trial court held that coverage was owed under the liability section of a homeowner's policy to an insured-husband, for claims arising
out of the death of a child that drowned while in a home daycare provided by an
insured-wife. *McIntosh v. Liberty Mutual Fire Ins. Co.*, No. Civ. A 01C-07–148CL,
2003 Del. Super. LEXIS 397 (Del. Super. Ct. Nov. 19, 2003). A policy exclusion
applied to bodily injury "arising out of or in connection with a 'business' engaged
in by *an* '*insured*.'" (emphasis added). The court rejected the insurer's argument that
there is no distinction between the use of "an" and "any" in the insurance policy
and held that, because there was evidence that the husband took no part in the care
of the child, there was a genuine issue of material fact as to whether the husband
was engaged in the "business" of providing daycare services. The opinion includes
no discussion of a severability provision. *See also Beazer Homes Corp. v. Selective Ins.
Group, Inc.*, No. 13-215, 2014 U.S. Dist. LEXIS 109593 (D. Del. Aug. 8, 2014)
("The provision by its very language applies to an employee 'of *the* insured,' not
any insured. Coupled with the separation of insureds provision, which requires that

the policy applies separately to each insured, it in fact appears that the employer's liability provision would only exclude coverage for suits by each respective insured's employee. While Defendants argue that there should not be an analysis of choice of article when the language is clear, the choice of article is part of the language. There is a difference between 'an,' 'any,' and 'the,' and it is up to the drafters of the policy to make that choice. Because Defendant Selective made that choice, it will be held to its decision.").

District of Columbia: A District of Columbia District Court held that the acts of one insured did not bar coverage for another insured under a prior acts exclusion. *F.D.I.C. v. Interdonato*, 988 F. Supp. 1 (D.D.C. 1997). The court concluded that the cases cited by the insurer were distinguishable because they involved "any insured" language, while the exclusion at hand did not contain any reference to whom the prior act exclusion applied. *Id.* at 12. "In the absence of a phrase expanding the clause's scope, as in the cases cited by [the insurer], the court finds that the prior acts exclusion, read in conjunction with the severability clause, should only apply to the prior acts of Mr. Interdonato." *Id. See also Athridge v. Aetna Cas. and Sur. Co.*, 351 F.3d 1166 (D.C. Cir. 2003) (Here, 'any person' is unambiguous and necessarily includes the named insured and his family members.").

Florida: The Court of Appeal of Florida held that coverage was owed under the liability section of a homeowner's policy to insured-parents, for negligent supervision of their insured-son, who sexually assaulted a child. *Premier Ins. Co. v. Adams*, 632 So. 2d 1054, 1057 (Fla. Dist. Ct. App. 1994). A policy exclusion applied to "bodily injury … which is expected or intended by *any* insured." *Id.* at 1055 (emphasis added). The court held that coverage was owed to the parents on account of the policy's severability clause. *Id.* at 1057. "In accordance with the rules of construction of a contract, the most plausible interpretation is that the exclusionary clause is to exclude coverage for the separate insurable interest of that insured who intentionally causes the injury. With this interpretation, all provisions in the policy are given meaning and one provision is not rendered meaningless by the other." *Id.*; *see also Kattoum v. New Hampshire Indem. Co.*, 968 So. 2d 602, 604–06 (Fla. App. 2 Dist. 2007) (rejecting argument that automobile policy's exclusion for any insured who intentionally causes property damage precluded coverage for insured-husband, whose wife intentionally damaged husband's car) ("NHIC's policy does not exclude coverage for losses intentionally caused by 'any insured,' it excludes from coverage '*any insured who*' intentionally causes bodily injury or property damage. The clause excludes a particular insured, not a particular loss, and the policy identifies which insured is excluded—it is the insured 'who intentionally causes' a loss.") (emphasis in original); *Valero v. Florida Ins. Gaur. Ass'n Inc.*, 59 So. 3d 1166 (Fla. App. 4 Dist. 2011) (distinguishing *Premier* and precluding coverage because *Premier's* exclusion "precluded coverage for bodily injury arising out of an intentional act *by any insured,* whereas the exclusion at issue [in *Valero*] preclude[d] coverage for bodily injury arising out of sexual molestation [interpreted as] *by any person*") (emphasis in original) (drawing further distinction by noting that the decision in *Premier* resulted from ambiguity of severability clause whereas the court in *Valero* found the exclusionary clause to be unambiguous); *State Farm Mut. Auto. Ins. Co. v. Menendez*, 70 So. 3d 566, 570–71 (Fla. 2011) ("In the text of the household exclusion itself—excluding coverage for 'any *bodily injury* to' 'any *insured* or any member of an *insured's* family residing in the *insured's* household'—the reference to 'the *insured's* household' cannot reasonably be understood as denoting only 'the *named* insured's household.' The interpretation advanced by the respondents ignores the preceding reference in the exclusion to 'any *insured* or any member of an *insured's* family.' The initial reference in the exclusion to 'any *insured*' governs the succeeding reference to 'an *insured's* family' and 'the *insured's* household.' In the last phrase, the word 'the' points back to the preceding reference to 'any *insured*' and 'an *insured's* family.' *The* is 'used as a function word to indicate that a following noun or noun equivalent refers to someone or something previously mentioned or clearly understood from the context or the situation.' *Webster's Third New International Dictionary* 2368 (1993). The exclusion's reference to family members 'residing in the *insured's* household' therefore encompasses family members residing in the household of any insured.") (italics in original); *Southern-Owners Ins. Co. v. Wiggins,* No. 10-390, 2012 U.S. Dist. LEXIS 15877 (M.D. Fla. Feb 9, 2012) ("[I]t is of no moment that the severability clause operates to create separate insurable interests in each insured. The Policy's liquor liability exclusion plainly applies to bodily injuries for which *any insured* may be liable where the Named Insured is 'in the business of manufacturing, distributing, selling, serving or furnishing alcoholic beverages.' The exclusion, therefore, acts to extinguish *all* of the Insurer's liability as to *any insured* where Sunshine Mart sells alcoholic beverages (which, according to the allegations of the state court action, it did). The language used in the liquor liability exclusion is clear, and it unambiguously applies the exclusion to the separate insurable interests of each insured.") (emphasis in original); *Dueno v. Modern USA Ins. Co.*, 152 So. 3d 60 (Fla. Ct. App. 2014) ("A policy may state that no coverage is provided to anyone who is connected with the insured who commits an act of sexual abuse. Under these circumstances, there is no coverage for all insureds under the policy for claims arising from an act of sexual abuse, even though the policy contains a severability clause providing that each insured would be regarded as having separate coverage.") (citation omitted); *Evanston Ins. Co. v. Design Build Interamerican, Inc.*, 569 Fed. Appx. 739 (11th Cir. 2014) (applying Florida law) (following *Premier*) ("Likewise here, Evanston's CGL policy contains an exclusion for bodily injury to 'an employee of any insured,' meaning that coverage is excluded only 'for the separate insurable interest of that insured' who is the employer of the individual who suffered the injury. Essentially, the exclusion's use of the term 'any insured' when read in conjunction with the severability clause creates a class of insureds who are excluded from coverage, i.e., employers of the injured claimant. Accordingly, as to other insureds who are not in the class of excludable insureds, but against whom a claim could be asserted, i.e., non-employers of the injured claimant, coverage is not precluded."); *Taylor v. Admiral Ins. Co.*, 187 So. 3d 258 (Fla. Ct. App. 2016) ("While the Absolute Employer's Liability Provision prevented Taylor from making a claim against Hello Florida [her employer], the Separation of Insureds provision permitted her to pursue her claims against additional insureds Villa Vizcaya and the County."); *Stettin v. Nat'l Union Fire Ins. Co.*, 861 F.3d 1335 (11th Cir. 2017) (noting that the phrase "any insured" created joint obligations because the policy in question did not contain a severability clause); *Walton v. St. Paul Fire & Marine Ins. Co.*, No. 17-61391, 2018 U.S. Dist. LEXIS 136434 (S.D. Fla. Aug. 10, 2018) ("[Insured] is a protected person under the policy, sued by Plaintiff, and, thus, the Employers liability exclusion can be interpreted to not apply to Plaintiff's claim, as she was not 'an employee of the protected person'"); *Alamo-Cruz v. Evanston Ins. Co.*, 369 F. Supp. 3d 1277 (S.D. Fla. 2018) (following *Design Build* and applying separation of insured provision to conclude that exclusion for bodily injury to "any independent contractor ... while performing work for you" did not preclude coverage for the party for whom an injured person was not performing work); *Maxum Indem. Co. v. Massaro*, 817 Fed. Appx. 851 (11th Cir. 2020) (noting that the court must read an exclusion for "bodily injury to an employee of the insured" in light of the policy's separation of insureds provision, which means substituting the name of the person seeking coverage for the term "insured" in the exclusion); *Aiello v. ASI Preferred Corp.*, No. 20-1078, 2021 Fla. App. LEXIS 4616 (Fla. Ct. App. Mar. 31, 2021) ("[T]he Watercraft Exclusion and severability clause at issue in this case use the term 'an insured' rather than 'the insured.' Courts have repeatedly recognized that 'an insured' and 'the insured' are distinct and have separate meanings; 'an' means 'any' and 'the' means a specific insured.").

Georgia: A Georgia District Court held that coverage was owed under a liability policy to an additional insured, for a claim by an employee of the named insured, who was injured in a motor vehicle accident. *Ryder Truck Rental, Inc. v. St. Paul Fire & Marine Ins. Co.*, 540 F. Supp. 66, 73 (N.D. Ga. 1982). A policy exclusion applied to "bodily injury to any employee of *the Insured* arising out of and in the course of his employment by the Insured or to any obligation of the Insured to indemnify another because of damages arising out of such injury." *Id.* at 71 n.1 (emphasis added). The Georgia District Court identified a conflict between various decisions from the Court of Appeals of Georgia concerning the interplay between, among other things, the employee exclusion and the severability of interests clause. *Id.* at 69–70. The court synthesized the decisions and determined that, on one hand, the term "the insured" can be read to mean *any insured*, thereby excluding coverage for all insureds when the injured person is an employee of any insured. *Id.* at 71. However, the court concluded that "when read in light of the severability of interests clause, 'the insured' can be interpreted to refer only to the party seeking coverage under the policy, excluding coverage only when the injured claimant is the employee of the party seeking coverage." *Id.* at 72.

Hawaii: A District of Hawaii court held that no coverage was owed under a comprehensive personal liability policy to insured-parents for failing to prevent their insured-son from committing an assault. *Allstate Ins. Co. v. Kim*, 121 F. Supp. 2d 1301, 1308 (D. Haw. 2000). A policy exclusion applied to "bodily injury … which may reasonably be expected to result from the intentional or criminal acts of *an insured person*." *Id.* at 1303 (emphasis added). The court sided with what it described as "the majority of courts" that have held that an exclusion that uses the terms "any insured" or "an insured" "expresses a contractual intent to create joint obligations and preclude coverage to innocent co-insureds, despite the presence of a severability clause." *Id.* at 1308. However, the court also suggested that its opinion may have been different if the severability clause had been specifically denominated as such, and not as a Limits of Liability clause (that contained a severability statement). *Id.* at 1308 n.5; *see also Allstate Ins. Co. v. Davis*, 430 F. Supp. 2d 1112, 1133–34 (D. Haw. 2006) (following *Kim*, but without any discussion of the potential effect of a severability clause); *Nautilus Ins. Co. v. K. Smith Builders, Inc.*, 725 F. Supp. 2d 1219 (D. Haw. 2010) (holding that a severability of insureds clause did not render meaningless an exclusion that used the term "any insured") (examining the history of the separation of insureds clause as support, in part, for its conclusion). *But see Tri-S Corp. v. Western World Ins. Co.*, 135 P.3d 82, 101 (Haw. 2006) ("[W]here an insurance policy contains a severability of interest clause, the phrase 'the insured' in a policy exclusion must be read to refer to the insured seeking coverage as opposed to the 'named insured' or 'any insured.'").

Idaho: The Supreme Court of Idaho held that, without regard to certain statutory considerations, no coverage was owed under the property section of a homeowner's policy to an insured-wife, for the destruction of the insured-residence, caused by a fire that was intentionally set by the insured-husband. *Trinity Universal Ins. Co. v. Kirsling*, 73 P.3d 102, 106–07 (Idaho 2003). A policy exclusion applied to "any loss arising out of any act committed: (1) by or at the direction of *an 'insured'*; and (2) with the intent to cause a loss." *Id.* at 104 (emphasis added). The court held that, based on the plain and unambiguous language of the policy, the intentional acts exclusion precluded coverage for an innocent co-insured. *Id.* at 106–07. The opinion includes no discussion of a severability provision. As an aside, the court ultimately concluded that coverage was owed for the innocent co-insured, otherwise the policy would have provided less coverage than Idaho's statutory standard fire insurance policy. *Id.* at 106.

Illinois: The Appellate Court of Illinois held that coverage was owed under the liability section of a homeowner's policy to an insured-defendant, who co-owned a building along with her insured-brother, for injuries sustained by her brother's wife in a fire at the insured-building. *State Farm Fire & Cas. Co. v. Hooks*, 853 N.E.2d 1, 8–9 (Ill. Ct. App. 2006). A policy exclusion applied to "bodily injury to [named insured] or any insured within the meaning of part a. or b. of the definition of insured." *Id.* at 3. The relevant definition of "insured" provided: "'insured' means [named insured] and, if residents of your household: a. relatives." *Id.* at 2. The court held that coverage was owed to the insured-defendant, notwithstanding that the injured party was an insured under the policy, on account of her status as the resident spouse of a named insured. *Id.* at 6. The court concluded that, on account of the policy's severability clause, the injured party's status as an "insured" is not determined once for the entire policy, but, rather, separately vis-à-vis both named insureds. *Id.* at 9. "[T]he clear import of the term 'applies separately to each insured' contained in the severability clause of the instant policy must be construed to modify the exclusion so as to render the insurer liable for claims brought by a related household member of one named insured against another named insured residing in a separate household." *Id.*; *see also James McHugh Const. Co. v. Zurich American Ins. Co.*, No. 1–09–2135, 2010 Ill. App. LEXIS 318 (Ill. Ct. App. Apr. 13, 2010) (interpreting "the insured," as used in an Employer's Liability exclusion, to mean "the insured seeking coverage," so that both the named insured and additional insured are equally subject to the exclusion) ("If 'the insured' referred only to the named insured … then the additional insured would receive more protection under the policy because the employer's liability exclusion could never apply to it."); *Archer Daniels Midland Co. v. Burlington Ins. Co.*, 785 F. Supp. 2d 722, 730 (N.D. Ill. 2011) (holding that additional insured not owed coverage for injury sustained by employee of named insured) ("[B]ecause the cross liability exclusion—which excludes coverage for suits brought by one insured against another insured—bars coverage for bodily injury to an employee of 'any insured,' the severability clause does not modify application of the exclusion to only the employer-insured, but to the non-employer-insured as well."); *Patrick Engineering, Inc. v. Old Republic General Ins. Co.*, 973 N.E.2d 1036 (Ill. Ct. App. 2012) (exclusion that precluded coverage for damage arising out of named insured's professional services did not bar coverage under policy, with separation-of-insureds clause, for additional insured for damages that arose out of its nonprofessional services); *Streit v. Metro Cas. Ins. Co.*, 863 F.3d 770 (7th Cir. 2017) ("The term 'the insured' is not defined in the Standard Fire Policy. But as noted by many states interpreting identical language, the inclusion of the word 'the' as opposed to 'an' serves as a limitation. If one insured party commits an intentional harm but another insured party is innocent of any wrongdoing, then the insurance coverage is suspended only as to the insured who caused the loss. An innocent coinsured may still recover.") (internal citations omitted) (policy that precluded coverage for "an intentional [fire] loss caused by any insured party" was "invalid and unlawful" pursuant to Illinois public policy); *Artisan & Truckers Cas. Co. v. A&K Rentals, LLC*, No. 17-00027, 2018 U.S. Dist. LEXIS 948 (S.D. Ill. Jan. 3, 2018) (following *Archer Daniels Midland* and criticizing other decisions) ("Artisan argues here that since Thessing is an employee of 'any' insured under the policy—American Complete—the exclusion still applies in respect to A&K. That interpretation is correct under the plain language of the policy. Even when you sever A&K away via the severability clause, Thessing is still an employee of 'any insured' of Artisan in this matter: American Complete. This interpretation makes even more sense given that American Complete is listed as an additional insured on A&K's policy—surely 'any' insured was meant by the parties to reach other named insureds on the policy at issue."); *Allstate Indem. Co. v. Contreras*, 109 N.E.3d 894 (Ill. Ct. App. 2018) (finding that an "expected injury" clause did not categorically preclude coverage for co-insureds despite the use of the phrase "any insured") ("[W]e decline Allstate's invitation to hold that Adan's intent to injure Janie and Janet categorically precludes a defense for the other insureds relating to claims for the same injuries. Instead, as in *Westfield National* [804 N.E.2d 601 (Ill. Ct. App. 2003)] we must look to the specific factual allegations asserted against Jasmine's Day Care and Alejandra in the underlying action to determine whether the 'expected injury' exclusion applies to their particular conduct.").

Indiana: The Court of Appeals of Indiana held that no coverage was owed under the liability section of a homeowner's policy to an insured-husband for molesting a child in his insured-wife's home daycare center. *T.B. v. Dobson*, 868 N.E.2d 831, 838 (Ind. Ct. App. 2007). A policy exclusion applied, in pertinent part, to "any claim made or suit brought against any insured by: (1) any person who is in the care of any insured because of child care services provided by or at the direction of: (a) *any insured.*" *Id.* at 835 (emphasis added). An exception to the exclusion applied, in pertinent part, to "the occasional child care services provided by *any insured.*" *Id.* at 836 (emphasis added). The court held that it was "undisputed that [the wife] provided non-occasional child care services to [the minor]. When [the minor] was molested, she was in [the husband's] care because of non-occasional child care services provided by [his wife]. As such, the coverage exclusion applies, and the exception to the exclusion does not." *Id.* at 838. The court rejected the argument that the policy's severability clause dictated a different result. *Id.* at 837; *see also Am. Family Mut. Ins. Co. v. Bower*, 752 F. Supp. 2d 957, 971 (N.D. Ind. 2010) (holding that insured-parents were owed coverage under homeowner's policy after son sexually molested minor girl) (surveying the issue nationally) ("[A] reasonable insured would believe from the severability provision that their insurance coverage and any exclusion of coverage would be judged on the basis of their particular conduct and acts within their control. To then exclude coverage on the basis of another insured's conduct creates a conflict between the two provisions and denies the reasonable insured the coverage protection which the severability provision affords. Accordingly, this court believes that Indiana would follow the reasoning of those courts that hold that a severability clause providing for separate coverage to named insureds applies despite language in an exclusion applying to 'any insured.'").

In 2013 this issue was addressed by the Indiana Supreme Court in *Holiday Hospitality Franchising, Inc. v. AMCO Ins. Co.*, 983 N.E.2d 574 (Ind. 2013) which held that "applying this abuse/molestation exclusion 'separately to each insured' does not change the analysis. The exclusion bars coverage for abuse or molestation of someone 'while in the care, custody or control of *any* insured,' or for the negligent hiring or retention 'of a person for whom *any* insured is or ever was legally responsible' and who commits abuse or molest. The use of the word 'any' in this provision means the fact that R.M.H. was in the care of Holiday Inn Express, and that Holiday Inn Express employed Forshey, bars coverage as conclusively for Holiday Hospitality and Megha as it does for Holiday Inn Express." (emphasis in original). *See also Warner v. United Farm Family Mut. Ins. Co.*, No. 23A04-1607, 2017 Ind. App. Unpub. LEXIS 614 (Ind. Ct. App. May 17, 2017) ("As to Exception (2)(a), the Warners argue because the undisputed evidence demonstrates the Ranger ATV was owned solely by David, and not Leah, Hayden, or Holden, the exception is satisfied because the Ranger ATV was not owned by 'an insured.'") ("[B]y the plain and ordinary meaning of the language, if any one of the insureds owns the Ranger ATV, Exception (2)(a) does not apply ["motorized land conveyance designed for recreational use off public roads, not subject to motor vehicle registration and: (a) Not owned by an 'insured'"]. Because David owned the Ranger ATV and was an insured under the homeowner's policy, Exception (2)(a) does not apply."); *United Farm Family Mut. Co. v. Matheny*, 114 N.E.3d 880 (Ind. Ct. App. 2018) ("Because the insurance policy states the exclusion applies to 'the intentional or criminal acts or omissions of any 'insured[,]'" this exclusion would apply to United's obligation or lack thereof for both Stacy and Earl even though only Stacy committed a criminal act, provided Stacy is considered an insured party.") (citing *Holiday Hospitality*). In *Am. Family Mut. Ins. Co. v. McCowan*, No. 14-46, 2018 U.S. Dist. LEXIS 53832 (N.D. Ind. Mar. 30, 2018), the court certified the following question to the Indiana Supreme Court: "Under Indiana law, does the American Family Policy serve to provide a duty to defend and indemnify an insured being sued only for negligence, notwithstanding any intentional or criminal acts of a co-insured which result in the exclusion of coverage for that co-insured, in light of the severability clause in the Policy?" The court observed that *Holiday Hospitality* "seem to be potentially inconsistent" with *Frankenmuth Mutual Insurance Co. v. William*, 690 N.E.2d 675 (Ind. 1997), which was relied upon by *Bower*. The Indiana high court accepted the question and the case was then dismissed by the parties shortly thereafter. (99 N.E.3d 625 (Ind. 2018)).

Iowa: The Supreme Court of Iowa held that no coverage was owed to an insured-father, under what appears to be the liability section of a homeowner's policy, for failing to prevent his insured-son from physically injuring a child while in a daycare center located in the father's home. *Am. Family Mut. Ins. Co. v. Corrigan*, 697 N.W.2d 108, 109 (Iowa 2005). The son was convicted of child endangerment. *Id.* at 109–10. The policy contained an exclusion for "bodily injury or property damage arising out of … violation of any criminal law for which *any insured* is convicted." *Id.* at 110 (emphasis added) (alteration in original). "Because the language of the exclusion clearly contemplates its applicability to multiple insureds under the policy, it would be unreasonable to interpret the severability-of-interests clause as the Corrigans suggest: that the clause calls for application of the policy as if [the father] were the sole insured. To interpret the policy in this manner would require this court to conclude the term 'the insured' means the same as 'any insured,' a conclusion we have rejected in the past." *Id.* at 116; *see also IMT Ins. Co. v. Crestmoor Golf Club*, 702 N.W.2d 492, 496–98 (Iowa 2005) (following *Corrigan*); *Deters v. USF Ins. Co.*, No. 10-0442, 2011 Iowa App. LEXIS 37 (Iowa Ct. App. Jan. 20, 2011) (affirming trial court that coverage was owed to the estate of president of insured-company because employees killed were not his employees, but, rather, employees of the insured company) ("Since the Estate of Leo Deters is an insured under the executive officer's provision and coverage is not excluded under the employer's liability exclusion, the separation of insureds provision does not defeat coverage in this case. The CGL separation of insureds provision requires USF to analyze coverage from the standpoint of not only [Tower Inc.], but also from the standpoint of Leo Deters as an executive officer and as an insured. … While coverage for [Tower Inc.] as the employer is excluded, coverage for Leo as an executive officer is not.") (quoting trial court and alteration in original); *Postell v. American Family Mut. Ins. Co.*, 823 N.W.2d 35 (Iowa 2012) ("David Postell, who set fire to the insured dwelling in order to commit suicide, had the requisite intent to cause a loss under the policy; that under the language of the policy [loss or damage arising out of any act committed by or at the direction of any insured], the innocent coinsured spouse, who did not participate in the intentional acts of the other coinsured, cannot recover due to the intentional loss exclusion; and that an innocent coinsured cannot recover under the recently amended Iowa standard fire policy in Iowa Code section 515.109.").

Kansas: The Supreme Court of Kansas held that coverage was owed under the liability section of a homeowner's policy to an insured-husband for negligence that contributed to his insured-wife's killing of a child in their care. *Brumley v. Lee*, 963 P.2d 1224, 1233 (Kan. 1998). A policy exclusion applied to "bodily injury … which is expected or intended by *any* insured." *Id.* at 1227 (emphasis added). The court held that the policy's severability clause created an ambiguity that required a construction that favored the insured. *Id.* at 1230. Looking at various dictionary definitions, the Kansas high court held that "the word 'any' is not materially different from the word 'a' or 'an,' and, contrary to the district court's ruling, [the insurer's] use of 'any' instead of 'an' in its policy does not eliminate the ambiguity created by the policy's severability clause." *Id.* at 1227–28. *See also Auto Club Family Ins. Co. v. Moroney*, No. 16-02789, 2018 U.S. Dist. LEXIS 24615 (D. Kan. Feb. 15, 2018) (insurer's severability clause clarified: "Where we use the phrase 'any insured,' we intend that such provisions not be limited to any one insured and that such provisions are applicable to any insured under the policy.") ("But broadening the scope of 'any insured' so that it is not 'limited to any one insured' actually narrows the scope of 'any other person' in the negligent-entrustment exclusion. ... [This] makes it logical to interpret 'any other person' in the exclusion as not including anyone insured under the policy. Because Conner Estrella was insured under the Policy, he is not 'any other person,' and under this interpretation, the Policy would therefore cover Defendants' claim of negligent entrustment against Benjamin and Suzanne Estrella.") (discussing *Brumley*); *Everest Indem. Ins. Co. v. Jake's Fireworks*, No. 19-2620, 2020 U.S. Dist. LEXIS 216634 (D. Kan. Nov. 19, 2020) ("[T]he parties have not cited and the Court has not identified any Kansas authority holding that a change from 'the insured' to 'any insured' in a coverage exclusion should be read to supersede a severability clause, and *Brumley* would seem to require the opposite result... [T]aking into account the *Brumley* holding—the Court assumes without deciding that the combination of the term 'any insured' in the [Employer's Liability] Endorsement with the Policy's separation-of-insureds clause creates ambiguity about the circumstances under which the [Employer's Liability] Endorsement will apply.").

Kentucky: The Court of Appeals of Kentucky held that no coverage was owed under a homeowner's policy to an insured–paternal grandmother, for failing to prevent her husband, an insured–step-grandfather, from sexually abusing their granddaughter. *K.M.R. v. Foremost Ins. Group*, 171 S.W.3d 751, 755 (Ky. Ct. App. 2005). The policy at issue contained, among others, an exclusion for bodily injury "[r]esulting from any act or omission that is intended by any of you to cause any harm or that any of you could reasonably expect to cause harm." *Id.* at 753. The policy defined "you" as the named insureds and family members and both grandparents were named insureds. *Id.* The court held that a clearly worded exclusion is not treated as ambiguous by the existence of a severability provision. *Id.* at 755; *see also Cincinnati Ins. Co. v. T. & T.R.*, 3:05-CV-792H, 2007 U.S. Dist. LEXIS 13171 (W.D. Ky. Feb. 23, 2007) (following *K.M.R.*) ("The exclusions unambiguously operate to preclude coverage to all insureds for liability attributable to the excludable acts of any one of the Insureds."); *see also Am. Nat. Prop. & Cas. Co. v. M. M.*, No. 4:09CV-00079, 2010 U.S. Dist. LEXIS 87298 (W.D. Ky. Aug. 24, 2010) ("[The insurer] carefully drafted its intentional act exclusion using the words 'any insured' which, despite the severability clause, unambiguously excludes coverage to any insured for liability based on the excludable actions of any other insured. Therefore, the Court does not find any ambiguity in [the insurer's] policy due to the severability clause included therein."); *Holzknecht v. Kentucky Farm Bureau Mut. Ins. Co.*, 320 S.W.3d 115, 122 (Ky. Ct. App. 2010) (exclusion for "'bodily injury' [a]rising out of or in connection with a 'business' engaged in by an 'insured'") ("John David May plainly falls within the scope of the policy's business-pursuits exclusion because it appears that he was involved in the enterprise. We agree that the policy exclusion is unambiguous and broad enough to encompass him. Since severability clauses are not drafted to negate policy exclusions, the existence of that clause in Farm Bureau's policy does not render the exclusion ambiguous."); *State Auto Prop. & Cas. Ins. Co. v. J.R.E.*, No. 13-974, 2014 U.S. Dist. LEXIS 111768 (W.D. Ky. Aug. 13, 2014) ("Here, the disputed intentional act exclusion removes from coverage '[b]odily injury' ... which is expected or intended by an 'insured.' By placing the indefinite article 'an' before the word 'insured,' the policy precludes coverage to all insureds for bodily injury intended by anyone insured under the Policy. Like the provision at issue in *K.M.R.*, this exclusion applies irrespective of whether the insured against whom the claim is brought is the intentional wrongdoer."); *Tower Ins. Co. v. Horn*, 472 S.W.3d 172 (Ky. 2015) ("Having determined that Horn is an insured, we apply the severability clause which states that 'the coverage afforded applies separately to *each* insured who is seeking coverage or against whom a claim or 'suit' is brought.' Because the language of the policy treats insureds individually, so too, must the ensuing analysis. Accordingly, by substituting Horn's name in place of the term 'the insured' it is clear that the employee exclusion does not apply to Horn. The policy 'does not apply to . . . [b]odily injury to . . .·[a]n employee of [Horn] arising out of and in the course of [e]mployment by [Horn]; or performing the duties related to the conduct of [Horn]'s business. . . .' Stafford was not an employee of Horn; Stafford's injury did not arise out of and in the course of his employment by Horn; and Stafford's injury and death did not arise out of his performance of duties related to the conduct of Horn's business. Therefore, the employee exclusion does not apply to Horn.") (emphasis added by court).

Louisiana: A Louisiana District Court held that coverage for employees of a title agent, under an errors and omissions policy, for negligence claims brought by a title insurer, alleging that the title agent's escrow accounts were deficient, was not precluded by a policy exclusion for "[a]ny damages arising out of any intentional, dishonest, fraudulent, criminal or malicious act, error or omission by or on behalf of or at the direction of (1) *the insured* or (2) any employee regardless of whether or not qualifying as an insured." *Stewart Title Guaranty Co. v. Kiefer*, 984 F. Supp. 988, 996–97 (E.D. La. 1997) (emphasis added). The court held that, because the exclusion at issue used the term "the insured," claims against an insured are not barred from coverage "solely on the basis of the [excludable] acts of other insureds." *Id.* at 996 (internal quotes omitted and alteration in original). However, the court also made clear that its decision would have been different if the exclusion at issue had used the term "any insured"—even with a separation of insureds provision in the policy. *Id.; see also Kleisch v. R&B Falcon Drilling U.S.A., Inc.*, No. Civ. A. 01–880, 2002 U.S. Dist. LEXIS 21006 (E.D. La. Oct. 29, 2002) ("'severability of interests clause' does not nullify the effect of the employer's liability exclusion which employs the '*any* insured' policy language") (emphasis in original). More recently, in *Petrozziello v. Thermadyne Holdings Corp.*, 211 So. 3d 1199 (La. Ct. App. 2017), the Court of Appeal of Louisiana addressed the applicability of an exclusion, for injuries sustained by an "employee of any insured," to an additional insured-non-employer of the injured party. Noting that "[t]he words 'any insured' mean just that—*any* insured," the court held that the exclusion applied: "The phrase 'any insured' in the employee-injury exclusion is clear and explicit. It is neither modified nor rendered ambiguous by any reasonable interpretation of the separation of insureds provision in the present policy." (emphasis in original). The court, citing *Stewart Title*, stated that "[c]ourts have recognized that [a separation of insureds provision] is intended to clarify which insured is 'the insured' when that phrase appears in a policy."

Maine: The Supreme Judicial Court of Maine held that coverage was owed under the liability section of a homeowner's policy to an insured-mother for failing to take steps to prevent an insured-father's sexual abuse of their daughter. *Hanover Ins. Co. v. Crocker*, 688 A.2d 928, 932 (Me. 1997). A policy exclusion applied to "bodily injury … which is either expected or intended from the standpoint of *the insured*." *Id.* at 931 (emphasis added). The court held that coverage was owed to the mother because the injury was not expected or intended from her standpoint. *Id.* "Our conclusion is consistent with the majority of other jurisdictions that have held that provisions excluding from coverage injuries intentionally caused by 'the insured' refer to a definite, specific insured, who is directly involved in the occurrence that causes the injury." *Id.* One month earlier in *Johnson v. Allstate*, 687 A.2d 642, 644 (Me. 1997) the Supreme Judicial Court of Maine held that no coverage was owed under the liability section of a homeowner's policy to a grandmother for failing to prevent her husband from sexually abusing their granddaughter. A policy exclusion applied to bodily injury intentionally caused by *an insured person. Id.* The court held that an exclusion for damages intentionally caused by "an insured person" excludes coverage for damages intentionally caused by any insured person. *Id.* The court rejected the argument that the policy's severability clause dictated a different result. *Id.*; *Huber Engineered Woods, LLC v. Canal Ins. Co.*, 690 S.E.2d 739, 748 (N.C. Ct. App. 2010) (applying Maine law) (discussing *Crocker* and *Johnson*) ("As the Supreme Judicial Court of Maine has determined that 'the insured' refers only to the person or entity seeking coverage, we must apply that definition to the facts of this case."); *Metro. Prop. & Cas. Ins. Co. v. McCarthy*, No. 12-151, 2013 U.S. Dist. LEXIS 80900 (D. Me. June 10, 2013) (because complaint did not allege that the perpetrator of sexual abuse was an insured, court did not reach the parties' arguments "whether 'you' as used in the abuse and intentional loss exclusions refers to 'the insured' or to 'any insured' or 'all insureds'") (citing *Crocker* and *Johnson*); *Peerless Ins. Co. v. K.F.H.*, No. 15-104, 2015 U.S. Dist. LEXIS 139505 (D. Me. Oct. 14, 2015) (distinguishing *Crocker* and *Johnson* on the facts -- here the injuries were all caused by the same person -- but reiterating their holdings).

Maryland: The Court of Appeals of Maryland held that coverage was owed under the liability section of a homeowner's policy to an insured-husband for injury to a child being babysat by his insured-wife. *Litz v. State Farm Fire & Cas. Co.*, 695 A.2d 566, 572 (Md. 1997). A policy exclusion applied to "bodily injury … arising out of business pursuits of *an insured." Id.* at 568 (emphasis added). The court held that "[i]n light of th[e] express severability clause, we construe the business pursuits exception in the Litzes' policy to mean that the business pursuits of 'an' insured disqualify only that insured from coverage in the event of property damage or bodily injury resulting from the business pursuit; other insureds, i.e., those not engaging in a business pursuit, remain covered under the policy." *Id.* at 572. In *Standard Fire Ins. Co. v. Proctor*, 286 F. Supp. 2d 567, 575 (D. Md. 2003), the court held that a homeowner's policy exclusion for bodily injury "which is expected or intended by any insured" precluded coverage for an innocent co-insured. The court distinguished *Litz* because it involved an exclusion for the business pursuits of *an* insured, while the exclusion in *Proctor* applied to bodily injury expected or intended by *any* insured. *Id.* at 574. The policy at issue in *Proctor* contained a severability provision. *Id.* at 574–75. *See also Emanuel v. Ace Am. Ins. Co.*, No. 11-875, 2011 U.S. Dist. LEXIS 135314 (D. Md. Nov. 23, 2011) (following *Litz's* rationale to limit the applicability of an exclusion) ("[T]he only operations that are excluded are 'retail used tires.'

Under a tenable interpretation of the Endorsement's language, only the retailing of used tires that constitutes an 'operation[]' conducted by or on behalf of the insured is excluded from coverage.").

Massachusetts: The Supreme Judicial Court of Massachusetts considered the distinction between the phrase "an insured" and "the insured" in *Aquino v. United Prop. & Cas. Co.*, 143 N.E.3d 379 (Mass. 2020). The *Acquino* court noted that the distinction, "although subtle on its face, is not without difference, and has been extensively analyzed by numerous courts and scholars, who have concluded that an intentional loss exclusion referencing 'the insured' offers more protection than an exclusion referencing 'an insured' or 'any insured'." *Id.* at 387. The court concluded that "by using the article 'the' and not 'an' before the word 'insured' in the statutory [fire] exclusion, the Legislature provided for several rather than joint rights and obligations. Had the Legislature intended to preclude recovery for innocent coinsureds, it would have drafted the statutory exclusion to apply to 'an insured' rather than 'the insured.'" *Id.* The Appeals Court of Massachusetts held that no coverage was owed under a personal umbrella policy to insured-parents for failing to prevent their insured–minor son from sexually assaulting other minors. *Hingham Mut. Fire Ins. Co. v. Smith*, 865 N.E.2d 1168, 1171 (Mass. Ct. App. 2007). The policy precluded coverage for "bodily injury … arising out of sexual molestation, corporal punishment or physical or mental abuse." *Id.* at 1173. The court rejected the parents' argument that coverage existed for them on the basis that the policy's severability clause required that each insured be treated as having separate coverage. *Id.* "Because the complaint in the underlying action alleges injuries due to sexual molestation, the exclusionary language in the definition of 'bodily injur[ies]' precludes coverage for claims against any insured, even when considered separately, where the claims brought against them would have no basis but for the molestation." *Id.* The *Hingham* Court also distinguished the Supreme Judicial Court's decision in *Worcester Mut. Ins. Co. v. Marnell*, 496 N.E.2d 158 (Mass. 1986), which held that, notwithstanding a homeowner's policy's exclusion for bodily injury arising out of the use of a motor vehicle operated by *any insured*, the policy's severability clause gave rise to coverage for a negligent supervision claim against parents who had supervised a party in which their son became intoxicated, subsequently causing the death of another while operating his motor vehicle. *Id.* According to *Hingham*, "the result in *Marnell* turned on the allocation of risks between homeowner's coverage and automobile liability insurance." *Id.*; *see also Miles v. Great Northern Ins. Co.*, 656 F. Supp. 2d 218, 224

(D. Mass. 2009) (provision upheld that bars coverage for an innocentco-insured spouse, through the inclusion of the term "any covered person"); *Rhoades v. Mass. Property Ins. Underwriting Ass'n.*, No. 09-11302, 2010 U.S. Dist. LEXIS 69870 (D. Mass. July 13, 2010) (discussing *Marnell* and holding that insured-father was not owed coverage under homeowner policy when minor-son struck and injured plaintiff with skid steer, a type of equipment within homeowner policy's motor vehicle exclusion, because the insured-father effectively owned skid steer, as he was president and director of corporation that owned the equipment) (explaining that exclusion "reflect[ed] the proper and anticipated allocation of risks developed by Massachusetts case law between an insured's homeowner's policy and other, more specific, insurance policies"); *Barnstable Mut. Ins. Co. v. Dezotell*, No. 200500361, 2006 Mass. Super. LEXIS 350 (Mass. Super. Ct. July 20, 2006) (granting motion to dissolve insurer's real estate attachment of property belonging to allegedly innocent insured-wife, whose husband reportedly paid man to burn down house, even though homeowner's policy included the phrase "an insured" in its exclusion for intentional loss because such policy language "may very well be construed as diminishing or diluting the coverage required under [the Massachusetts state insurance fire statute]," which incorporated the phrase "the insured" into its exclusion provision); *First Specialty Ins. Corp. v. Pilgrim Ins. Co.*, 990 N.E.2d 86 (Mass. Ct. App. 2013) (automobile exclusion applied "even if the claims against *any insured* allege negligence ... in the supervision[ ] [or] hiring[ ] ... of others *by that insured*," if the underlying claim involves an automobile "that is owned or operated by ... *any insured* ") ("In *Marnell*, the court construed a reference to 'any insured,' in light of the severability clause, to refer only to each insured who was sued. However, the policy at issue in *Marnell* did not have this [quoted] paragraph. Indeed, the [quoted] paragraph appears to be a response to the issues raised in cases like *Marnell*."); *A&W Maint., Inc. v. First Mercury Ins. Co.*, 91 F. Supp. 3d 113 (D. Mass. Mar. 17, 2015) (restating *Marnell*); *Liberty Mut. Ins. Co. v. Gonzalez*, No. 2015-1794, 2017 Mass. Super. LEXIS 67 (Mass. Super. Ct. June 12, 2017) ("Many courts have held that the policy unambiguously affords coverage to the innocent co-insured where the word 'the' is used to modify the word 'insured'...On the other hand, courts have generally held that a policy exclusion that uses the language 'an insured' or 'any insured' unambiguously creates a joint obligation as to all named insureds.") (noting that if a statutory policy "creates a several obligation by using 'the insured,' an insurance policy that uses 'an insured' or 'any insured'" will be reformed to meet the statutory requirement); *Phoenix Baystate Construction v. First Financial*

Insurance Company, No. 19-P-743, 2020 Mass. App. Unpub. LEXIS 411 (Mass. Ct. App. May 18, 2020) ("[I]f some exclusions refer to 'any insured,' while others refer to 'the insured,' there must be a difference between those two phrases.") (rejecting *Marnell* because it turned on the allocation of risks between homeowner's and auto policies); *Nagog Real Estate Consulting Corp. v. Nautilus Ins. Co.*, No. 19-11714, 2020 U.S. Dist. LEXIS 126737 (D. Mass. July 20, 2020) ("[T]he Policy envisions that the term 'that insured' and 'any insured' have different meanings, and because applying the separation of insured provision here would reject these different meanings, it was not intended to be applied to [the exclusion].") (noting that "the policy implications that animated the results in *Marnell* are not implicated here").

Michigan: The Supreme Court of Michigan held that no coverage was owed under the liability section of a homeowner's policy to an insured-husband for negligent entrustment of a firearm that led to his insured-wife shooting a neighbor. *Allstate Ins. Co. v. Freeman*, 443 N.W.2d 734, 754–55 (Mich. 1989). A policy exclusion applied to "bodily injury … which may reasonably be expected to result from the intentional or criminal acts of *an insured person* or which is in fact intended by *an insured person.*" *Id.* at 739 (emphasis added). The Michigan high court rejected the insured-husband's argument that the exclusion was ambiguous because "an insured" could mean "that insured," "the insured" or "any insured." *Id.* at 737. Instead, the court held that "an insured" unambiguously refers to "any insured." *Id.* The opinion includes no discussion of a severability provision. *See also Gorzen v. Westfield Ins. Co.*, 526 N.W.2d 43, 44–45 (Mich. Ct. App. 1994) (concluding that, even though the policy in *Freeman* did not contain a severability clause, the substance of it was considered by the supreme court and found not to affect the operation of the exclusion); *Vanguard Ins. Co. v. McKinney*, 459 N.W.2d 316, 318–19 (Mich. Ct. App. 1990) (distinguishing *Freeman* and finding coverage for an innocent co-insured, because the exclusion at issue applied to conduct of "the insured," which only precluded coverage for the particular insured that engaged in the conduct); *Castillo v. Wimpee*, No. 255605, 2005 Mich. App. LEXIS 3032 (Mich. Ct. App. Dec. 6, 2005) (citing *McKinney* and holding that insured-husband was not owed coverage under homeowner's policy for drowning of a child in insured-wife's daycare center because business pursuits exclusion applied to a business engaged in by "an insured"); *Home Owners Ins. Co. v. Selfridge*, No. 280112, 2008 Mich. App. LEXIS 2504 (Mich. Ct. App. Dec. 18, 2008) (holding that, despite existence of severability clause, false statement by one insured precluded coverage for all insureds where policy provided that it was void if "any insured" made a false statement).

Minnesota: The Court of Appeals of Minnesota held that no coverage was owed under the liability section of a homeowner's policy to insured-parents for their failure to prevent their insured-son from assaulting a neighbor. *SECURA Supreme Ins. Co. v. M.S.M.*, 755 N.W.2d 320, 329 (Minn. Ct. App. 2008). A policy exclusion applied to bodily injury which results "from the criminal acts of *any insured*." *Id.* at 322 (emphasis added). The court rejected the argument that the policy's severability clause dictated a different result. *Id.* at 328–29. The court relied on the Supreme Court of Minnesota's decision in *Travelers Indem. Co. v. Bloomington Steel & Supply Co.*, 718 N.W.2d 888 (Minn. 2006), which stated (admittedly, in *dicta*) that if an insurer wanted to preclude coverage for an innocent co-insured, it could have tied its intentional act exclusion to the conduct of "any insured" or "an insured" instead of "the insured," even with a severability clause contained in the policy. *Id.*; *see also Midwest Family Mut. Ins. Co. v. Cummings*, No. A10-1537, 2011 Minn. App. Unpub. LEXIS 508 (Minn. Ct. App. May 23, 2011) (warehouse owned by Cummings and leased to Shamrock Storage, LLC, a company owned by Cummings, burned down; Cummings and Shamrock Storage both named insureds) (coverage owed to Cummings) ("Midwest may have believed that the policy exclusions operated equally on Steven Cummings and Shamrock Storage. But the severability clause requires us to consider each insured separately and Midwest drafted the exclusion to apply to property in the care, custody or control of the insured rather than any insured.") (emphasis in original); *St. Paul Mercury Ins. Co. v. Order of St. Benedict, Inc.*, No. 15-2617, 2017 U.S. Dist. LEXIS 28103 (D. Minn. Feb. 28, 2017) ("The exclusion bars coverage for the intentional conduct of 'any' insured. The court is not persuaded that [because of the severability clause] there is any ambiguity to resolve or that the two provisions are in any way inconsistent.") (citing *M.S.M*).

Mississippi: A Mississippi District Court held that coverage was owed under a homeowner's policy to an insured-wife for damage caused by her estranged insured-husband's attack on the insured-residence with a baseball bat. *McFarland v. Utica Fire Ins. Co.*, 814 F. Supp. 518, 526 (S.D. Miss. 1992). A policy exclusion applied to "loss which results from an act committed by or at the direction of *an insured* and with the intent to cause a loss." *Id.* at 522 (emphasis added). The court held that the exclusion could be read two ways—that both insureds are denied coverage when one insured causes an intentional loss or that coverage is only precluded for the wrongful insured. *Id.* at 525. In finding that coverage was owed to the innocent-spouse, the court held that "[t]he [insurer] could have cured this ambiguity through clearer or more precise language … or, alternatively, through the addition of a non-severability clause. But, [the insurer's] policy contains no non-severability clause. Instead, on page 1 of the policy, there is found language which states that all insureds under the policy are 'separate insureds.'" *Id.* at 526 (citation omitted); *see also Nationwide Ins. Co. v. Clark*, No. 3:05CV615, 2006 U.S. Dist. LEXIS 90181 (S.D. Miss. Dec. 13, 2006) (distinguishing *McFarland* and concluding that no coverage was owed to an innocent insured because the intentional acts exclusion contained a nonseverability clause—"Such acts exclude coverage for all insureds").

Missouri: The Court of Appeals of Missouri held that no coverage was owed under the liability section of a homeowner's policy to an insured-wife for failing to prevent her insured-husband from molesting his step-granddaughter. *Am. Family Mut. Ins. Co. v. Copeland-Williams*, 941 S.W.2d 625, 629–30 (Mo. Ct. App. 1997). A policy exclusion applied to "bodily injury ... which is either expected or intended from the standpoint of *any insured*." *Id.* at 627 (emphasis added). The court held that, even in the face of a severability clause, the phrase "any insured" unambiguously established that the insureds' rights are jointly and not severally held when one insured intends or expects bodily injury to another. *Id.* at 629–30. *See also Argonaut Great Cent. Ins. Co. v. Valley Village, LLC*, No. 10-2247, 2013 U.S. Dist. LEXIS 145928 (E.D. Mo. Oct. 9, 2013) ("The acts of Bainsaeid [sexual abuse] were not within the scope of his employment, and thus he was not 'an insured' under the clear terms of the ... policy. Since Bainsaeid was not 'an insured,' the exclusion for intentional acts of an insured does not apply.") (exclusion for "bodily injury" or "property damage" expected or intended from the standpoint of *an* insured); *Yager v. Shelter Gen. Ins. Co.*, 460 S.W.3d 68 (Mo. Ct. App. 2015) ("As used in the 'non-owned auto' definition, the phrase 'owned by any insured' unambiguously excludes coverage for liabilities arising from the use of a vehicle, if one or another of the several persons listed as an 'insured' owns the vehicle in question, even though the vehicle owner is not the insured seeking coverage."); *Piatt v. Ind. Lumbermen's Mut. Ins. Co.*, 461 S.W.3d 788 (Mo. 2015) (upholding the distinction between an exclusion for bodily injury to an employee of the insured and an employee of a named insured); *Shelter Mut. Ins. Co. v. Brooks*, 693 S.W.2d 810, 811–12 (Mo. 1985) (holding that, based on a severability of interest clause, an automobile policy's liability exclusion for bodily injury to *the insured* only excluded bodily injury of the insured seeking coverage); *Safeco Ins. Co. of Am. v. Schweitzer*, 372 F. Supp. 3d 884 (W.D. Mo. 2019) ("Because Amanda is deemed as a matter of law to have expected or intended the harm to C.A., coverage for Jonah is also excluded by the 'any insured' language of the expected/intended acts exclusion. This is so despite the existence of a 'severability' clause, which separately insures each named insured.") (citing *Copeland-Williams*).

Montana: The Supreme Court of Montana held that no coverage was owed under a farm and ranch liability policy to insured-parents for failing to prevent their insured-son from committing a rape. *Farmers Union Mut. Ins. v. Kienenberger*, 847 P.2d 1360, 1361 (Mont. 1993). A policy provision stated that the insurer would pay damages for bodily injury caused by an "occurrence," defined as "an accident … neither expected nor intended from the standpoint of *the insured*." *Id.* (emphasis added). Notwithstanding that the coverage applied to damages neither expected nor intended from the standpoint of "the insured," the court held that no coverage was owed to the parents because the injuries "were caused by *an insured person's* intentional act, and the insurance contract clearly and unambiguously excludes coverage for intentional torts." *Id.* The opinion includes no discussion of a severability provision. However, another decision from the Supreme Court of Montana, involving a policy that contained a severability clause, concluded that policy provisions are interpreted from the standpoint of the insured seeking coverage. *See Swank Enters., Inc. v. All Purpose Servs., Ltd.*, 154 P.3d 52, 56 (Mont. 2007) ("The language of the exclusions at issue is clear and the reference pronouns are defined in the policy. The exclusions clearly refer to 'property damage' arising out of All Purpose's operations and 'property damage' to All Purpose's 'product.' The exclusions do not reference Swank. When strictly construed based on their plain language, the exclusions at issue do not exclude claims made by Swank, especially when considered in light of the severability of interests clause. On the other hand, the exclusion section is prefaced by the language '[t]his insurance does not apply to' with the list of exclusions following, which can be read to exclude coverage to *any* insured when the underlying damage triggers the exclusion.") (emphasis in original).

Nebraska: The Supreme Court of Nebraska held that no coverage was owed under the property section of a homeowner's policy to an insured-wife, for the destruction of the insured-residence, caused by a fire that was intentionally set by an insured-husband. *Volquardson v. Hartford Ins. Co.*, 647 N.W.2d 599, 606 (Neb. 2002). A policy exclusion applied to "any loss arising out of any act committed: (1) By or at the direction of *an insured*; and (2) With the intent to cause a loss." *Id.* at 604 (emphasis added). The court rejected the argument that only the phrase "any insured" contained in an intentional acts exclusion, and not "an insured," could serve to preclude coverage to an innocent co-insured. *Id.* at 605. The opinion includes no discussion of a severability provision. The Nebraska high court examined the impact of a severability of interest clause in *Am. Fam. Mut. Ins. Co. v. Wheeler*, 842 N.W.2d 100 (Neb. 2014), addressing coverage for a parent, for sexual abuse committed by his son, in the context of various exclusions that, generally speaking, barred coverage for injuries intentionally caused by "any insured" and injuries resulting from sexual abuse by "an insured" or "any insured." The court held: "We have in the past concluded that the 'an insured' language, and implicitly the 'any insured' language, is clear and unambiguous. Such language means what it says, and the severability clause does not operate to override this clear and unambiguous language. In other words, applying the insurance separately to each insured, as the severability clause requires, does not change that the exclusions reference 'an insured' or 'any insured.'" *Id.* at 107.

Nevada: A Nevada District Court held that no coverage was owed under the liability section of a mobile home policy to an insured-wife for her failure to prevent her insured-husband from sexually assaulting a minor. *Allstate Ins. Co. v. Foster*, 693 F. Supp. 886, 889 (D. Nev. 1988). A policy exclusion applied to "any bodily injury … which may reasonably be expected to result from the intentional or criminal acts of *an insured person* or which is in fact intended by an insured person." *Id.* at 887 (emphasis added). Noting that "A" or "an" is used in the sense of "any" and applied to more than one individual object, whereas "the" applies to the subject spoken of, the court held that "[s]ince the Allstate Mobilehome Policy excludes coverage for harm resulting from the intentional or criminal 'acts of *an* insured person,' the insurance policy excludes coverage to any other insureds … for liability arising from the harm which is directly attributable to the intentional or criminal act." *Id.* at 887. The opinion includes no discussion of a severability provision. *See also Colony Ins. Co. v. Kuehn*, No. 10–019432012, 2012 U.S. Dist. LEXIS 137071 (D. Nev. Sept. 25, 2012) ("In essence, Gibson asks the Court to interpret the term 'any insured' to mean 'the insured' so that the prior knowledge exclusion would only operate against the insured that had actual knowledge of the claim. This is the same strained interpretation that has been repeatedly rejected by other courts. In the context of a prior knowledge exclusion on a multi-party policy, courts adopt the ordinary definition of 'any' as the maximum or whole.") (no discussion of a severability provision); *Am Guarantee & Liab. Ins. Co. v. Flangas McMillan Law Group, Inc.*, No. 11–CV–188, 2012 U.S. Dist. LEXIS 24114 (D. Nev. Feb. 24, 2012) ("In the present Policy, no separation or severability clause exists. This absence makes it more likely that the intent of the phrase 'any insured' is to be applied as read, rather than to provide coverage for some insureds, but not others.").

New Hampshire: The Supreme Court of New Hampshire held that coverage was owed under the liability section of a homeowner's policy to insured-parents for failing to prevent their insured-son from assaulting a minor. *Pawtucket Mut. Ins. Co. v. Lebrecht*, 190 A.2d 420, 423 (N.H. 1963). A policy exclusion applied to "injury … caused intentionally by or at the direction of *the Insured*." *Id.* at 422 (emphasis added). Noting that the policy used the term "the Insured" in certain provisions and "any Insured" or "an Insured" in others, the court held that it was "of the opinion that the provisions excluding from liability coverage injuries intentionally caused by 'the Insured' was meant to refer to a definite, specific insured, namely the insured who is involved in the occurrence which caused the injury and who is seeking coverage under the policy." *Id.* at 423. The policy contained a severability of interest clause but the court did not address what impact it would have on an exclusion that applied to "any Insured" or "an Insured." *Id.* at 422. *See also Bianco Professional Ass'n v. Home Ins. Co.*, 740 A.2d 1051 (N.H. 1999) ("'The Insured' in the second paragraph plainly refers to the insured against whom a claim is asserted. The question is whether 'the insured' in the first paragraph also refers to the specific insured being sued or to any insured under the policy. It is reasonable to assume that while 'the Insured' in certain policy provisions may refer to different persons from 'an Insured' in other provisions, it refers to the same persons as 'the Insured' in other provisions unless defined otherwise.") (citing *Lebrecht*); *Mass. Bay Ins. Co. v. Am. Healthcare Srvs. Ass'n*, 172 A.3d 1043 (N.H. 2017) (finding phrase "any insured" in a malicious act exclusion was not ambiguous despite a separation of insureds clause) ("Triage argues that the malicious acts exclusion should not apply to Triage based upon the conduct of another insured. But because Triage's interpretation renders meaningless the word 'any' in the phrase 'any insured,' it is not a reasonable interpretation.").

New Jersey: The Supreme Court of New Jersey held that no coverage was owed under the liability section of a homeowner's policy to insured-grandparents for failing to prevent their insured-son from sexually assaulting his brother's daughter while in her grandparents' home. *Villa v. Short*, 947 A.2d 1217, 1224 (N.J. 2008). Policies at issue excluded coverage for "any bodily injury … which may reasonably be expected to result from the intentional or criminal acts of *an insured person* or which is in fact intended by an insured person." *Id.* at 1222 (emphasis added). The court held that the policy excluded coverage for all insureds for damages caused by the intentional or criminal acts of an insured. *Id.* at 1224. The court rejected the argument that the policy's severability clause dictated a different result. *Id.* at 1225; *see also D.R. v. Allstate Ins. Co.*, No. A-0180-08T1, 2010 N.J. Super. Unpub.

LEXIS 200 (N.J. Super. Ct. App. Div. Jan. 27, 2010) (holding that insured day-care owner was owed coverage for insured-son's sexual molestation because policy exclusion was for intentional acts of *the insured person*); *Farmers Mut. Fire Ins. Co. v. Zarate*, 2011 N.J. Super. Unpub. LEXIS 1033 (N.J. Super. Ct. App. Div. Apr. 27, 2011) (determining that insured-mother was not owed coverage under homeowner's policy for insured-son's murder of another because policy excluded coverage for *an* insured's willfully harmful act or knowing endangerment); *Arcelormittal Plate, LLC v. Joule Technical Services, Inc.*, 558 Fed. Appx. 205 (3rd Cir. 2014) ("In light of the severability clause, the reference to 'the insured' in the employee exclusion must be read, under New Jersey law, as referring to the insured making the claim."); *Atain Specialty Ins. Co. v. Lusa Construction*, No. 14-4356, 2016 U.S. Dist. LEXIS 80891 (D.N.J. June 21, 2016) ("[T]he parties agree that, when applying New Jersey law, the phrase 'the insured' refers to the insured seeking coverage, so the contract analysis functionally replaces the words 'the insured' with each individual entity seeking coverage to determine whether the exclusions apply to that entity.").

New Mexico: A New Mexico federal court held that knowledge of one insured was not imputed to other insureds for purposes of a policy's "prior knowledge" exclusion. *Evanston Ins. Co. v. Desert State Life Mgmt.*, No. 18-0654, 2020 U.S. Dist. LEXIS 7652 (D.N.M. Jan. 16, 2020). ["Prior to the effective date of this Coverage Part the Insured had no knowledge of such Wrongful Act(s) or Personal Injury(ies) or any fact, circumstance, situation or incident, which may have led a reasonable person in the Insured's position to conclude that a Claim was likely."] The insurer argued that, "because the definition of 'Insured' includes 'any' past or current principal, partner, officer, director, trustee, or shareholder, and because 'the term 'any' is unambiguously collective rather than several,' the Insured had knowledge of facts and circumstances that could reasonably give rise to a claim." *Id.* at *86-87. The court rejected the insurer's reliance on *Am. Family Mut. Ins. Co. v. Copeland-Williams* [*see* Missouri], which the court noted is "commonly cite[d] . . . for its interpretation of the phrase 'any insured' in exclusionary clauses rather than for an interpretation of 'any' across an entire Insurance Policy." *Id.* at *87. Thus, one insured's knowledge of wrongful acts or facts, circumstances, situations, or incidents that were reasonably likely to lead to a claim was not imputed to other insureds." *Id.* at *88.

New York: The Supreme Court of New York, Appellate Division, held that no coverage was owed under a commercial general liability policy to an additional insured for bodily injury to employees of the named insured. *Hayner Hoyt Corp. v. Utica First Ins. Co.*, 760 N.Y.S.2d 706, 706 (N.Y. App. Div. 2003). A policy exclusion applied to "bodily injury to an employee of *an insured* if it occurs in the course of employment." *Id.* (emphasis added). The court held that the term "an insured" is unambiguous and encompassed the named insured and the additional insured. *Id.* Thus, coverage was precluded for the additional insured for claims by employees of the named insured. *Id.* The dissent would have found coverage for the additional insured on the basis of the "separability of insureds doctrine" (although it did not cite to a severability provision in the policy). *Id.* at 707 (Piggott, Jr., P.J. and Pine, J., dissenting); *see also DRK, LLC v. Burlington Ins. Co.*, No. 5698, 2010 N.Y. App. Div. LEXIS 5576 (N.Y. App. Div. June 29, 2010) (upholding an exclusion for "bodily injury" to an employee of *any insured*) (specifically rejecting a separation of insureds provision as a basis to preclude the exclusion's applicability to a party that was not the underlying plaintiff's employer); *Howard & Norman Baker, Ltd. v. Am. Safety Cas. Ins. Co.*, 904 N.Y.S. 2d 770 (N.Y. App. Div. 2010) (same). *But see Shelby Realty, LLC v. National Surety Corp.*, No. 06 Civ. 3260, 2007 U.S. Dist. LEXIS 29482 (S.D.N.Y. Apr. 11, 2007) (reaching the opposite conclusion as *Hayner Hoyt* on the basis that the Employee Exclusion at issue must be read in conjunction with the policy's Separation of Insureds clause); *Ostrowski v. American Safety Indem. Co.*, No. 07-CV-3977, 2010 U.S. Dist. LEXIS 104874 (E.D.N.Y. Sept. 30, 2010) (following *Shelby*) ("The 'Separation of Insureds' Clause limits our reading of the Employee Exclusion to individual insureds, as though each is the only insured under the policy. Thus, the Employee Exclusion does not apply to [Hi-Tower] unless one of [Hi-Tower's] employees is injured during the course of his employment. Since [Ostrowski] worked for [ENY] and not for [Hi-Tower], his employment is not relevant to [Hi-Tower's] coverage.") (alteration in original); *385 Third Ave. Assoc., L.P. v. Metro. Metals Corp.*, 916 N.Y.S. 2d 95, 97 (N.Y. App. Div. 2011) (holding that property owner and general contractor were not owed coverage under subcontractor's commercial general liability policy for subcontractor's employee injured while in scope of his employment because policy's cross-liability exclusion precluded coverage for injury to employee of "any insured"); *Campoverde v. Fabian Builders, LLC*, 922 N.Y.S.2d 435, 436–37 (N.Y. App. Div. 2011) (holding that coverage was not owed to additional insured or named insured contractors, for injury sustained by an employee of one of their contractors, because policy's employee exclusion precluded coverage for damages arising out of bodily injury sustained by employee of any contractor hired by or for any insured in the course of employee's employment); *Richner Dev., LLC v. Burlington Ins. Co.*, 916 N.Y.S.2d 211, 212–13 (N.Y. App. Div. 2011) (upholding "any insured" provision in employee exclusion, despite separation of insureds clause); *Nautilus Ins. Co. v. Barfield*

Realty Corp., No. 11-7425, 2012 U.S. Dist. LEXIS 148714 (S.D.N.Y. Oct. 16, 2012) ("[T]his Court is persuaded by the latter view that a separation of insureds clause need not in fact preclude the applicability of unambiguous exclusionary language referring to 'any insured.'") (addressing several New York cases); *Citizens Ins. Co. of America v. Illinois Union Ins. Co.*, 964 N.Y.S.2d 131 (N.Y. App. Div. 2013) (separation of insureds clause did not negate the portion of the policy that precluded coverage to the additional insured when no coverage was extended to the named insured); *Endurance American Specialty Ins. Co. v. Century Sur. Co.*, 630 Fed. Appx. 6 (2nd Cir. 2015) ("Here, like the language 'any insured,' the language 'the named insured' evinces that the Action Over Exclusion clause specifically exclude coverage for bodily injury to employees of the named insured, Pinnacle. Hayden, in contrast, is not a named insured; rather, it is an additional insured."); *Hastings Dev., LLC v. Evanston Ins. Co.*, No. 14-6203, 2016 U.S. Dist. LEXIS 84346 (E.D.N.Y. June 29, 2016) ("[T]here are multiple Named Insureds under the policy and therefore, there is ambiguity as to what 'an employee of the Named Insured' means in the context of the Employers' Liability Exclusion. Hastings is a 'Named Insured' under the policy. Thus, it would appear that the separation of insureds clause which applies the insurance 'separately to each insured against whom claim is made or 'suit' is brought,' would require the Court to interpret the policy as if Hastings is the *only* 'Named Insured' under the policy. Under that logic, 'the Named Insured' in the Employers Liability Exclusion should be replaced with 'Hastings.' As Cohen was not an employee of Hastings, the Employers Liability Exclusion does not bar coverage to Hastings for the Cohen Action."); *Neth. Ins. Co. v. United States Underwriters Ins. Co.*, No. 14-3568, 2015 U.S. Dist. LEXIS 169443 (S.D.N.Y. Dec. 17, 2015) ("This argument, however, disregards a vital phrase in the liability clause: 'for which *any insured* may be held liable in any capacity.' . . . Because Valdez was retained by *one* of the insureds, the exclusion applies to *all* insured parties." (emphasis in original); *Flintlock Constr. Servs. LLC v. Technology Ins. Co.*, No. 652939/2017, 2019 N.Y. Misc. LEXIS 649 (N.Y. Sup. Ct. Feb. 15, 2019) (exclusion for "bodily injuries sustained by an employee of the insured") ("Plaintiffs' argument that this exclusion does not apply to Flintlock and Lexington, because Gutierrez was not their employee, is unavailing. While plaintiffs correctly argue that an insurer undertakes a separate obligation to the various insured parties, whether as a named insured or as an additional insured. . . nevertheless, nearly identical employee exclusionary clauses have applied to bar coverage to an additional insured for a claim by the named insured's employee."); *Buckingham Props., LLC v. Atl. Cas. Ins. Co.*, No. 17-6656, 2020

U.S. Dist. LEXIS 3153 (W.D.N.Y. Jan. 8, 2020) (rejecting argument that separation of insureds provision negated "any insured" language) (citing *Barfield*).

North Carolina: A North Carolina District Court held that coverage was owed under a liability policy to an additional insured, for a claim by an employee of the named insured, who was injured when he fell from a tractor-trailer owned by the additional insured. *Penske Truck Leasing Co. v. Republic Western Ins. Co.*, 407 F. Supp. 2d 741, 752 (E.D.N.C. 2006). A policy exclusion applied to "'Bodily injury' to: a. An 'employee' of *the 'insured'* arising out of and in the course of: (1) Employment by the 'insured.'" *Id.* at 750. (emphasis added). The court based its decision on the inclusion of a severability of interests provision contained in the policy. *Id.* However, the court also noted that "[i]f the exclusion barred coverage for bodily injury to an employee of 'any' insured, a different analysis may be required." *Id. See also Universal Ins. Co. v. Burton Farm Development Co., LLC*, 718 S.E.2d 665 (N.C. Ct. App. 2011) ("We agree with the reasoning of *Penske* and *Carbone* [937 F. Supp. 413 (E.D. Pa. 1996)] and adopt the majority rule. In this case, the exclusion at issue—the 'knowledge of falsity' exclusion—excludes coverage for personal injury 'done by or at the direction of *the insured* with knowledge of its falsity.' (Emphasis added [by court].) Since the exclusion refers to *the* insured rather than *any* insured, the separation of insureds clause requires that the exclusion be applied separately with respect to each insured.") (emphasis in original); *Cont'l Cas. Co. v. Amerisure Ins. Co.*, No. 14-529, 2017 U.S. Dist. LEXIS 313 (W.D.N.C. Jan. 3, 2017), *aff'd in part, vacated in part on other grounds* 886 F.3d 366 (4th Cir. 2018) ("If Amerisure had intended the exclusion to apply to the additional insureds, it could have easily drafted the provision to say so. *See Penske* (stating: '[t]he fact that [the insurer] could have drafted its policy to include the language 'any insured' together with the fact that it chose not to do so further support the court's interpretation of the language at issue.'")).

North Dakota: The Supreme Court of North Dakota held that no coverage was owed under the liability section of a homeowner's policy to an insured-wife for negligently failing to prevent her insured-husband from sexually assaulting a child in the wife's home daycare center. *Northwest G.F. Mut. Ins. Co. v. Norgard*, 518 N.W.2d 179, 183 (N.D. 1994). A policy exclusion applied to "bodily injury … arising out of sexual molestation … by or at the direction of *an insured*, an insured's employee or any other person involved in any capacity in the day care enterprise." (emphasis added). The court's decision rested on two rationales. First, the breadth of the sexual molestation exclusion—it applies when anyone connected to the operation of the daycare center commits an act of sexual molestation. *Id.* at 183. Second,

North Dakota law allows a contract to be explained by reference to "the circumstances under which it was made and the matter to which it relates"—"the increase in legal actions involving sexual abuse of children by adults who are not strangers to the children, including caretakers, is dramatic." *Id.* However, it appears that, without these rationales, the court could have found otherwise, stating that "we believe Northwest rolls the dice by insisting that the policy is clear on its face and by not attempting in the policy itself to more carefully reconcile the severability clause and the exclusions." *Id.* at 183. *See also Great West Cas. Co. v. Nat'l Cas. Co.*, 807 F.3d 952 (8th Cir. 2015) (concluding that the Supreme Court of North Dakota would apply *Norgard* and rule that fellow employee and employer's liability exclusions, "read together with the severability clause, do not apply to relieve [the insurer] of the duty to defend [an] additional-insured . . . from a negligence action by the named insured's employee").

Ohio: The Supreme Court of Ohio held that coverage was not precluded under a homeowner's or umbrella policy issued to insured-parents for their alleged negligence in failing to prevent their insured-son from stabbing a neighbor. *Safeco Ins. Co. of Am. v. White*, 913 N.E.2d 426 (Ohio 2009). The exclusions at issue applied, in part, to bodily injury "expected or intended by *an insured*" and "[a]ny injury caused by a violation of a penal law or ordinance committed by or with the knowledge or consent of *any insured*." *Id.* at 430 (emphasis added). The court concluded that its finding, that intentional-act and illegal-act exclusions are inapplicable to acts of negligence related to intentional torts, is a continuation of and consistent with its approach to "examine each act on its own merits." *Id.* at 436 (citation omitted). At least one of the policies at issue contained a severability of insurance clause, but it played no part in the court's analysis. *See also Crow v. Dooley*, No. 1-11-59, 2012 Ohio App. LEXIS 2269 (Ohio Ct. App. June 11, 2012) (distinguishing *White* in the context of an exclusion for "[b]odily Injury . . . arising out of sexual molestation") ("In the instant case, any language regarding the necessary knowledge or intent of the insured is remarkably absent from the Sexual Molestation exclusion. Therefore, the Sexual Molestation exclusion precludes coverage for any bodily injury arising out of sexual molestation *without regard* to the specific causal connection to the molester or the requisite mental state of the alleged tortfeasor. Because of the difference in the language of the operative exclusions in *White* and the present case, the holding in *White* is inapplicable to the instant case") (emphasis in original); *Sanders v. Nationwide Mut. Ins. Co.*, No. 95228, 2011 Ohio App. LEXIS 1658 (Ohio Ct. App. Apr. 21, 2011) (distinguishing *White* and holding that no coverage was owed to insured-mother after insured-son intentionally burned down house "because the coverage being sought here does not stem from the negligent actions of an insured, arising from the intentional act of another insured, for the benefit of a third party. Rather, plaintiff is seeking coverage for damages caused by the intentional actions of one insured for the benefit of herself, another insured"); *Goodell v. Motorists Mut. Ins. Co.*, 99 N.E.3d 1158 (Ohio Ct. App. 2017) ("In the case before us, the exclusions apply only to 'the insured.' Pursuant to the severability clause, 'the insured' is either the named insured or Pasquale as the omnibus insured. Each insured is considered individually as to whether the exclusion applies and the language clearly applies the exclusions to Wylie & Sons but not Pasquale because he is not Goodell's employer."); *Bedlion v. Travelers Indem. Co. of Am.*, No. 20-34, 2020 U.S. Dist. LEXIS 48395 (N.D. Ohio Mar. 20, 2020) ("The policy contemplates that Tracy Bedlion and Timothy Bedlion are jointly covered under the policy and that the intentional act of any insured precludes coverage for all insureds. Mr. Bedlion's admitted setting of the fire and causing loss precludes coverage under the policy and Defendant is well within its contractual rights to deny coverage.").

Oklahoma: The Supreme Court of Oklahoma held that no coverage was owed under a commercial general liability policy to an additional insured for bodily injury caused by a motor vehicle in which the named insured's employee was allegedly at fault. *BP America, Inc. v. State Auto Prop. & Cas. Co.*, 148 P.3d 832, 842 (Okla. 2005). The policy contained an exclusion for " 'bodily injury' … arising out of the ownership, maintenance, use or entrustment to others of any … 'auto' … owned or operated by or rented or loaned to *any insured.*" *Id.* at 833 (emphasis added). The court held that the term "any insured" in the Auto Exclusion precluded coverage for all automobile occurrences attributed to any of the insureds. *Id.* at 839. The court rejected the argument that the policy's separation of insureds clause dictated a different result. *Id.* at 841–42; *see also Farmers Alliance Mut. Ins. Co. v. Willingham*, No. 08-CV-0532, 2009 U.S. Dist. LEXIS 98482 (N.D. Okla. Oct. 20, 2009) (following *BP America* and holding that the term "one or more insureds," as used in an exclusion, means the same as "any insured"); *Trinity Universal Ins. Co. v. Jay*, No. CIV-08-1366, 2010 U.S. Dist. LEXIS 10827 (W.D. Okla. Feb. 8, 2010) (following *BP America* and precluding coverage for innocent insured-spouse) ("The policies clearly exclude coverage for bodily injury arising out of sexual molestation or a business engaged in by an insured. The conduct at issue encompassed both exclusions. Mr. Jay's business was the practice of law. He saw these clients, and others, in the garage apartment. Any bodily injuries arising out of that conduct would be excluded. Likewise, it is undisputed that Mr. Jay's conduct constitutes sexual moles-tation and therefore any bodily injury occurring as result is excluded under the pol-icies. Defendants ask the court to rewrite the policies to provide coverage for Mrs. Jay that is expressly excluded."); *Naylor Concrete Construction Co. v. Mid-Continent Cas. Co.*, 754 S.E.2d 259 (N.C. Ct. App. 2014) (applying Oklahoma law) (discussing *BP America* and rejecting the argument that a severability clause precludes an inter-pretation of an employer exclusion which treats multiple entities as "insureds").

Oregon: The Court of Appeals of Oregon held that no coverage was owed under the liability section of a homeowner's policy to an insured-wife, for negligently fail-ing to prevent her insured-husband, a convicted sex offender, from being alone in the house with the wife's granddaughter. *Ristine v. Hartford Ins. Co.*, 97 P.3d 1206, 1209 (Or. Ct. App. 2004). The husband sexually abused his wife's granddaughter during a sleep-over. *Id.* at 1207. The policy contained an exclusion for "bodily injury … arising out of sexual molestation." *Id.* The court concluded that the policy contained no wording that limited the exclusion to claims that arose out of sexual molesta-tion *by the insured. Id.* at 1208. To the contrary, the court observed that other policy exclusions were expressly predicated on the conduct of *the insured* or *an insured. Id.* at 1209. "The policy refers to claims arising out of sexual molestation without refer-ence to any limitation as to who committed the act of molestation. Thus, the policy appears to state that the exclusion is based on the nature of the act, not the identity of the actor." *Id.* The court rejected the argument that the policy's severability clause dictated a different result. *Id.* at 1209–10. *See also Am. Hallmark Ins. Co. of Texas v. Am. Family Mut. Ins. Co.*, No. 09–976, 2011 U.S. Dist. LEXIS 60695 (D. Or. June 6, 2011) ("It is undisputed that defendant's policy listed Popoff as an 'additional insured.' Accordingly, under the Separation of Insureds provision, Popoff has a contractual relationship with defendant independent from JRP. Thus, under Oregon case law and in accordance with the express language of defendant's policy, Popoff would be 'the insured' under the exclusion. Therefore, I find that the exclusion applies only when the injured employee is an employee of Popoff's."); *Kirk v. Mut. Of Enumclaw Ins.*, No. 18-02092, 2019 U.S. Dist. LEXIS 127704 (D. Or. July 31, 2019) ("The theft exclusion denies coverage when property is stolen by 'an' insured; only one insured need commit the theft for coverage to be barred for all policyholders. Kirk's interpre-tation requires the theft exclusion to only exclude coverage for theft 'committed by the insured.' In light of the specific provision at issue, this interpretation is implausi-ble. As one cannot commit a theft of one's own property, Kirk's interpretation would render the exclusion meaningless. The provision unambiguously excludes coverage for theft committed by any insured.") (noting that "if a distinction between 'an' and 'any' exists within the theft exclusion, it is a distinction without a difference").

Pennsylvania: The Superior Court of Pennsylvania held that coverage was precluded under a personal umbrella liability policy to insured-parents for allegedly failing to prevent their insured-son from going on a shooting spree in which he killed five people. *Donegal Mut. Ins. Co. v. Baumhammers*, 893 A.2d 797, 819 (Pa. Super. Ct. 2006), *aff'd in part, rev'd in part, on other grounds*, 938 A.2d 286 (Pa. 2007). Policy exclusions applied to bodily injury or damage "caused by the intentional or purposeful act of *any insured*" and bodily injury or damage arising out of a criminal act of "any insured" whether or not such insured is convicted of a crime. *Id.* at 805. The court held that "the criminal act exclusion clearly states that the insurance policy does not apply to bodily or personal injury arising out of a malicious or criminal act of any insured whether or not such insured is convicted of a crime. Similarly, coverage is excluded for bodily or personal injury caused by the intentional or purposeful act of any insured. The bodily and personal injuries suffered by Plaintiffs arose from the intentional, malicious, and criminal acts of an insured, Richard Baumhammers." *Id.* at 819. The opinion includes no discussion of a severability provision. *See also Strouss v. Fireman's Fund Ins. Co.*, No. Civ. A. 03–5718, 2005 U.S. Dist. LEXIS 2639 (E.D. Pa. Feb. 22, 2005) (holding that a severability clause did not render ambiguous an exclusion that applied to "bodily injury … which is expected or intended by one or more 'insureds'") ("as a matter of law … the obligations in the intentional injury exclusion are joint, rather than several"); *Becker v. Farmington Cas. Co.*, 1:08-CV-2228, 2010 U.S. Dist. LEXIS 73902 (M.D. Pa. July 22, 2010) (following Pennsylvania law that the phrases "any insured" or "an insured" plainly and unambiguously bar coverage for all insureds based on the actions of one insured, even when there is a severability clause); *Travelers Home & Marine Ins. Co. v. Stahley*, No. 15-6089, 2017 U.S. Dist. LEXIS 30787 (E.D. Pa. Mar. 3, 2017) ("[T]he intentional act exclusion of Travelers' policy [bodily injury expected or intended by an insured] precludes coverage for the Stahleys, even though the policy also contains a severability clause. As a result, the existence of a severability clause in the Policy does not override the clear and unambiguous language of the intentional act exclusion, and the terms of the Policy preclude coverage to all named insureds under these circumstances."); *Fid. Nat'l Title Ins. Co. v. Maxum Indem. Co.*, No. 16-1360, 2017 U.S. Dist. LEXIS 147134 (E.D. Pa. Sept. 12, 2017) ("[T]he exclusion is triggered as long as any insured commits a dishonest, fraudulent, criminal, or malicious act. It is of no significance that Lenders

Edge has not committed any of that conduct."); *Doe v. Liberty Mut. Fire Ins. Co.*, No. 18-1513, 2019 U.S. Dist. LEXIS 156827 (M.D. Pa. Sept. 13, 2019) ("Because the Policy's intentional or criminal act exclusion includes the phrase 'an insured,' the Court concludes that the exclusion bars coverage for the alleged negligent acts of D.H. as well as the intentional acts of N.H."); *Carrasquillo v. Kelly*, No. 2720, 2019 Pa. Super. Unpub. LEXIS 4229 (Pa. Super. Ct. Nov. 12, 2019) ("Here, the exclusionary language in the policy excludes coverage for the criminal act of 'an insured.' Indisputably, James Kelly is 'an insured' under the policy. Additionally, James Kelly committed a criminal act[.] . . . [W]e are constrained to conclude that the policy excludes coverage for Nancy Kelly based on the criminal act of James Kelly.").

The "innocent co-insured" issue in Pennsylvania also long-involved *Pa. Manuf. Assoc. Ins. Co. v. Aetna Cas. & Sur. Ins. Co.*, 233 A.2d 548, 550 (Pa. 1967) ("*PMA*"), where the Supreme Court, despite a severability clause, rejected the argument that an exclusion for "bodily injury … of any employee of *the insured*" only operated to exclude coverage for injury to those employees that were employed by the insured seeking coverage. (emphasis added). *See also* on the *PMA* issue *Scottsdale Ins. Co. v. The City of Easton*, No. 09–1815, 2010 U.S. App. LEXIS 9663 (3rd Cir. May 11, 2010) (applying Pennsylvania law) (following *PMA*); *Brewer v. U.S. Fire Ins. Co.*, 446 Fed. Appx. 506 (3rd Cir. 2011) (applying Pennsylvania law) (following *PMA*); *Endurance American Specialty Ins. Co. v. H & W Equities Inc.*, No. 12–693, 2013 U.S. Dist. LEXIS 99910 (M.D. Pa. July 17, 2013) (following *PMA*). *But see Luko v. Lloyd's London*, 573 A.2d 1139 (Pa. Super. Ct. 1990) (distinguishing *PMA*). In *Mutual Ben. Ins. Co. v. Politopoulos*, 115 A.3d 844 (Pa. 2015), the Supreme Court "decline[d] to extend *PMA's* expansive construction of the term 'the insured' to an instance in which a commercial general liability policy variously makes use of the terms 'the insured' and 'any insured.' Rather, we are persuaded that, at least where a commercial general liability policy makes varied use of the definite and indefinite articles, this, as a general rule, creates an ambiguity relative to the former, such that 'the insured' may be reasonably taken as signifying the particular insured against whom a claim is asserted." *Id.* at 853 (also noting that its decision is further supported by reference to the policy's separation of insureds provision).

Rhode Island: The Supreme Court of Rhode Island held that coverage was owed under a general liability policy to a real estate manager for damage to an owner's property under its management. *Metro Props. v. Nat'l Union Fire Ins. Co.*, 934 A.2d 204, 210 (R.I. 2007). The property owner, the named insured under the policy, sued the real estate manager, who also qualified as an insured. *Id.* at 206. The court held that a policy exclusion for "'Property damage' to: (1) Property you own, rent, or occupy" did not preclude coverage to the real estate manager beca use it did not own, rent, or occupy the property that experienced damage. *Id.* at 209. While the court was not required to interpret the scope of an exclusion that applied to "any insured" or "an insured," its decision was based on its observation that "[s] everal courts that have considered this issue extend coverage, despite exclusionary language, based upon either a cross-liability provision or a severability-of-interests clause." *Id.* at 209–10.

South Carolina: The Court of Appeals of South Carolina held that no coverage was owed under the liability section of a homeowner's policy to the estate of an insured-father for negligence that led to the drowning death of his insured-daughter (and himself). *Allstate Ins. Co. v. Mangum*, 383 S.E.2d 464, 466 (S.C. Ct. App. 1989). A policy exclusion applied to "bodily injury to *an insured person*." *Id.* at 465 (emphasis added). The court rejected the argument that, based on the policy's separability clause, the term "insured person" means only such person who is at fault and against whom the action is brought for negligence. *Id.* at 466. "Th[e] [separability] doctrine is not applicable to the policy before us because the obligation set forth in the insuring clause limits coverage to 'damages because of bodily injury … *covered by this part of the policy*.' The policy then clearly states that it does not cover bodily injury to an insured person and, under the terms of the policy, Inglis Paige Peurifoy [the daughter] is clearly an insured person." *Id.*; *see also Smith v. Travelers Cas. Co.*, C.A. No. 6:09-cv-02662, 2011 U.S. Dist. LEXIS 32673 (D.S.C. Mar. 28, 2011) (following *Magnum* and holding that coverage was not owed to insured-wife under husband's boat policy for injuries sustained after she became entangled with boat propeller because policy's exclusion was for liability to "your spouse or any insured," and wife fell under both categories) (concluding that even if severability clause had existed, it would not have altered result); *Auto-Owners Ins. Co. v. Taylor*, No. 17-02632, 2018 U.S. Dist. LEXIS 144980 (D.S.C. Aug. 24, 2018) ("The Intentional Act Exclusion excludes 'loss to covered property caused directly or indirectly by . . . an action by or at the direction of any insured committed with the intent to cause a loss.' [T]he issue is not whether Defendants are innocent co-insureds under the policy but whether Plaintiff can demonstrate Jeffery had an intent to cause a loss.") (discussing *Auto-Owners Ins. Co. v. Hamin*, 629 S.E.2d 683 (S.C. 2006)).

South Dakota: The Supreme Court of South Dakota held that coverage was precluded under the liability section of a homeowner's policy to insured-parents for bodily injury that their insured-son caused in a motor vehicle accident. *Great Cent. Ins. Co. v. Roemmich*, 291 N.W.2d 772, 775 (S.D. 1980). It was alleged that the parents failed to prevent their insured-son from operating the motor vehicle, when they knew of his propensity to do so in a reckless and careless manner. *Id.* at 773. A policy exclusion applied to "bodily injury … arising out of the ownership, maintenance, operation, use, loading or unloading of: … any motor vehicle owned or operated by, or rented or loaned to *any Insured.*" *Id.* at 774 (emphasis added). The court rejected the argument that the policy's severability of insurance clause dictated a different result. *Id.*; *see also EMCASCO Ins. Co. v. Diedrich*, 394 F.3d 1091 (8th Cir. 2005) (applying South Dakota law) (holding that homeowner's policy exclusion for bodily injury or property damage "which is expected or intended by *one or more* 'insureds'" precluded liability coverage to insured-parents for sexual assault committed by their insured-son and rejecting the argument that the policy's severability of insurance clause dictated a different result.); *Fedderson v. Columbia Ins. Group*, 824 N.W.2d 793 (S.D. 2012) (no coverage owed to an innocent co-insured spouse where her husband was convicted of conspiracy to commit arson of the insured premises restaurant) ("[T]he insurance contract explicitly voided the policy if 'any insured' misrepresented a material fact or committed fraud relating to the policy. This language is unambiguous. Gary's fraud and misrepresentation contractually voided the policy as to all coinsureds.").

Tennessee: The Court of Appeals of Tennessee held that coverage was not precluded under the liability section of a homeowner's policy to an insured-husband for the loss of a substantial amount of money that was intentionally burned by his insured-wife. *Tenn. Farmers Mut. Ins. Co. v. Evans*, No. 1, 1990 Tenn. App. LEXIS 356 (Tenn. Ct. App. May 18, 1990). The wife discovered the money in a safe deposit box, believed it to be illegally obtained and burned it. It was determined that the money did not belong to her husband. *Id.* A policy exclusion applied to "bodily injury or property damage expected or intended by *an insured person.*" (emphasis added). The court concluded that the exclusion was in "obvious conflict" with the policy's severability of insurance clause. Therefore, coverage was owed for the husband, unless it was later determined that he expected or intended the damage in question. *Id.*; *see also Tuturea v. Tennessee Farmers Mut. Ins. Co.*, No. W2009-01866-COA-R3-CV, 2010 Tenn. App. LEXIS 414 (Tenn. Ct. App. June 29, 2010) ("[A]n insurance company is generally not obligated to provide liability coverage to an innocent co-insured under an insurance policy that excludes coverage for losses resulting from the intentional act of 'an insured' or 'any insured' absent structural or textual ambiguity created by additional policy provisions."); *Allstate Ins. Co. v. Jordan*, 16 S.W.3d 777 (Tenn. Ct. App. 1999) ("The policy language in the instant case specifically excluded coverage for intentional criminal acts of any insured person. Not only is this language quite explicit, but also under the joint obligation clause it is clear that there can be no coverage for any insured when one of the insureds commits an intentional act for which coverage is sought. This clause provides that the acts of an insured person are binding on any other insured person. We find no ambiguity in the language of the policy that would lead an insured to believe that the insurance company would provide coverage for any insured resulting from the intentional acts of any other insured."). In *Spence v. Allstate Ins. Co.*, 883 S.W.2d 586 (Tenn. 1994) the Supreme Court of Tennessee addressed an exclusion for "[i]ntentional or criminal acts of an insured person." However, the case has unique aspects that make its applicability limited. In *Western World Ins. Co. v. Sanchez*, No. 14-1846, 2015 U.S. Dist. LEXIS 105953 (M.D. Tenn. Aug. 12, 2015), the Tennessee federal court cited *Spence* and *Tuturea* and declined to apply "innocent co-insured" case law to the interpretation of the Tennessee rescission statute; *Inman v. State Farm Fire & Cas. Co.*, No. 15-341, 2017 U.S. Dist. LEXIS 45023 (E.D. Tenn. Mar. 28, 2017) ("Upon review of this policy language, the Court finds that the innocent coinsured doctrine is inapplicable because, like the policy in *Jordan*, the insurance policy is not ambiguous on whether an innocent coinsured is covered. The policy here explicitly provides that if 'any person insured' engages in actions prohibited in the policy, the policy is void and defendant is not liable to any insured for losses. As such, the policy does not allow an innocent coinsured to recover for the losses resulting from the intentional acts of another insured.").

Texas: The Court of Appeals of Texas held that no coverage was owed under a commercial general liability policy to all insureds for bodily injury caused by a motor vehicle accident. *Bituminous Cas. Corp. v. Maxey*, 110 S.W.3d 203, 215 (Tex. Ct. App. 2003). Coverage was precluded on the basis of a policy exclusion for " 'bodily injury' … arising out of the ownership, maintenance, use or entrustment to others of any … 'auto' … owned or operated by or rented or loaned to '*any insured.*'" *Id.* at 209. The court concluded that the exclusion precluded coverage for bodily injury arising out of any conduct within the scope of the exclusion, by any entity or person insured by the policy, regardless of which insured is seeking coverage. *Id.* at 214. The court rejected the argument that the policy's separation of insureds clause dictated a different result. *Id.*; *see also Verhoev v. Progressive County Mut. Ins. Co.*, 300 S.W.3d 803, 810 (Tex. Ct. App. 2009) ("Although the policy does not contain a severability of interests clause providing that it is to be interpreted separately as to each insured, the common law 'doctrine of severability' holds that, even in absence of such a clause, where a policy uses the term 'the insured' when there is more than one insured, an exclusion is to be applied to each insured separately, with the term 'the insured' applying only to the insured seeking coverage.") (emphasis in original) (*opinion withdrawn*, 2009 Tex. App. LEXIS 9295 (Tx. Ct. App. Dec. 3, 2009)); *Hodges v. Safeco Lloyds Ins. Co.*, 438 S.W.3d 698 (Tex. Ct. App. 2014) ("We find no basis to distinguish *Maxey* simply because the policy excludes coverage for 'an insured,' rather than 'any insured.' The language of the policy does not limit the exclusion of personal injury coverage to simply the person making the claim, but also excludes bodily injury coverage to the named insured and all his relatives residing in his home with him."); *USAA Tex. Lloyd's Co. v. Doe*, No. 15-00673, 2017 Tex. App. LEXIS 5925 (Tex. Ct. App. Jun. 28, 2017) (following *Maxey* and rejecting insured's argument that the insured had a reasonable expectation of coverage) ("Like the court in *Maxey*, and contrary to the Doe's assertion, we conclude the severability clause has no effect on the exclusion provision.").

Utah: The Supreme Court of Utah held that no property coverage was owed under a homeowner's policy to an insured-wife for the destruction of her home on account of a fire that was intentionally set by her insured-husband. *Utah Farm Bureau Ins. Co. v. Crook*, 980 P.2d 685, 688 (Utah 1999). Coverage was precluded on the basis of a policy exclusion for "Intentional loss, meaning any loss arising out of any act committed: (1) By or at the direction of *an 'insured'*; and (2) With the intent to cause a loss." *Id.* at 687 (emphasis added). The court acknowledged that other courts have concluded that "an" is ambiguous, based on various dictionary definitions. *Id.* However, the Supreme Court of Utah concluded that, when reading the policy as a whole ("Insured" means you and residents of your household and "you" means the named insured and the spouse if a resident of the same household), "'an insured' in the … Policy may refer to multiple persons by definition, and intentional property damage by any insured is excluded under the Policy." *Id.* at 688. The opinion includes no discussion of a severability provision. *See also Allstate Ins. Co. v. Worthington*, 46 F.3d 1005 (10th Cir. 1995) (noting that, unlike cases involving exclusions that refer to "an insured," which courts read as "any insured," the exclusions at issue did not "explicitly state whether the triggering act or omission must be performed by 'the insured,' by 'any insured,' or by 'an insured'") ("[W]e agree with the district court's determination that the policy was ambiguous as to whether Allstate had a duty to defend and indemnify Brown when her coinsured husband was not covered because he engaged in an intentional or criminal act excluded by the policy. Based on Utah law that contracts of insurance are to be construed in favor of the insured, particularly exclusionary clauses, we hold that Allstate has a duty to defend suits alleging Brown's negligence and, if liability is imposed, to indemnify Brown even though her coinsured is denied coverage because of his intentional or criminal acts."); *West Am. Ins. Co. v. AV&S*, 145 F.3d 1224 (10th Cir. 1999) ("[W]e find that because the Separation of Insureds clause treats each named insured separately as the only insured, the term 'any insured' in the Auto Exclusion clause only applies to the single insured that actually owned the vehicle or whose employee operated the vehicle and the employees claiming insurance through that named insured.").

Vermont: The Supreme Court of Vermont held that coverage was not pre-cluded under a homeowner's policy to insured-parents for their alleged negligence in failing to prevent their insured-son from sexually abusing minors in the parents' home daycare business. *N. Sec. Ins. Co. v. Perron*, 777 A.2d 151, 166 (Vt. 2001). A pol-icy exclusion applied to bodily injury "expected or intended by *the insured.*" *Id.* at 155 (emphasis added). The Vermont high court acknowledged that "[c]ourts construing similar policy language have concluded that, when a provision uses the article 'the,' the provision applies only to claims brought against the particular insured named in the claim. Conversely, when the exclusionary language refers to intentional acts of 'an insured,' courts have uniformly concluded that the exclusion applies to all claims which arise from the intentional acts of any one insured, even though the claims are stated against another insured." *Id.* at 163. Based on this pronouncement, the court concluded that, because the exclusion precluded coverage for intentional acts of *the insured*, and not *an insured*, it did not preclude coverage to the parents for their son's acts of sexual abuse. *Id.* at 163–64. Despite the inapplicability of the "expected or intended" exclusion, coverage for the parents was ultimately precluded on the basis of the policy's "business-pursuits" exclusion. *Id.* at 164–66. In *Northern Sec. Ins. Co. v. Stanhope*, 14 A.3d 257 (Vt. 2010), the litigation at issue in *Perron* continued. The Supreme Court of Vermont held that coverage was owed to the insured-hus-band and insured-son, for the insured-son's sexual assault, even though the insured-wife made false representations to the insurance company "that no business pursuits were conducted on the premises" while she, in fact, operated a daycare center at her home. The homeowner's policy included an exclusion for fraud or misrepre-sentation that precluded coverage "for an insured who, whether before or after a loss, has: (a) intentionally concealed or misrepresented any material fact or circum-stance; (b) engaged in fraudulent conduct; or (c) made false statements; relating to this insurance." *Id.* at 259. The court concluded that the insurer was precluded from denying coverage to the insured-husband and insured-son based on the "coverage for innocent co-insured" doctrine. *Id.* at 260. The court refused to decide whether the policy's use of the language "an insured" could pertain to all insureds, and exclude the insured-husband and insured-son from coverage, because the argument was not preserved on appeal. *Id.* at 261. However, the court did "observe that the policy language could be construed to refer to the conduct of the specific insured who committed the fraud or misrepresentation, rather than the fraudulent act of any insured." *Id.*, n.3. In *Co-operative Ins. Companies v. Woodward*, 45 A.3d 89 (Vt. 2012), the Vermont high court held that a severability clause had no effect on, and could not override, an intentional acts exclusion for certain acts committed by "an insured." No coverage was owed to insured-wife, for negligent supervision of her insured-husband, for his act of kidnapping and murdering his niece.

Virginia: The Supreme Court of Virginia held that no coverage was owed under an umbrella policy to an insured-husband-passenger for bodily injuries sustained in an automobile accident in which his wife was the driver. *Gov't Employees Ins. Co. v. Moore*, 580 S.E.2d 823, 830 (Va. 2003). Coverage was precluded on the basis of a policy exclusion for "personal injury to *any insured*." *Id.* at 825 (emphasis added). The court rejected the argument that the policy's severability of interest clause dictated a different result, reasoning that "[t]o do so would contradict the obvious intention of the parties and … convert the umbrella policy from a third-party excess liability policy into a first-party personal injury policy. There is no authority for applying the severability clause in such a manner." *Id.* at 830. In *Montgomery Mutual Insurance Company v. Dyer*, 170 F. Supp. 2d 618, 625 (W.D. Va. 2001), the court held that property coverage was owed to one insured under a homeowner's policy for a fire that was intentionally set by another insured. The exclusion at issue was for "*an insured* who commits or directs an act with the intent to cause loss." *Id.* (emphasis added). The relevant section of the policy did not contain a severability clause. The court acknowledged that many courts have interpreted intentional loss exclusions to preclude coverage for innocent co-insureds. *Id.* at 624. However, the court held that, unlike exclusions in other cases, the exclusion before it placed emphasis on the person committing the act, not on the act itself. *Id.*; *Liberty University, Inc. v. Citizens Ins. Co. of America*, 792 F.3d 520 (4th Cir. 2015) ("[W]e conclude the Separation of Insureds provision does not displace Virginia's rule that an insurer has no duty to defend against a suit alleging the insured is liable for the intentional acts of its agents under a theory of respondeat superior.").

Washington: The Court of Appeals of Washington held that no coverage was owed under a homeowner's policy to an insured-wife, for failing to protect a foster child from physical abuse inflicted by her insured-husband. *Mutual of Enumclaw Ins. Co. v. Cross*, 10 P.3d 440, 445 (Wash. App. Ct. 2000). The policy contained an exclusion for bodily injury "which is expected or intended by *an insured.*" *Id.* at 441–42 (emphasis added). The court held that it agreed with those cases that have concluded that an exclusion that is clear and specific prevails over a severability clause. *Id.* at 445; *see also Truck Ins. Exchange v. BRE Properties, Inc.*, 81 P.3d 929, 933 (Wash. App. Ct. 2003) (citing *Cross* with approval but holding that an exclusion for bodily injury to "an 'employee' of *the insured* arising out of and in the course of employment" only excluded coverage for employees of "the insured" and not "an insured") ("When an insurance policy contains an exclusion for 'the insured,' each insured is entitled to read the policy as if applying only to that insured."); *Pacific Ins. Co. v. Catholic Bishop of Spokane*, 450 F. Supp. 2d 1186, 1202 (E.D. Wash. 2006) ("Washington courts seem to differentiate between exclusionary clauses written in terms of the '*the* insured' and similar clauses written in terms of '*an* insured.'") (emphasis in original); *Mut. of Enumclaw Ins. Co. v. Anderson*, No. 66337-2-I, 2012 Wash. App. LEXIS 2186 (Wash. Ct. App. Sept. 17, 2012) ("Unlike the … policy that excludes coverage for intentional acts that are expected or intended from the standpoint of *any* insured, where coverage and exclusions are defined in terms of '*the* insured,' the excluded act of one insured does not bar coverage for insureds who have not engaged in the excluded act.") (emphasis in original); *American States Ins. Co. v. Delean's Tile and Marble, LLC*, No. 69634–3–I, 2013 Wash. App. LEXIS 2793 (Wash. Ct. App. Dec. 9, 2013) (recognizing that Washington courts analyze coverage for multiple insureds separately when an exclusion refers to "the insured," and jointly when an exclusion refers to "any insured" but not willing to do so for purposes of an exclusion based on "any construction operations"); *IDS Prop. Cas. Ins. Co. v. Ivanov*, No. C18-1161, 2019 U.S. Dist. LEXIS 107979 (W.D. Wash. Jun. 27, 2019) (exclusion for "[b]odily injury . . . expected or intended by one or more insured persons") (citing *Cross* and concluding that because bodily injury was expected or intended by one insured, coverage was precluded for all insureds).

West Virginia: The U.S. Court of Appeals for the Fourth Circuit, applying West Virginia law, held that coverage was not precluded under an automobile policy to an omnibus insured for bodily injury sustained by an employee of the named insured. *Pepsi-Cola Bottling Co. of Charleston v. Indem. Ins. Co. of N. Am.*, 318 F.2d 714, 716 (4th Cir. 1963) (applying West Virginia law). A policy exclusion applied to "bodily injury to or sickness, disease or death of any employee of *the insured*." *Id.* at 715 (emphasis added). The Court of Appeals concluded that the exclusion did not apply as no reason was shown why an insured should not be indemnified against a claim of one outside *that insured's employment. Id.* at 716. The court also found it "strongly persuasive, if not conclusive" that the policy's severability of interests clause "compels consideration of each insured separately, independently of every other insured." *Id.* The severability of interests clause does not allow employment "to be attributed to another insured who in truth is not the employer." *Id.* More recently, the Supreme Court of Appeals of West Virginia, in *American National Prop. & Cas. Co. v. Clendenen*, 793 S.E.2d 899 (W. Va. 2016), addressed coverage for innocent co-insured parents and guardians of two friends who murdered a third friend. The two homeowners' policies at issue collectively contained exclusions for bodily injury or property damage "which is expected or intended by any insured even if the actual injury or damage is different than expected or intended," "arising out of any criminal act committed by or at the direction of any insured," and "bodily injury, property damage, or personal injury expected or intended by 'anyone we protect' . . . ." The court, following a comprehensive review of the issue nationally, held that the exclusions were unambiguous and precluded coverage for the innocent co-insureds. The court further held that "the severability clause's command to apply the insurance separately to each insured does not alter the intentional/criminal act exclusions' plain meaning or create ambiguity in its application. The purpose of severability clauses is to spread protection, to the limits of coverage, among all of the insureds. The purpose is not to negate unambiguous exclusions. The policies should be read as a whole with all policy provisions given effect." *See also Rector v. Rector*, No. 16-0867, 2017 W. Va. LEXIS 342 (W. Va. May 19, 2017) ("[G]iven that petitioner wholly fails to support his bald claim that the severability clause defeats the 'bodily injury or personal injury to any insured' exclusion, we cannot say that the circuit court erred in finding that the severability clause did not defeat that exclusion.") (discussing *Clendenen*); *Westfield Ins. Co. v. Matulis*, 421 F. Supp. 3d 331 (S.D.W.Va. 2019) (exclusion for "'[b]odily injury' or 'property damage' expected or intended from the standpoint of *the insured*" precluded coverage for an insured for its alleged negligent supervision of the insured who committed an intentional act) (discussing *Clendenen*).

Wisconsin: The Supreme Court of Wisconsin held that no coverage was owed under a homeowner's policy to an insured-wife for her alleged negligence in failing to prevent her insured-husband's intentional sexual contact with a minor. *J.G. &*

R.G. v. Wangard, 753 N.W.2d 475, 491 (Wis. 2008). Coverage was precluded on the basis of a policy exclusion for damages "arising out of an act intended by *any covered person* to cause personal injury." *Id.* at 480 (emphasis added). The court rejected the argument that the policy's severability clause dictated a different result. *Id.* at 487; *see also Wright v. Allstate Cas. Co.*, 797 N.W.2d 531 (Wis. Ct. App. 2011) (rejecting argument that *Wangard* is limited to sexual assault and holding that insured-mother was precluded from coverage under homeowner's policy after insured-son shot and killed neighbor where homeowner's policy's exclusion for intentional acts precluded coverage for "any bodily injury ... intended by ... *any* insured person"); *Estate of Dobry v. Wilson Mut. Ins. Co.*, 842 N.W.2d 536 (Wis. Ct. App. 2013) ("The criminal acts exclusion bars coverage for bodily injury resulting from a criminal act of 'any' insured. On appeal, it is undisputed that, if one insured committed a criminal act, coverage for bodily injury caused by that act is barred with respect to all insureds. Thus, Jordan's criminal act bars coverage for the Dobrys' claims against all of the Walker defendants, not just Jordan himself.") (citing *Wright*); *Kemper Indep. Ins. Co. v. Islami*, No. 2019AP488, 2020 Wisc. App. LEXIS 236 (Wis. Ct. App. May 27, 2020) (addressing policy's Concealment or Fraud provision; concealment of certain facts known before or after a loss) ("Here we are not dealing with an exclusion that bars coverage to 'an' or 'any' insured (or 'the insured' for that matter), but rather a provision that provides coverage to 'no insured' if an insured breaches the provision. Of at least equal importance, the policy in this case contains no severability clause."); *Fire Ins. Exch. v. Gibson*, No. 2020-810, 2021 Wisc. App. LEXIS 240 (Wis. Ct. App. May 18, 2021) (rejecting the insured's attempt to distinguish between "an insured" and "any insured" "as a matter of grammar, logic and common sense" because "an insured" is an indefinite article applicable to more than one individual object, and therefore is the substantial equivalent of "any insured").

Wyoming: The Supreme Court of Wyoming held that no coverage was owed under the liability section of a homeowner's policy to insured–cattle-handlers for accidentally shooting the named insured's minor son. *Page v. Mountain W. Farm Bureau Mut. Ins. Co.*, 2 P.3d 506, 509 (Wyo. 2000). A policy exclusion applied to "bodily injury ... [s]ustained by you [named insureds] or any insured as defined in paragraphs (1) and (2) of the definition of insured ['Insured means you and if residents of your household: 1. Your relatives; and 2. Minors in the care of those named above.'] (household exclusion)." *Id.* The minor child was neither a relative of the cattle-handlers nor a minor in their care. *Id.* The court rejected the argument that the policy's severability of interest clause limited the household exclusion to the household of the individual insured seeking coverage. *Id.* "Because [the injured minor] is so defined as an insured, the household exclusion clause clearly excludes the injuries he suffered from coverage … regardless of who is responsible for them." *Id. See also Peerless Indem. Ins. Co. v. Swanner,* 651 Fed. Appx. 785 (10th Cir. 2016) (finding itself bound by *Barnette v. Hartford Ins. Group,* 653 P.2d 1375 (Wyo. 1982), which the court noted has been rightly criticized, the Tenth Circuit held that "when a fellow-employee (or cross-employee) exclusion is combined with a severability clause, coverage will not be precluded when the insured in question is a fellow employee seeking policy protection"); *Am Nat'l Prop. & Cas. Co. v. Burns,* No. 16-301, 2018 U.S. Dist. LEXIS 241860 (D. Wyo. Jan. 3, 2018), *rev'd on other grounds* 922 F.3d 1045 (10th Cir. 2019) (agreeing with majority interpretation that "the phrase 'any insured' is distinct from the phrase 'the insured' when interpreting an insurance contract, and that the phrase 'any insured' unambiguously expresses a contractual intent to create joint obligations and to prohibit recovery by an innocent co-insured") (internal quotations omitted) ("After looking at the Policy from Dora's perspective, the Policy language excludes coverage because it excludes coverage if 'any insured' committed a criminal or intentional act. From Dora's perspective, she would be part of 'any insured'. Had the Policy language read 'the insured' and been interpreted from Dora's perspective, Dora would not be excluded from coverage because she was not the specific insured who committed the criminal and intentional acts.").

CHAPTER
11

Is Emotional Injury "Bodily Injury"?

It is axiomatic that a general liability insurance policy provides coverage for "bodily injury" and "property damage." Under many such policies, "bodily injury" is defined as "bodily injury, sickness or disease sustained by a person, including death resulting from any of these at any time." *See, e.g.*, INS. SERVS. OFFICE, INC., COMMERCIAL GENERAL LIABILITY COVERAGE FORM, No. CG 00010413, § V3 (2012).

In most general liability claim scenarios it is obvious whether the underlying claimant has sustained "bodily injury"—the blood or broken bones are a give-away. As such, whether damages are being sought for "bodily injury" is a non-issue. There are, however, situations where it is not so obvious. Most notably, when the underlying claimant alleges that he or she has sustained emotional injury, an issue sometimes arises whether such injury is "bodily injury." The issue also arises in the context of claims under the liability coverage part of homeowner's policies—which also provide coverage for "bodily injury." The legal issue is the same under both policy types, has arisen under a multitude of factual scenarios and courts have adopted several rationales for resolving it.[1]

In addition, the emotional injury/bodily injury issue also arises with frequency under automobile policies (especially uninsured and underinsured motorist), since, like general liability and homeowner's liability policies, automobile policies also provide coverage for "bodily injury." Whether emotional injury constitutes "bodily injury" usually arises under automobile policies in the context of a claimant alleging that he or she sustained emotional injury on account of witnessing—either from within or outside the vehicle—a loved one killed or injured in an accident.[2]

Claims often arise under this scenario for the following reason. Most automobile policies contain a limit of liability for "bodily injury" sustained by "each person" (such as $100,000) and a higher limit for bodily injury in "each accident" (such

---

1 As used herein, for convenience, the term "emotional injury" also includes such injuries as emotional distress, mental distress, humiliation, and the like.

2 As used herein, for convenience, such witnesses to the accident are referred to as "bystanders," regardless of their physical presence at the time of the accident.

as $300,000). When the claim by a person who unquestionably sustained "bodily injury" has exhausted the policy's "each person" limit of liability, the bystander will often seek to qualify as a person who *also* sustained bodily injury. This is so in an effort by the bystander to recover under a separate "each person" limit of liability available under the policy. Since the policy has a $300,000 "each accident" limit of liability, coverage remains available for other "persons" who also sustained "bodily injury." *See State Farm Mut. Auto. Ins. Co. v. Jakupto*, 881 N.E.2d 654, 656 (Ind. 2008) (describing the significance of this issue as "obvious").

Despite the obvious differences between general liability, homeowners, and automobile policies, they share a similarity concerning the fundamental question whether emotional injury qualifies as "bodily injury." For this reason, courts examining the issue under one policy type sometimes look for guidance from decisions that have addressed it under another policy type.

The majority of courts that have addressed whether emotional injury qualifies as "bodily injury," under a policy that defines such term as "bodily injury (or bodily harm), sickness or disease," have determined that it does not. *See Evans v. Farmers Ins. Exch.*, 34 P.3d 284, 286 (Wyo. 2001) (noting that the "overwhelming majority" of jurisdictions hold that bodily injury encompasses only physical harm) (citation omitted). A common rationale for this conclusion is that the term "bodily" suggest something physical and corporeal. *See Moore v. Cont'l Cas. Co.*, 746 A.2d 1252, 1254–55 (Conn. 2000). Other courts reach the conclusion on the basis that "bodily injury" is narrower than "personal injury," which covers an affront or insult to a person's reputation or sensibilities. *Smith v. Animal Urgent Care, Inc.*, 542 S.E.2d 827, 831 (W. Va. 2000).

A notable exception to the majority rule is the New York Court of Appeals, which held that emotional injury does qualify as "bodily injury." New York's highest court reasoned that the term bodily injury was ambiguous and declined to rewrite the definition to read *"bodily* sickness" and *"bodily* disease." *Lavanant v. Gen. Accident Ins. Co. of Am.*, 595 N.E.2d 819, 822 (N.Y. 1992).

While a substantial majority of courts have concluded that emotional injury does not qualify as "bodily injury," the issue is not always that simple nor is that general pronouncement always the last word. Rather, many of those same courts have also held that "bodily injury" encompasses emotional injuries that are accompanied by physical manifestation. *See Allstate Ins. Co. v. Wagner-Ellsworth*, 188 P.3d 1042, 1051 (Mont. 2008) ("Many courts have concluded in insurance interpretation cases like this one that the term 'bodily injury' is ambiguous when applied to physical problems arising from a mental injury.").

For example, in *Voorhees v. Preferred Mutual Insurance Co.*, 607 A.2d 1255, 1262 (N.J. 1992), the Supreme Court of New Jersey held that a claim under a homeowner's policy issued to parents, for emotional distress accompanied by physical manifestations suffered by their child's teacher, on account of disparaging comments made by the parents, qualified as "bodily injury." The policy defined "bodily injury" as "bodily harm, sickness or disease to a person, including required care, loss of services and death resulting therefrom." *Id.* at 1258. The court held that the teacher's headaches, stomach pains, nausea, depression, and body pains qualified as "bodily injury," concluding that such term was ambiguous as it relates to emotional distress accompanied by physical manifestations, and, therefore, should be interpreted in favor of the insured. *Id.* at 1261–62.

In some jurisdictions that have held that "bodily injury" encompasses emotional injuries accompanied by physical manifestation, a subsequent concern arises—how to define what constitutes adequate physical manifestation. *See Pekin Ins. Co. v. Hugh*, 501 N.W.2d 508, 512 (Iowa 1993) (noting that "every emotional disturbance has a physical aspect and every physical disturbance has an emotional aspect") (citation omitted). One court described the reason for such concern as follows:

> We have not been anxious to expand the availability of damages for emotional distress ... . This reluctance has arisen from the concern that claims of mental anguish may be speculative and so likely to lead to fictitious allegations that there is a potential for abuse of the judicial process ... . Thus, we have been careful to limit the availability of such damages to "those plaintiffs who prove that emotional injury occurred under circumstances tending to guarantee its genuineness."

Twin Cities Glaziers Architectural Metals & Glass Workers Local #1324 v. W. Nat'l Ins. Group, No. C3–96–1741, 1997 Minn. App. LEXIS 159 (Minn. Ct. App. Feb. 11, 1997) (quoting *Lickteig v. Alderson, Ondov, Leonard & Sween, P.A.*, 556 N.W.2d 557, 560 (Minn. 1996)); *see also Voorhees*, 607 A.2d at 1262 ("[A]lthough a few plaintiffs may be tempted to assert emotional distress with accompanying physical manifestations more often, that will not necessarily obligate insurers to undertake unbounded duties to defend and indemnify. When an emotional distress claim is not supported factually, the insurer can and should move to dismiss the meritless claims.").

In *SL Industries, Inc. v. Am. Motorists Insurance Co.*, 607 A.2d 1266, 1274 (N.J. 1992), the Supreme Court of New Jersey acknowledged the difficulty in distinguishing between mental and physical injuries and concluded that the phrase "bodily injury" "should be analyzed on a case-by-case basis to determine whether the alleged [mental] injuries are sufficiently akin to physical injuries to render the term 'bodily injury' ambiguous." Here, the court held that sleeplessness was an emotional, and not physical, injury. *Id.* at 1273. The *SL Industries* court distinguished this scenario from its companion case, *Voorhees, supra,* which concluded that headaches, stomach pains, nausea, depression, and body pains qualified as physical manifestation of emotional distress. *Voorhees,* 607 A.2d at 1262.

As *SL Industries* concluded, whether emotional injury rises to the level of physical injury should be, and, in fact is, analyzed on a case-by-case basis. *See Allstate Ins. Co. v. Wagner-Ellsworth,* 188 P.3d 1042, 1051 (Mont. 2008) ("Courts have struggled with these distinctions, focusing on the facts of each case.").

For example, in *Admiral Insurance Co. v. Hosler,* 626 F. Supp. 2d 1105, 1108 (D. Colo. 2009), the Colorado District Court addressed coverage for claims by condominium residents against the developer for construction defects that led to excessive noise on account of the residents' ability to hear sounds coming from other units. The court addressed whether the underlying plaintiffs had established physical manifestation of their alleged emotional harm to trigger coverage for "emotional harm." *Id.* at 1113.

Adopting *SL Industries*'s mandate, that the question whether emotional injury rises to the level of physical injury should be analyzed on a case-by-case basis, the *Hosler* court concluded that none of the plaintiffs' injuries qualified as physical. *Id.* at 1114–19. The court rejected the following conditions as physical manifestation of emotional injury: frustration, embarrassment, and dissatisfaction, *id.* at 1115; sleeplessness, *id.* at 1116–17; feelings of paranoia, anxiety, dazed confusion, lack of safety, and embarrassment. *Id.* at 1118; *see also Economy Preferred Ins. Co. v. Quanxi Jia,* 92 P.3d 1280, 1284 (N.M. Ct. App. 2004) ("We do not resolve what would be sufficient to constitute bodily injury; we simply hold that crying, shaking, and sleep difficulties are not enough."). *But see Trinh v. Allstate Ins. Co.,* 37 P.3d 1259, 1264 (Wash. Ct. App. 2002) (finding that genuine issues of material fact were raised whether weight loss, hair loss, fragile fingernails, loss of sleep, headaches, stomach pains, and muscle aches are physical manifestations of emotional injury); *State Farm Fire & Cas. Co. v. Westchester Inv. Co.,* 721 F. Supp. 1165, 1167 (C.D. Cal. 1989) (finding that dry throat, rise in body temperature, and knot in stomach were sufficient physical manifestations of emotional injury to constitute bodily injury).

While many courts hold that emotional injury, when accompanied by physical manifestation, qualifies as "bodily injury," at least one state has not been willing to go so far. *See Babalola v. Donegal Group, Inc.*, No. 1:08-CV-621, 2008 U.S. Dist. LEXIS 65207 (M.D. Pa. Aug. 26, 2008) (holding that a claim under a homeowner's policy issued to a hospital employee, for emotional distress, including physical manifestation, sustained by a co-worker who was allegedly subjected to inappropriate sexual touching by and interaction with the insured, did not qualify as "bodily injury") ("Pennsylvania courts have soundly rejected the contention that policy definitions of injury or bodily injury encompass mental or emotional harm … . Generally, a complaint alleging only physical manifestations of mental or emotional harm likewise fails to trigger coverage under a policy insuring against claims brought for 'bodily injury.'") (citation and internal quotation omitted). But see later Pennsylvania decisions, addressed in the fifty state survey.

Lastly, one consideration that may arise in the automobile context, that is not relevant when the issue arises in the general liability or homeowner's context, is that the bystander's claim may be viewed as derivative of, and not separate from, the injured party's claim. In other words, if bystanders are not considered separate *persons* who sustained "bodily injury," coverage for them would be precluded, even if emotional injury qualifies as "bodily injury." *See Farm Bureau Ins. Co. v. Martinsen*, 659 N.W.2d 823, 828 (Neb. 2003) ("There is no evidence or suggestion in the record that the [the parents] developed physical conditions causally related to the emotional distress they suffered as a result of the accident, and we do not consider whether this scenario, if established, could impose separate per-person liability on Farm Bureau whether or not the $300,000 per-person limit had been exhausted. Upon the record before us, we determine that the [parents'] emotional distress is a byproduct of and entirely dependent upon the bodily injury to [their son].")

50-State Survey: Is Emotional Injury "Bodily Injury"?

Alabama: An Alabama District Court held that a claim under a commercial general liability policy issued to a bank, for emotional injury suffered by an individual whose claim under a credit life policy was denied, on account of the bank's failure to ask certain questions on the policy's application, qualified as "bodily injury." *Am. Economy Ins. Co. v. Fort Deposit Bank*, 890 F. Supp. 1011, 1017 (M.D. Ala. 1995). The policy defined "bodily injury" as "bodily injury, sickness or disease sustained by a person, including death resulting from any of these at any time." *Id.* at 1015. The court concluded that "sickness" or "disease" encompassed mental anguish. *Id.* at 1017; *see also Nationwide Prop. and Cas. Co v. Lacayo*, No. 2:07cv809, 2008 U.S. Dist.

LEXIS 89341 (M.D. Ala. Nov. 3, 2008) ("Nationwide—by limiting its personal liability coverage to that arising out of an 'occurrence,' defining 'occurrence' to include only 'bodily injury' and 'property damage,' and defining 'bodily injury' to exclude emotional distress—has crafted a policy that protects it from ever having to pay damages for emotional distress."); *Owners Ins. Co. v. Shep Jones Const., Inc.*, No. 08-514, 2012 U.S. Dist. LEXIS 62095 (N.D. Ala. May 03, 2012) ("The policy defines 'bodily injury' as 'bodily injury, sickness or disease sustained by a person, including death resulting from any of these at any one time.' Under Alabama law, mental anguish qualifies as 'bodily injury' for purposes of a commercial general liability policy. *Am. States Ins. Co. v. Cooper*, 518 So. 2d 708, 710 (Ala.1987).") (However, note that the policy at issue in *Cooper* defined "personal injury" as "Bodily injury, sickness, disease, disability, shock, fright, mental anguish, and mental injury . . ."); *D.B.C. v. Pierson*, No. 13–00377, 2014 U.S. Dist. LEXIS 70295 (N.D. Ala. May 22, 2014) ("There is no indication in the policy definition of bodily injury [consult the definition at issue] that it covers physical injuries that arise out of mental injuries, without there first being some actual physical injury. The Alabama Supreme Court has not addressed whether the bodily injury policy term at issue covers physical injury or illness that arises out of mental injury. Several other courts, however, have interpreted the identical language at issue in this case and found that coverage does not exist where the physical injury was caused by a mental injury. . . . All of the claimed bodily illnesses and injuries in this care (sic) are physical manifestations of emotional distress. . . . Because the physical manifestations of emotional distress are not bodily injuries under the policies, Plaintiffs have presented no evidence that the exposure caused bodily injury."); *Auto-Owners Ins. Co. v. Small*, No. 16-01042, 2017 U.S. Dist. LEXIS 35119 (N.D. Ala. Mar. 13, 2017) (quoting *American Economy* and stating "[i]n construing the language of insurance contracts governed by Alabama law, tribunals have characterized mental anguish as 'bodily injury'"); *Monroe Guar. Ins. Co. v. Pinnacle Mfg. LLC*, No. 17-01630, 2018 U.S. Dist. LEXIS 113073 (N.D. Ala. July 9, 2018) (noting that, under a policy defining "bodily injury" as "bodily injury, sickness or disease sustained by a person, including death resulting from any of these at any time," "mental anguish or emotional distress may be considered bodily injury").

Alaska: An Alaska District Court held that a claim for emotional distress suffered by a mother, who did not witness her son's fatal collision, qualified as "bodily injury" for purposes of an automobile insurance policy. *Gov't Employees Ins. Co. v. Encelewski*, No. A94–0211, 1995 U.S. Dist. LEXIS 1107 (D. Alaska Jan. 13, 1995), *affirmed* 94

F.3d 651 (9th Cir. 1996). The policy defined "bodily injury" as "bodily injury to a person, including resulting sickness, disease or death." The court found that the definition of "bodily injury" was unambiguous and rejected the insurer's argument that "sickness, disease, or death" is only that which "result[s]" from a bodily injury and that emotional distress is a sickness that results from a mental or non-bodily injury. The court concluded that "[a]lthough 'painful study' of the insurance policy might lead to [the insurer's] conclusion, the objectively reasonable expectations of the insured are that this provision covers negligent infliction of emotional distress claims with physical manifestations." *See State Farm Mut. Auto. Ins. Co. v. Houle*, 269 P.3d 654 (Alaska 2011) and cases discussed therein addressing bystander-emotional injury claims under various language of automobile policies.

Arizona: The Court of Appeals of Arizona held that a claim under an underinsured motorist policy, for exposure to HIV-infected blood by trained medical professionals who were providing emergency medical care to automobile accident victims, did not qualify as "bodily injury." *Transamerica Ins. Co. v. Doe*, 840 P.2d 288, 291 (Ariz. Ct. App. 1992). While the policy did not define "bodily injury," the court found the term to be unambiguous and interpreted it according to its "ordinary meaning," namely, physical injuries, impairment of physical condition, sickness, disease, or substantial pain. *Id.* The court concluded that no "bodily injury" had been sustained within the meaning of the policy based on exposure to the blood because no physical injury, sickness, disease, or substantial pain resulted therefrom. *Id.* The court also rejected the argument that anxiety and emotional distress resulting from fear of contracting AIDS qualified as bodily injury. *Id.* at 292. "Appellant's failure to adduce evidence tending to establish the existence of any physical harm or medically identifiable effect from their exposure to a disease requires a finding that, as a matter of law, the necessary prerequisite for recovering damages for emotional distress is lacking." *Id.* (citation and internal quotation omitted). *See also Amari v. Scottsdale Healthcare Hosps.*, No. 1-CA-CV-17-0443, 2018 Ariz. App. Unpub. LEXIS 888 (Ariz. Ct. App. June 12, 2018) (non-coverage case) (using the rationale in *Transamerica* to conclude that a blood test [for possible HIV exposure] was an insufficient "physical invasion" to satisfy the "impact theory," which is that a plaintiff may recover emotional distress damages when he or she has sustained a contemporaneous physical impact or injury).

Arkansas: No instructive authority.

California: The Court of Appeal of California held that a claim under a general liability policy issued to a restaurant, for emotional distress suffered by an employee who was injured in an automobile accident, but whose health insurance application had not been submitted by her employer to the insurer, did not qualify as "bodily injury." *Aim Ins. Co. v. Culcasi*, 229 Cal. App. 3d 209, 220 (Cal. Ct. App. 1991). The policy defined "bodily injury" as "bodily injury, sickness or disease" (although it was not considered by the court as there was no record reference to support it). *Id.* at 218. Following a lengthy review of dictionary definitions and case law nationally, the court held that "[g]iven the clear and ordinary meaning of the word 'bodily,' we find the term 'bodily injury' unambiguous. It means physical injury and its consequences. It does not include emotional distress in the absence of *physical* injury." *Id.* at 220 (emphasis in original); *see also Chatton v. Nat'l Union Fire Ins. Co.*, 13 Cal. App. 2d 318, 327 (1992) (holding that "bodily injury" did not include "emotional distress"); *Waller v. Truck Ins. Exchange*, 900 P.2d 619, 632 (Cal. 1995) (holding that because the "occurrence" itself must directly cause any "bodily injury," emotional distress and attendant physical injury, caused by economic loss, did not qualify as "bodily injury"); *Treweek v. California Capital Ins. Co.*, No. B214671, 2010 Cal. App. Unpub. LEXIS 4075 (Cal. Ct. App. May 28, 2010) ("[T]he complaints filed by the small claims plaintiffs did not give rise to a potential for coverage. They alleged harm solely in the form of emotional and mental distress. That type of harm does not constitute 'bodily injury.'") (claims filed by neighbors against owner of apartment building alleging that people were playing basketball, drinking, making loud noise at night, and throwing their empty bottles into the neighbors' backyards.); *Shelton v. Fire Insurance Exchange*, No. B240775, 2013 Cal. App. Unpub. LEXIS 5279 (Cal. Ct. App. July 25, 2013) (policy defined "bodily injury" as "bodily harm, sickness or disease, including care, loss of services and death resulting from the injury") (noting that, under case law, "bodily injury, sickness or disease" is plain and unambiguous and coverage is limited to physical injury to the body and does not include nonphysical, emotional or mental harm, but that "bodily injury" includes physical injury resulting from emotional distress) (holding that testimony of appetite problems and sleeplessness, headaches, upset stomach, a mitral valve prolapse, and diverticulitis resulting in the removal of nine inches of colon, raised the possibility of coverage based on bodily injury arising from emotional distress caused by hedge and trees that allegedly blocked an ocean view, created a blind intersection and interfered with driveway sightlines); *Upansi v. State Farm General Ins. Co.*, 227 Cal. App. 4th 509 (2014) ("Although Kulkarni alleged he had suffered 'pain and suffering,' there were no allegations and there was no evidence that he had suffered bodily harm, physical injury, sickness, or disease as a result of the Upasanis' alleged actions. Kulkarni's injuries were emotional, not physical. 'The cases overwhelmingly hold that the phrase 'bodily injury, sickness or disease' is plain and unambiguous and that coverage under the bodily injury clause is limited to physical injury to the body and does not include nonphysical, emotional or mental harm.'") (citing *Chatton*); *Namo Co. v. Peerless Ins. Co.*, No. A132370, 2014 Cal. Unpub. LEXIS 4710 (Cal. Ct. App. June 30, 2014) (reiterating *Waller* and stating that commercial general liability policies "were never intended to cover emotional distress damages that flow from an uncovered 'occurrence'") ("[D]espite the more expansive definition of 'bodily injury' contained in the Xtend Endorsement, our conclusion remains the same. Because any claimed mental anguish resulted from business torts and economic loss suffered by the tenants, the emotional distress alleged by the tenants is not covered by the Travelers policy."); *Emerson v. Farmers Group, Inc.*, No. B262922, 2017 Cal. App. Unpub. LEXIS 2161 (Cal. Ct. App. Mar. 28, 2017) (expressing doubt that sleeplessness and shaking constitute bodily injury); *M.C. v. Princeton Excess & Surplus Lines Ins. Co.*, No. 16-6314, 2017 U.S. Dist. LEXIS 116278 (C.D. Cal. Jun. 1, 2017) (holding that it was a question of fact, involving medical or psychological proof, whether depression was a "real physical injury" based on depression being a disease or sickness with actual physical damage to the nervous system and manifestation through physical symptoms) (arguing that stress and trauma can suppress the production of neurons in the hippocampus); *Komin v. Travelers Prop. Cas. Ins. Co.*, No. F075381, 2019 Cal. App. Unpub. LEXIS 5713 (Cal. Ct. App. Aug. 27, 2019) (reiterating *Culcasi*).

Colorado: The Supreme Court of Colorado held that a claim under a comprehensive business liability policy issued to a city, for emotional distress suffered by a police officer on account of wrongful termination, did not qualify as "bodily injury." *Nat'l Cas. Co. v. Great Sw. Fire Ins. Co.*, 833 P.2d 741, 747 (Colo. 1992). The policy defined "bodily injury" as "bodily injury, sickness, or disease sustained by any person which occurs during the policy period, including death at any time resulting therefrom." *Id.* at 746. The Colorado high court declined to follow those few courts nationally that have determined that "bodily injury" includes emotional distress in the absence of physical impact, fear, or physical harm or physical manifestation of emotional distress. *Id.* at 747. Since no allegations of any physical injury, physical contact, or pain were made, the former police officer's claim for emotional distress was not within the bodily injury coverage provided by the policy. *Id.*; *see also Williams v. State Farm Mut. Auto. Ins. Co.*, 195 P.3d 1158, 1161 (Colo. App. 2008) (following *National Casualty Co.* and holding that emotional injury, without physical manifestation, did not qualify as "sickness" under Colorado's uninsured motorist statute); *Kreger v. Gen. Steel Corp.*, No. 07-575, 2009 U.S. Dist. LEXIS 88074 (E.D. La. Sept. 23, 2009) (applying Colorado law) ("[T]he Colorado Supreme Court has not ruled on the precise magnitude of the physical harm required to depart from the 'purely emotional harm' rule in *National Casualty Co.*") ("Whether Kreger's alleged loss of sleep is sufficient to constitute physical manifestations of emotional distress is also a close question. Although the factual evidence is slim, it is nonetheless enough to suggest that claim is for more than 'purely emotional' damages. Given the breadth of the duty to defend, the Court cannot hold as a matter of law that Colorado Casualty had no duty to defend in this case.") (citations omitted); *Am. Fire and Cas. Co. v. BCORP Canterbury at Riverwalk, LLC*, 282 Fed. Appx. 643, 650–51 (10th Cir. 2008) ("[I]n Colorado an insured must establish 'physical manifestations' of their emotional distress. But, aside from clarifying that claims for '*purely* nonphysical or emotional harm' do not trigger 'bodily injury' coverage, the Colorado Supreme Court has not spoken to what is required to meet the 'physical manifestation' requirement.") (addressing the "physical manifestation" requirement in detail but not answering the question in the case before it); *KF 103-CV, LLC v. American Family Mutual Ins. Co.*, No. 13–02875, 2014 U.S. Dist. LEXIS 124048 (D. Colo. Sept. 5, 2014), *rev'd on other grounds*, 630 Fed. App. 826 (10th Cir. 2015) (following *National Casualty* and holding that "the counterclaimants allege emotional distress and 'physical discomfort,' but those allegations are not sufficient to bring the claims within the definition of 'bodily injury' because there are no allegations of any physical manifestations of the alleged emotional harm."); *Colo. Cas. Ins. Co. v. Infinity Land Corp.*, No. 12-02748, 2015 U.S. Dist. LEXIS 113137 (D. Colo. Aug. 26, 2015) (restating *Nat'l Cas. Co.* and holding that "[h]ere, the Neighbors allege emotional distress, mental anguish, and physical discomfort. I find that these allegations fail to bring the claims within the Policy's definition of "bodily injury" because there are no allegations of any physical injury, physical contact, or pain."); *Peerless Indem. Ins. Co. v. Colclasure*, No. 16-424, 2017 U.S. Dist. LEXIS 22193 (D. Colo. Feb. 16, 2017) (citing *Nat'l Cas. Co.* that "the Colorado Supreme Court concluded that the term "bodily injury," which was defined in the subject insurance policy as 'bodily injury, sickness, or disease,' covers only physical injury and does not include claims for purely nonphysical or emotional harm") (construction defect case).

Connecticut: The Supreme Court of Connecticut held that a claim under a homeowner's policy, for emotional distress suffered by the insured's sister, on account of the insured obtaining a line of credit secured by a home that was jointly owned by his sister, did not qualify as "bodily injury." *Moore v. Cont'l Cas. Co.*, 746 A.2d 1252, 1257 (Conn. 2000). The policy defined "bodily injury" as "bodily harm, sickness or disease … including required care, loss of services and death resulting therefrom." *Id.* at 1254. The court reached its decision on the following bases: (1) "bodily," as used in the English language, strongly suggests something physical and corporeal; (2) nonbodily or noncorporeal torts are contemplated by "Personal Injury" coverage; and (3) the majority rule nationally is that bodily injury does not include emotional distress unaccompanied by physical harm. *Id.* at 1254–56. The Connecticut high court acknowledged that emotional distress might ordinarily be accompanied by some physical manifestations. *Id.* at 1257. Nonetheless, "[t]he question in this case is the legal meaning of 'bodily injury' as defined in the policy. It is not the medical or scientific question of the degree to which the mind and the body affect each other." *Id.*; *see also Taylor v. Mucci*, 952 A.2d 776, 781–82 (Conn. 2008) (following *Moore* and holding that emotional distress, without accompanying physical harm, did not constitute "bodily injury" for purposes of a bystander claim under an automobile policy); *Allstate Inc. Co. v. Burnard*, No. 3:08cv603, 2010 U.S. Dist. LEXIS 31535 (D. Conn. Mar. 31, 2010) (discussing *Moore* and concluding that it acknowledged the possibility that an allegation of emotional distress, with accompanying symptoms, such as psoriasis, could qualify as "bodily injury"); *Travelers Home and Marine Ins. Co. v. Zachs*, No. HHDCV126028347S, 2013 Conn. Super. LEXIS 775 (Conn. Super. Ct. April 3, 2013) ("The defendant can cite no Connecticut appellate authority holding or even suggesting that emotional distress, even when accompanied by physical symptoms, constitutes bodily injury under a homeowner's policy with language similar to that here.") (defining "bodily injury" as "bodily harm, sickness or disease, including required care, loss of services and death that results"); *Allstate Ins. Co. v. Wilson*, 18 F. Supp. 3d 156 (D. Conn. 2014) ("Courts have found that although claims for emotional distress alone may not constitute bodily injury, claims for the physical manifestations of emotional distress, such as sleeplessness, may constitute a bodily injury within the meaning of a policy.") (citing *Burnard* and *Peck v. Public Service Mut. Ins. Co.*, 363 F. Supp. 2d 137 (D. Conn. 2005)); *Mehta v. Ace Am. Ins. Co.*, No. 10-1617, 2015 U.S. Dist. LEXIS 39841(D. Conn. Mar. 30, 2015) (reiterating *Mucci* and holding that "bystander emotional distress not a separate and distinct bodily injury under the policy - defined as 'any bodily injury, sickness, disease or death sustained by any person' - notwithstanding accompanying physical manifestations of the distress"); *Cartier v. Shuff*, No. 156053465, 2016 Conn. Super. LEXIS 3475 (Conn. Super. Ct. Dec. 29, 2016) (holding that "[i]n the present case, the express terms of the policy similarly provide that a bodily injury 'includes *all* injury and damages *to others resulting from* that bodily injury.' As in *Galgano [v. Metropolitan Property & Casualty Ins. Co.*, 267 Conn. 512 (2004)] under the express terms of the policy, the bodily injury suffered by Amanda Cartier includes all injuries or damages sustained by others as a result of the bodily injury to her, including Anthony Cartier's claim for bystander emotional distress."); *Menard v. State*, No. HHDCV146051838S, 2018 Conn. Super. LEXIS 2066 (Conn. Super. Ct. Aug. 24, 2018) (relying on *Moore* to conclude that emotional distress, without accompanying physical harm, does not constitute "bodily injury" under the state's underinsured motorist statute); *Nationwide Mut. Fire Ins. Co. v. Damato-Kushel*, No. FBTCV186072099S, 2018 Conn. Super. LEXIS 6912 (Conn. Super. Ct. Dec. 11, 2018) ("Despite the allegations in the underlying complaint that the minor plaintiff suffered physical injuries, the only reasonable and plausible way to read the complaint is to conclude that he suffered only emotional injuries. Therefore, under the holding of *Moore* and similar cases, there is no coverage under the policy for emotional injuries."); *USAA Gen. Indem. Co. v. Sklanka*, No. UWY-CV196048058S, 2020 Conn. Super. LEXIS 457 (Conn. Super. Ct. Mar. 17, 2020) (harassment, potential violence, actual and substantial damages, and emotional distress are not "bodily injury").

Delaware: No instructive authority.

District of Columbia: The District of Columbia Court of Appeals held that a claim under a homeowner's policy, for defamation against an insured, for making false statements about the performance of an airline pilot, did not qualify as "bodily injury." *Washington v. State Farm Fire & Cas. Co.*, 629 A.2d 24, 26–27 (D.C. App. 1993) ("Washington's insurance policy defines 'bodily injury' as 'bodily harm, sickness, or disease.' The injury one suffers as a result of a defamatory statement, however, is something entirely different: an injury in one's trade, profession, or community standing, or one that lowers the injured party in the estimation of the community. We therefore hold that, as a matter of law, injury to reputation cannot be a 'bodily injury' as that term is defined in a homeowner's policy such as the one before us here.") (citing cases nationally); *see also Adolph Coors Co. v. Truck Ins. Exchange*, 960 A.2d 617, 623 (D.D.C. 2008) ("Psychological harm, however, is not bodily injury when there is no physical impact, fear of physical harm, or physical manifestation of emotional distress.") (citation and internal quotes omitted).

Florida: A Florida District Court held that a claim under a commercial general liability policy issued to a staffing company, for depression suffered by a client who was inappropriately touched by a temporary employee assigned by the staffing company, qualified as "bodily injury." *Prof'l Staffing v. Illinois Union Ins. Co.*, No. 8:04-cv-793-T-30EAJ, 2005 U.S. Dist. LEXIS 41006 (M.D. Fla. Sept. 19, 2005). The policy defined "bodily injury" as "bodily injury, sickness or disease sustained by a person, including death resulting from any of these at any time." *Id.* The court concluded that, notwithstanding that the victim never testified that she experienced any physical pain, the violation of one's person through sexual battery, which results in such debilitating conditions as depression and post-traumatic stress disorder, constitutes a "bodily injury." The *Prof'l Staffing* Court distinguished *Allstate Insurance Co. v. Clohessy*, 32 F. Supp. 2d 1333 (M.D. Fla. 1998), question certified by 199 F.3d 1293 (11th. Cir. 2000), *rev. dism.* by 763 So. 2d 1042 (Table) (Fla. 2000), which held that, while emotional distress did not constitute "bodily injury" under an automobile policy, such emotional distress did not involve direct physical harm. Rather, it arose from witnessing an accident involving a relative. *Id.* n.2. By contrast, *Prof'l Staffing* involved physical harm, irrespective of whether it manifested into physical pain. *Id.*

Georgia: A Georgia District Court held that a claim under a commercial general liability policy issued to a real estate developer, for emotional injury suffered by potential buyers of a lot in a residential development, on account of race discrimination, did not qualify as "bodily injury." *Auto-Owners Ins. Co. v. Robinson*, No. 3:05-CV-109, 2006 U.S. Dist. LEXIS 66551 (M.D. Ga. Sept. 6, 2006). The policy defined "bodily injury" as "bodily injury, sickness or disease sustained by a person, including death resulting from any of these at one time." The court held that no coverage was owed because the underlying plaintiffs did not allege that the humiliation, embarrassment, and emotional distress that they sustained were the result of a physical injury. Further, the court rejected the argument that "bodily injury" includes physical manifestation of emotional distress. *See also Nationwide Mut. Fire Ins. Co. v. Somers*, 591 S.E.2d 430, 435 (Ga. Ct. App. 2003) (holding that no coverage was owed under a general liability policy issued to a cemetery, for a claim brought by a mother, whose son's grave was not perpetually care for, because "bodily injury" is limited to physical injury to the body and does not include nonphysical, emotional, or mental harm); *Transportation Ins. Co. v. Selective Way Ins. Co.*, No. 11-01383, 2012 U.S. Dist. LEXIS 163007 (N.D. Ga. Nov. 14, 2012) ("Used in an insurance policy, the term 'bodily injury' means just that—'bodily injury.' It pertains to physical injury to the body. It does not include non-physical, emotional or mental harm. And it cannot be equated with the broader term 'personal injury.'"); *Doe v. Camp Dream Found.*,

Inc., No. 16-1323, 2017 U.S. Dist. LEXIS 150477 (N.D. Ga. July 21, 2017) (claim involved inappropriate touching of a camp counselor by a camper; policy at issued defined "bodily injury" as "bodily injury, sickness or disease sustained by a person, including death resulting from any of these at any time") (finding a genuine dispute of material fact as to whether the counselor's recovery was for "bodily injury" or only "mental damages" not extending to physical harm) (relying on *Presidential Hotel v. Canal Insurance Company*, 373 S.E.2d 671 (Ga. Ct. App. 1988) and *O'Dell v. St. Paul Fire & Marine Ins. Co.*, 478 S.E.2d 418 (Ga. Ct. App. 1996), which involved sexual harassment-related claims that the courts concluded did not seek damages for physical harm).

Hawaii: The Supreme Court of Hawaii held that claims by immediate family members, for negligent infliction of emotional distress on account of the death of their son, husband, and father, qualified as "bodily injury" under an automobile policy. *First Ins. Co. of Haw. v. Lawrence*, 881 P.2d 489, 494 (Haw. 1994). As the policy did not define the term "bodily injury," the court substituted "accidental harm," as used in the statute governing required automobile coverage. "Accidental harm" was defined as "bodily injury, death, sickness, or disease caused by a motor vehicle accident to a person." Hawaii's top court was persuaded by the Court of Appeals of New York's decision in *Lavanant v. Gen. Acc. Ins. Co. of Am.*, 595 N.E.2d 819, 822 (N.Y. 1992), which held that the average person reading an insurance policy would not conclude that mental anguish was excluded from the ambit of sickness. *Id.* at 494; *see also Allstate Ins. Co. v. Gadiel*, No. 07–00565 DAE KSC, 2008 U.S. Dist. LEXIS 90923 (D. Haw. Nov. 7, 2008) (citing *Lawrence*) ("Plaintiff additionally contends that Argus does not allege sufficient facts demonstrating physical injury and, instead, merely asserts a claim for emotional distress. Even if true, this argument is irrelevant. For purposes of insurance coverage in Hawai'i, bodily injuries include emotional distress."); *RLI Ins. Co. v. Thompson*, No. 09-00345, 2010 U.S. Dist. LEXIS 35979 (D. Haw. Apr. 12, 2010) ("[T]o the extent the underlying state-court complaint seeks damages for emotional distress caused by the Thompsons' alleged negligence in fixing rot or other damage, the Davises might be alleging a 'bodily injury' caused by accidental conduct.") (citing *Lawrence*) (noting that, based on the causes of action at issue, the underlying plaintiffs are unlikely to recover for their emotional distress damages; however, because a covered claim was asserted, a duty to defend was owed).

Idaho: An Idaho District Court held that a claim under a truckers occupational accident policy issued to a truck driver, for psychological counseling necessitated by an accident, qualified as "bodily injury." *Reyerson v. Nat'l Union Fire Ins. Co.*, No. CV-06–493-E-BLW, 2008 U.S. Dist. LEXIS 28759 (D. Idaho Apr. 8, 2008). The insured suffered nightmares, nausea, stomach pain, fatigue, and hypertension, among other ailments, on account of post-traumatic stress disorder brought on by the accident. The policy did not define "bodily injury." Noting that Idaho courts have not specifically addressed or defined "bodily injury," the court examined the split on the issue nationally. The District Court followed the Supreme Court of New Jersey's decision in *SL Industries, Inc. v. Am. Motorists Ins. Co.*, 607 A.2d 1266 (N.J. 1992) and held that the term "bodily injury," as used in the policy, was ambiguous as it was unclear whether "bodily injury" applied to psychological and/or emotional injuries resulting in physical manifestations; *Harn v. Scottsdale Ins. Co.*, No. 12-00633, 2014 U.S. Dist. LEXIS 132954 (D. Idaho Sept. 22, 2014) ("Defendant's reliance upon the holding in *Reyerson* goes too far. There, District Judge Winmill considered whether the term 'bodily injury' — which was undefined by the insurance policy in his case -- included emotional distress with attendant physical manifestations.") ("[T]his Court concludes that it is ambiguous whether or not the term 'bodily injury,' as used in the Policy [defined to include 'sickness'], embraces Plaintiff's allegations of emotional distress [even if unaccompanied by physical manifestations].").

Illinois: The Appellate Court of Illinois held that a claim under an automobile insurance policy issued to a medical transportation provider, for strong anxiety and fear suffered by a client that was sexually assaulted in the course of transport, did not qualify as "bodily injury." *SCR Med. Transp. Servs., Inc. v. Browne*, 781 N.E.2d 564, 571 (Ill. App. Ct. 2002). The policy defined "bodily injury" as "bodily injury, sickness or disease sustained by a person, including death that results from any of these." *Id.* at 570. Following a survey of Illinois decisions, the court concluded that, when a policy defines "bodily injury" as "bodily injury," and not "injury" alone, the definition is restricted to actual physical injury. *Id.* at 571. *See also Commercial Union Ins. Co. v. Image Control Prop. Mgmt.*, 918 F. Supp. 1165, 1171 n.8 (N.D. Ill. 1996) ("In light of the complaint's failure to allege physical injury, we need not decide whether emotional distress falls within the definition of bodily injury when the distress is manifested by physical injury."); *Health Care Indus. Liab. Ins. Program v. Momence Meadows Nursing Ctr., Inc.*, 566 F.3d 689, 696–97 (7th Cir. 2010) ("Momence makes two other arguments in favor of coverage, both of which lack merit. Momence maintains that Absher's and Mitchell's claims of emotional distress in counts three and four (the retaliation claims) are properly classified as claims for 'bodily injury' under CGL coverage A, which defines 'bodily injury' as 'bodily injury, sickness or disease sustained by a person.' Momence attempts to sidestep Illinois case law clearly hold-ing to the contrary.") (citing *SCR*); *Prof'l Sols. Ins. Co. v. Giolas*, 297 F. Supp. 3d 805 (N.D. Ill. 2017) (distinguishing *SCR*, which involved an auto policy and no physical injuries, but only fear and anxiety caused by allegedly negligent driving, and con-cluding that the allegations of sexual misconduct at issue were sufficient to allege bodily injury); *Pa. Manufacturers' Ass'n Ins. C. v. N. Am. Auto. Servs.*, 479 F. Supp. 3d 1287 (S.D. Fla. 2020) (applying Illinois law) (finding that the Plaintiffs' Office of Equal Opportunity claim, which alleged emotional and psychological injuries, including post-traumatic stress disorder, due to discrimination on the basis of sex did not allege "bodily injury" within the context of a Commercial Garage/Auto Dealers Liability policy, as "Illinois courts have found that mental harm does not constitute 'bodily injury'" under policies with nearly identical terms) (decision tied to policy's definition of "bodily injury," not stated in the opinion); *Taaffe v. Selective Ins. Co.*, No. 20-3417, 2020 U.S. Dist. LEXIS 195870 (N.D. Ill. Oct. 22, 2020) (not-ing that "bodily injury" requires actual physical injury and that "[e]motional distress is not a 'sickness' within the meaning of 'bodily injury'") (finding that "[b]ecause defamation concerns false statements and tortious interference concerns business relationships" the claims asserted against the insured did not allege "bodily injury" as defined in the insured's homeowners' insurance policy); *Scottsdale Insurance Co. v. Burks*, No. 17-668, 2021 U.S. Dist. LEXIS 172 (S.D. Ill. Jan. 4, 2021) (finding that a plaintiff, who alleged "no facts supporting a reasonable inference that he suffered any actual physical harm from his termination," failed to allege "bodily injury" cov-ered by a commercial general liability insurance policy, because although "Illinois courts have found 'bodily injury' defined only as 'injury, sickness or disease sustained by a person' could include any injury, including nonphysical harm," "where 'bodily injury' is defined—as in the Policy—as 'bodily injury, sickness or disease sustained by a person,' it is limited to actual physical harm (and possibly mental anguish aris-ing from that physical harm)".) (The court concluded that "without actual physical harm, 'bodily injury' as defined in the Policy does not include the kind of pain and suffering ordinarily suffered because of a wrongful termination").

Indiana: The Supreme Court of Indiana held that the emotional distress sus-tained by a wife and children, on account of being passengers in an automobile in which their husband and father was severely injured, qualified as "bodily injury" under an underinsured motorist policy. *State Farm Mut. Auto. Ins. Co. v. Jakupko*, 881 N.E.2d 654, 658–59 (Ind. 2008). The policy defined "bodily injury" as "bodily injury to a person and sickness, disease or death which results from it." *Id.* at 656.

The Indiana high court was persuaded by *Wayne Township Board of School Commissioners v. Indiana Insurance Co.*, 650 N.E.2d 1205 (Ind. Ct. App. 1995) and held that the average layperson would conclude that mental anguish comes within the ambit of "sickness." *Id.* at 658. However, the Supreme Court of Indiana also concluded that bodily injury does not include emotional injury unless it arises from a bodily touching—which was the case with the wife and children at issue as they were present in the automobile at the time of the accident. *Id.* at 658–59; *see also State Farm Mut. Auto. Ins. Co. v. D.L.B.*, 881 N.E.2d 665, 666 (Ind. 2008) (holding, on the same day as *Jakupko*, that emotional distress, even accompanied by physical manifestation, did not qualify as bodily injury under an automobile policy because the bystander seeking coverage did not suffer impact, force, or harm to his body); *Westfield Ins. Co. v. Hill*, 790 F. Supp. 2d 855 (N.D. Ind. 2011) (concluding that mother's claim for emotional distress upon learning of her son's sexual molestation was not "bodily injury" under a homeowners policy as her complaint did not allege that *she* suffered any direct, physical impact to her body as a result of the molestation); *Taele v. State Farm Mut. Auto. Ins. Co.*, 936 N.E.2d 306 (Ind. Ct. App. 2010) (following a lengthy review of the issue and holding that the insureds were "not entitled to recover UM benefits under the State Farm policy because they themselves were neither directly impacted nor directly physically injured by the accident that killed their daughter, notwithstanding the fact that they may have a valid NIED claim") ("The fact that John is claiming physical manifestations of his emotional distress also is irrelevant here. The *D.L.B.* opinion squarely holds that subsequent physical manifestations of emotional distress unrelated to a physical impact, force, or harm sustained in an accident is not a compensable 'bodily injury.'").

Iowa: The Supreme Court of Iowa held that a bystander claim for emotional distress qualified as "bodily injury" for purposes of an underinsured motorist policy. *Pekin Ins. Co. v. Hugh*, 501 N.W.2d 508, 511 (Iowa 1993). The policy defined bodily injury as "bodily harm, sickness or disease, including death that results." *Id.* at 510. The court held that "[u]nlike the loss of consortium claim, an injury the bystander suffers is not one that results from an injury to another person. Rather, the injury is directly to the bystander as a result of the bystander seeing the accident and reasonably believing that the direct victim of the accident would be seriously injured or killed. In addition, the emotional distress must be serious. That is, emotional distress should ordinarily be accompanied with *physical* manifestations of the distress." *Id.* at 511 (internal quotation omitted). The bystander claim was therefore subject to a separate "per person" limit of liability. *Id.*; *see also Moore v. Eckman*, 762 N.W.2d

459, 462 (Iowa 2009) ("Bystander recovery for emotional distress is strictly limited to situations which involve 'witnessing peril to a victim,' and which have produced emotional distress from '*sensory* and contemporaneous observance of the accident as contrasted with learning of the accident ... after its occurrence.'") (UIM claim) (quoting from *Barnhill v. Davis*, 300 N.W.2d 104 (Iowa 1981)).

Kansas: The Tenth Circuit Court of Appeals, applying Kansas law, held that a claim under a commercial general liability policy, issued to a real estate agency/financial advisor, for anxiety, worry, and mental and emotional distress suffered by clients from whom investment funds were misappropriated, did not qualify as "bodily injury." *ERA Franchise Sys., Inc. v. N. Ins. Co.*, 208 F.3d 225 (10th Cir. 2000) (table). The policy defined "bodily injury" as "bodily injury, sickness or disease." *Id.* at *10. The court held that emotional injury did not qualify as "bodily injury." *Id.* at *16. "We agree with the majority of courts and conclude the phrase 'bodily injury' standing alone or defined as 'bodily injury, sickness or disease' is unambiguous and extends coverage to physical harm only. The majority view that the term 'bodily' modifies the terms 'sickness' and 'disease' is the more logical interpretation." *Id.* In *Travelers Casualty & Surety Co. v. Rage Administrative & Marketing Services, Inc.*, 42 F. Supp. 2d 1159, 1168 (D. Kan. 1999), the court held that humiliation, embarrassment, emotional distress, and mental anguish, sustained as a result of race discrimination, did not qualify as "bodily injury," defined under a commercial general liability policy as "bodily injury, sickness or disease." While the court did not formally address whether physical manifestation of emotional injury qualified as bodily injury, the court did state that there was no evidence that the insurer "failed to undertake a good faith analysis of all information known to it or reasonably ascertainable by inquiry and investigation in order to determine the possibility of coverage for physical manifestations of [emotional] injury." *Id.; see also Partridge v. Mong*, 252 P.3d 640 (Kan. Ct. App. 2011) (declaring that amount of automobile insurance provided to a child, for mental distress that later manifested itself in physical symptoms as a result of witnessing a parent's injuries and death in an automobile accident, is included in the limit of coverage provided for the death of the parent) (noting that policy provided " 'Bodily injury to one *person*' includes all injury and damages to others resulting from this bodily injury, and all emotional distress resulting from this bodily injury sustained by other persons who do not sustain bodily injury."); *Heacker v. Safeco Ins. Co. of Am.*, 676 F.3d 724 (8th Cir. 2012) (applying Kansas law) (alleged post-traumatic stress disorder and alcoholism, suffered as a result of insured's negligent infliction of emotional distress, did not constitute "bodily injury," defined by homeowner's policy as "bodily harm, sickness or disease").

Kentucky: The Supreme Court of Kentucky held that no coverage was owed under a professional liability policy issued to a cemetery for claims that it interred bodies in already occupied graves. *Employers Ins. of Wausau v. Martinez*, 54 S.W.3d 142, 145 (Ky. 2001). The court based its decision on an exclusion for bodily injury caused by willful violation of a penal statute. *Id.* However, a dissenting opinion concluded that the majority erred by applying the exclusion. *Id.* at 146 (Johnstone, J., dissenting). Among other reasons, the dissent looked to the definition of "bodily injury"—"sickness or disease sustained by any person"—and noted that, under Kentucky law, the tort of infliction of intentional distress does not depend on the occurrence of bodily injury to be actionable. *Id.* Thus, the dissent concluded: "The exclusion in question applies only to 'bodily injury.' The exclusion does not, and cannot under Kentucky law, apply to the plaintiffs' claims for intentional infliction of emotional distress. A number of jurisdictions are in accord and hold that the term 'bodily injury' in insurance contracts does not encompass claims for mental injury." *Id.* at 147 (citations omitted). *See also Cincinnati Ins. Co. v. Roccanova*, No. 11–104, 2012 U.S. Dist. LEXIS 14021 (E.D. Ky. Feb 6, 2012) (holding that a negligent infliction of emotional distress claim was not covered under a CGL policy because damages sought for purported emotional distress were not for a "bodily injury" as defined by the policy) (court did not provide definition of "bodily injury" nor any support for its decision); *Auto Club Property-Casualty Ins. Co. v. Adler*, No. 14-00046, 2015 U.S. Dist. LEXIS 108667 (W.D. Ky. Aug. 18, 2015) ("The inclusion of 'personal injury' within the definition of 'bodily injury' -- so that under the insuring clause there is coverage for damages arising because of personal injury -- operates to provide coverage for damages arising because of emotional harm absent any physical injury. Without that inclusion, mental or emotional harm absent any physical injury does not constitute 'bodily injury' in the insurance context.") (citing non-Kentucky cases).

Louisiana: The Supreme Court of Louisiana held that a claim by a wife and her children, for emotional distress sustained on account of the death of her husband and the children's father, did not qualify as "bodily injury" for purposes of an underinsured motorist policy. *Hebert v. Webre*, 982 So. 2d 770, 777 (La. 2008). The policy defined "bodily injury" as "physical bodily injury to a person and sickness, disease or death which results from it." *Id.* at 773. In reaching its conclusion, the Louisiana high court looked closely at its decision in *Crabtree v. State Farm Ins. Co.*,

632 So. 2d 736 (La. 1994). *Id.* at 774. In *Crabtree*, the court held that mental anguish constituted "bodily injury" under an automobile policy that defined the term as "bodily injury to a person, and sickness, disease or death which results from it." *Id.* (quoting *Crabtree*, 632 So. 2d at 739). The *Crabtree* Court concluded that such definition was circular as the term being defined was used in the definition. *Id.* at 775 (quoting *Crabtree*, 632 So. 2d at 744). The *Crabtree* Court also concluded that, if the definition of "bodily injury" were intended to cover only external, physical injuries, then it could have been drafted in a more restrictive manner. *Id.* The *Hebert* Court, distinguishing the policy language before it from that which was at issue in *Crabtree*, concluded "that the addition of the word 'physical' is sufficient under *Crabtree* to differentiate a 'bodily injury' sustained in a physical manner, which would be entitled to separate per person limits, from an injury which is emotional in nature and, though might have physical consequences, is not a 'physical' bodily injury." *Id.* at 777. *See also Subervielle v. State Farm Mut. Auto. Ins. Co.*, 32 So. 3d 811 (La. Ct. App. 2009) (following *Hebert*) ("We are of the opinion that in the instant matter that the Subervielles are entitled to recover under the UEO limits of the State Farm policy, however their recovery is limited to their out of pocket expenses resulting from the accident. For additional expenses the Subervielles would have to prove that they suffered a 'bodily injury' as defined by the policy."); *Smith v. Thomas*, 2014 So. 3d 945 (La. Ct. App. 2017) ("Although the policy in this case does define 'bodily injury' as 'physical bodily injury' as did the policy in *Hebert*, the decision in *Hebert* did not rest solely upon that language and we do not believe that the Supreme Court meant for that language alone to control.") (claims of a fourteen-year-old daughter who was walking with her mother when her mother was struck by a passing motorist were entitled to a separate per-person limit); *Doty v. GoAuto Ins. Co.*, 251 So. 3d 706 (La. Ct. App. 2018) (following *Smith v. Thomas*).

Maine: The Supreme Judicial Court of Maine held that a bystander claim for emotional distress may qualify as "bodily injury" for purposes of an underinsured motorist policy. *Ryder v. USAA Gen. Indem. Co.*, 938 A.2d 4, 9 (Me. 2007). The policy defined "bodily injury" as "bodily harm, sickness, disease or death." *Id.* at 6. Finding that the definition of "bodily injury" was ambiguous, the court concluded that the words "sickness" and "disease" were not modified by the word "bodily," but, rather, served to expand coverage beyond "bodily harm." *Id.* at 7. Turning to the terms "sickness" and "disease," the court held that a bystander claim for emotional distress will qualify as "bodily injury," and trigger a separate per-person limit, if the claimant can "show that [it] suffered emotional distress that was serious" and that "the distress constitutes a diagnosable sickness or disease." *Id.* at 9. *See also Langevin v. Allstate Ins. Co.*, 66 A.3d 585 (Me. 2013) ("The Allstate policy at issue here defines 'bodily injury' in relevant part as 'physical harm to the body, including sickness or disease, and resulting death.' Unlike the definition of 'bodily injury' at issue in *Ryder*, this definition is unambiguous. . . . The definition in this policy quite clearly restricts 'bodily injury' to physical ailments and/or resulting death such that an ordinary person would understand that it does not encompass emotional pain and suffering."); *Lyman Morse Boatbuilding, Inc. v. Northern Assur. Co. of America, Inc.*, No. 12–313, 2013 U.S. Dist. LEXIS 139226 (D. Me. Sept. 27, 2013) ("[R]ecent Maine Law Court decisions have clarified Maine law on how to determine whether the bodily injury clause in an insurance contract covers emotional distress damages. If the adjective 'bodily' can grammatically modify each of the nouns following it (as in injury, sickness or disease), then emotional distress damages are not insured because they are not bodily injury, bodily sickness or bodily disease. But if grammatically the adjective 'bodily' can *not* apply to all the nouns that follow it (as in bodily injury, sickness or death, where 'bodily death' is nonsensical), then the adjectival limitation is ambiguous, ambiguities are resolved against the insurance company and emotional distress damages *are* covered.") (emphasis in original) (comparing *Langevin* and *Ryder*).

Maryland: The Court of Appeals of Maryland held that a parents' claim for emotional distress on account of the death of their son did not qualify as "bodily injury" for purposes of an automobile policy. *Daley v. United Servs. Auto. Ass'n*, 541 A.2d 632, 636 (Md. 1988). The policy defined "bodily injury," in pertinent part, as "bodily injury, sickness or disease, including death resulting therefrom." *Id.* at 633. Basing its decision entirely on the policy language, the court held that, since the parents suffered no separate and distinct bodily injuries of their own, the insurer's obligation for all damages suffered by the parents and their son was limited to the policy's "each person" limit. *Id.* at 636. The Maryland high court acknowledged that the Court of Special Appeals held in *Loewenthal v. Security Insurance Co. of Hartford*, 436 A.2d 493 (Md. Ct. Spec. App. 1991) that bodily injury encompasses a claim for pain, suffering, and mental anguish. *Id.* However, the court distinguished *Loewenthal* because it involved a broad duty to defend under a general liability policy and not the application of policy limits. *Id*; *Kivitz v. Erie Ins. Exch.*, No. 2015-2299, 2016 Md. App. LEXIS 1326 (Md. Ct. Spec. App. Apr. 29, 2016) (holding that "a reasonably prudent layperson could read the Policy as recognizing that the injuries for 'mental anguish' and 'loss of services' are personal to the Colton sons and separate from the injuries suffered by their mother. Incorporating that definition into the coverage provision, it follows that Erie has arguably promised to cover Baden's legal obligations to pay damages because of those injuries.") (defining bodily injury to mean "physical harm, sickness or disease including mental anguish, care, loss of services, or resulting death").

Massachusetts: The Supreme Judicial Court of Massachusetts held that a claim under a homeowner's policy issued to parents, for mental pain and anguish suffered by their daughter's teacher, on account of being defamed by the parents, did not qualify as "bodily injury." *Allstate Ins. Co. v. Diamant*, 518 N.E.2d 1154, 1157 (Mass. 1988). The policy defined "bodily injury" as "bodily injury, sickness or disease, including resulting death, care and loss of services." *Id.* at 1155. The court held that the term "bodily injury" was "unambiguous and understood to mean hurt or harm to the human body, contemplating actual physical harm or damage to the human body." *Id.* at 1157 (citation omitted). In *McNeill v. Metro. Prop. & Liab. Ins. Co.*, 650 N.E.2d 793, 796 (Mass. 1995), the Supreme Judicial Court of Massachusetts held that a bystander claim under an automobile policy, for emotional distress that exacerbated a father's diabetic condition, and led to his development of an ulcer, did not qualify as bodily injury. *See also Richardson v. Liberty Mut. Fire Ins. Co.*, 716 N.E.2d 117, 121 (Mass. App. Ct. 1999) (citing *Diamant* and *McNeill* and holding that bodily injury as used in an insurance policy includes only actual physical injuries to the human body and the consequences thereof); *Metropolitan Property & Cas. Ins. Co. v. Allan*, 945 N.E.2d 1005 (Mass. Ct. App. 2011) ("As a general matter, our case law has defined 'bodily,' as that term is used in insurance contracts, to exclude emotional trauma. . . . As *Richardson* makes clear, such mental suffering only constitutes a 'bodily injury' if it arises out of physical injuries. Here, the only physical injury that could potentially anchor E.E.'s emotional trauma claim in the definition of 'bodily injury' is the actual act of sexual molestation. Because sexual molestation is expressly excluded from the definition of 'bodily injury' in the insurance policies, we conclude that emotional trauma, which can only constitute a 'bodily injury' through its relationship with the actual act of sexual molestation, is also excluded from the definition of 'bodily injury.'"); *Modica v. Sheriff of Suffolk County*, 74 N.E.3d 1233 (Mass. 2017) (citing *Diamant* and holding that a state statute, providing compensation to correctional officers who sustain bodily injury caused by an inmate, requires physical impairment or damage, i.e., physical injury) ("As the plaintiff's sinus tachycardia is an impairment of function which has not led to structural heart damage, it is not a physical impairment or injury. Therefore, the plaintiff does not have a bodily injury within the meaning of the statute.").

Michigan: The Court of Appeals of Michigan held that a claim under a home-owner's policy, for emotional injuries caused by the insured's defamatory statements, did not qualify as "bodily injury." *Fitch v. State Farm Fire and Cas. Co.*, 536 N.W.2d 273, 275 (Mich. Ct. App. 1995). The policy defined "bodily injury," in part, as "physical injury, sickness, or disease to a person." *Id.* The policy also stated that "bodily injury" excluded emotional and mental disorder unless it arose out of actual physical injury. *Id.* The court held that "[u]nder Michigan law, when mental injury is alleged, at least some physical manifestation of the injury is required in order to bring it within the definition of 'bodily injury.'" *Id.* In *Meridian Mutual Insurance Co. v. Conti Development Corp.*, No. 1:97-CV-904, 1998 U.S. Dist. LEXIS 7133 (W.D. Mich. Apr. 22, 1998), the court followed *Fitch* and rejected the argument that the decision was based on the express exclusion from the definition of "bodily injury" for emotional distress unless it arose out of actual physical injury. "[T]he *Fitch* court only cited this portion of the policy [the emotional distress exclusion] as an alternative reason for finding in favor of the insurance company." *See also Paylor v. First Mountain Mortg. Corp.*, No. 278076, 2008 Mich. App. LEXIS 2006 (Mich. Ct. App. Oct. 9, 2008) ("Under the unambiguous language used to define 'bodily injury,' mental anguish must result from bodily injury. Here, there was no evidence of an actual bodily injury, but only evidence that the Paylors' mental anguish had physical manifestations. We therefore hold that the trial court erred as a matter of law in finding the requisite bodily injury for coverage under the policy."); *Hunter v. Sisco*, 843 N.W.2d 559 (Mich. 2014) (granting leave to appeal to decide "whether damages for pain and suffering and/or emotional distress may qualify as a 'bodily injury' that permits a plaintiff to avoid the application of governmental immunity from tort liability under the motor vehicle exception to governmental immunity, MCL 691.1405") (appeals court decision discussed the issue in the context of insurance coverage: "Our courts have interpreted coverage for 'bodily injury' in insurance policies as not encompassing those for mental suffering unless there exists some physical manifestation of the mental suffering." *Hunter v. Sisco*, 832 N.W.2d 753 (Mich. Ct. App. 2013)); *State Farm Fire & Cas. Co. v. Stone*, No. 16-12831, 2017 U.S. Dist. LEXIS 110283 (E.D. Mich. July 17, 2017) ("Looking to Heiney's counter-complaint and the alleged underlying conduct, this Court finds no allegation of physical injury. The counter-complaint lists a number of emotional injuries, including 'depression, emotional distress, humiliation, mortification and embarrassment, sleeplessness, [and] anxiety', and then, at the end of the list, includes the words 'physical damages' without any specification of what these physical damages are.

Just as courts have held that adding 'negligence' to the pleadings of an intentional tort claim is insufficient to cause the claim to sound in negligence, . . . adding the words 'physical damages' to pleadings alleging only emotional forms of injury is insufficient to give the claim a basis in physical damages.").

Minnesota: The Supreme Court of Minnesota held that a claim under a general liability policy, issued to an insurance agent, for emotional distress suffered by a customer upon learning, after a serious automobile accident, that the agent had not procured automobile insurance for her, did not qualify as "bodily injury." *Garvis v. Employers Mut. Cas. Co.*, 497 N.W.2d 254, 257 (Minn. 1993). The policy defined "bodily injury" as "bodily injury, sickness, or disease sustained by a person." *Id.* The court held that "emotional distress with appreciable physical manifestations can qualify as 'bodily injury' within the meaning of the insurance policy." *Id.* However, the court also concluded that the plaintiff's complaint did not allege any physical manifestation of emotional distress. *Id.*; *see also Mattson v. CSC Ins. Agency, Inc.*, No. C6–01–1409, 2002 Minn. App. LEXIS 186 (Minn. Ct. App. Feb. 5, 2002) (finding that claims of depression, anxiety, and sleeping problems constituted only emotional problems and did not satisfy the physical manifestation test, designed to assure the genuineness of the alleged emotional distress).

Mississippi: A Mississippi District Court held that a claim under a homeowner's policy issued to the director of the Mississippi Bureau of Narcotics, for emotional distress sustained by individuals on account of the insured's dissemination of false information about them to the press, did not qualify as "bodily injury." *Allstate Ins. Co. v. Melton*, 482 F. Supp. 2d 775, 782 (S.D. Miss. 2007). The policy defined "bodily injury" as "bodily harm, sickness or disease." *Id.* at 781. The insured argued that, under Mississippi law, because emotional distress damages for negligent infliction of emotional distress are available only if the plaintiff proves physical manifestation of injury or demonstrable physical harm, then a charge of negligent infliction of emotional distress must imply physical "bodily" injury of some sort. *Id.* at 782. The court concluded that, even if the insured's premise were correct, "physical manifestations of emotional distress, as contrasted with physical harm inflicted from some outside source, do not constitute 'bodily injury' under [the insurer's] policy." *Id.*; *See also Employers Mut. Cas. Co. v. Raddin*, No. 10–137, 2012 U.S. Dist. LEXIS 44649 (S.D. Miss. Mar. 30, 2012) ("No allegations of physical injury to the body are made in the Underlying Amended Complaint. [underlying plaintiffs alleged 'mental anguish, pain, suffering, duress, nervousness, depression, anxiety, embarrassment, humiliation and economic losses'] Even Darden's unwanted touching of the Underlying Plaintiffs would not constitute 'bodily injury.' The Underlying Plaintiffs allege that Darden touched them when he conducted unlicensed physical exams; however, the Underlying Amended Complaint does not contain any allegations that Darden's touching of the Underlying Plaintiffs actually caused them to suffer 'bodily injury.' Darden's unwanted touching of the Underlying Plaintiffs by itself does not constitute 'bodily injury.'").

Missouri: The Court of Appeals of Missouri held that a claim under a homeowner's policy, for emotional distress sustained by individuals, on account of the insureds' recommendation of a life insurance agent that ultimately committed fraud, did not qualify as "bodily injury." *Citizens Ins. Co. of Am. v. Leiendecker*, 962 S.W.2d 446, 452 (Mo. Ct. App. 1998). The policy defined "bodily injury" as "bodily harm, sickness or disease, including required care, loss of services and death that results." *Id.* at 451. The court cited a litany of cases nationally and followed the majority rule: "[T]he overwhelming majority of jurisdictions which have considered the issue hold that 'bodily injury' standing alone or defined in a policy as 'bodily injury [or harm], sickness or disease' is unambiguous and encompasses only physical harm." *Id.* at 452; *see also Am. Family Mut. Ins. Co. v. Wagner*, No. 05–4394-CV-C-NKL, 2007 U.S. Dist. LEXIS 23152 (W.D. Mo. Mar. 29, 2007) (rejecting the argument that emotional harm that includes a component of physical harm is "bodily injury," but decision based solely on the specific policy language); *Cairo Marine Service, Inc. v. Homeland Ins. Co. of N.Y.*, No. 4:09CV1492, 2011 U.S. Dist. LEXIS 49884 (E.D. Mo. May 10, 2011) ("Under prevailing Missouri law, the man's claim for emotional injuries does not fall within the [exclusion] for claims 'for bodily injury, sickness, disease or death.' ... The policy does not define any of the terms 'bodily injury,' 'sickness,' 'disease,' or 'death' and none of them unequivocally encompass emotional injuries such as those suffered by the man in the crane-injury case. Even if the term 'bodily' does not modify all of the terms following it in the exclusion, without more, it is at best merely possible that the terms 'sickness' and 'disease' could be construed to include mental injuries, such as post-traumatic stress disorder. However, given the plain meaning of the terms, it is at least equally probable that they do not."); *Derousse v. State Farm Mut. Auto. Ins. Co.*, 298 S.W.3d 891, 895 (Mo. 2009) (holding that claim for "anxiety attacks" and "severe mental and emotional distress" qualified as "sickness" or "disease" under uninsured motorist statute, and, therefore, there was no need to examine whether such claims met the definition of "bodily injury" in the insurer's policy); *State Farm Fire & Cas. Co. v. Dado's Café, Inc.*, 421 F. Supp. 3d 720 (E.D. Mo. 2019) ("Defendants argue in their response that the Underlying Plaintiffs allege that they were subjected to 'unwelcome physical contact' and 'where the claimant alleges sexual harassment involving physical contact, 'bodily injury' may be involved.' The Underlying Plaintiffs, however, admit that they have not suffered any tangible, physical injury. The Court holds that the Underlying Plaintiffs have not suffered 'bodily injury' under the Policy because the Policy's definition of 'bodily injury' does not extend to emotional or mental injuries that were not cause (sic) by a physical injury."); *Post Holdings v. Liberty Mut. Fire. Ins. Co.*, No. 18-1741, 2020 U.S. Dist. LEXIS 202832 (E.D. Mo. Oct. 30, 2020) (finding that the insurer had no duty to defend the insured in the underlying suit because that suit contained no claims for bodily injuries within the terms of the policies, where the insured's general liability policies defined the term "bodily injury" to "specifically cover 'mental anguish or other mental injury' only if it is caused by the 'bodily injury,' and that based upon this definition, "a reasonable person placed in the position of the insured would have understood the term 'bodily injury' to exclude coverage for any and all emotion type injuries, including any physical symptoms that might be caused by or tied to the emotional injury, unless the emotional injury was caused by actual physical bodily contact") (noting that "Missouri courts have concluded that the common meaning of the phrase 'bodily injury' 'refers to physical conditions of the body and excludes mental suffering or emotional distress'").

Montana: The Supreme Court of Montana held that a bystander claim for emotional distress, accompanied by stress, migraine headaches, and a rapid heartbeat upon hearing a siren, qualified as "bodily injury" for purposes of an automobile policy. *Allstate Ins. Co. v. Wagner-Ellsworth*, 188 P.3d 1042, 1051 (Mont. 2008). The policy defined "bodily injury" as "physical harm to the body, sickness, disease or death." The Montana high court overruled its decision in *Jacobsen v. Farmers Union Mutual Insurance. Co.*, 87 P.3d 995 (Mont. 2004), and held that "bodily injury" includes mental or psychological injury that is accompanied by physical manifestations. *Id.* at 1051. However, the court maintained that, in the case of purely emotional injuries, without physical manifestation, "bodily injury" connotes solely a physical problem. *Id.*; *see also King v. State Farm Fire and Cas. Co.*, No. CR 09-96, 2010 U.S. Dist. LEXIS 49029 (D. Mont. May 18, 2010), *aff'd on other grounds*, 500 Fed. Appx. 699 (9th Cir. 2012) ("The allegations in the underlying complaint and Montana's law at the time State Farm denied coverage preclude coverage for bodily injury. State Farm correctly concluded that under *Jacobsen* the emotional distress claims were not 'bodily injury.' Further, even under *Wagner-Ellsworth*, State Farm was not required to provide coverage. The underlying complaint alleges only that the Kings were distraught and suffered emotional distress, but does not include any allegations that the distress led to any 'physical manifestations.' ... Therefore, the underlying complaint did not allege 'bodily injury' within the scope of coverage under the Policy."); *State Farm Mut. Auto. Ins. Co. v. Freyer*, 239 P.3d 143 (Mont. 2010) (distinguishing *Wagner-Ellsworth* based on policy language); *Conley v. First Nat. Ins. Co. of America*, 494 Fed. Appx. 764 (9th Cir. 2012) ("Under Montana law, 'bodily injury' includes mental or psychological injury that is accompanied by physical manifestations. Such conditions include those which are susceptible to medical diagnosis and treatment in a manner which distinguishes them from mental injuries.") (quoting *Wagner-Ellsworth*) ("Even if anxiety typically includes such things as headaches, sleeplessness, muscle tension, and nausea, an insurer need not assume physical manifestations rising to the level of 'bodily injury' whenever 'anxiety' is alleged. At a minimum, there must be allegations of physical manifestations supported by sufficient documented evidence in order for insurance coverage to be triggered."); *Huckins v. United Services Automobile Association*, 396 P.3d 121 (Mont. 2017) (setting forth rule from *Wagner-Ellsworth* and concluding that no bodily injury alleged) ("[T]he Underlying Complaint does not allege such injuries, claiming only that Huckins experienced 'concern[] for the health and well being of her daughters as well as her own,' and 'pain, suffering, anxiety, stress, and emotional distress.' None of these are asserted to be 'physical manifestations' of physical injuries or actual 'bodily harm, sickness, or disease.' As such, Huckins did not plead a bodily injury."); *Walden v. Md. Cas. Co.*, No. 13-222, 2017 U.S. Dist. LEXIS 196180 (D. Mont. Nov. 29, 2017) (general discussion of what types of injuries are a physical manifestation of emotional distress) ("Houston alleges that as a result of her experience at Dahl's she became depressed, suffered from panic attacks that made her hands and arms shake, and that she was not able to mentally or physically function normally. Radford alleges that she suffered panic attacks which made it difficult to breathe. These attacks exacerbated her asthma and required additional medication. Additionally, she suffered from repeated bouts of insomnia and loss of appetite. The Court finds these symptoms are sufficient to raise an issue of fact, concerning whether Plaintiffs have physical manifestations of emotional distress.").

Nebraska: The Supreme Court of Nebraska held that a bystander claim for emotional distress did not qualify as "bodily injury" for purposes of an automobile policy. *Farm Bureau Ins. Co. v. Martinsen*, 659 N.W.2d 823, 827–28 (Neb. 2003). The policy defined "bodily injury" as "injury to a person's body and includes sickness, disease or death which results from it." *Id.* at 827. The court held that "a 'bodily injury' that could give rise to a separate per-person claim must be a physical, as opposed to a purely emotional, injury." *Id.* "There is no evidence or suggestion in the record that the [the parents] developed physical conditions causally related to the emotional distress they suffered as a result of the accident, and we do not consider whether this scenario, if established, could impose separate per-person liability on Farm Bureau whether or not the $300,000 per-person limit had been exhausted. Upon the record before us, we determine that the [parents'] emotional distress is a byproduct of and entirely dependent upon the bodily injury to [their son]." *Id.* at 828. The bystander claim was therefore not subject to a separate "per person" limit of liability. *Id. See also Addison Ins. Co. v. The Pink Palace, LLC*, No. 16-371, 2017 U.S. Dist. LEXIS 226463 (D. Neb. Sep. 25, 2017) (plaintiffs sought damages for, among other things, physical and emotional pain on account of being denied keno winnings because of a machine malfunction) (discussing *Martinsen* and holding that "the Policy's definition of bodily injury encompasses only physical injuries to the body, or a sickness or disease, but not emotional distress, generally," as well as concluding that the "conclusory allegation of physical pain does not, on its own, trigger Addison's duty to defend and potentially indemnify Pink Palace for a bodily injury").

Nevada: The Ninth Circuit Court of Appeals, applying Nevada law, addressed, but did not answer, whether a claim under a homeowner's policy for emotional distress sustained by a minor, on account of sexual abuse committed by her stepfather, qualified as "bodily injury." *State Farm Fire & Cas. Co. v. Pickard*, 849 F.2d 1220, 1222 (9th Cir. 1988). The policy defined "bodily injury" as "bodily harm, sickness or disease." *Id.* at 1221. The court acknowledged a split among courts nationally whether the term "bodily injury" includes emotional distress. *Id.* at 1222. However, the court concluded that it did not need to reach the issue because, even if "bodily injury" included emotional distress, coverage would be precluded by the policy's "household members" exclusion (denying coverage to relatives living in the same household as the named insured). *Id. See also Allstate Ins. Co. v. Foster*, 693 F. Supp. 886 (D. Nev. 1988) (concluding that, because coverage was excluded on other grounds, it was unnecessary to consider whether the term "bodily injury" included emotional distress); *Brewington v. State Farm Mut. Auto. Ins. Co.*, 45 F. Supp. 3d 1215 (D. Nev. 2014) ("[T]he court finds that State Farm's definition of 'bodily injury' is ambiguous. First, State Farm's definition is circular in that the term being defined is used within its own definition: '[b]odily injury means bodily injury to a person and sickness, disease, or death that results from it.' Such circular definitions are inherently ambiguous as they require additional information outside the definition to actually define the term being defined. . . . Second, State Farm's definition supports two reasonable interpretations: State Farm's physical injury interpretation and Brewington's broader mental injury and sickness interpretation. Where language of an insurance policy is subject to two or more reasonable interpretations the interpretation which favors coverage must be applied. . . . As such, the court interprets the term 'bodily injury' in the underlying insurance policy to include Brewington's emotional distress."); *Am. Reliable Ins. Co. v. Rodriguez*, No. 17-00740, 2018 U.S. Dist. LEXIS 133280 (D. Nev. Aug. 8, 2018) (addressing whether numerous types of damages, such as for breach of contract, fraud, slander and conspiracy, qualify as bodily injury).

New Hampshire: The Supreme Court of New Hampshire held that a claim under what appears to be a general liability policy, issued to a mobile home seller, for physical discomfort, emotional pain and suffering, aggravation, and embarrassment, sustained by owners of a mobile home, on account of the negligent design or installation of its vapor barrier that produced cold, dampness, clamminess, and a musty smell, did not qualify as "bodily injury." *Artcraft of N.H., Inc. v. Lumberman's Mut. Cas. Co.*, 497 A.2d 1195, 1196 (N.H. 1985). The policy defined "bodily injury" as "bodily injury, sickness or disease." *Id.* at 1195. Concluding that "sickness" or "disease" are "more than a mere temporary indisposition," the court held: "The record before us indicates that the Burnses sought no medical treatment either for the physical discomfort alleged, or for the emotional pain and suffering claimed. They also acknowledged that they suffered no loss of sleep, appetite, or weight or other physical consequences. They lost no time from work and incurred no out-of-pocket expenses related to the effects on them of living in their mobile home. Lack of any such physical manifestations precludes a finding that the physical discomfort and emotional pain and suffering complained of here can rise to the level of 'bodily injury' as defined in the policy." *Id.* at 1196; *see also Landy Veal Co., Inc. v. Employer's Mut. Cas. Co.*, No. C-93-150 (D.N.H. May 16, 1994) ("Ms. Day alleged that the conduct of the defendants and other Landy employees resulted in a hostile work environment from which she was constructively discharged. She claims that this atmosphere resulted in emotional distress however she fails to make any claim of resulting physical injury.") (relying on *Artcraft*).

New Jersey: The Supreme Court of New Jersey held that a claim under a homeowner's policy issued to parents, for emotional distress accompanied by physical manifestations suffered by their child's teacher, on account of disparaging comments made by the parents, qualified as "bodily injury." *Voorhees v. Preferred Mut. Ins.*

Co., 607 A.2d 1255, 1262 (N.J. 1992). The policy defined "bodily injury" as "bodily harm, sickness or disease to a person, including required care, loss of services and death resulting therefrom." *Id.* at 1258. The court held that the teacher's headaches, stomach pains, nausea, depression, and body pains qualified as "bodily injury," concluding that such term is ambiguous as it relates to emotional distress accompanied by physical manifestations, and, therefore, should be interpreted in favor of the insured. *Id.* at 1261–62; *see also SL Indus., Inc. v. Am. Motorists Ins. Co.*, 607 A.2d 1266, 1274 (N.J. 1992) (concluding that sleeplessness is not a physical injury for purposes of "bodily injury" and that purely emotional injuries, without physical manifestations, do not qualify as "bodily injury"); *Abouzaid v. Mansard Gardens Assocs., LLC*, 23 A.3d 338 (N.J. 2011) (addressing *Voorhees* and *SL Indus.* in detail); *Abouzaid v. Mansard Gardens Associates, LLC*, 23 A.3d 338 (N.J. 2011) ("[W]e presume that the extraordinary level of emotional distress required to support a *Portee* claim—'severe emotional distress,'—will, in most cases, bear with it a physical component. Thus, a policy providing coverage for claims of 'bodily injury' will be understood to require a defense from the filing of a *Portee* complaint unless such defense is specifically excluded by other contract language.") ("[U]nlike a garden-variety emotional distress claim, a *Portee* claim does not *require* the physical sequelae which, in *Voorhees*, we declared rendered the term 'bodily injury' in the policy ambiguous.") (A *Portee* claim (*Portee v. Jaffee*, 417 A.2d 521 (N.J. 1980) requires (1) the death or serious physical injury of another caused by defendant's negligence; (2) a marital or intimate, familial relationship between plaintiff and the injured person; (3) observation of the death or injury at the scene of the accident; and (4) resulting severe emotional distress.); *Sentinel Ins. Co. v. Benedetto*, No. 19-20142, 2021 U.S. Dist. LEXIS 53220 (D.N.J. Mar. 22, 2021) (stating that a plain reading of the insured's general liability policy indicated that lawsuit alleging "only emotional or psychological injuries" arising out of sexual misconduct did not allege "bodily injury") (noting that "mental anguish" was included as a form of bodily injury; however, the policy clearly did so "only in the context of mental anguish that 'aris[es] out of' physical injury, sickness, or disease," and no physical injury, sickness or disease was alleged in the lawsuit).

New Mexico: The Court of Appeals of New Mexico held that a bystander claim for emotional distress did not qualify as "bodily injury" for purposes of an uninsured motorist policy. *Economy Preferred Ins. Co. v. Quanxi Jia*, 92 P.3d 1280, 1284 (N.M. Ct. App. 2004). The policy defined "bodily injury" as "bodily harm, sickness or disease, including death that results." *Id.* at 1282. The Court of Appeals noted that the Supreme Court of New Mexico, in *Gonzales v. Allstate Insurance Co.*, 921 P.2d 944

(N.M. 1996), held that, by its plain meaning, "bodily injury" constitutes injury to the physical body and not mental and emotional injuries. *Id.* at 1283. However, the court also stated that *Gonzales* left open the possibility that physical manifestation of emotional injury might constitute bodily injury. *Id.* The Court of Appeals concluded that physical manifestation of emotional injury qualified as bodily injury. *Id.* at 1284. However, the court held that the specific maladies before it did not qualify as the requisite physical manifestation. *Id.* "We do not resolve what would be sufficient to constitute bodily injury; we simply hold that crying, shaking, and sleep difficulties are not enough." *Id.* In *Hart v. State Farm Mutual Automobile Insurance Co.*, 193 P.3d 565, 568 (N.M. Ct. App. 2008), the Court of Appeals of New Mexico characterized its decision in *Economy Preferred* as holding that an uninsured motorist policy affords no coverage for emotional damages unless the injury is physical in nature. Noting a similarity to *Economy Preferred*, the *Hart* Court likewise concluded that a claim for the physical, cognitive, or emotional manifestations of the effects of a sexual touching of a child (taking place in an uninsured vehicle) did not qualify as "bodily injury" under her parents' uninsured motorist policy. *Id. See also Arnold v. Farmers Ins. Co. of Arizona*, No. 09–0330, 2012 U.S. Dist. LEXIS 67262 (D.N.M. May 10, 2012) (summarizing New Mexico case law on the issue of emotional injury as "bodily injury" but in an unrelated context); *USAA Cas. Ins. Co. v. Calderon*, No. 18-588, 2019 U.S. Dist. LEXIS 106001 (D.N.M. Jun. 25, 2019), *aff'd* 818 Fed. Appx. 828 (10th Cir. 2020) (addressing number of limits available under an automobile policy) ("The language of the contract controls this dispute, and, pursuant to *Gonzales*, the Court must use the definition of bodily injury in the contract rather than the 'plain meaning' of the term. Under USAA's own definition, Ms. Calderon's loss of consortium claim is a bodily injury because it is a mental injury that arose out of physical injury to some person, i.e., her husband.").

New York: The Court of Appeals of New York held that a claim under a general liability policy issued to a landlord, for emotional distress sustained by tenants when a portion of the ceiling in their apartment collapsed, qualified as "bodily injury." *Lavanant v. Gen. Acc. Ins. Co. of Am.*, 595 N.E.2d 819, 822 (N.Y. 1992). The policy defined "bodily injury" as "bodily injury, sickness or disease." *Id.* at 820. The court concluded that the term "bodily injury" was ambiguous. *Id.* at 822. "We decline General Accident's invitation to rewrite the contract to add '*bodily* sickness' and '*bodily* disease,' and a requirement of prior physical contact for compensable mental injury. General Accident could itself have specified such limitations in drafting its policy, but it did not do so." *Id.*; *see also State Farm Mut. Auto. Ins. Co. v.*

Glinbizzi, 780 N.Y.S. 2d 434 (N.Y. App. Div. 2004) (holding that a definition of "bodily injury" in an automobile policy that was seemingly specifically drafted to avoid coverage for bystander claims under *Lavanant*—"bodily injury to a person and sickness, disease or death which results from it"—was ambiguous and could mean that any sickness, disease, or death to any person is covered if it results from bodily injury to the same or a different person); *Jewish Community Center of Staten Island v. Trumbull Ins. Co.*, 957 F. Supp. 2d 215 (E.D.N.Y. 2013) ("[T]he Spinelli complaint alleges that the then-minor plaintiff was 'humiliated' and 'emotionally ... injured,' that he 'felt ashamed' and 'helpless,' and that he became 'angry, defiant, erratic and withdrawn' as a result of the abuse he suffered. Neither Trumbull nor the JCC has disputed these allegations. But, they are significant on this point. New York courts have repeatedly held that emotional distress of the nature described in the Spinelli complaint constitutes 'bodily injury' for insurance law purposes."); *Inc. Vill. of Old Westbury v. Am. Alternative Ins. Corp.*, No. 15-7278, 2017 U.S. Dist. LEXIS 51963 (E.D.N.Y. Mar. 31, 2017) (distinguishing *Lavanant* on the basis that here the policy's definition of "bodily injury" stated that it included "mental anguish, mental injury, shock, fright, or death resulting from bodily injury, sickness, or disease" and, thus, the mental and emotional injuries at issue had to result from "an independent bodily injury" to be covered and rejecting the argument that "unwanted physical contact or physical confinement, without more, constitutes a 'bodily injury'").

North Carolina: The Court of Appeals of North Carolina held that a claim under a general liability policy issued to an employer, for emotional distress sustained by an employee (which would allegedly decrease his life expectancy), on account of wrongful termination and discrimination, qualified as "bodily injury." *Fieldcrest Cannon, Inc. v. Fireman's Fund Ins. Co.*, 477 S.E.2d 59, 72 (N.C. App. Ct. 1996). The policy defined "bodily injury" as "bodily injury, sickness or disease sustained by any person which occurs during the policy period, including death at any time resulting therefrom." *Id.* at 66. The court held that the employee made a *prima facie* claim for negligent infliction of emotional distress, which is "bodily injury" under the policy. *Id.* at 72.

North Dakota: The Supreme Court of North Dakota held that a claim for post-traumatic stress disorder, resulting in vomiting, weight loss, severe headaches, loss of sleep, night sweats, and nightmares, qualified as "bodily injury" under an automobile policy. *Hartman v. Estate of Anthony J. Miller*, 656 N.W.2d 676, 685 (N.D. 2003). The policy defined "bodily injury" as "bodily injury to or sickness, disease or death of any person." *Id.* at 677. The court agreed with the rationale of *Trinh v. Allstate Ins. Co.*, 37 P.3d 1259 (Wash. Ct. App. 2002) and held that the term "bodily injury" within the meaning of the policy included "post-traumatic stress disorder accompanied by nontransitory physical manifestations." *Id.* at 685.

Ohio: The Court of Appeals of Ohio held that an insured's claim for mental anguish, on account of the death of his brother, did not qualify as "bodily injury" under an uninsured/underinsured motorist policy. *Gilkey v. Gibson*, No. 97APE11–1477, 1998 Ohio App. LEXIS 3807 (Ohio Ct. App. Aug. 20, 1998). The policy defined "bodily injury," in pertinent part, as "physical injury to or sickness, disease, or death of any person." The court noted that, while the policy defined "bodily injury" broadly, to include in the terms "sickness" or "disease," the term under consideration was "bodily injury" not simply "injury." The court held that, because the word "bodily" must have some meaning in the context of the policy and cannot be ignored, "the injury, sickness, or disease under consideration must originate in the body as distinguished from the psyche. The definition does not encompass nonphysical, emotional, or mental harm originating in the mind, not the body."; *see also Allstate Ins. Co. v. Oldham*, No. 2002-P-0008, 2003 Ohio App. LEXIS 861 (Ohio Ct. App. Feb. 28, 2003) (holding that humiliation and embarrassment did not constitute "bodily injury" under a homeowner's policy); *Moore v. State Auto. Mut.*, No. H-98-012, 1998 Ohio App. LEXIS 4829 (Ohio Ct. App. Oct. 9, 1998) (following *Gilkey*); *Westfield Ins. Co. v. Porchervina*, No. 2008-L-025, 2008 Ohio App. LEXIS 5466 (Ohio Ct. App. Dec. 12, 2008) ("Pursuant to the language of the policy, 'bodily injury means bodily harm, sickness or disease, including required care, loss of services and death that result.' Generally, emotional distress does not qualify within the definition of bodily injury for the purposes of an insurance contract."); *World Harvest Church v. Grange Mut. Cas. Co.*, No. 13AP–290, 2013 Ohio App. LEXIS 5994 (Ohio Ct. App. Dec. 24, 2013) ("[E]ven in those jurisdictions in which emotional distress damages do not qualify as 'bodily injury' for insurance coverage, these damages may nevertheless be covered as damages *'because of'* bodily injury[.]") (emphasis added) (*rev'd on other grounds* 68 N.E.3d 738 (Ohio 2016)); *Grange Ins. Co. v. Sawmiller*, 11 N.E. 3d 1199 (Ohio Ct. App. Apr. 7, 2014) ("In light of the large body of longstanding case law, we join our sister appellate districts and hold that PTSD and physical symptoms stemming therefrom are not within the definition of 'bodily injury' as defined herein.") (addressing coverage under automobile policy for bystander from seeing her sister struck and killed by an automobile (sisters walking side-by-side at time of incident)) (policy defined "bodily injury" as "bodily harm, sickness or disease, including death that results"); *Cincinnati Specialty Underwriters Ins. Co. v. Larschied*, No. 1–14–01, 2014 Ohio App. LEXIS 4036 (Ohio Ct. App. Sept. 22, 2014) ("Even where, as here, the term 'bodily injury' is defined using the words 'bodily injury,' the term is not ambiguous and should not be construed against the insurer in favor of coverage for emotional injuries.").

Oklahoma: The Supreme Court of Oklahoma held that a husband's loss of consortium claim did not qualify as "bodily injury" under an underinsured motorist policy. *Littlefield v. State Farm Fire & Cas. Co.*, 857 P.2d 65, 70–71 (Okla. 1993). The policy defined "bodily injury" as "bodily injury to a person and sickness, disease or death which results from it." *Id.* at 67. The husband argued that his loss of consortium claim should be considered a separate "bodily injury," thereby invoking the policy's "per accident" limit. *Id.* at 68. The court held that, because the policy referred to "all damages due to bodily injury to one person," and because only the wife suffered "bodily injury," the "each person" limit applied. *Id.* at 70. Although the decision was based on the policy language, the Oklahoma high court also stated that "[w]hile the husband may have suffered emotionally, he has not incurred a bodily injury within the meaning of the policy." *Id.* at 70. *See also Nat'l Fire Ins. Co. v. NWM-Oklahoma, LLC, Inc.*, 546 F. Supp. 2d 1238 (W.D. Ok. 2008) ("The court concludes that the Oklahoma courts, when faced with the issue, would follow the majority view. In the underlying action, plaintiffs have only alleged that they suffered 'ridicule, extreme embarrassment and humiliation and severe mental distress.' With no allegations other than nonphysical or emotional harm, the court concludes that the allegations in the underlying action are not sufficient to constitute 'bodily injury.'"); *North Star Mut. Ins. Co. v. Henderson-Schultz*, No. 15-217, 2016 U.S. Dist. LEXIS 45268 (N.D. Okla. Apr. 4, 2016) ("[T]he Court finds that the language of the Policy defines 'bodily injury' to exclude coverage for physical injury which arises from emotional or mental injury. The undisputed facts evidence that Erwin sustained no physical injury during the shooting.") (decision tied to policy's definition of "bodily injury," which is not stated in the opinion); *State Farm Fire & Cas. Co. v. Aberdeen Enterprizes II*, No. 18-654, 2020 U.S. Dist. LEXIS 140658 (N.D. Okla. Aug. 6, 2020) ("Nowhere in their SAC do the Underlying Plaintiffs allege bodily injury, sickness, disease, or death. Instead, the Underlying Plaintiffs allege 'economic harm,' 'physical bodily confinement,' and 'physical restraint.' One of the Underlying Plaintiffs, David Smith, alleges he 'experienced stress and anxiety.' Physical confinement and physical restraint do not constitute 'bodily injury, sickness, or disease.'") (noting that "[e]ven emotional distress, which the Underlying Plaintiffs have not alleged, does not constitute 'bodily injury' in the insurance context").

Oregon: An Oregon District Court held that a claim under a general liability policy issued to property owner-sellers, for physical manifestation of emotional distress sustained by homeowners who purchased the property and then seemingly learned of the historic release of asbestos on it, qualified as "bodily injury." *Am. States Ins. Co. v. Bercot*, No. 03–637-CO, 2004 U.S. Dist. LEXIS 13057 (D. Or. July 1, 2004). The policy defined "bodily injury" as "bodily injury, sickness or disease sustained by any person." The court held that the physical manifestation of emotional distress, on account of the release of asbestos to the atmosphere and the environment which threatened the homeowners' health, qualified as "bodily injury."; *see also Klamath Pac. Corp. v. Reliance Ins. Co.*, 950 P.2d 909 (Or. Ct. App. 1997) (finding that, even if the insurer were correct, that emotional distress did not qualify as "bodily injury" unless it resulted from physical trauma to the body, the facts at issue—grabbing one's breasts and buttocks—could have caused the requisite trauma); *Allstate Indem. Co. v. Puzey*, No. 13-01520, 2014 U.S. Dist. LEXIS 184290 (D. Or. July 1, 2014) ("[B]oth commentators and tribunals alike identify the majority view to espouse that 'absent physical manifestations or physical contact, purely emotional distress allegations are insufficient to qualify as bodily injury. However, J.H. alleges that she suffered not only mental and emotional distress, but also physical symptoms as a result of defendants' alleged conduct. In particular, she alleges that she 'suffered severe mental and emotional distress which triggered a stress related heart condition requiring her to have to undergo heart surgery' and 'has endured, and will continue to endure, permanent pain.' That allegation of harm falls within the definition of 'bodily injury' in the Policy."); *Zweizig v. Northwest Direct Teleservices, Inc.*, 331 F. Supp. 3d 1173 (D. Or. 2018) (interpreting Oregon statute that caps non-economic damages and not citing coverage cases) ("[T]he Court's interpretation--that emotional distress is a type of bodily injury--is not inconsistent with Oregon case law, which has recognized that certain claims for purely emotional distress are considered claims for injury to one's person under Oregon law.").

Pennsylvania: In *Lipsky v. State Farm Mut. Auto. Ins. Co.*, No. 565 EDA 2010 (Pa. Super. Ct. Sept. 1, 2011) all three judges on a panel of the Superior Court addressed differently whether emotional injury qualified as "bodily injury." The majority concluded that claims of "physical complaints" and "great detriment and loss" from emotional and mental anguish brought negligent infliction of emotional distress claims within the ambit of the "bodily injury to a person" definition of "bodily injury" in an automobile policy. *Id.* at 10. The Pennsylvania Supreme Court affirmed, but on the basis that the Justices eligible to vote were equally divided. As a result, the court ruled that, by operation of law, the Superior Court's decision was affirmed. *Lipsky v. State Farm Mut. Auto. Ins. Co.*, 84 A.3d 1056 (Pa. 2014). In *Steadfast Ins. Co. v. Tomei*, No. 2014 - 477, 478, 479, 2016 Pa. Super. Unpub. LEXIS 1864 (Pa. Super. Ct. May 24, 2016), the court addressed several cases on the emotional injury as bodily injury issue and concluded: "[S]ome of the underlying plaintiffs alleged vague physical symptoms brought on by their emotional distress after learning that offensive videos [of them in varying states of undress in a tanning booth] had been posted to the internet. Even the 12 plaintiffs who at least alleged some physical symptoms associated with emotional distress did not allege any antecedent physical injury or impact, to themselves or anyone else. Nor did they allege anything resembling a 'disease' as in *Glikman* [*v. Progressive Casualty*, 917 A.2d 872 (Pa. Super. Ct. 2007)]. The trial court correctly held that the underlying plaintiffs' claims for emotional distress, humiliation and embarrassment did not qualify as claims for 'bodily injury' under either the Steadfast or Nationwide policy, and therefore, they were not required to provide a defense under Coverage A." *Id.* at *13-14. The *Tomei* court also cautioned that *Lipsky*, an unpublished memorandum decision from the Superior Court, cannot be relied upon or cited by a court or party in any other proceeding, and that *Lipsky*, involving a bystander negligent infliction claim, in which plaintiffs witnessed the vehicular homicide of a family member, was factually distinguishable. *See also Allstate Property and Cas. Ins. Co. v. Winslow*, 66 F. Supp. 3d 661 (E.D. Pa. 2014) (discussing the issue in detail, including *Lipsky*, and making a decision involving non-typical policy language); *Evans v. Travelers Ins. Co.*, 226 A.3d 96 (Pa. Super. Ct. 2019) (issue of fact whether plaintiff's PTSD resulted from bodily harm in motor vehicle accident); *Doe v. Liberty Mut. Fire Ins. Co.*, No. 18-1513, 2019 U.S. Dist. LEXIS 156827 (M.D. Pa. Sept. 13, 2019) (undertaking comprehensive look at Pennsylvania decisions on the issue) ("Here the definition in the Policy, expressed in the alternative, provides that bodily injury includes more than physical injury—it also includes 'disease or sickness' and 'disease or sickness can encompass mental and psychological disorders which either have been or may be diagnosed. In sum, consistent with *Glikman, Becker* [*v. Farmington Cas. Co.*, No. 08-2228, 2010 U.S. Dist. LEXIS 73902 (M.D. Pa. July 22, 2010)], and *Winslow* the term 'bodily injury' in the Policy does not require a physical harm to trigger coverage, and conditions caused by mental distress can qualify as 'bodily injury.'") ("Though the allegations in the underlying complaint do not allege that John Doe 1 has a diagnosis of post-traumatic stress disorder as in *Glikman*, the allegations include physical manifestations of stress including stomachaches and sleep disruption which may be deemed sickness and/or support the diagnosis of a disease such as the PTSD diagnosed in *Glikman*.").

In *Glikman v. Progressive Cas. Ins. Co.*, 917 A.2d 872 (Pa. Super. Ct. 2007), the court held that PTSD qualified as "bodily injury," under an auto policy that defined the term as "bodily harm, sickness, or disease, including death that results from bodily harm, sickness, or disease." *Id.* at 873. "We agree with Appellant that pursuant to Appellee's policy, there are four separate types of 'bodily injury': bodily harm, sickness, disease, and/or death that results from the first three. 'Disease' is a separately identified bodily injury in the policy. As the policy language clearly states that 'bodily injury' includes any 'disease' caused by an automobile accident, we must give effect to the language of the contract. Thus, under the language of Appellee's policy, contraction of a 'disease' caused by an accident arising out of the maintenance or use of a motor vehicle is a specifically covered bodily injury under the policy. As Appellee neither disputes that post-traumatic stress disorder is a disease nor the cause of Appellant's suffering, we find she has sustained a bodily injury within the meaning of the policy." *Id.* The court distinguished *Zerr v. Erie Ins. Exch.*, 667 A.2d 237 (Pa. Super. Ct. 1995), where "bodily injury" was defined as "accidental bodily harm to a person and that person's resulting illness, disease or death. *Id.* at 873-74. For additional cases addressing the issue, with some discussing *Glikman, see Babalola v. Donegal Group, Inc.*, No. 08-621, 2008 U.S. Dist. LEXIS 65207 (M.D. Pa. Aug. 26, 2008); *Nationwide Mut. Ins. Co. v. Garzone*, Nos. 07-4767 and 08-3895, 2009 U.S. Dist. LEXIS 85528 (E.D. Pa. Sept. 17, 2009); and *State Auto. Mut. Ins. Co. v. Angellilli*, No. 11–3425, 2013 U.S. Dist. LEXIS 11508 (E.D. Pa. Jan. 29, 2013).

Rhode Island: The Supreme Court of Rhode Island held that a claim under a homeowner's policy issued to a doctor, for humiliation, shame, emotional distress, and mental anguish sustained by a patient whose blood alcohol level became public, did not qualify as "bodily injury." *Mellow v. Medical Malpractice Joint Underwriting Ass'n of R.I.*, 567 A.2d 367, 368 (R.I. 1989). The policy defined "bodily injury" as "any physical harm, sickness, or disease and includes any care that is required or any services that are lost or death that results from bodily injury." *Id.* The court concluded that the complaint "allege[d] an invasion of privacy that led to emotional, rather than physical harm." *Id.*; *see also Aetna Cas. & Sur. Co. v. Wannamoisett Country Club, Inc.*, 706 A.2d 1329, 1330 (R.I. 1998) (holding that a claim under the employer's liability section of a workers' compensation policy, for battery and non-consensual touching, did not allege bodily injury).

South Carolina: A South Carolina District Court held that a claim under a general liability policy issued to a beer distributor, for loss of reputation, mental anguish, humiliation, and loss of enjoyment of life sustained by an employee for a racially motivated firing, did not qualify as "bodily injury." *Jefferson-Pilot Fire & Cas. Co. v. Sunbelt Beer Distribs., Inc.*, 839 F. Supp. 376, 379 (D.S.C. 1993). The policy defined "bodily injury" as "bodily injury, sickness, or disease sustained by a person, including death resulting from these at any time." *Id.* The court held that it was "not prepared to extend the interpretation of 'bodily injury' to include purely emotional damage absent some objective indication of physical symptoms." *Id.* In reaching its decision, the *Sunbelt* Court declined to follow the District of South Carolina's decision in *Allstate Ins. Co. v. Biggerstaff*, 703 F. Supp. 23 (D.S.C. 1989) or the Supreme Court of South Carolina's decision in *State Farm Mut. Ins. Co. v. Ramsey*, 374 S.E.2d 896 (S.C. 1988), which the *Sunbelt* Court characterized as recognizing that emotional trauma may constitute bodily injury for purposes of insurance coverage. *Id.* at 379. According to the *Sunbelt* Court, both *Biggerstaff* and *Ramsey* in fact involved physical manifestation of emotional injury, since they were addressing claims for negligent infliction of emotional distress, which has, as an essential element, "emotional distress [that] must both manifest itself by physical symptoms capable of objective diagnosis and be established by expert testimony." *Id.* at 379 n.3.

South Dakota: A South Dakota District Court held that a claim under a commercial general liability policy issued to a municipality, for high blood pressure sustained by the wife of a cancer-stricken municipal employee, on account of the municipality's group health insurance policy being cancelled, qualified as "bodily injury." *Western Cas. & Sur. Co. v. Waisanen*, 653 F. Supp. 825, 832 (D.S.D. 1987). The policy defined "bodily injury" as "bodily injury, sickness, or disease sustained by any person which occurs during the policy period, including death at any time resulting therefrom." *Id.* The court's opinion suggests that it may have ruled otherwise if the wife's injuries were solely emotional, which had been alleged in addition to high blood pressure. *Id.* (distinguishing *Rolette County v. Western Cas. & Sur. Co.*, 452 F. Supp. 125 (D.N.D. 1978), which held that coverage was denied because allegations were limited to mental anguish and emotional distress and there were no allegations of physical harm).

Tennessee: The Court of Appeals of Tennessee held that a claim under a commercial general liability policy issued to an employer, for emotional distress suffered by a female employee who was subjected to gender and racial discrimination, did not qualify as "bodily injury." *American Indem. Co. v. Foy Trailer Rentals, Inc.*, No. W2000–00397-COA-R3-CV, 2000 Tenn. App. LEXIS 794 (Tenn. Ct. App. Nov. 28, 2000). The policy defined "bodily injury" as "bodily injury, sickness or disease sustained by a person, including death resulting from these at any time." The court relied on, among other cases *Guardian Life Ins. Co. of Am. v. Richardson*, 129 S.W.2d 1107 (Tenn. Ct. App. 1939), which held that, when "disease" is unrestricted by anything in context, it includes disease of the mind as well as the body. However, when disease is restricted by the word "bodily," and when "bodily" grammatically modifies "disease" and "injury," it was inserted for the purpose of excluding mental disease. *Id.* In *Garrison v. Bickford*, 377 S.W.3d 659 (Tenn. 2012), the Supreme Court of Tennessee held that "a bystander claim for negligent infliction of emotional distress . . . is not a claim for bodily harm. Accordingly, we conclude that in the context of purely emotional injuries, the phrase 'bodily injury' as defined in the policy before us, is unambiguous. Its ordinary meaning connotes a physical injury. Thus, we hold that, as applied to this case, 'bodily injury' does not include damages for emotional harm alone. We further conclude that the definition of 'bodily injury' in the policy does not conflict with the uninsured motorist statute, section 56–7–1201(a).") (court provided a lengthy national survey of the issue and noted that its conclusion was in accord with the "overwhelming majority of jurisdictions which have considered the issue [and held] that 'bodily injury' standing alone or defined in a policy as 'bodily injury' [or harm], sickness or disease' is unambiguous and encompasses only physical harm."). *See also Nationwide Affinity Ins. Co. of Am. v. Richards*, No.19-02357, 2020 U.S. Dist. LEXIS 14685 (W.D. Tenn. Jan. 29, 2020) (discussing *Garrison*) ("The Miller Policy contemplates liability for emotional distress or mental anguish that is 'the direct result of bodily harm.' Nationwide does not assert that Defendants are barred from recovering damages for emotional distress or mental anguish resulting from their physical injuries in the January 7, 2018 accident -- which is the only type of damages for emotional distress or mental anguish Defendants seek.").

Texas: The Supreme Court of Texas held that a claim under a homeowner's policy issued to a clerk at a photo developing store, for severe mental pain, loss of privacy and humiliation, sustained by a customer whose revealing photos were disseminated to others, did not qualify as "bodily injury." *Trinity Universal Ins. Co. v. Cowan*, 945 S.W.2d 819, 820 (Tex. 1997). The policy defined "bodily injury" as "bodily harm, sickness or disease." *Id.* The court held that, "absent an allegation of physical manifestation of mental anguish, a claim of mental anguish is not a 'bodily injury' as defined in the policy for purposes of invoking the duty to defend." *Id.*; *see also Haralson v. State Farm Mut. Auto. Ins. Co.*, 564 F. Supp. 2d 616, 626–27 (N.D. Tex. 2008) (holding that extreme emotional distress accompanied by headaches, migraines, stomach aches, nausea, and sleeplessness, qualified as bodily injury for purposes of a bystander claim under an uninsured motorist policy); *East Rio Hondo Water Supply Corp. v. Am. Alternative Ins. Corp.*, 748 F. Supp. 2d 636, 647 (S.D. Tex. 2010) ("[T]he Court finds that the underlying plaintiffs and intervener potentially seek damages for mental anguish without physical manifestation. Thus, the underlying pleadings potentially allege at least one covered pure mental anguish claim which is not cognizable as 'bodily injury' under *Cowan*, 945 S.W.2d at 821. Consequently, because the intentional acts exclusion applies only to 'bodily injury' and 'property damage' as the insurance policy defines those terms, it does not negate coverage of these potential mental anguish allegations."). In *Evanston Ins. Co. v. Legacy of Life, Inc.*, 370 S.W.3d 377 (Tex. 2012), the Supreme Court of Texas held that an insurance policy providing coverage of 'personal injury,' defined as 'bodily injury, sickness, or disease including death resulting therefrom sustained by any person,' did not include coverage for mental anguish, unrelated to physical damage to or disease of the plaintiff's body. The court based its decision on *Cowan*, concluding that it contained definitions that were virtually identical as well as grammatical rules. At issue was coverage for a claim by a woman – who did not sustain physical injury -- against an organ donor charity, for its sale of her mother's tissue to a for-profit enterprise. *See also McClain v. State Farm Fire & Cas. Co.*, No. 02-16-00315, 2017 Tex. App. LEXIS 1788 (Tex. Ct. App. Mar. 2, 2017) ("Covered bodily-injury damages were specifically defined in the policy: 'Bodily injury' means bodily injury, sickness, or disease sustained by a person, including death resulting from any of these at any time. 'Bodily injury' includes mental anguish or other mental injury caused by the 'bodily injury.'") (rejecting argument that allegations of emotional distress are sufficient to constitute bodily injury on the basis that the phrase "caused by the 'bodily injury'" modifies only mental injury, not mental anguish, so, therefore, mental anguish does not have to be a result of a physical injury to be covered under the policy); *Metro Lloyds Ins. Co. v. Werkstell*, No. 16-00280, 2017 U.S. Dist. LEXIS 168826 (E.D. Tex. May 16, 2017) (definition of "bodily injury" excluded "emotional distress, mental anguish, humiliation, mental distress, mental injury, or any similar injury unless the direct result of physical harm") (plaintiffs alleged that "[t]he mothball smell has exacted a steep toll on [them] - emotionally, financially and physically") (holding that this was sufficient to allege "bodily injury"; however "any claims against Defendants for emotional or mental anguish damages would be barred by either the express Policy language for "bodily injury" and/or the Emotional and Mental Anguish Exclusion"); *Evanston Ins. Co. v. Alden Roofing Co., LLC*, No. 16-2626, 2017 U.S. Dist. LEXIS 81845 (N.D. Tex. May 30, 2017) (stating that "mental anguish, loss of consortium, and other economic injuries" were not injuries covered by the policy because "[u]nder Texas law, emotional injuries such as mental anguish are not considered bodily injuries in a commercial general liability policy") (citing *Cowan*); *Centauri Spec. Ins. Co. v. Hansen*, 369 F. Supp. 3d 796 (S.D. Tex. 2018) (citing *Cowan* in support of a finding that the plaintiff in the underlying lawsuit, who alleged "emotional pain, mental anguish, medical care expenses, and humiliation" did not allege "bodily injury" as defined in the insured's policy because "bodily injury 'does not include purely emotional injuries . . . . and unambiguously requires an injury to the physical structure of the human body'").

Utah: A Utah District Court held that a claim under a homeowner's policy issued to an individual, for emotional distress sustained by his minor-niece on account of his sexual touching, qualified as "bodily injury." *Am. Nat. Prop. and Cas. Co. v. Jackson*, No. 1:07-CV-00163, 2010 U.S. Dist. LEXIS 61514 (D. Utah June 21, 2010). The policy defined "bodily injury" as "bodily harm, sickness or disease, including required care, loss of services, and death resulting therefrom." "To be sure, most jurisdictions hold that the term 'bodily injury' does not encompass *purely* emotional harm. Nevertheless, many of these jurisdictions also recognize that 'emotional distress with appreciable physical manifestations can qualify as a 'bodily injury' within the meaning of [an] insurance policy.' Thus, if appreciable physical manifestations accompany the PTSD, OCD and emotional distress alleged in the Complaint, they too, in addition to the injuries from Michael's sexual misconduct, constitute cognizable bodily injuries within the Policy's definition." (emphasis in original). The court went on to conclude that, based on medical information, symptoms of PTSD and OCD include those that are physical. *In Progressive Cas. Ins. Co. v. Ewart*, 167 P.3d 1011 (Utah 2007), the Supreme Court of Utah held that a Utah statute, requiring mandatory liability limits for bodily injury, did not require an insurer to pay a separate policy limit for a loss of consortium claim brought by the spouse of an insured driver. *Id.* at 1015. The court noted that the question whether claims for emotional or psychological injuries are claims for "bodily injury" was not before it. *Id.* at n.15. However, the court commented that "'bodily' is commonly understood to refer to, simply, the 'body,'" and the spouse's loss of consortium claim in no way involves a bodily injury to her. *Id.* at 1014. *See also Cannon v. State Farm Mut. Auto.*

Ins. Co., No. 13–186, 2013 U.S. Dist. LEXIS 145598 (D. Utah Oct. 7, 2013) (taking guidance from *Ewart* and holding that "loss of consortium is not a bodily injury and therefore not covered within the policy's UIM Insuring Agreement.") ("According to the definitions provided by the policy [Bodily Injury means bodily injury to a person and sickness, disease, or death that results from it], Mr. Cannon did not have a bodily injury and thus did not suffer sickness, disease, or death resulting from his loss of consortium."); *McKeen v. USAA Cas. Ins. Co.*, No. 14-00396, 2015 U.S. Dist. LEXIS 172281 (D. Utah Dec. 28, 2015) ("Ms. McKeen argues 'while there is no physical injury to [her] reproductive system that prevents her from conceiving, there is a physical injury to her brain that manifests itself in myriad [ways], all of which have combined to prevent her from rearing children.' Her ability to conceive is irrelevant, according to Ms. McKeen, because she 'is *not* seeking compensation for emotional harm . . . .' Instead, she argues, she is seeking compensation for the consequences flowing from her brain injury. This is the correct analysis, and USAA's attempt to classify Ms. McKeen's injuries as 'purely emotional' is rejected.") ("[E]ven if Ms. McKeen were seeking compensation for emotional harm, it is not certain that she would be unable to show appreciable 'physical manifestations' resulting from her alleged emotional harm. Ms. McKeen has asserted that she experiences 'chronic migraine headaches and neck pain; sensitivity to noise and light; irregular sleeping patterns and physical and mental fatigue; dysnosmia and anosmia; impaired executive functioning and memory; diminished concentration, thought and speech processing; and chronic vertigo and nausea.' It is unclear whether these conditions are physical manifestations resulting from emotional harm, or are independent physical injuries in and of themselves.").

Vermont: The Supreme Court of Vermont held that a claim for emotional distress, as a result of exposure to formaldehyde gas, qualified as "bodily injury" under a homeowner's policy that provided coverage for damages "because of" bodily injury. *American Protection Ins. Co. v. McMahan*, 562 A.2d 462, 466 (Vt. 1989). "We held above that 'bodily injury' includes exposure to a toxic product. It follows that American is under a duty to defend and indemnify the McMahans for any damages incurred *because of* exposure to such product. This duty includes the emotional distress damages claimed by the Livaks." *Id.* (emphasis in original). In *Knutsen v. State Farm Fire & Cas. Co.*, 375 F. Supp. 3d 514 (D. Vt. 2019), the Policy at issue defined "bodily injury" as "physical injury, sickness, or disease to a person" and explicitly excluded "[e]motional distress . . . unless it arises out of actual physical injury to some person." Noting that the Vermont Supreme Court has not addressed the specific issue, the court looked to cases nationally. The federal court concluded that allegations of tingly fingers and trouble sleeping are not "bodily injury," but "slight physical manifestations may offer insight into the severity or extent of [the plaintiff's] emotional harm." *Id.* at 522.

Virginia: A Virginia District Court held that a claim under a general liability policy issued to a bank, for emotional distress sustained by an employee on account of wrongful termination, did not qualify as "bodily injury." *W. Am. Ins. Co. v. Bank of Isle of Wright*, 673 F. Supp. 760, 765 (E.D. Va. 1987). The court did not state whether the policy contained a definition of "bodily injury." Relying on a then recent Virginia District Court decision, *American & Foreign Insurance Co. v. Church Schools*, 645 F. Supp. 628 (E.D. Va. 1986), and the prevailing rule in other jurisdictions, the court held that coverage for "bodily injury" was limited to physical injury to the body and did not include claims for emotional harm. *Id.* The opinion does not address whether physical manifestation of emotional injury can qualify as bodily injury. *See also Rockingham Mut. Ins. Co. v. Davis*, No. CL01–12576, 2002 Va. Cir. LEXIS 163 (Va. Cir. Ct. Apr. 26, 2002) (distinguishing *Isle of Wright* because the underlying plaintiff's claim against the insured for inappropriate touching alleged, in addition to emotional injury, physical pain on account of the plaintiff's arm being grabbed, which constituted "bodily injury" under a homeowner's policy); *Liberty University, Inc. v. Citizens Ins. Co. of America*, 16 F. Supp. 3d 636 (W.D. Va. 2014) ("A deprivation of medical and dental health care, especially over time, could *lead to* or *result in* physical damage to a person's body, or to an unhealthy physical condition or illness. But the Jenkins Complaint did not allege these deprivations led to any specific physical damage, pain, or harm to Isabella. Therefore, the Jenkins Complaint did not allege 'bodily injury' as defined under Virginia law and as understood in its plain and ordinary meaning.") (emphasis in original); *Scottsdale Ins. Co. v. Doe*, No. 13–00342, 2014 U.S. Dist. LEXIS 153998 (W.D. Va. Oct. 30, 2014) ("[T]he facts of *Church Schools* do not begin to resemble the forcible sexual abuse alleged in this case. The allegations of forcible sexual assault resulting in psychological harm, including physical cutting, fall with the policy definition of 'bodily injury.'").

Washington: The Court of Appeals of Washington held that a bystander claim for emotional distress, accompanied by inability to eat, constant sickness to the stomach, vomiting, and hair loss, qualified as "bodily injury" for purposes of an uninsured motorist policy. *Trinh v. Allstate Ins. Co.*, 37 P.3d 1259, 1264 (Wash. Ct. App. 2002). The policy defined "bodily injury" as "bodily injury, sickness, disease or death." *Id.* at 1264. Following a review of a litany of cases nationally addressing the issue, and observing that the definition of "bodily injury" before it included sickness or disease, the court held that "bodily injury" includes emotional injuries that are accompanied by physical manifestations. *Id.* at 1264; *see also Daley v. Allstate Ins. Co.*, 958 P.2d 990, 998 (Wash. 1998) ("The term 'bodily injury' is unambiguous and does not include recovery for emotional distress unrelated to a physical injury."); *Grange Ins. Ass'n v. Roberts*, 320 P.3d 77 (Wash. Ct. App. 2013) ("Here, the record contains no evidence or allegation of physical injury. Instead, Brandis alleged purely emotional injuries due to Roberts's statements and actions. Grange has a duty to defend Roberts against claims asserting 'damages because of bodily injury.' As noted above, Grange's policy defines 'bodily injury' as 'bodily injury, sickness or disease sustained by a person, and includes death resulting from any of these at any time.'") (discussing and following *Daley*); *State Farm Fire & Cas. Co. v. El-Moslimany*, 178 F. Supp. 3d 1048 (W.D. Wash. Apr. 15, 2016) ("State Farm's insurance policy requires 'physical harm to a person' for coverage to apply, and expressly excludes coverage for emotional distress or similar injury 'unless it arises out of actual physical injury to some person.' Courts have concluded this definition of 'bodily injury' does not provide coverage for physical symptoms resulting from emotional distress, unless the emotional distress was caused by a physical injury.").

West Virginia: The Supreme Court of Appeals of West Virginia held that a claim under a general liability policy issued to a veterinary office, for emotional distress sustained by an employee on account of unwelcome sexual advances by a veterinarian, did not qualify as "bodily injury." *Smith v. Animal Urgent Care, Inc.*, 542 S.E.2d 827, 831 (W. Va. 2000). The policy defined "bodily injury" as "bodily injury, sickness or disease sustained by a person, including death resulting from any of these at any time." *Id.* at 829. The court examined case law nationally and concluded that the majority position—"bodily injury" is narrower than "personal injury," which covers an affront or insult to a person's reputation or sensibilities—was persuasive. *Id.* at 831. The West Virginia high court held that "in an insurance liability policy, purely mental or emotional harm that arises from a claim of sexual harassment and lacks physical manifestation does not fall within a definition of 'bodily injury' which is limited to 'bodily injury, sickness, or disease.'" *Id.*; *see also Tackett v. Am. Motorists Ins. Co.*, 584 S.E.2d 158, 166 (W. Va. 2004) (holding that "great embarrassment, consternation, mental pain and anguish, and emotional upset" did not constitute "bodily injury" under the insurance policy); *USF Ins. Co. v. Orion Dev. RA XXX, LLC*, 756 F. Supp. 2d 749, 755–56 (N.D. W.Va. 2010) ("The underlying lawsuit in this case alleges a long list of emotional and psychological damages, including humiliation, mental stress, and PTSD. However, this Court finds that none of the damage claims relate to a physical manifestation of any bodily injury arising out of Valecko's sexual misconduct so as to satisfy the definition of 'bodily injury' under the Policy. This Court's finding aligns with that of a majority of courts: absent some physical manifestation or physical contact, purely emotional distress allegations are insufficient to qualify as bodily injury.") (citing *Animal Urgent Care* and *Tackett*) ("This Court acknowledges that the underlying lawsuit contains allegations of unwanted physical contact, but these allegations are not tantamount to physical injury."); *Cherrington v. Erie Ins. Property and Cas. Co.*, 745 S.E.2d 508 (W. Va. 2013) ("The CGL policy at issue herein defines 'bodily injury' as 'bodily injury, sickness or disease sustained by a person, including death resulting from any of these at any time.' In her complaint, Ms. Cherrington avers that she 'has been subjected to emotional distress,' but she does not allege that she has suffered a 'bodily injury, sickness or disease' as a result of the defective workmanship. We previously have held that '[i]n an insurance liability policy, purely mental or emotional harm that ... lacks physical manifestation does not fall within a definition of 'bodily injury' which is limited to 'bodily injury , sickness, or disease.' (citing *Animal Urgent Care*) Because there is no indication that Ms. Cherrington's emotional distress has physically manifested itself, we conclude that she has not sustained a 'bodily injury' to trigger coverage under Pinnacle's CGL policy."); *State Farm Fire & Cas. Co. v. Kenney*, No.14-99, 2015 U.S. Dist. LEXIS 63994 (N.D.W.Va. May 15, 2015) (restating *Smith*) (claims of invasion of privacy and intentional infliction of emotional distress did not constitute bodily injury); *Grand China Buffet & Grill, Inc. v. State Auto Prop. & Cas. Co.*, No. 16-159, 2017 U.S. Dist. LEXIS 74255 (N.D.W.Va. May 16, 2017) (holding that "[h]ere, the Subject Policy defines 'bodily injury' as 'bodily injury, sickness or disease'. In light of clearly established West Virginia precedent, Ullom's underlying claims for statutory violations, 'emotional distress, embarrassment, [and] humiliation,' without more, do not fall within this definition. Ullom simply has not alleged any physical manifestation of these 'purely mental or emotional harm[s].' Therefore, coverage for 'bodily injury' is not triggered under the Subject Policy."); *Liberty Corporate Capital Ltd. v. Peacemaker Nat'l Training Ctr, LLC*, 348 F. Supp. 3d 585 (N.D. W.Va. 2018) ("Peacemaker argues that the Goldsteins have alleged potential bodily injury because in their response to an interrogatory they said they have experienced 'stress and anxiety at a time in their lives when they had hoped to enjoy a peaceful and pleasant retirement.' However, Peacemaker fails to state that the stress and anxiety was a direct result of 'bodily injury, sickness, disease or death' [as required under the policy's definition of "bodily injury"]. Therefore, coverage for 'bodily injury' is not triggered under Coverage A of the Policy."); *State Auto Mut. Ins. Co. v. Allegheny Med. Servs.*, No. 17-00283, 2018 U.S. Dist. LEXIS 64187 (S.D. W.Va. Apr. 17, 2018) (finding that insured's former patients did not allege "bodily injury" because, while they alleged a "a variety of emotional and psychological damages," they did not allege "physical manifestations of those damages," nor did they "contain specific factual allegations of physical injuries resulting from the sexual assaults"); *Cooper v. Westfield Ins. Co.*, 488 F. Supp. 3d 430 (S.D.W.Va. 2020) (noting, in the context of an employment lawsuit alleging "mental and emotional distress," that "[i]t is well-established under West Virginia law that mental and emotional injuries do not constitute 'bodily injury, sickness or disease' as required under the bodily injury portion" of Westfield's commercial general liability policies").

Wisconsin: The Supreme Court of Wisconsin held that a claim under a general liability policy issued to a radio station, for emotional injury sustained by a person against whom station employees filed a false security interest with the secretary of state, qualified as "bodily injury." *Doyle v. Ward Engelke*, 580 N.W.2d 245, 250 (Wis. 1998). The policy defined "bodily injury" as "any physical harm, including sickness or disease, to the physical health of other persons … includ[ing] any of the following that results at any time from such physical harm, sickness or disease[:] Mental anguish, injury or illness. Emotional distress. Care, loss of services, or death." *Id.* at 249. The insurer argued that emotional distress is insufficient to constitute "bodily injury" because of the "physical harm" requirement in the definition. *Id.* The Wisconsin high court disagreed, holding that "we are unable to separate a person's nerves and tensions from his [or her] body. It is common knowledge that worry and anxiety can and often do have a direct effect on other bodily functions." *Id.* at 250 (quoting *Levy v. Duclaux*, 324 So. 2d 1, 10 (La. Ct. App. 1975)) (alteration in original and internal quotation omitted). *See also Washington v. Krahn*, 440 F. Supp. 2d 911, 913–14 (E.D. Wis. 2006) (relying on *Doyle* and holding that emotional distress qualified as "bodily injury" pursuant to a definition that defined the term as sickness or disease); *Wosinski v. Advance Cast Stone Co.*, 901 N.W.2d 797 (Wis. Ct. App. 2017) ("Mental, emotional or psychological conditions are commonly considered as sickness or disease by both lay persons and medical professionals. Such conditions are routinely treated by medical personnel employing medical procedures. A reasonable insured would understand such conditions to be included within the concepts of 'sickness or disease' which the policy uses to define 'bodily injury.'") (relying on *Tara N. v. Economy Fire & Casualty Insurance Co.*, 540 N.W.2d 26 (Wis. Ct. App. 1995)).

Wyoming: The Supreme Court of Wyoming held that a bystander claim for emotional distress qualified as "bodily injury" for purposes of an underinsured motorist policy. *Evans v. Farmers Ins. Exch.*, 34 P.3d 284, 287 (Wyo. 2001). The policy defined "bodily injury" as "bodily harm to or sickness, disease or death of any person." *Id.* at 287. The court first concluded that, given such grammatical structure, the term "bodily" did not modify the terms "sickness" and "disease," as in the majority of cases on the issue that define "bodily injury" as "bodily injury, sickness or disease." *Id.* at 287. After reviewing dictionary definitions of the terms "sickness" and "disease," the court concluded that emotional injuries are neither expressly included nor expressly excluded. *Id.* The court therefore concluded that the term "bodily injury" was ambiguous and construed it in favor of coverage. *Id.*

Made in United States
Troutdale, OR
12/08/2023

15540403R00312